Facing Mount Kanchenjunga

THE COMPLETE WORKS OF SANGHARAKSHITA include all his previously published work, as well as talks, seminars, and writings published here for the first time. The collection represents the definitive edition of his life's work as Buddhist writer and teacher. For further details, including the contents of each volume, please turn to the 'Guide' on pp. 652–5.

FOUNDATION

1. A Survey of Buddhism / The Buddha's Noble Eightfold Path
2. The Three Jewels I
3. The Three Jewels II
4. The Bodhisattva Ideal
5. The Purpose and Practice of Buddhist Meditation
6. The Essential Sangharakshita

INDIA

7. Crossing the Stream: India Writings I
8. Beating the Dharma Drum: India Writings II
9. Dr Ambedkar and the Revival of Buddhism I
10. Dr Ambedkar and the Revival of Buddhism II

THE WEST

11. A New Buddhist Movement I
12. A New Buddhist Movement II
13. Eastern and Western Traditions

COMMENTARY

14 The Eternal Legacy / Wisdom Beyond Words
15 Pāli Canon Teachings and Translations
16 Mahāyāna Myths and Stories
17 Wisdom Teachings of the Mahāyāna
18 Milarepa and the Art of Discipleship I
19 Milarepa and the Art of Discipleship II

MEMOIRS

20 The Rainbow Road from Tooting Broadway to Kalimpong
21 Facing Mount Kanchenjunga
22 In the Sign of the Golden Wheel
23 Moving Against the Stream
24 Through Buddhist Eyes

POETRY AND THE ARTS

25 Complete Poems
26 Aphorisms and the Arts

27 Concordance and Appendices

COMPLETE WORKS 21 MEMOIRS

Sangharakshita
Facing Mount Kanchenjunga

EDITED BY KALYANAPRABHA

Windhorse Publications
169 Mill Road
Cambridge
CB1 3AN
UK

info@windhorsepublications.com
www.windhorsepublications.com

© Sangharakshita, 2018

The right of Sangharakshita to be identified as the author
of this work has been asserted by him in accordance
with the Copyright, Designs and Patents Act 1988.

Cover design by Dhammarati
Cover images: Back flap © Clear Vision Trust Picture Archive;
front: Kanchenjunga 1936, by Nicholas Roerich, courtesy
Nicholas Roerich Museum, New York.
Typesetting and layout by Ruth Rudd
Printed by Bell & Bain Ltd, Glasgow

**British Library Cataloguing
in Publication Data:**
A catalogue record for this book is
available from the British Library.

ISBN 978-1-911407-16-4 (paperback)
ISBN 978-1-911407-15-7 (hardback)

CONTENTS

Foreword, Kalyanaprabha   ix

FACING MOUNT KANCHENJUNGA

List of Illustrations   3
Maps   4

1 On My Own in Kalimpong   7
2 A New Gate Opens   23
3 Stepping Stones   40
4 The Spirit of the Hills   55
5 Widening Circles   82
6 Acceptance and Rejection   96
7 Burma Raja and the Devas   117
8 Repairing the Damage   137
9 Traditions and Individual Talents   148
10 Preparing to Receive the Sacred Relics   170
11 Pretexts and Processions   189
12 The Hermitage   216
13 Kindred Spirits   243
14 Contrasts in Kathmandu   263
15 A Big Setback   307
16 The Near and the Far   325

17 The Enemy of the Church   345
18 Discovering Dharmapala   367
19 A Re-enshrinement and a Reunion   390
20 Discussions in Bombay and Deolali   402
21 A Fresh Beginning   426
22 New Arrivals in Kalimpong ... and Dhardo Rimpoche   441

DEAR DINOO

Introduction, Kalyanaprabha   457

Letters   491

Appendix
The Monk and the Prophet, Kalyanaprabha   599

Notes   621
Index   637
A Guide to *The Complete Works of Sangharakshita*   647

FOREWORD

'Stay here and work for the good of Buddhism', Jagdish Kashyap said to the twenty-four year old Sangharakshita when he left him in Kalimpong in the eastern Himalayas. The first volume of Sangharakshita's memoirs concludes, 'I was left facing Mount Kanchenjunga.'

Now, in the second volume, which takes its title from those concluding words, we find out how the young *śrāmaṇera* or novice monk responded to the situation in which he found himself – or to which he had been led.

The book's title, subtitle, and opening words all give clues to the significance of the years recounted in its pages, beginning in March 1950 and taking us up to early 1953.

First, the title. What is meant by 'Facing Mount Kanchenjunga'? To understand that is to ask what did Kanchenjunga represent in the life, the inner life, of Sangharakshita? It is an image, a symbol – but what might it mean? There is a haiku that Sangharakshita wrote at this time called simply 'Kanchenjunga':

One white wave of snow
Towering against the blue
Sky, with clouds below.

To me there is a reflection here of the intense spiritual aspiration that was his, an awareness both of the infinite, the blue of the sky, and the purity and grandeur of the snows, even whilst from below clouds might dim their view.

The subtitle is 'An English Buddhist in the Eastern Himalayas' – an interesting juxtaposition. What does an English Buddhist see and experience in a world so different to the one in which he grew up? Perhaps he sees with more acute sensitivities since all that is around him is new. Certainly Sangharakshita found his new environment inspiring and even 'magical'.

What was he to *do* there in Kalimpong? The answer is straightforward. He follows his teacher's injunction to 'stay here and work for the good of Buddhism' – these are the words with which the present book begins and they tell us what the book is all about. But before exploring further what this meant in practice, let us look back to the first volume to remind ourselves from where the author had come. Like the poet Wordsworth's *Prelude*, which is addressed to his friend Coleridge, and explains the forces that shaped him, so *The Rainbow Road from Tooting Broadway to Kalimpong* tells what were the experiences of childhood and youth that influenced the emergence of Sangharakshita. Most pivotal of them all was his encounter at the age of sixteen or seventeen with *The Diamond Sūtra* when he realized he was a Buddhist 'and always had been'. The next eight years were crucial ones. His line of development was from 'a sort of spiritual falling-in-love' to something which had 'more of the nature of a reasoned conviction that included understanding as well as emotion, clarity as well as passion'. Aged twenty-one, by now in India, he left behind all worldly things, or in traditional Buddhist language he went forth. Meditation, study, deep reflection, meetings with great spiritual masters, and eventual ordination as a Buddhist monk characterized those years. But now, here in Kalimpong, his teacher's injunction ringing in his ears, 'a new gate opens'. It is a gate of gold, he tells us, and it opens onto a new path – that of responding to the needs of others.

But how best to respond to those needs, or, in the language of the Mahāyāna, how best to respond to the 'cries of the world'? Members of the Buddhist order which, eighteen years later, he would go on to found, sometimes see themselves each as a hand of Avalokiteśvara, the Bodhisattva of Compassion who, in his thousand-armed form, carries in each of his hands a different implement with which to respond to the suffering of humanity. Thus each Order member looks to his or her own capacities and talents to see what he or she is best able to offer the world. There was no order of this kind which Sangharakshita could join (the *bhikkhu* sangha did not share any such common archetypal myth) but in his own way, entering through the golden gate, seeking to respond to the world's predicament, he, too, draws on his particular talents and abilities – some of which he discovers as he goes along. His overriding response is to spread the Buddha's Dharma – really the master current of his whole life. At the same time he is aware of the more immediate needs of the people around him. And so, as he sets out to fulfil his teacher's injunction, we see his particular qualities or talents at work. There is his tremendous vision, the capacity to envision that which does not yet exist along with the ability to bring it into being – perhaps quite a rare combination. He describes the two 'iridescent balls' that hover above his head and which are called down into embodiment. The first is the Young Men's Buddhist Association of Kalimpong and the second, *Stepping-Stones,* a monthly magazine of Himalayan religion, culture, and education whose first edition appears within a few months of his arrival in the town. In the *Stepping-Stones* editorials he is able to express something of the force and purity of his aspiration and the strength of his vision for the significance of the Buddha's teaching for mankind. And surely it is this that communicates itself to some of the leading Buddhist writers of the time, Lama Govinda, Edward Conze, and others, who are soon contributing to its pages, even though the journal's editor is so young and, at this stage, unknown.

How does an English Buddhist get on in this town in the eastern Himalayas, this meeting place for individuals from so many different backgrounds? The local people include Newars, Lepchas, and others; most are Hindu or Buddhist, a few are Christian. There are the Europeans, including a number of eccentrics and oddballs, and there are the missionaries, some settled, some passing through. To people from all these backgrounds he offers the hand of friendship. All through the pages of this memoir are pen portraits, a few words describing appearance and habit that bring individuals alive before our eyes and give the memoir so much of its interest and even fascination.

A quality that Sangharakshita discovers as he goes along is his ability to organize. The logistics surrounding the reception of the Sacred Relics of the Buddha's two chief disciples, Śāriputra and Maudgalyāyana, prove to be quite a challenge not just logistically but politically. If all is to proceed smoothly he has to be one step ahead of local politics needing all the wisdom of the serpent whilst operating as far as he can with the gentleness of the dove. He has plenty of allies in the town but the uncompromising stance he takes on occasion, his willingness to speak out against that which he sees as wrong, including the bigotry he encounters among Christian missionaries, also make him one or two enemies.

Although the story is mostly about what lay beyond the golden gate, that is, the path of responding to others, we are offered now and then a glimpse of the unfolding of Sangharakshita's inner life, the personal struggles, the disappointments, as well as the inspirations, which are given fuller expression in his poems. Of one occasion he writes,

> On my return to the Hermitage with my three young friends I was silent and gloomy, some of Joe's remarks having depressed me, and the following morning, feeling that no one understood me or sympathized with what I was trying to achieve, and that I had no earthly refuge, I composed a poem of seven eight-line stanzas entitled 'Taking Refuge in the Buddha'.

One person who *could* understand, one in whom he found a kindred spirit, was the German-born Lama Govinda, writer, poet, and painter. They shared a sensibility which included an understanding of the basic unity of Buddhism and the value of art to the spiritual life. In fact, in the course of their first meetings they 'ranged over practically the whole field of Buddhist thought and practice' finding themselves in agreement to an astonishing degree. There are two others figures who stand out as exceptional individuals who come into the story. Towards the end of the memoir Sangharakshita 'discovers' Anagārika Dharmapala, the great Ceylonese *dharmadūta*. Although Dharmapala had by then been dead for almost twenty years, for Sangharakshita, to write about his life and work was to be moved and inspired by another kindred spirit. In the final pages of the memoir someone appears whose influence is to grow in the coming years and who will feature in the next volume: Dhardo Rimpoche.

Facing Mount Kanchenjunga is not the only work included in this volume of Sangharakshita's *Complete Works*. *Dear Dinoo* is unique among his published works as a collection of letters, written during the years 1955–1974, that is to say, beginning soon after the period covered by *Facing Mount Kanchenjunga* and extending to the beginnings of the Friends of the Western Buddhist Order (about which Sangharakshita writes to Dinoo from England).

A memoir is a life recalled by the maturer man looking back. Letters are a response in the present to a particular person. These letters afford us a very personal, even intimate glimpse of a friendship.

Dinoo Dubash came from a Parsi background. She lived in Bombay (Mumbai) where she ran a Montessori nursery school. She was an accomplished amateur artist, and had an interest in meditation. She met Sangharakshita on the occasion of one of his lectures. At the end, inspired and uplifted, she rushed up to meet him and invited him to tea. And so there sprung up between the Buddhist monk and the Montessori teacher a rather unusual friendship. In his letters we see Sangharakshita responding to his friend in many different ways so that he writes now as tour guide, as he helps Dinoo with her itinerary for a planned visit to Kalimpong, now as spiritual friend discussing matters of spiritual import. He sympathizes with her struggles and, knowing one or two of her foibles, sometimes allows himself a gentle tease. He also confides. It is to Dinoo that he writes about his momentous experiences at the time of the death of Dr Ambedkar.

Dinoo introduced Sangharakshita to Dr Mehta, former naturopathic physician to Gandhi. Dr Mehta had more recently founded what he called the Society of Servants of God. Dinoo was keen that the two men should meet. Meet they did, and they, too, became friends. (Dr Mehta, and his 'Scripts' – which he claimed came directly from God – feature in the next volume of memoirs.) The Appendix to *Dear Dinoo,* entitled 'The Monk and the Prophet', recounts more about the fascinating life of Dr Mehta, and explores the relationship between the two men.

The letters to Dinoo are presented here with a full set of notes providing more of the context and explaining references that might otherwise remain obscure. The Introduction tells more about Dinoo and her life, and her friendship with Sangharakshita. It also includes a section on the theme 'Sangharakshita, women, and friendship' and looks at the lives of two other women friends of his from those years: the poet Clare Cameron, and Kazini Elisa-Maria Dorje-Khangsarpa of Chakhung, both known to Dinoo.

But who wrote that Introduction, the notes, and the Appendix to *Dear Dinoo*? I must confess, it was myself! In the spring of 2010 I had no thought that I would ever work with Sangharakshita, nor become one of his literary editors. I was living abroad but difficult circumstances had led me to the conclusion that my best option was to return to England – though what I would do when I got there I did not know. Then came a message: 'Bhante (that is, Sangharakshita) has some work for you.' By this time I was living in Birmingham, near to where Sangharakshita then lived. Off I went to find out what that work might be. I came back with a blue file full of letters. And so began our happy collaboration. It drew from me far more than I realized was there in terms of writing and research, and has been one of the great joys of my life.

When it came to publishing the book Sangharakshita's usual publishers, Windhorse Publications, were unable to take on the project due to financial constraints. I was disappointed, but a day or two after receiving this news Sangharakshita turned up in the library where I was working and said with a twinkle in his eye that he had had an idea. We would publish it ourselves. And so Ibis Publications was born – its name a reference both to the well-known British publishers, Penguin (who also brought out Puffin and Pelican books) and to Thoth, the ibis-headed Egyptian god of wisdom.

Dear Dinoo sold rather more copies than was expected, aided by the launch which took place on 10 December 2011 at the Birmingham Buddhist Centre. I gave a twenty minute introduction and it was hoped that, if he was well enough, Sangharakshita, then already 86 years old, would say a few words. As it turned out the few words turned into ten, twenty, forty, nearly fifty minutes of an inspired talk. He took his audience first to Bombay with his recollections of Dinoo and her times but then he surprised us with a survey, a magnificent sweep over the whole history of the letter, from the clay tablets of Babylon to the shortest letter of all – the cheque (which gave him the opportunity for exposing with hard-hitting irony the empty shell of banking) – before returning to the personal letters of some of the famous including Byron, Coleridge, and Philip Larkin. It was a memorable talk; it was also, as it turned out, the last public talk that Sangharakshita has given (to date) – completing – if it is the last – a whole lifetime of Dharma talks and lectures.

In the course of preparing the Introduction and Appendix for *Dear Dinoo* I tried to find out a little more about both her, and about Dr

Mehta. I was grateful to be able to interview Dharmacāri Lokamitra about his memories of Dinoo in her later years, and Dharmacāri Suvajra for his memories of Dr Mehta and Sundri Vaswani. Ms Nazneen Dubash, Dinoo's niece and principal of the Casa Montessori in Mumbai, although she did not know her aunt very well, was able to furnish me with a little more information, and Ms Zarin Malva, Director of Mumbai's RTI Montessori Training Course, spoke to me on the telephone, recalling her time working with Dinoo at the Casa Montessori in the 1960s. For the rest I drew on published material, as well as some internet sources, as documented in the notes. But most of all I drew on the interviews I had with Sangharakshita during the latter part of 2010 and the early months of 2011.

I hope these words may have highlighted for you, the reader, some of the significance of these two works. They have much merit from a purely literary point of view – one can enjoy them just as literature. But for all those who share a spiritual aspiration, *Facing Mount Kanchenjunga* and *Dear Dinoo* have much to say that can inspire, encourage, and show the way.

Kalyanaprabha
Great Malvern
17 July 2017

Facing Mount Kanchenjunga

AN ENGLISH BUDDHIST IN THE EASTERN HIMALAYAS

LIST OF ILLUSTRATIONS

Map of the Eastern Himalayan Region   4
Map of Sangharakshita's Kalimpong   5
The first issue of *Stepping Stones*   50
After the *bhikṣu* ordination ceremony   110
Receiving a ceremonial scarf   111
Burma Raja and the princess   135
Speaking at a meeting in Kalimpong   174
Reception for the Sacred Relics   211
The Sacred Relics leaving Kalimpong   214
YMBA members outside the Hermitage shrine-room   219
With Lama Govinda and members of the YMBA   257
At the Swayambunath Stūpa   290
Speaking in Patan (Lalitpur), Nepal   294
With the Yellow Monk and others in Darjeeling   335
Anagārika Dharmapala   383
With Raj Kapoor, discussions for the film *Ajanta*   414
Dhardo Rimpoche   452

Eastern Himalayan Region, 1950s

Sangharakshita's Kalimpong

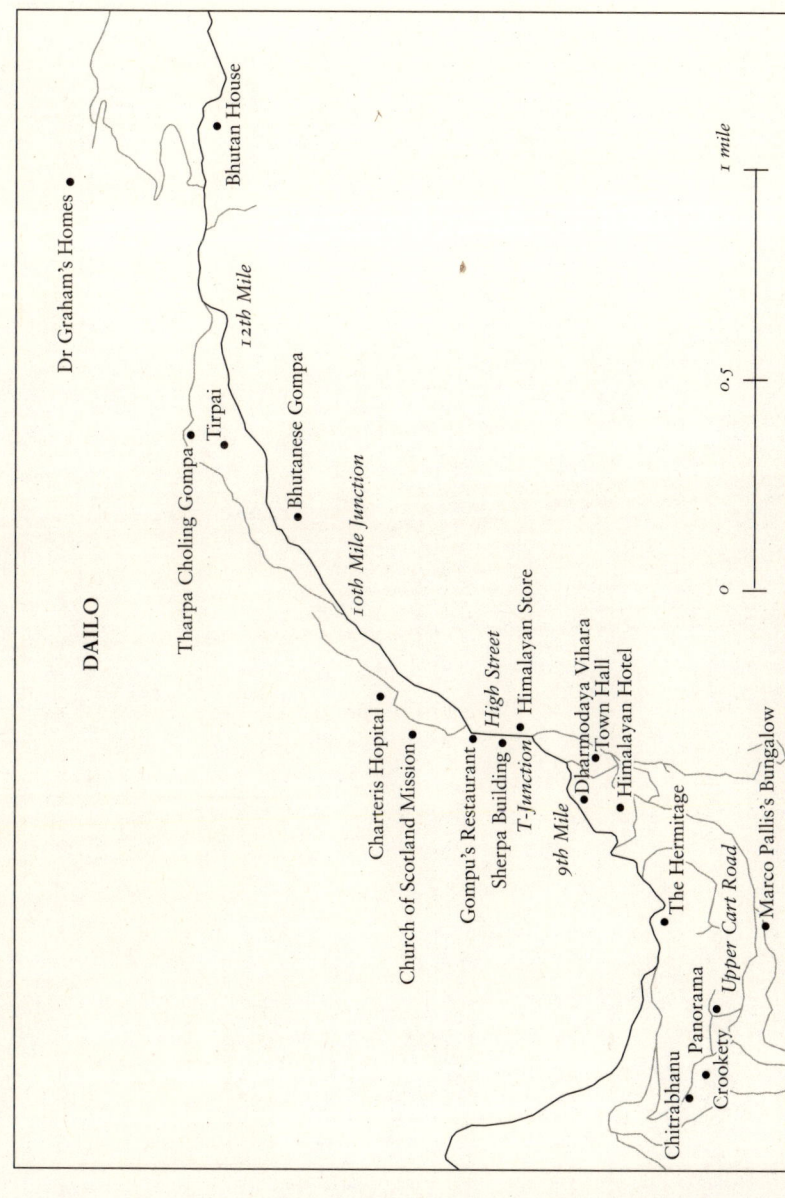

This map is based on descriptions in the text, information from the internet, and some 'best guesses'. Readers with any further information are requested to contact the publisher so that the map can be updated for any future edition.

1
ON MY OWN IN KALIMPONG

'Stay here and work for the good of Buddhism. The Newars will look after you.' As the jeep that was taking Kashyapji down to Siliguri disappeared round a bend, I was left standing at the side of the road with my teacher's parting words ringing in my ears. I was twenty-four years old. Since becoming Kashyapji's disciple seven months earlier I had not been separated from him for more than a few days, and now, barely three weeks after our arrival in Kalimpong, he had suddenly decided to leave me there. It was a brilliantly sunny day in March. Above me was the fathomless blue of the sky. Around me were the foothills of the eastern Himalayas, the great jagged ridges running together from all directions. In front of me, far away to the north, rising behind the exact middle of a gigantic saddleback, were the dazzling white peaks of Mount Kanchenjunga. For the first time in my life I was on my own. I had not been on my own in the army, which had originally brought me to India. I had not been on my own during my two years as a wandering ascetic. But now, left standing there at the side of the road in the sunshine that morning in March 1950, I was on my own at last, with no one to whom I could look up in any way, and with no one to help me but myself.

As I climbed the acclivity that led, in three sharp bends, from the road to the double-fronted, two-storey building where we had been put up, I thought about Kashyapji's parting words to me, 'Stay here and work for the good of Buddhism. The Newars will look after you.' The first part of this injunction presented no difficulty. Already the scenery and atmosphere of Kalimpong had made a deep impression on me, and I was perfectly willing to go on staying in such an inspiring and magical place. Working for the good of Buddhism was another matter. Less than a year had passed since my ordination as a *śrāmaṇera* or novice monk at Kusinara, and although I was willing to do everything in my power to carry out my teacher's instructions, I doubted whether I was as ready to work for the good of Buddhism as Kashyapji apparently thought – especially if, as seemed likely, I would be working on my own. I also doubted whether the Newars were ready to look after me. From what I had seen, they were not ready to look after Kashyapji himself. They had certainly shown no interest in making it possible for him to settle in the area, a step which for a time he appeared to be contemplating.

The Newars in question were of course the Buddhist – as distinct from the Hindu – Newars of Kalimpong. Like their counterparts in Butaol and Tansen, to whom U Chandramani had sent me to preach the Dharma immediately after my ordination, they came originally from the Kathmandu Valley, with which their social, economic, cultural, and religious ties were still very close. Some of them were merchants engaged in the highly lucrative import–export trade between India and Tibet. Others were goldsmiths and silversmiths. Others, again, were shopkeepers and petty traders. All, so far as they could, employed only fellow Newars, preference generally being given to blood relations. One of the town's most prominent Newar merchants was Gyan Jyoti, the second of the four brothers who made up the firm of Jyoti Brothers. Kashyapji had met him in Calcutta the previous year, when he had taken the opportunity of letting my teacher know that if ever he wanted to escape from the heat of the plains for a few weeks he would gladly make arrangements for him to stay in Kalimpong. As a true monk, as well as a genuine son of the soil, Kashyapji was not bothered by heat, but we were on holiday from Benares Hindu University, and after he had shown me some of the holy places of his native Bihar, the ancient Magadha, we boarded the train at Patna and from there made the three-hundred-mile journey to Siliguri, which was the railhead for Kalimpong.

Gyan Jyoti did not forget his promise. At Siliguri there was a jeep waiting for us outside the station, and on our arrival in Kalimpong three hours later we were driven straight to his home for lunch. When we had eaten and rested, our host, a smooth-faced smiling man of about thirty in semi-traditional dress – white jodhpurs and black English jacket –

took us to the Dharmodaya Vihara or 'Monastery of the Rise of the Teaching', as the building at the top of the acclivity was called, where he had made arrangements for us to stay. Before leaving he invited us, in the most cordial manner, to take our *bhikṣā* or almsfood – the polite term for the monk's single, pre-midday meal – at his home each day. For a week or more all was well. At ten-thirty every morning, having studied the *Dhammapada* together for a couple of hours, Kashyapji and I made our way to Nepali Building, which was situated on the other side of the town, less than a mile up the road from the vihara. Here, in the living quarters above the business part of the premises, we were given our meal. As the Newar custom was, the dishes were all strongly impregnated with garlic. The Newars themselves, in fact, were redolent of garlic. For three or four days we were served with full ceremony, in strictly 'orthodox' fashion, for the Newars of Kalimpong, like those of Butaol and Tansen, had in recent years come under the influence of a Ceylon- and Burma-based 'reform' movement, which in practice meant little more than that their own vulgarized and debased Vajrayāna had been to some extent overlaid with a veneer of imported Theravāda formalism. Before Kashyapji and I could eat, therefore, Refuges and Precepts had to be administered, verses of blessing recited, a short discourse delivered, and so on. Moreover, each dish had to be individually offered, that is to say, actually lifted up and placed in our hands. At the end of three or four days ceremony was first quietly abridged, then dropped altogether, our food being simply placed in front of us with a polite folding of hands and a smiling intimation that we should fall to without further ado. There were also fewer servants in attendance than before, and more often than not Gyan Jyoti himself was not present. This did not particularly surprise us: Gyan Jyoti was a busy man, his servants no doubt had work to do, and it was only to be expected that as people became accustomed to our presence they would treat us with less formality than at first.

On the ninth or tenth day after our arrival in Kalimpong we turned up at Nepali Building as usual only to find that no one was expecting us that morning. Though a meal was quickly prepared, something had evidently gone wrong. Later in the day Gyan Jyoti came flying along to the Dharmodaya Vihara full of apologies for the apparent discourtesy with which we had been treated, explained that there had been a misunderstanding, assured us that he had given the servants a good scolding for their remissness, and insisted that we should go on taking our meals at his place. We therefore gave the matter no further thought. A few days later the same thing happened again. Kashyapji and I found it difficult to believe that a second misunderstanding of this sort could occur so soon after the first. Had we outstayed our welcome? Or was there some disagreement between Gyan Jyoti and his servants? Were they his servants, anyway, or were they his elder brother's servants and, in that case, how much control over them did our smooth-faced host actually have? We did not know what to think. Only one thing was certain: the present ambiguous state of affairs could not be allowed to continue. Though further apologies and explanations were forthcoming from Gyan Jyoti, who appeared genuinely distressed by what had happened, Kashyapji decided that we should discontinue our morning visits to Nepali Building. In any case, it was not in accordance with the best monastic practice that, when there were so many Newar merchants in Kalimpong, we should rely on just one of them for our support. Come to think of it, it was strange that none of the other merchants had invited us to their homes or shown signs of wanting to share with Gyan Jyoti the responsibility – and the merit – of looking after us. (There was a reason for this apparent reluctance, but what it was I discovered only several months later.) Having decided on the course we should take, Kashyapji had a frank talk with Gyan Jyoti, explaining that since we had already given his servants more trouble than we ought, and felt reluctant to give them any more, we hoped that from now on he would excuse us from taking our *bhikṣā* at his home. At the same time, he thanked Gyan Jyoti warmly for all that he had done for us and was, in fact, still doing. Such was Kashyapji's tact, and so patent his sincerity, that we were able to discontinue our visits to Nepali Building without detriment to the cordial relations that had developed between our well-meaning host and ourselves.

As so often happens, the solution of one problem only resulted in the creation of another. The ambiguous state of affairs that had arisen in connection with our visits to Nepali Building was now resolved, but what were we to do about our *bhikṣā*? As a professor at the Benares Hindu University Kashyapji drew what by Indian standards was a handsome salary, and he had come to Kalimpong not unprovided with funds. What was more, he was quite prepared to dip into his own pocket whenever necessary in order to defray our expenses. We could take our meals at a brahmin – i.e. vegetarian – restaurant in the bazaar or, alternatively, we could buy provisions and get the old woman who lived in the outbuildings behind the Dharmodaya Vihara to do our cooking for us. She was already making our morning and afternoon tea, and would probably be glad to earn a little extra money. In the end we decided against both these courses. It would not do for monks to be seen eating in a public restaurant, and we did not really want to go to the trouble of setting up an establishment of our own – especially as we would not be staying in Kalimpong much longer. There was no doubt that the best course for us to take was the simplest. It was also the one that was the most traditional, and the most truly Buddhistic. Why had we not thought of it before? We would rely for our *bhikṣā* not on any one person, however charitable, but on the religious-minded general public. With our begging-bowls in our hands, we would go from door to door for alms. *That* was the solution to our new problem. We had, of course, recently gone for alms in the towns and villages of Bihar. Kashyapji at that time had no previous experience of the practice, at least not since his return from Ceylon twelve years earlier, and he doubted if the ancient Buddhist tradition of alms-gathering – as distinct from ordinary religious mendicancy – could really be revived in twentieth-century India. From my experience when walking from Kusinara to Lumbini, immediately after my ordination, I believed that it could be and managed to convince Kashyapji that we should at least make the attempt. For a few days we created a minor sensation among the good folk of Bihar. People wept with emotion to see yellow-robed Buddhist monks standing for alms outside the doors of their own homes – a sight that had not been seen for six or seven hundred years. Now that we had decided not to rely on any one person in Kalimpong for our *bhikṣā* we would see if what had been possible in one part of the country was possible in another. Next morning at ten-thirty, equipped with our begging-bowls, we therefore sallied forth from the Dharmodaya Vihara and made our way to the bazaar. Though we created less of a sensation than in Bihar, within an hour we collected as much food as we needed, and returned from our expedition well satisfied.

For the rest of the time that Kashyapji was in Kalimpong we went alms gathering together each day. The practice had many advantages. Besides solving the problem of what we were to do about our *bhikṣā*, it brought us into contact with people whom we might not otherwise have met. We even became acquainted with some of the other Newar merchants of Kalimpong, but though one or two of these invited us to their homes for a meal, and listened politely when Kashyapji spoke of his idea of starting an institute for the study of Pāli and Buddhist Philosophy 'at a suitable place in the hills', it soon became obvious that no one was interested in helping him stay on in Kalimpong, or prepared to do anything more for him than provide him with the occasional ceremonial *bhikṣā*. Thus it was not surprising that, ten or twelve days after the start of our alms gathering expeditions, and less than three weeks after our arrival in Kalimpong, my teacher should suddenly decide to return to the plains. In the course of our holiday he had at last made up his mind to resign from the Benares Hindu University, but not knowing as yet what to do after that he now wanted to stay quietly in Bihar until he found out. Fired by the prospect of freedom after twelve years of academic servitude, and anxious to be on his way, he paid a hurried visit to Gyan Jyoti and left Kalimpong the very next morning, directing his parting injunction to me from the jeep. 'Stay here and work for the good of Buddhism. The Newars will look after you.'

Whether Kashyapji ever seriously thought that the Newars would look after me I do not know. Probably he reckoned that as I was not only a stranger to the town, but also a European, my co-religionists would at least not allow me to starve, especially as I was a monk. Whatever he may have thought when he decided to leave me in Kalimpong, I had no wish to take advantage of my white skin and no wish to be a burden to anyone. After Kashyapji's departure I therefore continued to go alms-gathering as usual. So far as I was concerned, the almsround was an integral part of monastic life, and I had no wish to abandon the practice even if it had been possible for me to do so. A monk's robes and his bowl were his two wings, and equipped with them he was free to go, or to stay, wherever he pleased, dependent on all, and dependent on none. With robe and bowl, therefore, I made my way from the Dharmodaya Vihara to the bazaar at ten-thirty each morning, not walking at a respectful distance behind Kashyapji as before, but on my own. As the custom was, I went barefoot, with lowered head, and did not speak to anyone on the way. According to the most austere tradition, a monk should gather alms without omitting any house but accepting from all impartially, whether rich or poor, believing or unbelieving. Kashyapji had chosen not to follow this procedure. We had accordingly 'begged' – the Buddhist monk is not supposed actually to ask for alms, thus differing from his Hindu counterpart – exclusively from Buddhist Newars and such Hindu Biharis and Marwaris as Kashyapji had become acquainted with in the course of the week following our arrival. At first I continued to go for alms in this way, but as the weeks went by I gradually extended the scope of my operations, preferring to take smaller amounts of food from a number of houses rather than larger amounts from only two or three, even though this meant going further afield and, in consequence, spending more time out on my almsround. Such an extension of the scope of my operations would, I hoped, better enable me to act upon the Buddha's advice to the wandering monk and – as the *Dhammapada*, verse 49, puts it – 'gather alms in the village even as the bee, without injuring their colour or scent, collects honey from the flowers.'

For the greater part of the way my almsround lay along the road between the Dharmodaya Vihara and Nepali Building. This road, which was the main road, ran straight through Kalimpong, winding up from the plains of Bengal to join the middle of the saddleback along which the town was spread out and plunging down, a few miles farther on, into the valleys of southern Sikkim. My first halt after leaving the Dharmodaya Vihara was about halfway along the high street, at the open-fronted shop of a Marwari cloth merchant. This merchant was extremely kind to me. As soon as I took up my station outside his shop he would appear from the back part of the premises, where the living quarters were situated, with a brass tray piled high with rice, curried vegetables, and crisp, crinkled-up poppadams. Had I allowed him to do so he would have filled my bowl to the brim. At the end of the high street the road divided, the left-hand fork winding on up to Nepali Building and beyond, the right-hand fork falling steeply into the lower reaches of the bazaar. My way lay along the first of these. On the left, on the way up to Dailo, the pine-covered hill that formed the more northerly hump of the saddleback on which Kalimpong was situated, stood the buildings of the Church of Scotland Mission, the most prominent among them being a church, the square grey tower of which was one of the first things one saw on entering the outskirts of the town. On the right, backing onto the lower bazaar, stood a straggling row of open-fronted wooden shops, none of them more than a single storey high and all rather ramshackle. Indeed, they looked as though they might fall down at any time. Outside three of these shops in turn I halted for a few minutes. The first two, which were situated next door to each other, belonged to two Newar silversmiths, with furnaces and shabby display shelves both occupying the front part of the premises, facing onto the street, while the third shop contained the dispensary of a Bihari homoeopathic doctor. In contrast to the Marwari merchant, who wore a white shirt and dhoti and a bright yellow puggaree, the Bihari doctor wore a white dhoti, a long navy blue waistcoat, and a brown pillbox hat of the Nepalese type. As for the two silversmiths, they and their teenage sons and nephews were dressed in loose-fitting white jodhpurs and double-breasted Nepalese shirts that made them look as though they had just got out of bed, especially as they were all red-eyed from bending over the small charcoal furnaces. At each of the three shops I was received with folded hands and given a few spoonfuls of rice and curried vegetables. Depending on how much food I had already collected, I either went round to the back of the shops, where an old Newar woman lived, or on past Nepali Building to Kodamull Building, a cold, gloomy warren of a tenement block in different parts of which stayed four or five Newar merchants. Sometimes I did not go to either place, but went straight back to the Dharmodaya Vihara. All the way along the road there were, of course, plenty of shops and houses other than the ones at which I had stopped with my bowl, but some of these were occupied by Tibetans and Chinese, and not being sure of getting vegetarian food from them I did not include any of them in my almsround.

Since I went on my almsround with lowered head I did not see much of Kalimpong on such occasions. Apart from the road immediately in front of me, all I saw was legs. Some of the legs were short and thick, of the colour of weak tea, and with enormously developed calf muscles, almost like footballs. These, as I knew, were the legs of Nepalese coolies, dozens of whom could be seen at any hour of the day straining beneath the weight of enormous loads borne on their backs in cone-shaped wicker baskets. Others were black and stick-like, with ends of off-white dhotis flapping above bony knees. Some legs were sheathed in tight-fitting white jodhpurs or were encased in Western-style trousers, while others were decently concealed behind the skirts of black, brown, or blue gowns or heavy maroon robes. Besides human legs there were animal legs. There were the dun-coloured legs of the mules, and they sometimes passed by in such numbers, and raised such clouds of yellow dust, that I was forced to stand at the side of the road until they had passed. Some pairs of legs were going in the same direction as I was, others in the opposite direction. Some moved quickly and briskly, some slowly and saunteringly. For my own part, going and coming, I did my best to maintain the modest, measured gait considered appropriate to the alms-gathering monk.

Back at the Dharmodaya Vihara I washed the dust from my feet, rested for a few minutes, and then ate the food I had collected. Or rather, I ate part of the food. Though Kashyapji had left me on my own in Kalimpong, he had not left me alone. The fact that I was now responsible for myself did not mean that I was responsible for no one but myself. My begging-bowl was having to support not one person but two, and in the months to come would have to support even more. Tilakdhari Prasad Singh was a twenty-year-old Bihari whom we had met in Rajgir, where he was attending the training camp for village workers which Kashyapji and I had been invited to address on topics ranging from Buddhism to naturopathy. Like other young men we had met in the course of our tour, he was interested in Buddhism, at least to the extent that it formed part of the cultural history of his native Bihar, and he not only attended all our talks but spent a great deal of time in our company. By the conclusion of the training camp he was wanting to give up his job as a village worker and become a monk. However suited or unsuited to the monastic life Tilakdhari may have been, there was no denying the fact that he had developed a strong attachment to us. By nature he was, indeed, a warmly affectionate person. When the time came for Kashyapji and me to leave Rajgir he burst into tears and was so distressed at the idea of parting from us that my kind-hearted teacher invited him to accompany us to Kalimpong. Thus it was that, in the weeks following Kashyapji's departure, I came to be sharing with him each day the contents of my solitary begging-bowl.

The young man with whom I had been thrown into such close contact was of medium height and slightly built. He had a thatch of very thick, very wavy black hair from which protruded the knotted crown lock of the caste Hindu. Beneath the thatch was a brown pug face with a low, heavily corrugated brow and a pair of small, deep-set brown eyes the corners of which were quite yellow, as though with debauchery. Under a long navy blue waistcoat he wore a *kurta* or Indian collarless shirt and medium length dhoti. All three garments were of coarse hand-loom cloth, as befitted a member of the Congress Party and a village worker, and thus had a crumpled look, as if in need of ironing. His brown feet were stockingless, and thrust into a pair of down-at-heel shoes several sizes too large for him that slapped up and down when he walked. (Like many Indians, he walked with a curious forward jerk of the knee.) On the side of his head he wore a white hand-loom forage cap, thereby proclaiming his adherence to the Gandhian – and Congress – principles of truth and non-violence. By way of a concession to modernity he sported a cheap fountain pen, a pair of sunglasses, and a scarf thrown rakishly back over one shoulder. His mother tongue was the unpolished Hindi of rural Bihar, but he also spoke, or at least understood, a little English. Since our arrival in Kalimpong I had been giving him English lessons, and after Kashyapji's departure these lessons continued. Indeed, other subjects were added to the curriculum. Besides English, I taught him something of Buddhism, and introduced him to the practice of meditation. Not that the gains were all on his side. From time to time I practised my Hindi on him, getting him to correct the grammar and pronunciation. In this way we got on well together. He had always been more attached to me than to Kashyapji, and as the weeks went by his attachment turned into devotion. This did not mean that there was never any friction between us. His loud voice and uncouth manners often jarred on me, and no doubt there were times when he found my English reserve no less trying. Since he wanted to be a monk I did my best to disabuse him of his caste Hindu prejudices, which were still quite strong, as well as to make him realize that his faults and weaknesses were really such and ought to be got rid of as soon as possible. More often than not, he at first put up a show of resistance. Kayasthas really were superior to Shudras, even if not to Brahmins. It did not really matter if he smoked in the toilet and afterwards told me that he had not done so. If I thought he really meant what he said, or that there was a genuine misunderstanding to be dispelled, I went into the matter more deeply and argued with him until the truth was clear beyond doubt or cavil. His resistance would then suddenly collapse, he would admit he was wrong, and the brown pug face would be irradiated with a disarmingly innocent smile. At such moments I felt my efforts had not been wasted.

When I was not teaching Tilakdhari, or arguing with him, I sat cross-legged on my bed by the window, in one of the upstairs front rooms, either reading or writing. From where I sat I had an uninterrupted view of the hills, with Mount Kanchenjunga rising triumphantly above its saddleback, and whenever I became tired of concentrating on the printed page, or whenever inspiration flagged, I lifted up my eyes and allowed them to rest for a while on the gleaming white mass of the snow-peaks, all the whiter for being seen against a background of deep yet brilliant blue. The Dharmodaya Vihara was indeed an ideal place for study and literary work. Built originally as a European family house, it stood surrounded by its lawns and flower-beds on a ledge cut in the hillside. Below, but out of sight, was the road; behind, a series of steep terraces, some of them showing signs of cultivation. On the bazaar side of the vihara, half-hidden by a clump of large trees, could be seen the red corrugated roofs of the neighbouring bungalow, while on the other side there was a *jhora* or gully. In this *jhora*, which marked the boundary of the property on the western side, handsome thirty- and forty-foot bamboos grew so thickly as to form a living screen. Though well built, the vihara was not very big. There were two sizeable rooms both upstairs and downstairs, besides four smaller rooms. One of the pleasantest features of the building was the abundance of woodwork. The smaller rooms at the back were made entirely of dark brown wood, as was the gallery that ran the entire length of the building on the first floor. This gallery, to which there was access from both inside and outside the house, shed an interesting light on the domestic arrangements of the British in India, as well as showing the extent to which these were influenced by indigenous ideas. It was by means of this gallery that the sweeper gained entry to the back door of the upstairs toilets, which meant they could be cleaned without his actually entering the house and contaminating it with his unclean presence. The Dharmodaya Sabha, or 'Society for the Rise of the Teaching', the Newar Buddhist organization that had acquired the building a year or two earlier, had chosen to continue this arrangement. Once or twice a week, therefore, a dark, furtive figure could be seen – or heard – climbing the outside staircase, padding along the gallery, and swishing his stiff reed broom around inside the two toilets.

 The most important room in the vihara was the room next door to the one occupied by me. This room was, of course, the shrine-room. Here I performed my devotions each morning, reciting the salutation to the Three Jewels and other verses and meditating for a short period. An image of the Buddha had been installed in the octagonal bay window, between two orange curtains. It was a Burmese alabaster-and-gilt image, rather squat and square-featured, and it was planted in the middle of a small table. On the table, in front of the image, was a silver Tibetan butter-lamp, such as the Newar silversmiths themselves made, flanked by vases of flowers. Beneath the table stood a copper jug containing clarified butter, from which the lamps were replenished. On most days I was the only person to make use of the shrine. Apart from Tilakdhari and myself there was no one staying at the vihara, and such visitors as did come were of the talking rather than the worshipping type. Gyan Jyoti and fifteen or twenty other Newars came only on the occasion of the full-moon day and, though less regularly, on the new-moon day. Women and children came in the morning, bringing clarified butter to pour into the copper jug, flowers, packets of candles, paper twists of Nepalese incense, and handfuls of rice and small change which, in Newar fashion, they scattered over the image-table. They also offered me my morning *bhikṣā*, either bringing it with them in a tiffin carrier ready cooked or preparing it in one of the outbuildings with the help of the old woman, so that I did not have to go out on my almsround that day. In the evening came the men, who generally stayed quite late singing devotional songs to the accompaniment of a portable harmonium. Both morning and evening I would be requested to administer the Refuges and Precepts, perhaps to deliver a short discourse, and there would be a great deal of bowing down. On such occasions I was reminded of the happy weeks that, the previous year, I had spent with the Newars in Nepal, at the Padmagarbha Vihara, Butaol, and at the Mahachaitya Vihara, Tansen;[1] but though the general pattern of observance was the same, in Kalimpong, at the Dharmodaya Vihara, there were fewer people, the devotion was not so heartfelt, and I was conscious of strange undercurrents I could not understand.

Next to the shrine-room in importance was the library and reading room. This was situated downstairs, in the room below the shrine-room, and contained three or four hundred books. Among these were odd volumes of the Burmese and Thai editions of the Tipiṭaka, Hindi translations of Pāli Buddhist texts both canonical and non-canonical, works on Buddhism by modern Hindi writers, including Bhikkhu Kashyap, and books in the Newari language but printed – this was a recent development – in *devanāgarī* characters. Most of the books in the library, however, were Hindi romantic novels of the cheapest kind. On a table in the centre of the room lay a pile of newspapers and periodicals, among them two or three Buddhist magazines in English. Behind a smaller table, inside the door, sat the librarian. At least, he sat there when the library and reading room was open, which was from six till eight in the evening. Not more than ten or twelve people ever patronized the place in a single day. They consisted mostly of older men, who came to browse through the newspapers, and younger women and girls, who came to borrow Hindi romantic novels. All withdrawals were solemnly recorded by the librarian, who put on a pair of rimless spectacles for the purpose, and wrote in his book with much flourishing of the pen and many fatherly leers at the female borrowers. The librarian was, of course, a Newar. When Kashyapji and I first met him he greeted us with fulsome politeness, but he was clearly ill at ease in our presence, and after Kashyapji's departure it was obvious from his manner that he wanted as little to do with me as possible. He was about forty years of age, but quite bald, and with his close-set, rather prominent eyes, and wide trap-like slit of a mouth, he looked curiously like a bullfrog. When he stood up, his spindly legs and bloated belly made him look more like a bullfrog than ever, especially in the tight-fitting Nepalese garments he wore. When he spoke it was not with a deep, croaking sound, however, but in the high-pitched, yelping tones that I had come to recognize as characteristic of the male Newar.

Some weeks after Kashyapji had left Kalimpong I found in the glass-fronted wall cupboard in my room, behind some books, a framed photograph. The photograph showed a rather stern-faced Buddhist monk in Theravāda robes standing against an indeterminate background. I had seen that face somewhere before, but where it was I could not remember. Had it been in Nepal? Or in India? Eventually the truth flashed on me. The face in the photograph was the face of my bullfrog friend the librarian. Did the latter, then, have a brother who was a monk? Or had he once been a monk himself? Bit by bit I heard the whole story. Mahaprajna or 'Great Wisdom', as the librarian was called, had indeed once been a monk. He had been the best known of all the Theravāda Buddhist monks of Nepal – the best known of all the 'reformists' who were currently trying to replace a colourful but corrupt Vajrayāna with a pure but sterile Theravāda. He had been a Thera or elder monk, having completed ten years as a member of the monastic order, and many of the younger monks had been his disciples. He had travelled to Ceylon and Burma. He had practised meditation, especially the ten corpse meditations. He had been an accomplished and highly popular preacher in Newari, as well as being fluent in Hindi, Nepali, and Sinhalese. Above all, he had been a fearless opponent of the caste system, then still enforced by law in Nepal, and had had the honour of being personally flogged by the hereditary prime minister for daring to criticize it in public. On the opening of the Dharmodaya Vihara he was invited to come and stay there. Shortly after his arrival, he fell ill, being confined to the very bed by the window now occupied by me. Naturally, the Newars looked after him. Or rather, the Newar women looked after him. One of them, a widow with several young children, was particularly assiduous in her attentions, visiting the sick monk daily, spending hours at his bedside, and in short doing everything she could to assist his recovery. One day, a group of Newars came to see him, out of respect removing their shoes in the hall and stealing up the stairs in their stockinged feet. (As I knew, the sound of stockinged feet on the stairs could not be heard from inside the room.) On opening the door, they found Great Wisdom and the widow locked in an embrace typical of the Vajrayāna rather than of the Theravāda. As a result of this he had been forced to leave the vihara. Now, no longer a monk, he lived with the widow in the bazaar, where she kept a vegetable stall, and they already had, or were about to have, a child. In consideration of his past services to Buddhism, as well as of his present need, the Dharmodaya Sabha had appointed him as librarian and paid him a small stipend.

Apart from my almsround, I did not go out very much during the first few weeks that I was alone with Tilakdhari at the Dharmodaya Vihara, neither did I get to know many people. Gyan Jyoti called occasionally, as did his manager, who saw to it that I was kept supplied with milk for my morning and afternoon tea; Hindus sympathetic to Buddhism came to talk to the young English monk who was staying at the vihara, and that was about all. The first genuinely human contact I made in Kalimpong came about almost by accident. Returning from my almsround one day, I was accosted near the two silversmiths' shops by a tall, handsome Nepali, apparently a year or two older than myself, smartly dressed in immaculate Western-style clothes. Dropping to his knees directly in front of me, there in the road, he inclined his head in a deep reverence and remained in that position, with eyes closed, for several minutes. On rising to his feet he asked me who I was and where I came from. In accordance with monastic tradition, I did not speak to anyone when I was out alms-gathering, not even to the extent of returning a salutation, but so open and friendly was the young man's manner, and so alive his face with genuine interest and sympathy, that I willingly answered his questions. The result was that he subsequently came to the Dharmodaya Vihara and invited me to his house for lunch. In the course of the next few months I was to have lunch at his house a number of times, and in this way got to know him quite well. His name was Rudramani Pradhan. He came from a Hindu Newar family, and was the eldest of seven brothers. His father, his two uncles, and all his younger brothers, were engaged in the printing and publishing trade. He himself, much to his father's disgust, had decided to take up civil engineering, and he now worked as overseer to the Kalimpong Municipality. With his very beautiful wife, and infant son, he lived down a narrow lane between the silversmiths' shops and Nepali Building, in a three-roomed bungalow so tiny as to resemble a doll's house. As I came to know later on, when I had been in Kalimpong longer, and knew more people, Rudramani was well thought of by his superiors, highly popular with his contemporaries, and generally regarded as a rising young man. He had, moreover, a well deserved reputation for integrity and public spirit.

It was Rudramani's public spirit, in combination with his feeling for Buddhism, that gave me my first opportunity of carrying out Kashyapji's parting injunction and working for the good of Buddhism. A grand, government-sponsored agricultural exhibition was to be held at the village of Pedong, on the Bhutanese border, some fifteen or twenty miles from Kalimpong. Among the organizers of the exhibition were several of his friends and colleagues, and knowing how popular he was in the locality they appealed to Rudramani for his cooperation. His public spirit led him to respond to their appeal. His feeling for Buddhism – and his friendship for me – suggested to him the idea that, on the opening day of the exhibition, I should give a lecture on Buddhism. To Pedong then I went. Besides giving my lecture, I took the opportunity of visiting the local Buddhist *gompa* – a term which in the area indicated a temple rather than a monastery – and saw in the distance the low green hills of the dragon kingdom of Bhutan, of which, less than a century ago, the whole Kalimpong Subdivision had formed part. At the end of my lecture I was approached by a small, scowling man in a crumpled, ill-fitting khaki suit, with a pith helmet on his head and a Bible under his arm. So thoroughly had he been Europeanized, both within and without, that though he was very dark skinned it was impossible to tell whether he was an Indian or a Nepali, and whether he came from the hills or the plains. Addressing me in halting English, he asked whether I was an Englishman and whether I had been born a Christian. On my replying in the affirmative, he thumbed through his Bible, pointed an accusing finger at me, and in a voice thick with hatred declared, 'Your fate after death will be worse than that of other people. Not only have you gone astray yourself, but you are leading other people astray.'

In the coming months I was to lead more and more people astray.

2

A NEW GATE OPENS

One of the few things I had brought with me to Kalimpong in my small cloth carrier bag was a notebook. Into the front of this notebook I had been in the habit of copying the most inspiring passages from the books I came across in the course of my wanderings. Into the back I copied my poems. These poems were not always a record of my 'best and happiest moments', and I myself was in any case far from being one of Shelley's 'best and happiest minds',[2] but they certainly constituted a record of some kind or other. Some reflected my response to my changing environment. Others gave expression to passing moods and fancies, as well as to deeper insights and experiences. Now that I was on my own in Kalimpong I filled several pages in the front part of my notebook with passages from Śāntideva's *Śikṣā-samuccaya*, or 'Compendium of Instruction', an English translation of which I had found in the wall cupboard in my room. Several pages in the back part of the notebook were filled with haiku. From the images mirrored in these tiny poems it was clear that, seven or eight weeks after coming to Kalimpong, I had started to grow accustomed to the sights and sounds of the place – had even started to assimilate them. There were haiku with images of mountain and mist, of snow-peaks flushed with dawn and of blue hillsides gleaming, at eventide, with the orange jewels of village fires. There were haiku with images of cloudless blue sky, and of pink and white roses in bloom.[3] One haiku, however, did not mirror any external image. It simply gave expression to the fact that, in the weeks following

Kashyapji's departure, I had grown accustomed to the idea of working for the good of Buddhism – had even started to accept it. 'Behind me the old/Gate shuts,' declared the haiku. 'Before me opens/A new gate of gold.' For the last three years, perhaps longer, I had been concerned with the needs of my own spiritual life. *That* was the old gate that was shutting behind me. It was now time for me to start paying attention to the needs of others. *That* was the new gate that was opening before me – the new gate of gold. But what would I have to do before I could go through that gate? Would anyone be willing to go through it with me? What would I find on the other side?

An answer to these questions was not long in coming. It was now mid-April, and in mid-April it was hot even in Kalimpong, four thousand feet above sea level. Down in the plains it was much hotter, and the annual exodus to the hills had already begun. From all over northern India, from places like Benares and Calcutta, those who were in a position to do so had started making the long journey north, to the hill stations that were perched on spurs and ridges all the way along the southern slopes of the eastern Himalayas. Most of the people who came up from Calcutta went to Darjeeling, thirty-two miles west of Kalimpong, and a much bigger place. Only a few of them came to Kalimpong. Among those who came to Kalimpong that year was one who would help me go through the new gate that was opening before me, and even start to go through it with me. Colonel John Warren Swale Ryan, or Swale as he preferred to be called, had been a Buddhist for several years. I had, in fact, met him casually in Sarnath the year before, and seen him walking round the Mulagandhakuti Vihara hand in hand with Princess Pema Tsedeun of Sikkim, whom I also met then for the first time, and who was also now in Kalimpong. Swale was a member of the Maha Bodhi Society of India, and knew Devapriya Valisinha, the General Secretary. He also knew Maniharsh Jyoti, Gyan Jyoti's elder brother, who likewise was a member of the Society. It was Maniharsh Jyoti who had invited him to Kalimpong, and he was staying as the guest of the family at the house they had recently bought two or three miles up the road from Nepali Building. Before long he came to see me. Looking out of my window one afternoon I saw a tall, burly figure plodding up the last bend of the acclivity below and at once recognized him. He did not come alone. A short distance behind him came a slouching, dark-skinned Indian youth, and some way behind *him*, struggling up the steep slope, a stout figure in brilliant orange robes holding a big black umbrella.

Our first meeting must have been a success. At any rate, a few days later Swale Ryan came to see me again, this time accompanied only by the dark-skinned youth, who answered to the name of Damodaran. Soon he was dropping in at the vihara for a cup of tea and a chat nearly every afternoon, Damodaran always trailing along behind. Once or twice, at his invitation, I spent the day with him at his own quarters at the Jyoti brothers' house, where he had been assigned a first floor room at the far end of a broad gallery overlooking the garden. In this gallery we sat and talked, inhaling the fragrance of the jasmine that came floating up from below. Seeing as much of him as I did, I naturally got to know him quite well. My new friend was a man in his early forties, and due to an injury sustained during the war he walked with a slight limp. His face was square, pink, and freckled, with rather blunt features, and he had blue eyes and sandy hair. He wore – at least while he was in Kalimpong – a pair of khaki shorts and an open-necked shirt that, combined with stout shoes and full-length socks, made him look more like a retired scoutmaster than the former commanding officer. In manner he was hearty and hail-fellow-well-met, with a great deal of loud, almost aggressive joviality that was rather belied by the rigid set of his jaw and the hard look that sometimes came into his blue eyes. When that look was not there – and it was not there most of the time – the square, pink face wore an expression of cheerfulness and good humour. When he wished Swale could, indeed, be excellent company, being possessed of a ready laugh and a fund of anecdote that was not easily exhausted. Since he liked to talk, and I was happy to listen, I heard much of the story of his life. Though his manner suggested that he was speaking without reserve, I was nonetheless aware that there was a lot he did not tell me, and probably never would. He had evidently spent most of his life in India, much of it in the army. Indeed, it seemed that he had once commanded a regiment of Gurkhas. Through his family he had connections with South India, where a missionary aunt still worked to convert the heathen, as well as with Yorkshire – he was named Swale after a river in that county – and he also had business interests in Pakistan. Like the British soldier in Kipling's poem, however, he had heard the temple bells calling him back to Mandalay,[4] and after the war settled in Burma. In Burma he became interested in Buddhism. With two other Western Buddhists, an Englishman called Francis Story and an Australian called David Maurice, he engaged in Buddhist activities in different parts of the country. In particular, he helped run a Buddhist bookshop in the Shwe Dagon Pagoda. Unfortunately, something went wrong. – Burma was an independent country. – He made enemies. – Potshots were taken at him with a rifle, he did not know by whom. – In the end, realizing his life was in danger, he returned to India.

Back in India Swale established contact with the Maha Bodhi Society and spent some time at Sarnath, where we had first met. At Sarnath he had been ordained as an *anagārika*, or freelance, full-time worker for Buddhism observing the vow of celibacy. When I heard this I must have raised my eyebrows. He had not wanted to be ordained at all, Swale explained. He was quite content to remain an *upāsaka*, an ordinary lay devotee of the Dharma. But the monks of the Maha Bodhi Society had insisted. They had given him no peace until he agreed. At first they even wanted to make him a *bhikṣu*, or full monk – or at least a *śrāmaṇera* or novice. But a *bhikṣu* – even a *śrāmaṇera* – was the last thing he wanted to be. He was too fond of the fleshpots, he added, with a loud guffaw. In the end a compromise was reached. Colonel John Warren Swale Ryan would graciously allow the monks to ordain him as an *anagārika provided* he did not have to shave his head, or wear yellow robes, or in short live any differently from the way in which he had lived before. As an *anagārika*, therefore, he was ordained, being given the name of Sasana Ratana, 'Jewel of the Dispensation'. This name, as he pointed out, gave him the same initials as did the shortened form of his English name, which was the form he generally used. On hearing this bizarre account I thought of my own bitter experience at Sarnath the previous year, and wondered why the Maha Bodhi Society monks had been so eager to ordain Swale as a *bhikṣu* and so reluctant to ordain me even as a *śrāmaṇera*.

The monk under whose preceptorship Swale Ryan had been transformed into Sasana Ratana had come to Kalimpong with him and was likewise staying at the Jyoti brothers' house. He had accompanied Swale on his first visit to the vihara, and was the stout figure in brilliant orange robes whom I saw struggling up the slope behind Damodaran. Since his face was hidden then behind his big black umbrella, it was only when he entered my room and Swale introduced him to me as his guru that I recognized him. He was Bhikkhu Dhammajoti, one of the

Ceylonese monks who had refused my request for ordination. Indeed, it was he who was most anxious to assure himself of my strict Buddhist orthodoxy. Now that I was a *śrāmaṇera*, he seemed to be less bothered by this. Perhaps he thought that it could be taken for granted. Whatever the reason was, he responded cordially to my salutation, and I saw that he was a much less formidable character than I had imagined. Though scholarly, he was in fact a bit of a buffoon. Swale certainly did not take him very seriously. I soon noticed that though he had introduced him as his guru, he treated him with cheerful disrespect, and took every opportunity of poking fun at his foibles. 'Mind that schoolgirl complexion!' he would exclaim, as Dhammajoti put up his big black umbrella, which he did whenever there was the slightest risk of his face catching the sun. The point of the joke was that Dhammajoti's complexion was as black as the umbrella itself, and could hardly have been rendered blacker by any amount of exposure to the elements. Cheerful disrespect indeed seemed to be characteristic of Swale's dealings with the wearers of the yellow – or orange – robe. Some months earlier he had been a member of the Maha Bodhi Society delegation that had gone to Assam with the Sacred Relics of the Buddha's two chief disciples, Śāriputra and Maudgalyāyana. These relics – minute pieces of bone – had recently been returned to India by the Victoria and Albert Museum, and were being given enthusiastic receptions all over the country. One of the other members of the delegation was a small, self-important Ceylonese monk who was in charge of the Society's centre in Madras. When the time came for the Sacred Relics to be taken in procession from Government House through the streets of the state capital, this monk calmly seated himself in the Governor's car instead of in the car provided for the delegation. In vain the aides pleaded with him to move before His Excellency arrived. The monk sat there with his nose in the air, and took no notice. In the end Swale was called. Striding to the car he pulled open the door, thrust his head inside, and growled, 'You bloody fool! *Get out!!*' When he told me this story Swale laughed uproariously. He was as aware as I was that in Ceylon, as in all Theravāda countries, members of the monastic order were accustomed to being treated with the utmost deference, and it amused him to think of the self-important little monk crawling out of the Governor's car. Much as cheerful disrespect may have characterized his dealings with wearers of the yellow robe – myself he usually referred to as the Canary

– Swale was certainly not lacking in reverence for the Buddha. On one of my visits to his quarters in the Jyoti brothers' house he showed me the miniature shrine he had set up in his room and assured me that he and Damodaran offered flowers, incense, and lighted candles there every day. 'Don't we, Damodaran?' he added, turning to his young cook bearer for confirmation.

When he was not visiting me Swale was usually visiting somebody else. Despite his limp, which sometimes gave him trouble, he got around quite a lot in Kalimpong, always with Damodaran trailing along behind. On the days when he dropped in for a cup of tea he would tell me about the other visits he had made. Sometimes, though not very often, he brought people to see me. In this way I not only learned something of what was going on in Kalimpong but also became acquainted with several of its best known inhabitants, whether permanent residents or seasonal visitors. With his extrovert temperament, and gregarious habits, Swale was ideally suited to act as the intermediary between the world in which I lived at the Dharmodaya Vihara – a world of study, meditation, teaching, and the daily almsround – and the more brilliant world in which lived not, indeed, the rest of Kalimpong, but that part of it which was regarded as being the social élite and which included members of the Bhutanese and Sikkimese ruling families, Tibetan aristocrats, and Indian Government officers, as well as a sprinkling of European and American research scholars, explorers, and journalists. By this time I was becoming quite well known in the cosmopolitan little town. At least, I was becoming a well-known sight in the bazaar as, begging-bowl in hand, I went out each day on my almsround. It was therefore only natural that some of the people Swale visited should question him about me. Though I did not know it I had been the subject of a certain amount of curiosity – not to say gossip – ever since my arrival in Kalimpong. Some people were deeply impressed by the fact that, as it seemed, I took Buddhism seriously, and tried to practise it instead of just reading about it. Others thought I was simply being eccentric. When they asked Swale what the real explanation was, and what I was really like, he would laugh and offer to take them to the vihara so that they could find out for themselves.

Not many people took advantage of the offer. Most preferred to talk about me without knowing me. One of those who did take advantage of it, and who came to see me not once but several times, was Princess Pema Tsedeun, the eldest daughter of the Maharaja of Sikkim. In Sarnath she had been wearing a European-style frock. When she appeared at the Dharmodaya Vihara it was in the full glory of Tibetan traditional costume at its richest and most elegant. It was as if a beautiful and exotic butterfly had suddenly fluttered across my path. She possessed four qualities which are hardly ever found in one woman: beauty, charm, intelligence, and vitality. She possessed all of them to a higher degree than they often have when present separately. Moreover, all four qualities found expression in even her smallest actions – whether it was the quizzical way she looked up at one from under her long lashes, or slowly exhaled the smoke of a cigarette, or murmured a few words in her low, clear, musical voice. As if these things were not enough, they were perfectly set off by the splendid costume she wore, and by the unshakeable self-confidence that came from her consciousness that royal blood flowed in her veins. The total effect was subtly devastating. On her second or third visit she asked me, in the most delicate and respectful manner, if I would like to go with her to look at a set of Tibetan *thangkas* or painted scrolls that had been brought to Kalimpong from Lhasa and which, she thought, she might be interested in 'ransoming'. Off, then, we went together, she in her ankle length gown of Chinese silk brocade, with the magnificent 'rainbow apron' (as I mentally christened it) above, I in my yellow cotton robes. We did not have far to walk. The *thangkas* were on display in one of the annexes of the Himalayan Hotel, immediately above the vihara. With the jewel-like beauty of their colours and their fine detail they were indeed exquisite. I had never seen anything like them. Even Princess Pema Tsedeun, though she must have seen a great many *thangkas*, and seemed to know a lot about them, was clearly impressed by what she saw and was – I thought – toying with the idea of 'ransoming' them. What sort of 'ransom' was the fortunate proprietor of the *thangkas* hoping for, she enquired, murmuringly. Rubbing his hands together obsequiously, old Mr Macdonald, the father of the woman who ran the hotel, told her. This seemed to set her thinking, and a discussion ensued. Since this was carried on in Tibetan (despite his name the yellow, wizened old man looked more like a Lepcha than a Scot) I could not understand what was being said. After a few minutes, however, I noticed an abrupt change in the Princess's manner. From being gracious it became quite cold, almost distant, while her delicate eyebrows contracted slightly, as though in anger. Shortly afterwards we left. On our way back to the vihara she told me that, in response to her enquiries, the old man had explained that the *thangkas* were looted from Reting Monastery when it was sacked three years earlier, and were the personal property of Reting Rimpoche, the former Regent of Tibet. Out of respect for the memory of the Rimpoche, who had been murdered while in prison, no Tibetan – or Sikkimese – Buddhist could possibly think of touching them. As I was to learn later on, 'Daddy' Macdonald was far from having any such scruples.

Though I met some people through Swale, others I met independently, either because they came to see me or because I took the initiative and went to see them. Dhanman Moktan was one of these. He lived at Tirpai, a small bazaar about two miles up the road from the Church of Scotland Mission, on the way to Dailo. He came to see me soon after Kashyapji's departure, and before long invited me to lunch. In fact, in the course of the next few months he invited me a number of times. By occupation he was a dealer in food grains, and lived with his wife and teenage sons and daughters in the rooms above their open-fronted shop. In appearance he was slightly stocky, with a round, apple-cheeked face that was invariably wreathed in smiles. His eyes, though, were far from smiling. He was, in fact, a man of distinctly angry temperament. The main object of his anger – not to say his virulent hatred – was the Newars, particularly the Jyoti family and firm. He was himself a Tamang Buddhist. The Tamangs were one of the tribal peoples of Nepal, and they were said to be of Tibetan stock. In former times they could boast a language of their own, but few traces of this now survived, and almost without exception they spoke the dominant Nepali tongue. Like the Gurungs, Magars, Rais, and Limbus, they were found all over the Darjeeling District of West Bengal (of which the Kalimpong subdivision was a part), as well as in Sikkim, Assam, and Bhutan, having migrated there from Nepal at the turn of the century. By religion they were staunch followers of the Nyingma school of Tibetan Buddhism, though in the absence of contact with their spiritual roots in Tibet faith had become divorced from understanding to an alarming degree. English-educated Tamangs were, in fact, alienated from the ethnic cult into which it had degenerated, and spoke disparagingly of 'Lamaism' as a corruption of Buddhism. A small minority tended to favour a rationalistic Buddhism of the modern Sinhalese type. Others were more inclined to think in terms of reform and revival and, indeed, of a Buddhist movement that would unite all Nepali-speaking followers of the Dharma. Dhanman Moktan himself, in his younger days, had started, or helped to start, a Himalayan Buddhist Association which had, it seemed, been active in the district for a while.

It was partly in order to discuss the possibility of reviving this organization that he invited me to lunch so often. On each occasion, however, he soon turned from expatiating on the need for a revival of Buddhist activities in the area to explaining why such a revival had not, as yet, taken place. It was entirely the fault of the Newars, i.e. the Buddhist Newars. Besides being the meanest, they were the most selfish, narrow-minded, exclusive, sectarian, uncooperative set of people that it was possible to meet, and of all Newars the Jyoti brothers – and their father – were the worst. The family had come up in the world only yesterday. During the war old Bhajuratna could still be seen trudging the bazaar with his *tokri* on his back, looking for work. Since he had a reputation for honesty, Tibetans going on pilgrimage to Bodh Gaya got into the habit of depositing their spare cash with him till their return. While they were away he traded with this money on his own account. Now he and his sons were rolling in wealth. They had given the biggest donation towards the purchase of the Dharmodaya Vihara. *That* was why the other Newar merchants refused to have anything to do with the place, as I must have noticed. They regarded it as the personal property of the Jyoti brothers! In any case, the place was not really a Buddhist vihara at all. It was no more than a social centre for the Newars. Only Newars were welcome there. The Dharmodaya Sabha itself was an exclusively Newar organization. It had no interest in propagating the Dharma. All it wanted to do was to propagate the Newari language. The previous year, however, the Newars had been taught a good lesson. They had brought out, at the Jyoti brothers' expense, a book of useful sentences in Newari, English, and Tibetan. One of the sentences read, 'The rich Newari merchant gives money to the poor Tibetan beggar.' This had given great offence to the Tibetans. Indeed, it was regarded as a serious affront to the entire Tibetan community, which had thus been represented as a race of paupers. For weeks the bazaar was in an uproar. Tibetan merchants threatened to stop doing business with the Jyoti brothers, which probably would have ruined them. At the same time they were sneeringly advised not to forget the origins of their wealth.

The Tibetans had made them; the Tibetans could break them. In the end the Newars had been forced to withdraw the book from circulation. The Jyoti brothers made amends by giving a feast to the Tibetan community and presenting everyone with white ceremonial scarves. But though the Newars had been taught a lesson it was doubtful if they had benefited much from it. They were as arrogant as ever. I was wasting my time staying at the Dharmodaya Vihara. It would be much better if I stayed in Tirpai – or in Darjeeling. There was plenty of Buddhist work to be done all over the district. The Newars were only a hindrance....

When Dhanman Moktan went on in this way there was no stopping him. Having heard the same tirade two or three times I therefore came to the conclusion that he was interested not so much in the possibility of reviving the Himalayan Buddhist Association as in getting an opportunity of venting his hatred of the Newars. Nonetheless I could sense that he felt a genuine kindliness towards me and continued to accept his invitations. On one occasion he showed me the tiny, one-roomed wooden vihara that was situated only a few doors up the road from his own shop. Great Wisdom had once stayed there for a few months. Not only had he stayed there, he had covered the wall with crudely realistic paintings of corpses in various stages of decomposition, as well as of living bodies disfigured by enormous suppurating sores. Alas, they had not done him much good! Dhanman Moktan also took me to see the Tharpa Choling or 'Dharma-Island of Liberation' Gompa, the biggest Tibetan Buddhist monastery in Kalimpong. It was situated on a small spur a few dozen yards below the bazaar, and was built round the three sides of a grassy square. The fourth side of the square was open, and commanded, over the tops of the adjacent orange trees, a fine view of the brilliant white scattering of buildings that was the Kalimpong bazaar, as well as of the dark blue mass of Rinkingpong beyond, at the opposite end of the ridge. Passing through the main gate, which was at the rear of the premises, one emerged into the square with the *lhakhang* or temple on one's right, at the base of the square, and the abbot's quarters on one's left. Opposite the abbot's quarters, on the third side of the square, stood a row of hutments. It was very quiet in the square. There seemed to be nobody about. After exploring the gloomy interior of the temple, where wide-eyed images, packed close together, looked at us from behind panes of glass, we emerged into the sunlight and circumambulated the building, spinning as we did so the heavy *mani*-cylinders suspended along the wall. Though my Newar-hating friend never became closely associated with my work, we remained in fairly regular contact. Through him I became acquainted with Ari Bahadur Gurung, the local MP, who was a resident of Tirpai; through him, also, I became known down in the Dooars, where he had many friends and relations, and many business contacts, and later on two of his sons became my pupils.

Prominent among the more interesting people I met independently of Swale – though I met them not because they came to see me but because I took the initiative and went to see them – were Dr George Roerich, the distinguished Tibetologist, and the Hon. Mary Scott, a deaconess of the Church of Scotland who had been given an honorary degree in divinity by a Scottish university for her work among the Lepchas of Sikkim. The former lived in what was known as the Development Area, an area that corresponded to practically the whole of the southern half of the ridge, from the bazaar to Rinkingpong, and within which the Municipality permitted only pukka, or properly constructed, private dwellings to be erected. The latter lived on the other side of the main road into Kalimpong, almost immediately below the Dharmodaya Vihara. After a long walk in the hot sun, along well maintained roads that ran round the hillside in a complex system of loops, I reached Crookety, the house where Dr Roerich lived, more by accident than by design. Like several of its neighbours, the substantial, tree-girt house was built in what might be described as the Himalayan mock Tudor style of architecture. For some time after I rang the bell there was no answer. As at the Tharpa Choling Gompa, there seemed to be no one about. At length the door was opened a few inches by a youngish European woman who understood very little English. I gave my name, and she closed the door. After a few minutes the door opened again, I was admitted, and silently shown into a sitting room comfortably furnished in European style. When a few more minutes had passed, a plump, ruddy-faced man in riding boots and breeches strode into the room and greeted me with a great appearance of cordiality, though at the same time with marked formality. I noticed the frozen blue eyes, the rather fixed smile, the small red mouth, and the little waxen-pointed orange beard. It was George Roerich. He was, as I knew, the elder son of Nicholas Roerich, the Russian artist and explorer, and as a young man had travelled widely with his father in Tibet and Mongolia. When

I had introduced myself, and explained how I came to be in Kalimpong (he had already heard about me), we talked for an hour or more about the progress of Buddhist studies, especially Tibetan Buddhist studies, and about the condition of Buddhism in Kalimpong. Throughout the conversation I was conscious of a tremendous downward pressure in the room. It was not a physical but a psychic pressure and it came from the room overhead.

The Hon. Mary Scott, variously known in Kalimpong as Lady Mary (she was the daughter of a Scottish peer), Dr Scott, and Auntie Mary, proved to be much easier of access. She lived in the front part of the Blind School, which she had founded and still ran, and was always ready to welcome anyone who wanted to look round. One had only to walk in, and she would come almost immediately, having heard the ping of the bell as the door opened and closed. At first the dumpy, grey-haired little woman with the sagging Queen Victoria jowls was startled to find a young Englishman in yellow robes standing on her sitting room carpet, but she recovered herself almost immediately and was soon talking away energetically. As I afterwards learned, nothing could stop Mary Scott talking – or prevent her dispensing hospitality. I must have some tea, *and* a slice of cake. (Luckily I had called in the morning, before twelve o'clock!) She would put the kettle on. Would I like to see the Blind School first? Here it was. (We had passed to a courtyard at the back of the premises.) The boys were making wicker baskets. She had thirteen of them altogether, from all over the district. Would I like to hear them sing a hymn? (They sang a hymn in Nepali, Lady Mary vigorously beating time.) Did I know why they were blind? Congenital syphilis, *that* was the reason. The area was rife with it. There was so much immorality. The European tea planters were also to blame. Bastards everywhere – by local women, of course. Dr Graham was a kind-hearted man. He had rescued the poor, neglected, half-caste children and started the Kalimpong Homes. (This well-known institution occupied the hillside above the Tharpa Choling Gompa, just below Dailo.) But it was a great mistake. It only encouraged immorality. Girls who had been educated at the Homes went down to Calcutta, got pregnant – sometimes without being married – and then sent their children to the Homes to be brought up. The whole thing was self-perpetuating. She herself had nothing to do with it. For more than thirty years she had worked in Lachhen, in North Sikkim. When she arrived the Lepcha women didn't even know how to knit. I must have another cup of tea – *and* another slice of cake. (We were back in the sitting room.) The cake had been brought by Coocoola (i.e. Princess Pema Tsedeun). Did I know her? Coocoola wasn't her real name, of course. Nobody could pronounce her real name. Her Scottish nanny had called her Coocoola, and that was what everybody called her now. She had been a very nice child. The Sikkim family was a very nice family. During the last few years Coocoola had become rather wild. (Auntie Mary shook her grey head and Queen Victoria jowls disapprovingly over this.) Her younger sister Kula (i.e. Princess Pema Choki) was *much* more staid. I must have heard of the Maharani's goings on, but they were no concern of *hers*. *She* was concerned exclusively with the love of God. There was nothing like it. She experienced it all the time. Was I much of a reader? She herself was a great reader. She had just finished a wonderful book on St John's Gospel by the Archbishop of Canterbury. All about the love of God. I really must read it. She never lent books to Indians. They never returned them. But she could see that I was different. She was sure that I would return any book that she lent me.... Thus it was that I came away from my first visit to the Hon. Mary Scott with a book by William Temple and an invitation to call again whenever I liked.

By this time I had been in Kalimpong for about three months, Swale probably for as many weeks. Thanks to my daily almsround and his constant visiting we now had, between us, quite a number of contacts. Centred upon me at the Dharmodaya Vihara there was an informal network of English-knowing people who, for one reason or another, had some kind of interest in, or sympathy for, Buddhism, and who saw at least one of us on a fairly regular basis. Thus in less than two months from Kashyapji's departure I had reached the point where I could actually start working for the good of Buddhism as my teacher had directed. The new gate – the new gate of gold – was about to open before me. But just how was I to start working for the good of Buddhism? What specific steps must I take in order to go through the gate? Some kind of loose organizational framework was clearly essential. Swale was in any case inclined to think – perhaps too readily – in organizational terms. Out of the discussions that took place between him, Dhammajoti, and myself, the idea of starting a Young Men's Buddhist Association in Kalimpong eventually was born and hovered above our heads like a beautiful iridescent ball. The idea was not a new one. There was already a Young Men's Buddhist Association in Ceylon, and several of my articles had appeared in its English monthly journal *The Buddhist*. The more we talked about the idea, however, the more it took possession of our minds – at least, it took possession of my mind. I would bring the beautiful iridescent ball down to earth. I would embody it in an organization through which I would work for the good of Buddhism – work for the benefit of others – not only in Kalimpong but throughout the district, perhaps even beyond.

At the beginning of May, therefore, a meeting was convened at the Dharmodaya Vihara, the iridescent ball was invited to descend, and the Young Men's Buddhist Association, Kalimpong, came into existence. Either because I was so dazzled by the splendour of the ball itself that the process of its mundane embodiment made but little impression on me, or because my interest in things organizational was in any case minimal, the events of the day did not remain long in my mind. According to a report published two months later, 'On Sunday 6th May, 1950, the young men of Kalimpong assembled in the Dharmodaya Vihara under the chairmanship of Rev. Sangharakshita with the object of establishing a Young Men's Buddhist Association. After preliminary discussion, resolutions concerning the objects and activities of the Association were unanimously passed, and office-bearers elected. It was decided to open a recreation room for the use of members as soon as possible and to inaugurate a series of weekly public lectures and debates. At the end of the meeting about thirty young men enrolled themselves as members of the Association.'[5] The 'objects' adopted at the meeting were (1) to unite the young men of Kalimpong and (2) to propagate the teachings of Buddhism by means of social, educational, and religious activities. The office-bearers consisted of myself (President), Topsher Tshering (Vice-President), Nucche Bahadur (Secretary), Gyan Jyoti (Treasurer), Rudramani Pradhan (Publicity and Propaganda), and Anagārika Sasana Ratana (Manager). Topsher Tshering was a tall, thin young man of Tibetan origin who smiled nervously all the time but never said very much. After hovering uncertainly on the fringes of the organization for a year or more he slowly faded away. As in the case of the Cheshire Cat, the last part of him to go was his smile. Nucche Bahadur was a very different kind of person. He was a small, active Buddhist Newar whose intelligent, rather foxy face was deeply pitted by smallpox scars.

Though by birth a *vajrācārya* or 'Buddhist Brahmin' (the Newars of Nepal had accepted, or been forced to accept, the Hindu caste system) he was bitterly critical of the debased Vajrayāna of Nepal as well as of the narrowness and exclusiveness of his fellow Newars. For the months that he remained in Kalimpong he was of great assistance to me, and I was extremely sorry when he left.

The fact that our beautiful, iridescent ball had taken the form of a Young Men's Buddhist Association was an advantage in more ways than one. Since membership was limited to young men, which in practice usually meant school and college students, the Association could not be accused of setting itself up in rivalry to the existing Buddhist organizations, which were thus left free to regard it as a kind of junior counterpart of themselves. This was particularly important in the case of the Dharmodaya Sabha, as we were counting on being able to use the vihara for our activities. Moreover young men, especially English-educated young men, were less conscious of social differences than their elders, and less inclined to respect traditional observances that had outlived their usefulness. With a membership consisting exclusively of young men it should be possible to create an organization in which people from different ethnic and linguistic groups could work together to propagate the ideals of Buddhism in a way that would make them accessible to the modern world. The need for such an organization was demonstrated only a day or two before the Association was established, when the Newars celebrated Vaiśākha Pūrṇimā, the anniversary of the Buddha's Birth, Enlightenment, and *parinirvāṇa*, in the way that had, apparently, become traditional among them. While the Newar women and girls trooped upstairs to the shrine-room with their offerings, the Newar men and boys spent the day sitting around the place playing cards, gambling, and smoking country cigarettes. In Nepal itself, I was told, they would be drinking too, but since the Dharmodaya Sabha was part of the Ceylon- and Burma-based 'reform' movement alcohol was not permitted on the vihara premises.

Though it was not possible to open a recreation room for a couple of months, the YMBA Sunday lectures and debates began the following week with a symposium on 'The Role of Modern Youth' at which the speakers were myself and Swale, followed by Kashyapji and an Indian Catholic priest, or ex-priest, called Anthony Elenjimittam. Kashyapji, accompanied by the ex-priest, had arrived only a few days earlier. He had come to see how Tilakdhari and I were getting on in Kalimpong and to let me know what his own plans were. After spending three weeks in the jungles of Bihar, at the ashram of a Hindu yogi friend, he had decided to devote the rest of his life to reviving the ancient Buddhist monastic university of Nālandā, the very extensive remains of which we had seen earlier in the year, before coming up to Kalimpong. For the time being he would be staying at Rajgir, at the Japanese Buddhist temple. A young Bihari whom he had just ordained as a *śrāmaṇera* was setting up a nature cure clinic there under his guidance. Father Anthony would also be helping. When it came to the point, however, Father Anthony found the prospect of returning to Rajgir and nature cure with Kashyapji less attractive than that of staying on in Kalimpong with me and the YMBA.

Despite this defection, Kashyapji did not return to Rajgir unaccompanied. With him went Tilakdhari. During the last few weeks it had become increasingly obvious that, whatever his interest in Buddhism, our pug-faced young friend was not really suited to the monastic life. For one thing, he found it extremely difficult to meditate – not that proficiency in meditation was any longer regarded, in some Buddhist circles, as a necessary accomplishment for a monk. At first he was unable or unwilling to tell me why he found meditation so difficult. At length, on my cross-examining him, it transpired that he was troubled by lustful thoughts relating to his old, worldly life in Bihar. Indeed, he broke down and confessed that, far from his being celibate, as he had given me to understand he was, he had led a life of extreme debauchery. He had regularly used his position as a Congress Party organizer, working at district level, to intimidate village girls into having sexual relations with him. He had even kept one girl as a mistress for several years, supporting her out of money misappropriated from Congress Party funds. Altogether it was a sordid story he had to tell – a story of factionalism, chicanery, and exploitation at the lowest level of political life. Like charity, the white Gandhi cap covered a multitude of sins. Yet his own sexual misdemeanours had not made Tilakdhari any more tolerant of those of other people. A Jain ascetic was suspected of having a sexual relationship with a young boy. One night he and his fellow organizers had crept up to the ascetic's hut and peered through the window. After watching what was going on inside for as long as they wanted they suddenly burst in through the door and beat up the ascetic.

From the relish with which Tilakdhari recounted the incident it was clear that for him it had been no more than an excuse for indulging in voyeurism, physical violence, and righteous indignation. I saw that beneath the affectionate surface personality he was not much more than a bundle of instincts and ambitions of the grossest kind. He was certainly not suited to the monastic life, as he himself now realized. Back then to the plains of his native Bihar with Kashyapji he went, though not without a few tears at parting from me, to take Father Anthony's place and help with the setting up of the nature cure clinic. Once more I was left on my own in Kalimpong, even though again I was not left entirely alone. But this time the situation was different. Newars or no Newars, my work for the good of Buddhism had begun. With the help of Swale and other friends I had taken my first steps through the new gate that had opened before me and I would not look back.

3
STEPPING STONES

In June the rainy season began. The grey clouds came rolling up from the plains, first of all infiltrating the valley of the Teesta in loose, detached masses, then moving in across the hills in a solid wall of rain that at times blotted out the entire landscape. For days on end Mount Kanchenjunga could not be seen. Instead, even when the sky cleared, there was only thick white cloud piled up against the horizon. Though the rain fell heavily enough at times, the rainy season was much less severe in the hills than in the plains. In between the downpours the sun was hot and bright, and the sky intensely blue, though the thick white cloud hardly ever moved – hardly ever moved aside to reveal the snows of Mount Kanchenjunga sparkling through the rain-washed air. It was my fourth year in India. Already I had learned to love the rainy season. I loved the heavy drumming sound of the rain on the roof. I loved the sense of green things thirstily drinking up the rain and growing as they did so. Above all, I loved the way in which the rain insulated one from the rest of the world, weaving around one a silver-grey cocoon of silence within which one could sit, hour after hour, and quietly muse.[6] No wonder the Buddha had advised his monks not to wander about during the rainy season but to remain in one place, whether in a mountain cave, a woodland shrine, or a shed at the bottom of somebody's garden![7] No wonder the rainy season had come to be regarded, in the course of centuries, as a time of spiritual retreat – a time of more intensive study of the scriptures and more intensive practice of meditation!

The Dharmodaya Vihara was an excellent place in which to spend the rainy season, but for me it had one disadvantage. Though I could get on with my study and meditation there easily enough, I still had to go out on my almsround each day, and I still had to go at a certain time. (Had I gone earlier, food would not have been ready, and had I gone later there might not have been any left.) Sometimes it was raining at this time, sometimes it was not. Once or twice it was raining so heavily that my thin cotton robes were saturated in a couple of minutes and I returned to the vihara soaked to the skin. Nucche Bahadur saw this and undertook to do something about it. From the time we first met he had been a regular visitor to the vihara, and especially after his election as secretary of the YMBA I came to rely on him in a number of ways. He was my main source of information about the religious practices of the Buddhist Newars. From him I learned that Newar boys were initiated into the cult of one or another of the more esoteric Tantric deities – usually without understanding what it was all about – and that they were supposed thereafter to perform the ritual worship of the deity every day. Some of the older Newars actually did this. The majority, like Nucche himself, gave up the practice after a few years, or even after a few months. Newar boys were also initiated into the Buddhist monastic order – by married *vajrācāryas*! Heads shaved, and clad in yellow robes, for three days they lived as monks, going for alms each day to the houses of relatives and friends (who fed them sumptuously, Nucche said) and taking no solid food after midday. At the end of the period they returned to their preceptor, confessed that they found the life of a monk much too hard to bear, and asked to be released from their vows. Newar girls underwent an even stranger ceremony. They were married to the fruit of a bel tree, a tree which in Hindu tradition is sacred to the god Shiva. This meant that no Newar woman ever became a widow, her true husband being always living. Nucche himself, though by birth a *vajrācārya*, had little sympathy for the practices he described, seeing in them only signs of educational backwardness and being convinced that they were destined to disappear with the spread of modern knowledge, as indeed they probably were. For him the very fact that he could be a *vajrācārya* while knowing nothing of the Vajrayāna proved beyond all doubt that there was something radically wrong with the traditional Buddhism of Nepal. In his view education, modern English education, was the only remedy, and he was hoping to set up an English boarding school for boys in Nepal. Meanwhile, he was a highly efficient secretary, and helped me in as many ways as he could. Having seen that it was not easy for me to go out on my daily almsround during the rainy season he went and collected enough money from the Buddhists of Kalimpong to support me for that period. Altogether he collected 140 rupees.

For the second time since my arrival in Kalimpong the solution of one problem only resulted in the creation of another. Nucche absolutely insisted on handing over the money he had collected to me personally, so that I would be free to spend it on whatever I wished, whenever I wished. This put me in a quandary. For two years or more I had not touched money. Not to touch gold or silver was, indeed, one of the ten *śrāmaṇera* precepts, and I wanted to go on observing it, even though, as I well knew, it was nowadays honoured much more in the breach than in the observance. Indeed, the fact that others did not observe the precept seemed all the more reason why I should observe it. However, Nucche's good deed had put him in a quandary too. In Kalimpong, as elsewhere in India, there were only too many people who went round collecting money for this or for that worthy cause and who then, on one pretext or another, pocketed most of it themselves. If Nucche was to take care of the 140 rupees, and spend from it on my account as necessary – which is what I wanted him to do – he might well be accused of doing this kind of thing. After all, he had made enemies among the Newars by his outspokenness, and he was also without regular work. In the end, with the greatest reluctance, I allowed Nucche to count out the dirty notes and dull coins into my hand. How strange it was to be handling money again! How strange even the simplest monetary transaction felt! Indeed, the whole business of going into a shop, asking for what one wanted, and then handing over in exchange certain bits of paper and metal, seemed extraordinarily clumsy, artificial, and unnatural, even slightly absurd, and it was several weeks before I became accustomed to it all.

Reluctant as I was to handle money again, the change from the economics of the begging-bowl to the economics of the market place was not without its advantages. It was not simply that I no longer had to go out on my almsround during the rainy season. Though Tilakdhari had returned to Bihar, my begging-bowl still had to go on supporting more than one person. Indeed, by the time Nucche Bahadur handed over to me the money he had collected its capacities were being stretched to the limit and I was beginning to wish I had been given one of those giant, well-lacquered Burmese bowls that were capable of holding enough food for half a dozen people. Besides Anthony Elenjimittam, I had two young English travellers staying with me at the vihara, and several other visitors would be turning up before long. Some of them were able to support themselves. Others turned up penniless, or very nearly so, and had to be provided for. In the circumstances it was more convenient to be able to buy provisions than to have to distribute the contents of my begging-bowl. Anthony Elenjimittam stayed with me for only two or three weeks. His original intention was to help me organize the YMBA, but he spent most of his time in his room banging out articles on his portable typewriter. I had read two books by him a couple of years before. One was on Rabindranath Tagore, the greatest figure in modern Bengali – perhaps in modern Indian – literature, while the other was on 'Netaji' Subhas Chandra Bose, the founder of the so-called Indian National Army. Both books were written in a sort of rhythmic prose, and were couched in the most pompous and grandiloquent style imaginable. The style was indeed the man! Some months later I took Anthony Elenjimittam as the model for a pen portrait of the sort of person who mistakes concepts for realities, and who is unable to distinguish between the state of emotional intoxication with the *idea* of helping others and actually *feeling* love for them and helping them.

> Not long ago a gentleman was introduced to us who professed, with almost every other breath he drew, that his sole mission in life was to 'serve Humanity'. He spoke several languages fluently, had read widely in both Eastern and Western philosophy and religion, was a not unpractised journalist, and above all else was quite sincere in his professions.... Grandiose schemes for the regeneration of humanity, and for the amelioration of the lot of the Indian masses, together with the wildest generalizations and most impractically altruistic sentiments imaginable,
>
>   Full of sound and fury, signifying nothing,[8]
>
> flowed from his lips in an unending stream. He did his best to appear overwhelmed with work, and flew from one organization to another as a startled bird flies from tree to tree. After meeting him

twice or thrice, and having on each occasion fruitlessly endeavoured to elicit from him an unambiguous statement of what he truly believed and what he really was trying to accomplish, and having always found that it was his habit, when thus interrogated, to beat a hasty retreat behind a cloud of the most vapid generalities possible – much as a lamp-scared squid disappears into the darkness of its own effluvia – we concluded that he had completely lost the earth-touch of what are conventionally termed realities, and was floundering his bewildered way through a cloud-cuckoo-land of his own imagination, a realm of meaningless abstractions wherein he had by that time become completely lost. We were therefore hardly astonished when we found that none of his schemes had ever borne fruit, and that, despite the loftiness of his ideal of universal service, he had never succeeded in being of practical use to a single one of his fellow men in even the most ordinary and insignificant manner. Perpetually excited, invariably in a hurry, vapouring advice with the smuggest assumption of spiritual authority, he thrust upon our notice a striking illustration of the fate that can befall the sincerest spiritual aspirant, even, who forgets that he has not to love and serve some unreal abstraction, whether "Humanity" or any other conceptual symbol of the mind's own creation, but the concrete, individual men and women whom we see living and working and suffering round us every day of our lives.[9]

This was perhaps rather strong, at least as regards Anthony Elenjimittam. He must have irritated me considerably. Perhaps I did not make sufficient allowance for the fact that as an ex-Roman Catholic, and an ex-priest (he would never say what his ecclesiastical status actually was) he was in a state of chronic mental and emotional confusion. Like others in the same position, he was in fact floundering his way through religious universalism and romantic nationalism towards some kind of social work.

The two young English travellers were Leslie Turner and Donald Hofford. Though knowing nothing of the languages of most of the countries through which they passed, they had made the journey from London to Gangtok without mishap, travelling by road, by rail, and on foot, and meeting everywhere with kindness and hospitality, even in places which they had been warned by the authorities were unfriendly. In Gangtok they had pitched their tent on the palace lawn. Princess

Pema Tsedeun, who was then in Sikkim, gave them a note to me, and that was how they came to be staying with me at the Dharmodaya Vihara. Leslie Turner was blond, burly, and placid, Donald Hofford thin, dark, and intense. Neither of them was interested in Buddhism, though towards the end of their journey through Afghanistan they had taken the trouble of going to see the enormous rock Buddhas of Bamian, the largest of which was over 150 feet high.[10] In the course of a talk given as part of our regular Sunday lecture series Donald Hofford gave a vivid description of the valley of Bamian, and of the colossal Buddhas standing sentinel at the bottom of the cliff. Like Anthony Elenjimittam the two travellers did not stay at the vihara long. This was just as well. Probably because they had been in each other's company day and night for more than three months there was quite a lot of tension between them, and this sometimes resulted in vicious squabbles.

Major Joseph E. Cann, or Upāsaka Joseph E. Cann as he preferred to be styled, was not only interested in Buddhism but even more intense than Donald Hofford. Swale had met him the previous year in Lucknow, where he had settled after the war and where he had become the President of the local branch of the Bengal Buddhist Association. Thinking that, as the YMBA expanded, we would need more full-time workers, my organizationally-minded friend had suggested that he should invite him up to Kalimpong to join us, and to this I readily agreed. Soon afterwards the *upāsaka* arrived, and was given a room at the vihara. Since he was drawing an army pension, as Swale also was, his presence did not impose any additional strain on my slender resources. On the contrary, from the very first he contributed generously – even lavishly – to the expenses of our little establishment. Though neither of us then knew it – indeed, it was not even possible for us to think in such terms – he was to stay in Kalimpong for very much longer than Swale, and even for longer than me. Throughout the whole of his stay, however, he would never admit to any other age than the one he put down on his YMBA membership form on his arrival: 'Over fifty'. In appearance Joe, as he liked to be called, was of medium height and build, with hair rather longer than Swale's and more silver than brown. His most extraordinary feature were his eyes, which had a haunted look, and stared out from a white, haggard face with alarming intensity. When speaking he constantly crossed and uncrossed his legs, like a schoolgirl who wants to go to the toilet but is afraid to ask, while from time to time he let out a high-pitched nervous cackle that ended, more often than not, in a kind of screech. Nervousness was indeed Joe's outstanding characteristic, and I was not surprised to find that, as his nicotine-stained fingers indicated, he was an inveterate chain-smoker. The clothes he wore were of American make, obviously quite expensive, and both rather too big for him and rather too young (the reason for this I learned later), and when he went out he either wore a light blue homburg hat or carried a multi-coloured golf umbrella.

Despite his almost cockney accent, Joe was in fact in many ways more American than English. Part of his early life had indeed been spent in Canada, though he gave no details and was altogether more reluctant to talk about his family and professional background than Swale, apparently, was to talk about his. About his immediate background he was more communicative. In Lucknow he lodged with an Anglo-Indian (i.e. Eurasian) Christian family who refused to take his Buddhism seriously and were always trying to persuade him to accompany them to church. He himself took his Buddhism very seriously indeed, up to a point, though I never succeeded in learning from him how or on what grounds he had become a Buddhist. There were two Buddhist viharas in Lucknow, one belonging to the local branch of the Bengal Buddhist Association, the other to the Maha Bodhi Society – though in neither case was the legal position really so straightforward as these words suggest. Joe was more closely associated with the Bodhisattva Vihara, as the Bengali vihara was called. Formerly there had been much conflict between the two viharas, but thanks to Joe's efforts peace had been restored and they now worked together harmoniously for the advancement of Buddhism in Lucknow. The founder and presiding genius of the Buddhist Temple, as the Maha Bodhi Society's vihara was called, was a redoubtable ex-Brahmin monk of Bengali origin named Bodhananda Maha Sthavira, about whom I had already heard from Kashyapji. Bodhananda's policy was to make Theravāda Buddhism acceptable to the non-Buddhist Indian layman by providing him with a complete set of *saṃskāras* or domestic rituals on the orthodox Hindu model, with verses from the Pāli scriptures instead of Sanskrit Vedic mantras, and Buddhist monks taking the place of Hindu Brahmins. There were – as I saw in the thick Hindi book he had compiled – rituals for birth, rituals for taking one's first rice, rituals for piercing the ears (for earrings), rituals for commencing one's studies, rituals for marriage, and rituals for death. There were rituals for every conceivable stage and activity of human existence. It was also the old monk's policy, Kashyapji had explained, to encourage Sinhalese Buddhist men living and working in Lucknow to marry local girls, instead of importing their brides from Ceylon. 'What is there so wonderful about the Sinhalese girls?' he would ask. 'Are their private parts made of *gold*? Marry Indian girls and produce some good Indian *upāsakas* who will look after me in my old age!' Joe had an amusing story of his own to tell about Bodhananda Maha Sthavira. On calling at the Buddhist Temple one morning he had found the old man sitting beneath an enormous full length portrait of himself, evidently a recent acquisition. The head of the portrait was surrounded by a halo. Slowly Joe looked from Bodhananda to the portrait, then from the portrait back to Bodhananda, and at length said, 'I don't see any halo.'

'My devotees put it in,' explained the old monk, not without irritation.

'You vain old man,' Joe screeched indignantly, 'you had it put in yourself!'

Perhaps there really was a halo round the old monk's head, for he died not long afterwards, full of years and honours, and was cremated by his devotees with all due ceremony.

Besides restoring peace between the two viharas, Joe had also restored peace within the Bodhisattva Vihara itself, where two factions of Bengali Buddhists were fighting for control of the place. He had been able to restore peace there, however, only at a price, the price being that the 'Major Saheb' himself should assume the presidency of the local branch of the Bengal Buddhist Association, to which the vihara belonged, and in this way preserve the balance between the two factions and prevent either of them from dominating the vihara's affairs. So far the arrangement had worked quite well, though Joe soon found that the President was also expected to be the principal donor. Most of the two or three dozen members of the Association were poorly paid cooks and bearers working either for high-ranking government officers or in big European-style hotels. As the pampered lodger in an Anglo-Indian Christian family and the respected leader of the local Bengali Buddhist community Joe was in Lucknow a comparatively big fish in a comparatively small pond. In Kalimpong the pond was a bigger pond, and the fish therefore a proportionately smaller fish, and it was this fact that was partly responsible for Joe's extreme nervousness – though it was easy to see that he would be nervous in almost any situation. One tangible result of his association with the Bengali Buddhists was that he was well drilled in orthodox Theravāda manners and customs, particularly in those relating to the treatment of monks, and this certainly made it less difficult for him to adapt to life at the Dharmodaya Vihara than might otherwise have been the case. Despite the sharpness of his reaction to Bodhananda's halo, Joe was in fact most punctilious in paying his respects to the yellow robe, and always did so with full traditional ceremony. Though his behaviour later underwent a change, this was only after he had been in Kalimpong for some length of time and had seen, perhaps, how 'ordinary' monks (i.e. monks who were not incarnate lamas) were treated by Tibetan Buddhists, especially by members of the aristocracy. Meanwhile, the question was: what was he to do in Kalimpong? Swale had suggested, in his letter, that Joe might help with administrative work, but of this kind of work there was as yet very little to be done. I myself thought he might help by doing some lecturing and perhaps collaborate on the various literary projects we had in mind, on one of which, in fact, I was already working. Joe had not been long in Kalimpong, however, before it became obvious that he would not be of much use in either of these fields. The preparation of a short talk threw him into agonies of anxiety, while his spelling and grammar were distinctly shaky: he had no idea how to construct a sentence. However much he might be able to help with the work of the YMBA it was clearly not going to be through giving lectures and collaborating on literary projects. Something else would have to be found for him to do.

The literary project on which I was already working was that of a monthly magazine of Himalayan religion, culture, and education. It would not be just another scholarly publication but a journal of living Buddhism. It would be imbued with the all-embracing spirit of the Mahāyāna and would include articles on the Buddhist traditions of Tibet, of Sikkim, of Bhutan, and of Nepal. There would be poetry and short stories, extracts from the great Mahāyāna *sūtras*, and news of YMBA activities. We would send it out not only all over the district, but all over India, all over the world. Thus above the beautiful iridescent ball that was the idea of the YMBA there hovered a second ball, in some ways even more beautiful and iridescent than the first – a ball that would send out even more brilliant flashes and be seen even farther afield. This second ball too was invited to descend, and in the month of July, either shortly before or shortly after Joe's arrival, the monthly magazine *Stepping Stones* came into existence. (Friends subsequently persuaded me that 'Stepping-Stones' was the more correct form so from the third issue onwards the name was hyphenated.) In format the magazine was a twenty page octavo with cream-coloured wrappers printed in red ink. On the front cover was a Tibetan block print of the Buddha delivering his first discourse to the five ascetics in the deer park at Sarnath, near Benares, and below this the Contents. The principal contents were two articles and a short story. Perhaps predictably, the first article was by Dr Roerich, and perhaps equally predictably it was on the celebrated mantra *oṃ maṇi padme hūṃ*. Since my first meeting with Dr Roerich I had seen him several times and he had not only given a Sunday afternoon lecture on 'The Introduction of Buddhism into Tibet' but had agreed to be one of the office-bearers of the YMBA, with the title of Adviser – though on the clear understanding that he would not be expected to do any organizational work. Each time I saw him he was wearing riding boots and breeches, and whenever I visited him at Crookety I was conscious of the same tremendous downward pressure coming from the room overhead as on my first visit.

The first of these mysteries was cleared up more quickly than the second. In the course of his travels in Tibet and Mongolia Roerich's father, Nicholas Roerich, had been told of ancient prophecies relating to the coming of Maitreya, the future Buddha. These prophecies had impressed him deeply, and he had come to believe that the coming of Maitreya was imminent and that it would be preceded by certain events of world-shaking significance in which he and his family would play an important role. George Roerich, it seemed, shared this belief. The most important of the events preceding Maitreya's advent was the appearance of the King of Shambhala. This mysterious personage would come riding forth from his hidden kingdom in the heart of Central Asia accompanied by a host of warriors on horseback and would conquer the whole earth. Those who wanted to help prepare the way for the coming of Maitreya must be ready to ride with the King of Shambhala and his men. He might appear at any minute. They must be prepared – prepared to mount and ride. They must be always booted and spurred. Though I never discussed his father's beliefs with Dr Roerich, and had no idea how literally the distinguished Tibetologist took these prophecies,

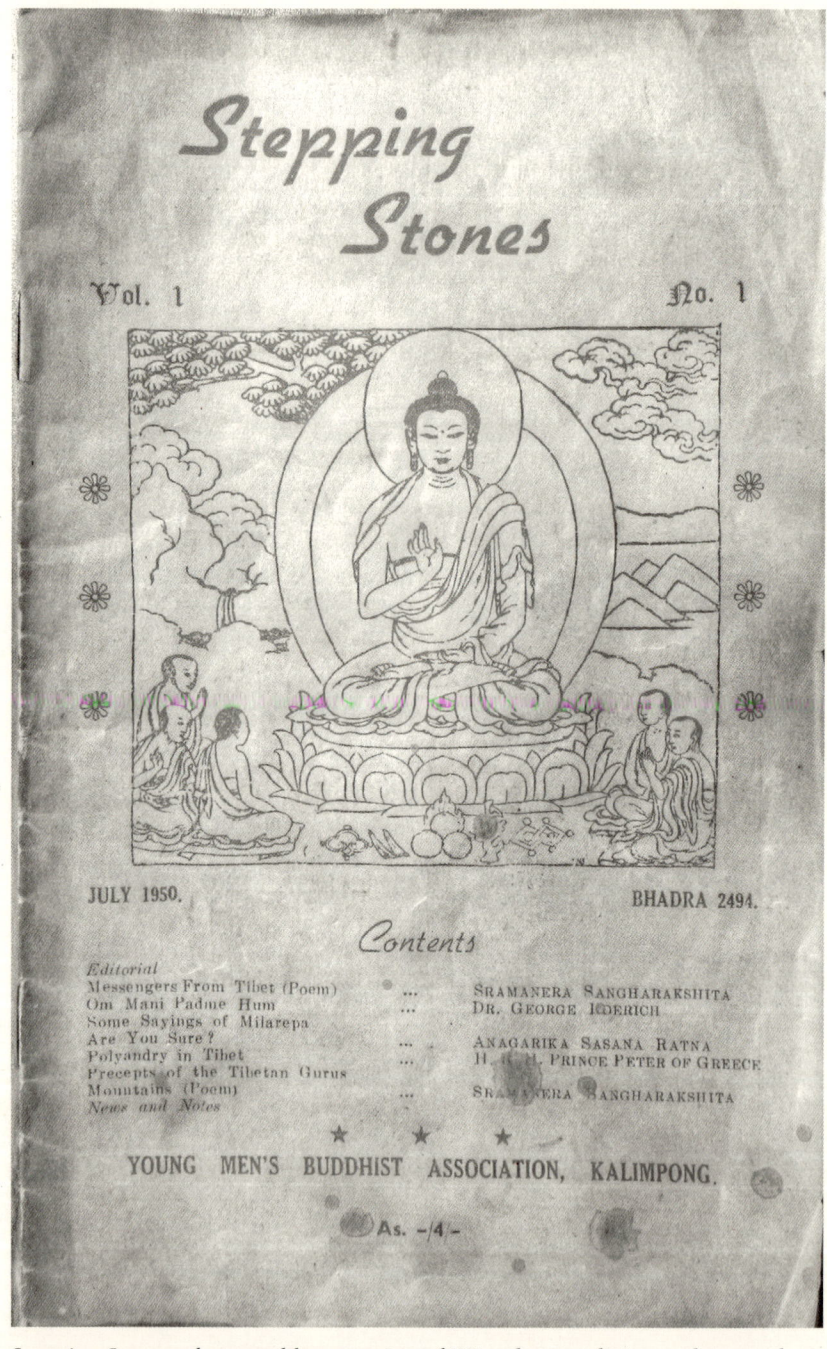

Stepping Stones, *the monthly magazine of 'Himalayan religion, culture and education', first appeared in July 1950*

or to what extent his father had enlarged upon them, there was no doubt that Nicholas Roerich had announced the coming of Maitreya in numerous articles and poems, and had also made it the subject of some remarkable paintings. There was no doubt, either, that George Roerich was always booted, even if not spurred. Whether or not this meant that he was actually waiting to ride with the King of Shambhala, he passed his time quietly enough, working on his translation of *The Blue Annals*[11] and acting as adviser to the YMBA.

The second of our two main articles was by Prince Peter of Greece and dealt with 'Polyandry in Tibet'. This was appropriate, in a way, as Prince Peter lived practically next door to Roerich, in an even bigger example of the Himalayan mock Tudor style of architecture, and had also given a Sunday afternoon lecture for us, on 'Western Tibet'. He was, in fact, a well-known anthropologist, and specialized in the study of polyandrous peoples. A tall, well-built man in his early forties, already beginning to go bald, he mixed easily with all sections of Kalimpong society, from the coolies and the beggars to the aristocracy, and was well liked on account of his unassuming, friendly behaviour. The short story that came in between the two main articles was by Swale. Entitled 'Are You Sure?' it featured, perhaps rather unfortunately, a haunted Tibetan *gompa* and a talking figure of the Buddha. Joe subsequently made much of the fact that the Buddha-figure, speaking to the hero of the story, who clearly represented Swale himself, said, 'You've been a long time in gaining the summit, and I have been waiting for you. Your path has been long and steep. Full of pitfalls at times, but you have made it at last.' According to Joe, Swale was nowhere near the summit, and whatever the pitfalls might have been was guilty of the grossest presumption in claiming that he had made it at last. Be that as it may, Swale was an inveterate writer of short stories, some of which, he averred, had been published in *Blackwood's*,[12] and on this occasion may have allowed his imagination to run away with him.

In addition to the articles by Dr Roerich and Prince Peter and the short story by Swale, our first *Stepping Stones* contained some 'Sayings of Milarepa', taken from *Tibet's Great Yogī Milarepa*, and some 'Precepts of the Gurus', taken from *Tibetan Yoga and Secret Doctrines*,[13] as well as two poems by me, an editorial (which came at the front of the magazine), and a 'news and notes' section (which came at the back). Like the haiku I had written earlier, and was still writing, each of the poems reflected images drawn from my immediate surroundings. One of them was quite short, consisting of only two verses, the other rather longer. The first poem was entitled simply 'Mountains', the second 'Messengers from Tibet'.[14] I must have thought quite highly of 'Messengers from Tibet', for a few years later I made it the title poem of a small collection of poems. At any rate, I composed it in a mood of unusually intense inspiration. It was about three o'clock in the afternoon. The sun was shining brightly. Swale and I were walking in the direction of Bong Busti, which lay on the other side of the ridge, below the Development Area. We were on our way to see Mr Shen, the headmaster of the Chinese School. Suddenly the first verse of the poem came into my mind, then the second, and then slowly, at much longer intervals, the rest of the verses. I hardly saw Mr Shen. I hardly heard what he and Swale were saying. I hardly knew what I was saying myself. As in a dream, I was conscious of verses struggling one by one into my mind and being helped to emerge undamaged from wherever it was they came. By the time we returned to the Dharmodaya Vihara the poem was complete and I wrote it down.

The editorial and the 'news and notes' section were both written by me. (I had constituted myself the editor of *Stepping Stones*, while Swale printed and published it on behalf of the YMBA.) In the editorial I struck what I hoped would be an unambiguously 'spiritual' note. I spoke of the Way, and of the Buddha's discovery of the three great stepping-stones of moral conduct, meditation, and transcendental wisdom, by leaping from one to another of which a man could safely cross over the raging torrent of desire, hatred, and delusion and reach the Further Shore of Enlightenment which is also Compassion and Perfect Bliss. Seeing that men were running more blindly than ever up and down the Hither Shore, our little magazine sought, I declared, to draw the attention of the modern world to those great stepping-stones which the Buddha had discovered.

But producing *Stepping Stones* involved much more than collecting articles and stories and writing editorials. There were printers to be found, galleys and page proofs to be read, papers to be selected, illustrations to be chosen, and advertisements to be procured – not to mention subscribers. In the first issue of *Stepping Stones* there were two full-page advertisements. Gyan Jyoti, who of course was Treasurer of the YMBA, took the inside back cover for Jyoti Brothers, while a young

Marwari well-wisher took the outside back cover for his own firm. When the advertisements appeared, I was dismayed to find that both of them featured musk, which was an animal product, and one of the three principal exports from Tibet to India, the other two being yak tails and wool. (Yak tails were used for making the fly-whisks waved in Hindu ritual worship.) The inside front cover was taken by a Lahore publishing concern in which Swale had some kind of interest – or rather, we gave them the space, the advertisement being one of the unpaid variety. Announced as 'Out Shortly' were *Smile Awhile!* a book of lyrics in lighter vein by 'Swale', and *The Introduction of Buddhism into Tibet* by Dr George Roerich. Neither of these publications ever appeared. The second of them of course comprised Dr Roerich's lecture of the previous month, and the question of its publication had already given me some trouble. Indeed, it was responsible for the most unpleasant experience I had yet had in Kalimpong.

Among those present at the lecture had been Suresh Chandra Jain, a tall, portly Bihari in his late thirties. He was a well-known figure in Kalimpong, being the manager of the Himalayan Store, the town's principal emporium, a member of the Municipal Council, and editor of the *Himalayan Times*, a paper which described itself as 'the only English Weekly serving Tibet, Bhutan, Sikkim, The Darjeeling Hills, Tea-Gardens & Dooars.' He had apparently attended in his editorial capacity. After the meeting he approached Dr Roerich for permission to publish the lecture in his paper. Dr Roerich referred him to me, saying that he had already handed the manuscript over to me for publication by the YMBA. The wily Jain therefore approached me. Would I mind lending him the manuscript for a few days so that he could write a short summary of the lecture for the *Himalayan Times?* Nothing loth, I at once agreed. Distrusting the man's oily manner, however, I stipulated that the summary should be very short, and that it should not include any verbatim extracts from the lecture. Oh yes, it would be very short, purred Jain. A few days later I heard, quite by chance, that the whole lecture had been set up in type and was about to be printed. Thinking that there must have been a mistake, I went to see Suresh Babu. Oh no, he assured me, the lecture was *not* being printed. All that was being printed was a short summary, just as he had promised me. The following afternoon the brother of a YMBA member who worked as a compositor in the Himalayan Times Press came to the vihara with an urgent message. The lecture *had* been set up in type, and was being printed that very evening. If I wanted to do anything about it, I must act quickly. Once again I went to see Jain. This time he did not deny that the lecture had been set up in type. Dr Roerich had given him permission to publish it, he told me smoothly. I at once telephoned Roerich. No, said the Tibetologist in astonishment, he had not given any such permission. In fact, he had not spoken to Jain since the day of the meeting. Back then again to Jain I went, having first taken the precaution of asking Roerich to telephone Jain and confirm that he did *not* have his permission to publish the lecture. Once again Jain insisted that he *did* have Roerich's permission. Had Roerich not telephoned him, then? No, he had not. This meant another telephone call to Roerich. Yes, he *had* telephoned Jain, the Tibetologist told me, unable to understand what was going on. Not only that, Jain had assured him that the lecture had *not* been set up in type and that he would *not* be publishing it. There was now nothing for it but to have a showdown with Jain. He was not at the Himalayan Store. Eventually I tracked him down at a small office he had recently opened at the entrance to the high street and called him out into the road. 'You are nothing but a liar,' I told him, as his face purpled with indignation, 'nothing but a dirty, despicable liar,' and ignoring his splutterings I continued in this strain for several minutes. What made matters worse, from his point of view, was that four or five of his employees were standing in the doorway behind him, grinning broadly, and apparently by no means averse to hearing their lord and master being taken to task in this unceremonious fashion.

As I might have expected, Jain took his revenge. Before the rainy season was out he had spread round the bazaar the story that I was a Communist spy. Five or six years later he died tragically, in a motor car accident. Long before his death the breach between us had been more or less repaired, but the story of my being a Communist spy lingered on, and in the politically sensitive state of the border area this did me no good.

4
THE SPIRIT OF THE HILLS

Two months after the founding of the YMBA a small, three-roomed building to the rear of the Dharmodaya Vihara was opened for recreational purposes, and a month later evening tutorial classes were started. Until the opening of the Recreation Hut, as we called it, our activities consisted mainly of lectures and educational film shows. In addition to Prince Peter, during the first three or four months of our existence the main 'outside' speakers were Professor N. C. Ahuja, a lecturer in agriculture from the Benares Hindu University, and Kanwal Krishna, a well-known Punjabi artist. Ahuja had had a wide experience of different methods of agriculture and dairying in England, Denmark, and South America, and we had become acquainted the previous year while I was staying with Kashyapji on the Benares Hindu University campus. He was a tall, fair-skinned, rather anglicized Punjabi Hindu with scarlet cheeks and black eyebrows and a bright, strangely wooden smile. Beneath the smile lurked a diabolical temper, and it was because he was worried about this temper that he first came to see me. I advised him to meditate, and thereafter he visited me regularly. He had come up to Kalimpong partly for a holiday, partly in order to renew his acquaintance with me, and partly to cast a professional eye on the agronomics of the area. The subject of his lecture was 'The Development of the Himalayas'. He began by giving a geographical survey of the Himalayan region, comparing it with the Andes and the Alps, and then enthusiastically declared that with proper agricultural development there could be a dozen Switzerlands in the Himalayas. The audience was suitably impressed. Though I could see there was a need to improve the economic position of the Himalayan peoples, personally I was not sure if I wanted to see even one Switzerland in the Himalayas. On the contrary, I was perfectly content with them as they were.

Kanwal Krishna's lecture was on 'Art and Education'. Besides hearing him speak, I also saw the paintings he had brought with him to Kalimpong, as well as those of his wife Devayani. On the whole I preferred Devayani's more sensitive and restrained work to the bold and colourful studies of local scenes and local people in which Kanwal Krishna had just done such a brisk trade in Gangtok. Perhaps I could not help showing my preference. Before their departure Devayani presented the YMBA with a watercolour depicting Tibetan devotees before an image of the Buddha. With assistance from me as to spelling and grammar, Joe attempted a pen-picture of this painting for *Stepping-Stones*.

> In the foreground, in rich maroon-coloured garments are six devotees; five are seated, whilst the sixth is walking to the image to offer puja. Upon the altar – which is painted in yellows and carries the main light of the picture – are blue bowls and a pot wherein incense sticks are burning. From the altar the sight is drawn upward to the image of Lord Buddha. He rests upon a lotus seat, in a preaching attitude, and is painted in dark colours, the form being outlined in bold strokes of yellow where the light falls; the background holds the half-lights, with brilliant touches of red to accentuate the head. On either side of the image, gay silken banners hang – yellow, blue, green, orange, and red. The whole picture has a definite atmosphere of dignified reverence and is sufficiently mysterious to convey fully the impression of a temple interior. The colours though vivid have a harmony and quietness that pervades the whole work and leaves one with a feeling that the artist was never in doubt of the inner feeling the subject gave her.

When framed and hung this beautiful painting gave great offence to our Tibetan friends. As Joe's pen-picture failed to make clear, the artist had shown only the lower half of the Buddha's face, the rest not being included in the picture. What this was meant to convey was obvious. The devotees were worshipping That which ultimately transcended their understanding. The mystery of Enlightenment was not to be confined within any conceptual framework. Our Tibetan friends saw things quite differently. According to them what Devayani had done, plainly and simply, was to chop the Buddha's head in two. Thus she was guilty of the offence of *wounding the body of a Buddha*, which according to Buddhist tradition was one of the five most heinous offences anyone could possibly commit, along with killing an *arhant*, patricide and matricide, and causing schism within the monastic order. Throughout the rest of the Buddhist world 'wounding the body of a Buddha' was understood to mean shedding the blood of a Buddha (a Buddha could not be killed), as Devadatta had done in the case of Śākyamuni, and it was therefore possible to commit the offence only while there was a Buddha actually alive in the world. As I now discovered, the Tibetans had a different interpretation. According to them, 'wounding the body of a Buddha' was to be understood not just literally but also metaphorically, even symbolically. Any image or other representation of the Buddha was itself a 'body' of the Buddha, and cutting or tearing it, or defacing or disfiguring it in any way, was in their eyes as much tantamount to 'wounding the body of a Buddha' as stabbing the Host was, in the eyes of Roman Catholics, tantamount to stabbing the body of the Saviour himself. Yet though Devayani's painting gave such offence to our Tibetan friends, they did not react with the outrage – even the violence – with which Roman Catholics might have reacted in similar circumstances. Diffidently, but with evident disquiet, they drew our attention to the gravity of the offence – as they held it to be – that Devayani had committed, and left it to us to deal with the matter in whatever way we thought best.

Educational film shows proved even more popular than lectures. At Swale's request, the United States Information Service lent us a projector, a screen, and other equipment and sent a regular supply of films. Thus it was that twice a week Nepalis, Tibetans, Sikkimese, Bhutanese, Indians, and Chinese of all ages and every degree of literacy crowded into the big downstairs room next to the library to see such films as 'Home Demonstration Work' and 'All Around Arkansas', as well as the latest newsreel. So many people came, in fact, that after a few weeks we had to limit admission to YMBA members and associate members (associate membership was open to women and to boys under the age of twelve). Eventually the Town Club invited us to hold the shows at the Town

Hall, which we did for quite a long time, showing the films once instead of twice a week and attracting more and more people. Unfortunately, the fact that the films were supplied by the USIS, and that Swale was given to making cheery remarks about YMBA activities keeping young men off the streets and away from Communism, led to a story going round the bazaar that we were American agents. (Joe had by this time revealed himself as virulently anti-American, at least as far as words went.) This story too did me no good, though far from cancelling out Jain's story it seemed to combine with it in some people's minds and to make them more suspicious of me than ever – or at least to give them a *pretext* for being suspicious.

Besides lectures and educational film shows our activities during the first three months of our existence included a debate on the motion 'that the State should immediately enforce temperance' (it was defeated by one vote) and a tree planting festival. The latter took place, appropriately enough, shortly after Professor Ahuja's lecture, and was our contribution to the government-sponsored tree planting week. A number of trees, both useful and ornamental, were planted within the precincts of the Dharmodaya Vihara, the ceremony being inaugurated by Moti Chand Pradhan, the Subdivisional Officer of Kalimpong, who planted the first tree. I had already met him more than once, usually on YMBA business. He was a tall, thin man of about sixty, short-sighted, with a thatch of white hair and a stoop so pronounced he always seemed in danger of overbalancing. Most of the time he lived in a sort of cloud, a cloud from which he emerged dimly from time to time to rub his hands together and do whatever was required of him. The cloud was Theosophy and Krishnamurti. He was, in fact, one of those lifelong Theosophists whose brains, not very strong to begin with, had been seriously weakened by contact with Krishnamurti and his teaching. Like a lot of other people, when I went to see him at his office I found it almost impossible to get him to attend to the business on which I had come. All he wanted to do was to talk in a vague, woolly, wandering sort of way about Krishnamurti. Before becoming SDO he had been Second Officer in Darjeeling, and his appointment to a post formerly occupied by a European had given great satisfaction to his fellow Nepalis, by whom he was widely esteemed for his inoffensiveness and his freedom from corruption. Whether because the Government of West Bengal found that the Kalimpong Subdivision did not run very well on Theosophy and

Krishnamurti, or for some other reason, Moti Chand was not only the first Nepali SDO but also the last. During my stay in Kalimpong I was to see many more SDOs come and go, but all of them were Bengalis.

The Recreation Hut was tucked away behind the kitchen building, at the foot of the vertical clay bank where the hillside had been cut away to form the ledge on which the vihara stood. It was really no more than a wooden shack, and in the days when the vihara was a European family residence must have been the servants' quarters. At one time chickens had been kept there. Before it could be used for recreational purposes the whole place had to be cleaned out, repaired, and decorated. There were chicken-droppings to be removed, leaks in the roof to be stopped up, walls to be scrubbed down and whitewashed. There was a wooden partition to be taken down in order to make a room big enough to hold the ping-pong table, and the ping-pong table itself to be made, to our specifications, by a local carpenter. At length everything was done, and the Recreation Hut declared open. Since electricity had not, as yet, been installed, it could be used only from four o'clock to six o'clock every afternoon, that is to say, from the time school and college finished to the time it grew dark. Before long YMBA membership had more than doubled. The young men of Kalimpong felt that they now had a place of their own. In theory the older youths, at least, could have joined the Town Club, and played ping-pong and badminton in the Town Hall, but few of them could afford the monthly subscription (more than twice the cost of YMBA membership for a whole year), and in any case they did not feel wholly at ease there, as the Club was patronized mainly by government officers and members of the Bengali ruling élite. To the YMBA then, in ever-increasing numbers, the young men came.

Much as they enjoyed playing ping-pong and carrom-board in the Recreation Hut, and badminton on the court we had marked out on the patch of ground beside the kitchen, our school- and college-going members were not unmindful of more serious matters. Little victims they might be, and play they certainly did, but they were little victims who did not play regardless of their doom.[15] In their case doom meant the examinations for which they had to sit towards the end of the year. Examinations were important because passing was important. Passing was important because passing gave you, eventually, a scrap of paper stamped 'qualification'. A qualification was important because it secured you, if you were lucky, a job, that is to say, a white-collar job, preferably in government service, that not only lifted you from the 'uneducated' and insolvent masses to the 'educated' and relatively solvent classes but also ensured that you and your family would be provided for for the rest of your days. Education was not so much the gateway to knowledge as the bridge to success in life. Below the bridge yawned the abyss – the abyss of poverty, degradation, and despair. In Calcutta, when the examination results were announced, there was always a crop of suicides. Failed matriculates, IAs and BAs would throw themselves into the waters of the Hooghly or under the wheels of trains, unable to face the reproachful – or despairing – looks of parents and elder brothers who had slaved and starved to keep them at school or college for another year and who would not be able to repeat the effort. In the hills the economic situation was not as bad as that, and the pressure to pass examinations not nearly so great. Most Nepalese families lived in a wattle-and-daub hut they had built themselves and owned a plot of land on which they could grow maize and squash, raise chickens, and, if they were of sufficiently low caste, even fatten a few pigs. Nevertheless, though the pressure to pass examinations and obtain the magic 'qualification' was not nearly so great as it was in the cities of the plains, it was strong enough, and as the weeks went by the cheerful faces of our young friends became more and more clouded with gloom. Most of them were convinced that they stood little chance of passing their examinations unless they received private tuition. Such tuition was available in the evenings, for a consideration, from the selfsame teachers who taught them at school or college during the day.

To me it was strange that private tuition should be so necessary, and stranger still that the students should have to take it from their own school and college teachers. One would have thought that the teaching they received in class during the day would have been quite sufficient. If it was not, why did their teachers not improve their methods of teaching? Why did they not give their students more homework? The school- and college-going members to whom I put these questions only met them with smiles of incredulity. More homework? Their teachers never gave them *any* homework. They did not even teach them properly in class, during the day. All they were interested in was getting students to take private tuition from them in the evenings – for a consideration. Some students maintained that however well they did in the internal (i.e. the school or college) examinations their teachers would fail them unless they were going to them for private tuition, and if they failed the internal examinations they could not sit for the external examinations, which of course were the ones that mattered. All of them believed that, with few exceptions, their teachers regarded school and college classes simply as recruiting grounds for private pupils. One teacher had even fitted up a room in his bungalow like a classroom, complete with desks, and he had so many pupils and had made so much money that although he had been in Kalimpong for only a few years (he was a Bengali from Calcutta) he had been able to buy two substantial properties. Private tuition really was necessary. They all felt the need of it, and they were all prepared to take it if they could get it, even if this meant having to sacrifice all their free evenings from now up to the time of the examinations. There was only one difficulty. In most cases they – or rather their parents – could not afford to pay for private tuition. They already had to pay the school or college fees, as well as to provide their own text books and writing materials, and the additional expense was simply beyond their means.

Once they were assured of a sympathetic hearing the young men voiced their grievances quite freely, but though they spoke reasonably enough I sensed that beneath their growing gloom there was a strong undercurrent of bitterness and resentment. Life had stacked the odds too heavily against them, they seemed to feel. Without a 'qualification' you could not get a decent job. Without passing your examinations you could not get a 'qualification'. Without private tuition you could not pass your examinations. Without money you could not pay for private tuition. Everything depended upon money. Money was the greatest of all blessings, lack of money the greatest curse. With money you could do anything, without it you could do nothing. Usually you – or rather your parents – did not have money. Even if they did have, usually they would refuse to spend it on private tuition for you. You just had to study harder. The only reason why students failed to pass their examinations, you would be told, was laziness. A student had no business to be doing anything, day or night, except studying. Parents always refused absolutely to listen to any complaint against the teachers. This undercurrent of bitterness and resentment was strongest in the Nepali- and Tibetan-speaking students, most of whom came from communities officially regarded as being socially, economically, and educationally 'backward'. Besides having to suffer on account of their parents' poverty or lack of understanding, they were the victims of communal prejudice and religious bigotry. Bengali teachers tended to favour Bengali students, while Christian teachers tended to favour students who were either Christians already or who were at least willing to go to church. (Most of our student members attended the Scottish Mission High School, the undeclared policy of which was to appoint Christian rather than non-Christian teachers.) Life could be difficult if you were a student in Kalimpong. It could be still more difficult if you were a student and poor, and most difficult of all if you were a student and poor *and* a Nepali- or Tibetan-speaking Hindu or Buddhist. Clearly we would have to give whatever help we could to our school- and college-going members, but for the time being at least that help would have to be given within the framework of the existing educational system.

In the first week of August, therefore, a month after the opening of the Recreation Hut, and three months after the establishment or the YMBA, evening tutorial classes were started and continued for the next four months. Their original purpose was to assist YMBA members preparing for the matriculation and intermediate arts examinations, but very soon, in response to popular demand, we had to enlarge them so as to include Class VIII and Class IX students, who wanted help in preparing themselves for their own examinations. The subjects in which *all* the students were weakest were English, mathematics, and (in the case of IA students)[16] logic, and on these we decided to concentrate. Joe took Class VIII and Class IX students for English (he could at least give them conversational practice, which they badly needed), Swale took students of all classes for mathematics, while I took the matriculation and IA students for English and logic. Classes were held from four o'clock to six o'clock in the afternoon, and no fees were charged. Most students came to the vihara straight from school or, if they happened to live in the bazaar, after dashing home and gulping down a cup of tea. Initially about forty students attended the different classes each day, but as the weeks went by and examinations, both internal and external, drew ever nearer, numbers rose first from forty to fifty, then from fifty to sixty. With so many students coming for tuition each day we were rather hard pressed for space. In the end Joe took his students in the room he had been given downstairs, while Swale used the big room next to the library where we held our lectures. As for me, I took my students in the corresponding room upstairs which was my bedroom, study, editorial office, dining room, and reception room. At the close of the two hour session there would be a general stampede to the Recreation Hut. Having devoted themselves to their studies for the greater part of the day, most of the students felt that they could now throw aside their books and enjoy themselves for a while with a clear conscience. Gradually some of them got into the habit of spending, altogether, anything from four to six hours at the vihara every evening. This was not just because they enjoyed playing ping-pong, carrom-board, and draughts, and the other games we provided. It was not just because they enjoyed one another's company. In some cases, it was at least partly due to the fact that, when they went home, it would be to a hut full of younger brothers and sisters, where the only light was that of a paraffin lamp, where there was no quiet corner, and where, more likely than not, a stern father would expect them to sit up studying long after the rest of the family had gone to bed.

The opening of the Recreation Hut, and the starting of the tutorial classes, made quite a difference to life at the vihara, especially during the latter part of the day. Mornings remained more or less unchanged. When I had finished my puja and meditation Joe and I had breakfast together in my room, after which I studied, or got on with editorial work, or wrote letters, while he either went curio-hunting in the bazaar or smoked and typed in his own room. Sometimes we spent the morning talking. Since we were not only working together for the YMBA, but also staying in the same building, I soon got to know him quite well – much better than I had been able to get to know Swale. Like me he had had little formal education, the difference being that he had not had it for a much longer time and *minded* that he had not had it. His appreciation of the cultural achievements of humanity and his feeling for beauty in all its forms were both unusually intense, though he had a tendency to think of culture in terms of what was rare and costly, even simply luxurious. No less intense was his desire to make a personal contribution to culture, to create something beautiful himself; but here he was badly handicapped by his lack of the basic techniques. Whether he tried to compose a haiku, or write an article for *Stepping-Stones*, or paint a picture, it simply would not go right, and he was left feeling frustrated and emotionally exhausted. He was also left feeling bitter and resentful. Because he had not had the 'advantage' of a proper education, and lacked basic creative skills (the two things seemed to be connected in his mind) Joe in fact suffered from acute feelings of inferiority and inadequacy and cherished a strong sense of grievance against society – especially against those who were better educated or technically more competent than he was. As in the case of Philoctetes, his very defects were not without their corresponding advantages. Oversensitive as he was in matters of education and artistic technique, he was quick to detect – indeed to pounce upon – any attempt to use these to conceal poverty of thought or failure of inspiration. Technical virtuosity for its own sake particularly enraged him: it was 'clever' – one of the most damning words in his vocabulary. With this ability to see through pretence and insincerity in a poem, a novel, a play, a picture, or even in a person (not that he did not have his blind spots) Joe excelled in destructive criticism of the more ferocious type. He was never happier than when tearing something to pieces. If he could also trample on the fragments so much the better. Destructive criticism gave him an outlet for his feelings of frustration, bitterness, and resentment in a way that nothing else did. It enabled him to express emotions of indignation, scorn, contempt, and disgust, as well as to indulge in irony, ridicule, sarcasm, and invective. Destructive criticism permitted him to 'be himself'. To a greater extent than anyone I had yet known he was most creative when he was most critical. In fact it was only by being critical that he could be creative at all.

Besides indulging his penchant for destructive criticism, and relating anecdotes of his life in Lucknow with the Anglo-Indian family, Joe from time to time alluded to the facts of his army career. These allusions were so rare, and couched for the most part in such vague and general terms, that I was left with the impression that the whole subject of the army and his connection with it made Joe quite uneasy and that he was being deliberately evasive about it. On one occasion or another I gathered that he had joined the British Regular Army at an early age, that he had served in India as an ordinary ranker, that he had been commissioned during the war, and that he had spent the war years doing some kind of administrative work in Assam: and that was about all. Though he had lived in India for most of his life, unlike Swale – who was fluent in several Indian languages – he spoke only a few words of Hindi, all of which he habitually mispronounced. He also mispronounced – deliberately, it seemed, not to say defiantly – such

Pāli Buddhist words as he knew. The vihara, for instance, was always 'the *wee*-har'. To pronounce the words of a foreign language correctly – even to pronounce one's own language correctly – was simply being 'clever'! Though his allusions to his army career were for the most part couched in vague and general terms, there was one part of it about which he reminisced repeatedly, and at considerable length. This was the mess Christmas party. The mess Christmas party always ended with a dance. At the dance they always wore fancy dress. Joe himself, then a sprightly young ranker, had always dressed up as a woman, wearing a tight-fitting silk dress, high-heeled shoes, and lots of rouge, lipstick, and mascara. Not only that: he had danced with the officers! Whenever he reached this point in the story, Joe went off into a series of high-pitched cackles, crossing and uncrossing his legs, hugging himself, and rocking violently backwards and forwards in his chair. Dancing with the officers was not, however, the climax of the story. The climax came later, with someone whispering in his ear – and apparently someone always did whisper – 'Joe, you've got the face of an angel and the eyes of a devil!' – a description which despite his grey hair and gaunt features Joe seemed to think entirely appropriate even now.

Appropriate or not, there was no doubt that Joe's reminiscences of Christmas Day in the mess related to a period of his life that had ended some years, even some decades, earlier. This was not to say that he had undergone a complete transformation during the interval. In some respects the young ranker who had dressed up as a woman and danced with the officers was still very much alive, and though he may not have been much in evidence at our morning talks he certainly showed himself on other occasions. Generally the old woman who lived in the kitchen building prepared breakfast and lunch for us. This did not involve much more than boiling a pot of rice, and sometimes Joe did the work instead. When this happened I could be pretty certain that for breakfast, at least, I would get a brass goblet filled with rice into which he had stuck, upright, half a peeled banana. This dish, which was of his own invention, he called 'phallic rice'. He always carried it up the stairs to me himself, depositing it in front of me with a flourish, and glaring at me through his spectacles as he did so as if to say, 'Refuse it if you dare!' Soon after getting to know me Joe had come to the conclusion that I was not only young but very naive, that I had no experience of things 'in the raw', and badly needed to be taught the facts of life.

In the afternoon, after an early lunch (I still took no solid food after midday), I did more editorial work, talked with Swale and anybody he might have brought with him to see me, and prepared my lessons for the evening. One afternoon, sitting on my bed as usual, I looked out of the open window to see Swale assisting a peppery-looking old gentleman of about seventy up the last of the steps. This was Dr Joseph Rock, a noted American anthropologist, who had recently returned from the jungles of western China and was now staying at the Himalayan Hotel with his Austrian secretary. As soon as he caught sight of me the old gentleman called out, 'Colonel Ryan says he's a monk just like you. Is it true?'

'No, it isn't,' I called back promptly. 'He's an *anagārika*.'

'There, I told you so!' exclaimed Dr Rock triumphantly, turning to Swale. 'You're not a monk.'

'I belong to a different order from him,' Swale protested, rather weakly I thought.

From half-past-three the vihara started filling up with young men. Despite the fact that they already had a day of school or college behind them they were rarely late, and indeed seemed to look forward to their evening tutorial classes. Having left shoes and sandals in the back hall, and having leapt up the stairs two at a time in their bare or stockinged feet, the students of each of my own two classes came crowding into my room with broadly smiling faces, most of them bidding me a cheerful 'Good evening, Sir,' as they took their places on the floor in front of me and pulled out their books and notebooks. Sitting on my bed with my back to the window, I took first the Class x or matriculation students for English, then the Intermediate students for English and logic, one class playing ping-pong and carrom-board in the Recreation Hut while the other studied with me. Altogether I had not less than thirty students, the greater number of them being in the lower class. Most of the students were in their late teens. Ethnically, religiously, and linguistically, they were quite a mixed lot, as were the students in the classes taken by Joe and Swale. Features ranged from the definitely Mongoloid (high cheekbones, slant eyes, and hairless faces) to the definitely Aryan (prominent noses and incipient beards and moustaches), while complexions varied from blue-black to pinkish white, and from dark brown to light yellow. Some students were high caste Hindus, others tribal Buddhists. There were locally born Nepalis and Tibetans, as well as Sikkimese from the Protectorate of Sikkim and Indians from the states of Bihar, East Punjab, and Rajputana. Some students had Nepali for their mother tongue, some Tibetan, and some Hindi: several spoke two of these languages, or even three. Among the Hindus (who overlapped with the Nepalis and Indians) there were a dozen different castes, and among the Nepalis (who overlapped with the Hindus and the Buddhists) a dozen different tribes. The typical student, however, tended to be Mongoloid rather than Aryan in appearance, light brown rather than dark brown in complexion, Hindu rather than Buddhist, speaking Nepali as his mother tongue rather than Tibetan or Hindi, and occupying a lower rather than a higher place in the caste system.

Despite the diversity of their ethnic, religious, and linguistic backgrounds, our student members were characterized by a surprising unanimity of outlook. This was not only because they all belonged to approximately the same age group and were in any case all students and, as such, all undergoing the same educational process. It was mainly because they were all subject to powerful influences emanating, ultimately, from the urban, industrial, and secular civilization of the modern Western world. These influences reached them partly through the educational process itself (English was still the medium of instruction at high school and college level), partly through the third-rate 'English' (i.e. English and American) films shown at the local cinema, and partly through the mass-produced consumer goods sold in some of the local shops – as well as in a hundred other more indirect ways. Almost without exception, they saw these influences as entirely beneficent. For them the modern Western world was a world of 'progress', and its civilization was the glittering culmination of centuries of human effort. America in particular was heaven upon earth. It was everybody's dream come true – a place of unrestricted personal freedom and unlimited affluence. If any of them ever looked to Russia, it was because Communism seemed to offer a speedier way of bringing to the people of India the kind of material prosperity already enjoyed by the people of America. Yet bedazzled though they all were by the brilliance of the results achieved by modern Western science and technology, the students had by no means lost contact with their own particular cultural traditions. In fact they were more deeply influenced by them than they realized. For them their own cultural traditions represented the past, and the past was something that they took for granted. Modern Western civilization represented the future, and the future they did not – indeed could not

– take for granted. Thus although they stood with their backs to the past they had their faces turned to the future. It was with the future, as represented by modern Western civilization, that they sought to identify. It was the future they wanted to inherit.

One of the ways in which they showed their unanimity of outlook, and the extent to which they sought to identify with modern Western civilization, was in the matter of dress. Almost without exception, they had discarded the Nepalese, or Tibetan, or Indian traditional costume still worn by the majority of their elders and adopted a simplified version of modern Western dress, which meant that they wore long trousers ('pants' they always called them, American fashion) and an English-style shirt with, as the weather grew colder, a pullover or jacket. Practically the only students to resist the rising tide of sartorial conversion were a Nepalese Brahmin youth who wore jodhpurs and a long, double-breasted Nepalese shirt, and a young Marwari who wore a dhoti. In *Peaks and Lamas*, the book that had so much impressed me five years earlier, when I was in Singapore, the author Marco Pallis (who was living in Kalimpong, and whom I was soon to meet) had much to say on the subject of traditional costume or national costume, as he also called it, though the two expressions are not really synonymous. According to him, the question of costume, external though it might appear at first sight, was a crucial one for India, China, Japan, and other nations too. He believed it had become 'a symbol of something far more deep-seated, a touchstone by which the traditional and anti-traditional souls could be distinguished'. By this criterion our students were as a body decidedly among the anti-traditionalists. When I asked them why they did not wear their traditional costume, whether Nepalese, Tibetan, or Indian (at that time, and for some years afterwards, I tended to adhere to Marco Pallis's rather simplistic views on the subject) they generally replied that traditional costume was uncomfortable and inconvenient, and took a long time to put on. Western dress, on the contrary, was both comfortable and convenient, and one could slip into it in a few minutes. Though not the whole truth, this was not altogether a rationalization. It took quite a long time to squeeze into the tight-fitting Nepalese jodhpurs, while the double-breasted Nepalese shirt had quite a lot of tapes that needed tying together, some of them right under the armpit where they were difficult to get at. In the Tibetan *chuba* one could not move one's limbs freely, and it was difficult to run. As for the Indian dhoti, the way in which it revealed the inside of the leg right up to the crotch was positively indecent – a verdict with which I was inclined to agree.

Though their insistence that traditional costume was uncomfortable and inconvenient was not wholly a rationalization, there was little doubt that the real reason for the students' wholesale adoption of Western dress was simply that it was Western. By adopting it they identified themselves, at least to some extent, with modern Western civilization. It was the uniform of the army under whose banner they wished to march – the banner on which was inscribed the magic word 'Progress' – and as such they were proud to wear it. While Marco Pallis was right in seeing in the abandonment of national costume a symbol of alienation from tradition – from traditional culture and traditional spiritual values – nonetheless the students' preference for Western dress was not altogether a bad thing. Tradition, or what passed for tradition, was by no means an unmixed blessing. In any case it existed not in one form but in many different forms. Consequently there were many *different* traditional cultures in existence, and as many different types of traditional costume. Was it necessarily a good thing that one's dress should immediately identify one as a Nepalese Hindu, or an Indian Muslim, or a Tibetan Buddhist – or proclaim to the world that one belonged to a higher or a lower caste? The students did not think so. As recently as 1947 differences of 'nationality' and culture, acutely felt, had been responsible for inflicting untold misery on millions of people in India and Pakistan – had, in fact, been responsible for the eventual partition of the subcontinent – and in their view the less such differences were given prominence by the wearing of a distinctive 'traditional costume' the better. All that dress should do was to make it clear that one was an educated human being.

Though they may not have consciously thought in such terms, the students preferred Western dress not only because they wanted to identify with modern Western civilization but because they wanted to identify with one another. Unlike traditional costume, which in effect meant many different traditional costumes, Western dress was a means of emphasizing what they had in common with one another, rather than what separated them. What they had in common – what united them – was that they were all young men, all students, and that having come under the influence of modern Western civilization they all shared the same 'progressive' outlook – all looked forward to the same secular millennium. Western dress also served to remind them that they were all primarily human beings, and only secondarily members of the particular ethnic and cultural group into which they had been born. One of the reasons why they had been drawn to the YMBA in the first place, in fact, was that it aimed to unite the young men of Kalimpong, as well as to propagate the teachings of the Buddha by means of social, educational, and religious activities, and that membership was open to all who accepted these objects, regardless of race, caste, economic position, and nominal religious affiliation. What they had not yet realized – perhaps I had not yet realized it fully myself – was that genuine unity was not possible on the basis of any secular notion of 'equality' but only on the basis of common commitment to a common spiritual ideal.

Since the students were coming to the vihara every day (as examinations drew near, they came even on Saturdays and Sundays) I soon got to know my own matriculation and IA students quite well. First I became familiar with their faces, then I learned their names, and finally I tried to find out more about their backgrounds than it was possible to infer from their cognomens and agnomens and from their actual physical appearance. Sometimes my efforts produced unexpected results.

'Who is your father?' I enquired one day of a determined-looking youngster with a protruding underlip who might have been either Tibetan or Sikkimese. (People I already knew sometimes stopped me in the bazaar to ask how their sons were getting on and it was important to be able to connect the right offspring with the right parent.)

'My father is Mr Lha Tsering,' replied the youngster promptly, though with a grin that could have indicated either defiance or embarrassment.

At the name of Mr Lha Tsering there was a burst of good-natured laughter from the rest of the class. Mr Lha Tsering, as everybody knew, was the head of the Kalimpong branch of the Central Intelligence Bureau. But it was not this circumstance that was responsible for the laughter, as I then thought, but something of a quite different character, about which I learned only months later, after I had become acquainted with Lha Tsering himself. Another student who, judging from his appearance, might also have been of either Tibetan or Sikkimese stock, turned out to be the grandson of someone much better known, and certainly far more distinguished, than the formidable boss of the local intelligence network. A gentle, fair-skinned youth, he was the son of an inspector in the West Bengal police force who, in his turn, was the son of the famous Lama Kazi Dawa-Samdup, whose translations of the *Tibetan Book of the Dead*, *The Life of Milarepa*, and other works formed the backbone of Dr W. Y. Evans-Wentz's celebrated Oxford Tibetan Series. Alas! young Samdup could tell me little about his illustrious grandfather, and indeed did not appear to be particularly well-versed in Buddhism, though it may have been that he gave this impression simply because he was not accustomed to expressing himself in English on the subject. At least he was studying classical Tibetan and it was to be hoped that one day he too would be a translator of Buddhist texts.

Among the students who came most regularly, and whom I got to know best (this may have been partly due to the fact that they were more fluent in English than many of the others), there were five or six who seemed to be on particularly friendly terms with one another and who, since they formed a fairly closely knit group, seemed to give a lead to the other boys. The members of this little fraternity were all between sixteen and eighteen years of age, they all lived in the bazaar, and all attended the Scottish Mission High School. Jungi Bahadur Gautam, the youngest of the group, was a short, cheerful Nepali about whose background I never learned very much. Though the son of a Brahmin (his mother belonged to a lower caste), he was fonder of sports and games than of his books, and eventually gave up his studies to pursue a career in professional football. Padamlal Periyar was the handsomest of the group. In complexion he was extremely dark, but with 'lotus eyes' and finely cut features such as one sees in the Ajanta frescoes. His father was a tailor, and had a little shop on the way down to the lower bazaar. Whenever I passed by I would see the grey-headed old man sitting behind his antiquated sewing machine, facing the street, and he always rose to his feet and smilingly saluted me with folded hands. Lachuman Gazamair was the group's pessimist. Though his expression was cheerful enough, he always looked on the gloomy side of things. This may have been due to the fact that, though tall and well built, he had a sickly, yellowish-brown complexion, and was not really very healthy. His father worked for the Kalimpong Municipality, and was a bent, wizened little man who looked about sixty but was probably much younger.

Unlike Jungi, Padam, and Lachuman, who were all Hindus by birth, Karka Bahadur Lama belonged to a Tamang Buddhist family. Tall and thin and gaunt, with clothes that seemed to flap upon him, he had a pale face and was of a somewhat choleric disposition. He was also the oldest member of the group. His family background was rather complicated. His father, a retired police inspector even more advanced in years than Lachuman's father, was conducting a liaison with the Hindu Newar widow of a Sikkimese liquor-shop keeper. The liaison was so well established that it probably would be more correct to speak of old Mr Lama as living polygamously, with one wife up at Tenth Mile (localities along the main road were generally known after the ordinals of their miles up from Teesta Bridge: the vihara was situated just above Ninth Mile) and the other down in the lower bazaar, except that owing to Christian missionary influence polygamy was rather frowned upon in the area and English-educated people, at least, did not usually admit to practising it. The situation was further complicated by the fact that, according to popular report, his father supported one wife, Karka's mother, and her children, with the help of money derived from the other, who had a grown-up son of her own together with whom she managed the liquor-shop and ran a motor transport service. Despite his years, and the stiffness with which he moved, old Mr Lama was in many ways sprightly enough. Unlike most of his contemporaries he wore a Western-style suit and a trilby hat which he raised ceremoniously whenever he met Joe or me in the street. What was more, alone among his contemporaries, he refused to submit to the indignity of a toothless, mumbling old age, and had instead invested in a complete set of false teeth, some of them made of gold. Dawa Tsering Bhutia, the only other Buddhist member of the group, was a 'Darjeeling-born' Tibetan who had lost his father at an early age. His mother was away in England with an English family for whom she worked as an ayah. In her absence Dawa lived with an 'uncle' who stood *in loco parentis*. Though he was a friendly, good-natured youth, Dawa's smooth face often wore a worried look, as though he was trying to work something out, and he was inclined to be secretive. He also had a streak of hot temper, which he claimed he had inherited from his mother, a lady for whom he felt a mixture of love and terror. She was a strict disciplinarian, and beat him frequently: very hard. Her two great fears were that he would become a drunkard like his father, and that he would marry a non-Tibetan girl.

Just as the little fraternity gave a lead to the rest of the students, so there was one member of the group who seemed to give a lead to the group itself. This was a seventeen-year-old Nepali called Sachindra Coomar Singh. In appearance he was of medium height, with a slender, graceful figure, and features that were a perfect blend of the Mongoloid and the Aryan. He had not been coming to the vihara long, or been in my matriculation class for more than a few days – even a few hours – before I was made aware of the qualities which, as I soon discovered, gave him so much influence over his contemporaries and made him such a general favourite. Besides being extremely lively, and full of fun and mischief, he was possessed of such extraordinary charm that it was quite impossible to refuse him anything. At the same time, he was well spoken and well mannered, with a natural modesty that added to his charm – if that was possible – and only half concealed an equally natural self-assurance. His only faults were that he was, as one might have expected, rather too fond of his own way, and a little too inclined to play the tyrant. Sometimes he played the tyrant to such an extent that the other members of the group rebelled, but he had only to exercise his charm and they once again submitted to his rule, though at times not without a few grumbles.

Years later, in a book by Rumer Godden called *Black Narcissus*, I encountered a character who, in respect of his effect upon other people, reminded me very much of Sachin when I first met him. The character in question is a young Nepalese prince whose family sends him to a European school in the green, jungle-clad foothills of the eastern Himalayas 'somewhere near Darjeeling'. With his beauty and his charm, he appears to the nuns who have started the school, and who are trying to make a success of the venture, to be the very incarnation of the spirit of the hills – the dangerous, pagan spirit they are seeking to overcome with their Christian teaching. Every day the young prince arrives at the school wearing a different coat of colourful silk brocade – each one more dazzling than the last. Sachin was not a prince, and he did not wear coats of colourful silk brocade, but from the effect he produced when he appeared at the vihara he might just as well have done. Once again it was as if a beautiful and exotic butterfly had fluttered across my path – or rather, this time it was as if the butterfly was fluttering along the path with me, now alighting on my hand, now alighting on my shoulder, and now dancing on ahead of me down a sunlit track bordered with brilliant orange marigolds and multicoloured zinnias. With a beauty and a charm that in his case did not need to be set off by splendid costume, or by the consciousness of distinguished social position, Sachin too appeared to be the very incarnation of the spirit of the hills. It was the spirit of the hills that fluttered along the path with me, and danced on ahead down the sunlit track, for was not the butterfly, according to the ancients, the symbol of the psyche, the soul, and could there not be a 'soul' or spirit of a place as well as of a person? This spirit, the spirit of the hills, was not dangerous and pagan, as Rumer Godden's nuns believed – or rather, it was dangerous only when thwarted, and pagan only in the sense of being the source of life and joy.

Sometimes Sachin seemed to incarnate something more than the spirit of the hills. Just turned seventeen, he was at the age when, according to Indian Buddhist tradition, the male human form is at the peak of its development and when – strong without being clumsy, graceful without being weak – it can most fittingly represent the ideal of the infinitely wise and boundlessly compassionate bodhisattva who, with Nirvāṇa seemingly within his grasp, renounces for ever his 'own' Enlightenment and turns back to the world of suffering humanity to succour and to save. Thus it was that the young Nepali sometimes appeared strangely bodhisattva-like, as though one of the beautiful golden figures that one saw in the dimness of Tibetan temples had stepped down from its lotus-throne, where it had been pensively sitting beside the greater golden figure of the Buddha, and had wandered among the hills, and through the streets of Kalimpong – to the vihara.

In actual fact, of course, Sachin's origins were much more mundane, though his background still differed somewhat from that of the other members of the group. He came from a rather Westernized Hindu family and lived not so much in the bazaar as on the edge of it, in a bungalow attached to the Scottish Mission hospital, where his father worked as a doctor. Both his parents were originally from Darjeeling, and several female relations on his mother's side had married Bengalis.

The better I got to know Jungi, Padam, Lachuman, Karka, Dawa, and Sachin, and the better they got to know me, the more there developed between us something akin to friendship. The reason for this development was not so much that they were fluent in English, or were members of a closely knit group, but rather that they gradually got into the habit of staying on after their class and talking with me. Sometimes we continued our talk in the Recreation Hut, and sometimes I challenged one or another of them to a game of ping-pong (carrom-board, which was a great favourite with most of the boys, I thought boring). Usually I played either Sachin or Lachuman, as the three of us were fairly evenly matched and able to keep one another on our toes. According to 'orthodox' Buddhist ideas it was not at all proper for a monk to play games, and I well knew that in the most rigidly correct Buddhist circles my conduct would be severely reprehended. Yet I could not really believe it was morally wrong for me to play ping-pong with my students, or even that it was simply unbecoming for one who had 'gone forth' to spend time in this way. Playing ping-pong with the students helped me to develop a closer relationship with them (a rigorous Theravādin might have questioned the utility of this), and also gave me an outlet for my physical energies – an outlet I probably needed more than I realized. Such is the influence of convention, however, and such the pressure of group attitudes on the individual, that even though I could not really believe it was morally wrong, or even unbecoming, for me to play ping-pong, the fact that I knew my behaviour would meet with widespread disapproval gave me a certain amount of uneasiness. Sometimes instead of playing ping-pong we went for a walk, on one occasion going as far as Fourteenth Mile, where the main road became a dusty yellow mule track and the houses on either side gave way to clumps of tall bamboo. More often than not we would be joined in our talks and excursions by Joe, who had also got to know Jungi, Padam, and the rest of the five or six members of the little fraternity. It was noticeable that Joe's relations were closest with Jungi, Padam, and Karka, whereas mine were closest with Sachin, Lachuman, and Dawa. It was also noticeable that within the fraternity itself relations were closest between Sachin, Lachuman, and Padam. This may or may not have had something to do with the fact that, as I discovered later, they belonged to the same Nepali Hindu caste, and that this was a very low one. The subject of caste was, in fact, quite a sore one with them, and one of the reasons why they were attracted to Buddhism, and to the YMBA, was that it was well known that the Buddha had criticized the brahminical system of hereditary caste, teaching that what really counted was not birth but worth. One of Padam's sisters was indeed married to the celebrated Indian Buddhist scholar Rahul Sankrityayan, who had once been a Buddhist monk, and who had spent a few weeks at the Dharmodaya Vihara the previous year. Kamala Periyar had come to the vihara each day to type for Rahulji, as he was universally known, and one day the two of them were found in the same compromising embrace in which Great Wisdom and the Newar widow had been discovered. Such was the outcry that Rahulji, who had disrobed some years earlier and was now in his fifties, was obliged to abandon the vihara and take refuge in a hotel. When he left Kalimpong he took Kamala with him and subsequently married her. Once again the Newars' pious custom of removing their shoes in the hall and stealing upstairs in their stockinged feet had had unlooked for results.

Talks after class and walks along the road were not the only means by which something akin to friendship developed between me and the five or six members of the little fraternity. Some of them took to inviting me to their homes for tea and in order to meet their parents and other members of the family. Joe was invited too. Sometimes we would be invited together, sometimes on separate occasions. In this way we had tea in the room behind the tailor's shop where Padam lived, in the two-storey wooden building at Tenth Mile which was Karka's home, and the hospital bungalow near the church where Sachin resided. At first these occasions tended to be formal and somewhat constrained, with our hosts doing their best to make us feel at home by giving us an English-style tea and being on tenterhooks lest they should do anything wrong. After one or two such visits, however, the atmosphere relaxed, and we not only gained a better understanding of the students themselves by seeing them in their own homes but also made the acquaintance of parents, brothers and sisters and other relations, neighbours, and anybody else who happened to look in. It soon became evident what a wealth of goodwill existed towards us among people we had not met before, and of whom we had not even heard. Parents, especially, could not sufficiently express their gratitude for what the YMBA was doing for the students, and were always so delighted to see us that we ended by getting to know some of the fathers almost better than we knew their sons. Joe struck up with old Mr Lama, Karka's father, an acquaintance that was to have important consequences both for me personally and for the YMBA, while I developed with Dr Ravi Das Singh, Sachin's father, a friendly understanding that lasted until his death at a relatively early age five or six years later.

Nonetheless the principal means of developing our relationship with the students, including even those we knew best, was still the evening tutorial classes. Though the fact that they were now getting private tuition meant that their faces were no longer clouded with gloom, the examinations for which they had to sit towards the end of the year were still their doom, a doom of which they did not play unmindful, and passing their examinations was therefore still the major preoccupation of their lives. This preoccupation did not altogether exclude the cultivation of other interests, especially those which could be regarded as overlapping with their examination subjects. Sachin, Padam, and Lachuman were all keen amateur musicians, which meant they were capable of performing on the box harmonium, an instrument that must have been introduced by missionaries during the Victorian period in order to provide an accompaniment for Christian hymns but which nowadays was more often found giving the same support to Hindu devotional songs. Sachin not only played but sang, accompanying himself on the harmonium with various trills and arpeggios that he did not always get quite right. He was extremely fond of performing in this manner, and once he got hold of the harmonium it was difficult for anyone to get it away from him. Though his voice was not very strong, he sang quite well, and I never tired of listening to him as he poured out song after devotional song at the end of the full-moon day pujas we held in the shrine-room every month. His main interest outside his studies, however, was not so much music as literature, especially English poetry, an interest that overlapped not only with one of his examination subjects but with my own interests as well. Poetry in fact came to form an enduring bond between us and to provide an important element in a steadily growing friendship.

Besides being the principal means of developing our relationship with the students, the evening tutorial classes also proved to be an important means of teaching Buddhism. This was particularly true of the English classes, which were devoted not so much to grammar and composition as to English literature as represented by the matriculation and IA poetry and prose selections. It was not that I deliberately set out to teach Buddhism by this means, or even that I had any prior idea that such a thing was possible. I made the discovery that one could teach Buddhism while teaching English literature, especially English poetry – that teaching English poetry *was*, in fact, teaching Buddhism – entirely by accident. Whoever had compiled the matriculation and IA poetry and prose selections, a portion of which was set by the examiners each year, must have been a great admirer of the Romantic poets – or else have thought they were particularly well suited to the Indian temperament. Wordsworth, Keats, and Shelley all figured prominently in the pages of the slim, paper-bound volume, though Herrick, Browning, Wilfred Owen, and Rupert Brooke were also represented. (The main prose authors were H. G. Wells and Oscar Wilde.) What most of the students wanted from me was simply a paraphrase of such poems as 'The Cloud', or 'To a Skylark', or 'To Daffodils' – a paraphrase they could learn by heart and then reproduce on paper in the examination hall when invited by the question paper to give the meaning of the poem 'in your own words'. Thus I had to dictate 'paraphrases' beginning in some such manner as 'The Cloud, speaking like a human being, declares that he brings fresh showers of rain from the seas and the streams'; or, 'The poet, greeting the skylark enthusiastically as a happy spirit, tells him that he was not ever a bird'; or, 'The poet informs the daffodils, whom he addresses as beautiful, that he and others like him are unhappy to see them run away so quickly.' *That* was the kind of thing the students expected from me. *That* was the kind of thing that was acceptable to the examiners, and earned good marks.

Once I had done my duty by the students, however, and provided them with the sort of paraphrase they wanted, I felt free to go beyond the examination requirements. Taking the paraphrase I had dictated as my starting point, I tried to communicate to them something of the real meaning of the poem as the expression of an intense emotional and intellectual experience – an experience that was of universal significance and value. This involved exploring the connotation of key words, elucidating idiomatic expressions, explaining mythological allusions, pointing out parallels in ordinary human experience, and so on. Many of the students appreciated this kind of approach. Some, especially Sachin, found it intensely stimulating. One day, when the class was particularly attentive, and I was feeling more than usually inspired, I was explaining the last verse of Shelley's 'The Cloud',[17] and discovering in it greater and greater depths of meaning, when suddenly I realized *I was teaching the students Buddhism.* It was not that I had forgotten about the poem I was supposed to be explaining, and had unconsciously slipped into teaching Buddhism instead. In explaining the poem I *was* teaching Buddhism. This could only mean that at a certain level of experience poetry and Buddhism – poetry and the Dharma – were the same thing. There was a sense in which Beauty *was* Truth, and Truth

Beauty, and even if this was *not* all that I needed to know on earth it had at least become clear to me that my interest in poetry was not incompatible with the spiritual life, as I had sometimes felt, or had been made to feel, but that the two things were complementary aspects of the same process of higher human development.

What with sponsoring lectures and educational film shows, opening the Recreation Hut, and starting evening tutorial classes, the YMBA's achievements during the first three or four months of its existence were not negligible. Swale and I were pleased that it had been possible to do so much since the time when he and I and Dhammajoti (now safely back in Sarnath) had held our first discussions and the idea of starting a Young Men's Buddhist Association in Kalimpong had hovered above our heads like a beautiful iridescent ball. Gyan Jyoti was pleased that the Dharmodaya Vihara was at last being put to good use. Parents were pleased that their sons were being kept off the streets and given help with their studies. The young men of Kalimpong were pleased that they had a place of their own to which they could go, where they could meet their friends, play games, and receive private tuition. The illiterate were pleased that there were educational film shows for them to see. The literate were pleased that there were interesting lectures for them to attend. Buddhists generally were pleased that there were signs of Buddhist revival in Kalimpong. The only person who was not pleased with what we were doing (with the possible exception of the Christian missionaries, whom I had not yet met) was Great Wisdom. He sat behind his little table in the library with a more and more vindictive smile on his bullfrog face, and spent more and more of his time writing letters on long rolls of paper that curled over the edge of the table and dropped in great coils onto the floor. At first I did not take much notice of him. Ever since my arrival he had shown no disposition to be friendly, and had in fact ignored me as much as possible. It was only when I overheard Nucche arguing hotly with him one day that I realized something was amiss. What the argument was about Nucche would not say. Eventually I learned that Great Wisdom had been abusing the YMBA to the people who patronized the library and sending false reports of what was happening at the vihara to his former disciples in Nepal, and that Nucche, on coming to know of this, had decided to have the matter out with him. The reason for the ex-monk's interminable letter-writing was now clear. What was not so clear at this stage, even to Nucche, was the harm the long rolls of paper were doing. Uncoiling from the library floor, they were carrying all over Nepal the same lying message. The Newars had lost control of the Dharmodaya Vihara. It had been overrun by low caste people from the bazaar who were using it for parties and dances. They were in fact tearing the place down over his head. If some of the monks did not come soon and help him drive the intruders out the vihara would soon be completely destroyed.

Even when it became clear what harm Great Wisdom's letters had been doing I found it difficult to understand how anyone could have taken his allegations seriously. After the establishment of the YMBA I had written to the Dharmodaya Sabha asking for permission to use the vihara for our activities until we were able to acquire a place of our own, and this permission we had received and had gratefully acknowledged in the first issue of *Stepping Stones*. Our presence in the vihara was thus perfectly legitimate and there was no reason for any misunderstanding about it. As for what actually happened at the vihara, and whether anyone was really tearing the place down over Great Wisdom's head, these were things that could be easily ascertained by anyone living in Kalimpong who cared to interest himself in the matter. (The 'tearing down' apparently referred to the removal of a wooden partition in the Recreation Hut.) What was *really* upsetting Great Wisdom, it seemed, was the fact that the vihara was being used to such an extent by non-Newars, particularly by 'low caste people from the bazaar', by which he apparently meant Sachin, Padam, Lachuman, and other students belonging to the same low-ranking Nepali Hindu caste. Though as a monk he had opposed the caste system in Nepal, in reality he had opposed it only to the extent that it discriminated against the Newars. Like many other people, he resented being discriminated against by those who were 'above' him, but had no objection to practising discrimination himself against those who were 'below' him. It was not so much that he disbelieved in the caste system, as that he wanted a higher place in it for the Newars.

Sectarian narrow-mindedness was not the only reason why Great Wisdom was not pleased with what we were doing. There were also reasons of a more personal nature. Before my arrival on the scene, and particularly before the establishment of the YMBA, not much happened at the vihara, not many people came there, and he had more or less complete control over the place. This meant that he was able to let out rooms, and sell off bamboos from the *jhora*, without anyone being any the wiser. He was also able to pocket the proceeds. Now that there were so many people around, and the rooms were all being used, he could no longer do either of these things. Moreover, he was afraid that the YMBA might take over the running of the library, with the result that he would lose his job, and with it the stipend that was his sole remaining source of income.

All this I came to learn only much later. Even if I had known it at the time it might not have given me so much cause for concern as did the fact that there was disharmony within the YMBA. Since practically the day of Joe's arrival in Kalimpong he and Swale had not got on well together. Swale professed himself extremely disappointed with Joe. He had met him only once in Lucknow, he explained, and had no idea what he was really like. Had he known, he would never have invited him up to Kalimpong to join us. Joe, for his part, professed himself extremely disappointed with Swale – as well as with the YMBA. Had he known that we did not have premises of our own, and that a wealthy local Buddhist had *not* promised to give us 20,000 rupees, as Swale had written and told him (Swale denied this), he would never have left Lucknow, where in any case he had all the Buddhist work he wanted. In private each confided to me what he thought of the other. According to Swale, Joe was not a gentleman. According to Joe, Swale was not a Buddhist. When they met, they sometimes found it difficult to be polite to each other. Swale's attitude towards Joe was one of cold antipathy, as though Joe was a kind of poisonous reptile. Joe's attitude towards Swale was one of icy revulsion, as though Swale was a kind of obscene monster. It was clear that if things continued in this way there would be room in the YMBA for only one of my two helpers, and that I would have to choose between them.

5
WIDENING CIRCLES

The YMBA had been established in May as the Young Men's Buddhist Association, Kalimpong, and its objects were to unite the young men of Kalimpong and to propagate the teachings of Buddhism by means of social, educational, and religious activities. Towards the end of the year the name of the organization was changed to the Young Men's Buddhist Association (India), while its two objects were combined and enlarged into the single object of disseminating the teaching of the Buddha among the young men of India by means of social, cultural, and religious activities. (The head office of the Association remained in Kalimpong.) These changes reflected our recognition of the fact that although the work of the YMBA was confined to Kalimpong it was in principle capable of a much wider extension. Indeed, they reflected our recognition of the fact that the process of extension had already begun. A few months earlier, Kashyapji had paid a brief visit to the city of Ajmer, in Rajputana, on the other side of India. In consequence of this visit members of the Koliya Rajput community, who claimed to be the modern descendants of the Koliya clan to which belonged Māyādevī, the mother of the future Buddha, had formed a YMBA of their own, and in October or November this organization affiliated itself to us as our first branch. The moving spirit behind the affiliation was Ram Singh Chhawara, a pushing young man who later studied Buddhism for a few months in Burma and changed his name to Rahula Suman Chhawara. As secretary of the Ajmer branch he tried to start activities there on the model we had already established and brought the work of the YMBA to the attention of a growing number of people in north-west India. Both inside and outside Kalimpong we were becoming better known.

In Kalimpong itself we were becoming better known partly on account of the lectures I was giving under the auspices of the Institute of Culture. The 'Institute' was the darling brain-child of a middle-aged Bengali named Mr Indra, who with his stick, Bengali shawl, and almost obsequious politeness, was a well-known figure in Kalimpong. Meetings were held once a month, in a small hotel, or rather boarding house, of which Mr Indra was the proprietor, and before long I was a favourite speaker. My first lecture, the first of many, was given towards the end of September, and was on the subject of 'The Way to Nirvāṇa.'

> Stressing that religion was not the negation, but the fulfilment, of life, the speaker said that the Way to Nirvāṇa, the Middle Way or Noble Eightfold Path taught by the Buddha, was the Path of the Higher Evolution, which led men from humanity to superhumanity, to Buddhahood, just as the path of the lower evolution had led him from animality to humanity. Religion was therefore a perfectly natural thing, the finest flowering of life. It consisted in complete unfoldment of the latent spiritual faculties of man. It was a matter of being and becoming, not of mere blind faith or unintelligent acceptance. Moreover, it was a process in which every individual human being participated, for every single action, whether of thought, word or deed, was fraught with spiritual significance, and carried the doer either upwards towards Nirvāṇa or downwards away from it.[18]

So far as I know, this was the first time I had spoken of Buddhism as the path of the Higher Evolution and the first time I had distinguished this from the path of the lower evolution. From what obscure corner of my reading I produced these terms, or indeed whether I coined them – or thought I coined them – myself for the occasion, I no longer recollect. In any case, it was not until a quarter of a century later that I took them up again and attempted to give a more detailed and systematic interpretation of Buddhism along 'evolutionary' lines. Meanwhile, I almost always wrote and spoke of it in purely traditional terms. The reason why in my first lecture at the Institute of Culture I departed from my usual practice was that its membership consisted, for the most part, of Westernized and secularized Bengali Hindus who might conceivably find Buddhism more intelligible, and perhaps more acceptable, if it was presented to them in terms of modern thought. This was not to say that such an approach was not liable to misunderstanding. Among the thirty or more people who attended the lecture were two newly arrived Seventh Day Adventist missionaries, one American and one Dutch. As I left I heard one of them say to the other, with a dismissive nod of the head, 'It's a form of Naturalism.' Perhaps he had taken too literally what I had said about religion being a perfectly natural thing. By this I did not mean to reduce it from a spiritual to a mundane activity, or to deny the existence of the transcendental element in religion (religion itself being, indeed, nothing but the science and the art of the Transcendental), but only to draw attention to man's inherent affinity with that element, which was in truth not something imposed upon him from without (as in Christian supernaturalism) but rather something developed from within.

One of the first signs that we were becoming better known outside Kalimpong was the appearance on the veranda of the Dharmodaya Vihara, one day towards the end of the rainy season, of two tired and footsore young aspirants to Enlightenment and monastic ordination. They had come to us from Sarnath. Indeed, they had been sent to us from Sarnath. Whether the Maha Bodhi Society monks there really believed we were in a position to provide them with the facilities they required, or whether they had merely found it a convenient way of getting rid of them, I did not know. The fact was that the monks had assured the two young aspirants that Kalimpong was the best possible place for them, the YMBA the best possible organization, and Sangharakshita the best possible 'guide, philosopher, and friend'.[19] To Kalimpong, therefore, had they come. They were an oddly assorted pair. By coincidence they had arrived at Sarnath at the same time, and for the same purpose, and finding themselves treated with equal indifference by the resident monks spent most of their time together and became good friends. Their names were Wee and Saraswati. Wee was a smiling but taciturn Straits Chinese of about twenty, with the usual plump face and gold-filled teeth, Saraswati a slender, worried-looking North Indian Brahmin of about seventeen. The former wore a crumpled Western suit, the latter the more traditional white dhoti and shirt. As they stood forlornly there on the veranda, dripping with rain, I remembered my own difficulties and disappointments in connection with ordination, and decided to take them in. During the time that they were at the vihara they gave me no cause to regret this decision. They joined me in my morning puja and meditation, studied the Dharma together, helped Joe with the cooking and shopping, sat in on the evening tutorial classes, and made friends among the students. In short, they were model disciples. Unfortunately, they had been at the vihara only three weeks when the world they thought they had left behind for ever caught up with them. At least, it caught up with Saraswati. Late one afternoon there appeared on the veranda an elderly Indian Brahmin wearing a white dhoti and shirt and carrying a black umbrella. It was Saraswati's father. As soon as Saraswati saw him the colour left his face, he fell at the old man's feet with a cry, the old man bent down to embrace him, and both of them burst into tears. The upshot of this affecting scene was that, after a brief argument, Saraswati reluctantly agreed to accompany his father home and to go back to college. They left the next morning. Deprived of the company of his friend, Wee became sad and restless, and on my advice eventually returned to Malaya and entered a Chinese monastery in order to undergo the traditional training.

Wee and Saraswati were not the only persons I had to take in during that rainy season. There was at least one more. He came not from Sarnath but from Rajgir, and had been sent not by the Maha Bodhi Society monks but by my own teacher Jagdish Kashyap. Far from being an aspirant to Enlightenment and ordination, the newcomer already wore the yellow robes of the *śrāmaṇera* or novice monk, having been ordained by Kashyapji himself at Rajgir a few months earlier. Kamalashila, as my teacher had named him, was a very thin, very dark, very talkative Bihari of about my own age. Why Kashyapji had named him Kamalashila was not immediately apparent to me. The original Kamalaśīla had been a celebrated Buddhist philosopher of the Sautrāntika-Vijñānavāda school, the author of a commentary on the encyclopaedic *Tattvasaṃgraha* of his master Śāntarakṣita, and one of the brightest ornaments of the ancient Buddhist monastic university of Nālandā. The latter-day Kamalashila had no interest in Buddhist philosophy whatever. Indeed, he seemed to have no interest in Buddhism. His real interest was in nature cure, and it was he who had set up the nature cure clinic at the Japanese Buddhist temple about which Kashyapji had told me on his last visit. Reading between the lines of the letter of introduction with which Kashyapji had provided him, and listening to his own rather negative account of how the clinic was being run, I could not help thinking that there had been a disagreement between him and his teacher, and it was on account of this disagreement that he had left Rajgir. Be that as it may, before long there was certainly a disagreement between him and me, and it was certainly on account of this disagreement that he left Kalimpong. The disagreement was over Buddhism itself. Kamalashila declared that such things as puja and meditation and the study of Buddhist texts were a waste of time. What was really needed was social work. Buddhist monks ought to be social workers. Whether he went so far as to say that social workers were the true Buddhist monks I cannot be sure, but he certainly said enough to leave me wondering why Kashyapji had ordained him, especially as he had never ordained anybody before, and might have been expected to exercise extreme caution in the selection of the first of his own *śrāmaṇera* disciples. In any case, Kamalashila had only the haziest of ideas about what constituted social work. So far as I could make out, it meant little more than going from place to place exhorting everybody to work hard for the good of the nation. Though he was less well educated, there was more than a touch of Anthony Elenjimittam about Kamalashila.

Despite our disagreement over Buddhism, which made it difficult for him to stay long at the vihara, the talkative Bihari *śrāmaṇera* and I parted quite amicably, and he left Kalimpong for Assam with a large bundle of *Stepping-Stones* to distribute. As it happened, this was the best thing he could have done. The Barua, Tai, and Tamang Buddhists of Assam, who had very little contact with the rest of the Buddhist world, were glad to see him on account of his robe, on account of the news he brought of Buddhist activities in Kalimpong, and on account of the copies of *Stepping-Stones* he distributed so lavishly among them. As for Kamalashila himself, with his restless spirit he was glad to be constantly on the move, glad to be continually meeting new people, glad to be doing something useful. In the course of a couple of months he covered practically the entire state, penetrating into remote Buddhist villages, spreading news of the YMBA, and enrolling subscribers to *Stepping-Stones*. In this way we became well known to the Buddhists of Assam. On his way back to Rajgir Kamalashila spent a few days with us in Kalimpong. For the next two years this was to be his regular programme. After spending a few months at the Japanese Buddhist temple with

Kashyapji and nature cure, he would come up to Kalimpong, collect a bundle of *Stepping-Stones*, and be off with them to Assam, visiting us on the way back to report on the success of his mission. Thanks to his efforts, by the time I visited Assam myself a few years later the ground was well prepared.

Though Kamalashila was our only colporteur, and though his travels, extensive though they may have been, were confined to a single state of the Indian Union, it was in fact mainly through *Stepping-Stones* that the YMBA was becoming better known outside Kalimpong. The flashes sent out by the second beautiful iridescent ball we had invited to descend were indeed more brilliant than those sent out by the first and were indeed being seen even farther afield. The second ball was in fact now illuminating the first. At the same time, the second ball itself, as refracted through the medium of *Stepping-Stones*, was shifting its colours slightly, incorporating here a brighter hue, there a more delicate tint, so as to create a richer and more harmonious effect. In the course of the first six months of its existence our monthly journal of Himalayan religion, culture, and education, had attracted not only more and more readers and subscribers but also a number of gifted new contributors, each of whom was helping to make it a more adequate embodiment of the idea with which it had been started. The first of our new contributors was Dr René de Nebesky-Wojkowitz, a young Austrian anthropologist who had arrived in Kalimpong with Dr Rock, and who was staying with him at the Himalayan Hotel and functioning in a secretarial capacity. He was gathering material for a book on the Oracles and Demons of Tibet, as he called them, and in order to do original research in the subject was studying Tibetan, both classical and colloquial. For one reason or another, the life he led with Dr Rock was not an easy one, and he sometimes relieved his feelings towards that peppery old gentleman by telling stories about him that were not always to the latter's credit. One of his favourite stories was of how Dr Rock had, in the interests of anthropology, once spent several months as the third wife of a Lolo chief. Among our other new contributors were Lama Anagārika Govinda and Alfred Sorensen, alias Shri Shunyata, as he also called himself. Lama Govinda had hailed the appearance of *Stepping-Stones* with great enthusiasm, sending me letters of advice and encouragement after every issue, and promising support and cooperation. The cooperation was not long in coming, taking first the form of a parable entitled 'Look Deeper!', in which a Thera of Nālandā is taught by Avalokiteśvara, the Bodhisattva of Compassion, to see a village girl not as a 'bag of bones' but as a living and suffering fellow-creature,[20] and afterwards that of a whole series of brilliant and inspiring articles. The first of these articles, which appeared in the November issue, was entitled 'The Universal Perspective of the Bodhisattva Ideal'. In it Lama Govinda struck a characteristic note, declaring,

> The surest way to [get rid of the ego] is to see ourselves in the proper perspective to the rest of the world, that is, in the universal perspective which has been opened by the teachings of the Enlightened Ones, illustrated by their lives and emphasized by the teachers of the Great Vehicle. As long as we see life only through the pin-point of our ordinary human consciousness, it seems to make no sense, while if we could see the whole 'picture' of the universe, as mirrored in the mind of an Enlightened One, we would discover its meaning.[21]

Alfred Sorensen, alias Shri Shunyata ('Mr Emptiness'), was a Dane who had become an Indian sadhu or holy man. Prince Peter had written an article about him for the October issue of *Stepping-Stones* and it was through this article that he had come to know of our existence. Thereafter he was a regular correspondent, sending me long rhapsodizing letters about the Himalayas and the spiritual life. Sometimes the letters were accompanied by richly poetic articles and stories. Sometimes the letters themselves turned into articles. In either case, what he had written needed a good deal of rather drastic editing, not to say pruning, before it was fit for publication.

My own contribution to *Stepping-Stones* consisted mainly, and most importantly, of the editorials that appeared at the front of the issues. In these editorials I continued to strike the same unambiguously 'spiritual' note that I had struck in the first issue. Not unnaturally, my choice of topic was generally determined by my own current preoccupations, both as an individual Buddhist and as a member of the Buddhist spiritual community. Having spoken, in the first issue, of the Way, I went on to speak, in subsequent issues, of 'Unity' and of 'The Voice Within', besides asserting that 'Everything That Lives is Holy', dealing with 'The Problem of Desire', and describing 'The Awakening of the Heart'. In connection with each of these topics I tried to give direct expression to my deepest experiences and most dearly held beliefs. I tried to communicate, in fact, my vision of Buddhism – sometimes in contradistinction to the various erroneous 'views' about it current in various quarters. 'Unity' was a plea for selflessness and 'mutual interpenetration' among the followers of the Buddha; 'The Voice Within' an indictment of 'the intolerable weight of the external', whether secular or 'religious'; 'Everything That Lives is Holy' a reminder that the presence or absence of ego-consciousness was the true criterion of the spiritual value of an action, and so on.[22]

With so much of my time being taken up by the YMBA and *Stepping-Stones*, I was unable to do much in the way of literary work, and for months together the editorials were my sole literary productions. That is to say, they were my sole literary productions in prose. Inspired as I was by the sights and sounds of Kalimpong the writing of poems went on without interruption. Haiku and other verse forms continued to mirror external images and internal moods. Besides writing the poems, I was also getting some of them published. If the YMBA was becoming better known outside Kalimpong mainly through *Stepping-Stones*, I myself was becoming better known outside Kalimpong – better known outside the small world of Indian Buddhist revival – mainly through my poems. For the past several years I had contributed both poems and articles to journals like the *Maha Bodhi* (Calcutta) and the *Vedanta Kesari* (Madras), but as the 'house' journals of particular religious movements these publications had a limited appeal and, therefore, only a small circulation. In the same month that *Stepping Stones* came into existence my poems started appearing in the *Illustrated Weekly of India*. This was the leading magazine of its kind in the whole country. Published from Bombay under the editorship of C. R. Mandy, an English littérateur, it circulated widely among the English-educated 'middle class', being read literally 'from the Himalayas to Cape Comorin'. Copies were even available in Kalimpong. The first of my poems to appear in the *Illustrated* was 'Village India',[23] which I had written in Bihar a few weeks before coming to Kalimpong; the second was 'The Bodhisattva',[24] written in Kalimpong itself and reflecting the deep influence that was being exerted upon me by the bodhisattva ideal, especially as depicted in Śāntideva's *Śikṣā-samuccaya*. For many years this was one of my most popular poems, being reprinted in Buddhist magazines all over the world. In it the bodhisattva, speaking in his own person, gives expression to his determination not to enter into the bliss of Nirvāna until all beings, down to a blade of grass, have entered into it first. He is willing to postpone his 'own' Nirvāna, and even to endure endless torments, so long as even one living being remains undelivered from suffering.

Was it a coincidence that I wrote this poem only a few weeks after establishing personal contact, through correspondence, with one who was widely hailed as a bodhisattva after his death, and who did, in effect, deliver millions of people from suffering? The name of Dr B. R. Ambedkar, the great Scheduled Caste leader of western India, had been familiar to me since the previous year, when I had first heard of it in connection with the controversies over the proposed Hindu Code Bill which he, as Law Minister, was drafting for presentation to the Indian Parliament. More recently, I had read the characteristically pungent article on 'The Buddha and the Future of His Religion' that he had contributed to the Vaiśākha number of the *Maha Bodhi*.[25] In fact, towards the end of June I had written to him expressing my appreciation of this article, and telling him about the formation of the YMBA, and about ten days later had received an encouraging reply. This exchange of ours was to have momentous consequences. Through 'Village India' and 'The Bodhisattva' and the rest of the poems that appeared in the *Illustrated Weekly* over the years I became known to tens of thousands of cultivated middle-class people who appreciated English poetry of the more traditional type. As a result of my contact with Dr Ambedkar I became known, towards the end of the decade, to hundreds of thousands of despised and rejected ex-Untouchable people who, inspired by the example of their great leader, had burst asunder the age-old shackles of orthodox Hinduism and gone for Refuge to the Buddha, the Dharma, and the Sangha. In the concluding paragraph of his letter Ambedkar wrote:

> Great responsibility lies on the shoulders of the Bhikkhus if this attempt at the revival of Buddhism is to be a success. They must be more active than they have been. They must come out of their shell and be in the first rank of the fighting forces. I am glad you have started the YMBA in Kalimpong. You should be [even] more active than that.

Three months later I took Ambedkar's words quite literally. If Kalimpong was my shell, I came out of it. At the beginning of October, the YMBA having apparently been established on a sufficiently secure footing to be able to function without me for a few days, I paid a brief visit to Darjeeling 'for the purpose of establishing personal contact with representatives of religious and humanitarian organizations.'[26] I did not go alone. With me went Sachin. A few weeks earlier he had been elected Assistant (Games) Secretary, and this not only involved him more deeply in the work of the YMBA but had also brought him into closer personal contact with me. When I decided to go to Darjeeling he therefore decided to go too. He would give me what help he could in my mission, and also pay a surprise visit to his maternal grandmother and other relations.

Darjeeling was thirty-two miles from Kalimpong by road but only fifteen miles away, so I was told, 'as the crow flies'. It was scattered along a ridge, at a height of 8,000 feet, on the other side of the River Teesta. This meant that in order to get there from Kalimpong one first plunged *down* 4,000 feet to the valley (or rather, to the bottom of the crack between the two hillsides), crossed over Teesta Bridge, then shot *up* 8,000 feet through tropical jungle, tea gardens, and tracts of pine forest to Ghoom by a series of hairpin bends even longer and more acute than those by which one had come down from Kalimpong to Teesta Bridge – all in the space of two to two-and-a-half hours, depending on the precise degree of impatience and recklessness on the driver's part. This was altogether too much for my stomach, and between Ghoom and Darjeeling I was violently sick. Hardly without exception, this was to be my experience on nearly all my subsequent visits to Darjeeling, at least until I discovered car sickness tablets, and the fact may have accounted for the somewhat mixed feelings with which I came to regard the Queen of the Hill Stations. On the present occasion, having recovered from the effects of the journey, and adjusted to the change of altitude, I started looking about me.

Darjeeling was much bigger than Kalimpong, much closer up (apparently) to the snows of Mount Kanchenjunga, much more definitely Nepalese in character – and also much less Europeanized than at the time of my previous visit. (This visit had taken place in 1945, when I was still in the army, and I had vivid recollections of the Chowrasta and Observation Hill, as well as of the Tibetan monastery at Ghoom.)[27] Whether on account of the rarified atmosphere of the place, or whether because, the rains being over and gone, the festival season – the season of the autumn pujas – was now coming upon us, a marked sense of exhilaration prevailed. The rose-cheeked young men seemed more animated than in Kalimpong, as well as healthier and happier. Seeing their cheerful Mongoloid faces, I could not but feel more animated myself. So much so, indeed, that before long I had seen all the things I wanted to see, and met all the representatives of religious and humanitarian organizations I was supposed to meet.

At least half the people I met in this capacity seemed to be called Mr Lama. Tall or short, fat or thin, wearing traditional Nepalese costume or a version of Western dress, there were Mr Lamas by the dozen in the town, the only difference between them in this respect being a bewildering variety of initials. Nor was this all. Not only were there Mr Lamas by the dozen: there were Mrs Lamas by the dozen too, as well as an even greater number of Master Lamas and Miss Lamas. Now 'Lama', I had always understood, meant '(spiritual) superior', and signified a spiritual teacher, or guru. Was there, then, a whole tribe of gurus in Darjeeling, gurus of both sexes and all ages, from the lean and slippered pantaloon to the mewling and puking infant? The mystery was soon cleared up. The Mr Lamas were the hereditary priests of the Tamang Buddhist community. Once upon a time they – or their ancestors – had been real lamas, real gurus. But corruption had set in. They had married, founded families, and adopted secular occupations. Now they knew no more about Buddhism, no more about the distinctive teachings of the Nyingma school, to which they traditionally belonged, than did the rest of the eighteen septs into which the Tamang community was divided. A few of them still officiated in the temples on a part-time basis, but most of them had not functioned even as hereditary priests – even to this very limited extent – for several generations. Far from signifying a spiritual teacher, the word 'lama' was no more than a family surname.

Most of the Mr Lamas were well aware of the true nature of the situation. Some reacted to it by wanting to throw away the ritual bathwater along with the doctrinal baby. Others looked away from the Nyingma tradition altogether and in the direction of Bengali-Burmese Theravāda, a small outpost of which existed on the outskirts of the town in the form of the Gandhamadan Vihara, a branch of the Bengal Buddhist Association. Mr Lamas of this type were, however, comparatively rare. Like the rest of the Tamang community, nearly all the Mr Lamas, as well as all the Mrs Lamas and most of the Master and Miss Lamas, had a strong sense of ethnic and religious identity, and thought of themselves as being definitely Tamangs and definitely Nyingma Buddhists. Weak as they may have been in knowledge, there was no doubt that they were strong in faith and devotion – to the extent that devotion can, in fact, be thus separated from knowledge. At all events, their devotion was sufficiently strong – and their material resources sufficiently plentiful – for them to have built in the heart of the bazaar area a Nyingma temple of the typical Nepalese pagoda type, and it was this temple that gave me the experience that was, spiritually speaking, the climax of my entire visit. I had never seen an image of Padmasambhava before, perhaps not even a painting. As I entered the temple, all the greater was the shock, therefore, when I saw in front of me, three or four times larger than life, the mighty sedent figure of the semi-legendary founder and inspirer of the Nyingma tradition, a skull cup in his left hand, a staff topped with skulls in the crook of his left arm, and the celebrated 'wrathful smile' on his moustached face. All this I took in instantly, together with the 'lotus hat', the richly embroidered robes, and the much smaller flanking figures of his two consorts, one Tibetan and one Nepalese. Having taken it in, I felt that it had always been there, and that in seeing the figure of Padmasambhava I had become conscious of a spiritual presence that had in fact been with me all the time. Though I had never seen the figure of Padmasambhava before, it was familiar to me in a way that no other figure on earth was familiar: familiar and fascinating. It was familiar as my own self, yet at the same time infinitely mysterious, infinitely wonderful, and infinitely inspiring. Familiar, mysterious, wonderful, and inspiring it was to remain. Indeed, from then on the figure of the Precious Guru – Guru Rimpoche – was to occupy a permanent place in my inner spiritual world, even as it played a prominent part in the spiritual life and imagination of the entire Himalayan region.

Though seeing the figure of Padmasambhava was the climax of my visit, there was another experience in store for me before my departure. This experience took place not in a temple but in a bookshop. Browsing round the shelves of either the Oxford or the Cambridge Bookshop with Sachin (there were no bookshops in Kalimpong), I came across a dozen or more slim volumes in light blue covers. It was the cheap, Indian edition of the works of Rabindranath Tagore. A glance was enough to tell me that here was a treasure indeed, and since the volumes were so moderately priced that even a penniless monk could afford them I at once bought *Fruit-Gathering* for Sachin, as a Puja present, and *Stray Birds* for myself. *Stray Birds* was a series of more than three hundred poetic aphorisms. Some of these aphorisms moved me deeply, though others I found jejune. Subsequently I learned that they were not really aphorisms at all but Tagore's own adaptations of the Japanese haiku, and that he had started writing them on his visit to Japan, where he was frequently called upon to contribute 'a few lines' to the album of some friend or admirer. Adaptations or not, the form of these little effusions appealed to me greatly, and not long after my return to Kalimpong I started producing 'poetic aphorisms' of my own. Like Tagore's, these aphorisms were the spontaneous overflow of some of my more intimate thoughts and emotions – thoughts and emotions that might otherwise have found no outward expression. As Tagore himself put it, in the opening aphorisms of the book:

Stray birds of summer come to my window to sing and fly away.
    And yellow leaves of autumn, which have no songs, flutter and
fall there with a sigh.[28]

In the course of the next two years I was to produce more than a hundred of these free adaptations of, or variations on, the traditional Japanese haiku, stricter imitations of which, both rhymed and unrhymed, I continued to write. While not producing nearly so many of them as Tagore, in one respect at least I went one better than the great Bengali poet. Though each of my aphorisms was complete in itself, I arranged the majority of them into a sequence in such a way as to tell a kind of story.[29] This development did not take place until nearly three years after my experience in the bookshop, when I had made the journey from Kalimpong to Darjeeling at least three more times. Meanwhile, my first – or rather my second – visit to Darjeeling was at an end. Some of the people I had met, including three or four of the ubiquitous Mr Lamas, had suggested that a branch of the YMBA should be started in Darjeeling. I had bought myself a copy of *Stray Birds*. Above all, I had seen the figure of Padmasambhava. I therefore returned to Kalimpong well content with the success of my mission.

    While I was taking Ambedkar's advice to heart and 'coming out of my shell' Joe stayed firmly put in his. During the four days that Sachin and I were away he did his best to keep the evening tutorial classes going (Swale had dropped out some time before), but it was not easy for him to do this single-handed, and upon my reappearance in my accustomed place on the bed by the window I was greeted not only with broad smiles of welcome but also with sighs of relief. The matriculation and intermediate arts examinations were now close at hand, there were only a few more weeks left for preparation, and the students were anxious not to lose any more time. By popular request, the duration of the classes was increased, so that they encroached on the time hitherto reserved for ping-pong and carrom-board, while additional classes were held on Sunday afternoons. Soon I was more deeply immersed than ever in the teaching of English and logic, and what with this and other YMBA work was kept fully occupied. Indeed, during the rest of October and until well into November it sometimes seemed that I had settled at the Dharmodaya Vihara for good and that there stretched before me an unending vista of classes, lectures, and editorial work. But this was not to prove the case. Though the YMBA was to continue becoming better known, both inside and outside Kalimpong, there was to be a temporary setback, and I myself was not only to come further out of my shell but to be thrown out of the nest altogether.

6
ACCEPTANCE AND REJECTION

According to the most ancient Buddhist traditions, there were three levels of monkhood. There was the *śrāmaṇera* or novice monk, the *bhikṣu* or full monk, and the *sthavira* or elder monk. The novice monk observed ten precepts and could be ordained by a single elder monk, provided the consent of the other monks had been obtained. The *bhikṣu* or full monk observed (according to the Theravāda) 227 precepts, seventy-five of which were really rules of etiquette and seven rules of procedure to be observed by the *bhikṣus* collectively, and could be ordained (outside the 'Middle Country') by a minimum of five full monks in good standing among whom there was at least one elder monk to act as president. The elder monk was simply one who had been a full monk for at least ten years, or rather, one who had observed at least ten 'rains residences'. Ordination as a novice monk was often known, in English, as the lower ordination, and ordination as a full monk as the higher ordination. There was no special ceremony for the elder monk. On completing his tenth rains residence the full monk automatically became entitled, provided he was otherwise qualified, to preside at *bhikṣu* ordinations and to accept junior monks as personal disciples.

I was of course a novice monk, and more than a year-and-a-half had passed since my ordination at Kusinara. In the Theravāda countries of South-East Asia, as I well knew, only a short time usually elapsed before the novice monk became a full monk. Indeed, if he was over twenty (age being reckoned from conception, not birth) the likelihood was that the higher ordination would follow immediately upon the lower, often as part of one and the same ceremony. Had I become a *śrāmaṇera* in Ceylon or Burma instead of in India there was little doubt that I would have been a *bhikṣu* by now. I certainly wanted to be a *bhikṣu*. When the idea had first taken root in my mind I could not say: probably it was quite soon after I became a *śrāmaṇera* – perhaps as soon as I grasped what being a *bhikṣu*, as distinct from being a *śrāmaṇera*, really meant. Since that brilliantly sunny day in March when Kashyapji had enjoined me to stay in Kalimpong and work for the good of Buddhism, and especially since the YMBA had come into existence, the idea of being a *bhikṣu* had taken firmer root than ever. Indeed, it had flowered into a definite wish for the higher ordination. Though a *śrāmaṇera* had 'gone forth' from home into the homeless life he had not won 'acceptance' (as the word *upasampadā*, signifying *bhikṣu* ordination, was sometimes translated) and was not, therefore, really a member of the monastic order. In a sense he was neither monk nor layman. He dwelt in a kind of intermediate state between two worlds, the spiritual and the secular, at best occupying a place on the fringes of monasticism. For me this was no longer enough. I wanted to be a *real* monk, not a hanger-on of the monastic order. I wanted to identify myself with Buddhism and the spiritual life as fully as I possibly could, and to know that the fact that I had so identified myself was acknowledged by other Buddhists. This meant, in effect, receiving the higher ordination – meant becoming a *bhikṣu*, a full monk. As a full monk I would not only be able to commit myself more firmly to the goal of Enlightenment, but also to work more effectively for the good of Buddhism. Eighteen months after my ordination as a novice monk so much, at least, was clear to me. But where could I be ordained? Who would be willing to admit me to the monastic order? There were no Theravāda monks in Kalimpong, and I did not know enough about Tibetan Buddhism to be able to think of asking for the higher ordination in that quarter.

A few weeks after my visit to Darjeeling, when I was still deeply immersed in English and logic, there came a letter that seemed to point to a way out of the difficulty. The letter was from Venerable M. Sangharatana Thera, the Secretary of the Sarnath Centre of the Maha Bodhi Society, and was an invitation to the nineteenth anniversary celebration of the opening of the Mulagandhakuti Vihara. The Mulagandhakuti or 'Original Perfumed Chamber' Vihara – so named after the room or hut occupied by the Buddha, especially the one made for him by Anāthapiṇḍika – was the temple that Anagārika Dharmapala, the founder of the Maha Bodhi Society, had built on the site of the Deer Park where the Buddha had delivered his first discourse, and I knew that the anniversary of its opening was celebrated each year by hundreds, even thousands, of people from all over the Buddhist world. Among these people there would surely be many *bhikṣus*, some of whom might be willing to make up the quorum of ten *bhikṣus* needed to confer higher ordination in the Middle Country. I therefore wrote to Venerable Sangharatana accepting his invitation, and to U Chandramani formally requesting the higher ordination, as I knew that in most years the old man came down to Sarnath for the anniversary celebration. I also took the precaution of writing to U Kittima, U Chandramani's seniormost disciple, who was in charge of the Burmese temple in Sarnath, asking him to intercede with 'Babaji' – as our teacher was affectionately called – on my behalf. The letters having been sent, there was nothing more I could do except hope that by the time I reached Sarnath arrangements for my higher ordination would have been made.

I did not have to leave at once. This was fortunate, as it meant I could keep the tutorial classes going right up to the eve of the examinations, as well as bring out the November issue of *Stepping-Stones* and make arrangements for the running of the YMBA during my absence. It also meant that for a few more weeks I could enjoy the perfect autumn weather, which brought not only continual sunshine and an abundance of flowers but the daily unveiling of the sublime spectacle of Mount Kanchenjunga. Whenever I looked out of my window I could see afar off the dazzling-white mass of the great snow range rising from behind its saddleback against a backdrop of dark blue sky – the topmost peak wearing a plume of white smoke. As I knew by this time, the name Kanchenjunga meant 'the Five Treasures of the Snow', the five treasures being gold, silver, gems (or weapons), grain, and sacred books. According to local belief, the mountain was the abode of many gods – was itself a god. To set human foot upon it would be an act of sacrilege, and it had therefore never been climbed by anyone.[30]

With autumn had come the Pujas, the great series of Hindu religious festivals that celebrated, among other things, the victory of the hero Rama over the ten-headed tyrant Ravana and of the goddess Durga over the ferocious Buffalo Demon – celebrated, that is to say, the victory of the forces of good over the forces of evil. Like the Christmas season in the West, the Pujas were a time of general rejoicing, of family reunions, of giving and receiving presents and blessings, as well as being, of course, a time of eating, drinking, and making merry. Like Christmas, too, the Pujas were a time for worship – in *their* case the colourful and sanguinary ritual worship of the great Mother Goddess in her various forms, both benign and terrible. In a small, out of the way place like Kalimpong, where there was in any case a substantial Buddhist minority, the Pujas naturally were not celebrated on anything like the scale on which they were celebrated in Calcutta and Kathmandu, or even in Darjeeling. Certain minor festivals were in fact omitted. Nevertheless, even in Kalimpong, despite their comparatively modest scale, the Pujas could not be ignored. From a loudspeaker in the heart of the bazaar there floated up the lilting melody of the latest popular film song. That year, I think, it was *Tu pyara ke sagara ho*, 'You are the Ocean of Love', a song that in the film itself was addressed to Sri Krishna but which was generally given a wider and more romantic application. Along the main road below the vihara, and through the streets of the town, there strolled bands of happy, carefree people, the majority of them Nepalese. Most of the people were dressed in new clothes, with many of the men and boys wearing garlands of marigolds round their necks and red *tika*-marks on their foreheads. Occasionally a cow or a dog with a garland of marigolds and a red *tika*-mark could also be seen. The cow wore its garland and *tika*-mark with dignity, the dog with a raffish air.

I myself took no part in the Puja celebrations, being well content to observe them from a respectful distance. I did, however, buy myself a bright red woollen shawl. This was on account of the season not in the socio-religious but in the meteorological sense, for despite brilliant sunshine and blue skies autumn could be quite cold in the hills – cold enough to make me shiver in my two thin cotton robes. The shawl was of the cheapest kind, costing me only twelve rupees, and I bought it at the Himalayan Store. Twelve rupees being quite a large sum to me then, before making the purchase I debated the pros and cons of the matter anxiously with myself for several days. Did I really need the shawl? What was the justification of spending so much money merely for the sake of comfort? Was it, in fact, merely for the sake of comfort? Ought I to run the risk of catching a chill and thus possibly endangering my health? In the end prudence prevailed over asceticism and I bought the shawl. The bright red colour was the same as that of the poinsettias, or christmas-red as the shrub was called in Kalimpong, great clumps of which were already lifting their scarlet crowns beside the road. Walking through the bazaar I was conscious of being a more conspicuous figure than ever.

Though I myself was content to observe the Pujas from a respectful distance, my students certainly were not. Most of them were eager to participate in the celebrations as fully as their preoccupation with the forthcoming examinations allowed. For some of the more important festivals Sachin, Lachuman, and Padam even appeared in traditional Nepalese costume – seemingly no less self-conscious in their pastel green and pastel blue shirts and jodhpurs, and their conical embroidered caps, than I was in my bright red shawl. Eager as they were to participate in the Pujas, however, the students did not trouble their heads very much about their religious significance. So far as they were concerned, the significance of the various festivals was social and cultural rather than religious. They knew what good Hindus were supposed to do when the Pujas came round, but had no idea why they were supposed to do it. This was particularly the case with a festival, or observance, that came towards the end of the Puja season, and which thanks to the students themselves became a means of raising funds for the YMBA. The festival in question was known as Dewsay or Dewsay Ray. Why it was celebrated, and what the name itself meant, no one in Kalimpong seemed to know. Some thought the words 'Dewsay Ray' were a corruption of Deva Sri Rama, but even this was not certain. All that was certain was that Dewsay was celebrated and that it was celebrated in a particular way. Parties of young men and boys went from door to door singing songs and collecting money. Originally the money thus collected was devoted to religious and charitable purposes, but in recent times things had changed, at least in Kalimpong. Dewsay parties now tended to be made up of very small boys who were out simply to collect sweet money for themselves. For this reason people no longer took Dewsay seriously and gave the boys hardly any money when they called – just a few annas for old times' sake. Some of the students thought it a great pity that Dewsay had degenerated in this way and that money was no longer being collected for religious and charitable purposes. Perhaps the ancient practice could be revived. Why should we not have a YMBA Dewsay party and why should it not go from door to door collecting funds for YMBA activities?

Whether the idea came from me, or from the students themselves, I no longer recollect. It may simply have crystallized 'out of the air' in the course of discussion without being attributable to anybody in particular. At any rate, no sooner was the idea of our sending out our own YMBA Dewsay party put forward than it met with an enthusiastic response, and Sachin undertook the responsibility of forming the party and organizing rehearsals. On 10 and 11 November, therefore, under Sachin's leadership, some fifteen members of the YMBA made the rounds of the town and the Development Area calling at the houses of a number of our friends and sympathizers. Most of these friends and sympathizers were Nepalese Hindus of various castes and tribes, but there were also a few Tibetan Buddhists among them, as well as a few Europeans. Everywhere it went the party received a warm welcome. Nepalese Hindus in particular were overjoyed that the ancient practice had been revived and that Dewsay was again being celebrated in a befitting manner. When a few songs had been sung, the women of the house would smilingly come forward with the traditional ceremonial offering of a trayful of rice on which were flowers and, sometimes, a lighted oil lamp. Among the flowers would be tucked a currency note. At some houses, especially those (not a few) where Sachin was personally known, the party would be invited in for refreshments, or laughingly requested to sing another song. All fifteen students thoroughly enjoyed collecting funds in this way. Accompanied by a small double-headed drum, they sang not only various popular songs but the customary 'Dewsay song'. The latter was a vigorous, not very tuneful chant in which the soloist's appeals for money alternated with a full-throated chorus of '*Dewsay Ray!*' from the rest of the party. From time to time the appeals for money were replaced by nonsense words and phrases which allowed the introduction of an element of buffoonery that set the women tittering. By the time Dewsay was over Sachin and the rest were all suffering from sore throats, but nearly 200 rupees had been collected and everybody was well pleased. Our friends and sympathizers were pleased to have had an opportunity of showing their appreciation of what the YMBA was doing, especially in the way of providing tutorial classes for students. Our members were pleased to have been able to do something for the YMBA themselves, and thus to help me help them.

As usual, the only person who was not pleased was Great Wisdom. Since Nucche's argument with him he had had less to do with me than ever. In fact, even when I was in the library looking at the Buddhist magazines and he was sitting at his little table behind the door he did his best to pretend that I was not there – that I did not exist. This did not, of course, prevent him from abusing the YMBA behind my back as much as ever or from continuing to send false reports of what was happening at the vihara to his former disciples in Nepal. For a long time these reports had met, as it seemed, with no better success than they deserved. No one heeded his call to come and help him drive the low-caste intruders from the bazaar out of the vihara before they destroyed it completely. Probably the monks of Nepal were observing the rains residence. Possibly they were all asleep. Recently, however, there had been a change. Things were at last beginning to move in the direction the ex-monk wanted. Though not pleased with the success of our Dewsay party he was, therefore, not quite so displeased with things in general as he had been, and even permitted himself a triumphant smirk. My first intimation that there was anything wrong came quite unexpectedly. Either shortly before or shortly after the idea of our sending out our own Dewsay party had been put forward (probably before), one of the students, a Nepalese Brahmin, on happening to look out of the window suddenly exclaimed, 'How can such an angry looking man be a Buddhist monk!' Several of the other students rushed to the window, while I turned my head round to look. Sure enough, stomping up the path below was a man in yellowish-brown robes and with an expression of habitual ill-temper on his face. Great Wisdom's call for help had been answered. The reinforcements had at last arrived.

The Venerable Aniruddha, as the angry-looking monk was called, was in his mid-thirties and was, of course, by origin a Newar Buddhist. After being ordained a novice monk by U Chandramani he had gone to Burma for a few years and there received the higher ordination. With his angry look, rough speech, and uncouth ways, he was, in fact, much more like some of the Burmese monks I had seen than their Newar counterparts, Burmese members of the monastic order being a byword for irascibility. The Venerable Aniruddha indeed could be said to exemplify, in many points, Buddhaghosa's classic description of the person of angry temperament.[31] Such a person digs his toes into the ground when walking, is of rigid demeanour, performs any action in a rough and violent manner, eats his food hastily and without pleasure, and (if he is a monk) wears his robes tightly fastened and awry. All this – and more – was true of the Venerable Aniruddha. When we met, his first act was to thrust into my hand a letter from the Secretary of the Dharmodaya Sabha, Venerable Mahanama, informing me that the bearer had been appointed as monk-in-charge of the vihara and that I should carry out whatever instructions he gave me. This was of course only right and proper. The new arrival was a full monk, almost an elder; I was only a novice monk. It was for him to guide me, not for me to guide him. By both actions and words (Venerable Aniruddha spoke a little Hindi) I therefore sought to convey to him that in my eyes he was not just the monk in charge of the vihara but my own immediate monastic superior and that, as directed by Venerable Mahanama, I was ready to carry out all his instructions. For the moment, however, Venerable Aniruddha had no instructions to give. The truth of the matter was, he had arrived fully prepared to do battle on Great Wisdom's behalf, and the discovery that the vihara was *not* being torn down over the ex-monk's head, and *not* being used for parties and dances, had rather disconcerted him. He therefore contented himself with scowling at any student he came across and shouting threateningly, to nobody in particular, 'This place is a vihara, yer know!' and, 'Some people don't know how to show proper respect to a *bhikṣu*!' Showing proper respect meant making the traditional prostrations. Most of the students did not think it necessary to take Venerable Aniruddha very seriously, and I did not feel justified in disillusioning them. Some of them even thought him a little crazed. Before the week was out we had grown more or less accustomed to his irate presence about the place and were no longer perturbed by the violent quarrels he was having with Great Wisdom, mostly about money.

By the time this happened I was already preparing to leave for Sarnath. With the start of the examinations the tutorial classes had come to an end, the November issue of *Stepping-Stones* was out, and I was free to go. Swale agreed to collect the mail from the post office each day while I was away and deal with urgent letters, while Sachin undertook to see to the running of the Recreation Hut. As for Joe, *he* had already left for Lucknow, after promising to meet me in Sarnath. Since the day of his arrival he had been utterly fascinated by the 'fantastic' sights and 'exotic' inhabitants of Kalimpong, and despite his initial disappointment with the YMBA he had now decided to settle in the little Himalayan township for good. He had also formed a strong attachment to an eighteen-year-old Nepalese artist, a worker in the Kalimpong Arts and Crafts, whose talents – in Joe's opinion – were being wasted on lampshades and fire-screens, and this fact too may have had something to do with his decision. Before he could settle in Kalimpong, however, Joe had to wind up his affairs in Lucknow, and this, he thought, would take him three or four weeks. While there he would try to arrange a few lectures for me and I could accompany him back to Lucknow after we had attended the Mulagandhakuti Vihara opening-anniversary celebrations.

Though in fact free to leave Kalimpong somewhat earlier, it was not until the third week of November that I set out on my journey. Nearly ten months had passed since my coming up into the hills with Kashyapji, and during that time I had almost forgotten what life in the plains was like. Going from Kalimpong down to Siliguri, which was the nearest railhead, was like entering into another world. It was a world of oppressive heat, of all-pervading dust, and of well-nigh universal poverty. It was also a world of politics. Though Kalimpong was no Shangri-La, during my stay there very little outside news had reached me, most of it relating to Tibet, where the Chinese Communist troops were steadily advancing on Lhasa, or to Nepal, where an armed uprising against the autocratic Rana regime had broken out. In the plains one could not get away from politics. Three years after Independence there was still considerable tension between India and Pakistan, particularly over the 'link' line that connected Assam with the rest of India. Between Siliguri and Calcutta this line ran not only through *West* Bengal, which was part of India, but also through *East* Bengal, which was part of Pakistan. When a train halted at stations in West Bengal, Muslim passengers were liable to be attacked by local Hindus, and when it halted at stations in East Bengal, Hindu passengers were likely to be attacked by local Muslims. Of late the number of such incidents had increased, and there had been several deaths. The Government of India was therefore thinking of closing the line. Knowing nothing of all this, I bought an intermediate class ticket for the overnight train. There were very few passengers on board, but though this was highly unusual in India, I did not give the matter much thought. In the middle of the night the train stopped at the Pakistan border. Hindu passengers were made to alight, and their luggage was thoroughly searched. Shortly afterwards a Pakistani customs officer, obviously a Muslim, entered the compartment and asked me how much money I had on me in Indian currency. 'Eighty rupees,' I replied, quite truthfully. He seemed rather taken aback by this information, but passed on without saying anything. Later I learnt that fifty rupees was the maximum amount of Indian currency one was permitted to import into Pakistan, and that to try to import more was a serious offence. At the Indian border things were more relaxed. Indeed, as day dawned, and as the train penetrated deeper into West Bengal, the compartment gradually filled up and a lighter atmosphere prevailed.

I had once been told that all the most interesting people in India travelled by intermediate class. If one went first class one met only members of the upper classes (princes, millionaires, ICS officers,[32] and top military brass), if second class only members of the middle classes (doctors and lawyers, the moderately rich, and lower-ranking civil and military officers), and if third class only members of the working classes (peasants, factory hands, domestic servants, and the *hoi polloi* generally). If one travelled intermediate, however, one met members of the (relatively) classless and casteless intelligentsia; one met the more cultured minority. To what extent this was true of the occupants of my own compartment I could not say. With one exception, they consisted of English-educated Hindus, neither particularly old nor particularly young. The exception – a very striking one – was a tiny old man wearing a long black gown and big white turban. He was a *moulvi*, or Muslim 'priest', and could hardly have been less than eighty. Before long most of the people in the compartment were engaged in conversation. Not unnaturally, their main topic was the tension between India and Pakistan and the continuing violence on that particular section of the railway. Since much of the conversation was in Bengali, I could follow what was being said only in a general way, but a serious argument had, it seemed, developed between three or four of the educated Hindus and the old *moulvi*, and they were pressing him pretty hard. Why, they wanted to know, was it necessary for the subcontinent to be divided? Why did the Muslims have to be so different from the Hindus? What was the reason for their intransigent attitude? To all these questions the old man had only one answer. '*Khudda ka hukkum hai!* It is God's *will*!' he exclaimed, laying tremendous stress on the word 'will', and bringing his clenched fist down onto his knee with tremendous force to emphasize the point. '*Khudda ka hukkum hai!*' So overcome was he by his sense of the divine omnipotence, and its absolute over-ridingness in all human affairs, that he more than once shed tears. At length one of the Hindus, perhaps growing impatient with all these references to the divine will, and not convinced that God was as responsible for everything as the *moulvi* believed, demanded, 'Why can't you Muslims live at peace with the Hindus?'

The old man looked at him steadily for a minute. Then in a quiet, dangerous voice, and the air of one producing a dagger, he slowly asked, 'Have you heard the word *acchut*?' *Acchut* meant 'untouchable'.

'Of course I've heard it,' replied the Hindu, 'but what has that...?'

'Say no more!' roared the old man, his eyes blazing and his whiskers bristling with indignation. 'SAY NO MORE!!!' There was, indeed, no more to say. That was the end of the argument, and of our journey. Shortly afterwards the line was closed.

On my arrival in Sarnath (I had spent a night or two in Calcutta before continuing on my way) I lost no time in going to the Burmese temple and meeting U Kittima. The Burmese temple was situated about a quarter of a mile from the Mulagandhakuti Vihara, on the opposite side of the archaeological area. It was a somewhat gloomy place. Three or four solidly constructed but rather unsightly buildings – among them the temple proper, which contained the *sīmā* or ordination area – stood amidst big trees within a compound entirely surrounded by a crumbling stone wall. Access was by a sort of causeway across a moat filled not with water so much as with semi-liquid mud on the surface of which was a dried up layer of brilliant green scum. I had stayed at the Burmese temple once before, on my return from Nepal, and had already made U Kittima's acquaintance. He was a taciturn but not unfriendly man of about fifty, more scholar than monk, who sat in a cane armchair quietly puffing endless Burmese cheroots. Beside him was a big brass spittoon into which, every now and then, he spat. He had no disciples, his entire household consisting of a Brahmin woman who did the cooking and the woman's teenage son, who acted as a sort of manager. U Kittima was not above joking about his little ménage, maintaining that the scriptures were full of references to '*śramaṇa-brāhmaṇa*', i.e. *bhikṣus* and Brahmins, and that he was only being faithful to the ancient ideal. Faithful or not, his household had apparently expanded since my last visit. Washing clothes at the well and lounging beneath the trees were a number of people, most of them Burmese and most of them pilgrims. U Kittima himself was in the library. When I had paid my respects he told me, in his usual unhurried way, that he had good news for me. Yes, U Chandramani had consented to my receiving the higher ordination and had directed him to make arrangements for the ceremony. Unfortunately, he added, Babaji himself would not be attending, as he was ill in bed at Kusinara. But I was not to worry. Two distinguished elder monks were arriving from Rangoon, and one of them would act as preceptor and preside over the ceremony in Babaji's place.

On 24 November 1950, being the full-moon day, at nine o'clock in the morning, I therefore received the higher ordination in the Mahawijitawi Sima of the Ariya Sangharama, as the Burmese temple was officially called. Four or five dozen people were present. Within the ordination area, which was marked off by means of a number of low posts of a special kind, were seated fourteen full monks from Burma, Ceylon, Nepal, and India. I was seated in the midst of the monks, directly facing (for the greater part of the time) the *upādhyāya* or preceptor. Outside the ordination area, though still within the temple, sat the lay community or, more strictly speaking, all those who were *not* full monks, i.e. who were either lay disciples or novice monks, or who were not full monks *according to the Theravāda tradition*. The most important person inside the *sīmā* was, of course, the preceptor, U Kawinda Sayadaw, the senior of the two elder monks who had come from Rangoon. He was a softly spoken, mild-mannered man of about fifty who, I afterwards learned, was a celebrated preacher. The most important person *outside* the *sīmā* was Kusho Bakula, the well-known Ladakhi 'incarnate lama', an aloof, mysterious figure with a strangely triangular face and an expression of remarkable thoughtfulness and refinement. He was in Sarnath for the opening-anniversary celebrations, and had been invited to attend the ordination. Having been ordained according to the Tibetan Mahāyāna (properly Sarvāstivāda) tradition, it was not possible for him to be seated inside the *sīmā*, it being considered important to keep different lines of monastic ordination distinct. Instead, he sat at the head of the lay community, immediately behind the (other) monks, and right up against the *sīmā*. He thus occupied, in a sense, a position midway between the lay community and the monastic community – a position not inappropriate in the case of one who was a follower of the bodhisattva ideal of being 'in the world but not of it' and who was himself widely regarded as a veritable embodiment of that ideal.

The actual ordination was a straightforward, almost businesslike affair. U Kawinda, as *upādhyāya*, put before the monks the motion that the novice monk Sangharakshita wished to receive the higher ordination from the assembly with Venerable Kawinda as his preceptor and that the assembly should, if it so wished, grant him the ordination. Three batches of three monks in turn then requested the assembly to agree to the motion that the novice monk Sangharakshita be granted the higher ordination from the assembly with Venerable Kawinda as his preceptor, each batch repeating the request in unison once. The assembly remaining silent, the motion was declared carried. I was now a *bhikṣu*, a full monk, a member of the monastic order. Immediately before the ordination, i.e. before the putting of the motion, I had been reordained as a *śrāmaṇera*, and interrogated with regard to various disabilities. The first batch of monks reciting the request consisted of U Kawinda himself, Yetanapon U Zagaya, and Venerable Dharmarakshita. U Zagaya was a thick-set, beetle-browed man of about forty who was General Secretary of the Mahasanghas of Burma, Venerable Dharmarakshita an Indian disciple of U Chandramani who had joined the Maha Bodhi Society and was now editor of *Dharmadut*, the Society's Hindi monthly. The second batch consisted entirely of Sinhalese monks. There was stout, amiable Sasanasiri, thin, voluble Sangharatana, and silent, smiling Sivali. All three belonged to the Sarnath Centre of the Maha Bodhi Society, of which Venerable Sangharatana was, of course, Secretary. The third batch consisted of monks of three different nationalities. Foremost among them was Kashyapji, who had come from Bihar Sharif for the occasion and who had acted as *ācārya* or teacher at the ceremony, reordaining me as a *śrāmaṇera* and interrogating me with regard to the disabilities. With him were Saddhatissa, a youngish Sinhalese monk who was studying for a degree at a local college, and Amritananda, a Nepalese (Newar) monk whom I had met in Rajgir the previous year. After the ordination U Kawinda, who spoke a little English, explained to me in a gentle, kindly manner what were known as the *nissayas* or 'reliances' of the monk. He should rely on alms for food, on dust-heap rags for robes, on the roots of trees for lodging, and on cow's urine for medicine. Nonetheless, allowances were made. A monk could also accept invitations to meals, wear robes made of various materials, live in a house or cave, and take ghee, butter, oil, honey, and sugar when sick.

Since much of the ordination was conducted in 'Burmese Pāli', i.e. in Pāli chanted in the gutteral Burmese fashion with many mispronunciations (e.g. *tissa* for *tassa* and *gissami* for *gacchāmi*), I was unable to follow it very well. Only some time later, when I had studied the relevant texts and 'reconstructed' the ceremony stage by stage, did I really understand what had happened. At the time, however, my inability to follow the ordination procedure did not bother me very much. Whilst the ceremony was in progress I experienced an extraordinary sense of peace, satisfaction, fulfilment, acceptance, and belonging. It was a feeling such as I had not experienced before, and in subsequent years I was never surprised when an elderly monk told me that receiving the monastic ordination had been the greatest experience of his whole life.

The day following the ordination I left for Lucknow. Joe, who had been present at the ceremony, was anxious that we should be off. Before our departure U Kawinda took me aside. Since I would not be staying with him, he explained, it would be necessary for me formally to renounce my *nissaya* or 'reliance' on him. Generally a monk stayed with his preceptor for ten years, or at least for five. Renouncing my *nissaya* meant that I was effectually 'on my own'. U Kawinda also gave me his card – gilt-edged and bright pink in colour. If ever I visited Burma, he smilingly assured me, I could stay with him at his monastery for as long as I liked.

So far as ancient monuments were concerned, Lucknow was a Muslim rather than a Hindu city. Joe lost no time in taking me on a rapid tour of the principal buildings of interest, among which were the eighteenth-century Imambara or mausoleum, one of the largest rooms in the world, and the great Jamma Masjid or Friday Mosque. For the better part of the day we traversed vast empty courtyards, climbed enormous flights of stairs, and gazed up at floating domes and soaring minarets. Once again I admired, as I had admired in Delhi six years earlier, the grandeur, simplicity, and refinement of the Moghul style of architecture, where red sandstone and white marble meet in perfect harmony and where 'all below is strength, and all above is grace'.[33] Most of my time during the four days I spent in Lucknow was devoted not to seeing buildings, however, but to meeting members of the city's tiny Buddhist community, as well as Hindu intellectuals sympathetic to Buddhism. Joe had arranged for me to stay at the Bodhisattva Vihara, which belonged to the Lucknow branch of the Bengal Buddhist Association, of which he was still President. This made it possible for me to see the local Bengali

After the bhikṣu *ordination ceremony, Sarnath, 24 November 1950, with Yetanapon U Zagaya (left) and U Kawinda Sayadaw, who acted as preceptor (right)*

Buddhists, many of whom came to take the Refuges and Precepts from me each morning and to make the usual ceremonial food-offering. He had also arranged for me to visit the Buddhist Temple, as the Maha Bodhi Society's Lucknow Centre was called. Had he not done this, it might have been thought that I was being deliberately kept away from the place. Conflict between the two viharas was fortunately a thing of the past, but a certain amount of rivalry persisted, and it was necessary to avoid misunderstandings. At the Buddhist Temple, where there was a more cosmopolitan atmosphere than at the Bodhisattva Vihara, I met

After the bhikṣu *ordination ceremony, with Jagdish Kashyap (seated) and Lama Kusho Bakula offering a ceremonial scarf*

people from a number of different communities. Among them was the Venerable Prajnananda, the friendly, English-educated young Sinhalese monk who, on the death of Bodhananda Maha Sthavira, had succeeded to the incumbency of the vihara. His main interest, he told me, was publishing Buddhist literature in English and Hindi.

Besides meeting people individually and discussing Buddhism with them, while in Lucknow I gave three lectures. Mindful of the promise he had given before leaving Kalimpong, Joe had arranged for me to give two lectures at the Bodhisattva Vihara and one at Lucknow University. The lecture I gave at the University was the means of bringing me into contact with two outstanding scholars, one of whom was then at the beginning of his career, the other very near its close. It also marked the beginning of my doubts concerning the general intellectual level among university students. The scholar who was at the beginning of his career was Dr Herbert Vignāntaka Guenther. Austrian by birth, and about thirty years of age, he had left Europe for personal reasons a year or two earlier and was now a lecturer in the university's Department of Philosophy. Joe was on friendly terms with him and his Austrian-born wife Sarojani, and in Kalimpong I had heard much from him about them. Dr Guenther was undoubtedly a man of great intellectual brilliance. He had read an extraordinary number of Buddhist texts in the original Pāli and Sanskrit and could quote from them to illustrate a point, or reinforce an argument, with astonishing readiness and fluency. Before leaving Europe he had published a book in German on 'The Soul-Problem in Ancient Buddhism',[34] a book which I believe he afterwards repudiated. His current love was the Vajrayāna, about which he held forth at great length with tremendous enthusiasm and wonderful eloquence – so much so, indeed, that I invited him to contribute articles on the subject to *Stepping-Stones*. As well as being a man of great intellectual brilliance, Dr Guenther was a man of great intellectual arrogance. I soon found that it was not possible, in his presence, to mention the name of any other scholar working in the field of Buddhist studies, however eminent, without his instantly pouring forth the vials of his wrath upon the unfortunate man's head. Professor X? He didn't know a word of Sanskrit. Hadn't read a *single* text in the original language. Doctor Y? A complete ignoramus. Had got absolutely *nothing* right. And so on. His strongest expressions of contempt were reserved for a very distinguished historian of Indian philosophy, risen to high office in the state, who according to Dr Guenther had not personally examined a single Sanskrit manuscript and was forced to rely entirely on English translations. The man was in fact nothing but an out and out charlatan – not a scholar at all but a politician. Sweeping denunciations of this kind disfigured Dr Guenther's conversation in much the same way that they afterwards disfigured some of his books, and I found his hypercritical stance not very much to my liking. Joe, I could see, felt differently. Arms clasped round his knees, blue eyes gleaming, he leaned forward eagerly, drinking in every intemperate word. It was clear that he liked hearing 'clever' people being given (as he thought) their comeuppance, and that he saw Guenther as a sort of hero, slaying the intellectual dragons in a way he would have liked to do himself had he been able.

The only living scholar for whom Dr Guenther appeared to have any regard at all was Dr Surendranath Dasgupta, who was the other outstanding scholar with whom I came into contact in Lucknow. If anything, he seemed to have too high a regard for him, as though he was compensating for his underestimation of all other scholars by overestimating this one. According to Guenther, the account of Buddhist philosophy contained in the first volume of Dr Dasgupta's standard work *A History of Indian Philosophy* was not only thoroughly reliable but the only reliable one available in English at all. With this I strongly disagreed. To me it seemed that Dasgupta's discussion of the Madhyamaka school was quite inadequate, and that he had not only relied for his understanding of *The Awakening of Faith* on *an English translation* (an unforgivable sin in Guenther's eyes), but had uncritically accepted this well-known text as a Chinese translation of an original Indian work.[35] In comparison with the magnitude of his total achievement, however, these were minor blemishes, and there was no doubt that with the possible exception of one or two Indian scholars of the old type he was supreme in his field. There was also no doubt that he was approaching the end of his career. He had returned to India from Cambridge a very sick man, and not knowing how much time he had left was now hard at work on the fifth and final volume of his *History*. In this he had the collaboration of his wife Surama, a scholar in Indian philosophy in her own right, who was a former student of his and considerably younger than he was. Though they must have been busy, both husband and wife received me with great kindness, and Dasgupta and I had a long discussion on Buddhism. Despite the fact that he was a Hindu by birth, his attitude towards Buddhism was both sympathetic and fair-minded, and I found him more willing to recognize the extent to which Buddhism had influenced Hinduism than Hindu scholars usually were. When I asked him if he agreed with Swami Nikhilananda, the translator of the *Māṇḍūkya Kārikās*, that their author Gauḍapāda was neither a Buddhist nor influenced by Buddhism he shook his head. Regardless of whether or not Gauḍapāda was a Buddhist, the influence of Buddhism on his thinking could not be denied. The great Śaṅkara himself – grand-disciple of Gauḍapāda and the brightest ornament of the Advaita Vedanta school – was influenced by Buddhism. The conception of *saṃsāra* as beginningless, which Śaṅkara had adopted, was of Buddhist origin. Buddhism had profoundly influenced popular Hinduism too. Saraswati, the goddess of learning, for instance, was first mentioned in a Mahāyāna Buddhist *sūtra*, in which she undertook to help the Buddhist monks not to forget the scriptures which they had committed to memory.[36]

In this way two or three hours passed very agreeably. While we were talking Surama, who had joined in the discussion from time to time, brought us tea. She also showed me the two thick manuscript volumes of her Ph.D thesis on 'The Concept of Karma in Indian Thought', in which the Hindu, Buddhist, and Jaina philosophies of karma were examined in considerable detail. Though Dasgupta and I found ourselves in agreement on most topics, the venerable old scholar was plainly worried by what he considered my excessively 'dynamic' interpretation of Buddhist philosophy and spiritual life. Unfortunately, the word dynamic was my own. I had been trying to explain the nature of *pratītya-samutpāda* or conditioned co-production as an all-embracing reality that included both the cyclical process of mundane existence and the spiral process of spiritual life and growth, and in this connection had described Buddhism as seeing reality in dynamic rather than in static terms and as being, therefore, a dynamic religion. Oh no, the old man protested, with something like a shudder. Buddhism was not dynamic at all. Spiritual life was not dynamic. Spiritual life was peace. It was *rest*, profound rest. Evidently, after his five years in Europe, the connotation of the term 'dynamic' was for Dr Dasgupta anything but positive. 'Dynamic' to him suggested restlessness, assertiveness, ambition, and 'dynamic Buddhism' a religion that was either the oriental counterpart of muscular Christianity or else aggressively 'missionary' in character. This was not at all what I had meant to convey, but seeing the look of sadness and suffering in the dark eyes, and the expression of profound weariness on the deeply furrowed face, I did not pursue the matter further. Besides, even when dissenting from what he understood me to have said, the saintly old scholar expressed himself with such childlike simplicity and gentleness, and such an entire absence of arrogance, that I did not think there was any real need for me to clear up the misunderstanding and justify my use of the word. Great scholars, I had found, were often intellectually arrogant. The very greatest scholars were never so, and to this select band Surendranath Dasgupta undoubtedly belonged.

The lecture which Joe had arranged for me at Lucknow University was held in the Philosophy Department under the auspices of the University Philosophical Association, with Dr Dasgupta himself in the chair. My subject was the bodhisattva ideal. Thinking that the general intellectual level among university students would be much higher than that to which I was accustomed (I had not spoken at a university before), and not wishing to disappoint my audience by failing to do justice to the subject, I had prepared my talk quite carefully. After summarizing the standard 'exoteric' presentation of the bodhisattva ideal, I plunged into an exposition of the bodhisattva's compassionate activity as the expression of his experience of *śūnyatā* or voidness. As my text, so to speak, I took that well-known section of the *Diamond Sūtra* in which the bodhisattva is represented as vowing to lead countless sentient beings to Nirvāṇa and yet, at the same time, realizing that there existed no sentient beings for him to lead to Nirvāṇa. When the meeting was over I asked Dr Dasgupta what the students and faculty members had made of the lecture. The old scholar smiled. He believed he was the only person present who had understood it, he said. It was after this experience that I began to doubt whether the intellectual level among university students – even those who were students of philosophy – was quite so high as hitherto I had, in my ignorance, supposed it to be.

My four days in Lucknow were soon over, and it was not without feelings of regret that, having reached the farthest point of my itinerary, I said goodbye to Joe and started on the long journey back to Kalimpong. On the way I halted in Calcutta, where I spent a few days looking up old friends. This pleasant duty accomplished, I made the journey from Calcutta to Siliguri by the longer route, which involved crossing the River Ganges by paddle-steamer and catching another train on the other side. On 5 December, more than twenty-four hours after I had left Calcutta, the Landrover in which I had travelled up from Siliguri deposited me at the foot of the well-known acclivity that led from the main road up to the Dharmodaya Vihara. I was back at last: back in Kalimpong, back in the hills, back facing Mount Kanchenjunga. My joy knew no bounds. I had been away for two weeks. During those two weeks much had happened. Above all, the dearest wish of my heart had been granted: I had received the higher ordination. I had left Kalimpong a *śrāmaṇera*, and now returned to it a *bhikṣu*, a full monk, a member of the monastic order established by the Buddha. Even though the Newars did not look after me, I was in a better position than ever to work for the good of Buddhism.

At the top of the acclivity a shock awaited me. All was not well at the Dharmodaya Vihara. All was not well with the YMBA. Taking advantage of my absence, Aniruddha had closed the Recreation Hut, nailing wooden boards across the door to prevent anybody getting in. Students turning up at the vihara were told that all YMBA activities had been shut down, that the place did not belong to them, and that they were not wanted there. As for the English monk who had had the effrontery to encourage low-caste people to use the place, *he* would be thrown out as soon as he arrived. True to his word, Aniruddha had not only moved into my old room but had hurled my few belongings downstairs into the back hall. Swale, visiting the place a few days later, found my books and papers and a spare robe or two still lying scattered about on the floor. Gathering them up, he kept them in the downstairs back room formerly occupied by Joe. In this room I now installed myself. Before long Aniruddha came banging on the door. If I wanted to stay at the vihara, he bawled, I would have to pay him a hundred rupees a month rent. Otherwise, I could clear out.

7

BURMA RAJA AND THE DEVAS

Kalimpong was a small place. The news that the YMBA had been shut down and that the English monk who had done so much for the youth of the town was in danger of being thrown out for his pains spread rapidly. Most people's reaction was one of surprise, bewilderment, and, in some cases, indignation. For several months prior to my arrival on the scene the Dharmodaya Vihara had been practically deserted. Now, those very activities which had at last made the place useful to the public had been suddenly and savagely curtailed, indeed abolished altogether, and the vihara was apparently being allowed to revert to its previous desolate and neglected condition. Among those most disturbed by these unfortunate developments were the parents and guardians of the YMBA members, especially those whose sons had been attending the evening tutorial classes. To them it was unbelievable that a Buddhist monk should have behaved in the high-handed and unsympathetic fashion that Aniruddha had done, and that students turning up at the vihara should have been sent away with rough words. Yet such was the case, and they could only exclaim, as the Nepalese Brahmin student had exclaimed on the day of Aniruddha's arrival, 'How can such an angry-looking man be a Buddhist monk!' or rather 'How can such an angry-speaking and angry-acting man be a Buddhist monk!' This was unfortunate in more ways than one. Not a few of the good people of Kalimpong, both Buddhist and Hindu, had hitherto supposed that only Tibetan 'lamas' were capable of rough and quarrelsome behaviour. *Real* Buddhist monks, they had believed –

monks who wore yellow cotton robes instead of red woollen ones – were different. It now seemed as though the yellow-robed monks were as bad as their red-robed Tibetan brethren.

Whether the honours were in fact so evenly divided I had no means of telling. For the time being I was having to go on living with the yellow-robed Aniruddha. It did not take me long to realize just how desperate the situation was. However indignant people might feel about the shocking way in which the YMBA had been treated there was nothing they could really do about it. Even the parents of YMBA members were completely powerless. They had no control over the vihara, which of course was the property of the Dharmodaya Sabha, and no means of influencing what Aniruddha did in his capacity as monk-in-charge. None of them even knew Aniruddha. The only person who might, I thought, be able to help was Gyan Jyoti. When I visited him at his office in Nepali Building the smooth-faced, smiling merchant received me with many expressions of sympathy, and much shaking of the head in wonderment at Aniruddha's outrageous behaviour. Not that it really surprised him, though. Aniruddha had a reputation for that sort of thing, he told me, and his father, who was also a yellow-robed monk, was even worse. It was lucky for me that they had not *both* arrived at the same time. Then I would *really* have had something to complain about. Despite the bantering tone in which he spoke, Gyan Jyoti was not really disposed to make light of what had happened. He was, I could see, genuinely distressed at the trouble I was experiencing, and genuinely dismayed at the way in which Aniruddha was carrying on. At the same time, as I could also see, his loyalties were divided. On the one hand, he was treasurer of the YMBA, and did not want to see its activities shut down after such a successful start. On the other hand, he was a Newar, and did not want to find himself in open opposition to a monk of his own community, especially when that monk appeared to be acting with the support of the Dharmodaya Sabha, the treasurer of which was his elder brother Maniharsha and the secretary their cousin Venerable Mahanama. Another person whose loyalties were divided was Swale. As manager of the YMBA he could hardly approve of what Aniruddha had done. At the same time, as the guest of the Jyoti family, as he still was, he could not very well come into direct conflict with him. Between the divided loyalties of these two friends, therefore, I was left with plenty of personal sympathy but no real help either for the YMBA or for myself. Gyan Jyoti counselled patience and hoped that things would somehow turn out all right in the end. Swale breezily commented that I would just have to 'grin and bear it'.

The only real sympathy I received – apart from that of my students, who considered themselves below rather than above the battle – came from two Hindu Newars. Gopal Pradhan and Madan Kumar Pradhan were cousins (or perhaps it was brothers-in-law). Both were about forty years of age and both lived quite near the vihara, in bungalows situated at opposite ends of the same compound. There the resemblance between them ended. Gopal Babu, as he was universally known, was stout, cheerful, and ebullient, and when he went out wore baggy, unpressed Western-style clothes and an old pork pie hat. Madan Kumar Babu was slim, quiet, and thoughtful, and wore a smart three-piece suit when he went out and Indian (not Nepalese) dress at home. Gopal Babu, though always busy, seemed to have no regular occupation, but functioned as a kind of agent or general factotum to a variety of private individuals and business concerns. Madan Kumar Babu was a successful lawyer who had the largest practice in Kalimpong. He was, moreover, Vice-Chairman of the Kalimpong Municipality (the Subdivisional Officer was Chairman, *ex officio*), and well known for his public spirit. In recognition of his services to the community the previous government had awarded him the title of Rai Sahib. On any given day Gopal Babu might be anywhere in the bazaar or the Development Area. Madan Kumar Babu was almost certainly either in the *cutchery* or court or at home in his office, besieged by clients. Gopal Babu smoked *bidis* or country cigarettes. Madan Kumar Babu smoked English or American cigarettes, which he drew from a gold cigarette case and inserted in a long holder. Gopal Babu was comparatively poor. Madan Kumar Babu was comparatively rich – as with ten or twelve children to support, to his cousin's (or brother-in-law's) four or five, he had every need to be. Which of these two allied but dissimilar Pradhans I had met first it would be difficult to say: probably Gopal Babu. Whichever of them it was, by the time of my trouble with Aniruddha I had come to know both of them fairly well, and had been invited to each of their homes for a semi-ceremonial food-offering on more than one occasion. Gopal Babu's eldest son had in fact been attending the evening tutorial classes, and both men knew quite well what the YMBA had been doing. Having realized that no help could be looked for from Gyan Jyoti, it was therefore to Gopal Babu and Madan Kumar Babu that I turned, not for sympathy but for advice, or at least the opportunity to talk things over.

Such an opportunity they certainly gave me. Their two bungalows being so close to the vihara – only a quarter of a mile up the road, and then 150 yards down the crooked path on the left – I went and saw them several mornings in quick succession. In the course of those visits I received, besides real sympathy, a little advice and quite a lot of information. So far as the YMBA was concerned, Madan Kumar Babu told me kindly, our position was hopeless. It was with the permission of the Dharmodaya Sabha that we had been using the vihara for our activities, and that permission having been withdrawn, as it now seemed, those activities had been shut down, and there was nothing we could do about it. However roughly and ungraciously Aniruddha might have behaved in the matter, as the official representative of the Dharmodaya Sabha he was perfectly within his rights in doing what he had done. The best thing for *me* to do would be to find the YMBA premises of its own and restart our activities there as quickly as possible. All the same, he added, with a thoughtful exhalation of cigarette smoke, he could not *quite* understand why the Dharmodaya Sabha should have taken such strong exception to what I was trying to do at the vihara, especially as it had originally given us permission to use the place for our activities. Perhaps Aniruddha had exceeded his authority. Perhaps Great Wisdom had alarmed everybody with his lying reports. (I had told my two sympathizers about the ex-monk's incessant letter-writing.) Perhaps there had been a difference of opinion within the Sabha itself. Or perhaps, what was most likely, it was all simply a case of ordinary human jealousy. Oh yes, didn't I know it? In starting the tutorial classes I had done what the Dharmodaya Sabha itself had promised to do a couple of years back. I had succeeded where they had failed. Jyoti Brothers had given the biggest donation: granted; but the truth of the matter was that the building now known as the Dharmodaya Vihara had been purchased with money collected from the general public of Kalimpong and collected, moreover, not for a Buddhist monastery at all *but for a school*. He knew. He was one of the people who had been approached for a donation and who had given something. And who had done the collecting? Why, those two prize beauties the Venerable Amritananda and the Venerable Mahanama. Arriving in Kalimpong one fine day, the pair of them went around collecting money for a school, as they said, and at length purchased the present building. After organizing a grand opening ceremony, for which dozens of yellow-robed monks were invited, they stayed on at the vihara – as the building was now called – for a few months without doing anything and then, having spent the rest of the money that had been collected on luxurious living, departed as suddenly as they had arrived. Neither of them had been seen in the town since, and of course no school of any kind was ever started. *That* was why people had been so pleased when the YMBA had started evening tutorial classes – and so surprised and bewildered when Aniruddha had shut our activities down. *That* was why he himself did not *quite* understand why the Dharmodaya Sabha should have taken such strong exception to what I was trying to do. They should have been grateful to me. I was doing their work for them.

By the time I had talked things over with Gopal Babu and Madan Kumar Babu I had been back at the vihara for two weeks or more, and life with Aniruddha had become increasingly difficult. He had now abandoned all pretence of wanting rent, and what with the scowls, the constant angry mutterings, and the periodic outbursts of rage with which he favoured me, I was left with no doubt whatever that the one wish of his heart was to have me out. So disturbed was the atmosphere of the vihara, in fact, and so filled with hate, that at times it made me feel quite ill. One day, his patience apparently exhausted, Aniruddha's outbursts of rage became more than usually violent. He would have me *thrown* out of the vihara, he stormed, his small eyes red with fury. He would have me thrown out by force. He didn't care what anybody said. I would be thrown right out of the front door and down the veranda steps. There were people who would do the job for him. He was sick and tired of waiting for me to go. Genuinely alarmed by his threats, I at once went to see Gyan Jyoti. The situation was becoming serious, I told him. Would he please come to the vihara and remonstrate with Aniruddha. Gyan Jyoti shrugged his shoulders. It was not for him to interfere between two *bhikṣus*, he said, shifting uneasily in his seat. They would have to settle their differences themselves. I therefore went straight from Nepali Building to the two bungalows at the end of the crooked path. Fortunately Madan Kumar Babu was in. When I told him what had happened he looked grave. The best thing I could do, he said, was to go the *thana* or police station and 'give an information'. I had never heard of this procedure before. All I had to do, he explained, was to tell the officer-in-charge that Aniruddha had threatened to evict me from the vihara by force, which of course was against the law. An entry to that effect would then be made in the station diary and if Aniruddha attempted to carry out his threat, and if there should be a breach of the peace, the fact that I had already given an information would be useful in helping to establish that I was the innocent party. Besides, he added, reassuringly, Aniruddha was sure to hear that I had been to the *thana* and this in itself would cause him to think twice about resorting to violence. Madan Kumar Babu's advice was sensible and shrewd enough, but I nonetheless felt a strong reluctance to act upon it. A police station was surely the last place in which a Buddhist monk should be seen, for whatever purpose. It was like being seen in a brothel, or a butcher's shop. Moreover, that one Buddhist monk should be forced to seek the protection of the secular authority against the violence of another Buddhist monk was a dreadful thing. It was not for this that I had received the higher ordination a few weeks ago. By giving an information against Aniruddha I would be bringing discredit not upon Aniruddha alone but upon the whole monastic order. Yet suppose Aniruddha *did* try to throw me out of the vihara. Surely *that* would bring even greater discredit upon the Order. In the end, it seemed that giving an information was the lesser of the two evils.

Regaining the main road, and walking up it as far as the T-junction, I therefore slowly climbed the flight of steps on the right hand side that gave access to the police station. At the top of the steps stood an enormously fat man in khaki shirt and shorts whom I at once recognized. It was Inspector Subba, the officer-in-charge, who from this favourite vantage point was accustomed to look down on the main road, and along the high street, in order to assure himself that no crimes were being committed within his jurisdiction. He showed no surprise at seeing me, and after greeting me with pompous cordiality led the way into the small wooden building – hardly more than a shack – that was the Kalimpong Police Station. Here he seated himself ponderously behind his desk, a handsome young Sikkimese sub-inspector brought me a chair, and I told my story. When I had finished Inspector Subba's broad red face creased into a benevolent smile. I had absolutely nothing to worry about, he boomed. Nobody could throw me out of the Dharmodaya Vihara. It was against the law. As a Buddhist monk, I had a perfect right to stay at the vihara for as long as I pleased, and while *he* was Inspector Subba, and in charge of the Kalimpong Police Station, that right would be upheld. There was no real need to make an entry in the station diary, but he would do so all the same. That Newar monk seemed to be a hot-headed sort of fellow, and if necessary he would have a quiet word with him himself. The handsome young Sikkimese sub-inspector was even more cordial. He had wanted to meet me for some time, he said, as I left the *thana*. Could he come and see me one day? He was a Buddhist, and wanted to talk about Buddhism. Though it seemed strange that I should have encountered more friendliness at the police station than at the Dharmodaya Vihara, I felt glad that I had acted on Madan Kumar Babu's advice, and returned to the vihara feeling more at ease in my mind than I had done for several days.

Whether Inspector Subba did have a quiet word with Venerable Aniruddha I had no means of knowing, but the fact was that the irascible Newar monk's threat to throw me out of the vihara was not repeated and, what was even more important, no attempt to carry it out was made. This certainly did not mean that Aniruddha was now reconciled to my continued presence at the vihara. His determination that I should go was as strong as ever. He had only changed his tactics. If I could not be driven out I must be squeezed out. One afternoon, shouting that *he* wasn't going to pay *my* bills any more, he disconnected my electricity and water supply. Being without electricity was no great hardship: electric light could always be replaced by candles. Being without water was a much more serious matter. I had no water for washing or drinking, and the toilet could not be flushed. My situation was parlous in the extreme. I did not know what to do next. One or two of the Newars who occasionally came to the vihara saw the results of Aniruddha's action with a certain amount of unease, but they said nothing. After all, it was not for them to question the wisdom of what had been done by one of their own monks. Had there been anywhere else for me to go I would have gone. But I was in a quandary. According to the Vinaya or Monastic Code it was not proper for a full monk to live in the same house with lay people, as Aniruddha well knew (he was a strict observer of the Vinaya). At the same time, there was no other vihara in Kalimpong in which I might take refuge. Unless I took to the open road, or went and lived under a tree, I had no option but to stay where I was regardless of consequences.

At this point Burma Raja intervened. Hearing that he had called to see me, I at once went to the front of the vihara, where I found the magnificently beturbaned old man standing stiffly on the veranda, ignoring Aniruddha's clumsy attempts at polite conversation. 'I have come to take you back with me,' he announced, tapping the ash from his big Burmese cheroot with his forefinger. 'My guest cottage is at your disposal. The taxi is waiting.'

I had met Burma Raja once before, when he came to the vihara with Prince Peter to hear Dr Roerich's lecture, and we had then exchanged a few words. Swale had met him a number of times, and knew him quite well, as did Gopal Babu. In Swale's case, he had got to know Burma Raja mainly on the strength of his fluent Burmese. The old man was naturally delighted to meet someone with whom he could converse in his native tongue – someone who had, moreover, spent much of his life in Burma, and who enjoyed a good Burmese cheroot. As for Gopal Babu, in former days he had been Burma Raja's manager. Even as a boy, in fact, he had run errands and done odd jobs for him. It was from these two people that I had learned what little I knew about the personage who had intervened thus dramatically in my affairs, and who now awaited my response to his generous proposal with a smile of such warmth and understanding. From Swale I had learned that he was the nephew of King Thibaw, the last king of Burma, and that his wife was the second daughter of King Thibaw and the notorious Queen Supayalat, known to history as the Cobra Woman. Had Burma now been a kingdom instead of a republic, Burma Raja – as he was popularly known – would in all probability have been king. As things were, however, he remained Prince K. M. Latthakin. From Gopal Babu I had learned that for many years Burma Raja had been a leading figure in the social life of Kalimpong, taking a prominent part in everything that went on, from tennis parties to tiger hunts. In the case of his wife the princess, however, there had been no question of any social life, and hardly anybody ever saw her. Burma Raja was emphatic that until she could appear in society in a manner befitting her position she would not appear in society at all. Since 1947, the year of Independence, there had been no question of either of them appearing in society. The new Indian government having cut their modest allowance by more than half, the old couple were now living in greatly reduced circumstances, and Burma Raja himself led a quiet, semi-retired life. His life was not so quiet as to prevent his seeing his friends, however, nor so retired that he did not know what was going on in the world. Both Swale and Gopal Babu visited him regularly, as I knew, and it must have been from one or the other of them – perhaps from both – that he learned of my predicament. Being as impulsive as he was generous, he came at once to the vihara to place his guest cottage at my disposal.

It did not take me long to make up my mind to accept his offer. Apart from bundles of unsold *Stepping-Stones* I had very little luggage, and everything was soon stowed away in the back of the taxi which was waiting below at the roadside. While I was packing Burma Raja remained standing on the veranda, sternly ignoring Aniruddha's requests that he should come in and sit down. 'He *can't* be a real monk!' he exclaimed in disgust, when we were seated in the taxi. But I did not want to think about Aniruddha. I was too glad to be leaving him and the Dharmodaya Vihara behind me. Turning right at the T-junction we passed the *thana*, the post office, the town hall, the jail, and then, swinging slowly round bend after bend, drove along the Upper Cart Road, through the Development Area, until we came, after about two miles, to the top of a narrow lane flanked by dense evergreens. Turning right down this lane, we eventually emerged into a small, grass-covered compound on the open hillside. At the rear or hillward end of this compound there stood a red-roofed bungalow of modest dimensions. Beyond, on a slightly lower level, there was another compound, and another bungalow, also red-roofed. Both bungalows faced north-west, and commanded much the same view as the Dharmodaya Vihara. Burma Raja lived in the first bungalow, which was appropriately named Panorama. The second bungalow was the guest cottage, and to this he now led me. It consisted of four or five small rooms, the most attractive of which was the front sitting room, where there hung several oil paintings. In this pleasant retreat I soon made myself at home, monastically speaking. A glassed-in veranda at the back became the *Stepping-Stones* editorial office. A bedroom was transformed into a shrine and meditation room, the first separate one of my own I had ever had. In this room I placed all the shrine equipment I then possessed – a large Tibetan-style colour print of the Buddha and a miniature stupa or reliquary. At night the bungalow – or guest cottage, as Burma Raja preferred to call it – was strangely quiet. The only sound to be heard was the intermittent tinkle of the tiny wind-bells hanging from the eaves of the little Burmese pavilion outside. Sometimes I could hear the silvery chime through my dreams. Life is sweet, the wind-bells seemed to be saying, but not lasting. It passes away, even as the sound of the wind-bells passes away on the breeze.

Before the week was out the unpleasant happenings at the Dharmodaya Vihara had started to take on a shadowy and insubstantial character, as if they had never really occurred. Burma Raja was an excellent host, and despite his limited means did everything in his power to make my stay at the guest cottage happy and comfortable. Nearly every morning he came down to see that I was all right, and that I had everything I wanted, and if he saw I was not busy he generally stayed on talking for a while. Gradually I started looking forward to these visits, and whenever I saw the sarong-clad figure squeezing through the gap in the hedge and eagerly descending the two or three steps into my compound I would put aside whatever I was doing and pretend I was not busy that morning. 'What, not busy?' he would exclaim, his face lighting up with a smile, after he had poked his turbaned head enquiringly round the door. 'Well, in that case...' And he would come quickly in and sit down. In this way we spent a lot of time together, and since Burma Raja was of a frank, communicative disposition I soon learned a great deal more about his background and present position than Swale and Gopal Babu had been able to tell me. As was perhaps only natural, he often talked about the deposed King Thibaw, and about what it had been like to live in the famous Golden Palace in Mandalay before the annexation of the Kingdom of Ava in 1885. Oh the dazzling profusion of riches! Oh the endless intrigues! Oh the appalling massacres, when princes and princesses of the blood were trampled to death by elephants in red velvet bags specially imported from Antwerp! But King Thibaw was not a bad man, Burma Raja hastened to assure me. I must not believe everything that had been written about him, especially by the British – if I did not mind him saying so, he added quickly. King Thibaw was a very good man, a very kind man, and extremely religious. *He always fed the monks.* Hundreds of them at a time would be invited to the palace for this purpose. Since Burma Raja spoke rather rapidly, and tended to jump breathlessly from one topic to another, especially when he spoke about King Thibaw, it was difficult to tell what had really happened in those far off days. It was also difficult to tell how much Burma Raja himself actually remembered, how much he had heard from

King Thibaw (or from Queen Supayalat, though *her* name was never mentioned), and how much he had learned from Burmese books about the period, of which there was a good collection in the sitting room, many of them illustrated with photographs of members of the royal family and palace officials in the magnificent court '*deva*' costume, with 'flames' rising from their shoulders, elbows, and knees. 'Look, look!' he would exclaim excitedly, pointing to one of these illustrations, '*That's how we used to dress in those days!*'

So far as I was able to make out, Burma Raja could not have been more than two or three years old at the time of King Thibaw's deposition from the Lion Throne, and when the royal family was exiled to India he had been taken with them. On the long voyage from Rangoon to Bombay there occurred an incident about which Burma Raja spoke more than once. King Thibaw owned a magnificent ruby, the size of a pigeon's egg, which he prized above all his other possessions. This ruby he entrusted for safe keeping to the British officer who was escorting them. When they reached their destination, however, the officer denied all knowledge of the ruby, and despite anything he could say the king never saw his ruby again. Burma Raja used to shake his head sadly over this incident. He was not so much sorry for the loss of the ruby. He was sorry that a British officer and gentleman could behave so badly.

From Bombay the royal family was taken to Ratnagiri, 200 miles further down the coast, and here they all remained until King Thibaw died. Burma Raja and the princess had moved – or had been moved – to Kalimpong some years before the war. There was another princess living in Calcutta, I gathered, and yet another living in Rangoon. *She* had married an Australian who owned the local racecourse. From the way in which Burma Raja told me this it was clear that, while he recognized the princess's right to marry whoever she pleased, there was no doubt in his mind that by marrying a foreigner and a commoner she had automatically forfeited her position as a member of the Royal House of Alompra. He himself was proud of the family to which he belonged, proud of the royal blood that flowed in his veins, proud of being Burmese. Indeed, considering how small a fraction of his life he had spent in his native land it was surprising how intensely Burmese he was. King Thibaw had taught him to write the Burmese language in its more difficult literary form, and he invariably wore Burmese dress. The latter consisted of a kind of Norfolk jacket, grey or purple in colour, worn over a deep crimson or green or gold sarong of heavy hand-loom silk. His head was swathed, indoors and outdoors alike, with a silk turban of some matching colour, of the type associated with the late Queen Mary – lofty rather than low, and broader at the top than at the bottom. The only part of his costume that was of Western origin were his black leather shoes. One day I asked him where his magnificent sarongs came from, as they were certainly not available in Kalimpong, or perhaps even in Calcutta, and he seemed to have quite a stock of them. His eyes sparkled. 'Friends send them to me, friends send them to me,' he said laughingly, dismissing the subject with a wave of the hand, as though he had a network of loyalist agents and supporters all over Burma who were only too happy to send him such trifles. Besides wearing his colourful Burmese dress, which made him look picturesque enough already, Burma Raja also sported a pair of fierce handlebar moustaches of truly regal dimensions, which he cheerfully admitted to dyeing. Indeed, whereas his moustaches were black, the wisps of hair that escaped from beneath his imposing turban were grey in colour, if not actually white.

As intensely Burmese as he was, when his native land gained independence in 1948 Burma Raja had been in no hurry to return. Independent Burma might be, but it had proclaimed itself a republic, and he had no idea where he stood under the new dispensation. Or rather, he had a very good idea where he stood. Yes, the rascals who were now in power had indeed invited him to go back: they had made all sorts of promises; but he was too old a bird to be caught with such chaff. He knew why they wanted him back. They wanted him back so that they could have him put quietly out of the way. (Clearly Burma Raja had not forgotten the red velvet bags and the elephants.) If he went back he would go back on his own terms. They had offered him a *pension*. Let them give him his *rights*. Never mind if they didn't want to have him back as king: that was *their* business. He didn't particularly want to be king. But let them give him what was his own. Let them give him his gold mines and ruby mines – or at least the ruby mines. These had been King Thibaw's personal property. They were not the property of the state. Oh yes, he had written to the President of Burma, as the fellow called himself. Give me back my ruby mines, you thieves, you rascals, he had told them. Oh yes, he had written plainly and straight-forwardly enough. There was no point in beating about the bush. Right was right. Who *were* these upstarts, anyway? He had never heard of them before. They still had not replied to his letters; he couldn't think why: he thought he had written plainly enough. Probably they were too ashamed of themselves to write. Or probably not. Such people were completely shameless. They had stopped paying his allowance. Or rather, they had not even started paying it. Originally the Government of India had paid, i.e. the old imperial government: 1,000 rupees a month for himself and the princess. When India became independent the new government stopped paying. They said the Government of Burma ought to pay. The Government of Burma refused to pay unless he returned to Burma – *there* was the rub. For a year or more he had received no allowance from anyone. If good friends like Prince Peter had not rallied round he and the princess would have been in serious trouble. In the end something had been sorted out. Other good friends like Madan Kumar Babu and Gopal Babu had written to the Government of India and the Government of India now gave him 400 rupees a month, which barely covered the necessities of life for himself, the princess, their adopted son, and the maidservant. *That* was why he no longer took part in the social life of Kalimpong. He was unwilling to accept hospitality he was not in a position to return. But he had not forgotten about the ruby mines, he added, his face brightening. Only the other week he had written another letter to the President of Burma, ordering him and his fellow gangsters to hand over his property forthwith. He had given the letter to Gopal Babu to send by registered post. This time there would certainly be a reply.

The stopping of his allowance was not the only unpleasant experience Burma Raja had to endure after India became independent. Only a year before I met him there had been the painful matter of the confiscation of his rifles and shotguns. As a keen amateur sportsman, the old man possessed quite a collection of these weapons. Indeed, from the stories he told me I sometimes thought he must have kept a small arsenal at Panorama. Either because he had not paid his licence fees, or because they wanted to reduce the number of firearms held by members of the public, the authorities had decided that all Burma Raja's weapons should be confiscated and had directed him to hand them in at the police station. This Burma Raja flatly refused to do. A sub-inspector was therefore sent to Panorama to take possession of the weapons. Burma Raja took a pot-shot at him from a window and he was forced to withdraw without carrying out his mission. The next thing that happened was that a party of armed police arrived on the scene and took up position in the lane. Burma Raja's response to this development was to barricade himself in the bungalow and threaten to open fire if anyone came too near. Oh yes, he would have shot them all right, he assured me cheerfully. They had no right to enter his compound without his permission. First he would have shot the princess, then he would have shot as many policemen as he could before *they* shot *him*. That was the important thing. The princess must not be touched: she was sacrosanct. Any views that the princess herself might have had about being despatched in this summary fashion Burma Raja did not, apparently, think it necessary to take into consideration. He seemed to look upon her as a kind of dynastic fetish that had been entrusted to his care and which must at all costs be protected from profanation. Fortunately the authorities had no wish to drive matters to an extremity. The police remained out of sight behind the evergreens, Burma Raja did not carry out his threat to open fire, and the princess survived to be shot by her protector on some other occasion. Madan Kumar Babu and Gopal Babu had intervened in good time, so it seemed, and thanks to their good offices Burma Raja had at length been persuaded to hand over his rifles and shotguns peacefully. The truth was, however, that the idea of killing the princess in order to protect her from being touched by profane hand was something of an obsession with the old man, and he often spoke of it. 'I'd *kill* the princess,' he would say, his eyes gleaming, after describing some imaginary crisis, 'and *then* I'd kill everybody else. They could kill *me* if they wanted to. I wouldn't mind.' So evident was the enthusiasm with which he expressed himself on the subject that I sometimes thought that the idea of falling across the dead body of the princess, mortally wounded, after killing a hundred men single-handed, rather appealed to Burma Raja. He seemed to think it would be a glorious death.

Despite Burma Raja's obsession with the idea of killing her, the princess had somehow managed to survive, and one morning, after we had talked as usual, the stout-hearted old man took me up to Panorama to see her. She was much shorter than he was and (as I knew already) several years older. Like him, she wore Burmese dress, which in her case consisted of a silk sarong and a short silk jacket. Her hair was drawn tightly back from her face, thus accentuating the sloping forehead which, together with the heavily lidded eyes, gave her the well-known 'cobra-headed' look characteristic of all members of the House of Alompra. Her head was not, however, the princess's only striking feature. Besides having a pronounced stoop, on account of which her head was almost lower than her shoulders, she had a way of swaying her body from side to side as she walked and darting her beady black eyes suspiciously in this direction and that. One almost expected to see a forked tongue flickering out from between her lips. When she spoke it was in a rapid confidential whisper, and she kept glancing over her shoulder as if afraid of being overheard. Though Burma Raja must have told her who I was, and why I was staying at the guest cottage, her pleasure in seeing the yellow robe was strangely mingled with doubt, distrust, and apprehension. It was almost as though she suspected Burma Raja of having commissioned me to make sure, once and for all, that the fetish could never be profaned, and that the unknown person in the yellow robe whom he had brought to see her was not a monk at all but an executioner in disguise. When I had been up to Panorama a few times, however, and she had made the usual ceremonial food-offering without being stabbed or strangled afterwards, she lost much of her nervousness and started confiding in me. At least, that is what she seemed to be doing. Whenever Burma Raja's back was turned, she would start giving me what appeared to be urgent messages for various people, not without many nods and gesticulations to the effect that Raja Sahib, as she always called him, must on no account be told anything about the matter. What the messages actually were was by no means clear, as on the occasions on which she confided in me in this way the princess's customary whisper sank so low, while the mixture of Hindi and Nepali in which she spoke became so rapid and intense, that it was virtually impossible for me to make out what she was saying. Some of the messages seemed to be meant for Madan Kumar Babu and Gopal Babu, however, and seemed to have something to do with money. Whether such was actually the case or not, I nodded understandingly to everything she said, and with this she appeared satisfied.

Besides the princess herself, on my visits to Panorama I also saw the two other members of Burma Raja's little household. These were the old couple's adopted son and the Nepalese maidservant who was his real mother. The adopted son was a sullen, graceless youth of about nineteen who had been given the Burmese name of Alaungyi. He was supposed to be going to school, but I knew from my students that such was not in fact the case, and that he spent the whole day loafing about the bazaar and getting into bad company. Even had news of this reached Panorama it is doubtful if Alaungyi would have been given anything more than a mild scolding. Both Burma Raja and the princess doted upon the boy, who as a result had been thoroughly spoiled. I also knew from my students that Alaungyi had not been doing well at school, and that he was far from popular with the other boys. They had, in fact, changed his name from Alaungyi to Aluji, which was Hindi for 'Mr Potato'. On account of the airs he gave himself as Burma Raja's son, despite the fact that he hardly ever had any money, they also called him Ek Paisaka Raja or 'Prince One Farthing'. The most remarkable thing about Alaungyi, however, was his unmistakable resemblance to Burma Raja and the princess – especially the latter. The same sloping forehead, the same heavily lidded eyes! What could it mean? The Nepalese maidservant, Alaungyi's mother, was a flattering, wheedling, ingratiating woman who danced constant attendance on the Rani Sahiba, as she always called her, and who functioned not only as her cook, housekeeper, and confidante but as the entire royal court as well. Burma Raja seemed to take very little notice of her.

One of the few occasions on which the court was not present was when the Rani Sahiba performed her devotions. This she always did quite alone. According to Burma Raja the princess was a devout Buddhist who in addition to her morning and evening devotions spent much of her time in meditation. One day, at his suggestion, she showed me her shrine-room. This was the smallest room in the bungalow and contained little more than a meditation mat and a low wooden table. On the table were five or six Buddha images, none of them more than four or five inches in height, and all so thickly covered in gold leaf as to present a distinctly fat and lumpy appearance. Besides performing her devotions to the Buddha, Dharma, and Sangha the princess also made offerings to the *devas* or 'shining ones'. This did not surprise me. Worship of the *nats* or *devas* was, I knew, an integral part of Burmese popular Buddhism – indeed, a part of popular Buddhism in all the Theravāda countries of South-East Asia. It was well understood, though, that the *devas* – the gods and spirits – were not able to help one in the attainment of Nirvāṇa: only the Buddha could do that; but being more powerful and more long-lived than men they were able to help one in the acquisition of material things. They were mundane by nature, not transcendental. Theirs was the glory that passes away, not the Peace that abides for ever. Nonetheless, the *devas* worshipped by the princess were no ordinary *devas* of hill or plain, tree, or lotus pond. They were, so Burma Raja solemnly assured me, the guardian *devas* of the Royal House of Alompra. They had dwelt with King Thibaw among the crimson pillars of the Golden Palace in Mandalay. They had accompanied him to his place of exile at Ratnagiri. Now they lived with the princess and himself at Panorama. He had never seen them with his own eyes, of course, but the princess saw them every day. They were no more than two or three inches in height, had butterfly-like wings, and when they flew through the air they emitted a brilliant golden radiance.

This was surprising enough, but more was to come. As I had no doubt observed, Burma Raja continued, with an appreciative chuckle, the princess was not just a devout Buddhist, not just an advanced meditator: she possessed magical powers of a high order. Whenever they were really short of money, as indeed happened from time to time, all that the princess had to do was to make offerings to the *devas* and they gave her money, usually in the form of hundred rupee notes. When she went into the shrine-room the next morning, there the money was, underneath the Buddha images. The *devas* had put it there during the night. This was so extraordinary a circumstance that the next time I saw Gopal Babu I told him exactly what Burma Raja had said. The former manager was inclined to be amused. He knew all about the princess's magical powers, he assured me, with a short laugh. He knew more about them than Burma Raja did. The princess was certainly visited by the *devas*, but they were five or six feet in height, and they wore white dhotis and yellow turbans. The truth of the matter was, he explained, taking pity on my ignorance, that as Burma Raja had told me he and the princess were from time to time very short of money. When this happened the princess borrowed from the Marwaris, who as I knew were great money-lenders. Burma Raja himself absolutely refused to borrow money from anybody, and had he known what the princess was doing he would have been very angry. The princess therefore told him that the *devas* had brought the money, and since he had implicit confidence in her he believed what she said. Sometimes though, he added, with a mischievous expression, the thought occurred to him that perhaps Burma Raja only *pretended* to believe. Perhaps he simply turned a blind eye to the princess's machinations. But the *devas* certainly visited Panorama. They usually came late in the evening, when Burma Raja was either reading or dozing. The princess slipped out of the back door and met them in the lane, having arranged everything beforehand through the maidservant. Sometimes her plans miscarried. A message might be delayed, or misunderstood, and the *devas* would either not turn up or turn up late. Sometimes, therefore, the princess would have to stand waiting in the lane for hours on end. To me it seemed both pitiable and ironic that the daughter of a woman who had intrigued her way to absolute power over a whole kingdom should be reduced to intriguing with money-lenders for the sake of a few hundred rupees, and that she should have to stand waiting for the money in the dark at the bottom of a deserted lane.

Whether Burma Raja really believed the princess's story about the *devas* putting money underneath the Buddha images in the shrine-room, or whether he only pretended to believe, was difficult to tell. Sometimes I thought that at the very *bottom* of his mind he knew what was going on but refused to admit that he knew even to himself. There was no doubt, however, that he believed in the occult. Indeed, he was very interested in it. Some time before the war he and Moti Chand Pradhan, who was a great friend of his, had established in Kalimpong a lodge of the Theosophical Society. They had rented a room in the High Street and organized weekly meetings and discussions. The favourite topic of discussion was the occult – though later this was superseded by the teachings of J. Krishnamurti. Burma Raja himself was particularly interested in occult physiology and occult cosmology, and there were books on these arcane subjects in the sitting room of the guest cottage, most of them bearing the stamp of the now defunct lodge. Occult cosmology included occult geography, and here Burma Raja's interest had come to centre on the Sumeru system. He was fascinated – indeed obsessed – by the image of Kailas, the mountain generally regarded as the earthly embodiment of the axis of that great system. He had not seen Kailas, which was situated in the south-western corner of Tibet, a hundred miles or so from the Indian border, but he had seen photographs of the holy mountain and knew exactly what it looked like. Indeed, he had tried to depict it in numerous paintings. Two of these hung on the wall of the sitting room, and there were others elsewhere in the guest bungalow, as well as up at Panorama. Burma Raja was not a skilled artist, but he had received a few lessons from Kanwal Krishna on

Prince K. M. Latthakin (Burma Raja) and his wife, the princess

one of his visits to the area and had captured the main features of Kailas quite well. There at the centre of the painting, either flanked by lesser mountains or surrounded with rainbows, was the white dome-shaped mass, looking as though it was indeed the abode of gods, as ancient legend maintained. Burma Raja was dissatisfied with all these efforts. None of them really succeeded, he told me, in depicting Kailas as he saw it in his mind's eye. But he would try again. One day he would succeed.

Not all Burma Raja's paintings were devoted to the subject of Kailas. Some of them reflected his more mundane interests. One of the most striking of these, which also hung on the wall of the sitting room, showed Burma Raja himself, wearing his usual Burmese dress, in the act of shooting an enormous Bengal tiger that had reared up on its hind legs and was about to spring on him. What with the vivid green of the surrounding jungle, the dull orange of the enraged beast, and the rich reds and purples of the erect figure of the huntsman, it was a sufficiently colourful piece of work. But the subject? Sometimes it seemed as though Burma Raja's interests were of a rather contradictory nature. One day, therefore, when our talk had ranged more widely than usual, I asked him when it was that he had enjoyed life most of all. The old man did not hesitate. 'When I've *meditated*,' he said emphatically, 'and when I've *killed* something.'

Though Burma Raja no longer meditated very much, any more than he went tiger hunting, he was fond of talking about the subject. He was also fond of talking about the *devas*, especially the guardian *devas* of the Royal House of Burma. One did not have to be a member of the Alompra family in order to see them, he explained. Anybody could see them, whether king or commoner. In my own case, it was surprising that I had not seen them already. After all, I meditated regularly, I lived near Panorama, and the *devas* were, he knew, well disposed towards me. Something would have to be done about the matter. He would go and speak to the princess. He would ask her to send one of the *devas* down to the guest cottage at once. Before I could stop him he had jumped up from his chair, was out of the door and scrambling up the steps between the two compounds. 'Stay where you are,' he called out over his shoulder, as he disappeared through the gap in the hedge, 'I shall be back in half an hour.' It was four o'clock in the afternoon, and since it was pleasant to sit there simply enjoying the peace and tranquillity of the place I did exactly as I had been told. After what I had heard from Gopal Babu I did not expect to see anything. I did not expect anything to happen at all. Ten minutes passed … twenty minutes … half an hour. Suddenly I heard Burma Raja coming down the steps. 'Have you seen anything? Have you seen anything?' he demanded excitedly, before he had even entered the door. 'The princess has just sent one of the *devas* down.' I had not seen anything. But something had happened. Two minutes before Burma Raja's arrival the room had suddenly filled with the strong, unmistakable scent of roses.

8
REPAIRING THE DAMAGE

The little Burmese pavilion was only big enough to hold one person. It stood not far from the guest cottage, on the angle formed by the two banks that marked the boundary in that corner of the property. Burma Raja had built it some years previously, and already much of the gilding had worn off the little pinnacled roof. What was left of it still gleamed in the sunlight, and the tiny wind-bells that hung from the eaves still tinkled merrily – or mournfully – in the breeze. Sometimes I sat there in the evening, if the weather was not too cold, watching the sun as it sank behind the dark blue Darjeeling hills. It was very peaceful on that side of the town, and as one more day ended I was gladder than ever to be staying there. By placing his guest cottage at my disposal Burma Raja had certainly rescued me from a dilemma, at least for the time being. There was no longer any question of the freedom of the open road, or the shelter of a kindly tree, being the only alternative I had to the hate-ridden atmosphere of the Dharmodaya Vihara. Thanks to the generosity of a warm-hearted old man who had troubles of his own to bear I was now provided with a pleasant retreat where I could study and meditate, where I could get on with my literary work, and where I could receive Sachin and the other students whenever they came to see me. But though Burma Raja's dramatic intervention had solved the most pressing of my problems, it was far from having solved them all. There were new premises to be found for the YMBA, and funds to be raised to cover the extra expense that this would involve. At all costs the damage Aniruddha had done to our activities must be repaired as quickly as possible.

Banshi's Godown was a large wooden warehouse with a corrugated iron roof that stood a short distance below the main road, on the way down to the bungalows of my two Hindu Newar sympathizers. It was called Banshi's Godown after its owner, Banshilal Agarwala, a Marwari merchant well known in the town for his tight-fistedness. Since trade between India and Tibet was practically at a standstill the place was more or less empty, and with Gopal Babu's help I was able to rent six small rooms on the ground floor for a hundred rupees a month. Our members were overjoyed. Once again the beautiful iridescent ball, that for the last few weeks had seemed in danger of hovering permanently above our heads, or even of floating away altogether, could be invited to descend and take fresh mundane embodiment. Once again the YMBA had a place for its activities and one that was, moreover, even nearer to the centre of the town than the vihara. It did not take us long to adapt the new premises to our requirements. Two of the rooms were de-partitioned so as to make a large room for ping-pong (we salvaged our old ping-pong table from the former Recreation Hut), one room became a reading room, one the YMBA office, while the two remaining rooms were set aside for the evening tutorial classes. Within a matter of days all the old faces had reappeared and our activities were flourishing vigorously. Indeed, they were flourishing more vigorously than ever, for the new premises in Banshi's Godown were ours in a sense that the Dharmodaya Vihara had never been. Nonetheless, the change was not without its drawbacks. The immediate surroundings of the warehouse were not nearly so attractive as those of the vihara. Instead of lawns and flower beds there were mounds of rubbish and the heavily rusted chassis of old cars. Moreover, although they were only a few hundred yards from the centre of the town, the new premises were more than two miles from Panorama. For me this meant that whenever I wanted to take part in YMBA activities I had a long walk each way – a walk along what was at night a dark and deserted road. There was also the question of raising funds to meet the extra expense we were now incurring in the way of rent, as well as the continued expense of running our usual programme of activities. Membership subscriptions did not even cover the cost of the ping-pong balls. Where was all the money to come from?

For help in solving this problem I turned to Madan Kumar Babu and

Gopal Babu, as I often did at that time. Raising funds in Kalimpong was no easy matter, they warned me, however deserving the cause for which they were being raised might be. All sorts of organizations were going around fund-raising all the time, and the public had naturally grown tired of being perpetually taxed in this way. Besides, Kalimpong was a trading centre. It was dependent for its prosperity on the wool trade with Tibet. Now that very little wool was coming through from Lhasa there was very little money circulating in the town. If I had come to Kalimpong a few years earlier.... Eventually a plan of action was decided upon. Madan Kumar Babu would go out collecting donations with me every morning after breakfast for the next two or three weeks. Starting with the more well-to-do members of the community, and confining ourselves to the bazaar area, we would try to see at least four or five people each day. If one substantial donation was forthcoming, others would follow. That was the way things were done in Kalimpong. In all probability two or three weeks would be sufficient for us to raise several thousand rupees. We might even be able to collect enough money to build or buy a permanent headquarters for the YMBA.

A day or two later we started putting our plan into execution. At least, we tried to start putting it into execution. When I turned up at Madan Kumar Babu's bungalow at eight o'clock in the morning, as we had arranged, it was only to find that several clients had already come to see him on urgent business. By the time he had finished with them it was too late for us to do anything, since at ten o'clock he had to be in court, and he had not even had his breakfast. Much the same thing happened the next day, and the next. Despite the earliness of the hour there were always people waiting to see Madan Kumar Babu. If it was not clients it was witnesses, and if it was not witnesses it was other lawyers, and their business was always urgent. Clearly there were disadvantages as well as advantages attached to being a successful lawyer with the largest practice in Kalimpong. While I waited for Madan Kumar Babu to finish I studied the faces of his visitors. Almost without exception they were of a particularly villainous and evil cast. Perhaps there really was a criminal type, as Lombroso contended in a book I had read many years before, except that here the criminals tended to be traders, commission-agents, and big landowners. So villainous-looking were the faces of some of Madan Kumar Babu's visitors, indeed, that I was not surprised that he seemed relieved when he was rid of them at last. I would not have been surprised if he had gone and washed his hands after talking to them – or taken a bath. Compared with giving *them* consultations, going round the bazaar collecting donations for the YMBA seemed a very innocent occupation. It was not until I had turned up at Madan Kumar Babu's bungalow for the third or fourth time, however, that he succeeded in extricating himself from the clutches of his clients and we could actually make a start. Even so, despite the abandonment of an important consultation he had less than an hour at our disposal. In that time we saw three or four High Street traders, all Marwaris, and succeeded in raising a couple of hundred rupees. It was not a very propitious beginning, and I began to wonder if there was not something wrong with our plan of action.

There certainly was something wrong with it. During the next two or three weeks Madan Kumar Babu was able to go out collecting with me only three or four times, with the result that we saw only ten or twelve people and raised in all no more than four or five hundred rupees. This was extremely disappointing. It was all the more disappointing because, as I had soon realized, it was not Madan Kumar Babu's intention that we should approach all the more well-to-do members of the community, but only those who were his clients, and with whom he had a certain amount of influence. Yet even with this more selective approach we had not done as well as expected. While it was true that there was very little money circulating in the town the main reason for our failure – for failure it undoubtedly was – lay in the fact that, much as he might want to help us, Madan Kumar Babu was in reality far too busy to give to the work of collecting donations the time and thought it required. After we had raised four or five hundred rupees, therefore, I stopped turning up at his bungalow in the morning and our plan of action was by tacit agreement shelved.

Though the problem of raising funds with which to meet the expense of running the YMBA had not been solved, or solved only to a very limited extent, I was not sorry that I no longer had to go out collecting donations. The experience of approaching people who, for the most part, had no desire to give, and who only yielded to pressure, of one kind or another, was not one that I found particularly pleasant. Indeed, during the three or four times I had gone out with Madan Kumar Babu, as well as on the one or two occasions I had gone out with Gopal Babu, or on my own, it had become more and more distasteful to me. Not that I had any regrets.

In less than three weeks we had raised enough money to keep the YMBA going for three or four months (excluding the cost of publishing *Stepping-Stones*). Besides, I had learned something about the way things were done in Kalimpong, and had come into contact with several people I might not otherwise have met. I had also been left with some very vivid personal impressions. The most vivid were those relating to our most reluctant donor, our most generous donor, and our most procrastinating donor.

Our most reluctant donor happened to be our first. Madan Kumar Babu having extricated himself from the clutches of his clients, it had taken us no more that five minutes to reach the High Street. Our first call was at a shop of the traditional open-fronted Indian type, situated on the right hand side of the road, only a few doors down from the Himalayan Store. Here, on an enormous expanse of grubby white mattress, the mouthpiece of a hubble-bubble between his aged gums, reclined the grossly fat figure of Banshilal. On top of the spherical body there rested, neckless and completely bald, a spherical head, in the middle of the spherical head there was a small spherical nose, and on either side of the spherical nose there were two button eyes. In his grubby white shirt and dhoti he looked for all the world like an enormous baby. There was nothing baby-like, however, about his expression, which was one of unfathomable shrewdness, meanness, and greed. Many were the stories that were told in Kalimpong about Banshilal. He had made his fortune during the war, as so many people had done. There had been a shortage of washers. Banshilal had quietly accumulated several thousand rupees worth of the old copper *lal paise* or 'red farthings', which were of course perforated, had sandpapered them down a bit, and then sold them to the American army at more than four times their face value. But Madan Kumar Babu had no time for personal reminiscences that morning. 'Bhikshuji has come for a donation,' he announced crisply as he seated himself on the edge of the mattress. Banshilal's fat frame quivered like a jelly with the shock. No, no, he protested hoarsely, removing the mouthpiece of the hubble-bubble, that was quite out of the question. He could not possibly give any donation – not so much as a rupee. Times were bad. Business was very slack. He was barely able to feed himself and his dependants. But in the grip of his own lawyer (as Madan Kumar Babu was), who knew most of his secrets, and who had a good idea how much he was worth, the dissembling old man was quite helpless. 'Give him a receipt for a hundred rupees,' said Madan Kumar Babu coolly. 'You can take it out of the rent.' Banshilal threw up his hands in horror at this, and his button eyes rolled wildly in his head, as though looking for some means of escape. But Madan Kumar Babu had risen to his feet, and was already on his way to the next shop. After a moment's hesitation I wrote out the receipt, deposited it on the mattress, and followed after him, leaving our reluctant donor sitting there with an expression of mingled indignation and reproach on his flabby countenance.

Our most generous donor was Raja S. T. Dorji, the Bhutan Agent in Kalimpong, and I went to see him not with Madan Kumar Babu but with Gopal Babu. He lived at Twelfth Mile, in a large house with a red tiled roof and cream-coloured roughcast walls that seemed to belong to the Home Counties rather than to the foothills of the eastern Himalayas. Above the front gate was an enormous *dorje* or 'thunderbolt sceptre,' more than six feet in length, which somehow gave the place a sinister and threatening look. I had been to Bhutan House, as it was called, once or twice before, and had met Raja Dorji's wife, Rani Chuni Dorji, a small, stony-faced woman of about fifty who was the sister of the Maharaja of Sikkim and, therefore, aunt of the fascinating Princess Pema Tsedeun. Either because she had heard what Swale had supposedly told Joe about a wealthy local Buddhist – namely herself – promising to give the YMBA twenty thousand rupees, or, what was more likely, because she was naturally of a frigid and unexpansive disposition, she did not give me a particularly friendly reception. However, she thawed sufficiently to show me her magnificent chapel, which I had wanted to see ever since I first saw a photograph of it in Marco Pallis's *Peaks and Lamas*. Judging by the amount of gold and silver it contained the Dorji family was immensely wealthy. But though there was a silver butter-lamp burning before the principal showcase the atmosphere of the chapel was cold and sterile, like that of a drawing room that is used only on formal occasions. Some time later Rani Chuni, with her elder daughter, Tashi Dorji, attended our Dharmacakra Day celebrations. Since then I had not seen her and she had taken no further interest in our activities. When I turned up at Bhutan House with Gopal Babu I was fortunate enough to meet Raja Dorji himself, as well as Rani Dorji and the rest of the family, and received a much friendlier reception than I had done before. Topgay Raja, as he was generally called, was a man of about fifty-five or sixty, and like his wife and other members of the family wore traditional dress. In his case it consisted of a simple, Bhutanese knee-length gown, dark blue in colour, and sufficiently full in the bosom to serve as both pocket and shoulder bag. When Gopal Babu spoke about the YMBA's need for funds he listened in a grave and kindly fashion, and from time to time nodded sympathetically. I noticed that although he was of noble and dignified appearance he entirely lacked his wife's more aristocratic graces. Despite his present power and wealth he was, in fact, of comparatively humble origin, his grandfather having been a syce. When Gopal Babu had finished speaking Raja Dorji turned and said something to one of his sons, whereupon the young man at once left the room, returning a few minutes later with 201 rupees. This time I did not have any qualms about writing out the receipt. It was not exactly a princely donation, but there was little doubt that had we met Rani Dorji rather than her more open-handed spouse the YMBA would not have received anything.

Our most procrastinating donor did not live in Kalimpong at all, and I went to see him on my own. Shantabir Lama was a successful government contractor who lived in Siliguri, where he had built himself a big new house on the flat, marshy land not far from the new but as yet unopened railway station. I had met him in Kalimpong, perhaps through Dhanman Moktan, and he had invited me to spend a few days with him and his family whenever I wished to do so. Thinking that now was the time to take advantage of his invitation, as well as to approach him for a donation, I decided to pay a short visit to the hot, dusty, insanitary little town that was Siliguri. Shantabir Lama was a stout, energetic man in his early forties with two wives, one old and one young, and a correspondingly large number of children of different ages. He could hardly have entertained me more hospitably, but it soon became evident that parting with *cash* was another matter. Much as I tried to bring him to the point of actually making a donation, he kept evading the issue by pressing me to stay another day. In the end I had to fix the day of my departure regardless, but fortunately, just before I left, he gave me twenty-five rupees.

While I was still busy raising funds for the YMBA Joe, having finished winding up his affairs in Lucknow, returned to the 'fantastic' sights and 'exotic' inhabitants of his now beloved Kalimpong. He already knew what had happened at the Dharmodaya Vihara, as I had written and told him about Aniruddha's closure of the Recreation Hut and his determination to have me out, but he had returned nonetheless and with Burma Raja's permission I gave him a room in the guest cottage. Here he would stay until such time as he could find somewhere suitable for himself and Dil Bahadur, the young Nepalese artist, to live and work. Now that I had Joe staying with me the guest cottage was not so quiet or so peaceful as before. Burma Raja did not come down so often, either, since for one reason or another he had never taken to Joe in the same way that he had taken to Swale and often shook his head over him, as if unable to make him out. Still, though he could be very prickly at times Joe was on the whole lively and stimulating company and I was not sorry to have him staying with me for a while. Indeed, his presence enabled me to set up some kind of establishment. Since my arrival at the guest cottage Burma Raja and the princess had been sending lunch down to me each day, besides inviting me up to Panorama from time to time for a ceremonial food-offering. Knowing how short of money they were, and not wanting to take advantage of their generosity more than was absolutely necessary, I ate out whenever I could, that is to say, whenever anybody invited me. Now that Joe was staying at the guest cottage and there were two of us to share the expense I decided that the time had come for me to take on a cook bearer, and Rudramani found a Pradhan boy he thought would be suitable for the post. Gopal (as the boy was called) thus became the first of a whole succession of cook bearers who were to serve me during the coming years. Plump and fair-skinned, he had a fixed, vacuous smile on his face, and he laughed softly to himself every few minutes. Though a reasonably good cook, he was painfully slow, and lunch was very often late, especially when he had been to market. However, we did not expect wonders for twenty rupees a month all found and put up with him as best we could.

Besides enabling me to set up some kind of establishment, Joe's presence at the guest cottage also made it necessary for me to come to a decision about a more serious matter. There was still disharmony within the YMBA. Though more than six months had passed since Joe had been invited up to Kalimpong as a full-time worker he and Swale were as far from getting on well together as they had ever been. This was certainly not because they had tried and failed. To do the two men justice, they had not even tried. By the time of Joe's departure for Lucknow it was therefore obvious that there was room in the YMBA for only one of my two helpers and that if Joe did return to Kalimpong I would have to choose between them. It was not even that they simply disagreed between themselves. Each tried to turn me against the other, and resented the fact that I could not be turned. To each of them the fact that I could not see how evil and despicable the other was simply showed my own gullibility, my lack of maturity, and my need for more experienced guidance. Swale was unable to understand why I could not see that Joe was an upstart, a social climber, and an outsider. Why, he had not even belonged to a decent regiment. He had been commissioned at all only because it was war time and there was a shortage of officers. His substantive rank was probably only that of captain, anyway, and even if he *had* managed to become an officer, technically speaking, he was certainly not a gentleman and never would be one. Joe, for his part, was unable to understand why I could not see that Swale was a con man, a poseur, and a snob. Was he not abusing the hospitality of the Jyoti brothers in the most shameless manner? Did he not always refer to his hostess, their mother, as 'that old bitch' and openly boast of smuggling beef into the house despite her religious objections? The fact of the matter was that there was *some* truth in what each man said about the other, but it was not the whole truth. I could see Joe's weaknesses as well as Swale, and Swale's no less clearly than Joe, but I could also see, in both my helpers, the positive qualities that the other could not see.

This did not, of course, make it any easier for me to choose between them, now that Joe was back in Kalimpong and the time for a decision had come. If it had been at all possible I would have liked to keep both my pig-headed helpers, despite the trouble they gave me, but I could not ignore the fact that the disharmony within the YMBA had begun to spread from the higher to the lower levels of the organization and was causing a certain amount of disquiet. Our members simply could not understand how it was that two Englishmen, both ex-army officers, both Buddhists, both working for the YMBA, and both on friendly terms with me, should be unable to get on well with each other – should, in fact, be on terms of more or less open hostility. In the end I decided that Swale would have to be the one to go. Though I found him easier to get on with than Joe, he had been taking less and less interest in YMBA activities, and hardly ever put in an appearance at Banshilal's Godown. Joe, on the other hand, despite his tendency to prickliness, had taken classes and helped with office work right up to the time of his departure for Lucknow. At the guest cottage he was again doing my typing for me. There were also considerations of a more general nature to be taken into account. I had noticed that Joe was much more generous than Swale, and often made donations to the YMBA, whereas Swale had never given as much as a rupee. Somewhere among the thorny tangles of Joe's nature there bloomed a redder rose of devotion to the Three Jewels than anything Swale could show. What weighed with me most, perhaps, was the fact that although the icy revulsion Joe had come to feel for Swale was no less strong than the cold antipathy Swale had come to feel for him, it was Swale who had been the original aggressor. Swale, therefore, would have to be the one to go.

Fund-raising and disharmony within the YMBA were not the only things with which I had to concern myself during the first two months of the new year. Fortunately there were more peaceful things to think about – things more in keeping with the atmosphere of the place in which I was now staying. The second, still more iridescent ball that had descended when *Stepping-Stones* came into existence had been in no danger of floating away and had not needed, therefore, to take fresh embodiment like the first. Through all vicissitudes our little monthly magazine of Himalayan religion, culture, and education continued to be edited, printed, and distributed. Neither in the editorial articles nor in the Notes and News section was there the slightest reference either to the shutting down of the Recreation Hut or to the unpleasant way in which I had been squeezed out of the Dharmodaya Vihara. So far as *Stepping-Stones* was concerned Aniruddha did not exist. The editorial articles continued to strike their unambiguously spiritual note with such topics as 'The Awakening of the Heart' and 'Rights and Duties',[37] while the News and Notes section confined itself to reporting such matters as my recent visit to the plains and the activities of our Ajmer branch, as well as announcing the forthcoming arrival in Kalimpong of the Sacred Relics of the *arhants* Śāriputra and Maudgalyāyana, the two chief disciples of the Buddha. The only item that could possibly be understood as referring to recent events at the Dharmodaya Vihara was an extract from the *Sūtra of Forty-Two Sections* entitled 'On Returning Good for Evil' which I included in the January issue.

As refracted through the medium of *Stepping-Stones*, our second, still more beautiful iridescent ball was indeed incorporating brighter hues and more delicate tints than ever, thus creating a still richer and more harmonious effect. Both Lama Govinda and Dr Guenther were now among our regular contributors, the brilliant blues of the one and the subtle purples of the other forming a valuable addition to our total range.

Within the first three months of the year Lama Govinda contributed a poem entitled 'The Temple of Sunyata,' which appeared in the January issue, and the first instalment of a ten part article on 'The Significance of "OM" and the Foundations of Mantric Lore,' which appeared in the issue for March. In an introductory note to the poem, which had originated from a dream, I wrote 'The symbolical language of Poetry is often able to convey the intuitions of the spirit more vividly and clearly than the conceptual language of Philosophy.' Some years later the article on 'The Significance of "OM" and the Foundations of Mantric Lore' reappeared, in slightly enlarged form, as Part One of Lama Govinda's book *Foundations of Tibetan Mysticism*. Within the same three months Dr Guenther contributed an article on 'Ahankara and Selflessness', which appeared, in two instalments, in the February and March issues. Beginning with the issue for January he also contributed to our 'Lotuses of the Mahāyāna' section a series of excerpts that he had selected and translated from the *Gaṇḍavyūha Sūtra*, the principal text of the Avataṃsaka school of Buddhism, which arose in China during the second half of the sixth century CE, and of the Kegon sect of Japan. As he explained in his Introduction, the text describes the ideal of a bodhisattva.

> The youth Sudhana travels all over India on the advice of the bodhisattva Mañjuśrī, in order to achieve the highest knowledge of Enlightenment. He goes to all kinds of men, women, and deities. Finally, by the help of the bodhisattva Samantabhadra, the highest knowledge is revealed to him, which is essentially the vision and experience of the interpenetration of each and every thing. In the course of his travels he is sent from one teacher to another, because everyone, with the exception of bodhisattva Samantabhadra, has only a limited knowledge.

In the course of the last few years I, too, had travelled all over India, and like Sudhana I had met with all kinds of men, women, and (very nearly) deities. Unlike Sudhana's teachers, most of the people I encountered did not have even a limited knowledge of Enlightenment. Nonetheless, though they were unable to teach me, I had learned from them. Sometimes the process was a painful one. In Kalimpong, too, I had been meeting people and learning from them. No doubt the process would continue.

9
TRADITIONS AND INDIVIDUAL TALENTS

Staying at Burma Raja's guest cottage had both advantages and disadvantages. The principal disadvantage was that I was so far from the bazaar, and from the YMBA. Unless I actually went along to Banshilal's Godown in the evening and took part in the activities I hardly ever saw our members, which was certainly not good for the development of our work. Two miles was not a long way to walk, especially for a hill-man, but people who lived in the bazaar were not accustomed to paying visits in the Development Area, to them another world, and it seemed that the majority of my students were simply unable to overcome their habit of *not* walking in that particular direction. Even Sachin, Lachuman, and Dawa came to see me only very occasionally. The principal advantage of staying at the guest cottage was, of course, that I could enjoy the peace and quietness of the place, but it also brought me into closer contact with several well-known Kalimpong residents who lived in that quarter of the town. During the six months that I spent with Burma Raja I came to know two or three of these quite well and, through them, a number of other people of different religious traditions and different individual talents.

Some of the people I came to know lived in quite splendid houses. Beyond the guest cottage, on a lower level still, at the far end of a lawn flanked by fruit trees, stood Manjula, with its own guest cottage – in this case a medium-sized house – even farther down. Manjula was the summer residence of Mrs Charu Mitter, otherwise known as the

Queen of Kalimpong. The lady's right to this title was not altogether undisputed, some people disloyally maintaining that she was not Queen of Kalimpong at all but only queen of the local Bengalis. Be that as it may, there were undoubtedly Bengalis in the town, especially during the summer months, and if there was such a thing as Bengali society Mrs Mitter was undoubtedly its leader, or even its queen. Every year she came up to Kalimpong for the hottest part of the season, bringing with her her small daughter Manjula (after whom the house was named), her Bengali cook, and her Nepalese ayah. Her husband, who was an architect, arrived later than she did and left earlier, staying altogether only two or three weeks. Once settled at Manjula Mrs Mitter gave tea parties, entertained women friends and relations from the plains, and pulled numberless small strings in the world of (predominantly) Bengali officialdom. She had even succeeded in getting a whole section of road between the Lower Cart Road and her own front gate tarred and gravelled by the Municipality. Now that the British had gone the local Bengalis regarded themselves as the ruling class, not to say the master race, and expected everything to be done for their convenience. Some of them in fact looked down on the hill people as an inferior breed ('They're so backward!' was the usual cry), an attitude the hill people themselves deeply resented. It was with reference to this arrogant and overbearing attitude on the part of the Bengalis that Mrs Mitter had been given the title by which she was generally, if ironically, known, for if she was queen of the Bengalis, and if the Bengalis ruled Kalimpong, then Queen of Kalimpong she must assuredly be.

I had met Mrs Mitter the previous year, when she attended one of our Sunday lectures at the Dharmodaya Vihara, but this had been my only contact with her. Swale, on the other hand, knew the lady quite well. When visiting Panorama he had always made a point of calling at Manjula too, and from him she had not only learned how the YMBA was progressing but also imbibed a strong dislike for Joe. Now that I was staying at the Panorama guest cottage, and she herself was back in Kalimpong for the season, she was forever sending her elderly Nepalese gardener up to me with messages and with Bengali curries and sweetmeats in little covered dishes. In these circumstances it was inevitable that I should become better acquainted with her and be drawn, to some extent, into her social circle. Not liking to refuse all her invitations, which were often quite pressing, I used to go down to see her in the morning sometimes, when she would entertain me very hospitably with tea and Bengali sweetmeats. Once or twice I put in an appearance at her afternoon tea parties, though I disappointed her by not bringing with me Burma Raja and the Princess, who had also been invited, so that she had to content herself with having captured Prince Peter. (Dinner parties were, of course, out of the question for me, as I still adhered to the rule of not taking solid food after midday.) My hostess was a woman of about forty, inclining to stoutness, with a round, rather ugly face on which there at times appeared an expression of extreme hardness. Though she was in many ways quite Westernized, and spoke excellent English, Mrs Mitter invariably wore the graceful Bengali sari. In the morning this was of white cotton, with the red border that denoted a married woman whose husband was still living. In the afternoon it was of heavy silk, hand-printed in what I came to recognize as the Santiniketan style – a style based on motifs adapted from Bengali folk art. When she went out Mrs Mitter draped the edge of her sari over her head, which together with her attendant ayah, and her formidable expression, made her look for all the world like a Roman matron of senatorial family on her way to a good seat at the gladiatorial shows. Mrs Mitter was, in fact, of a somewhat domineering disposition. I had not been to see her more than a couple of times before she was trying to pull a few strings in the little world of the YMBA. I should make *much* more use of that *nice* Colonel Ryan, she told me, and get rid of that *dreadful* Major Cann, whom nobody liked. By this time I was accustomed to my older friends thinking that I was young and inexperienced and in need of their advice, and I therefore kept my own counsel. I knew quite well, however, that strong as was Mrs Mitter's dislike for Joe it was fully reciprocated. When they happened to meet he was always careful to be extremely polite to her, raising his hat and enquiring after her health in the most solicitous manner – all of which she acknowledged with a stiff half smile – but as soon as she was out of hearing it was another story. 'She's a *very hard* woman,' he would breathe, half to himself, absentmindedly twisting an imaginary neck.

    Domineering and hard though she might be, Mrs Mitter was meekness and gentleness itself when her husband was around – at least in public. This was illustrated by an amusing incident that occurred soon after the latter's arrival in Kalimpong, when Swale and I were talking with him on the veranda. Happening to want a box of matches Mr Mitter, a gross-featured, corpulent man who spent the day lounging about in singlet and lungi, suddenly raised his voice and shouted for his wife, who was inside the house. In an instant she was in the doorway, her mouth full of food, without even pausing to wash the hand with which she had been eating. 'Just see how obedient these Hindu wives are!' exclaimed Mr Mitter in mock deprecation, as Swale let out a hearty guffaw. 'They come whenever we call them.' Then turning to his wife, he added in a milder tone, 'I'm sorry, my dear, I didn't know you were taking your meal.' Mrs Mitter blushed like a girl at this, and there was a good deal of laughter at her expense, in which she herself could not help joining. After this incident Swale was forever joking with Mrs Mitter about her being a model of wifely obedience, always coming the instant her lord and master called. Strange to say, that formidable lady never seemed to mind him joking with her in this way, even though he sometimes carried the joke so far as to put even a Hindu wife on the defensive, so that she felt constrained to justify herself. 'It's the way we've been brought up,' she would protest, with an apologetic laugh. Swale's only reply to this was an enormous guffaw. Observing them together, it was soon clear to me that far from minding the way in which he joked with her Mrs Mitter actually quite enjoyed it, and that his boisterous jocularity was very much to her taste. Unlike the unfortunate Joe, my gregarious friend was in fact extremely popular with her, and there was no doubt that if the Queen of Kalimpong had a court then Swale was the favourite courtier.

Such was Swale's popularity with Mrs Mitter, indeed, that she viewed the prospect of his leaving Kalimpong with considerable dismay. When she learned that her string-pulling in the world of the YMBA had not been as successful as her string-pulling in the world of Bengali officialdom, and that I had decided to get rid of nice Colonel Ryan rather than the dreadful Major Cann, she was extremely displeased, and lost no time in telling me so. Though I continued to see her, the lady's attitude towards me underwent a marked change, cordiality being replaced by coolness, and when she came up to Kalimpong in subsequent years she always took good care to let me know that she had still not forgiven me for preferring Joe to Swale and probably never would. As for her attitude towards Joe himself, whom she regarded as being at the bottom of all the mischief, this underwent a marked change too, her dislike for him becoming more deeply rooted than ever. His politeness was now acknowledged not with a stiff half smile but with a disapproving stare or a look of pronounced distaste. There was, of course, no reason why Swale should not have stayed on in Kalimpong even after ceasing to work for the YMBA (there was no interruption of our friendly personal relations), but his ties with the place were loose, he was conscious that he had outstayed his welcome as guest of the Jyoti family, and before the summer was out he was gone. Damodaran wanted to see his family in Malabar, he told me cheerily before his departure. They would spend some time in South India, then return to Calcutta. After that, he did not know what he would do. Perhaps he would go back to Burma and let them take a few more pot-shots at him. Perhaps he would get a job in Assam.

Though the change in Mrs Mitter's attitude towards me was so marked, I found it as difficult as ever to account for her extreme displeasure at my getting rid of Swale rather than Joe. Clearly, she believed that it was his ceasing to work for the YMBA that had been mainly responsible for his departure from Kalimpong, but it seemed strange nonetheless that she should take the loss of her favourite so much to heart that she could become cold to me and positively rude to Joe. Did she enjoy his company to such an extent that she resented being deprived of it? Or was she a woman who was so accustomed to having her own way that she resented being thwarted when once she had made her wishes known? Had the little YMBA puppets given offence by not dancing in the way she wanted them to dance when she had, as she supposed, given a good jerk on the right strings? There was no doubt that the answer to these questions was in the affirmative, but in the end I concluded that the real reason for Mrs Mitter's change of attitude was to be found in a region the importance of which I, as a monk, had tended to overlook – the region of matchmaking. Not long after her arrival in Kalimpong Mrs Mitter had been joined by her school-teacher niece Miss Bose, a short, extremely plump girl with a toothy smile and an incipient moustache. The fact that Miss Bose was still unmarried must have been very much on her aunt's mind. Even I knew that twenty-five or thereabouts was very late indeed for a girl to be lingering in the marriage market, and perhaps I should have attached greater significance than I did to the fact that Swale was permitted to associate with Miss Bose far more freely than was customary even in quite Westernized Hindu families. He even took her out for a walk once or twice unchaperoned!

However, though Swale plainly enjoyed the plump niece's company, and she apparently his, and though in a moment of enthusiasm he once went so far as to describe her as 'bedworthy' (an expression I had not heard before), I gave no more thought to the matter than if Miss Bose had been an English girl. Only in retrospect did I see that, from Mrs Mitter's point of view, things must have seemed to be moving in a certain direction – a direction of which she herself must have approved, if not actively encouraged. Indeed, it was more than likely that the solicitous aunt had been indulging in a little unobtrusive matchmaking on her niece's behalf, and had actually contrived to bring the whole situation about. If such was indeed the case, and if Mrs Mitter had been relying on Swale's work for the YMBA to keep him in Kalimpong long enough for things to be brought to a successful conclusion, then my decision to get rid of the nice Colonel rather than the dreadful Major must have ruined all her plans. No wonder she was so displeased with me! At the same time, I knew quite well that from Swale's own point of view there had been no question of things moving in a certain direction, or indeed in any direction. Even if some of the things Joe said about him were *not* true, I was convinced that, lightly as he seemed to take his *anagārika* ordination, he would never forget himself so far as to espouse Miss Bose, however 'bedworthy' the plump girl might be. Indeed, I was inclined to think that, unobtrusive as Mrs Mitter's matchmaking had been, it had not escaped Swale's notice, and that he left Kalimpong partly in order to avoid complications.

Whatever the truth of the matter may have been, before my decision to get rid of Swale became generally known, and when Mrs Mitter's attitude towards me was still one of cordiality, she introduced me to a number of people in her circle. The most interesting and important of these was Mrs Pratima Tagore, the niece and daughter-in-law of the poet, who lived practically next door to Mrs Mitter, in a house called Chitrabhanu. I soon realized that Pratima Devi, as she was generally called, occupied a position of special pre-eminence in the local Bengali community and that if Mrs Mitter was the Queen of Kalimpong *she* was the Queen Mother. This was due not merely to the fact that she was related to the poet both by blood and by marriage (for Bengalis Tagore was the Poet in much the same way that for the medieval schoolmen Aristotle was the Philosopher) but also to the fact that she was a woman of unusual beauty of character who from girlhood onwards had been especially close to him. It was in order to make sure of not losing her companionship that Tagore had, so I gathered, arranged for her to marry his son Rathindranath. Since the great man's death ten years earlier Pratima Devi had come to be revered as the guardian of his memory, as the upholder of his ideals, and as the protectress of Santiniketan, the complex of educational and cultural activities which Tagore had created some ninety miles north of Calcutta. Santiniketan was, in fact, a sort of shrine to which admirers of the poet resorted not only from all over Bengal but from many parts of the world, and Pratima Devi was the high priestess of the shrine, who kept the lamps burning and safeguarded the purity of the cult. Every year, however, she passed the summer months in Kalimpong, just as Mrs Mitter did, and the two ladies were on terms of intimacy. Mrs Mitter in fact spent a good deal of her time with Mrs Tagore, often running down to Chitrabhanu with something she had cooked, or with an item of gossip, as many as three or four times in the course of a single day. Whether they were on terms of intimacy because they were neighbours, or because they were the two most prominent figures in local Bengali society, it was difficult to tell. Probably each of these circumstances played a part. There was also the fact of their common religious background. Both Mrs Mitter and Mrs Tagore belonged to families long connected with the Brahmo Samaj, the Hindu reformist movement started by Raja Rammohan Roy more than a hundred years earlier. The poet's father Debendranath Tagore, popularly known as the Maharshi or 'Great Sage', had in fact been one of the leaders of the movement, the influence of which was still widely if thinly diffused throughout Bengal. Whatever the reason may have been, on terms of intimacy the two ladies undoubtedly were, and thus it came about that one afternoon Mrs Mitter took me down to Chitrabhanu to see Pratima Devi, who had more than once expressed a wish to meet me.

  Even away from her shrine Pratima Devi looked not unlike a high priestess. Like Mrs Mitter she wore the Bengali sari, but in her case it was predominantly white or cream in colour, and slightly starched, so that it fell to her feet in stiff, straight folds. Though still in her middle fifties, she was not only rather emaciated but quite frail, as if recently recovered from a long illness, and when she rose from the Santiniketan-style couch on which she had been sitting and advanced towards me it was evident that she moved with some difficulty. Soon we were talking, while Mrs Mitter bustled about supervising the serving of tea. Despite her thin face and rather sharp features Pratima Devi had a complexion like the petal of a magnolia flower, and it was not difficult to see that as a young woman she must have been quite beautiful. One of her first questions was the one that was, plainly, uppermost in her mind. Had I been to Santiniketan? From the way in which she put the question it was clear that, often as she must have asked it, for her it was no mere formality. She really wanted to know. Unfortunately, I had to admit that I had not been to Santiniketan, adding, quite truthfully, that I hoped to go there before very long. 'Oh you *must* go!' she responded fervently, a rapturous look transfiguring her worn face. 'I am sure you would like it there. Even though it isn't what it was when Gurudev was alive Santiniketan is a wonderful place.' The high-pitched, rather quavering voice in which Pratima Devi uttered these words made them sound all the more impressive, as though the high priestess had momentarily become the inspired prophetess. I also noticed that she pronounced the word Gurudev or 'Divine Master', as she called her father-in-law, with profound reverence, though, at the same time, in a manner that was wholly spontaneous and natural. Her devotion to the poet's memory was, in fact, wonderful to behold. Whenever his name was mentioned, or his work referred to, her pale features would be suddenly illumined with an inner glow. It was as though an alabaster lamp had been lit in the shrine. Even when Tagore was not the theme there was a quality of transparency and luminosity about Pratima Devi which, combined with her dignity and sweetness, her perfect courtesy, and her refined, aristocratic manners, created the impression of a being from another world. Beside her poor Mrs Mitter looked thoroughly coarse and plebeian.

When we had talked for about half an hour, and I was drinking my second cup of tea, we were joined by a tall, thin man of about sixty with shoulder length grey hair and a decidedly melancholy look. This was Mrs Tagore's husband Rathindranath, the poet's son. Though the house had been built to his own design, and though he had made the Santiniketan-style furniture with his own hands, it somehow seemed as though he did not really belong to the place. After a few minutes he left us, and I never saw him again, though I continued to see Mrs Tagore for a good many years. Being the poet's son was much more difficult than being his daughter-in-law. Rathindranath had not only grown up very much in his great father's shadow, but grown up almost entirely lacking in talent in a family where talent – not to speak of genius – was the rule rather than the exception. His sole talent was for woodwork and leatherwork and this, despite the poet's own more enlightened attitude, was not to be compared, in caste-ridden India at least, with a talent for the more liberal arts of poetry, music, and painting. No wonder the clean-shaven brown face had such a melancholy look! Lack of talent had not been Rathindranath's only problem, however. As Mrs Mitter had already told me, though not in so many words, the poet's son had never had a career of his own. Until recently, in fact, he had not had a life of his own. Even his marriage to Pratima Devi had been arranged more with a view to providing his father with a daughter-in-law than himself with a wife. Although arranged marriages were customary in Bengal, as elsewhere in India, and usually turned out quite well, it was not surprising that this union had not been a success. Indeed, a few weeks after our brief encounter I heard that he had run away from Santiniketan with a woman much younger than himself, and that the couple had settled in Dehra Dun. Perhaps Rathindranath had come out from his father's shadow at last. As for Mrs Tagore, she bore the shock of her husband's defection without complaint, and was duly invested by her women friends with a halo of martyrdom, which she wore with her usual dignity.

Morals were indeed changing in West Bengal, in more ways than one. The fact that Mrs Mitter could think of Swale as a possible husband for her niece showed that the old caste barriers had crumbled to some extent. Interracial marriages were not unknown among the Westernized professional classes, and it was therefore not surprising that through Mrs Mitter I should come to know two European women who had married Bengali Hindus. Both Eta Ghosh and Irene Ray had, in their different ways, completely identified themselves with the society and the culture into which they had married and of which they were, in a sense, now part. Indeed, I sometimes thought they were more Bengali than the Bengalis. Both wore Bengali saris, both spoke the Bengali language, both cooked and ate in Bengali style, and both were, for all practical purposes, Bengali Hindus. Eta Ghosh's sari was, however, pure white, without the traditional red border. Her husband, a well-known doctor, had suddenly collapsed and died at Manjula itself, only two years earlier, when they were staying with Mrs Mitter for the summer holidays. A plump, brisk, motherly woman, she was now a teacher at Santiniketan, and warmly invited me to stay with her when I paid my promised visit to the place. She would cook me a goulash, she declared, on learning that I was of partly Hungarian descent. She herself had been born in Hungary, not far from Budapest, and she had not forgotten how to make the national dish. Irene Ray had been more fortunate than Eta Ghosh. She was still entitled to wear the red border. Her husband, another doctor, was still living, but had been left behind in Calcutta to look after his practice while she spent a few weeks in the cooler air of the hills. She was taller and slimmer than Eta, besides being more serious-minded, and like myself she had been born in England. What was more, she was a native of south London; in fact, a native of Tooting. It seemed strange to be sitting there in Mrs Mitter's garden, within sight of Mount Kanchenjunga, talking to someone who knew Tooting Broadway as well as I knew it myself.

While Eta was content with pujas and devotional songs, Irene was a serious student of Indian philosophy and religion, and a regular contributor to the house journals of various religious movements. Though she knew something about Buddhism, her real interest was in the Advaita or 'Non-Dualist' tradition of the Vedanta as popularly expounded by the swamis of the Ramakrishna Mission. She was, in fact, a devotee of the mission, as well as being an active supporter of the mission's Institute of Culture in Calcutta, with which I had myself been associated some four or five years earlier. Since then the Institute had moved from its old home in Wellington Square to spacious new premises in Russa Road, and activities had expanded considerably. Besides attending lectures and anniversary celebrations, Irene helped with administrative work, and in this way she had come to know several people whom I had known. Among these were Swami Nityaswarupananda, the scheming and ambitious Secretary of the Institute, and Kantaraj, his ever-helpful assistant, both of whom still remembered me. Despite her practical involvement with the Institute, however, Irene Ray was no mere 'organization woman'. Her interest in the contemplative disciplines of the Advaita Vedanta was deep and genuine. Though I had met her through Mrs Mitter she had come up to Kalimpong not to enjoy a holiday but to make a spiritual retreat, and she was staying not at Manjula, as Eta was, but at the local Ramakrishna ashram.

The ashram was situated at the highest point of the Development Area, three or four hundred feet above Panorama. Though no more quiet and secluded than my cottage, it commanded an even finer view of Mount Kanchenjunga, as well as of several adjacent peaks. Irene was staying not at the ashram proper but in the very comfortable guest house, and before leaving she invited me for tea there. I had visited the ashram once or twice before, and had already met both the swami in charge and his assistant, who was still a *brahmacārī*. (In the Ramakrishna Order a swami was equivalent to a *bhikṣu* or full monk and a *brahmacārī* to a *śrāmaṇera* or novice.) While the *brahmacārī*, a comparatively young man, was a very popular figure in the town, the swami was almost universally disliked. The reason for this strange state of affairs was that whereas the *brahmacārī* was a person of great warmth and friendliness, Swami Gangeshwarananda, as the older man was called, was not only rude and intolerant in the extreme but seemingly consumed by a black hatred for everything and everybody. He was, in fact, an even better example of Buddhaghosa's 'person of angry temperament' than was Venerable Aniruddha himself. Aniruddha, it could be said, was merely bad-tempered. Though he became angry easily enough, in between the bouts of anger he could be quite cheerful and, in his own rough way, even friendly. Gangeshwarananda, however, had an evil temper. He was never cheerful and never friendly, for the black demon by which he was possessed gave him no respite. If Aniruddha's anger was like the sudden blazing up of fire, Gangeshwarananda's was like the constant dripping of poison from the fangs of a cobra. Why he should be in such a state after more than thirty years in the Ramakrishna Order one could only speculate. Yet in it he was. The authorities of the mission had indeed posted him to Kalimpong only because his evil temper could do less harm there than elsewhere. Since the Kalimpong ashram had been built as a place of rest and recuperation for senior swamis and well-to-do devotees, it conducted no public activities, and all the swami in charge had to do was to keep the buildings in good repair and make sure that guests did not leave without paying. This Swami Gangeshwarananda certainly did. He also lectured occasionally, besides visiting the few Bengali houses where he was still welcome. One of these was Manjula. Though Mrs Mitter disliked him, her husband was a devotee, or at least a supporter, of the Ramakrishna Mission, and according to Joe the swami never left without a hundred rupee note being slipped into his hand. Whether I first met him at Manjula or at the ashram it is no longer possible for me to say. Wherever it was, we had not talked for more than a few minutes before I realized that he nursed a particular hatred for Buddhism. So strong was this hatred that, two years later, it burst forth at a public meeting in a virulent personal attack on the Buddha – an attack which gave great offence to Buddhists and Hindus alike and lost him what little sympathy people still felt for him.[38] As a member of the Ramakrishna Mission the swami was, of course, a believer in Universalism. He subscribed to the view that all religions are one and all worthy, therefore, of the same respect and admiration. This made his hatred for Buddhism all the more unaccountable. In the circumstances I could only suppose that, though all religions were one, some were more – and some less – one than others.

Universalism of a more sophisticated kind was, however, also to be found in the neighbourhood – not to speak of more amiable Universalists. During my stay with Burma Raja I came into contact with someone who, though connected with the Tibetan Buddhist tradition, was at the same time a follower of the 'élitist' Universalism of René Guénon and his school. This was none other than Marco Pallis, otherwise known as Thubden Tendzin, the London-born author of *Peaks and Lamas*. I had first heard of him in Singapore, when my old friend Arnold Price wrote me an enthusiastic letter about the then little-known book, which he strongly urged me to read.[39] Read it I did, thus getting my first real insight into Tibetan Buddhism, and my first glimpse of one of its most attractive and inspiring personalities – the eleventh-century poet-saint Milarepa. Since then I had very much wanted to meet Marco Pallis, and it was with both surprise and delight that I learned, shortly after my arrival in Kalimpong, that he was actually living in the town. He was not, however, a very easy man to approach. Though he attended one of Prince Peter's lectures he disappeared immediately afterwards and for the whole of the time that I was at the Dharmodaya Vihara my wish to meet him remained unfulfilled. Some time later, when we had come to know each other quite well, he admitted that he had been avoiding me. The reason for this rather strange behaviour was that, having read the short stories Swale had contributed to the first two issues of *Stepping Stones*, he had been afraid that my interest in Tibetan Buddhism might be limited to its more sensational 'occult' and 'psychic' aspects! A perusal of some of the more recent issues of the magazine had, fortunately, convinced him that this was not in fact the case, and hearing that I was now staying in the Development Area, not far from where he himself lived, he lost no time in seeking me out.

From that time onwards we met frequently, and became good friends. Usually we met at the guest cottage (he rightly thinking it more in accordance with Buddhist etiquette that he should visit me than that I should visit him), though he did once invite me up to his bungalow for a meal. The bungalow was situated at the top of a flight of irregular stone steps, and what with trees looming up behind and shrubs pressing in on either side it was a sufficiently quiet and secluded place. Here Thubden La, as he liked to be called, lived with his friend Richard Nicholson, otherwise known as Thubden Shedub, the companion of the travels recorded in *Peaks and Lamas*. As lunch was not quite ready, he showed me round the place. Tibetan painted scrolls hung on the walls, and the polished wooden floors were covered with Tibetan rugs. There were silver butter-lamps on the altar, and massive copper teapots on the sideboard, all gleaming in the shuttered semi-darkness. In one room I could just make out the unfamiliar shape of a harpsichord. What it was doing there I could not imagine, and neither Thubden La nor Shedub La offered any explanation. Only years later, long after they had left Kalimpong, did I come to know that the two men were accomplished musicians, with a special interest in early music. There was, in fact, quite a lot about Marco Pallis that I did not know at that time, and the semi-darkness in which he seemed to live was perhaps not without significance. One was conscious that there were gleams other than those of silver and copper piercing the dense atmosphere of the place, and unfamiliar shapes other than that of the harpsichord rising up out of obscure corners. There were movements and currents in the air, as of unseen fish in deep waters, and even though one had no idea what it might be one was vaguely aware of something going on 'behind the scenes'. The bungalow was, in fact, very much like a cave, with treasures heaped just inside the entrance, but with a tunnel running from the back of the cave into the darkness – a tunnel down which Marco Pallis disappeared from time to time and which was the venue for all kinds of mysterious activities.

Frequently as we now met, the author of *Peaks and Lamas* and I always had a good deal to say to each other, and our talk covered an increasingly wide range of topics. Both of us were deeply concerned about the state of Buddhism in Kalimpong and the surrounding area, as well as about the decline of spiritual values in the modern world. On this latter topic Marco Pallis, in particular, felt very strongly (I felt less strongly perhaps because I had seen less of the world than he had), and his ideas as to why such a decline had taken place were clear and definite. It had taken place, so he believed, because of a growing lack of respect for tradition – 'tradition' being the whole body of thoughts, practices, and institutions coming down to us from remote antiquity *insofar as these are informed by principles belonging, ultimately, to the metaphysical order*. (What made Marco Pallis a Universalist, as well as a 'traditionalist', was the fact that he also believed that the different individual traditions, such as Buddhism, Christianity, and Islam, had all issued from one Primordial Tradition.) It was in connection with his ideas about tradition, I think, that my new friend first mentioned to me the name of René Guénon, who together with Ananda K. Coomaraswamy had been, so it transpired, the immediate source of these ideas, as well as the main inspiration behind his thinking. He and Richard Nicholson had, in fact, translated several of Guénon's books into English, and copies of these works were soon put into my hands. As might have been expected, I found them of great interest. The idea of religion being a special form of tradition appealed to me strongly, and enabled me to see the whole subject in a new light. Unfortunately, despite his Universalism the French savant was a victim of the same kind of selective blindness as the Bengali swami, and some of his references to Buddhism showed actual prejudice against that religion. Perhaps he too was an example of 'a person of angry temperament'! On my drawing Marco Pallis's attention to the references in question he promised to raise the matter with the author and to see that corrections were made in future editions of the volumes concerned. He was as good as his word, and some years later this was actually done. Meanwhile, though it featured in my writings for a time the idea of religion as a special form of tradition lost some of its initial appeal, and I came to attach less importance to such matters as the wearing of traditional dress – or rather, came to see that the issues involved were less straightforward and simple than had at first appeared. In one respect at least, however, Marco Pallis's ideas about tradition continued to influence me long after our meetings at Burma Raja's guest cottage had come to an end. This was in connection with the comparatively humble subject of handicrafts, and in particular that of the superiority of natural dyes such as were traditionally used in Tibet over their modern aniline substitutes. If in future years I was able to distinguish the subtler and richer effects of the one from the cruder and bolder effects of the other it was largely owing to my contact with Marco Pallis. For me this was not so small a matter as it might seem. Colour is an integral part of our perception of the external world, but the quality of the colour perceived depends upon the degree of awareness and emotional sensitivity in the percipient. Only a beautiful soul can perceive beautiful colours.

Much as I enjoyed my talks with Marco Pallis, his visits to the guest cottage were attended by one drawback. This was the effect they had upon Joe, who was still staying with me. Though he did not feel for Marco Pallis the almost physical revulsion he felt towards Swale, in the older man's company he was extremely ill at ease and tended to behave with an abruptness that at first rather puzzled the visitor. The truth of the matter was that Marco Pallis possessed those very advantages which Joe himself was so painfully conscious of lacking and which were, therefore, most likely to activate his morbidly acute feelings of inferiority and inadequacy – feelings that in any case were never far from the surface. Marco Pallis was the son of a diplomat, had been to public school and university, knew four or five languages, was highly articulate, and had written a book which, though by no means a best-seller, had won for the author a modest degree of fame. In these circumstances it was not surprising that Joe, being the sort of person he was, should feel the way he did. At the same time, Marco Pallis was so kind and courteous, and beamed at Joe with such evident good will, that the latter had no excuse for one of his usual petulant outbursts or even for a display of prickliness. The result was that he felt more frustrated than ever, and as soon as Marco Pallis had gone I was treated, more often than not, to a variety of jeering comments on our unoffending visitor's opinions, personal appearance, and mannerisms – or even to an angry tirade. Only one of Joe's comments had any real basis, and even that related to what was no more than a rather embarrassing habit. When expounding his favourite ideas Marco Pallis was liable to be so carried away by enthusiasm that not only did he get as close as possible to the person he was addressing but actually thrust his face right up into theirs, so that they were compelled to back away, Marco Pallis following, until he had them pinned against the back of a chair or against a wall, there to be overwhelmed with more argument, fresh enthusiasm, and a pair of gleaming eyes.

A painful consciousness of his own lack of advantages was not the only reason for the feelings with which Joe regarded Marco Pallis. He did not have much difficulty in convincing himself that I enjoyed my talks with 'old Marco', as he always called him, far more than I enjoyed my talks with *him*. This was only natural, he was at pains to assure me, brushing aside my protests with an irritable wave of the hand. After all, Marco Pallis and I had a lot in common. We had both read all sorts of difficult books that *he* had not read, and knew all sorts of learned words that *he* did not know – and probably never would. *Naturally we got on well together. Naturally* I preferred his company to that of someone who had only seen life in the raw and who could only speak from his own experience. When Joe was in that sort of mood there was little one could do, except wait for the storm to blow over. As he himself recognized in his more reasonable moments, the fact that I enjoyed Marco Pallis's company did *not* mean that I did not enjoy his. Different as the two men were in so many respects, I appreciated them both, liked them both, wished them both well, and only regretted that owing to Joe's difficult temperament they were unable to get on better together. Not for the first and certainly not for the last time in my life I found myself in the uncomfortable position of being friends with two people who, for one reason or another, could not or would not be friends with each other.

Having come to know Marco Pallis, it was not long before I came to know some of the people in his circle. One of the most likeable of these was a flat-faced, shaven-headed young Tibetan in brown *chuba* and yellow sash who greeted me with a smile of unusual friendliness and intelligence. His name was Lobsang Phuntshok Lhalungpa, and from the way in which Marco Pallis introduced him it was clear that he regarded the young man with particular approval. (The meeting took place in the cave-bungalow, on the day that I had been invited for lunch, and on my arrival the brown-clad figure rose to depart, but was prevailed upon to stay for a few more minutes.) As I could see from his dress, Lobsang Phuntshok was a monk official in the Tibetan government, and he had been sent to Darjeeling to look after the Tibetan boys who were studying there on government scholarships. Since his English was no better than my Tibetan we did not have much to say to each other, but when, a few years later, the young Tibetan – no longer shaven-headed – moved to Kalimpong, we became fast friends. Thus our chance meeting at Marco Pallis's bungalow eventually bore good fruit.

Another likeable person whom I came to know through Marco Pallis, but with whom I became at all well acquainted only at a much later date, was the colourful and contradictory Mr Tharchin. He had been born not in Tibet but in Ladakh, and was not a Buddhist but a Christian – in fact, a Scottish Presbyterian. Nonetheless, he had an excellent knowledge of Tibetan, both colloquial and classical, and was in great demand as a teacher, especially among the growing number of Western scholars who came to Kalimpong in order to pursue their researches into Tibetan Buddhism. His principal claim to celebrity, however, was the fact that he was the editor, proprietor, printer, and publisher of the *Tibet Mirror*, which proudly proclaimed itself to be the only Tibetan language newspaper in the world, and which was read from the monastic colleges of Lhasa to the oriental departments of major Western universities, not to mention the foreign offices of Washington, Pekin, London, and Moscow, and the Ministry of Home Affairs in New Delhi. The reason it was so widely read was that Mr Tharchin was violently anti-Communist and anti-Chinese, and denounced Chairman Mao and all his works with unsparing vigour in every issue of his paper. Not that the *Tibet Mirror* came out very frequently. It was certainly not a daily; it was not even a weekly or a monthly. The truth was, it came out whenever Mr Tharchin had the time – and the money – to write, print, publish, and distribute the shiny tabloid sheets. There had been periods in its history, indeed, when the *Tibet Mirror* did not appear for months together, or even for a year or two. When the paper did appear, therefore, it was quite an event in the Tibetan-speaking world, both inside and outside Tibet, even though only four or five hundred copies were printed, and even though some of these took weeks to reach their destination. Now that China had invaded Tibet, however, and Communist troops occupied Lhasa, Mr Tharchin had redoubled his efforts. At least two issues of the *Tibet Mirror* had appeared in recent months, and Chairman Mao had been denounced more vigorously than ever. For Mr Tharchin his paper was now no less than the voice of Free Tibet, a fact which was not without political significance, especially so far as relations between India and China were concerned.

When not actually engaged in the production of the *Tibet Mirror*, Mr Tharchin printed such things as Bible texts and religious tracts for the Church of Scotland Mission, in which he was a lay preacher, besides doing a certain amount of job work for local traders. In this way he kept quite busy, so that unless he was out somewhere explaining the mysteries of Tibetan grammar to a budding Tibetologist (as the breed was beginning to be called) one could usually count on finding him at his compositor's bench, or his editorial desk, in the small wooden building at Tenth Mile which was the home of the Tibet Mirror Press. It was to the home of the Tibet Mirror Press, therefore, that Marco Pallis took me to meet Mr Tharchin one morning, some time after we ourselves had become better acquainted. Despite the fact that I belonged to what Mr Tharchin's missionary colleagues regarded as the enemy camp, the lay preacher received me with a combination of cordiality and courtesy that, as I afterwards came to recognize, was thoroughly characteristic of the man. By sight, at least, he was already well known to me. Though this was our first actual meeting, I had seen him several times before, usually when making my way to Nepali Building, and he had no doubt seen me. As if to demonstrate the truth of everything Marco Pallis had ever said about the unsuitability of Western dress for the peoples of the East, he habitually wore a shabby, ill-fitting three piece suit, complete with watch chain, and a greasy felt hat which he doffed repeatedly whenever he met anybody he knew. So badly did his clothes fit him, indeed, that they did not seem to belong to him at all, and it was with some surprise that one saw the scraggy neck emerging from the soiled, collarless shirt. With the head on the neck there was nothing wrong, however, nor with the cheerful and good-humoured expression of the rather foxy-looking face. Despite his bristly grey eyebrows and bad teeth – not to mention the shabby three piece suit – Mr Tharchin in fact presented a thoroughly agreeable picture as he stood bowing and rubbing his hands in the centre of his little office. The ostensible purpose of our visit was to purchase a few back issues of the *Tibet Mirror*, which Marco Pallis wanted for a friend in England. These Mr Tharchin was only too happy to supply, and the purchase having been made, and many compliments exchanged, we therefore took leave of him without further ceremony. Though the meeting had been a brief one, I was left with an impression of genuine warmth and good will, and looked forward to seeing the editor of the *Tibet Mirror* again before long. On our way back to the Development Area Marco Pallis confided to me his belief that, despite his connection with the Church of Scotland Mission, Mr Tharchin was still very much a Buddhist at heart.

Someone I did not meet through Marco Pallis, but whom I heard about from him, and who was decidedly *not* a Buddhist at heart, was the Austrian climber Heinrich Harrer. At the outbreak of war he had been in Karachi, waiting for the ship that was to take him back to Europe, and he had been interned. After making his escape he crossed the border into Tibet and with one companion walked all the way to Lhasa, where he lived for five years and became the confidant and tutor of the young Dalai Lama. As the Chinese extended their hold on the country he decided to leave for India, and was now staying with Marco Pallis, writing the account of his experiences afterwards published as *Seven Years in Tibet*. When I asked Marco Pallis what sort of man the young Austrian was he replied, with an air of cheerful finality, 'He's a better type of Nazi.'

At the same time that I was coming to know people through Mrs Mitter and Marco Pallis I was also meeting them through Joe. Since his return to Kalimpong the prickly *upāsaka* had been giving private tuition in the bazaar and already had a number of pupils, including several wealthy Tibetans. One of these was Yugyel Sadutshang, the youngest of the five Sadutshang brothers. As the suffix *tshang*, meaning 'nest' or 'house', indicated, the brothers were from Kham in eastern Tibet, and the import–export firm bearing their name was one of the biggest in the town. Technically Yugyel was a *getsul* or novice monk, and had spent some time in a monastery, but the only sign of this was that he was still shaven-headed, or at least short-haired. In all other respects he was very much the would-be English gentleman. Suit, shirt, tie, and shoes were all of the very best, and for him 'the best' meant English. 'But is it the *best*?' he would enquire anxiously, whenever he was buying anything. 'Is it *English*?' One of the comparatively un-English things about him was his inability to speak more than a few words of the English language, and this was where Joe came in. Joe was his English tutor, in the double sense of being the tutor who taught him English and the tutor who was himself English. Joe was the *best*. Like all Tibetans, Yugyel was convinced, perhaps not unreasonably, that English could be learned only from an Englishman – not from a Bengali or a Nepali. It could be learned all the more easily if you went and stayed with the Englishman, or, better still, if the Englishman came and stayed with you. Yugyel had therefore invited Joe to move into his spacious flat at Tenth Mile, and Joe was still trying to decide whether or not to accept the offer. Such was Yugyel's insistence that everything about him should be English that, when Joe brought him to the guest cottage to see me, I could not help wondering if he had come in search of an English domestic chaplain – someone who would light butter-lamps and recite prayers for him every day, preferably in English. In appearance the technical *getsul* was a podgy, unattractive little man of about thirty, with a receding hairline and a Hitlerian moustache. While Joe was out of the room he squeezed my hand and started rubbing himself against me. I decided that I did not want to be his domestic chaplain, however English it might help him to be. Some weeks later Joe moved into the flat at Tenth Mile, and stayed there with Yugyel for a few months before moving into a place of his own. During this time he was able to convince the would-be Englishman that he ought to support the English monk's efforts to propagate the Dharma through the medium of the English language, and eventually he donated a hundred rupees to the YMBA.

It was not through Joe, I think, that I met the young Newar who became associated with us at about this time. Ratnaman had heard about the YMBA in Lhasa, and being of an alert, enquiring turn of mind, on his arrival in Kalimpong made a point of coming to see me. Round-faced and rose-cheeked, he had rather black eyebrows and a pair of close-set eyes the expression of which I described as shrewd and Joe as suspicious. Though little more than twenty, he already had considerable business experience, having helped his father run the family business in Lhasa for the past three or four years. Since he had been educated in Darjeeling his English was quite good. He also spoke Tibetan, his mother in fact being Tibetan. Like many Newar traders who spent much time in Lhasa, his father had two wives, one in Nepal and one in Tibet, and Ratnaman had elder brothers in Kathmandu whom he had never seen. Before long he was taking an active part in the running of the YMBA and eventually replaced Gyan Jyoti as Treasurer.

That news of the YMBA had penetrated as far north as Lhasa was highly encouraging. It had also penetrated as far south as Madras. Since the end of the previous year I had been receiving letters and poems from a Sinhalese Buddhist girl who was training to be a nurse at the Christian Medical College, Vellore, one of the best known medical institutions in the country. Sujatha Hettiarachchi, as she signed herself, proposed that an organization of the young women of India similar in aim and scope to the YMBA should be started under the name of the Visakha Fellowship, and in this connection she wanted to come and see me. By the time she arrived in Kalimpong, however, she had changed her mind about the Visakha Fellowship and had decided to start a Buddhist nursing order instead, and on this subject we therefore had several talks, besides discussing poetry, the revival of Buddhism in India, and a number of other topics. Since she had been brought up as an 'orthodox' Theravāda Buddhist she refused to sit on a chair in my presence, so that Joe was obliged to spread a carpet for her on the floor. This led to his making caustic remarks about Mary Magdalene sitting at the feet of Jesus Christ. No one ever wanted to sit at *his* feet, he declared, with mock indignation. *He* was only a humble *upāsaka*, and had no time to spare for all the wonderful and idealistic things that *we* were interested in talking about. Sometimes Sujatha wore her special 'Kandyan' dress. This was a chiton-like affair of white silk gathered in at the waist and bosom with slender silver chains, thus producing a slightly flounced effect. It was worn, so she informed us, only by women belonging to the Sinhalese aristocracy. But though the style suited her well enough, the unrelieved whiteness of the dress made her dark brown face and arms look almost black in comparison. After spending about a week in Kalimpong, and discussing all her plans and projects with me in great detail, Sujatha returned to Vellore. Though nothing ever came of the Buddhist nursing order, I continued to receive letters and poems from her for a long time to come.

Perhaps my strangest encounter during the time I spent at Burma Raja's guest cottage was one that took place at the beginning of the year. 1951 was the year of the census, the first to be held in India since Independence, and one fine January day I received a visit from the official enumerator. He was a Bengali and, as it transpired, an orthodox Hindu, and there took place between us an exchange along some such lines as the following.

'What is your religion?'

'Buddhist.'

'That is impossible. You cannot be Buddhist. Buddhism is not a separate religion. It is part of the great Hindu religion. Buddhist is what you are by *caste*.'

'I cannot agree with that. Buddhism does not believe in the caste system, and therefore a Buddhist has no caste – especially not a monk. Besides, I was born in England, and we don't have any caste system there.'

'Don't teach me how to enumerate you! Your religion is Hindu, and your caste is Buddhist, and I shall enter you in the form accordingly.' (The greater part of the population being illiterate, it was the enumerator who completed the census return, not the enumerated.)

'In that case I must protest.'

Much as I protested, however, the enumerator remained adamant. As a Hindu by religion and a Buddhist by caste was I therefore officially enumerated. How many orthodox Hindu enumerators were there at work in West Bengal, I wondered, and how had all the Bhutia (i.e. locally born Tibetan), Newar, Tamang, Lepcha, Bhutanese, and Sikkimese Buddhists in Darjeeling District been enumerated? If my own case was anything to go by, the census returns for 1951 would not be very reliable, at least so far as the figures for Buddhists were concerned. Not for the first time in recent years I realized how implacable the opposition was, and how determined was orthodox Hinduism to 'contain' its hated rival. It was not going to be easy to revive Buddhism in the land of its birth.

10
PREPARING TO RECEIVE THE SACRED RELICS

'Know thyself' was the injunction of one of the sages of Ancient Greece, an injunction that was also inscribed on a pillar in the Temple of Apollo at Delphi, but neither in the ancient nor in the modern world has it ever been easy for a man truly to know himself. At the time that I was staying at Burma Raja's guest cottage, and becoming better acquainted with such traditions and individual talents as were represented in the little town of Kalimpong, I was still far from knowing myself. In particular, I was far from knowing the extent of my own capabilities. This was in part due to circumstances. Having spent much of my childhood as an invalid, and my three years in the army doing work for which I was quite unsuited and which I cordially detested, I had come to think of myself as an essentially impractical kind of person whose real interests and real life lay in a completely different world. Like Baudelaire's albatross, I felt more at home in the sky than on a ship's deck, even though my wings were as yet far from being fully developed.[40] This impression of myself as lacking in practicality had been reinforced during my two years as a wandering ascetic. Satyapriya, the companion of my wanderings, was an exceptionally active and capable person, with more than a touch of the desire to lead and to dominate. He it was who took all the decisions and made all the practical arrangements, leaving to me the role of admiring spectator of his energy and ability. The contemplation of my impracticality in comparison with his own extreme competence indeed gave him a pleasant sense of superiority.[41]

In Kalimpong I was threatened with a repetition of the same kind of pattern. Though deferring to me in all matters of a purely religious nature, both Joe and Swale were inclined to regard me as hopelessly impractical where mundane affairs were concerned and as quite incapable of running the YMBA without the advice and guidance of my older and more experienced friends. They only differed as to which of these older and more experience friends I should allow myself to be advised and guided by. Since they could not agree on this all-important point, and between them often gave me contradictory advice, I usually did whatever I myself thought best. Indeed, I had no alternative. Nevertheless, despite the modest success that the YMBA in general and *Stepping-Stones* in particular had already achieved, I still tended to think of myself as an impractical rather than a practical person. It was only in connection with the arrival of the Sacred Relics in Kalimpong in March 1951 that Joe and Swale were proved wrong about me, and I was able to come to a better knowledge of my own capabilities and, to that extent, to a truer knowledge of myself.

The Sacred Relics in question were those of the *arhants* Śāriputra and Maudgalyāyana, the two chief disciples of the Buddha. They had been discovered in the middle of the previous century, when General Sir Alexander Cunningham opened the stupas or memorial mounds at Sanchi, in central India. In one of these stupas he found two small steatite boxes containing fragments of bone and inscribed respectively 'Sāriputta's' and 'Moggallāna's' in Brahmi characters of the time of Aśoka. These important finds were taken to England and deposited in the Victoria and Albert Museum, where they remained until 1947. In that year the British Government handed them over to the Maha Bodhi Society for enshrinement in the land of their origin, and after spending two years in Ceylon the Sacred Relics (as they were now universally called) were the occasion of public rejoicings on an unprecedented scale. Their arrival in India was, in fact, treated as a state function, with the Prime Minister, Pandit Nehru, coming specially to Calcutta to receive them and hand them over to the President of the Maha Bodhi Society for safe keeping until such time as they could be properly enshrined. The brilliant and historic ceremony took place in the presence of some half a million people, among whom were representatives of the Buddhist countries of Asia in colourful national costume, and the ensuing festivities lasted a whole month.

Originally the Maha Bodhi Society had intended to enshrine the Sacred Relics in New Delhi, but later it had second thoughts, and in this case second thoughts proved to be better than first thoughts. The Sacred Relics would be enshrined in Sanchi, which had already been their home for more than 2,000 years, and they would be enshrined not in the stupa where General Cunningham had found them but in a brand-new temple! Work on the Chetiyagiri Vihara, as the new temple was to be called, had in fact started in 1946, but the building would not be ready until 1952. In the meantime the relics of the two *arhants* were to remain in Calcutta. They were far from remaining there uninterruptedly, however. Invitations came pouring in from all over India, as well as from different parts of the Buddhist world, and the Sacred Relics had already been taken to Bihar, the United Provinces, Assam, Burma, and Ladakh. Everywhere they went they were received with tremendous popular enthusiasm. I had paid my own respects to them in Benares, the citadel of Hindu orthodoxy,[42] and when Kashyapji and I visited the holy places of Bihar we found that their presence there a few months earlier had resulted in a great upsurge of devotion and given rise to a demand for the revival of Buddhism.[43] Now, having returned from their triumphal tour of Ladakh, the Sacred Relics were to be given a state reception by the Government and people of Sikkim, the dark blue foothills of which could be seen away to the north, on the other side of the River Teesta.

As soon as I heard the news I realized that here was a wonderful opportunity. If the Sacred Relics were visiting Gangtok there was no reason why they should not visit Kalimpong too. All we had to do was invite them. A visit from the Sacred Relics would undoubtedly give Buddhism in Kalimpong a tremendous boost and, in this way, make the work of the YMBA much easier. I therefore wrote at once to Devapriya Valisinha, the General Secretary of the Maha Bodhi Society, enquiring if the Sacred Relics could be brought to Kalimpong for exposition immediately after their visit to Gangtok. Valisinha replied that they could, provided that a 'strong representative committee' was set up and provided this committee undertook to bear the entire cost of the visit. The Sacred Relics would be in Sikkim at the end of February, and I could expect them in Kalimpong at the beginning of March. This was all I needed. With the help of Madan Kumar Babu a public meeting was convened at the Town Hall, and my proposal that the Sacred Relics should be invited to visit Kalimpong having been carried unanimously the 'strong representative committee' was set up as required, with Rani Chuni Dorji as Chairman, the abbot of Tharpa Choling Gompa as Vice-Chairman, Gyan Jyoti as Treasurer, and myself as General Secretary.

While I was thus engaged I received a letter from Venerable Sangharatana. He and Kashyapji would be accompanying the Sacred Relics to Sikkim (he wrote), together with Dr Madhuram Soft, one of the Vice-Presidents of the Maha Bodhi Society. Would I like to accompany them as part of the official delegation? Two monks were not really sufficient to look after the Sacred Relics, and they would be glad of my company. This offer came like the answer to an unspoken wish. Though I had been in Kalimpong for more than ten months, I had as yet not visited the tiny Himalayan principality on the other side of the river, and the prospect of establishing contact with the Sikkimese Buddhists and, perhaps, seeing Mount Kanchenjunga at closer quarters, was one that appealed to me considerably. Moreover, the fact that I would be going to Sikkim with the Sacred Relics, as well as in the company of Venerable Sangharatana and my teacher Kashyapji, made the idea of such a visit doubly attractive, especially as I had not seen or heard from Kashyapji since my ordination at Sarnath, and wanted to talk to him about events that had led to my departure from the Dharmodaya Vihara. I therefore wrote to Venerable Sangharatana thanking him for his kind offer and assuring him that I would be delighted to be with him and Kashyapji in Gangtok at the end of February. Already I could see in my mind's eye the curved yellow roofs rising above the tree-tops, and red-robed figures blowing a deep-throated welcome to the Sacred Relics from giant copper trumpets.

But there was little time for such dreams. Though the strong representative committee had been set up, and though at least some of its two dozen members could be relied upon to attend the meetings I called at the Town Hall from time to time, I very quickly discovered that by far the greater part of the actual work of organizing the reception of the Sacred Relics would devolve on the General Secretary. Indeed, it was *expected* that it would devolve on him. Most of the public-spirited citizens who had constituted themselves into the Sacred Relics Reception Committee, Kalimpong, or who had allowed themselves to be co-opted onto it, were evidently of the opinion that being a member of the committee indicated not that one was prepared to work for it but only that one gave it one's moral support and, of course, the benefit of one's

Speaking at a meeting in Kalimpong, Madan Kumar Pradhan on the far left

advice. Even the Chairman of the committee, I soon realized, was no exception to the general rule. Rani Dorji had not accepted the position of Chairman out of any great desire to help, as I at first hoped was the case, despite my previous experience of her marked lack of interest in Buddhist activities, but only because she had been pressed by her fellow-citizens to such an extent that she could hardly refuse without giving a good deal of offence. For their part, the fellow-citizens had pressed her to accept the position not because they really expected her to do anything but because, as the head of the most prominent Buddhist family in the locality (Raja S. T. Dorji was away in Bhutan), she was expected to take the lead – at least nominally – in all matters affecting the Buddhist community. As Madan Kumar Babu remarked, that was the way things were done in Kalimpong.

For the next few weeks I was therefore busier than I had been since my arrival in the town. Nearly every morning I made my way from the peace and seclusion of Burma Raja's guest cottage to the comparative noise and bustle of the bazaar, where more often than not I spent the greater part of the day, sometimes with no other refreshment than the cups of Indian or Tibetan tea (and biscuits, if it was before noon) that I was given at the various houses, shops, and offices at which I called. Not only did I get much less help from the other members of the committee than I had expected, but the actual work of organizing the reception proved to be much greater than anyone had foreseen. There were posters and handbills to be distributed, vehicles to be hired for the conveyance of the Sacred Relics and the accompanying delegation, arches of welcome to be erected all along the route by which the Sacred Relics would pass, permission to take out the procession to be obtained from the police, correspondence to be conducted with Devapriya Valisinha and Venerable Sangharatana, as well as with friends and well-wishers throughout the Subdivision, and of course funds to be collected. All this was in addition to my usual work of running the YMBA, which included taking the evening tutorial classes at our new premises on the ground floor of Banshi's Godown and producing an issue of *Stepping-Stones* every month and despatching it to our subscribers. Fortunately, Gyan Jyoti took his duties as Treasurer quite seriously, and not only kept the accounts but did the greater part of the fund-raising. I also had a certain amount of help from two other members of the committee. These were Marco Pallis, who was in any case a regular visitor to the guest cottage, and Mr Lha Tsering, the formidable boss of the local branch of the Central Intelligence Bureau, the mention of whose name as his father by one of the boys in my matriculation class some months previously had occasioned so much laughter among the rest of the class. Marco Pallis and Lha Tsering knew each other quite well, but although relations between the two men were amicable enough I had the impression that neither took the other very seriously. Whenever Lha Tsering mentioned Marco Pallis it was with a snort of good-natured contempt, while whenever Marco Pallis referred to Lha Tsering it was with uplifted eyebrows and eyes that twinkled with amusement. Marco had, in fact, playfully christened Lha Tsering 'The Long-Lived Deva', this being the literal translation of his Tibetan name, and as the Long-Lived Deva we always spoke of him, especially when we were not sure who might be 'listening in' to our conversation, since there was a feeling in Kalimpong that in view of Lha Tsering's position as head of the local intelligence network it was not wise to be overheard talking about him – especially if one happened to be a foreigner.

Marco Pallis helped me mainly by functioning as my 'guide, philosopher, and friend' – as well as my interpreter – whenever I had to have dealings with the Tibetan Buddhists, which was quite frequently. The *khenpo* or abbot of the Tharpa Choling Gompa having been elected Vice-President of the Reception Committee, it was necessary to keep him informed about what was happening, as well as to consult with him and his monks about the arrangements for the procession, the success of which would depend largely on their cooperation. At least once a week, therefore, Marco and I walked from the Development Area to the bazaar, and from the bazaar up the winding dusty track that led to Tirpai and the Tharpa Choling Gompa, my companion usually discoursing all the way on Tradition, Tibetan Buddhism, the regrettable tendency of local youth to adopt Western dress, the corruption of the modern world, and other favourite topics. No sooner had we arrived at the *gompa* than it was clear that Marco Pallis – or Thubden Tendzin, as perhaps I should now start calling him – was a regular visitor there. It was also clear that he was well liked by the monks, who on account of his devotion to the Dharma, the fluency with which he spoke Tibetan, and his familiarity with their manners and customs, indeed held him in high regard. Probably there was no other person in Kalimpong – certainly no other European – whose companionship would have ensured me a more favourable reception at the *gompa*.

On the occasion of my first visit Thubden Tendzin provided me with the usual *khata* or white ceremonial scarf to offer to the abbot, who received us in the upstairs room of his modest quarters on the northern side of the grassy square in front of the temple. It was quite a small room, with a glass-fronted shrine at the far end and a row of square Tibetan cushions down either side, the abbot's cushion – actually two or three cushions piled one on top of the other – being higher than the rest and situated next to the carved and gilded shrine, behind the panes of which was a strange assortment of images, photographs, biscuit tins, and artificial flowers. The abbot could not have been much less than sixty, which I knew was quite an advanced age for a Tibetan. A gaunt, almost emaciated figure, he sat up very stiff and straight in his maroon-coloured woollen robes with the projecting shoulder-pieces and the hint of red and gold brocade underneath. With his bald head and sunken cheeks, and his prominent, strongly aquiline nose, he looked for all the world like a weather-beaten old eagle perched alone on his solitary crag. At first the conversation was mainly between him and Thubden Tendzin, who evidently knew him quite well, and on whom he beamed with considerable satisfaction. Though he nodded and chuckled from time to time, he did not say very much, being seemingly content to allow Thubden Tendzin to do most of the talking. Eventually he turned a friendly and sympathetic but, I thought, slightly ironic gaze on me. To which honourable country did the honourable monk belong and was his honourable body free from affliction? Whereupon there ensued, with Thubden Tendzin acting as interpreter, a conversation which gradually took on a more informal tone, and in the course of which the abbot showed signs of increasing interest and goodwill. He was particularly intrigued by the colour and pattern of my robes, which of course were not red but yellow, and made not of wool but of cotton, uttering exclamations of surprise and delight when it was discovered that the number of patches of which they consisted corresponded to the number of patches on the yellow silk robes which the Tibetan monks themselves wore on ceremonial occasions over their more customary maroon-coloured garments.

While we were talking, one of the abbot's monk attendants shuffled in and out with a huge Tibetan teapot, filling and refilling the delicate Chinese cups which he had previously placed on the low carved tables before us. He carried the teapot in shoulder-high, and as he bent down to serve each person he gave it a vigorous sideways shake before pouring out the tea, which naturally was Tibetan buttered tea, and of the finest quality I had yet tasted. In contrast to the cups that had been given Thubden Tendzin and myself, the abbot's cup, which stood in readiness on his own much higher and more elaborately carved table, was provided with an ornate gold and silver stand, and a still more ornate gold and silver cover, on the pointed top of which was a large semi-precious stone by way of a knob.

Having compared notes on the subject of robes, it was only natural that we should proceed to discuss the Vinaya or Monastic Code in general, and here too the abbot was surprised and delighted to find that we had much in common. Though not really surprised, I was no less delighted than he was. I already knew that the Tharpa Choling Gompa was a Gelugpa establishment, and that the so-called 'Yellow Hat' monks of the Gelug order observed a version of the Hīnayāna Monastic Code that was not substantially different from that of the tradition into which I had myself been ordained. Thus I knew that they were celibate, that they were supposed to abstain from alcohol and from taking solid food after midday, and so on. But though I knew at least something about them, they did not really know anything about me. While the abbot and the other inmates of the Tharpa Choling Gompa had often seen me going on my almsround (a practice that was followed only by the 'poorest' and least respected Tibetan monks), all that they as yet knew – or thought they knew – about me was that I was a follower of the Hīnayāna or 'Little Way' of Emancipation and not of the Mahāyāna or 'Great Way' and not, therefore, a follower of the bodhisattva ideal; but which version of the Monastic Code I followed, or whether I followed the Monastic Code at all, they had no idea. With my shaven head, my yellow cotton robes, and my black begging-bowl (Tibetan monks, I subsequently learned, hardly ever possessed begging-bowls), I was in their eyes an antiquated figure out of the remote, legendary Indian past of Buddhism – a figure such as they had seen, if at all, only in paintings of episodes from the life of the Buddha. Now that they had actually met me, and had some idea who and what I was, their natural suspicions were allayed, and by the end of that first conversation with the abbot I had been able to secure their cooperation in carrying out my plan of taking the Sacred Relics in a grand procession through the streets of Kalimpong. Indeed, the abbot assured me that he and his monks were willing to do anything that would help enhance the prestige and extend the influence of the Dharma in the region.

In the course of my subsequent visits to the Tirpai Gompa, as it was popularly known, I drank many more cups of Tibetan buttered tea with the old abbot, and discussed many more subjects, Thubden Tendzin always interpreting. It was not long before we passed from the minutiae of the Monastic Code to doctrinal and spiritual issues of a more general and more fundamental nature. Thubden Tendzin enjoyed these discussions immensely, translating from Tibetan to English, and English to Tibetan, with tremendous zest, and from time to time interposing comments of his own for the benefit of one or the other of us. For him they were, perhaps, reminiscent of the Spituk Debates, that is to say, of the discussions he and his two mountaineering companions had had with the Venerable Dawa, Bursar of Spituk, in Ladakh fifteen years earlier, as described in the pages of *Peaks and Lamas*. Perhaps the most fundamental issue to be touched upon by the abbot and myself in our discussions at the Tharpa Choling Gompa was that of the bodhisattva ideal, which Thubden Tendzin rightly regarded as the 'presiding idea', as he termed it, of Tibetan Buddhism,

'The Presiding Idea' indeed being the title of the extra chapter that he was to add to a later edition of his famous book. Though it was the abbot himself who first referred to the bodhisattva ideal, from the cautious and tentative way in which he approached the subject I could see that he was unsure what my own attitude towards it might be and that he was, in fact, sounding me out. Since the bodhisattva ideal had come to occupy a more and more central place in my spiritual life, I had no hesitation in assuring the abbot that I accepted it unreservedly and that in:

> the conception of Bodhisattvahood, the state of the fully awakened being who, though under no further restraint by that Law of Causality which he had transcended, yet freely continues to espouse the vicissitudes of the Round of Existence in virtue of his Self-identification with all the creatures still involved in egocentric delusion and consequent suffering

(as Thubden Tendzin was to describe it)[44] I found a source of constant inspiration. This assurance the venerable old man received with exclamations of surprise and delight even more emphatic than those that had greeted the discovery about the number of patches on my robes. If I accepted the bodhisattva ideal I was a follower of the Mahāyāna, and if I was a follower of the Mahāyāna then, despite outward differences, I was 'one of them'! All this was conveyed, not so much in words, as by the truly wonderful expression of benign satisfaction that lit up the abbot's careworn countenance and sparkled in his red-rimmed eyes. It was as though he rejoiced that yet another human being had, however imperfectly, dedicated himself to the cause of universal emancipation.

The fact that I was now known to be 'one of them', despite my yellow cotton robes, made my dealings with the Tibetan Buddhists easier than they might otherwise have been, even with the help of Thubden Tendzin. I experienced no difficulty in finalizing with the abbot and his monks the arrangements for the procession, and no difficulty even when it came to securing their cooperation in a matter of still greater importance. This was the actual exposition of the Sacred Relics. Devapriya Valisinha had informed me that the Sacred Relics could stay in Kalimpong for four days, and I had therefore proposed to the Reception Committee that during this period they should by kept at the Tharpa Choling Gompa and be exposed there each day for the veneration of the public. The

Tharpa Choling Gompa was the biggest and most important Buddhist monastery in Kalimpong, and to me it was obvious that the Sacred Relics could be kept there and nowhere else. To keep them anywhere else would be an affront to the Tibetans, who were the major Buddhist community in Kalimpong, and for whom the *gompa* was the centre of their religious and cultural life. At first the committee was inclined to agree with me, but as the discussion proceeded dissentient voices were raised and I became aware that there was a strong undercurrent of opposition to the idea of keeping the Sacred Relics at the Tharpa Choling Gompa and holding the exposition there. This opposition eventually came out into the open, and was found to consist mainly of Rani Dorji and Gyan Jyoti. Why they objected to keeping the Sacred Relics at the Tharpa Choling Gompa was not clear, though Mr Tharchin (who had somehow got onto the committee) expressed concern lest the monks of the *gompa* should start fighting over the custody of the Sacred Relics – a concern that the bursar and precentor, who were attending the meeting as representatives of the abbot, indignantly declared to be totally without foundation. Discussion then shifted to the question of access. Was the *gompa* not situated at a considerable distance from the Kalimpong bazaar, and would it not be a cause of great hardship to people if they had to walk all the way up to Tirpai in order to have *darshan* of the Sacred Relics? Why not keep the Sacred Relics at the Dharmodaya Vihara, which was near the centre of the town, and have the exposition *there*? This last suggestion was made by Rani Dorji, who made it with an air of bland impartiality, as though she was only trying to be helpful, and it was eagerly taken up by Gyan Jyoti, who expatiated at length on the advantages of holding the exposition at the vihara and having the Sacred Relics practically on people's doorsteps, so to speak. Aniruddha, who was also present, gave his support to Rani Dorji's suggestion in his own rough way. 'That's right!' he shouted, 'Why should they be kept up at the *gompa*? Let's keep them at Dharmodaya. *That's* the proper place.'

It was now clear that I was not going to get my proposal accepted by the committee without a struggle, since although the majority of its members were in favour of keeping the Sacred Relics at the Tharpa Choling Gompa, they hesitated to oppose so prominent and influential a person as Rani Dorji, especially as many of them did not have very strong feelings about the matter anyway. I therefore told them bluntly that the idea that the religious-minded people of Kalimpong would not be prepared to walk the two miles from the bazaar up to Tirpai in order to pay their respects to the Sacred Relics was ridiculous. Why, small children walked three or four miles to school every day of the week, and thought nothing of it! Hill people were born walkers. These sentiments met with general approval, one elderly Tamang Buddhist going so far as to declare that, speaking personally, he would be happy to walk a hundred miles in order to have the opportunity of worshipping the Sacred Relics. The opposition was forced to change its ground. Why should the Sacred Relics be kept either at the *gompa or* at the vihara, or in fact in any place that was identified with a particular section of the community? Why not keep them at the Town Hall, which belonged to *all* the people of Kalimpong, and where everybody would feel free to go? This suggestion seemed to find greater favour with the committee than had the previous one, and I was careful to refute it at some length. Though the Town Hall was nearer to the centre of the town, and though it indeed belonged to all the people of Kalimpong, it was in a dirty and dilapidated condition, as they all knew very well (this was a reference to recent unsuccessful attempts to clean up the place), and it would not be fitting for the exposition of the Sacred Relics to be held in such dingy surroundings. Moreover, the Town Hall was used for all sorts of secular purposes, and was hardly the most suitable venue for a function of a purely religious nature. Above all, people smoked *bidis* and cigarettes in the Town Hall, and for the purity of the Sacred Relics to be polluted by their being kept for four days in the smoke-laden atmosphere of the place would be deeply offensive to the religious feelings of all Buddhists. To this last argument, in particular, even Rani Dorji had nothing to say, since it was a matter of common knowledge that the very thought of tobacco was abhorrent to the traditionally-minded followers of Tibetan Buddhism, whether Tibetans, Bhutanese, Sikkimese, or Nepalese (the Thirteenth Dalai Lama had actually forbidden the import of cigarettes into Tibet), and after I had headed off a last-minute attempt by the opposition to revive the claims of the Dharmodaya Vihara it was finally decided that for the four days that they would be in Kalimpong the Sacred Relics would be kept at the Tharpa Choling Gompa.

The meeting at which the debate over where to keep the Sacred Relics took place was the longest and liveliest of all the meetings of our Reception Committee. Unfortunately, it was also the most unpleasant, for although the amenities were observed – Rani Dorji, in particular, treated everyone with scrupulous politeness – there was a growing tension in the atmosphere which could, I felt, easily result in an explosion. This tension was connected with the fact that while Rani Dorji carefully refrained from saying anything detrimental to the Tharpa Choling Gompa she was clearly determined that the Sacred Relics should not be kept there, and lost no opportunity of giving her support to any alternative proposal. Why this should be the case I was unable to tell. Gyan Jyoti wanted the Sacred Relics to be kept at the Dharmodaya Vihara not out of any actual hostility to the *gompa* but simply because he was a Newar and wanted the honour to go to the religious and cultural centre of his own community. As for Aniruddha, he was not only a Newar but also a staunch Theravādin, and thought it was only right and proper that the remains of two Theravādin *arhants* – as he regarded them – should be lodged at the Theravādin vihara. But Rani Dorji was nominally, at least, a follower of Tibetan Buddhism, in its Bhutanese (Dukpa Kagyu) form, and why she should be so opposed to the idea of keeping the Sacred Relics at the Tharpa Choling Gompa was a mystery. Opposed, however, she undoubtedly was, for as the claims of the vihara and the Town Hall were gradually demolished the little woman's stony face became stonier still, her bloodless lips more tightly compressed, while her eyes began to glitter with a look that was positively baleful. By the time the meeting was over, and my proposal at length accepted, it was evident that, despite the frozen ceremoniousness of her departure, Rani Dorji was very, very angry at the way things had turned out, though the reason for her anger – as for her opposition – still remained a mystery.

The mystery was cleared up two or three days later, when I happened to visit Mr Lha Tsering. The abode of the Long-Lived Deva was not far from Tenth Mile, down the same lane as that in which Rudramani Pradhan's modest bungalow was situated, and I had got into the habit of calling there quite frequently, partly because the weather was at that time bitterly cold, and I was glad to be able to warm myself at the glowing charcoal brazier that stood in the middle of the room, and partly because he was always glad to see me and always ready to lend a sympathetic ear if I wanted to discuss anything. Sikkimese by birth, he had spent the war years as an officer in the British Army, from which he had only recently retired. With his short, well-brushed hair, shining pink face, and generally spruce appearance, he was – despite his slant eyes and gold teeth – very much the ex-army officer. As I soon discovered, he was strongly pro-British. I also discovered that, although of a frank and open disposition, he was prone to violent outbursts of temper. During one of my early visits he had been so enraged by the mistakes a clerk had made in typing out a report that he had flung the bulky file at the man's head with fearful imprecations. On another occasion – it was that of my first visit – I had myself come very near to provoking a similar outburst. Thinking the news would please him, I told him that his son was one of the most promising students in my Matriculation class, and that he would be sure to do well at college. To my amazement, the Long-Lived Deva's face turned first scarlet, then purple, and he seemed about to explode. Controlling himself with a tremendous effort, and swallowing hard two or three times, he abruptly changed the subject and I realized that I had somehow committed a serious *faux pas*. Only later did I learn that although Namgyal, as the boy was called, was indeed the son of the Long-Lived Deva, the latter – despite the extraordinary facial resemblance between them – obstinately refused to recognize him as such. Fortunately, the incident did not interfere with the growth of our friendship, and we were soon on quite confidential terms. If he was busy when I called he would hand me a batch of intelligence reports and ask me to 'check the English' for him while I waited. Most of the reports, I noticed, related to people living or staying at the Himalayan Hotel. This did not surprise me very much, since I knew the place had a bad reputation in more ways than one and that the Long-Lived Deva himself often looked in there of an evening, just to keep an eye on things. Why he should have taken such a strong liking to me it was difficult to say, but a strong liking to me he undoubtedly had taken. There were times when his attitude towards me was positively protective, even fatherly, which seemed strange in view of the way in which he chose to treat one of his own sons. Years later, when he had long ceased to be the much-feared boss of the local intelligence network, a friend we had in common offered a possible explanation. A few months after my arrival in Kalimpong, she said, he had seen me going for alms in the bazaar, and had been deeply moved by the sight, remarking, 'There goes someone who really believes in Buddhism.'

Such was Mr Lha Tsering, the Long-Lived Deva, the remaining member of the committee from whom, as from Gyan Jyoti and Thubden Tendzin, I had a certain amount of help in the work of organizing the reception to the Sacred Relics. When I told him about the decision to keep the latter at the Tharpa Choling Gompa, and about Rani Dorji's strange behaviour, he threw back his head and laughed until the tears ran down his cheeks. How he wished he had been there! he exclaimed, slapping his thigh with delight. How he wished he could have seen Rani Dorji's face when, for once in her life, she did *not* get her own way! What a pity he had to attend another meeting that afternoon! He would willingly have given a hundred rupees to have been able to hear our discussion. Seeing that I did not share his mirth, however, and was evidently in the dark about certain matters, he wiped the tears from his eyes with a pocket handkerchief and suddenly became quite serious, even grim. *Of course* the Sacred Relics should be kept at the Tharpa Choling Gompa. It was the only place where they possibly *could* be kept. There was absolutely no question of keeping them either at a hotbed of Newar selfishness and sectarianism like the Dharmodaya Vihara, where I myself had been so shabbily treated, or in a filthy hole like the Town Hall. As for Rani Dorji's determination that the Sacred Relics should not be kept at the Tharpa Choling Gompa, this was not in the least surprising. She had very good reasons of her own for not wanting them to be kept there. If they were kept there then, as Chairman of the Reception Committee, she would be obliged to go to the *gompa* in order to receive them on their arrival, whereas it was well known that she had vowed never to set foot in the *gompa* again. If she were to go to the *gompa* it would, therefore, mean that she was being made to eat her own words, so to speak, with consequent loss of prestige, and prestige, as I had lived long enough in the area to know (the Long-Lived Deva added smilingly) was something to which Tibetans, and people of Tibetan religion and culture, attached tremendous importance. No, it was not in the least surprising that Rani Dorji had not wanted the Sacred Relics to be kept at the Tharpa Choling Gompa, or that she had been so ready to support any alternative proposal.

The reason for the stony-faced little Rani's behaviour at the meeting, as well as for the state of suppressed fury in which she had departed, was now explained. But why had she vowed never to set foot in the Tharpa Choling Gompa again? Far from having been cleared up, the mystery had only deepened. While thoughts like these were passing through my mind, my violent-tempered friend was evidently trying to decide how much about local politics I really needed to know. At length he appeared to have made up his mind to tell me at least enough to enable me to understand the situation in which, all unwittingly, I found myself involved. Shortly before my arrival in Kalimpong, he explained, there had been some trouble at the Tharpa Choling Gompa. Parties had been formed among the monks, and some of the lay supporters of the monastery had been drawn into the conflict – among them Rani Dorji. Eventually the trouble became quite serious and actual fighting broke out, and in the course of this fighting a monk was killed. The situation was, of course, extremely complicated, and it was difficult to apportion blame, but Rani Dorji had been deeply involved in the conflict and – rightly or wrongly – it was widely believed in Kalimpong that she was morally responsible for the monk's death and people criticized her accordingly. Rani Dorji herself acknowledged no responsibility for what had happened, but the fact that her association with the *gompa* had led to her being criticized had infuriated her to such an extent that she had publicly vowed never to set foot in the Tharpa Choling Gompa again.

In the light of these disclosures I saw that I had, perhaps, made a second enemy in Kalimpong, and one much more formidable than the portly, lying editor of the *Himalayan Times*. I was also worried in case there was, after all, some basis to Mr Tharchin's concern lest the monks of the *gompa* should start fighting over the custody of the Sacred Relics. But the Long-Lived Deva was quick to reassure me on this point. The troubles at the *gompa* had long since been settled, he declared emphatically, and a formal ceremony of reconciliation would take place as soon as the necessary officials of the Tibetan government arrived from Lhasa. This, at least, was good news, but it could not disguise the fact that what my presumably well-informed friend had just told me about the politics of Kalimpong revealed a state of affairs that was deeply disturbing. In particular, it was disturbing that a conflict at the *gompa* should actually have resulted in the death of one of the monks, and hardly less dreadful that the repercussions of the tragedy should still be felt within the Buddhist community and had even threatened to disrupt our arrangements for the reception of the Sacred Relics. It was also disappointing – to say the least! – that someone in Rani Dorji's position should have meddled in the affairs of the *gompa* in such a way as to earn for herself the execrations of the public. Though she did not have a very attractive personality, I had hitherto been under the impression that she was well respected in Kalimpong and even quite popular.

When I told the Long-Lived Deva this his reaction was one of scornful amusement. Rani Dorji respected? Rani Dorji *popular*? If I was under *that* impression then the sooner I corrected it the better. She might be popular with the Europeans who hobnobbed with her at Bhutan House, or with the Church of Scotland missionaries whose work she was always praising, but she was certainly not popular with the local people. In fact, she was decidedly unpopular – and with good reason. Though it hurt him to have to criticize Rani Dorji, who was by birth a Sikkimese princess, and the sister of his own Maharaja, the truth was that she was the most cold, selfish, narrow-minded, hard-hearted, grasping, avaricious, miserly person that anyone could possibly meet. She was even worse than the Marwaris and the Newars, which was saying a good deal. All she cared about was money. She was so mean that if she saw a red farthing lying in the filth of the gutter she would bend down and pick it up. Did I know that she was a licensed moneylender? (I did not, any more than I knew that a moneylender had to have a licence.) Not only did she lend money to the local peasantry at high rates of interest on the security of their land, but the minute they failed to keep up with their repayments – as they usually did, sooner or later – she either had them sold up or seized their land and put in her own people as tenants. She was utterly without mercy, and provided she could make a bit more money thought nothing of driving honest folk from their homes and turning them and their children into paupers and beggars. It wasn't as though she didn't have more than enough money already. The Dorjis were the richest family in the whole area. They were multi-millionaires. Practically the whole of the trade between India and Bhutan was in their hands. Next to the royal family itself, they were the biggest landowners in Bhutan. But Rani Dorji always wanted more.

While he was delivering this tirade the Long-Lived Deva's initial scornful amusement changed to undisguised hatred and contempt, and I could see that his feelings towards Rani Dorji were much the same as Dhanman Moktan's feelings towards the Jyoti brothers and the Newars. (There were certainly a lot of animosities within the Kalimpong Buddhist community!) Those feelings did not extend to Rani Dorji's husband, Raja S. T. Dorji. The Raja Saheb, so the Long-Lived Deva assured me, was a completely different type of person from his wife. He was as generous as she was tight-fisted, and as warm and open-hearted as she was cold and reserved. It was, therefore, hardly surprising that whereas *she* was unpopular with the local people *he* was very popular with them. There were, indeed, those who treated Rani Dorji with respect only on account of their regard for Raja Dorji and because she herself was connected by birth with the ruling house of Sikkim. The Raja Saheb was, in fact, both a popular and a respected figure in Kalimpong, as well as the object of much affection to those who knew him personally. He was highly approachable, and in time of need could be a true friend, as he himself (the Long-Lived Deva declared with some warmth) had found on more than one occasion. As a young man, he had spent quite a lot of time with Raja Dorji. They had gone shooting together. But that was many years ago, before the war, and now they hardly ever saw each other. Despite his noble qualities, the Raja Saheb was very much under his wife's thumb, and since he (the Raja Saheb) knew what he (the speaker) thought of Rani Dorji it seemed better that they should not meet.

To me it was dreadful that two men who had been as close to each other as the Long-Lived Deva and Raja Dorji had evidently been in their youth should be kept apart by a woman like Rani Dorji, and for the next few days the story gave me hardly less food for thought than did my irascible friend's revelations about local politics and about Rani Dorji's unpopularity. Not that I really had much time to think about any of these matters, however, even for that short period. Now that the committee had finally decided that the Sacred Relics should be kept at the Tharpa Choling Gompa I was busier than ever, and my visits with Thubden Tendzin to the wind-buffeted old eagle-abbot became more frequent and more prolonged. As before, discussion was by no means limited to the details of the procession or – now that the Sacred Relics were to be kept at the *gompa* – to the arrangements that would have to be made for their exposition, as well as for the accommodation of the accompanying delegation. On one occasion the abbot continued the process of sounding me out, this time on the subject of Madhyamaka dialectics. 'What is the cause of *śūnyatā*?' he abruptly demanded, with a severe expression. I replied that *śūnyatā* or Voidness being the ultimate reality the conception of causality was inapplicable. But the abbot shook his head decisively: that was not the answer. The result was that during the next ten or twelve years I spent quite a lot of time puzzling over the meaning of the old man's question. It stuck with me like a Zen koan, and in much the same way as the Zen disciple asks himself, with ever-increasing intensity, 'What is the sound of one hand clapping?' I kept asking myself, 'What is the cause of *śūnyatā*?' The reply I had given the abbot was not incorrect, but it was obviously not the last word that could be said on the subject.

Preparations for the reception of the Sacred Relics were still under way when I received two letters that materially altered our plans. The first letter was from Devapriya Valisinha. Interest in the Sacred Relics having spread like wildfire throughout the entire eastern Himalayan region, he wrote, invitations had now been received from the people of Darjeeling, as well as from His Holiness the Dalai Lama, who was at present staying at Yatung, in southern Tibet, not far from the border between Tibet and Sikkim. The Sacred Relics would therefore be going from Gangtok to Yatung, which meant that they would arrive in Kalimpong two or three weeks later than originally planned. The second letter was from Venerable Sangharatana. Since I would in any case be joining the delegation in Sikkim, and helping him and Kashyapji look after the Sacred Relics there, would I like to accompany them to Tibet, as well as to Darjeeling? The news seemed too good to be true. It was as though another unspoken wish had been answered. Deeply moved, I spent the two or three weeks that followed ensuring that my absence from Kalimpong for so long a period would not jeopardize the success of our reception and making ready for my journey to Sikkim – and Tibet.

11

PRETEXTS AND PROCESSIONS

I reached Gangtok late in the evening, when darkness had long since fallen. The journey from Kalimpong had taken much longer than I had expected, and when the Landrover set me down at the motor stand only a few dimly lit shops and stalls were still open and the centre of the village capital, as it was called, wore a strangely deserted and desolate look. Engaging a coolie to carry my bedding-roll, I somehow made him understand that I wanted to be taken straight to the Royal Palace, and after a short delay we set off together in what I hoped was the right direction. The Sacred Relics were, I knew, being kept at the palace temple, and the palace seemed to be the most likely place in which to find Venerable Sangharatana and the other members of the delegation.

After the coolie and I had plodded on in silence for half an hour the path suddenly became very steep and soon we were climbing up what seemed to be the hillside. Moreover, it was pitch dark. Surely there must be some mistake. We did not seem to be getting any nearer to the Royal Palace. Indeed, all buildings had long since been left behind. The coolie, however, seemed quite confident that we were going in the right direction, and I had no alternative but to follow in his footsteps, forcing my way between bushes and stumbling over the rough ground. Eventually we emerged into the open and I found myself on the edge of a sort of plateau, with the dark mass of a building standing silhouetted against the night sky only a few dozen yards away. From a pair of french windows in the centre of the mass streamed a brilliant light, and towards this light I made my way. Before I could reach it, however, I was intercepted by an astonishing figure in red and black and white who carried a rifle and wore a pink hat with feathers in it. This was one of the soldiers of the royal bodyguard, and his uniform was based on what I was afterwards told was traditional Lepcha dress. Taking me round to a veranda at the front of the building, he called an aide-de-camp, and the aide-de-camp called the Crown Prince. The Sacred Relics were indeed being kept at the palace temple, the Crown Prince explained, but the delegation was staying at the state guest house. He would drive me there in the jeep immediately.

A few minutes later, therefore, we were speeding down a series of hairpin bends which the Crown Prince, judging by the speed and skill with which he negotiated them, knew very well indeed. Though short, the journey gave us an opportunity of becoming better acquainted, and not having met the Crown Prince before I scrutinized the figure at the wheel with considerable interest. He was dressed in an off-white *chuba*, and whenever he turned his head to speak to me I saw an intelligent-looking Mongolian face in which there twinkled a pair of beady black eyes. The most noticeable thing about the Crown Prince, unfortunately, was his stutter, which was so pronounced that he at times had to struggle for half a minute or so before he was finally able, with a tremendous effort, to ejaculate the word that was giving him trouble.

Having arrived safely at the state guest house, which was a small bungalow situated on the hillside within a leisurely bend of the road, I found Venerable Sangharatana and the other members of the delegation clustered round the English-style fireplace in one of the bedrooms and warming themselves at the blaze – the first of its kind I had seen for several years. Accustomed as they were to the sweltering heat of the plains, both Venerable Sangharatana and Kashyapji were feeling the cold quite badly, and despite their balaclava helmets and woollen jerseys were still shivering violently. Dr Madhuram Soft, whom I had not met before, apparently felt the cold much less than his two yellow-robed companions. He was a very tall, hardy Punjabi of about sixty, clad in the white homespun garments – in his case loose-fitting trousers and long Indian overshirt – that betokened the orthodox Gandhian believer. Head and face alike were covered with a white stubble, while his toothless gums were parted in a smile of genuine warmth and friendliness that contrasted strangely with the rather angry expression in his eyes. As

I was to learn when I knew him better, Dr Soft was a very kindly man indeed, but he was also, by his own oft-repeated confession, the possessor of a truly vile temper that he was at times quite unable to control. Also clustered round the fireplace were the three assistants to the delegation. These were Brahmacārī Munindra, the young Bengali Buddhist in whose company Buddharakshita and I had travelled from Nautanwa to Lumbini only two years previously, Tashi Dorji, a young Darjeeling-born Tibetan who had formerly worked in the Maha Bodhi Society's Calcutta office, and Geshe Sangpo, a graduate from one of the great monastic universities of Lhasa. By birth the *geshe* or 'Doctor of Buddhist Divinity' was a native not of Tibet but of Mongolia, which was said to produce the greatest scholars in the whole Gelugpa Buddhist world. How great a scholar Geshe Sangpo was I had no means of telling, but I noticed that he was never without a big Tibetan xylograph volume in his hands and usually sat cross-legged on his bed reading while the rest of us talked.

As soon as greetings had been exchanged, and the bearer ordered to bring more tea, Venerable Sangharatana told me the latest news from Sarnath, as well as all about the reception that had been given the Sacred Relics on their arrival in Gangtok earlier in the day. As a matter of fact, he explained, in his usual enthusiastic, excitable manner, they had brought with them not two sets of relics but three. After all, they were going to Tibet, to meet the Dalai Lama, and they might as well do the thing properly. Besides the relics of the two *arhants* they had brought with them, in a brand-new reliquary, some very authentic relics of the Lord Buddha which had been presented to the Mulagandhakuti Vihara some years ago. He was sure the Dalai Lama would be delighted, though he *was* rather young. Did he know anything about Buddhism? Anyway, the people of Sikkim were certainly delighted. At Bagdogra, where the plane had arrived two hours late, the relics had been received by the Crown Prince, and in Gangtok they had been received at the palace temple by the Maharaja. In between there had been a grand procession. Thousands of people had taken part. It had been a very busy day. Probably tomorrow would be even busier. By the way, was the Maharaja quite right in the head? Instead of greeting him in the usual manner, with folded hands, he (the Maharaja) had taken both his (Sangharatana's) hands in his own and had asked, in a confidential undertone, 'Do you want a woman?' As he told me the story Venerable

Sangharatana laughed uproariously. Like most Sinhalese monks, he was by no means prudish, and was inclined to treat the whole thing very much as a joke. For my part, I knew that a mystery of some kind surrounded the person of the Maharaja of Sikkim. According to one account, he was a mystic of an advanced type who spent most of his time in meditation. According to another, he was an alcoholic. Whatever the truth may have been, he in fact led the life of a recluse, appearing in public only on the most important occasions.

One such occasion was that of the first public exposition of the Sacred Relics, which took place the following morning in the palace *lhakhang* or temple. This was not a mere chapel within the palace, as I had thought (thinking, perhaps, of Rani Dorji's chapel at Bhutan House), but a very new, very square, dazzlingly white, yellow-roofed building of traditional Sikkimese type that stood at the opposite end of the ridge from the palace which, I could now see, was a medium-sized country house built after the English pattern. More than that I did not have time to observe. With Sangharatana and Kashyapji I was ushered up the narrow staircase and into the first-floor chamber in which the Sacred Relics – both those of the two *arhants* and of the Buddha – were being kept. Here too the impression was one of light and colour. Crimson pillars with elaborately carved and painted capitals supported the roof, while the walls were covered with frescoes of the most brilliant hues. At the far end of the chamber the enormous golden figures of Buddhas and bodhisattvas gleamed from behind panes of glass. The reliquaries containing the Sacred Relics were placed on a kind of throne that stood immediately in front of the central image, leaving only a little gangway behind. The silver-gilt reliquary containing the remains of Śāriputra and Maudgalyāyana was the more interesting of the two. It had been presented by the Buddhists of Ceylon, and was a replica of the stupa in which the Sacred Relics of the Buddha's two chief disciples had been found by General Cunningham. After the three of us had chanted the Refuges and Precepts in Pāli, followed by some verses of blessing, Venerable Sangharatana took out two small keys and proceeded to open the reliquaries and remove the lids. The lid of the reliquary containing the Sacred Relics of the two *arhants* was modelled after the dome, *harmika*, and umbrella-spire of the stupa, while its base, which was about sixteen inches in diameter, was modelled after the stupa's railed circular plinth. On the raised middle portion of this base were the two steatite boxes in which the Sacred Relics had originally been found and two golden lotuses, the boxes being situated to the north and south and the lotuses to the east and west. On the lotuses stood two gold-rimmed glass capsules, circular in shape. These capsules were about half an inch thick, and about two inches in diameter, and each was attached to its lotus by a little golden ball. The greyish crumbs of bone on which all this artistry had been lavished, and which the Government and people of Sikkim were receiving with so much enthusiasm, lay at the bottom of the capsules – all that was left, humanly speaking, of the two lifelong friends who had been the Buddha's chief disciples.

By the time we had finished arranging the opened reliquaries on their brocade cushions the chamber was full, and presented a more colourful appearance than ever. Sikkim being a Buddhist kingdom, and its ruler not an ordinary Maharaja but a Chogyal or Dharmaraja, that is to say, a Righteous Monarch, the first exposition of the Sacred Relics was being attended not only by the reclusive Maharaja but also by the royal family, the royal court, and members of the clergy and nobility, all resplendent in traditional costume. Since for the laity this costume was the *chuba* (long-sleeved for men, sleeveless for women), and since on occasions like this the *chuba* had to be of Chinese silk brocade, the two or three hundred people ranged on the right hand side of the throne supporting the Sacred Relics and down the side of the chamber were an unforgettable sight. There were *chubas* of every imaginable hue – magenta, bottle green, chocolate brown, orange, peacock blue, royal purple, and violet, all shimmering and glittering in the sunlight that streamed in through the lattices of the big square windows. There were ruby *chubas*, sapphire *chubas*, and amethyst *chubas*. There were even *chubas* of silver and *chubas* of gold. Amidst all this magnificence it was easy to forget that Sikkim was a country a third of the size of Wales, that its capital, Gangtok, contained 2,000 souls, and that its entire population numbered less than 150,000.

After the Maharaja and his entourage had paid their respects to the Sacred Relics by prostrating themselves and offering, one by one, the usual silk *khata* or ceremonial white scarf, the doors of the palace temple were opened to the public, and for the next few hours Sangharatana, Kashyapji, and I were kept very busy indeed. In front of the Sacred Relics passed a stream of people, all desirous of paying homage to the Buddha and his two chief disciples. Besides the Sikkimese themselves, who in any case were of quite mixed descent, there were Tibetans, Bhutanese, and

Nepalese, all in their distinctive national costumes. There were even a few Indians, mainly Marwaris and Punjabis. Most of the worshippers were content simply to press their foreheads to the edge of the throne on which the two reliquaries had been placed, offer their silk or cotton *khata* together with some money, and then pass on. The more orthodox, or the more devout, retreated a few paces from the throne in order to make a triple prostration, after which they would insist on having the reliquary containing the remains of Śāriputra and Maudgalyāyana, which was the larger of the two, lifted up and placed on the top of their heads by way of a blessing. Followers of Tibetan Buddhism, it seemed, attached great importance to actual physical contact with sacred objects. Every few minutes, therefore, Sangharatana and I, who were stationed on either side of the throne (Kashyapji found it difficult to remain standing for very long) had to grasp the base of the reliquary firmly in both hands and then, between us, lift it up a few inches before gently lowering it onto the bowed head of the devotee, who would receive the blessing with hands resting on the edge of the throne and tongue respectfully protruded. Whenever there were a number of such worshippers in quick succession, this process of raising and lowering the reliquary was apt to degenerate into the administration of a series of rapid bumps on the bowed heads that appeared in front of us. Sometimes, for one reason or another, the bump would be quite a hard one, whereupon Sangharatana would laugh heartily. As for the recipient of the bump, from the pleased expression with which he or she looked up at us afterwards it was clear that they were only too happy to be blessed in this emphatic and unmistakable manner.

When not actually attending to the needs of the worshippers, Sangharatana and I had to keep clearing away the *khatas* that had been laid along the edge of the throne, immediately in front of the Sacred Relics, since otherwise the two reliquaries would have been completely buried beneath them. We were helped in this task not only by Dr Soft but also by a jovial young Sikkimese nobleman in a blue brocade *chuba* who had been dashing about the chamber taking a large number of photographs with a whole battery of expensive-looking cameras. This was Tseten Tashi, the Maharaja's good-natured and obliging Private Secretary, with whom we very quickly made friends, and who lost no time in telling us that his two great passions were photography and orchids. In fact, he had a photographic studio in the bazaar, he proudly informed us, and also ran an orchid nursery as a sideline. If our reverences wanted our photographs taken before leaving Gangtok, or if we wanted a few orchids for our friends, then Tseten Tashi was at our service! From the comical way in which he said this it was clear that he did not really expect us, as monks, to take his offer very seriously. But if he did not really expect to be of service to us where photographs and orchids were concerned, he was certainly of great service to us there in the chamber. Indeed, he stayed with us until the last worshippers of the day had passed in front of the Sacred Relics and helped us to clear up afterwards. He tied up the *khatas* into great bundles, swept the coins and currency notes into bags, and gathered up the pieces of jewellery that had been offered by some of the women worshippers, all the time keeping up a cheerful commentary on the events of the day.

In the evening Kashyapji and I delivered discourses in the spacious music room adjoining the palace temple. Why it was called the music room was not clear, since there was no sign of any musical instruments, whether Eastern or Western, or indeed of any arrangements for the playing of music. Perhaps the lamas attached to the temple used the place for practising on their drums and trumpets, or perhaps a Western-style concert had once been held there. In any case, it was surely not without significance that whereas there should be a palace *lhakhang* or 'House of Divinities' of the utmost magnificence for the ritual worship of the Buddhas and bodhisattvas, there should be no corresponding provision for the teaching of the Dharma, that is to say, no proper Dharma hall. If this state of affairs was at all representative of conditions in the kingdom as a whole it would seem to indicate a serious imbalance in contemporary Sikkimese Buddhism. Though I did not know it at the time, such an imbalance between faith and wisdom did in fact exist and, as Thubden Tendzin (who knew Sikkim well) pointed out in an article he wrote for the special Sikkim number of *Stepping-Stones* that I brought out two months later,[45]

> On the negative side of the balance sheet it must be said that the strictly intellectual element in the tradition, that of doctrine, both in its more theoretical form and as actualised by method and experience, has largely disappeared [from Sikkim] and this is a matter for very serious misgiving, since the loss affects the most essential element of all, Knowledge, starting point and final term of all spiritual endeavour.[46]

It was also significant that whereas in the course of the day several thousand people had paid their respects to the Sacred Relics, only a few dozen people turned up to hear Kashyapji and myself deliver our discourses. For the most part these belonged to the Western-educated minority, and included a number of Hindus. As for the Maharaja and his court, on this occasion they were conspicuous by their absence, though the Crown Prince was there and followed the discourses with close attention.

For the remainder of the week that the Sacred Relics were in Gangtok the days passed in much the same way that the first one had done. In the morning and afternoon Sangharatana, Dr Soft, and I – assisted, more often than not, by the ebullient Tseten Tashi – watched over the Sacred Relics in the upstairs chamber of the palace temple and attended to the needs of the worshippers, many of whom had come on foot from distant parts of Sikkim and Bhutan. In the evening Kashyapji and I delivered our discourses in the music room. By the end of the seventh day of the exposition 10,000 people, it was estimated, had paid their respects to the Sacred Relics, and Sangharatana and I had blessed – and bumped – at least one third of that number on their respectfully bowed heads with the silver-gilt reliquary. It was noticeable, though, that as the week went by the stream of people slowly abated, and that whereas on the first day of the exposition several thousand worshippers had passed through the upper chamber of the palace temple on the last day there were fewer than a thousand. In the case of the evening discourses, however, exactly the opposite happened. Day by day our little audience steadily grew, with the result that by the end of the week it numbered nearly a hundred. Younger Sikkimese Buddhists, in particular, responded to the discourses with great enthusiasm. They had no idea, they declared, that Buddhism taught such wonderful things. Since Kashyapji and I had been discoursing mainly on such basic topics as the Four Noble Truths and the Noble Eightfold Path this was rather surprising, and constituted further evidence of the disastrous decline in respect of doctrinal knowledge that had overtaken Sikkimese Buddhism in recent years. Clearly there was an urgent need for a revival of Buddhism throughout the entire kingdom, and perhaps the YMBA could be of some help in this connection.

Since Sangharatana, Dr Soft, and I spent so much of our time together (Kashyapji was generally absent on business of his own), it was inevitable that the three of us should become better acquainted day by day, especially as both of my fellow delegates – Sangharatana particularly – were of a warm-hearted and communicative disposition. Dr Soft was never tired of telling Sangharatana and myself how, only a few weeks earlier, he had accompanied the Sacred Relics to Ladakh, where they had had to struggle through the snow with their precious burden from one remote monastery to another. What a reception the people of Ladakh had given them! How devout they were! As the old man reminisced, his face lit up, and his eyes filled with tears. To have witnessed such devotion, he declared, was one of the greatest experiences of his life. Sangharatana, for his part, had quite a lot to say about how, a few months previously, he had accompanied the Sacred Relics to Burma, where they had been received by the Prime Minister, U Nu, and taken for exposition to many different parts of the country. The Burmese Buddhists too were very devout – much more devout than the Sinhalese. In fact, until he came to Sikkim he had never seen such devotion as he saw in Burma. The faith of the Burmese Buddhists was so strong it could even work miracles. In one of the places to which the Sacred Relics had been taken (a small town in the interior, I think he said it was) he himself had actually seen with his own eyes the tiny fragments of bone rotating in a clockwise direction within their respective capsules while there emanated from them a brilliant rainbow-coloured light. Two thousand people had been present and had seen the miracle – if it really was a miracle, he added with a laugh. That is to say, two thousand people had seen the rainbow-coloured light, and several hundred – including himself and the other members of the delegation – had seen the Sacred Relics rotating within their capsules. No doubt it was all due to the especially intense devotion with which the Burmese Buddhists had been worshipping the Sacred Relics on that occasion.

Though Venerable Sangharatana was a man of fervently devotional temperament, he was also truthful and outspoken to an unusual degree, and I therefore saw no reason to question the complete accuracy of his account. According to the Theravāda tradition 'miracles' of the kind he had described could be produced in three different ways. They could be produced as a result of an exercise of *iddhi* or supernormal power, especially by a Buddha or an *arhant*; they could be produced by the intervention of the *devas* or gods; and they could be produced by the faith of the worshipper. Since neither the Buddha nor, presumably, any *arhant* had been present on the occasion, and since no one had seen any *devas* (not that they might not have been invisibly present) it seemed wisest to assume – with Sangharatana – that the 'miracle' had been produced as a result of the collective faith of the worshippers, who were undeniably present in large numbers and, apparently, deeply moved by the presence among them of the actual bodily remains of the Buddha's two chief disciples.

But although all this was quite clear to me, I was not so clear about my own personal attitude towards the Sacred Relics, which was in fact rather ambivalent. I was deeply touched by the simple faith and unaffected piety of the people who, every day, came to pay their respects to the Sacred Relics, and I could even empathize with that faith and that piety; at the same time, I was quite unable to feel towards the Sacred Relics the kind of devotion that they so evidently felt. For one thing, I was not even sure that the tiny fragments of bone lying at the bottom of the capsules really had belonged to Śāriputra and Maudgalyāyana. True, they had been discovered by General Cunningham in Stupa No. 3 at Sanchi, and there seemed no reason to doubt that the inscriptions on the steatite boxes in which he had found them were in Brahmi characters of the time of Aśoka; but how could one be sure that these same fragments of bone really were the relics of the two *arhants*, as the builders of the stupa apparently believed? Between the time of Śāriputra and Maudgalyāyana, who had predeceased the Buddha, and the time of Aśoka, there was an interval of more than 200 years, and there was no record of the whereabouts of the relics of the two great disciples – if indeed relics there ever were – during that period. I had to admit to myself that although the relics *might* be those of Śāriputra and Maudgalyāyana, and although the idea that I *might* possibly be in contact with a portion of their actual bodily remains did give me a more vivid sense of their actual historical existence, the sight of the tiny fragments of bone lying at the bottom of the capsules was far from making me feel – as judging by their rapt expressions many of the worshippers felt – that I was in the actual living presence of the two *arhants*. For me the principal value of the exposition consisted in the fact that it was a means of awakening in the hearts of thousands of people devotional feelings which could, if properly channelled, eventually be directed to the actual study and practice of the Buddha's teaching. That was why I had been so eager to invite the Sacred Relics to Kalimpong. That was why I had joined Sangharatana and Kashyapji in Gangtok, and it was one of the reasons why I was going to accompany them to Tibet.

Arrangements for our departure had been going on all the week. The two officials of the Tibetan government who were to act as our escort had arrived some time previously, and with their help the delegation had been provided with warm clothing, a sufficient number of mules, and a palanquin for the conveyance of the Sacred Relics. We were to set out at the beginning of March, only two days after the end of the week-long exposition of the Sacred Relics in the palace temple. Almost on the eve of our departure, however, an unexpected setback occurred, at least as far as I was concerned. Word reached us that the Government of India was refusing to allow me to cross the frontier between Sikkim and Tibet. In my excitement at the prospect of visiting the Land of Snows I had either forgotten that there were such things as frontier permits, or had assumed that they were only a formality. I soon discovered my mistake. When I went to see the Political Officer, as the Government of India's representative in Sikkim was called, he told me that he had received definite instructions from Delhi not to allow me to enter Tibet by way of Sikkim and was, therefore, unable to issue the necessary permit. The three other members of the delegation, who had accompanied me to the Political Officer's residence, all protested vigorously, saying that I was a Buddhist monk, that I would be going to Tibet as the guest of the Tibetan government, which had already granted me a visa, and that my mission was of a purely religious nature. All this was, of course, perfectly true. It was also true – as my companions thought it advisable *not* to point out – that the Sikkimese authorities, who one would have thought were the ones most directly concerned, had no objection whatever to my entering Tibet from Sikkim. But in matters of this sort the truth did not, it seemed, carry much weight. Nothing that Dr Soft, or Sangharatana, or Kashyapji could say was of any avail, and Mr Dayal, the Political Officer, continued to insist that he was unable to issue me with the permit. Their repeated protests and expostulations did, however, have the effect of embarrassing him, at least in his personal capacity. Having heard some of my discourses, and apparently not wanting me to think that he was acting on his own initiative, instead of simply obeying orders, he therefore took me aside and showed me a letter he had received from the Ministry of External Affairs. The letter was to the effect that I was not to be given a permit (apparently the Political Officer had referred the matter to Delhi) and that foreign nationals were not to be allowed to cross the border between Sikkim and Tibet 'on any pretext'. It was signed 'Jawaharlal Nehru'.

That of course settled the matter. Dr Soft, who was the official leader of the delegation to Tibet, thanked the Political Officer for seeing us, and we all parted on friendly terms. It was now quite clear that I would not be able to accompany the Sacred Relics to Tibet, and quite clear that the decision not to give me the necessary permit had been taken at the very highest level and for purely political reasons. Though I did not understand the situation very well at that time, I knew that the Chinese armies that had invaded Tibet the previous autumn were preparing to march on Lhasa and that on the advice of his ministers the Dalai Lama had withdrawn to Yatung so as to be out of harm's way in the event of any fighting. It was therefore conceivable that if the delegation accompanying the Sacred Relics happened to include an English Buddhist monk the Chinese might take the view that the supposed Buddhist monk was, in reality, a British agent sent to establish secret contact with the Dalai Lama. It was also conceivable that they might regard it as an unfriendly act on the part of the Government of India to have allowed a British agent disguised as a Buddhist monk to enter Tibet via Sikkim (which was an Indian protectorate), and to risk upsetting the Chinese was almost the last thing that Nehru and his pro-Chinese advisers wanted to do. Though the heady days of 'Hindi-Chini Bhai-Bhai' or 'Indians and Chinese are Pals' were yet to come, India seemed intent on preserving good relations with Communist China at almost any cost. After feeble initial protests, it had come to acquiesce in the Chinese occupation of Tibet, and only a few weeks earlier had actually allowed the Chinese general who had been placed in command in Tibet to travel to Lhasa via Calcutta, Kalimpong, and Gangtok. No wonder I did not get my permit! If the Government of India was willing to sacrifice the freedom and independence of Tibet on the altar of Sino-Indian friendship, it was unlikely that it would hesitate to make a similar sacrifice of my own chance of accompanying the Sacred Relics to Tibet. Having swallowed so enormous a camel, it could hardly be expected to strain at a gnat.

Naturally it was a great disappointment to me that I would not, after all, be able to visit the Land of Snows, especially as I knew that I might well not have the opportunity again. But disappointment was not the only emotion I felt on leaving the Political Officer's residence. I was also extremely annoyed by the implied suggestion, in Pandit Nehru's letter, that my reasons for visiting Tibet might not be what they seemed and that, consequently, I myself might not be what I seemed. Foreign nationals, the Political Officer had been told, were not to be allowed to cross the border *on any pretext*. Was the fact that I wanted to accompany the Sacred Relics to Tibet officially regarded as a pretext, then, and if so a pretext for what? Apparently it was conceivable that if the delegation happened to include an English Buddhist monk the Indians, no less than the Chinese, might take the view that the supposed Buddhist monk was in reality a British agent. Indeed, in the case of the Indians it seemed more than conceivable, for had I not been refused a permit and had not Pandit Nehru's letter spoken of *pretexts* for crossing the border? It was, of course, possible that I was attaching too much significance to a single word or a single phrase. 'On any pretext' might well mean no more than 'on any grounds' or 'for any reason'. Nonetheless, I could not quite dispel the suspicion that the word pretext had been used quite deliberately, and reflected the Government of India's inability to imagine that a foreigner could possibly have settled in a 'sensitive border area' for purely religious reasons. My annoyance at what I took to be a slur on my good faith therefore lasted considerably longer than my disappointment at not being able to visit Tibet.

At the time, however, I put these and all other personal feelings aside and with the rest of the population of Gangtok prepared to give the Sacred Relics – and the delegation – a fitting send-off on their departure for Tibet. Since it would take them four days to reach Yatung, and another day to reach the Donkara Gompa or 'White Conch Shell Monastery', where the Dalai Lama was staying, they set out early. The day was cold but clear, and the morning sun shone down brightly from a sky of cloudless blue on a picturesque and colourful scene as the Sacred Relics, after being deposited in a yellow-curtained palanquin provided by the Tibetan government, were carried in procession as far as the outskirts of the town. First, in single file, walked the lamas, some in magnificent ceremonial robes, some bearing the enormous multi-coloured, many-flounced cylinders know as 'banners of victory', and some bearing giant Tibetan trumpets whose deep and mournful notes seemed to express – if I was not being too fanciful – the sorrow of the people at the departure of the Sacred Relics. Next came the yellow-curtained palanquin, borne on the shoulders of six bearers, on either side of which walked the Maharaja and the Crown Prince, members of the royal family, nobles, officials, and delegates. In the rear followed the Guard of Honour provided by the Sikkim State Police Force, and members of the public. On reaching the huge *maṇi*-wall, or wall painted with the mantra *oṃ maṇi padme hūṃ* in the six traditional colours, which marked the beginning of the road to Tibet, the delegation mounted their ponies, the palanquin was shouldered by a fresh party of bearers, and amid shouts of farewell the Sacred Relics slowly disappeared up the winding mountain trail that led to Yatung.

Once again I was left standing at the side of the road, and though this time I was not alone I felt the departure of Sangharatana, Kashyapji, and Dr Soft for Yatung no less keenly than I had felt Kashyapji's departure for Siliguri exactly a year ago. This time there were no parting words of admonition ringing in my ears. I knew what I had to do. After standing there beside the huge *maṇi*-wall for a few minutes, wrapt in thought, I turned round and with the help of a lift from the Crown Prince was soon back at the state guest house. There I made arrangements to return to Kalimpong the same day. I had been away for little more than a week, instead of for a month as I had expected, and Burma Raja and the rest of my friends would be surprised to see me and surprised to learn that I had not been able to accompany the Sacred Relics to Tibet.

But not being able to accompany the Sacred Relics to Tibet was not the only disappointment I suffered in Gangtok. I also suffered a disappointment of a more strictly personal nature, and it was in connection with Kashyapji. Quite apart from the prospect of visiting the Land of Snows, one of the reasons why I had welcomed Sangharatana's invitation to join the delegation in Gangtok was that this would give me an opportunity of telling Kashyapji – indeed, of complaining to him – about the way in which I had been treated by Aniruddha. Since our days were taken up with looking after the Sacred Relics and our evenings with delivering discourses, and since Kashyapji was often absent on business of his own, it was not very easy for me to find a suitable occasion on which to speak to my teacher, and it was only towards the end of the week that I was able to unburden myself of the feelings of distress and indignation that had weighed on me since my enforced departure from the Dharmodaya Vihara – feelings which until then I had kept to myself. Or rather, it was only towards the end of the week that I was able to *begin* to unburden myself. Unburden myself fully I could not. After a few minutes Kashyapji cut me short and abjured me, in the strongest terms, not to feel any ill will towards Aniruddha and to forget all about the matter. We were *bhikṣus*, he said, and it was our duty to put up with ill treatment without complaining. This was, of course, sound doctrine, and it was no doubt right and proper that he should remind me that, in the words of the *Dhammapada* verses we had studied together, hatred did not cease by hatred but only by love. But what if one *bhikṣu* ill-treated another? What if the ill treatment came not from a hostile king or an unsympathetic householder but from a fellow member of the monastic community, from whom one was entitled to expect sympathy, support, and encouragement, especially if one was very much the junior of the two? This aspect of the matter Kashyapji absolutely refused to consider, and would not even allow me to talk about it. He even refused to consider the possibility that Aniruddha had acted wrongly in any way. All he would say was that I should forgive and forget. While I agreed wholeheartedly that I should forgive, however difficult I might still find it to do this, I was by no means convinced that it was possible or even desirable for one to overlook the way in which one had been treated by another monk – or for one's teacher to overlook it. Though I did not have as clear an understanding of the nature of the Buddhist spiritual community as I had later, it was obvious to me that disharmony within the sangha was a serious matter and could not be ignored, regardless of who was and who was not at fault. Kashyapji's attitude seemed to suggest that there was, in fact, no effective spiritual community, and that if you were ill-treated by another monk you should simply keep out of his way, being only careful not to feel ill will towards him. The second disappointment I suffered in Gangtok was therefore due not so much to Kashyapji's lack of sympathy for the way in which I had been treated by Aniruddha (though I felt that too) as to his apparent failure to understand the emotional shock I had experienced on discovering that the monastic order was not the kind of spiritual brotherhood that I had been led to suppose. This original disappointment the disappointment I experienced in connection with Kashyapji only served to compound. It was as though Kashyapji accepted the lack of a Buddhist spiritual community, at least so far as the Theravāda tradition was concerned, and believed that one should simply keep one's own nose clean. If that was really the case, I was even more alone than I had thought.

Thinking things over in the Landrover on the way back to Kalimpong, I remembered a conversation that had taken place between Kashyapji, Sangharatana, and Brahmacārī Munindra one day in the jeep that was taking us from the state guest house up to the palace temple – a conversation that perhaps threw some light on Kashyapji's attitude towards disharmony in the sangha. The three of them were discussing a serious breach of the Vinaya or Monastic Code of which an elderly and highly respected *bhikṣu* had recently been guilty, and about which nothing, apparently, was going to be done. The breach was so serious – nothing less than making one of his female disciples pregnant – that I could not help asking Kashyapji, in some astonishment, 'But is the story really true?' In tones of great sadness Kashyapji had replied, 'Yes, it's true. I'm afraid our old friend is no better than the rest of them.' Since 'the rest of them' were the other Theravāda Buddhist monks in India I could not help wondering whether my teacher had not suffered disappointments of his own in connection with the monastic order. I already knew that the Maha Bodhi Society *bhikṣus* at Sarnath were extremely jealous of him and that, with the exception of Sangharatana, they spoke disparagingly of him behind his back, even though none of them had a hundredth part of his learning or generosity of spirit. But while he never referred to the jealousy of the Sarnath *bhikṣus*, Kashyapji must have been well aware of it, and it was highly unlikely that their constant disparagement of him was the only unkindness he had had to put up with from his brother monks, or the least. Indeed, the more I thought about the matter the more likely it seemed that Kashyapji had had quite a lot to put up with from them, and might well have suffered disappointments no less bitter than my own. Like me, he was not that living contradiction in terms, a 'born Buddhist'. Born into a Hindu family, and educated and trained as an orthodox Hindu scholar and ascetic, he had embraced Buddhism out of personal conviction, and his entry into a monastic order as formalistic and spiritually moribund as that of Theravādin Ceylon must inevitably have been followed by a period of disillusionment. If that was the case, and if Kashyapji himself really had suffered the equivalent of being thrown out of the Dharmodaya Vihara, it was understandable that the subject of disharmony in the sangha should be quite a painful one for him and one that he was not willing to discuss. This would account for the peremptory manner – so unusual for him! – in which he had stopped me unburdening myself to him, and for his refusal to allow me to talk about Aniruddha's misdeeds. Having long ago made up his mind that there was no such thing as a Buddhist spiritual community he would naturally see no point in listening to complaints that assumed that there was and no point, therefore, in giving me any other advice than he had done. Despite his apparent failure to understand the emotional shock I had experienced Kashyapji was, I knew, deeply concerned for my welfare, and if he had exhorted me to forgive and forget it must have been because he genuinely believed that, in the circumstances, it was the best thing for me to do. Having come to this conclusion I felt much easier in my mind, and by the time the Landrover crossed Teesta Bridge, and started on the steep climb that constituted the last stage of the journey, the keenness of the second disappointment I had suffered in Gangtok had begun to abate.

Once back at Burma Raja's guest cottage, and within sound of the reassuring tinkle of the wind-bells, it did not take me long to pick up the threads of my various activities. Since I had completed most of the arrangements for the reception of the Sacred Relics before my departure for Gangtok I did not have to make my way to the bazaar, or up to Tirpai, on quite so many mornings as before. What with the running of the YMBA and the bringing out of the next issue of *Stepping-Stones* there was, however, quite enough work to keep me busy, especially as the next issue of our monthly journal of Himalayan religion, culture, and education was to be a special Sikkim number. The longest and most important article in this Sikkim number, which also contained contributions by Lama Govinda, Dr Guenther, and Dr de Nebesky-Wojkowitz, was Thubden Tendzin's article on 'Sikkim Buddhism Today and Tomorrow'. Since Thubden Tendzin was an extremely scrupulous and conscientious person, and something of a perfectionist, the writing of this article gave him – and me – quite a lot of trouble. There was much discussion, and many anxious consultations, before it was at last finished, and even when it had been given to the printer and was going through the press the author continued to make extensive alterations and additions. So lengthy did his article in fact become that the Sikkim number grew to twice the size of an ordinary issue, thus doubling our printer's bill for the month. With his usual generosity, Thubden Tendzin came to the rescue with a cheque to cover the difference.

By this time the Sacred Relics had returned to Gangtok, and the delegation was taking a short rest before setting out for Kalimpong. They were expected to arrive towards the end of March. After calling a final meeting of the Reception Committee, I therefore went round making quite sure that all our preparations were in order and that the reception would go off without a hitch. While I was thus engaged I received news of a very disturbing nature. The procession in which the Sacred Relics were to be taken on their arrival in Kalimpong was to start at Eighth Mile, where there was a straight stretch of road, pass through the town via the High Street, and then proceed (past the Church of Scotland Mission!) up to Tirpai and the Tharpa Choling Gompa. This meant that it would have to pass in front of the Dharmodaya Vihara, or rather, in front of the acclivity that led to those now deserted premises. The news I had received was to the effect that a group of Newars were planning to station themselves at the foot of the acclivity with the idea that, when the palanquin containing the Sacred Relics drew abreast, they would seize hold of it and forcibly divert the procession to the Dharmodaya Vihara. Greatly alarmed, I at once went to see the Long-Lived Deva. But my irascible friend only told me I was worrying unnecessarily and scornfully pooh-poohed the notion that the weak and cowardly Newars (as he termed them) would dare to divert the procession in this way. Despite his assurances, I was not completely convinced that the attempt would not be made, and eventually persuaded him to accept the responsibility of walking in front of the procession and making sure that it kept to the appointed route. Perhaps I should also arrange for a few policemen to be stationed at the foot of the acclivity leading to the Dharmodaya Vihara. But such a precaution the Long-Lived Deva roundly declared to be quite unnecessary, and when I asked him what he would do if the Newars did, in fact, seize hold of the palanquin, he only stabbed himself in the chest with his forefinger and, lapsing into Tibetan, roared, '*Nga pompa re!* I am the boss!' With him in charge, his words clearly implied, no one would dare to seize hold of anything.

It was therefore with a comparatively light heart that, two or three mornings later, I drove down to Teesta Bridge to meet the jeep in which Sangharatana and the rest of the delegation were bringing the Sacred Relics from Gangtok. Before leaving I made sure that the procession was drawn up in proper order on the left hand side of the road at Eighth Mile, and as I got into my car I had the satisfaction of seeing the Long-Lived Deva marching up and down and making sure that nobody moved from his place. An hour or so later I returned with the Sacred Relics, which were immediately transferred from the decorated jeep in which they had travelled from Gangtok to the palanquin that would take them to the Tharpa Choling Gompa. As soon as the jeep and the other vehicles had fallen into line behind the palanquin, I gave the order to start and, with a tremendous roar from the twelve foot long Tibetan trumpets, the entire procession started moving slowly up the road. After more than two months of preparation, the Sacred Relics had actually arrived in Kalimpong, and our arrangements for receiving them appeared to be functioning like clockwork. Having done what I had to do, and having nothing further to worry about (though the thought of possible disruption by the Newars still lingered at the back of my mind), I was therefore content to sit back in the jeep with Sangharatana and Kashyapji and admire the beauty of the spectacle of which we were a part.

Since the procession was more than half a mile long, and since the road into the town was not only very steep but twisted round the hillside in a series of sharp bends, I could see large sections of it at a time. Right in front of the procession moved the tiny figure of the Long-Lived Deva, very upright and walking with a kind of military strut. Behind him, walking in single file, came a long line of red-robed Tibetan monks, about fifty in number, and mostly from the Tharpa Choling Gompa. Some of the monks carried musical instruments, while about a dozen others bore aloft the multi-coloured, many-flounced 'banners of victory', which had been spaced out in such a way as to produce the maximum effect. Immediately behind the monks, and in front of our own jeep, came the palanquin containing the Sacred Relics. This was bright yellow in colour, and shaped like a Chinese-style pavilion, with curved roof and curled-up eaves, and it was borne on the shoulders of eight stalwart Tibetans, who were relieved, at intervals, by eight other stalwart Tibetans, so that the merit of carrying the Sacred Relics could be shared by as many people as possible. Behind us followed the vehicles that had accompanied the Sacred Relics from Gangtok, which were in turn followed by an ever-growing number of local people. The whole procession moved to the slow, heavy beat of an enormous Tibetan drum, while the almost continuous sound of the shrill, harsh *geylings*[47] was punctuated from time to time by the prolonged roar of the twelve-foot trumpets, the echoes of which reverberated from the hillside.

After we had gone about a mile I saw ahead, on the right hand side of the road, the sheltered spot that Tibetan mule-drivers sometimes used as a camping ground. Beyond this, I knew, was the Dharmodaya

Vihara. But there was no sign of any trouble. Indeed, as we passed the vihara the light 'auspicious shower' that had started when the Sacred Relics arrived from Gangtok suddenly stopped, the sun came out, and the dazzling white peaks of Mount Kanchenjunga were revealed looking down on the scene. As the procession turned left into the High Street – the Long-Lived Deva still marching ahead, and the *geylings* and twelve-foot trumpets making a tremendous racket – we found ourselves moving between the densely packed ranks of the cheerful and excited people that lined it on either side. Smiling faces looked down from the windows and balconies of the two- and three-storeyed buildings. On the steps in front of many of the shops stood braziers, from which the smoke of burning juniper-twigs drifted across the street in dense white clouds. *Chuba*-clad figures prostrated themselves in the path of the procession, while others, detaching themselves from the crowd, darted between the legs of the eight stalwart Tibetans and passed underneath the palanquin to the other side – thus obtaining, as they believed, the blessing of the Sacred Relics, or at least good luck. By the time the procession had debouched from the High Street into the more open road that led to Tenth Mile the crowd had thinned out considerably, and I could see the figure of Thubden Tendzin walking incense-stick in hand beside the palanquin, the black *chuba* that he had donned for the occasion contrasting strangely with the intense pallor of his face. On their arrival at the Tharpa Choling Gompa the Sacred Relics were received by the abbot and, no doubt, by Rani Dorji. I had noticed that as we drew near to Tirpai the monks carrying the twelve-foot trumpets detached themselves from the procession and rushed on ahead. As we entered the *gompa* there they were, inside the gate, blowing for all they were worth on their prodigious instruments, the mouthpieces of which rested on the shoulders of red-robed novices.

During the four days that the Sacred Relics remained in Kalimpong the delegation and I were kept busy in much the same way that we had been in Gangtok. In the morning and afternoon the Sacred Relics were exposed for worship in the *lhakhang* or temple of the *gompa*, which though darker and gloomier – and dustier – than the palace temple in Gangtok was somehow a more impressive place, with a more intensely vibrant atmosphere that was due, no doubt, to the fact that it was used more frequently and by a greater number of people. As in Gangtok, Sangharatana and I had to bump hundreds of heads each day, as well as clear away thousands of *khatas* or white ceremonial scarves. In fact there were more heads to be bumped and more *khatas* to be cleared away than there had been in Gangtok, as well as more money to be collected by Gyan Jyoti. Both Sangharatana and Dr Soft remarked on the fact that whereas the Indians who came to pay their respects to the Sacred Relics offered only the smallest coins the Tibetans always offered currency notes. Was this because the Indians were poorer, or because the Tibetans were more devout? It was difficult to say which was the case, but I knew that the Tibetans regarded the Indians – that is, the modern Hindus – as very irreligious, an opinion which, had they known of it, would have shocked the latter greatly. Again, as in Gangtok, Sangharatana and Dr Soft had told me how they had accompanied the Sacred Relics to Ladakh and Burma, so now they told me about their experiences with the Sacred Relics in Tibet (Kashyapji had either left Kalimpong early, or was away most of the time). Both of them had received a stronger impression than ever of the faith and devotion of the Tibetan Buddhists – an impression that was being still further reinforced in Kalimpong. They also spoke in the most glowing terms of the fifteen-year-old Dalai Lama, whose appearance Dr Soft described as 'charming and energy-personified'. The Dalai Lama had not only received the Sacred Relics on their arrival at the Donkara Gompa, but after they had been exposed for four days for the veneration of the public he had preached, in their presence, a sermon (as Dr Soft called it) that had lasted three days and at the end of which he had personally blessed every one of the thousands of people present by touching them on the head with a golden jar. So interesting were the reminiscences of my two friends that I asked Dr Soft to write an article about the Sacred Relics' visit to Tibet for the Vaiśākha number of *Stepping-Stones*. This he did, after he had returned to Calcutta, and the article appeared in our little magazine two months later. Meanwhile, colour pictures of the Dalai Lama receiving the Sacred Relics on the steps of Donkara Gompa had appeared in the American *Life* magazine, and were seen by millions of people.

In the evening there were no discourses as there had been in Gangtok. (I had delivered a public lecture on Śāriputra and Maudgalyāyana at the Hill View Hotel a few months earlier.) Instead, the Sacred Relics were taken on short visits to the Bhutanese *gompa* and the Dharmodaya Vihara, as well as to the houses of some of the more prominent Buddhist families of the town. The Bhutanese *gompa* was a small building situated amid pine trees a short distance beyond Tenth Mile. I had visited it several times since my arrival in Kalimpong but had always found it locked. Nothing ever seemed to happen there, and no one seemed to live there except a couple of caretakers who might have been either monks or laymen and who were in any case not usually to be seen. Thus when Sangharatana, Dr Soft, and I accompanied the Sacred Relics to the Bhutanese *gompa* it was the first time I had seen the place open, and the first time I had been able to enter. Within, the general layout was much the same as that of the *lhakhang* at the Tharpa Choling Gompa, and we had the satisfaction of exposing the Sacred Relics for the veneration of a hundred or so crop-headed Bhutanese Buddhists, all barefoot and all wearing baggy striped *chubas* which, in the case of the men, were kilted to the knee. At the Dharmodaya Vihara we performed a similar service for the more excitable white-clad Newars. It was the first time I had been there since Burma Raja had whisked me away in his taxi three months earlier. Quite a number of the Newars were plainly glad to see me again and, despite Aniruddha's scowls, came and paid their respects to me in the usual manner. Some of my friends had been of the opinion that in view of the way in which Aniruddha had shut down the activities of the YMBA and thrown me out the Dharmodaya Vihara could no longer be regarded as a Buddhist centre and it would not be fitting for the Sacred Relics to be taken there. With this I did not agree. Though Aniruddha had certainly behaved badly, many of the Newars were not at all happy with his conduct, and it did not seem fair that they should be penalized on his account. When I saw the smiles with which many of them greeted me on my reappearance at the vihara I was more than ever convinced that in allowing the Sacred Relics to visit the Dharmodaya Vihara I had done the right thing.

The private houses to which the Sacred Relics were taken were situated quite far apart. Thus Sangharatana and I found ourselves chanting the Refuges and Precepts and opening the two reliquaries in the coldly magnificent chapel of Bhutan House at Twelfth Mile, in the very new, Tibetan style shrine-room of the Jyoti brothers' very new house at Eleventh Mile, and in the sitting room of Mrs Rose Samdup's flat on the third floor of Chung Building, the tallest building in the High Street. Who Mrs Rose Samdup was I did not know. In fact I had not heard of her before, but Sangharatana assured me that she was a

Reception for the Sacred Relics at the home of Gyan Jyoti, Sangharakshita at the back, Bhikkhu Aniruddha to his left, Dr Soft front right

staunch supporter of the Maha Bodhi Society, as her father had been before her, and that it was only right and proper that the Sacred Relics should be taken to the home of such a distinguished devotee. The distinguished devotee turned out to be a small, plump Tibetan woman in her early forties, apparently Darjeeling-born, with an ingratiating manner and a rather winning smile, who sat on her haunches in front of the Sacred Relics with a dazed expression on her face, as if hardly able to credit her good fortune, while her friends and neighbours came and made offerings. Not long after the Sacred Relics had left Kalimpong I discovered that, in the estimation of the public, Mrs Rose Samdup was not quite such a distinguished devotee as I had been led to believe. Indeed, the fact that the Sacred Relics, which had been considered too pure to be kept in the polluted atmosphere of the Town Hall, should have been taken to the home of a woman like Mrs Samdup occasioned a good deal of surprise.

Sangharatana and I also chanted the Refuges and Precepts and opened the two reliquaries in the Burmese Princess's tiny shrine-room at Panorama. Knowing that Burma Raja dearly wanted to see and worship the Sacred Relics, but that the proud old man hesitated to invite them on account of his inability to make what he considered to be the proper offerings, with Sangharatana's consent I told him that we would bring the Sacred Relics to Panorama after dark and that we would not bring anyone else with us. Burma Raja and the Princess thus had the satisfaction of having the Sacred Relics entirely to themselves for an hour. While they were busy worshipping them in evident fullness of heart I took Sangharatana down to the guest cottage and gave him something to eat. By this time I knew that the Maha Bodhi Society *bhikṣus* at Sarnath all ate at night, and that one of the reasons they had kept Buddharakshita and myself so very much at arm's length two years earlier was that they were afraid we might find this out. Sangharatana, however, no longer made any secret of his post-meridional repasts. Indeed he considered them perfectly justified. With his weak stomach (so he had confided to me in Gangtok), and only half his liver in working order, it was quite impossible for him to eat before noon a sufficient quantity of food to sustain him throughout the day. All the same, he had quickly added, it was better not to let the laity know what one was doing. Some lay people found it difficult to understand such things, and it was important to keep up their faith in the *bhikṣu* sangha. At the guest cottage, however, there was no need for him to bother about matters of this sort, and Venerable Sangharatana therefore tucked into the omelette Gopal eventually cooked for him with a clear conscience.

When he had finished we made our way back to Panorama and prepared to take the Sacred Relics back to the Tharpa Choling Gompa. I was touched to see that during our absence Burma Raja and the Princess had placed in front of the reliquaries, by way of an offering, thirty rupees in currency notes and some packets of gold leaf. Thirty rupees! Compared with the three hundred rupees that Mrs Samdup had given, and the larger amounts offered by Rani Dorji and the Jyoti brothers, it was a pitifully small sum; but knowing Burma Raja's proud and generous spirit I was well aware that it probably represented all the ready money that he and the Princess had in the house at the time. Had he received the Sacred Relics as King of Burma, as might well have been the case, there is no doubt that he would have been happy to offer thirty *lakhs* of rupees. It was a sobering thought, and one that I could not help sharing with Sangharatana after we had deposited the Sacred Relics on their throne in the *lhakhang* of the Tharpa Choling Gompa and were walking through the monastery orange grove towards the small stone building in which the delegation had been accommodated and where I too was staying. Indeed, I was anxious that Sangharatana should understand Burma Raja's position and not think that he was lacking in generosity. But I need not have worried. My warm-hearted friend knew from his own experience that the Burmese were hardly less generous than the Tibetans, and in any case he had seen enough of Burma Raja, even in the course of a short visit, to know what sort of man he really was. By the time we reached the steps leading up to the back entrance of the building, therefore, Sangharatana had assured me that he fully understood Burma Raja's position and that, having met him and the Princess, he was more glad than ever that we had taken the Sacred Relics to Panorama.

Though I did not know it at the time, the building in which the delegation had been accommodated had in fact been – and in a sense still was – the private residence of the celebrated Tomo Geshe Rimpoche, who besides being the virtual founder of the Tharpa Choling Gompa was also the founder of the Donkara Gompa, in the Chumbi Valley, where the Dalai Lama was now staying. Though the Rimpoche had been dead for many years, his was still a name to conjure with not only in southern Tibet but throughout the entire Himalayan region. Many people in the Darjeeling District still remembered him, and many were the stories that were told about his learning, his asceticism, and, above all, his extraordinary miraculous powers. There was an image of him in the bottom left-hand corner of the glass-fronted showcase that occupied the entire back wall of the *lhakhang* in which the Sacred Relics were being kept. There was also, just above the image, a photograph of his naked embalmed body sitting erect and cross-legged. It was difficult to tell, either from the image or the photograph, what Tomo Geshe Rimpoche had really looked like, but there was no mistaking the fact that the broadly grinning face in the photograph, at least, was that of an exceptionally strong and determined personality.

Two days after Sangharatana and I had taken the Sacred Relics to Panorama their visit to Kalimpong came to an end. It was now the people of Darjeeling's turn to give them a reception and, as originally planned, I accompanied the delegates to the Queen of the Hill Stations in order to help them look after the Sacred Relics there too. Once again,

The Sacred Relics leaving Kalimpong

therefore, I saw the Sacred Relics taken in procession (though in a far less orderly fashion than in Kalimpong), and once again Sangharatana and I bumped heads and cleared away white ceremonial scarves – this time in the small shrine-room that occupied the top floor of the Tamang Gompa, as the Nyingma temple in the centre of the bazaar was popularly known. This shrine-room was dedicated to Amitābha, the Buddha of Infinite Light, just as the big shrine-room on the ground floor was dedicated to the Great Guru Padmasambhava, and the medium sized one on the middle floor to the eleven-headed and thousand-armed form of Avalokiteśvara, the Bodhisattva of Compassion. It was the first time I had been on the second and third floors of the temple, and the first time I had seen this particular arrangement of images. According to Nyingma tradition, Padmasambhava represented the *nirmāṇakāya* or Created Body of the Buddha, Avalokiteśvara his *sambhogakāya* or Body of Glory, and Amitābha his *dharmakāya* or Body of Absolute Reality. Thus the whole pagoda-type temple, with its shrine-rooms on three floors, and its three principal images, was in fact a three-dimensional representation of the *trikāya* or Triple Body of the Buddha – the same

Triple Body that, in the form of body, speech, and mind, was potentially present in every human being.

Having parted from Sangharatana and Dr Soft for the second time in little more than a month, I again crossed Teesta Bridge and again felt the Landrover swaying from side to side as we climbed up through the clouds to Kalimpong. I was well content with the week's work – so content, indeed, that the disappointments I had experienced in Gangtok now hardly seemed to matter. As a result of organizing the reception of the Sacred Relics I knew myself better than I had done three months ago and had a better understanding of my capabilities. It also seemed likely that the visit of the Sacred Relics had given Buddhism in Kalimpong the kind of boost it so badly needed – and that the work of the YMBA had been made correspondingly easier. If this was indeed the case there was no time to be lost. Our various social, cultural, and religious activities would have to be carried on more vigorously than ever and expanded in as many directions as possible. Contacts I had made through my work as General Secretary of the Reception Committee would have to be followed up, and more members and supporters enlisted. Above all, perhaps, we would have to start looking for more suitable premises from which to operate.

12
THE HERMITAGE

The Hermitage was situated at a bend of the road a few hundred yards short of Ninth Mile. I must have passed it more than once, but could not remember having noticed it before. This was not surprising, since it stood well back from the road, and on looking up all one saw against the hillside was a small wooden bungalow that had evidently known better days. It had not always been called the Hermitage. What it was originally called I do not know, but it had been built twenty years earlier by an Englishman, probably a missionary or a retired army officer, and had been untenanted for some time. Joe had come to know about it through Karka Bahadur, who had heard about it from his father, who had heard about it from his Hindu Newar mistress and her half-Sikkimese son, to whom it jointly belonged. It had first been offered to Joe himself, but since he did not like the place he had suggested it might do for me and the YMBA. So far as I was concerned, it would more than do. In fact I fell in love with the place as soon as I saw it. Joe therefore discussed the question of rent with Mrs Bishnumaya Pradhan and her son Tashi Tsering, who were so delighted with the idea of their bungalow being occupied by the English Buddhist monk who had recently organized the reception of the Sacred Relics that they declared themselves happy to take only sixty-five rupees a month. They also declared that they intended to rename the bungalow in my honour. In future it would be known as the Hermitage.

Like so many other buildings in Kalimpong, the bungalow into which I moved at the beginning of June stood on a narrow ledge that had been cut out of the hillside. In this case the ledge was rather broader than usual and was bounded at each end by a *jhora* or ravine in which grew clumps of bamboos. The Hermitage was situated at one end of the ledge (the one that was nearer the town), while at the other end stood an octagonal summer house. Between the Hermitage and the summer house, as well as all the way along the front of the property, was an extensive garden – or what had once been a garden – in which grew a variety of fine ornamental trees. There were magnolias and tulip trees, besides camellias and chocolate palms and a number of other trees whose names I did not yet know. There was also an ornamental pond in front of the summer house, circular in shape, and surrounded by a parapet.

The Hermitage itself was a simple frame building with a corrugated iron roof that had once been painted red. What colour the walls had been painted it was difficult to tell, for the paint had peeled off long ago, both inside and outside. Moreover, many of the boards that comprised the exterior walls of the bungalow had warped and shrunk to such an extent that light penetrated through the chinks into the rooms. There were also cracks between the floorboards, through which one could see the bare earth only a few inches below. Despite its semi-derelict condition, however, I was delighted with the place. It seemed to suit our requirements exactly. No sooner had the question of rent been settled, therefore, than the YMBA moved in from Banshi's Godown, and I moved in from Burma Raja's guest cottage.

There were five rooms, three of which opened directly onto the veranda, which was scarcely big enough to accommodate three chairs. In the middle one of these three, which extended from the veranda to the back of the house, we installed our ping-pong table, which filled practically the entire room, leaving only a narrow gap on either side and barely space enough at each end for the players. The front room on the left, which contained a plank bed, a rickety gate-legged table, and a kind of settle, became my bedroom and study, while the corresponding room on the right, which contained a small cabinet which had once been glass-fronted, became our library and reading room. The two smaller rooms at the back were reserved for guests. As for the summer house at the far end of the garden, which unlike the Hermitage was a pukka building, that is to say, constructed of reinforced concrete, this naturally became the shrine-room. Here I pinned up my Tibetan colour print of the Buddha, which apart from the miniature stupa was still the only religious object I possessed, and here I performed my devotions each morning and evening and meditated.

Before many days had passed I had settled in and was following much the same routine as I had followed before my departure from the Dharmodaya Vihara. I did not, however, go alms-gathering each morning. Gopal had moved to the Hermitage with me, and continued to do the cooking and shopping, though he was more painfully slow than ever and it was becoming obvious that I would soon have to start looking for a new cook bearer. Meanwhile, I had no alternative but to be patient with the old one and to get on with my work as best I could despite late breakfasts and even later lunches. As before, my day was divided into two approximately equal parts. The morning and early afternoon was taken up with my Buddhist studies and with literary work, including the work of editing and publishing *Stepping-Stones* (bundles of back issues of which were stacked on the floor of the library and reading room), while the late afternoon and early evening was devoted to giving individual tuition in various school and college subjects, as well as to developing my friendship with Sachin, Dawa, Padam, Lachuman, Jungi, and the other more regular members of the YMBA, all of whom were soon dropping in for a chat with me, or a game of ping-pong with one another, or even for a quiet browse through the Buddhist magazines we were receiving in exchange for *Stepping-Stones*, almost every evening of the week. By the time the next full-moon day came round, therefore, YMBA activities were flourishing even more vigorously at the Hermitage than they had done at Banshi's Godown, so that when we crowded into the shrine-room for our inaugural puja there was a sense of elation in the air. Our members were happy that we had more attractive premises, and that I was more easily accessible than I had been for a long time. I was happy that the YMBA and I were back under one roof, and that we had a place which could, I hoped, be developed into a spiritual centre the influence of which would be felt not only in Kalimpong but far afield.

But there was one thing about which I was not happy. Though glad to have moved into the Hermitage, I was not happy that my departure from Burma Raja's guest cottage should have upset Burma Raja and the Princess as much as it had done. On the morning of my departure they had invited me up to Panorama for a farewell meal. After taking the Refuges and Precepts they offered the various dishes one by one,

Members of the YMBA outside the Hermitage's octagonal shrine-room

in the traditional manner, and I spoke a few words about the Dharma. Then, when I had finished eating, and had chanted the usual verses of blessing, the Princess offered me some packets of gold leaf and Burma Raja his big, four-volume *Webster's New International Dictionary of the English Language* (Second Edition). I knew this dictionary very well, having frequently had occasion to consult it during the last six months. I also knew that it would be difficult for Burma Raja to manage without it, since he was a keen solver of crossword puzzles, and consulted the dictionary even more often than I did. But it was impossible to refuse the gift. It was also impossible to thank Burma Raja for it, that not being the Burmese Buddhist custom on such occasions. I therefore accepted the dictionary in silence, but I was deeply moved, and Burma Raja was moved too. Throughout the meal (which they did not, of course, share with me), both Burma Raja and the Princess had in fact been strangely silent, and Burma Raja had more than once wiped his eyes with the back of his sleeve. When I rose to go they both wept openly. For my part, though as a *bhikṣu* I was not expected to show any emotion, or even to feel any, I could not help a lump forming in my throat, and tears coming into my eyes, when I thought how much I owed to Burma Raja and the Princess. Despite their own troubles, they had taken me in when I was in difficulties and had nowhere to go. They had looked after me, they had treated me like a son, and I would be grateful to them for as long as I lived.

Though the farewell meal had further strengthened the bond between us, the fact that I was no longer living at the guest cottage naturally meant that I saw much less of Burma Raja and the Princess than before. It also meant that I saw much less of Mrs Mitter and Mrs Tagore and my other neighbours in that part of the Development Area. But if I saw less of my old neighbours I made up for it by making contact with the new neighbours that I had acquired by moving to the Hermitage. My nearest neighbour was Mrs Hamilton, who lived at Glengarry, on the opposite side of the road from the Hermitage. Since Glengarry was situated as much below the road as the Hermitage was above it, all I could see of the place was a strip of red-tiled roof that showed above the tall, neatly trimmed hedge. On the first few occasions that I encountered the grim-faced, grey-haired old woman standing at her front gate, or toiling up the road, she ignored me completely. Subsequently she glared at me through her spectacles, then she gave me a very distant nod, and finally she bestowed on me a frosty 'Good morning!' After that we got on extremely well. She showed me round her very English garden, where I saw a very un-English krait wriggling along between the pansies and petunias, and actually invited me into her very English bungalow for a very English tea. The contrast between the interior of Glengarry and the interior of the Hermitage could hardly have been more striking. I might have been in a drawing room in the Home Counties – except for the hovering Nepalese bearer and the ayah, not to mention the *mali* or gardener who came in with a bunch of roses for me to take back to the Hermitage with me.

After that I used to go down to Glengarry for my elevenses (which suited me better than afternoon tea) at least once every two or three weeks, and in her grim way Mrs Hamilton always seemed pleased to see me. Though she was not exactly communicative, I gathered that she lived alone (the five servants did not count, of course), that she was seventy-three years of age, and that she had a daughter in the UK High Commission in New Delhi and a son in the Pakistan Air Force. I also gathered that she had very decided views on the subject of servants, who were apparently getting more unreliable every year. Servants should be seen but not heard. They should know their place. Though one should, of course, always treat them fairly, one should never permit the slightest familiarity or, indeed, allow one's relationship with them to be anything other than that of master – or mistress – and servant. In particular, one should never *accept* anything from servants – by which she meant never accept the sweetmeats that Hindu servants were accustomed to offer their employers on the occasion of certain religious festivals. *She* never accepted anything from them. She refused even to *touch* what they brought, or even to allow it inside the house. If a servant of hers ever brought her anything she ordered them to give it to the beggars immediately. Accepting things from servants could prove disastrous. It placed one under an obligation to them, and if one allowed *that* to happen they would be sure to take advantage of it sooner or later.

But if Mrs Hamilton had very decided views on the subject of servants she also had no less decided views on the subject of their employers – especially if these happened to be Bengalis. I was walking with her in her garden one day and admiring the flowers, when Mrs Mitter's elderly Nepalese gardener – the same man who had brought me the curries and sweetmeats when I lived at the guest cottage, and was still in the Queen of Kalimpong's good books – came with a bundle of seedlings. They were from Mitter Memsahib, he explained, salaaming. Mrs Hamilton glared at him. 'She is *not* Mitter Memsahib,' she said sternly. 'She is Mitter *Babuni*.' 'Memsahib' was, of course, the term of respect used of a European married woman, and although some of the more Westernized Bengalis considered themselves to have succeeded to the social position formerly occupied by the British, people like Mrs Hamilton were not prepared to let them get away with such presumption. Not that she herself was really British. From her complexion, which was almost as dark as

Mrs Mitter's and much darker than Mrs Tagore's, her accent, and the fact that she appeared to have no memories of Britain, it was evident that Mrs Hamilton was in fact an Anglo-Indian, a person of mixed British and Indian descent, and most likely had never set eyes on the country to which she considered herself as belonging and with whose manners and customs she so strongly identified. But although it was evident that Mrs Hamilton was an Anglo-Indian, I knew there was no question of my ever alluding to the fact, much less still asking her about it. For most Anglo-Indians, the subject of their racial provenance was an extremely delicate one, and many of them still regarded it as a deadly insult to be treated as anything other than one-hundred-per-cent British in every respect.

Another delicate subject was that of religion. Being British Mrs Hamilton was naturally a member of the Church of England, but since there was no Anglican church in Kalimpong (which was divided fairly equally between the Church of Scotland Mission up near Tenth Mile and beyond and the Roman Catholic Mission down at Seventh Mile) she was dependent on the ministrations of the Anglican clergyman who came over from Darjeeling once every two or three months to take tea with, and give Holy Communion to, the town's four or five Anglican inhabitants. He was a very nice man, Mrs Hamilton assured me. *He never talked about religion.* This information she imparted to me quite early on in our acquaintance, from which I gathered that her views on the subject of religion were no less decided than her views on the subject of servants and on that of their uppity Bengali employers. Religion was something that nice people never talked about. The message was clear. If I wanted her to think me a nice man the subject of religion must never be mentioned between us. She would ignore the fact that I was a Buddhist, or whatever it was, and that I wore those strange yellow robes. We would talk about other things – like the growing unreliability of servants. Since I took the hint and never spoke about religion she must have thought me a nice man. All the Anglicans in Kalimpong, in fact, must have thought me a nice man, even though the Presbyterians and Catholics did not. At any rate, that other nice man, the Anglican clergyman from Darjeeling, came to see me not long afterwards. On this occasion he was not staying at Glengarry, he explained, as he usually did, but at the Blind School. He had heard quite a lot about me. Before he had set out from the Blind School, however, he added with a smile, Auntie Mary had warned him about me. 'Be very careful of that

English Buddhist monk,' she had said. 'He can be very charming.' Since we were both nice people, and inclined to be ecumenical, the elderly Anglican clergyman and I laughed heartily at this little joke at Auntie Mary's expense.

Not all my new neighbours were of the opinion that religion was something nice people never talked about. Mrs Crisp, for instance, talked about it a lot and in fact seemed to have quite an interest in the subject. She had changed her religion seventeen times, she told me airily. She had been a Roman Catholic, a Muslim, a Christian Scientist, and a lot of other things. She had even been a follower of the Ramakrishna Mission, although so far, she added thoughtfully, she had not been a Buddhist. Not that she had any intention of becoming one, of course. At present she and her son Esmond were Seventh Day Adventists, and she really believed she had at last found what she was looking for. How I came to know Flossie Crisp I no longer recollect. A short, plump, rather pig-faced woman of about fifty, with an abundance of greasy brown hair, she lived up the road from Mrs Hamilton, in a tiny cottage situated a short distance down the hillside, and in her usual unceremonious fashion must have accosted me on my way to or from the bazaar. Mrs Hamilton probably would not have thought her a nice person at all. Not only did she talk quite freely about religion, but she wore shabby old dresses, with down-at-heel shoes, and was obviously poorer than it was proper for a European to be in India. But Flossie Crisp did not care. She was an artist, she assured me in her rich Irish brogue, over a cup of tea at the Hermitage. She had painted hundreds of pictures. In fact, mother was an ARA, wasn't she, Esmond? Oh yes, her son responded eagerly, mother was an ARA all right. Flossie Crisp's accounts of herself and her doings were apt to punctuated in this way by appeals to Esmond for confirmation – confirmation that was invariably forthcoming and constituted her son's only contribution to the conversation, except for an occasional boyish remark. Tall and stooping, he wore a grey flannel suit that he had long outgrown, and from which his arms and legs protruded to a painful extent, together with an unpressed shirt, collar, and tie. He was also completely bald. How old he was it was difficult to tell: probably between twenty-five and thirty. Eventually it dawned on me that Esmond was, in fact, mentally retarded, and that his mental age was probably not more than twelve. But this was another delicate question, and I could no more ask Mrs Crisp about it than I could ask

Mrs Hamilton if she was an Anglo-Indian – though the former did once volunteer the information that 'poor old Esmond' was not very bright and had experienced difficulty finding a job. It also eventually dawned on me that even if Flossie Crisp was not Irish – for in the end I even doubted the genuineness of the rich Irish brogue – she must certainly have kissed the Blarney Stone not once but a hundred times.

Nonetheless, she was cheerful, good-natured, and amusing; her habit of romancing about herself and her doings did no harm to anyone – except, perhaps, the romancer, and I was always glad to see her and Esmond at the Hermitage and glad to have tea with them sometimes in the homely living room of their cottage. On one of these latter occasions she talked at length about the tiny Adventist Mission down near Seventh Mile of which she and Esmond were members, and about the elderly Dutch couple who were now running it. The Janssens, I gathered, were not nearly such nice people as their youthful American predecessors, whom I had myself met shortly after my arrival in Kalimpong and whom I had found much friendlier than any of the missionaries there. The Janssens just wanted to make life difficult for everybody. Though she and Esmond attended services every week, Mrs Crisp complained, with some bitterness, the Janssens were forever criticizing them, and accusing them of backsliding. In particular, they were forever criticizing them for drinking tea. (As I knew from my contact with the Janssens' American predecessors, the Seventh Day Adventists prohibited stimulants of every kind.) Nor was this all. When she had asked Mr Janssen what she should drink instead of tea, he had replied, 'Drink Ovaltine, Mrs Crisp. Drink Ovaltine.' She had nearly exploded. Did I know how much a tin of Ovaltine cost in a place like Kalimpong? (I didn't.) Well, it cost far more than she and Esmond could afford. It was easy enough for Mr Janssen to talk. He and his wife received enormous food parcels from America every month, and could drink as much Ovaltine as they liked without having to spend a *pie*.[48] But no one sent food parcels to her and Esmond. They had to drink tea, because that was all they could afford to drink. Anyway, even though she was a Seventh Day Adventist she liked her cup of tea, she added defiantly, replenishing our cups. These brave words were hardly out of her mouth when there came a sudden loud knock at the door. Mrs Crisp turned pale. 'My God!' she exclaimed, in a terrified whisper, 'It's the minister' – and promptly *hid the teapot*.

The incident gave me considerable food for thought, not only at the time but long afterwards. It was a perfect illustration of the way in which people can be controlled through the imposition of more or less arbitrary taboos the breaking of which gives rise to irrational feelings of guilt. If the taboo is of such a nature that it is almost certain to be broken, sooner or later, then the task of control is made much easier, for the power that imposes the taboo is also the power that absolves the breaker of the taboo from his feelings of irrational guilt – for a price. Drinking tea may not be very good for one's health, but it can hardly be considered a sin. Yet Mrs Crisp had been made to feel that it was a sin, or something so very much like a sin that the difference hardly mattered. When she heard Mr Janssen's knock she had actually experienced fear, at least for a moment: fear of being caught breaking a taboo; and to the extent that he could make her feel fear – fear based upon guilt – the minister had her under his control. It was also interesting that Mr Janssen had advised Mrs Crisp to drink Ovaltine, which he could afford and she could not. Evidently there were some taboos which could not be observed without money, and if they could not be observed without money then only the rich could be virtuous. The rich were, in fact, the virtuous, just as the poor were the sinners. Wealth was virtue, poverty was vice – equations that Joe regarded as typically American.

Typically American or not, they were equations with which at least one person whom I came to know at this time would have disagreed. This was Miss Rao. She was not a neighbour, and I came to know her not so much because I had moved to the Hermitage as because I had organized the reception of the Sacred Relics – or rather, because I had accompanied them on their visit to Mrs Samdup's flat in Chung Building. Like Mrs Crisp, Miss Rao talked about religion with a freedom that would have horrified Mrs Hamilton, though unlike Mrs Crisp she had never changed her religion. She had no need to. She was a Hindu, and firmly believed that all religions were the same because (as she was fond of explaining to her Buddhist and Christian friends) they were in fact nothing but different forms of Hinduism. Since Miss Rao lived in a flat on the second floor of Chung Building, it was therefore only natural that when the Sacred Relics were taken to Mrs Samdup's flat on the third floor Miss Rao should have been among the friends and neighbours who came and made offerings. It was also natural that she should have spoken to Sangharatana and myself, and still more natural that, a few weeks later, she should have invited me to have tea with her and her ailing mother, whom she very much wanted me to meet.

Though the shabby and congested flat at the back of Chung Building, overlooking the *mela* ground, bore little resemblance to Chitrabhanu, Mrs Rao herself was in certain respects the South Indian counterpart of Mrs Tagore. Like Mrs Tagore she was a woman of great dignity and sweetness of character who had evidently suffered much, and like Mrs Tagore she was rather emaciated. She was, however, not only considerably older than the high priestess of Santiniketan but also much more frail, though not as if recently recovered from a long illness but as if slowly succumbing to its effects. She had, in fact, not much longer to live, and though I did not know this it was obvious that the gentle, quietly spoken old Brahmin lady from Mysore was glad to be able to talk to someone about more serious matters, as well as to share her fears and anxieties with regard to her unmarried daughter and the unemployed son whom I had not yet seen.

As I listened to Mrs Rao, I could not help thinking how little resemblance there was between her and Miss Rao. Mother and daughter were, in fact, exact opposites in almost every respect, and it was difficult to believe that they were related at all. One could only assume that Miss Rao resembled her father, who had died some years previously and about whom she often spoke. Daddy had been the manager of a large and important bank. They had been extremely rich and had moved in the highest social circles. She herself had been brought up with the daughters of the Maharaja of Mysore, and was in and out of the Palace day and night. But Daddy had died and they had lost all their wealth – or nearly all of it. They had been swindled. Banks in which they had deposited their money had failed. Now they were as poor as church mice. That was why they were having to live in a place like Chung Building, and put up with a landlady like Mrs Samdup. Oh yes, didn't I know? Mrs Samdup was the owner of Chung Building. She had been married for a while to Mr Chung, the Chinaman who had built the place – though that was a long time ago, and no one knew what had happened to Mr Chung. But as she was saying, now they were as poor as church mice and she and her mother could hardly make both ends meet. She only wished I could have seen them in Mysore, before Daddy's death, when I would have been astonished by their pomp and grandeur. Why, in those days they had been simply *rolling* in wealth. This was a favourite phrase of Miss Rao's, and one with which she so often concluded her accounts of the past glories of the House of Rao, that I was eventually left with a mental picture of the whole Rao family actually rolling in enormous heaps of gold, kicking their heels in the air with delight as they did so.

But although Mrs Rao and her daughter were opposites in almost every respect, it was in personal appearance that they differed most strikingly. Whereas there was nothing in the least unusual about Mrs Rao, Miss Rao presented a truly extraordinary sight. To begin with, she was hardly more than four feet tall, with a head that was a little too big for her body, and was invariably swathed in a gaudily coloured sari that was much too large for her. She was, indeed, the only Indian woman I had ever seen who did not wear a sari elegantly. On top of her sari she wore a woollen cardigan, also gaudily coloured, while her head and shoulders were completely covered by a kind of wimple, from which there looked out a little black face with quick-darting, suspicious eyes and a large, sensual mouth. On special days, such as when Miss Rao came to see me at the Hermitage, the little black face would be thickly covered with white powder, which gave it a purplish tinge, and the large, sensual mouth liberally smeared with bright red lipstick. Miss Rao also wore a pair of brown plimsolls, and when she went out her costume would be completed by a battered leather handbag, gloves that had split at the seams, various rings, brooches, and necklaces, a knitted scarf or two, and, occasionally, an old fur boa.

Cutting the fantastic figure that she did, it was hardly surprising that Miss Rao should be well known to quite a number of people in Kalimpong, at least by sight. It was also hardly surprising that she should be the subject of a certain amount of speculation. According to my students, the speculation centred on her wimple, which was held in position by hairpins, and which no one had ever seen her without. Some people were of the opinion that Miss Rao wore the wimple because she was bald, others that she wore it because her hair was, in fact, only a wig. A third school of thought, which was the one most favoured by the students themselves, maintained that Miss Rao wore the wimple because she had no ears. Which of these explanations was the right one, or whether they were all wrong and Miss Rao wore the wimple for an entirely different reason, it was really impossible to say. It was also impossible to ask Miss Rao herself to clear up the mystery, for it was obvious that here was yet another of those delicate questions I had already encountered with Mrs Hamilton and Mrs Crisp. Not that I was particularly concerned to know why Miss Rao wore a wimple. That was her own affair. But knowing as I did how upper caste Hindus felt about any kind of physical blemish or defect, especially in a woman, I was well aware that life might have been made difficult for her in more ways than one. I therefore resolved that, even though there was something about Miss Rao that I found quite repulsive, I would go on seeing her and her mother and help them in whatever way I could.

While I was busy making new friends, however, I was suddenly deprived of an old friend. One morning Thubden Tendzin arrived at the Hermitage with the news that within the next few days he would be leaving Kalimpong and returning to England. Why he was leaving he did not say, and I did not ask, though I knew he was well settled in Kalimpong and had been looking forward to staying there indefinitely. It was only too evident that the whys and wherefores of his departure belonged with all the other delicate questions I had recently encountered in Kalimpong and which seemed to crop up there with such frequency. In any case, from remarks that had been made by the Long-Lived Deva I knew that the Government of India was well aware that something was going on 'behind the scenes' at Thubden Tendzin's bungalow and that it was not very happy with what my universalist friend did when he disappeared down the tunnel that led from the back of his 'cave of treasures' into the darkness. Like my own chance of accompanying the Sacred Relics to Tibet, Thubden Tendzin's continued stay in Kalimpong was being sacrificed along with the freedom and independence of Tibet on the altar of Sino-Indian friendship. The mysterious activities of which the tunnel was the venue were ultimately connected with the Tibetan resistance movement, and since this was a connection that the Government of India was not prepared to tolerate Thubden Tendzin had been asked to leave Kalimpong.

I was sorry to see him go. Since the departure of the Sacred Relics we had seen quite a lot of each other and had paid several more visits to the Tharpa Choling Gompa. On one of these visits we had witnessed the ceremony of reconciliation between the two parties that, as I had heard from the Long-Lived Deva, had been formed among the monks some time previously, with such disastrous results. The ceremony took place in the grassy courtyard in front of the monastery temple. Somewhat to my surprise, if not to Thubden Tendzin's, the forty or fifty monks, headed by our old friend the abbot, all sat together on the bare ground, while the Tibetan government officials sat on richly carpeted chairs – something that would have been quite unthinkable in a Theravāda Buddhist country. One of the officials read out a letter from the Dalai Lama, white ceremonial scarves were exchanged, and after the monks had been harangued at great length by Mr Tharchin, who of course was a Christian, everybody filed into the temple for a puja. On another visit we had the opportunity of meeting the Gyalmo Chenmo, or Great Royal Mother, that is to say, the mother of the Dalai Lama, who was spending a few weeks in Kalimpong before carrying on with her pilgrimage to Bodh Gaya. We met her in the abbot's room. A tall, stout woman of great natural dignity and evident kindliness, she was magnificently dressed in a *chuba* of Chinese silk brocade and wore on her head a tall gold brocade cap with enormous projecting earflaps lined with fur. Thubden Tendzin was thoroughly captivated by her, and afterwards spoke of her with tremendous enthusiasm – and indeed she was all that one would expect the mother of a Dalai Lama to be. Apparently Mr Tharchin had also been captivated by her. According to Thubden Tendzin he had come away from a meeting with her shaking his head and exclaiming, 'What a wonderful woman! Just think, she is the mother of *three* incarnations!' – the Great Royal Mother having given birth not only to the Dalai Lama himself but to two other sons who had also been recognized as 'incarnate lamas'. Thubden Tendzin was inclined to think that Tharchin's outburst showed that he was, at heart, very much a Buddhist, but personally I found this difficult to believe. So far as I could see, the editor of the *Tibet Mirror*, though amiable enough, was a victim of chronic mental confusion, and did not really know where he stood.

Before Thubden Tendzin left Kalimpong we agreed to correspond, and he presented me with a Tibetan rug, a Bhutanese copper-and-brass jug, a silver coffee pot, and seven battered aluminium puja bowls. The Tibetan rug, which was predominantly dark blue in colour, was beginning to fray at the edges; but Thubden Tendzin explained that it was a rather special rug, since it had been made for him in Gyantse before the War, and was the first one he had commissioned from the master rug-maker with whose help he had subsequently tried to revive what was by that time a rapidly dying art. It was, of course, made of wool, and the dyes that had been used in its manufacture were all of natural origin. He also offered me a choice of *thangkas* or painted scrolls. I could either have a set of three *thangkas* depicting the Buddha with Śāriputra and Maudgalyāyana and the sixteen *arhants*, the brocade mounts of which were badly torn, or a single *thangka* depicting the wrathful Vajrapāṇi, which was in somewhat better condition. Though I was very much attracted by the figure of the wrathful Vajrapāṇi, which indeed affected me in much the same way as the giant image of Padmasambhava I had seen in Darjeeling, on reflection I decided to take the set of three *thangkas* instead. The wrathful Vajrapāṇi or 'Thunderbolt-in-hand' was, as I knew, a specifically Tantric divinity, and pictorial representations of him were, like the pictorial representations of other such divinities, not works of art in the modern Western sense but aids to the visualization of his flame-encircled and awe-inspiring form in meditation. Since I was not practising this kind of meditation, which I was indeed not qualified to practise (not having received the appropriate Tantric initiations), and since the *thangkas* were in any case not to be treated simply as decorations, it did not seem right for me to have in my possession a *thangka* depicting the wrathful Vajrapāṇi or any other specifically Tantric divinity. The *thangkas* depicting the Buddha with Śāriputra and Maudgalyāyana and the sixteen *arhants* were another matter. Representing as they did not Tantric deities but historical personalities the beautifully painted scrolls were not aids to visualization so much as an incitement to the living of the spiritual life in the widest sense, and as such they were well suited to my present needs. Beneath the benign gaze of the Buddha who, flanked by his two chief disciples, occupied the upper half of the centre scroll, the sixteen shaven-headed, yellow-robed *arhants* were travelling across the sea on the backs of all kinds of strange land and marine monsters. According to legend, they had been forced to leave Kashmir due to persecution and were now on their way to China to preach the Dharma to the people of that country.

In choosing the *thangkas* depicting the Buddha with Śāriputra and Maudgalyāyana and the sixteen *arhants*, rather than the one depicting the wrathful Vajrapāṇi, I was of course acting in accordance with Buddhist tradition; but there was at least one Western Buddhist in Kalimpong to whom tradition meant very little, and who had no qualms whatever about using *thangkas* of Tantric divinities as decorations, or even for stranger purposes. Joe was by this time living up at Tirpai, with a well-to-do Sherpa family, and visited the Hermitage only occasionally, usually for the full-moon day puja or when I gave a lecture. The first time he saw my newly acquired *thangkas*, which I had hung on the wall beside my bed (the summer house shrine was too damp for them at that time of year) he turned away with a contemptuous sniff and a dismissive wave of the hand after only a cursory inspection. I should have taken the other *thangka*, he declared irritably, with an air that suggested that in his usual headstrong fashion the youthful and inexperienced Sangharakshita had once again done the wrong thing due to lack of proper advice and guidance. Anyone could see with half an eye that a single large figure would have looked better on the wall than a number of small ones. Not that *he* cared what *thangka* I chose, he added sharply, glaring at me through his spectacles as though I had accused him of such a weakness. So far as he was concerned I could choose what *thangkas* I liked. But I should not think I was the only one in Kalimpong who was acquiring *thangkas*. He too had started acquiring them, though in his case, of course, there was no one to give them to him, much less still offer him a choice. If *he* wanted a *thangka* he had to buy it himself. In fact he had recently commissioned a small painted scroll from a Tibetan artist who lived at Tirpai. Next time I passed by on my way to the *gompa* I should drop in and have a look at it. It might broaden my outlook.

On my next visit to the Tharpa Choling Gompa, therefore, I made a point of calling on Joe at the downstairs flat he and Dil Bahadur occupied in Sherpa Building. The *thangka* he had commissioned was not mounted on brocade but framed in Western style, and it hung just inside the door of the flat, where it was most likely to catch the eye of the visitor. Like the single *thangka* that Thubden Tendzin had offered me, it depicted the wrathful Vajrapāṇi, and it depicted him in much the same way. There was the same stout, dark blue body, naked except for a garland of skulls, the same aureole of flames, the same expression of terrific anger. The only difference was that Joe's Vajrapāṇi was depicted with an erect penis. This was, I knew, a perfectly traditional way of representing the bodhisattva of Power and, in fact, a number of other wrathful as distinct from peaceful Tantric divinities as well. The erect penis symbolized the arisen or awakened *bodhicitta*, the aspiration to Supreme Enlightenment for the sake of all living beings, but from Joe's cackle of amusement as I stopped to look at the painting it was clear that he had commissioned it not as a means of reminding himself about the *bodhicitta* but rather in order to shock the unwary visitor. To him the erect blue penis was simply an erect penis, and since erect penises of whatever colour were not usually depicted in art the sight of the painting could be expected to have all sorts of interesting effects on people.

What effect it had on me, apart from broadening my outlook, it would be difficult to say. Certainly I was not shocked, and Joe had to be satisfied with telling me, over a cup of tea, how extremely shocked some of his other visitors had been when they set eyes on his wrathful Vajrapāṇi. A woman missionary from Dr Graham's Homes who had seen it had been so shocked that she actually screamed. As he told me the story Joe crossed and uncrossed his legs, and rocked himself backwards and forwards in his chair, with undisguised glee; but though I could share his amusement at the missionary's reaction to the painting, at least to some extent, I was far from sympathizing with his underlying attitude. The use to which he had put his wrathful Vajrapāṇi represented a serious devaluation of the sexual symbolism of the Tantras, not to say a degradation. Unfortunately, it was a devaluation that was to become increasingly common among Western Buddhists as the artistic expressions of that symbolism became more widely known. In Joe's case the devaluation was obviously mixed up with all sorts of personal factors, the precise nature of which was a delicate question. I therefore confined myself to assuring him that contrary to what his remarks at the Hermitage had implied I had started acquiring *thangkas* only in the sense that I had not acquired any previously. How long it would be before I acquired others I did not know. *Thangkas* were extremely expensive, and I could certainly not think of commissioning a Tibetan artist to paint one for me as he had done.

But if I had not started acquiring *thangkas* I had started acquiring religious objects of a more modest kind. I had started acquiring Tibetan wood blocks of the various Buddhas and bodhisattvas and other divinities. Most of them were about ten inches long and eight inches wide and less than an inch in thickness, and they were used for producing crude prints for the household shrines of those who were too poor to afford anything more elaborate. I had started acquiring them – even, it must be admitted, collecting them – partly because I was attracted by their very roughness and simplicity and partly because I was not in a position to buy either images or *thangkas*. I bought them from the same little Tibetan curio shop in Darjeeling where, only six years earlier, when I was still in the army, I had bought a Moghul miniature painting to send to Clare Cameron, the enigmatic editor of the *Middle Way*, the quarterly journal of the London Buddhist Society.[49] Though the ink-stained blocks cost no more than seven or eight rupees apiece, even this modest sum was often beyond my means, and I had to leave the shop without having bought anything. Not that the grey-haired Tibetan proprietor seemed to mind. He always greeted me with a bow and a warm smile when I entered his shop, and gave me a bow and an equally warm smile when I left.

The reason why I was able to buy Tibetan wood blocks at Tashi Pemba's little shop in Mackenzie Road was that shortly before moving into the Hermitage I had started paying regular visits to Darjeeling. The purpose of these visits was not to add to my collection of wood blocks, however, or even to add to my collection of books. As a result of the reception that the town had given the Sacred Relics at the beginning of April there had been in Darjeeling, as in Kalimpong, a definite upsurge of interest in Buddhism, and I wanted to take advantage of this upsurge before it had time to subside. While the Sacred Relics were still in Darjeeling I had, in fact, called a preliminary meeting of young Buddhists (that is, Buddhists under forty) to consider the possibility of opening a branch of the YMBA there. After I had briefly outlined the aims and objects of the Association it was unanimously resolved that a branch of the YMBA should be established in Darjeeling and that a second meeting should be held for the election of office-bearers. At this second meeting, which took place two weeks later, I again outlined the aims and objects of the Association and a committee was elected with one of the ubiquitous Mr Lamas as President and another as Secretary. The committee then resolved that regular meetings should be held, if possible every Sunday, and that efforts should be made to secure premises at an early date. On my next two visits to Darjeeling, which took place in June and August, I gave two public lectures on Buddhism at the Brahma Samaj Hall, as well as a lecture on 'The Purpose of Education' at the Government College, with the Bengali principal of which I was soon on friendly terms. The two public lectures, in particular, aroused considerable interest. They were the first I had given in the town and, I suspected, the first that had been given there on Buddhism for a very long time. At any rate, they were of sufficient rarity for the town's leading citizens to be there in force, from the Bengali Deputy Commissioner and his wife downwards. In the first lecture I took a very broad view, and besides attempting to cover the whole field of Buddhism surveyed its relation to the modern world in general and India in particular. In the second lecture, confining myself to a more specific theme, I sought to elucidate the threefold significance of the term 'Dharma'.

Yet despite these visits, and despite the undoubted success of my lectures – despite committee meetings, and talks with the Mr Lamas and other friends – the Darjeeling branch of the YMBA never succeeded in establishing itself in the way I had hoped. Not a single Sunday meeting was held, and no premises were ever secured. So long as I was actually there in Darjeeling, and in personal contact with people, it was all right. There would be plenty of enthusiasm, and many promises to organize this or that activity. But no sooner was I back in Kalimpong than everything would collapse like a house of cards – until my next visit. Strange to say, it was much the same story in Gangtok. There too a definite upsurge of interest in Buddhism had taken place as a result of the reception given to the Sacred Relics, and there too a branch of the YMBA had been formed, with no less a person than the Crown Prince as President. The Crown Prince had, in fact, given the branch the use of a room in the bazaar. But after a few months everything had collapsed in Gangtok too. The young Sikkimese who had been appointed Assistant Secretary, and who was effectively in charge, stopped replying to my letters, and I subsequently learned that he was generally too drunk to do either that or anything else. In these circumstances I could not help wondering how long even the Kalimpong YMBA would survive if I was away for any length of time. Joe was fast losing interest, and our members were as yet too young and too inexperienced to be able to manage on their own. Sooner or later I would have to give serious thought to the whole question of the future of our activities in the area.

Giving lectures and attending committee meetings was not the only purpose of my visits to Darjeeling, however. *Stepping-Stones* was now being printed not at the Mani Press, Kalimpong, but at the Mani Printing Press, Darjeeling, and though our new printers were not only cheaper than the old ones but more efficient I thought it best to see them personally from time to time. Unfortunately, in transferring our custom in this way I had unwittingly become embroiled in a bitter family feud. The Mani Press had been started by three Hindu Newar brothers, all of whose personal names terminated in 'mani', meaning jewel or pearl. After they had carried on the business together for a few years, a split had occurred between the two younger brothers and the eldest brother, and the former, after a particularly violent quarrel, had driven the eldest out and deprived him of his share of the business. Vowing revenge, this brother had moved to Darjeeling and founded the Mani Printing Press. Since he was a man of considerable energy, and moreover one who combined business acumen with literary talent, he had soon built the new press up into one of the leading printing and publishing houses in the district. Having done this, he had started systematically enticing his brothers' customers away from them and was now, by this means, steadily achieving his declared objective of driving them out of business. He had enticed his brothers' customers away from them by the simple expedient of offering to do their work at the Calcutta rate, which was considerably less than the local rate, and the YMBA was one of those that had been so enticed. When they heard that they had lost our custom to their elder brother, and that *Stepping-Stones* would in future be printed not in Kalimpong but in Darjeeling, the two brothers at the Mani Press were not only very dismayed but even quite angry. But I soon pacified them. Assuring them that there was no question of our being dissatisfied with their work, I told them frankly that the financial position of the YMBA was such that I had no alternative but to get our printing done as cheaply as I could. Since they had no difficulty in appreciating this, and since I settled their bill without too much delay, before many months had passed friendly relations had been restored, though it was noticeable that the elder of the two brothers never treated me with quite the same cordiality as he had done in the days when *Stepping-Stones* was being printed in Kalimpong.

Compared with some of the other customers that the enterprising founder of the Mani Printing Press had succeeded in enticing away from his two brothers, the YMBA was of very little consequence; but Parasmani Pradhan (as he was called) was pleased to be printing *Stepping-Stones* all the same, and for reasons that were not entirely connected with the family feud. In the first issue that he had printed for us there had appeared an announcement to the effect that from the following month a special Nepali section, containing articles on Himalayan religion, culture, and education, besides translations of the teachings of the Buddha, would be published in *Stepping-Stones* every month. This was exactly the kind of project that Parasmani Pradhan, as a zealous champion of Nepali language and literature, was most anxious to encourage, and besides printing our now bilingual magazine he therefore also made sure that the Nepali Section was up to standard from the literary point of view. We had started publishing this Nepali section for very definite reasons. Though Nepali was the *lingua franca* of the Darjeeling district, as well as the national language of Nepal, so far as I had been able to ascertain there existed in Nepali not a single book on Buddhism and not a single Buddhist magazine. A deficiency as serious as this clearly had to be made good without delay, at least to a limited extent, for it was obvious that unless the millions of Nepali-speaking Buddhists were able to study the Buddha's teachings in their own language there was little hope of their being able to understand and practise those teachings, and little hope that the YMBA or any other Buddhist organization would be able to make much headway among them.

The expansion of *Stepping-Stones* into a bilingual magazine naturally entailed a certain amount of extra work and, therefore, a certain amount of reorganization. After some rather protracted discussions and negotiations an editorial board had been set up consisting of myself as editor, Bhaichand Pradhan as assistant editor, with special responsibility for the Nepali section, and Rudramani Pradhan and Sachindra Coomar Singh as members. Rudramani Pradhan was the public-spirited young civil engineer who had accosted me on my almsround more than a year earlier and who had arranged for me to give a lecture at Pedong. Though not one of our regular members, he came to see me from time to time, and I could always rely on his help in an emergency. As the eldest of Parasmani's eight sons (the one who was *not* engaged in the printing and publishing trade), there were at least a few drops of printer's ink in his veins, despite the fact that he preferred inspecting roads to checking proofs, and he was glad to cooperate with us in our new undertaking. Bhaichand Pradhan was not a member of the YMBA at all. Sachin, Padam, and various other friends had more than once tried to persuade him to join but hitherto he had always refused. So far as I could tell, his aloofness was due partly to the fact that he was eight or ten years older than the majority of our members, and had no wish to be seen associating with a pack of boys, and partly because he was afraid of falling under my influence and thus compromising his independence. In appearance he was not only extremely tall but so thin that the tight-fitting Nepali costume he invariably wore made him look positively skeletal. His face was long and cadaverous, with deep furrows down either side of the mouth, but his eyes were bright and his expression was one of exceptional intelligence and good humour. Since he was an arts graduate, he had naturally gravitated to teaching, and in fact taught Nepali at the local Government High School, which was situated next door to the Hermitage (on the bazaar side) but hidden away behind so dense a screen of bamboos, and so thick a mass of giant rhododendrons, that I rarely heard any other sound than that of the school bell. Though not yet thirty, Bhaichand Pradhan was already known as something of a littérateur, and much of his spare time was spent writing articles and poems for Nepali magazines and attending Nepali literary conferences. His companion in these pursuits was a small, meek-looking Nepali poetess called Sanumati Rai, whom he visited every evening at her home behind a vegetable shop in the High Street, and with whom he was reputedly carrying on a highly platonic love affair.

Love affair or no, his connections with the Nepali literary scene made Bhaichand Pradhan the obvious choice as editor of the Nepali section of *Stepping-Stones* and his name came up more and more frequently in our discussions. But how was the stand-offish young littérateur to be persuaded to accept the position? In the end Rudramani undertook to approach him and, with the help of a certain amount of cajolery, eventually succeeded in overcoming his resistance and inducing him to accept our invitation to join the editorial board of *Stepping-Stones*. Bhaichand did not accept the invitation without laying down certain conditions, the chief of which was that he should not have to join the YMBA and not be expected to take part in any of its activities. On the whole this arrangement worked quite well. Though he continued to be extremely wary of any personal contact, Bhaichand was a conscientious and reliable editor, and the Nepali section of *Stepping-Stones* was soon well known to the Nepali-speaking Buddhists of the area. Despite the fact that it consisted of no more than eight or ten pages, it was quite varied in content. There were translations from the Pāli Buddhist scriptures, articles on various aspects of Tibetan Buddhism (some of them translated from English), editorials, news items, and a generous sprinkling of poems by Sanumati Rai.[50]

Among the Pāli Buddhist texts that I was most anxious to see translated into Nepali was the *Dhammapada*, and it was not long before excerpts from this celebrated scripture began appearing in the

Nepali section of our little magazine. Space, however, was limited; only half a dozen verses could be published in each issue, and I calculated that at this rate it would take us seven or eight years to bring out the entire work. This was much too long. Since Bhaichand was making good progress with the translation, I therefore decided that we would bring it out in book form, together with the original Pāli text, without further delay. But from where were we to get the necessary funds? At least 2,000 rupees would be needed; we had no wealthy backers, and I already knew how difficult it was to collect donations for our work. In these circumstances I bethought myself of the distinguished devotee and staunch supporter of the Maha Bodhi Society to whose flat on the third floor of the Chung Building Sangharatana and I had taken the Sacred Relics. Perhaps Mrs Rose Samdup would help. I accordingly went to see her. She received me with much fluttering of eyelashes and a good deal of confusion at the honour I had done her by visiting her humble abode, and after we had talked about the Sacred Relics, and she had offered me tea, I explained the purpose of my visit. The small, plump Tibetan woman was all sympathy, and listened to me wide-eyed, her clasped hands pressed tightly to her bosom. How wonderful it would be to have the *Dhammapada* in Nepali! She would be able to read it herself at last. She had to admit that she was really rather naughty, she added, wriggling her broad hips; though she was Tibetan (well, a Darjeeling-born Tibetan!) she was unable to read or write Tibetan properly and therefore could not study the Tibetan Buddhist scriptures. They were very difficult anyway, weren't they? It would be such a comfort to have the *Dhammapada* in Nepali. Of course she would help me. But 2,000 rupees was an awful lot of money; she was very poor, and had all sorts of expenses to meet. Buildings had to be repaired. Tenants didn't pay their rent. Anyway, she would think about the matter and see what she could do. Would I mind coming again in two or three days time?

Two or three days later, therefore, I again climbed the flights of dirty stone steps that led to Mrs Samdup's flat. Again she received me with much fluttering of eyelashes, though this time with only a fair amount of modest confusion, and after she had given me tea we had the same conversation, with minor variations, that we had had on my previous visit. In the course of the following month this performance was repeated at least five or six more times, and I began to wonder if the distinguished devotee and staunch supporter of the Maha Bodhi

Society was really quite so sympathetic as she appeared. Perhaps in some ways I *was* rather young and inexperienced, not to say naive, as Joe had always maintained. Anyway, since she continued to ask me to come again 'in two or three days time' I continued to climb the stairs of Chung Building, though I now did so at somewhat longer intervals, sometimes combining a visit to Mrs Samdup on the third floor with a visit to Miss Rao and her mother on the second. In the course of these visits I not only drank innumerable cups of tea, and stayed to lunch once or twice, but also came to know a little more about Mrs Samdup. Her name was not really Rose, she informed me, simperingly. Rose was what she had been called at school, on account of her beauty, and the name had stuck to her ever since. And indeed, though her black hair was now streaked with grey, though she had bad teeth, and though her pink cheeks were wrinkled like an old apple, the dumpy, bespectacled little woman in the shabby blue *chuba* and the faded and stained rainbow apron really did look as though she had once deserved her name. But if the flower itself had faded its perfume lingered on. The perfume was charm. The fact was that despite her comparatively advanced years Mrs Samdup possessed charm to a truly extraordinary degree, though perhaps it would be more correct to say not that she possessed charm but that she emanated it. It emanated not only from the ingratiating manner and the winning smile, but from every coaxing, wheedling word she spoke and every shy, shrinking, submissive, insinuating movement of her now somewhat corpulent person. Whether leaning her head to one side as she listened to what one was saying, or bending forward to offer one a toffee, or even asking one for the fifth or sixth time if one would mind coming again 'in a few days' time' Mrs Samdup emanated charm from her very fingertips. It was in fact amazing that so much charm could co-exist with so much scruffiness, both in her own person and in her immediate surroundings.

This charm was not very much in evidence in the three members of her family who lived with her at Chung Building. Indeed, they did not resemble Mrs Samdup in any way and had one not known that they were, in fact, closely related to her, one would never have guessed. This was particularly true in the case of her son, a bright and intelligent-looking twelve-year-old with typically Bengali features and complexion who was evidently growing up very fast. 'The Tibetan women have already started taking an interest in him,' his mother informed me, with an air of great complacency, though the boy himself only scowled. In the case of her daughter, a thin, shy little girl of about six, the features and complexion were not typically Bengali but typically Chinese, and her lank black hair was cut straight across the forehead in Chinese fashion. Both son and daughter wore Western dress. Not so the third other member of the family. This was a stooping, lantern-jawed crone who shuffled around in a *chuba* that was even shabbier, and a rainbow apron that was even more faded and stained, than Mrs Samdup's own, and she clearly had never possessed either beauty or charm at any stage of her career. From the fact that she seemed to be responsible for such cooking and cleaning as were carried on in the establishment, as well as from the fact that Mrs Samdup spoke to her quite sharply at times, I concluded that the toothless old creature was a servant of some kind; but on my second or third visit to Chung Building the supposed servant was introduced, with all Mrs Samdup's usual charm, as her respected mother. Having been introduced (or rather identified) the respected mother stood grinning and bowing for a minute and then shuffled back into the kitchen.

Her twelve-year-old son, her six-year-old daughter, and her old mother, were not the only members of Mrs Samdup's family. As I learned some time later, she had two grown up sons living in Darjeeling but so deeply ashamed were they of their mother that they refused to have anything to do with her. These sons, who by all accounts were very decent young men, were Mrs Samdup's sons by her first husband, a Sikkimese nobleman who had divorced her after she had committed adultery with his Bengali lawyer. It was this Bengali lawyer who was the father of the twelve-year-old son who lived with Mrs Samdup at Chung Building. The six-year-old daughter's father was a certain Mr Chung of Calcutta, though Mr Chung had denied this, and Mrs Samdup had had to go to the *cutchery* and swear to the fact of his paternity in order to get possession of Chung Building on behalf of her daughter. Since this had involved admitting in open court that she had had sexual relations with Mr Chung while still married to another man, Mrs Samdup had in effect publicly proclaimed herself a whore, a piece of brazenness for which she had been roundly condemned in Kalimpong. She was a shameless woman, and her morals were those of the barnyard. But Mrs Samdup cared no more about what people thought of her morals than Mrs Crisp cared what people thought of her shabby old dresses and her down-at-heel shoes. Like her good friend Rani Dorji, all Mrs Samdup really cared about was money.

Though the Sikkimese nobleman might have been the first of Mrs Samdup's conquests, Mr Chung of Calcutta had certainly not been the last. According to local report, Mrs Samdup had been married, in one way or another, no fewer than thirty-seven times. Strange to say, she had emerged from every one of these matrimonial adventures the better off by a house, or some valuable pieces of jewellery, or a substantial cash settlement. She was thus quite a rich woman, and all the more so because she never spent any money if she could help it and never parted with anything she had acquired except on terms highly advantageous to herself. Though only a Darjeeling-born Tibetan, and the daughter of a Darjeeling-born Tibetan (her father had been a pork butcher), Mrs Samdup had all the strong commercial instincts of her native Tibetan ancestors. Buying and selling were in her blood, so to speak, and she had the reputation of being an even better businesswoman that Rani Dorji, for whereas Rani Dorji was sometimes restrained by considerations of social prestige Mrs Samdup never was. Indeed, Mrs Samdup had the reputation of being such a good businesswoman that she could cheat even the Marwaris – which in Kalimpong business circles was the ultimate accolade. Whether she managed to cheat the Marwaris by exclusively commercial means, or whether she also employed some of her other skills, it was difficult to say. In any case, Mrs Samdup handled all her complicated business and financial transactions herself, and could often be seen hastening either up the High Street in the direction of the bazaar or down it in the direction of the *cutchery*. On these occasions she would be clad in the same shabby blue *chuba*, and the same faded and stained rainbow apron, that she wore indoors, though with the addition of a pair of men's black lace-up shoes. She always walked with her head bent forward, as though she was deep in thought, and with her rather large rump jutting out behind. Such was her reputation in the town that she was rarely accosted by anybody. Nepalese and Indians (though not Tibetans) often spat as she passed by. Indeed, it was said that the more orthodox among them held her in such abhorrence that if they happened to meet her first thing in the morning, when they were on their way to settle any matter of importance, they turned back and went home. The sight of an immoral woman – especially a woman as immoral as Mrs Samdup – was an inauspicious omen, and brought bad luck for the rest of the day.

But long before I learned all these things I had stopped visiting

Chung Building, or at least stopped visiting the flat on the third floor. After I had been there seven or eight times, and had been asked seven or eight times if I would mind coming again 'in two or three days time', Miss Rao happened to mention that when she had gone upstairs the previous day to pay the month's rent Mrs Samdup had spoken to her about me. 'That English monk keeps coming to see me,' she had tittered, no doubt with her usual charm. 'I'm sure I don't know what he wants.' Realizing that the distinguished devotee and staunch supporter of the Maha Bodhi Society was trying to spin some kind of web around me, and that she was not really interested in helping me bring out the Nepali *Dhammapada* in book form, I stopped going to see her and started looking for help elsewhere. I was still doing this, not very successfully, when Gyan Jyoti came and told me he had finished writing up the accounts of the Sacred Relics Reception Committee and that there was a surplus of nearly 2,000 rupees. What were we to do with the money? It did not take me long to call a meeting of the Committee and to propose that the amount should be donated to the YMBA for the purpose of bringing out a Nepali translation of the *Dhammapada*, nor did it take the committee long to agree to my proposal. A few months later, therefore, the translation of the *Dhammapada* made its appearance in book form, and Nepali-speaking Buddhists were at last able to study the whole of this celebrated scripture in their own language. In the meantime, however, Mrs Samdup had sent me a bundle of grubby currency notes and a few lines scribbled in pencil on a scrap of paper torn from a school exercise book. 'Here is fifty rupees for your Nepali *Dhammapada*,' she wrote. 'I am sure the printers will do the work for this amount if you bargain with them a little.'

13
KINDRED SPIRITS

At the time of my moving into the Hermitage the two owners of the property were engaged in constructing at the other end of the garden, between the summer house and the road, a small wooden chalet. About a month later it was finished; the corrugated iron roofing had been painted the usual dark red and the walls a pleasant lime green. Flanked as it was by the summer house, and backed by the thirty- and forty-foot bamboos that grew in the *jhora*, it presented an idyllic appearance. But by whom would it be occupied? If it was occupied by a family – and Bishnumaya Pradhan and her son had obviously constructed the chalet as a source of income – there was every possibility that the peace and seclusion of the place would be seriously disrupted. With Joe as an intermediary, I therefore entered into negotiations with the two owners and eventually succeeded in renting the chalet from them for twenty rupees a month, so that we were now paying them eight-five rupees a month. The additional expenditure would certainly stretch our resources, but by this time I had conceived the idea of withdrawing to some extent from local YMBA activities and devoting more of my time to the work of editing and publishing *Stepping-Stones* and establishing branches of the YMBA elsewhere. As long ago as April, when we were still operating from Banshi's Godown, I had set up an Activities Committee to manage the activities of the YMBA in Kalimpong, thus leaving what I called the Headquarters Committee to concentrate on wider issues affecting the Association as a whole. This Activities Committee consisted of nine members, with Joe as Chairman, Padam as Vice-Chairman, Sachin as Secretary, Lachuman as Treasurer, and Dhan Bahadur as Librarian, and it was to them that I now entrusted the responsibility of running the games room and the library and reading room, as well as the responsibility of raising at least part of the rent of the Hermitage, where of course the day-to-day activities of the local YMBA were being conducted. Having done this, I moved into the chalet, which consisted of two tiny rooms, one behind the other, with a tiny veranda at the front and a tiny bathroom (that is, a room with a cement floor and a tap) at the back.

Hardly had I become accustomed to my Lilliputian new quarters, however, than I had to move back to my old room at the Hermitage for a few days in order to accommodate two guests. This was an inconvenience to which I was more than happy to submit, for the two guests were Lama Govinda and his wife Li Gotami.

Lama Govinda and I had been in correspondence for more than a year, and he had long been a member of that small but brilliant team of regular contributors whose articles had done so much to bring *Stepping-Stones* to the notice of English-speaking Buddhists all over the world. Since the appearance of the third and last instalment of his ten-part article on 'The Significance of "OM" and the Foundations of Mantric Lore' he had contributed an article on 'Buddhism as Living Experience' that revealed, even more clearly than his previous contributions, the depth and maturity of his thought and the extent to which he had succeeded in grasping the spirit as distinct from the letter of the Buddha's teaching. In this article he in fact sounded, as though on some mighty organ, notes that struck a responsive chord in my own heart and set up there reverberations that were to grow rather than diminish in volume as the years went by. For Lama Govinda, Buddhism was not to be identified with any particular conceptual expression. Buddhism was a matter of spiritual experience, and spiritual experience was something that could be put into words only to a very limited extent. The Buddha had, therefore, confined himself to showing his disciples how they might experience the truth of the Dharma for themselves. He had not laid down any system of philosophy, for this would have been to create a dogma and thus prevent individual development. No formulation of the Buddha's doctrine was final. He himself had been obliged to have recourse to the 'language' of his day, and had he lived later would doubtless have expressed himself differently. To cling to outmoded forms of spiritual life and thought was disastrous. Spiritual things could not be 'fixed'. Where there was growth there was life, and spiritual growth depended upon our rediscovering spiritual truths for ourselves instead of trying simply to 'take over' the existing conceptual formulations of these truths. Through this process of spiritual growth the individual would become a link between the past and the present; history would become part of life, rather than an object of scholarly study or blind religious veneration. Having understood that spiritual life was a process of organic growth, we would cease to judge the various phases of Buddhist history as 'right' or 'wrong'. We would develop genuine tolerance for all schools of Buddhism, even though we might be more strongly attracted to one school than to another. Just as the real nature of the tree lay in the organic development and relationship of all its parts, so the essential nature of Buddhism could be found only in a development in time and space that included all its different schools, and there was no justification for trying to reconstruct the 'original' Buddhism of the Buddha from the knowledge of a single school, however ancient. 'It is far better,' the article had concluded, 'to approach all forms of Buddhism and of Buddhist life with an open and unprejudiced mind and to accept whatever leads towards the realisation of Enlightenment. This is the only criterion of Buddhism.'[51]

These sentiments were very much my own. Since my initial contact with the Dharma ten years earlier I had always regarded myself not as a follower of this or that school of Buddhism but simply as a Buddhist. Though the abbot of the Tharpa Choling Gompa had apparently taken my acceptance of the bodhisattva ideal to mean that I was a follower of the Mahāyāna, I was a follower of the Mahāyāna rather than of the Hīnayāna only in the sense that I agreed with the Mahāyāna in accepting the Hīnayāna, too, as the teaching of the Buddha, rather than with the Hīnayāna in not accepting the Mahāyāna as such. In the person of the modern Theravāda the Hīnayāna indeed went so far as to reject the Mahāyāna completely, and I had in fact for some months past watched with growing concern as this bigoted attitude found increasingly violent expression in the pages of a new Buddhist periodical.

The periodical in question was the notorious *Buddhist World* (not to be confused with the later and more ecumenical *World Buddhism*): a fortnightly paper in English edited and published by Major-General Tun Hla Oung, a Burmese military man who had been forced to leave Burma for political reasons and who was now living in exile in Ceylon.

At first I welcomed the appearance of the new periodical, which seemed to fill a gap, and at once gave it an exchange advertisement in *Stepping-Stones* – as I continued to do until *Stepping-Stones* ceased publication. Though rather belligerent in tone, the paper at least had the merit of being unambiguously Buddhist, in that it did not seek to mix Buddhism with other religions in the way that more than one 'Buddhist' magazine did, and I hoped that it would live up to its name and eventually become the mouthpiece of the entire Buddhist world. Unfortunately, for the Burmese Major-General and his Sinhalese collaborators such as Soma Thera and the former Dr Cassius Pereira (now Bhikkhu Kassapa) the Buddhist world meant the Theravādin world, just as Buddhism meant the Theravāda. The Theravāda was what they were pleased to call 'the pure Dhamma' (sometimes 'the pristine Dhamma', or even 'the pure, pristine Dhamma'), all other forms of Buddhism being regarded as so many corruptions and degenerations of the one true faith which, having been delivered once and for all to the *arahants* (in Pāli, of course!), had been preserved absolutely unchanged in Ceylon ever since.

But though the aggressive Theravāda fundamentalism of the *Buddhist World* filled me with dismay, it at least served to sharpen my awareness of my own more ecumenical attitude – as well as my awareness that it was an attitude I shared with Lama Govinda. It also served to highlight the fact that the sentiments to which Lama Govinda had given such clear and forceful expression in his article on 'Buddhism as Living Experience' were less widespread in the Buddhist world than I had supposed. It was therefore not enough that one should regard oneself simply as a Buddhist, not enough that one should approach all forms of Buddhism and of Buddhist life with an open and unprejudiced mind, not enough that one should accept whatever led towards the realization of Enlightenment. What one also had to do was to bear public witness to the fact that the only truly Buddhist attitude towards other schools of Buddhism was the ecumenical one, and that the narrowness and dogmatism displayed by Tun Hla Oung and his collaborators was totally at variance with both the spirit and the letter of any form of Buddhism – not excluding the Theravāda as represented by its own Pāli scriptures.

Such witness Lama Govinda had indeed borne in his article, which had appeared in the July issue of *Stepping-Stones*. Reading between the lines of the article, it was not difficult to see that in writing it Lama Govinda had had the *Buddhist World* very much in mind. Short though it was,

'Buddhism as Living Experience' was not only a vigorous statement of the 'Mahāyāna' point of view for its own sake, so to speak, but at the same time also a trenchant, point by point refutation of the historical, logical, and spiritual tenability of the Theravāda fundamentalism that Tun Hla Oung and his collaborators were so anxious to promote. Coincidentally, my own editorial article for the July issue of *Stepping-Stones* was entitled 'The Parable of the Raft', and in it I had reminded my readers that the Dharma was not an end in itself but a means to an end, the end being Enlightenment or Buddhahood. Reading between the lines of this article, also, it was not difficult to see that in writing it I too had had the *Buddhist World* very much in mind. Indeed, if strength of language was anything to go by I must have had it even more in mind than Lama Govinda did. After enlarging on the significance of the Buddha's 'Parable of the Raft' (found, incidentally, in the Pāli scriptures themselves), and emphasizing the primacy of Enlightenment as the one constant factor in the history of Buddhism, I continued by saying,

> 'One might think that these statements would be clear and incontestable enough in the eyes of those who had a superficial acquaintance, even, with the contents of the Scriptures; that having, as followers of the Buddha, accepted Enlightenment as their ultimate goal, they could hardly fail to understand that the Dharma was simply the means of attaining that supreme end, or help appreciating the fact that it might be necessary for this means to be adapted from place to place and from time to time, in accordance with the widely varying temperaments of different classes of aspirants. But such is, unfortunately, not always the case. Those are not wanting who, despite the fact that their own "shrunken and aberrant" form of Buddhism had been for centuries unable to produce even a single *arahant*, clamorously insist that they alone possess what they are pleased to call "the Pure Dhamma", and that all other forms of Buddhism whatsoever are "degenerations" of the primitive and authentic teaching. Such an attitude smacks far more strongly of insular prejudice and Protestant "fundamentalism" (wherein lies, perchance, its true origin) than of the Dharma of the All-Enlightened and All-Compassionate One.'[52]

And so on.

The 'shrunken and aberrant' form of Buddhism referred to was not, of course, the Theravāda as represented by the Pāli scriptures (a quotation from which concluded my article) so much as the Theravāda as represented by a selective and literal-minded reading of those scriptures. Both Lama Govinda and I were of the opinion that the narrowness and one-sidedness of the modern Theravāda, as I sometimes called it (though it was at least a thousand years old), was one of the principal obstacles that had to be overcome if there was to be a real understanding of the Buddha's teaching and if that teaching was actually to function as a means of spiritual development. It was not surprising, therefore, that Lama Govinda and I should have been in correspondence for more than a year, or that he should have become a regular contributor to *Stepping-Stones*. It was not surprising that our respective articles in the July issue of *Stepping-Stones* should have sounded such very similar notes, even though Lama Govinda had sounded a greater variety of notes and sounded them more skilfully. It was not surprising that Lama Govinda and Li Gotami should now be coming to Kalimpong to spend a few days with me and not surprising that I should be more than happy to submit to a trifling inconvenience in order to be able to accommodate them. Even from the contact that Lama Govinda and I had already had with each other I felt that we were kindred spirits, and that our forthcoming meeting would be a meeting not of bodies only but of hearts and minds. Small wonder, then, that the editorial I wrote for the September *Stepping-Stones* should have been entitled 'The Good Friend',[53] or that I should have spent the greater part of the month in eager anticipation of the moment when, on looking out of the window, I at last saw the picturesque figures of the German-born lama and his Indian wife alighting from the Landrover and making their way up the path to the gate of the Hermitage.

Lama Govinda was at that time a little over fifty. In appearance he was of medium height, and his very slight corpulence was virtually concealed by the brown *chuba* that fell in loose folds to his feet, on which he wore Indian-style sandals. The *chuba* was made not of the usual heavy woollen cloth but of some light material more suited to the Indian climate. Over one shoulder he wore an embroidered bag of the type carried by South-East Asian Buddhist monks, while round his neck there hung a Tibetan rosary with the usual attachments. His costume was completed by a kind of stole which he wore over the rosary and which hung down on either side almost to the hem of his *chuba*. Being a married lama he was not shaven-headed, and his light brown hair was brushed straight back from a forehead of unusual loftiness and intellectuality. His forehead was, in fact, the dominating feature of his face, contrasting strongly with his rather full lips and weak, receding chin. In manner he was mild and conciliatory in the extreme and, as I soon discovered, courteous almost to the point of ceremoniousness, with an air of distinction as though he had always moved in good society. Only the subtlety of the smile that played about his lips, and the keenness of the glance that occasionally shot from his deep-set eyes, gave one any indication of the extent of the life – and the fire – that lurked within. Li Gotami was about twenty years younger than Lama Govinda, as well as shorter and plumper. Apart from the fact that her *chuba* was sleeveless (she wore a long-sleeved blouse underneath), she was clad in much the same hybrid but artistic costume as her distinguished husband. Though her dark hair was bobbed in Western style, she had the creamy complexion, the prominent nose, and the large black eyes that, at a later date, I came to recognize as typical of the Parsi stock from which she sprang. Besides being extremely vivacious, she was sociable and talkative, and possessed a clear, ringing laugh that was very infectious.

When one has looked forward to meeting two people as much as I had been looking forward to meeting Lama Govinda and Li Gotami – and as they, apparently, had been looking forward to meeting me – there is always the possibility of mutual disappointment. In the event, this was far from being the case. Within half an hour of their arrival at the Hermitage a definite rapport had been established between us and we were talking as freely as though we had known each other for years. As might have been expected, I felt a greater rapport with Lama Govinda than I did with Li Gotami, who in any case had only a fraction of the wisdom and insight that was manifest in almost every word that Lama Govinda spoke. Nevertheless, I appreciated Li Gotami for her liveliness and intelligence, as well as for her delightful outspokenness, which at times bordered on the outrageous. Though her religious affiliations were by no means exclusively Buddhist, she knew enough about Buddhism to be able to take a serious interest in the subject and there was, therefore, no question of her being excluded from the lengthy discussions in which Lama Govinda and I soon became involved.

What these discussions were about it would be difficult to say. It was as though in the course of the five days that my two guests spent with me in Kalimpong, as well as the seven days that I spent with them in Ghoom immediately afterwards, Lama Govinda and I ranged over practically the whole field of Buddhist thought and practice. On whatever topic we happened to touch, we found ourselves in agreement to an extent that would have been surprising had we not been familiar with each other's writings and had we not already exchanged ideas in a number of letters. Indeed, as the cloudless autumn days went by, my feeling that we were kindred spirits received more abundant confirmation than I had dared to hope, and I was left in no doubt whatever that despite the fact that he was a married lama and I was a celibate monk I had more in common with Lama Govinda than with any other Buddhist I had ever met.

One of the most important topics on which we touched, and in fact touched more than once, was that of the relation between Buddhism and the spiritual life, on the one hand, and literature and the fine arts, on the other. Besides being a Buddhist by conviction, Lama Govinda was himself an artist and poet of no small repute. He had held exhibitions of his paintings in a number of major Indian cities, and had brought out two small volumes of poetry in his native German.[54] For my part, I had written poetry since the age of eleven or twelve, and was even now thinking of putting together some of my more recent poems for publication in book form. A few of these poems had already appeared in the pages of the *Illustrated Weekly of India*, which had financed Lama Govinda's expedition to Tsaparang in Western Tibet and afterwards serialized Li Gotami's account of their experiences, and from the nature of these poems he was well aware that I was no more indifferent to the claims of Beauty than I was to those of Truth or Goodness.

The fact that Lama Govinda and I cultivated literature and the fine arts did not, however, mean that he painted pictures or that I wrote poems *in addition to* doing such specifically Buddhist things as observing the precepts, meditating, studying the Dharma, and giving lectures. For him as for me the painting of pictures and the writing of poems was an integral part of the spiritual life itself. The relation between Buddhism and the spiritual life, on the one hand, and literature and the fine arts, on the other, was not, therefore, one that was merely external, as between different material objects. On the contrary, there was a deep inner connection between them. For this reason there could be no question of the cultivation of literature and the fine arts being inconsistent with the practice of Buddhism and the living of the spiritual life, as I had for a time supposed (or had been led to suppose), much less still of the one being actually inimical to the other. Thanks largely to his intimate acquaintance with Tibetan Buddhist art in all its forms, Lama Govinda's understanding of this important truth was at that time much clearer and more explicit than my own. In particular he had a deep appreciation of the relation between art and meditation. 'Art and meditation are creative states of the human mind,' he had written in a little book on the subject that he afterwards gave me,

> Both are nourished by the same source, but it may seem that they are moving in different directions: art towards the realm of sense-impressions, meditation towards the overcoming of forms and sense-impressions. But the difference pertains only to accidentals, not to the essentials. First of all, meditation does not mean pure abstraction or negation of form – except in its ultimate illimitable stages – it means the perfect concentration of mind and the elimination of all unessential features of the subject in question until we are fully conscious of it by experiencing reality in a particular aspect or from a particular angle of vision. Art proceeds in a similar way: while using the forms of the external world, it never tries to imitate nature but to reveal a higher reality by omitting all accidentals, thus raising the visible form to the value of a symbol, expressing a direct experience of life. The same experience may be gained by a process of meditation. But instead of creating a formal (objectively existing) expression, it leaves a subjective impression, thus acting as a forming agent on the character or the consciousness of the meditator.[55]

Since Li Gotami too was an artist, and had almost as intimate an acquaintance with Tibetan Buddhist art as her more celebrated husband, she naturally had more to contribute to the discussion when Lama Govinda and I touched on the relation between Buddhism and art than when we touched on more abstruse topics. At such times it seemed as though all three of us were kindred spirits, and that there was a meeting of three hearts and minds as well as of three bodies. With her hearty good humour, and her readiness to say – especially in connection with certain prominent figures in the Buddhist world – things that Lama Govinda only permitted himself to think, Li Gotami indeed enhanced the rapport that had been established between us and made it possible for us to talk more freely than ever.

But though much of the time that Lama Govinda and Li Gotami spent with me in Kalimpong was spent in discussion, we did not spend all of it in this way. Even before their arrival I had, with their consent, arranged a number of engagements for them. Thus it was that on the second day of their stay Lama Govinda gave a talk on his journey to Tsaparang, a journey that had taken place four years earlier and on which he had been accompanied by Li Gotami. Though I had read about this journey in the articles Li had written for the *Illustrated Weekly of India*, and though I was to read the more detailed account that appeared in *The Way of the White Clouds*[56] fifteen years later, it was the story of the Tsaparang expedition as I heard it from Lama Govinda's own lips that left the most vivid impression on my mind. This impression was heightened by the fact that Lama Govinda illustrated his talk by showing a number of his paintings and sketches, many of which he had executed on the spot. Quite a high proportion of them depicted massive, cubiform fortresses or monasteries in a setting – or against a background – of still more massive and hardly less cubiform mountains. Fortresses, monasteries, and mountains, together with the occasional *chorten*, indeed seemed to be the artist's favourite subjects, and ones to which his simple, monumental style was well adapted. At the conclusion of the talk, which took place at the Hermitage, a tea party in honour of Lama Govinda and Li Gotami was given for all YMBA members, and Sachin and another musically inclined young Nepali entertained the gathering with their songs.

The main object of the Tsaparang expedition had been to make, before it was too late, as complete a record as possible of the priceless works of art that the long-deserted temples of the ruined city contained. Among the most important of these works were some exceptionally fine frescoes, including two series depicting the life of the Buddha. Since it was not possible to remove the frescoes bodily from the walls on which they were painted, both Lama Govinda and Li Gotami had spent much of their time making tracings of those that were still in good condition. Li Gotami had, it appeared, concentrated on the frescoes depicting the life of the Buddha. On the day after Lama Govinda's talk she accordingly showed these tracings, and Lama Govinda gave a running commentary on the different episodes in the Buddha's career that they depicted. Besides making tracings of the frescoes, Li Gotami had noted down in the corner of each tracing a detailed colour-key to the original painting. With the help of the tracings and the colour-keys, she explained, she hoped to be able to produce copies of all the frescoes depicting the life of the Buddha that had still been in good condition at the time of their visit. Since there were about thirty of them altogether, it would be the work of a lifetime.

This meeting, at which Li Gotami also showed a number of her black-and-white photographs of Tsaparang, was smaller and more intimate than the one that had taken place the previous day. Such regular contributors to *Stepping-Stones* as resided in Kalimpong were naturally well represented. Prince Peter of Greece, Dr Roerich, and Dr Nebesky were all eager to meet Lama Govinda and Li Gotami and to see the tracings, as well as to ask all sorts of archaeological, historical, geographical, ethnological, and linguistic questions relative to Western Tibet in general and Tsaparang in particular, and all three of them therefore turned up at the Hermitage in good time in Prince Peter's well-known green American limousine. As for the artists of Kalimpong, they were represented by Mrs Crisp and Esmond (and perhaps by Joe, who had recently added to his frustrations by trying to paint), though it was noticeable that Mrs Crisp had much less to say for herself than usual and made no reference whatever to being an ARA.

But if Mrs Crisp had less to say for herself than usual, there was a third lady present of whom this could not be said, and who obviously had no intention of allowing Li Gotami to monopolize the attention of the gathering. This was Princess Irene of Greece, who had arrived with Prince Peter, Roerich, and Nebesky in the green American limousine. Though pleased to see her at the Hermitage, I was a little surprised, since I knew from Nebesky that I was in her bad books and had therefore not expected her to come. But no doubt her curiosity to see Li Gotami's tracings had triumphed over her dislike of me. She was a tall, rather heavily built woman of about forty, with a puffy white face and a mass of frizzy hennaed hair. Probably she had once been quite beautiful, but now the wrinkles were beginning to show through the powder, while crow's-feet between the eyes gave her an unpleasantly bad-tempered expression. When she spoke it was in a harsh, guttural voice that every now and then rose to a screech that could set one's teeth on edge. Mentally I compared her to a peacock, which despite its beautiful plumage has an extremely raucous voice. When she came to the Hermitage to see the tracings it was only the second time that we had met. The first time had been when, about a year earlier, she had invited me to a tea-party at Tashiding, the Himalayan mock Tudor residence that she and Prince Peter occupied at Ringkingpong, not far from Crookety where Dr Roerich lived. At this tea-party I had been offered a piece of cake, but since I took no solid food after midday I had refused it. Unfortunately, Princess Irene overheard me refusing the cake and screeched across the room, 'I made that cake myself!' – and from that moment I had been in her bad books.

From the way things were going on the present occasion it looked as though Li Gotami would soon be in the Princess's bad books too. In order that we could see the tracings more clearly they had been spread out on the ping-pong table, which occupied the greater part of the games room. Princess Irene sat at the head of the table, so to speak, while Lama Govinda and Li Gotami sat facing each other across it farther down. Partly because of the shortage of chairs, and partly because of the lack of space, the rest of us either stood round the lower end of the table or looked over Princess Irene's shoulder as Li Gotami showed the tracings and Lama Govinda gave his running commentary. In the case of some of the tracings quite a lot of commentary was required, since the original frescoes depicted several episodes from the Buddha's life at the same time and it was not always easy to make out which details belonged to which episode, even when one looked quite closely. At one point, when Li Gotami was showing her third or fourth tracing and was pointing out something of particular interest, Princess Irene suddenly jerked the tracing out of her hand and pulled it towards herself in order to take a better look at it through her thick-rimmed spectacles. Li Gotami bristled. Not being the sort of person who was prepared to put up with rudeness, however exalted the quarter from which it came, and not being in the least intimidated by the Princess's haughty, overbearing manner, she reached across the corner of the table and with a loud 'Thank *you*!' promptly hauled the tracing back, whereupon it was Princess Irene's turn to bristle. For a moment it seemed as though there was going to be a tug-of-war between the two ladies for possession of the tracing, and high words might even have passed between them, but Lama Govinda diverted Li Gotami's attention by a timely question and Prince Peter directed towards Princess Irene a look of mild reproof, to which that lady responded by making an ugly face at him. But if Li Gotami was now well and truly in Princess Irene's bad books, Princess Irene herself was no less in Li Gotami's. 'I certainly wasn't going to let her get away with *that*!' the pugnacious little Parsi woman told Lama Govinda and myself afterwards, laughing heartily at the recollection of how she had paid Princess Irene back in her own coin. 'Who does she think she is, anyway?'

That was a question indeed. Though I did not know it at the time, Princess Irene was not a princess by birth at all, or even of royal blood, and this fact may have accounted for the notorious rudeness of her behaviour, on account of which she was as unpopular in Kalimpong as Prince Peter was popular. But having paid Princess Irene back in her own coin, Li Gotami was not disposed to give the matter any further thought. There were plenty of other things for her to think about. She and Lama Govinda had only one more full day in Kalimpong left, and they had not yet called on Mrs Tagore, whom they both knew quite well, Lama Govinda having been a lecturer at Santiniketan and Li Gotami a student. The next morning, therefore, they called not only on Mrs Tagore but also, for good measure, on Mrs Mitter, and in the afternoon both ladies came rustling along to the Hermitage in their best saris to see the tracings. Since I knew Mrs Mitter had not forgiven me for preferring Joe to Swale (not that the preference had done me much good, anyway!) I was hardly less surprised to see her at the Hermitage than I had been to see Princess Irene there. In the case of the Queen of Kalimpong, too, her curiosity to see the tracings – and her sense of its being her duty to accompany Mrs Tagore – had no doubt triumphed over whatever displeasure she still felt with me. As we all talked together I noticed that Mrs Tagore addressed Li Gotami not as Li but as Rati, having originally known her as Rati Petit and afterwards as Rati Khandelawala. Later on in the afternoon Lama Govinda and Li Gotami were entertained to tea by Sachin at the bungalow in the Scottish Mission compound and met his parents. I had been invited to the place a number of times since moving into the Hermitage and now knew Sachin's self-effacing, hard-working doctor father quite well, and was beginning to know his mother and other members of the family too.

It may have been on that same afternoon that, accompanied by Sachin and Indranarayan (Rudramani's nephew, and the other musically inclined young Nepali who had entertained the gathering with their songs after Lama Govinda's talk), Lama Govinda, Li Gotami, and I walked up the track to Tirpai as far as Sherpa Building. The purpose of the visit was not so much to see Joe, however, as to see the elderly couple to whom the double-storeyed house belonged. Twenty years earlier

Lama Govinda had stayed with them for a while, either in Kalimpong itself or in Darjeeling, and very glad indeed they were to see him again after such a long time. Since Joe occupied the other downstairs flat (a Tibetan incarnate lama occupied the whole of the upstairs floor), Lama Govinda and Li Gotami could hardly avoid calling on the cantankerous *upāsaka*, even though Li Gotami had taken something of a dislike to him almost at first sight ('What a strange man!' she had commented to me afterwards), and though he, for his part, had been noticeably ill at ease both with her and – to a lesser extent – with Lama Govinda. However, when we all knocked on his door he received us graciously (probably he did not expect either Lama Govinda or Li Gotami to be shocked by his wrathful Vajrapāṇi), and though he commented in his usual scathing fashion on whatever topics were raised I could see that he was secretly gratified by the visit. After he had given us tea, we all went out into the garden and Li Gotami took a number of group photographs, though she absolutely refused to have her own photograph taken.

These photographs were the visible record of what had, in fact, been a highly successful visit. Lama Govinda and Li Gotami had clearly enjoyed their contact with me, as well as their contact with the members and friends of the Kalimpong YMBA, who for their part felt very much encouraged by the friendly and sympathetic interest that the two distinguished visitors had taken in our activities. Both Lama Govinda and Li Gotami were by nature extremely warm-hearted, and the simple, unpretentious way in which they behaved made it easy for them to get on well with young people and win their confidence. For my part, I had enjoyed my contact with them even more, perhaps, than they had enjoyed their contact with me, and was already looking forward to accompanying them to Ghoom, where they had invited me to spend a week with them at the bungalow in which Lama Govinda had lived before the war with his German foster-mother, who had been well known in the locality for her devotion to Anagārika Brahmacārī Govinda (as he was then known), as well as for her age and eccentricity.[57] This foster-mother had (I think) recently died. At any rate, Lama Govinda, who had not visited Ghoom for many years (perhaps not since the beginning of the War, when he had been interned), was now going there in order to sort out his books and papers and other belongings and take away with him such as were still of any use. He and Li Gotami had recently found a place of their own in the form of the Gate Lodge,

With Lama Govinda and members of YMBA: (left to right) Sachin, Indra, Lama Govinda, Sangharakshita, Padam, Dil Bahadur, and Joe Cann

as it was called, of a school in Deolali, a cantonment town about 100 miles north-east of Bombay, and he naturally wanted to have all his possessions in one place.

The Pines was small and dark, and set among pine trees the foliage of which was inky black rather than dark green. There was mist everywhere. The name Ghoom was indeed said to mean mist or fog, and it was well known that however clear a day it might be down at Teesta Bridge, or in Darjeeling, on passing through Ghoom one would be sure to encounter anything from a thick blanket of white cloud, through which the grey-blue shapes of the pines loomed like the shadows of giants, to a veil of mist so fine as to be almost invisible. Surrounded by mist as it was, The Pines was naturally both cold and damp, especially as the place had not been lived in for a while, and the three of us spent much of our time huddled round the tiny charcoal fire trying to keep warm. We also spent much of our time talking, and in the greater silence and isolation of Ghoom the rapport that had been established between us in Kalimpong was considerably deepened. One morning, however, when the weather was brighter than usual, we paid a visit to the famous Ghoom Monastery, which was only a short distance away. This monastery occupied an important place in Lama Govinda's spiritual history, for it was here that he had met his guru who, as I knew from the articles that had appeared in the *Illustrated Weekly of India*, was Tomo Geshe Rimpoche.[58] The monastery also occupied a place in my own spiritual history, though not nearly so important a one as in the case of Lama Govinda. I had been to see it six years earlier, on the occasion of my first visit to Darjeeling, and had vivid recollections of the golden face of the colossal seated image of Maitreya, the coming Buddha, looking down at me through the gloom.[59] Now I was happy to be able to visit the monastery – or rather, the monastery temple – with Lama Govinda and Li Gotami.

As we lifted the heavy felt curtain that screened the entrance I saw the same colossal figure seated there in the semi-darkness, the same golden face glimmering beneath the great jewelled tiara. Smaller figures gleamed from behind the glass doors of showcases and glowed with a subdued richness from the frescoed walls like reflections seen in deep water. Rosary in hand, Lama Govinda and Li Gotami moved clockwise round the chamber, pausing for a moment in front of each image or *thangka* and reciting the appropriate mantra, and I followed in their wake. Some of the mantras were new to me, and of these two in particular – the mantra of Śākyamuni and the mantra of Padmasambhava – not only sounded strangely familiar but also set up reverberations that made themselves felt in the remotest corners of my being. The whole experience affected me deeply. There was the rectangular chamber itself, dimly lit from above by the light that filtered in at a kind of skylight, there was the brooding presence of the images, with the colossal Maitreya silently dominating the rest, and there was the sound of the mantras as the two dark figures in *chubas* made their way with bowed heads round the chamber. What affected me most deeply, however, was the evident devotion with which Lama Govinda and Li Gotami recited the mantras and the way in which they seemed to feel, behind each image, the living spiritual presence of which the image was the representation or, indeed, even the veritable embodiment.

It was therefore only natural, perhaps, that of all the discussions Lama Govinda and I had in Kalimpong and Ghoom the only one to leave a distinct and separate impression on my mind should have taken place after our visit to the Ghoom Monastery and should have related to meditation and, in particular, to meditation on the different Buddhas and bodhisattvas. While I listened enthralled, Lama Govinda explained how one took up first one kind of spiritual practice, then another, in accordance with the various needs of one's developing spiritual life. It was not, however, that on taking up a new practice one discarded the old practice and put it behind one, so to speak. What one did was add the new practice to the old and incorporate both in a higher unity. In this way one's meditation or spiritual practice would, over the years, gradually become an ever richer and more complex thing. As Lama Govinda spoke, I had a vision of petal being added to petal, or facet to facet, until one had a thousand-petalled rose or a thousand-faceted crystal ball complete in all its glory. What Lama Govinda was doing, of course, was speaking of meditation or spiritual practice – indeed, of the spiritual life itself – in terms of the gradual building up of a mandala. In other words, he was speaking of it not only in terms of time but in terms of space. Hitherto I had thought of it as a progression from stage to stage, or level to level. Now I also saw it as an unfolding from an ever more truly central point into an ever increasing number of different aspects and dimensions.

Before my return to Kalimpong (Lama Govinda and Li Gotami were staying on for another two weeks, sorting out and packing) we also paid a visit to Darjeeling. It was a clear, bright autumn day, and Lama Govinda and Li Gotami donned for the occasion the silk brocade *chubas* in which they had been married in Bombay some four years earlier. Lama Govinda's was, I think, a deep violet. As we walked up Mackenzie Road in the direction of the Chowrasta the three of us must have presented a colourful appearance for we attracted a good deal of attention. So much attention did we attract that I felt slightly embarrassed, though my two companions seemed to take it as a matter of course or even to regard it as their due. On the way we met a number of people who knew Lama Govinda – that is, who had known him twenty years earlier – as well as a number of people who knew me, and we had to stop and talk, or at least exchange greetings, so many times that our progress was very slow. One of the people we met in this way was Mr Tendufla. Mr Tendufla was that rare phenomenon, a thoroughly Westernized – or rather, a thoroughly anglicized – Tibetan. He invariably wore Western dress, and it was said of him that he was unable to speak Tibetan properly (like Mrs Samdup, he was a 'Darjeeling born' Tibetan). Certainly he could not read or write the language. I had met him in the course of my previous visits to Darjeeling and had tried, without much success, to enlist his support for the YMBA. He was a tallish, thin man of about forty, with a toothbrush moustache – rather like a Guards officer – and hair brushed straight back from his forehead. As the proprietor of a Western-style hotel, he mixed a good deal with Europeans and Americans and was said to be fonder of their company than of that of his own people. Nonetheless, Mr Tendufla was a prominent figure in Darjeeling, being generally regarded as the leading Tibetan – and the leading Buddhist – citizen of the town. He was chairman of a dozen *gompa* committees, and of a score of other bodies, for none of which had he ever been known to do anything. The sole reason for Mr Tendufla's prominence was that he was the son-in-law of Sardar Bahadur Laden La, the much-decorated police inspector who, in the days of the British Raj, had been the town's most famous son. As if to emphasize the fact that he was the legitimate successor to the honours of the late Sardar Bahadur, Mr Tendufla had incorporated into his own name the honorific suffix which his grateful fellow-citizens had accorded Laden La for his many services to the community. Thus it was that plain Mr Tenduf had become Mr Tendu*fla* – a solecism for which he was ridiculed behind his back by other Tibetans. It was rather as though the son-in-law of that distinguished citizen John Brown, esquire, should start calling himself Mr Smithesquire.

With someone like Mr Tendufla being regarded as the leading Buddhist citizen of the town, it was hardly surprising that Buddhism had not made much progress in Darjeeling since Lama Govinda's time. Neither was it surprising that, despite the enthusiasm aroused by the visit of the Sacred Relics, it had not been possible for the YMBA to establish itself there in the way that I had hoped. Mr Tendufla represented one of the main difficulties by which we were confronted. As a thoroughly Westernized Tibetan, he represented alienation from, and indifference to, Buddhism and Buddhist culture, just as some of the other people Lama Govinda and I met on our way to the Chowrasta represented over-identification with, or blind attachment to, a particular form of ethnic Buddhism or even to a particular ethnic Buddhist community. Whether in Darjeeling, or Kalimpong, or Gangtok, there seemed to be very few Buddhists who were devoted to Buddhism simply as a spiritual tradition, or a means to the attainment of Enlightenment. There seemed to be very few who had any understanding of spiritual friendship as distinct from a sense of ethnic solidarity and very few, therefore, who were capable of being spiritual friends. In these circumstances I was all the more grateful for the contact I had had with Lama Govinda, and all the more sorry when the time came for me to say goodbye to him and Li Gotami.

Shortly before I left, Lama Govinda presented me with a standing image of the Buddha. It was about a foot-and-a-half in height, and though the rather flat wooden body was carved and painted with a simplicity that was almost primitive, the gilded face, hands, and feet, which were of clay, were of unusual delicacy and refinement. The image was not unfamiliar to me. It featured in a painting by Li Gotami depicting Lama Govinda 'in his hermitage at Ghoom' that had been reproduced in the *Illustrated Weekly of India*. In this painting Lama Govinda was shown sitting cross-legged at a kind of lectern before the window, pen in hand, and surrounded by books and *thangkas* and various souvenirs of his travels. The image stood in the right hand corner, next to the shrine. It had been carved in Darjeeling, Lama Govinda told me, by an old Tibetan monk he had known many years ago. Though he was very fond of the image, he had decided not to take it to Bombay, since one finger was already broken and he feared that in the course of the long train journey further damage would be done. He was therefore happy to give it to me. He was also happy to give me some fifteen or twenty volumes of Pāli texts and translations which he no longer needed. A number of these volumes bore the signature of Earl Brewster, the American Buddhist, whom he had known in Capri (and, I think, in Ceylon). Earl Brewster, in his turn, had known D. H. Lawrence, and it was with Brewster and his wife Achsah that Lawrence had stayed in Ceylon on his way to Australia. It seemed strange that through the grey-covered Pali Text Society volumes I should be in contact with someone who had been a personal friend of the author of *The Rainbow*, which I had read when I was sixteen or seventeen and which had struck me with the force of an emotional revelation.[60]

On my arrival at the Hermitage I installed the standing image of the Buddha in the octagonal shrine-room and added the volumes of Pāli texts and translations to my small but steadily growing collection of books. Both the red and gold image and the grey-covered volumes would be a constant reminder of the twelve memorable days that two – and at times three – kindred spirits had spent together.

14
CONTRASTS IN KATHMANDU

After their return to Calcutta from Tibet the Sacred Relics of the *arhants* Śāriputra and Maudgalyāyana, the two chief disciples of the Buddha, were to make only two more journeys outside India before their re-enshrinement in the new temple that was being built for them in Sanchi. The first of these journeys was to the Hindu kingdom of Nepal, and thus it was that for the second time that year I received a letter inviting me to accompany the Sacred Relics as part of the official delegation. This time the letter came from Devapriya Valisinha, the General Secretary of the Maha Bodhi Society, whom I had met in Gangtok when he put in a brief appearance there during the week that the Sacred Relics had spent in the village capital six months earlier. Venerable Sangharatana would not be going this time (Devapriyaji wrote), since with the pilgrim season fast approaching his presence would be required at Sarnath, but Dr Soft would be going, as well as several prominent members of the monastic order, and if he could spare the time he hoped to go himself.

Though the prospect of visiting Nepal did not affect me nearly so deeply as the prospect of visiting Tibet had done, and though Devapriyaji's letter certainly did not come like the answer to an unspoken wish, I was glad to accept the invitation and at once started making preparations for my departure. I had, of course, spent a few weeks in Nepal two-and-a-half years earlier.[61] Immediately after our ordination as *śrāmaṇeras* or novice monks in May 1949 my friend Buddharakshita and I had walked from Kusinara, the scene of the

Buddha's final passing away, to Lumbini, the place of his birth, which was situated a few miles inside Nepalese territory. From Lumbini we had walked up through the jungle to Butaol, and from there had made our way across the first range of foothills to Palpa-Tansen. In both places we had stayed with the Newar Buddhists and had seen for ourselves the way in which Buddhism was persecuted under the orthodox Hindu despotism of the hereditary Rana prime ministers who, for the last hundred years, had governed Nepal in the name of the King. But now everything was changed. In the course of the last twelve months there had been armed uprisings against the Rana regime in several parts of the country, the King and other members of the royal family had taken refuge in the Indian embassy, from where they had been flown to New Delhi in an Indian Air Force plane, the Rana government had capitulated to a combination of insurrectionary tactics on the part of the Nepali Congress and diplomatic pressure on the part of the Government of India, the King had returned in triumph to Kathmandu, and the last hereditary Rana prime minister had become the first prime minister of the new interim government.

These developments – which my Nepalese friends in Kalimpong and Darjeeling followed with the keenest interest – had naturally affected the position of the Newar Buddhists and even, to some extent, the position of Buddhism itself. Under the autocratic rule of the Ranas the Newar Buddhists had been subjected not only to the same political oppression as their Hindu neighbours but to a certain amount of religious persecution as well. Buddhist activities in the wider sense were officially prohibited, as was the ordination of monks and the publication of books and magazines in the Newari language. In short, the free and open practice of the Buddha's teaching was virtually impossible. It was therefore not surprising that many of the more educated and influential members of the Newar Buddhist community should have been strongly opposed to the Rana regime or that they should have supported the King in his efforts to regain the powers which, for the last hundred years, had been exercised on his behalf by the hereditary Rana prime ministers. The result was that when the King returned in triumph to Kathmandu in February 1951 the Buddhist Newars found themselves very much on the winning side and very much in the King's favour. Though the anti-Buddhist laws had not been repealed they were no longer so strictly enforced, and the Newar Buddhists were freer to practise and propagate their religion than they had been at any time within living memory. This meant that the headquarters of the 'reformist' Dharmodaya Sabha, which had been founded six or seven years earlier, could be transferred from Calcutta to Kathmandu. It meant that the handful of Ceylon- and Burma-returned monks and their wealthy Newar Buddhist supporters could make ambitious plans for the revival of Buddhism in Nepal along strictly Theravādin lines. Above all, it meant that with the consent of the King – who was reputed to be personally sympathetic to Buddhism – the Sacred Relics of the *arhants* Śāriputra and Maudgalyāyana could be invited to pay a two-week visit to the land in which their great master had been born and brought up and from which, at the age of twenty-nine, he had 'gone forth' into the jungles of north-east India in search of Supreme Enlightenment.

Since the Maha Bodhi Society and the Dharmodaya Sabha were in regular contact with each other, and in fact had more than one leading member in common, the governing body of the Society had readily accepted the invitation, which was extended in the name of the government and people of Nepal, though arrangements for the actual reception of the Sacred Relics were in the hands of the Dharmodaya Sabha. Moreover, since this would be the first real contact between the Buddhists of Nepal and the Buddhists of other Asian countries for many centuries the governing body had decided that the delegation accompanying the Sacred Relics should, on this occasion, be as large and as representative as possible. Invitations were accordingly sent out, with the result that by early November there had assembled at the Maha Bodhi Society's Calcutta headquarters some fifteen or twenty monks and laymen from India, Ceylon, Greece, and England who, on the morning of 6 November, left Dum Dum Airport for Nepal carrying with them the Sacred Relics of the two *arhants* in their familiar silver-gilt casket.

It was the first time I had travelled in an aeroplane, and though my stomach reacted violently to the change of altitude I felt strangely exhilarated. The weather was bright and clear and the sunlight that streamed in through the windows on my right lit up the yellow and orange robes of the monks and sparkled on the hemispherical golden lid of the reliquary. Most of the other members of the delegation were already known to me, at least by name. Prominent among the lay delegates was the tall figure of Dr Soft, who did not stay long in his seat beside Devapriya Valisinha but moved up and down the aisle talking to the other passengers, including the Nepalese government officials who were accompanying us on the flight. Not far from Valisinha sat Venerable Jinaratana, a Sinhalese monk of about forty who was one of the two joint secretaries of the Maha Bodhi Society, the other being Venerable Sangharatana. I could see the back of his bald head gleaming above his seat and hear his harsh, cracked voice as he exchanged remarks in Sinhalese with a monk on the other side of the aisle. Though we had as yet not really spoken to each other, that harsh, cracked voice was very familiar to me indeed. Some five years earlier, before taking up the life of a wandering ascetic, and while Valisinha was still in Ceylon, I had spent a month at the Sri Dharmarajika Vihara (as the Maha Bodhi Society's Calcutta headquarters was called) and had been the witness of some rather unmonklike behaviour on the part of His Holiness the High Priest, as Jinaratana had instructed me he was to be styled, and now that I was myself a monk there was a feeling of awkwardness between us that neither of us had found a way of resolving.[62]

In other parts of the cabin sat Venerable Silabhadra, Reverend Dhammaratana, Bhadant Anand Kausalyayan, and Venerable Narada Thera. I could see the backs of their bald heads gleaming above their seats, though none of them gleamed as brightly as Jinaratana's, which like the tonsured head of Chaucer's monk 'shone as any glass'.[63] Silabhadra was a Bengali ex-Hindu who had been ordained rather late in life after a career at the Rangoon Bar; Dhammaratana a Sinhalese novice who was studying for a degree and who seemed to prefer smiling to speaking. Both of them stayed at the Sri Dharmarajika Vihara and helped Devapriya Valisinha with the work of editing the *Maha Bodhi* journal. Anand Kausalyayan, or Anandji as he was generally called, was the youngest member of the once famous trio of Anandji, Kashyapji, and Rahulji – a trio that had been broken up when Rahul Sankrityayan, its most distinguished member, gave up the robes after a series of episodes similar to that which had led to the downfall of Great Wisdom. A Punjabi by birth, he was a tall, rather striking figure, though his woollen cap and his carelessly draped upper robe made him look more like a Hindu sadhu than a Buddhist monk. As I had known since the time when Aniruddha was trying to throw me out of the Dharmodaya Vihara, and I was wondering to whom I could turn for help, he was the Vice-President of the Dharmodaya Sabha and had, moreover, the reputation of being very anti-British. To what extent this reputation was justified

I had no means of telling, but on meeting him and the other delegates at the Sri Dharmarajika Vihara a few days before our departure I had been relieved to find no trace of any anti-British bias in his attitude towards me. On the contrary, he took a friendly but detached interest in the young English monk who had been invited to accompany the Sacred Relics to Nepal and showed no awareness whatever of the unhappy events that had taken place at the Dharmodaya Vihara a year earlier.

Anandji's interest in me was shared by Venerable Narada Thera, who sat near the Sacred Relics in the forward half of the cabin, somewhat apart from the other monks. We had already talked more than once since my arrival at the Sri Dharmarajika Vihara. Indeed, had I been wearing a Western style suit instead of the traditional monastic robes the middle-aged Sinhalese monk with the curiously high-pitched voice and the rather simian features could be said to have buttonholed me. Besides being the seniormost monk on board the aeroplane Narada Thera was, as I well knew, the doyen of the English-speaking monks of Ceylon. In great demand as a lecturer both inside and outside his own country, he was the author of innumerable simply written pamphlets on (Theravāda) Buddhism or, as he preferred to call it, 'the pure Dhamma'. Tens of thousands of these pamphlets had been printed for free distribution by his lay admirers, but though I had come across a good many of them in the course of my travels they had not added much to my understanding of (Theravāda) Buddhism.

Whatever his limitations as an exponent of Buddhism, however, Narada Thera undoubtedly had a genius for buttonholing people. We had not been in the air for many minutes before he succeeded in buttonholing Prince Peter of Greece, who had gone to take a closer look at the Sacred Relics, or rather, at the silver-gilt reliquary in which they were contained. Both before and after the meeting at which Li Gotami had shown her tracings of the Tsaparang frescoes, and at which she and Princess Irene had very nearly been involved in a tug-of-war over one of them, Prince Peter had occasionally dropped in at the Hermitage for a cup of tea and a chat. On such occasions he invariably came riding on a chestnut-coloured horse – which he tethered to a tree near the gate – and wearing a sort of cowboy costume complete with red check shirt, neckerchief, and stetson. In this way we had gradually become more closely acquainted, though without ever really becoming friends, and he had told me about such things as his visit to South India, where he had studied polyandry among the Todas and where Princess Irene had added to her already extensive collection of love charms. I was therefore hardly surprised when, having heard that I was going to Nepal with the Sacred Relics, he sent me a note enquiring if I thought there was any chance of his going too. He was very interested in the country, and would like to see it before, as now seemed likely, it was modernized out of all resemblance to its former traditional self. On receiving this note I immediately wrote to Devapriyaji, who in turn wrote to Prince Peter inviting him to accompany the Sacred Relics as a member of the official delegation. Thus it was that among the fifteen or twenty monks and laymen who had assembled at the Maha Bodhi Society's Calcutta headquarters there had been someone from Greece (and Denmark!), and thus it was that Prince Peter was with us on the aeroplane and being buttonholed by Narada Thera.

But I soon ceased paying much attention to my fellow delegates. After we had been in the air for about half an hour, and my stomach had adjusted to the change of altitude, I started looking out of the window. As I peered through the thick glass I saw a panorama such as, before the twentieth century, had been visible to none but gods and those favoured mortals whom the gods had caught up bodily into the air. Far below me was a green patchwork of fields, with here and there a tiny village or grove of trees. I was reminded of the time when, two years earlier, I had climbed to the top of the Vulture's Peak, near Rajgir in Bihar, and had seen a thousand feet below me a similar green patchwork.[64] On the present occasion I was looking down from a height many times greater than that of the Vulture's Peak, and without having any connection with the earth, and the green patchwork below me consisted not of hundreds but of thousands of fields. Some of the fields were light green in colour, others dark green, while through them there wound ochre-coloured rivers which, though many times wider than even the biggest field, from the height from which I was surveying them looked no more than streams.

An hour and a half later, when all the monks on board had been fed, and the laymen had started on their own meal, the green patchwork of the Gangetic plain gave way to the continuous dark green of the Nepalese Terai. At the same time, huge masses of cumulus cloud came floating past, every now and then engulfing us in a rush of spectral vapours that blotted out the blue sky and the sunshine. We also got into an air pocket and for several appalling minutes were tossed about in a manner that threatened to tear apart the quivering and groaning walls of the cabin and expose us all to the fury of the elements. When the aeroplane finally righted itself, however, I saw on the distant horizon, dazzlingly white against the intense blue of the sky, the long line of the Himalayas. For so many hundreds of miles did they seem to extend that I fancied I could see, far away to the east, the familiar double peak of Mount Kanchenjunga. In a matter of minutes we were over the first range of foothills and making a rapid descent into the Kathmandu Valley. According to tradition, the valley had originally been a lake, but Mañjuśrī, the Bodhisattva of Wisdom, had cleft the hills to the south with his sword, thus draining away the waters and turning the whole area into a green and fruitful garden. As the aeroplane banked and circled, we could see Kathmandu spread out below us, with the white dome and golden spire of Swayambhunath just visible to the west of the town. A few minutes later came the sudden jolt of touchdown. We had arrived. For the second time in my life I was visiting the land of the Buddha's birth, and I was visiting it, moreover, under circumstances very different from those of two-and-a-half years ago. Then I had entered the country on foot, with a single companion, and without official permission, whereas now I was entering it by the most modern form of transport, with the Sacred Relics and the other members of the delegation, and as the guest of the government and people of Nepal.

On emerging from the aeroplane into the crisp, sunlit air of the valley – so different from the smoke-laden atmosphere of Calcutta – we found a great crowd of people waiting at the aerodrome. Most of them were Newars, and most of them were clad – men and women alike – in pure white garments, the whiteness of which contrasted in the most striking manner with the drab khaki of the Gurkha policemen who were engaged in holding them back and preventing them from surging forward onto the tarmac and surrounding the aeroplane. Though I did not know it at the time, this contrast of white and khaki, Newar and Gurkha, was the first of the many contrasts that I was to encounter in the course of the next two weeks. When the delegates had formed themselves into a sort of procession, with the monks in the van and the lay members bringing up the rear, the Sacred Relics were taken from the aeroplane to a marquee that had been pitched nearby. Here they were received by King Tribhuvan, a plump, pleasant-looking man of about forty whom I had seen some five years previously in Calcutta, strolling in Eden Gardens with ten or twelve members of his entourage.[65] On that occasion he had been wearing, like them, a dark Western-style suit, but now he wore traditional Nepalese costume, consisting of double-breasted shirt, jodhpurs, and conical cap, though with the addition of a Western-style jacket.

From the marquee the Sacred Relics were taken in procession to the Narayanhiti or 'Abode of Narayan', as the Royal Palace was called. It was so called because the King was popularly regarded as the incarnation of the god Vishnu, the second member of the Hindu trinity of Brahma the Creator, Vishnu the Preserver, and Maheshvara (or Shiva) the Destroyer. Indeed, the ten monarchs of the Shah dynasty, from Prithvi Narayan to King Tribhuvan, were collectively known as the Das Avatar or 'Ten Incarnations', and prints depicting all ten of them together were often seen in the homes of pious and patriotic Nepalis. This Nepalese set of ten incarnations was, of course, quite different from the standard Hindu set, but this fact had not prevented the Rana prime ministers – otherwise rigidly orthodox – from encouraging the cult of the (Nepalese) Das Avatar. If the King was the incarnation of Vishnu he was far too sacred a person to be concerned with the government of the country, which was best left in the hands of ordinary mortals. He was far too sacred to be exposed to the gaze of his subjects, and except for the occasional brief visit to Benares or Calcutta should remain secluded in the Narayanhiti. But now all that was changed. Since the upheavals of nine months ago the King had become actively involved in the process of transition from autonomy to democracy, and was showing himself in public more and more frequently. This was why he could receive the Sacred Relics on their arrival at the aerodrome and ride in procession with them to the Narayanhiti. This was why he could see for himself the enthusiasm with which they were welcomed by his subjects.

The enthusiasm indeed was immense. Thousands of people lined the streets through which the procession passed, all eager to pay their respects to the memory of the two *arhants*. As at the aerodrome, most of them were Newars, and as at the aerodrome most of them were clad in spotless white garments, the whiteness of which again contrasted strikingly with the drab khaki of the Gurkha policemen who were holding them back and preventing them from getting in the way of the procession. Such was people's enthusiasm that it took us some time to reach the wrought iron gates of the Narayanhiti. Here I was disappointed to find not a grander version of the pagoda-type buildings I had glimpsed on our way through the town but a neo-classical structure which, with its pillared façade and lateral flights of steps, was more like a provincial town hall or a city bank than the abode of the incarnation of Vishnu. Between the ancient and the modern architecture of Kathmandu, as between the King and his official residence, there in fact was a contrast no less striking than that between the white of the Newar worshippers and the khaki of the Gurkha policemen.

Since the Sacred Relics were to be kept, for the time being, at the Royal Palace, the members of the delegation were taken from the Narayanhiti straight to the quarters which they would be occupying for the duration of their stay. The monks were taken to the Ananda Kuti Vihara, a small monastery on the slopes of the Swayambhunath hill that had been constructed only a few years previously and which, as the headquarters of the Dharmodaya Sabha, was the centre of 'reformist' Theravāda Buddhism in Nepal. On our arrival there, however, it soon became obvious that the place was not big enough to accommodate all of us. Arrangements were therefore made for Anand Kausalyayan and me to stay a short distance round the hill at a place called Santiniketan, though we would eat at the vihara with the other monks – except, of course, when we were all invited to the house of a lay supporter for a ceremonial food-offering. As it turned out, this suited me admirably. Santiniketan, or 'the Abode of Peace', was neither a monastery nor a layman's house but the abode of a Vajrayāna or 'Tantric Buddhist' guru who, as I afterwards learned, had a considerable following in the Kathmandu Valley among both Buddhists and Hindus. As he was ill in bed when we arrived Anandji and I did not see him, but we were warmly welcomed by his four sons, all of whom were clad in white and whose ages ranged from sixteen to twenty-two or twenty-three. At first they were a little shy, but there was no mistaking the interest and goodwill with which they regarded the two foreign Buddhists (I was probably the first Westerner they had ever seen) and it did not take us long to win their confidence. By the time Anandji and I retired for the night, in fact, a definite feeling of warmth had sprung up between the four young hermits and ourselves and I looked forward to getting to know them better. It was indeed fortunate that for the next two weeks I would be staying not amidst the noise and bustle of Ananda Kuti but in the peaceful atmosphere of Santiniketan.

The next morning I was awoken before dawn by the sound of distant singing. The sound was of indescribable sweetness, and seemed to be the product not of a single voice but of scores, even hundreds, of voices. It also seemed to move in waves up the hillside, so that no sooner had one wave reached the top than another started from the bottom, or even from halfway up. As I afterwards discovered, the singing – which I heard every morning of my stay – proceeded from the bands of worshippers who, while it was still dark, made their way up the flights of stone steps leading to the spacious platform where, from amidst a hundred lesser shrines, the great white dome and gilded spire of the Swayambhunath Stupa towered aloft into the heavens. As the worshippers made their way up the steps, and as they circumambulated the stupa, they sang a variety of traditional devotional songs, all of them of such extraordinary sweetness that, on hearing them for the first time, one might well think that choirs of invisible angels were hovering round the sacred hill singing the praises of the Buddha, Dharma, and Sangha. It was an ideal way to be woken up, and the effect of the singing lasted until long after I had risen and long after Anandji and I had left for Ananda Kuti. It lasted until, at about ten o'clock, we went with the other monks to the house of Bhajuratna – the father of Gyan and Maniharsh Jyoti – for our first ceremonial food-offering in Nepal.

Here there was bad news awaiting us. The procession and public meeting that had been planned for the afternoon would probably have to be cancelled. What had happened was that the previous evening – the evening of the very day of the arrival of the Sacred Relics in Nepal – there had been a student demonstration against the interim government's recent security order and ten of the demonstrators had been arrested. When their comrades had attempted to storm the police station to which they had been taken the police tried to disperse them with tear gas and, when this proved ineffectual, opened fire with their rifles. As a result, one student had been killed and two injured. Once again I was confronted by a contrast, this time between violence, as represented by the demonstrators and the police, and non-violence as represented by the Sacred Relics. It seemed a pity that the forces of democracy and the forces of autocracy could not agree on a truce at least for the two weeks that the relics of the Buddha's two chief disciples would be spending in the land of their great master's birth. Unfortunately, it appeared more likely that both parties would try to manipulate the visit in their own interests.

While we were discussing the situation the leader of the students, a youngish Newar Buddhist named Dharmaratna, came to see us. Since the students would be taking out a procession of their own that afternoon, he told us, it would not be possible for them to join the procession that would be taking the Sacred Relics to the parade ground for the public meeting, and if we insisted on holding the procession as planned there might be a clash. Whether he was simply pointing out possible consequences or threatening us with them it was difficult to tell. Perhaps he did not know himself. Be that as it may, we replied that whether or not the Sacred Relics were taken in procession that day depended entirely on His Majesty's wishes. As soon as we had finished our meal, therefore, and had chanted the usual verses of blessing, we went in a body to the Narayanhiti and told the King what Dharmaratna had said. It did not take him long to decide that the wisest course would be to postpone both the procession and the public meeting until the following afternoon, by which time the passions aroused by the shooting would have cooled down. During the half hour or so that we were with King Tribhuvan I was able to observe him much more closely than had been possible in the comparatively crowded marquee where he had received the Sacred Relics the previous day. The dark curls that peeped out from beneath his conical Nepalese cap and framed his rather puffy face gave him a distinctly youthful appearance, particularly as the cap was made of soft, gaily patterned material and was worn at a slightly rakish angle. Despite his rather anxious expression, it was clear that he was a good-natured, well-meaning man who genuinely wanted to do what was best for his country. At the same time, I gained the impression that he was possessed of no great strength of character and could easily be influenced by other people. It was noticeable that in the course of our discussion with him he kept turning for advice to his Private Secretary, a smooth-faced, smiling young Newar Buddhist who wore the same traditional Nepalese costume as the King, except that his cap was made of an even more gaily patterned material and was worn at an even more rakish angle.

Since there would be no procession that day, and no public meeting, the members of the delegation accompanying the Sacred Relics had more time at their disposal than they had expected. On our leaving the Narayanhiti a small party of us, consisting of Anand Kausalyayan, Silabhadra, Dhammaratana, Jinaratana, and myself, therefore decided to pay a visit to the temple of Pashupatinath, the biggest and most important Hindu shrine in Kathmandu, to which pilgrims came from all over Nepal and, indeed, from many parts of India. On our way to the temple we called in at the rest house in which the lay delegates were staying, where we knew we would find Dhammaloka and Mahanama, the two monks who we hoped would be able to accompany us to Pashupatinath and, in Mahanama's case, act as our interpreters. Dhammaloka was a young Sinhalese monk with protruding ears and a toothy smile, while his friend Mahanama, with whom I had corresponded the previous year in his capacity as Secretary of the Dharmodaya Sabha, was the rather effete nephew of Bhajuratna and cousin of the Jyoti brothers. Unlike the other Newar monks, he wore his hair quite long (for a *bhikṣu*) and sported a silk robe that he threw back over one shoulder in a decidedly elegant fashion.

The temple that we had decided to visit was situated on the outskirts of Kathmandu, on the banks of the Bagmati River, and consisted of a cluster of buildings dominated by a pagoda with a golden roof. Though the place as a whole was of no great architectural interest, there was much for us to see and admire as Dhammaloka and Mahanama led our little party through the maze of halls, courtyards, and corridors that occupied the area between the main entrance and the *sanctum sanctorum*. On the way we were particularly impressed by the magnificence of the ornamentation which, usually in the form of wood carving and beaten metalwork in copper, silver, and brass, confronted us at every turn. We were rather less impressed by the dirty and neglected condition of the place, parts of which were so badly in need of repair as to be in danger of tumbling down, and impressed least of all by the seven or eight Brahmin *pūjāris* or officiating priests who glared at us from the depths of the *sanctum sanctorum* as we approached. They were, in fact, the most villainous-looking crew I had ever seen, and with their unkempt hair, bloodshot eyes, and general attitude of suspiciousness, resembled a gang of dacoits rather than a band of *pūjāris*. What was even more surprising, they were not Nepalese but South Indians of some kind. Their complexions were, indeed, so dark as to be almost black, and their blackness was heightened by the bright red of the robes they wore. (Presumably they were red so as not to show the blood with which they were splashed during the animal sacrifices.) At first they were extremely unwilling that we should set foot in the *sanctum sanctorum*, but after Mahanama had expostulated with them for a few minutes – apparently pointing out that we were state guests and had come straight from the Narayanhiti – they not so much allowed us to enter as refrained from preventing us when, seeing that they had begun to waver, Jinaratana strode boldly in and the rest of us followed. It was not that they objected to the presence of Buddhists. In Nepal it was quite usual for Buddhists and Hindus to frequent each other's places of worship. What they objected to was the presence of people who, like the English and the Ceylonese, had come to India – and Nepal – from beyond the *kālapāni* or 'black water' and who as Mlecchas or 'barbarians' were automatically in a state of ritual pollution. In the case of Indians and Nepalese who had travelled abroad such pollution could always be removed by the performance of the appropriate ceremonies; but where we were concerned the *pūjāris* had no means of telling whether or not those ceremonies had been performed or – in the case of at least some of us – whether it was even possible for them to be performed. They had, consequently, no means of telling whether or not our presence polluted the *sanctum sanctorum*. As we wandered round the place they therefore muttered to themselves and scowled.

Apart from the ornamentation there was not much to see. The principal object of interest was the image, two or three feet in height, that stood in the centre of the chamber. Since it was smothered in garlands of red and yellow flowers, and since the *pūjāris* had grouped themselves round it as though to protect it from profanation, I was not able to see it very clearly; but it appeared to have four faces, one fronting each of the chamber's four entrances. It was, in fact, not a fully anthropomorphic image at all but a representation of the god Maheshvara or Shiva, the third member of the Hindu trinity, in the form of a four-faced *linga* or phallus – Pashupati or 'the Lord of Beasts', to whom the temple was dedicated, being one of the many different aspects of Shiva.

Having seen what there was to see in the *sanctum sanctorum*, we were not sorry to leave the villainous-looking *pūjāris* and make our way to the steps that led down to the Bagmati, which was considered to be the Ganges of Nepal just as Pashupati – the district in which Pashupatinath was situated – was considered to be its Benares. These steps extended for quite a distance, and Mahanama described how it was the custom of pious Hindus to be brought here to die. They were set down at the bottom of the steps in such a manner that their feet were covered by the water of the sacred river. To die in this way was regarded as highly auspicious. A Hindu who died in this way would be sure to go straight to heaven. It was also considered necessary for the welfare of the state that the King should expire in the same orthodox fashion, even though in his case it was not a question of going to heaven as a result of merit so much as of returning by virtue of his inherent divinity to the supernal abode from which he had descended for the benefit of the people of Nepal. As Mahanama spoke, I saw in my mind's eye a picture of King Tribhuvan being carried down to the water's edge to die and lying there, perhaps, day after day and night after night until his eyes finally closed for ever. But this was not to be. Less than four years later King Tribhuvan died not on the banks of the Bagmati but, more prosaically, in a hospital in Zurich.

This picture of King Tribhuvan lying at the bottom of the steps with his feet immersed in the water is associated with an actual image I saw that afternoon in or near the precincts of the Pashupatinath temple. The image was of the god Vishnu. The second member of the Hindu trinity was not standing upright but lying flat on his back, and he was lying in a kind of tank, the waters of which scarcely covered his finely moulded torso. They certainly did not cover his diademed head, or his well-braceleted arms, or the great cobra's hood that arched protectively above him – a hood that belonged to the serpent on whose invisible coils he lay stretched out as though on a bed. The god's eyes were closed, but not in ordinary slumber. They were closed in the aeon-long sleep that succeeds the destruction of the universe and precedes its re-creation, and on his face there was an expression of passionless calm.[66]

Twenty-four hours later the expression on almost every human face was one of joy. As the King had foreseen, the passions aroused by the police shooting had cooled down, and it was possible to go ahead with the procession and public meeting, albeit one day later than originally planned. Nevertheless, the fact that only two days earlier a student had been killed could not but make a difference, and the procession was not quite so successful as the organizers had hoped. The public meeting, however, was a complete success. Thousands of people were present, and listened with varying degrees of attention to speeches in Nepali,

Newari, and English. On the platform with the Sacred Relics and the accompanying delegation sat the King and the Crown Prince, the Prime Minister and other members of the interim government, and sundry notabilities. Among these was a mild-looking man in Gandhian dress who, I was told, had been freed at the time of the 'democratic revolution' after spending eighteen years in jail for opposing the Rana regime. To me the most interesting figure on the platform, however, was that of the Prime Minister, Mohan Shamser Janga Bahadur Rana, a dignified old man in a Moghul-style *sherwani* or long coat and a black pillbox hat. Paying no attention to the proceedings, he sat with hands clasping the top of his stick and head sunk on his chest. As Prince Peter remarked to me afterwards, he looked like a beaten old lion.

While opinions may have differed as to whether he looked like a lion, there was no doubt that the last of the hereditary Rana prime ministers of Nepal was beaten. The forces of democracy had triumphed over the forces of autocracy. Indeed, only three days later Mohan Shamser was forced to resign as Prime Minister of the interim government, his place being taken by M. P. Koirala, the titular head of the Nepali Congress and one of the two famous Koirala brothers. Both brothers were on the platform that afternoon, and inevitably one of them was called upon to speak. As the preternaturally thin figure in light blue Nepalese dress strode purposefully to the microphone one might have been forgiven for thinking that if Mohan Shamser looked like a beaten old lion at least one of the Koirala brothers looked remarkably like a triumphant young jackal. The contrast between the representative of autocracy and the representative of democracy was, in fact, as striking as any I had yet encountered in Kathmandu. It was not simply that whereas Mohan Shamser had completed his three score years and ten the Koirala brother was only halfway through his, or that whereas one was clad in black and grey the other was dressed from top to toe in light blue. The real contrast was between the respective attitudes of the two men. Mohan Shamser was not only defeated but exhausted and demoralized by his defeat, as well as profoundly pessimistic about the future of the country. The Koirala brother, on the other hand, was not only victorious but stimulated and elated by victory, as well as highly optimistic about the future of the country. Watching the blue-clad figure at the microphone as he harangued the crowd, and seeing the way in which his meagre frame was dilated with pride, arrogance, and ambition, I could not help wondering whether Nepal would, in fact, be better off under democracy than under autocracy. Were Messrs M. P. and B. P. Koirala *really* an improvement on Mohan Shamser? Would they use their newly acquired power for the benefit of the people whose interests they claimed to represent, or would they use it for their own aggrandizement?

Time alone would tell. Meanwhile, as I looked from the beaten old lion to the triumphant young jackal I had to acknowledge that, so far as present appearances went, my sympathies were with the former rather than with the latter. This was partly owing to the fact that, almost regardless of the goodness or badness of his cause, a man not unoften is a nobler figure in defeat than in victory. Indeed, it might even be argued that whereas victory frequently brings out the worst in people, defeat no less frequently brings out the best. Not that defeat had brought out the best in Mohan Shamser. As the old Prime Minister sat there with hands clasping the top of his stick and head sunk on his chest he was not even a noble figure, but at least he was a dignified one and to that extent deserving of respect. When the time came for me to speak, therefore, I addressed myself not only to the monks, the King, the Crown Prince, and the other members of the audience, but also to the Prime Minister, whose presence on the platform the previous speakers had ignored. 'Venerable Sirs, Your Majesty, Your Royal Highnesses, *Your Highness*,' I began in my most formal manner, turning to each of them as I spoke. As I turned to the Prime Minister, who was officially styled His Highness the Maharaja (the King was known as the Maharajadhiraja), the old man acknowledged the courtesy with a stately inclination of his head.

In my speech I emphasized the fact that the Buddha had been born and brought up in Nepal, and that Nepal was a country with a long and glorious tradition of Buddhist civilization and culture. In particular, I emphasized the importance of its art and architecture, and said how impressed I was by what I had already seen of these. I also exhorted Buddhists and Hindus alike to remember that the best way of honouring the memory of the Buddha – and his two great *arhant* disciples – was by actually practising his teaching. In all this there was nothing that the other Buddhist speakers, especially those belonging to the delegation accompanying the Sacred Relics, might not have said, and, in fact, did say. Towards the end of my speech, however, I struck a more original note. It was a note of warning. In places like Darjeeling and Kalimpong, I said, there were people who had their eye on Nepal and who followed developments there with very great interest. These people were the Christian missionaries, and the reason they followed developments in Nepal with so much interest was that they wanted to enter the country and proselytize it. Both Buddhists and Hindus should beware of them. On no account should they be allowed to set foot on the soil of Nepal. Besides being cunning and unscrupulous they were extremely determined, and once they had succeeded in establishing themselves anywhere it was very difficult to get rid of them and very difficult to stop them undermining the indigenous religion and culture.

In striking this note of warning I was motivated by an intense desire that Nepal should be spared the havoc that Christian missionaries had wrought in other Asian countries. Though conditions in Nepal were far from perfect, and though there were plenty of things that needed changing or abolishing (for instance, the caste system and animal sacrifice), Nepal was one of the few traditional societies still left in the world and it would be a thousand pities if it should be overrun by Bible-thumping fanatics who knew of no better way of propagating the Gospel than by abusing other religions and inducing potential converts to change their faith by offering them such things as modern education, medical treatment, employment, and even hard cash. That Nepal had not been overrun by such fanatics years ago was entirely due to the fact that under the Rana regime Christian missionaries had not been permitted to enter the country. When I struck my note of warning, therefore, I referred to what I did not hesitate to call 'the wisdom of the previous regime' in keeping the missionaries out and urged the government and people of Nepal not to depart from that policy. The fact that I could refer to the Rana regime in these complimentary terms, and that I was willing to give even the devil his due, did not go unnoticed, either on or off the platform. Out of the corner of my eye I saw Mohan Shamser, who had looked up when I started speaking, was regarding me with an expression of mild surprise on his thin, care-worn face. He had certainly not expected to hear any words of praise for the detested Rana regime that afternoon, least of all from a Buddhist monk.

But though I had spoken out loud and clear on the subject of Christian missionaries I was far from being satisfied that I had done enough. A warning that is given in public must be followed up in private, and in this case what better person was there with whom to follow it up than King Tribhuvan, who besides being the connecting link between the old regime and the new, autocracy and democracy, was the embodiment of the collective identity of his people and the guardian of the traditional values on which their lives were based? That same evening, therefore, I went to the Narayanhiti with three other members of the delegation accompanying the Sacred Relics, all of whom were in strong agreement with what I had said in my speech and wanted to express to the King their own concern lest Christian missionaries should be allowed to enter Nepal. These were Narada Thera, Devapriya Valisinha, and the well-known writer Sri Nissanka. As Sinhalese Buddhists all three of them knew far better than I did the kind of damage that Christian missionaries were capable of inflicting on an Asian country. Had not the Portuguese, Dutch, and British emissaries of the Church and the Gospel descended on Ceylon in three successive waves, and had not each of them in turn striven to eradicate the indigenous religion and culture?[67] As Sinhalese Buddhists my three companions could, therefore, give expression to their concern not just with a full knowledge of the facts but with considerable warmth of feeling. In these circumstances it was not surprising that the King heard us with close attention, and appeared to take our private warnings as seriously as the one I had already given in public. At all events, Lok Darshan (as the smooth-faced, smiling young Private Secretary was called) was told to make a note of the matter, and we were left with the impression that something would actually be done. This was all the more reassuring inasmuch as we had heard rumours to the effect that, taking advantage of the politically unsettled condition of the country, Roman Catholic missionaries had already infiltrated some of the more outlying districts from their bases in India and were at work among the unsuspecting tribal people. It was on account of these rumours, in fact, that I had decided to strike my note of warning that afternoon and draw attention to the danger before it was too late.

Besides expressing our concern about missionaries to the King we raised the question of government support for a Buddhist school. (The two subjects were, of course, closely connected, since missionaries were often able to gain a foothold by means of their educational work.) Only that morning Narada Thera and I had been to see the proposed site of a school that the Dharmodaya Sabha was planning to build. On our way back, however, we found that a Buddhist school had already been established in the neighbourhood of Swayambhunath by a *vajrācārya* who, we were informed, had actually manufactured the bricks for the building with his own hands. This unexpected discovery both surprised and delighted us, and on our return to the Ananda Kuti Vihara Narada Thera suggested to the leading members of the Dharmodaya Sabha that, instead of trying to build a school of their own, they should join forces with the enterprising *vajrācārya* and help develop *his* school. Since the Dharmodaya Sabha was supported by only a minority of Newar Buddhists (mainly by Bhajuratna and his sons) the suggestion was a sensible one, but it was soon evident that Mahanama, Maniharsh Jyoti, and the rest did not find it acceptable. The followers of 'reformist' Theravāda Buddhism had no intention of cooperating with a follower of the Vajrayāna. Naturally, Narada Thera and I said nothing to King Tribhuvan about these divisions among his Newar Buddhist subjects. We were concerned simply to obtain from him a promise of government support for 'a Buddhist school' and this we had no difficulty in doing. I also took advantage of the opportunity to ask the King if there would be any objection to my returning to Nepal. Since the day of my arrival I had been talking to people about the possibility of forming a YMBA in Kathmandu, but mindful of what had happened in Darjeeling (and Gangtok) I did not want to take any definite steps in that direction without being sure I would be able to spend some time there whenever necessary. Fortunately, the King said there would be no objection to my coming again, and the four of us left the Narayanhiti well satisfied with our evening's work.

From the following morning the Sacred Relics were exposed for the veneration of the public. The first exposition took place at the Ananda Kuti Vihara, to which the Sacred Relics had been taken after the public meeting and where they were to be kept for the following week. Eager to show their respect for the memory of the Buddha's chief disciples as well as to obtain whatever blessings they could from the relics themselves, hundreds of white-clad Newars had been pouring into the vihara since dawn and were waiting in a jostling, excited mass for the inauguration of the worship of the Sacred Relics to begin. Once again I realized how lucky I was to be staying in the peaceful atmosphere of Santiniketan. That morning the worship was inaugurated by Prime Minister Mohan Shamser, and as was customary he inaugurated it by unlocking the silver-gilt reliquary so that the lid could be removed and the capsules containing the relics exposed to view. When Venerable Amritananda handed him the key, however, the old man looked doubtfully at the reliquary and asked, 'Do I have to touch it?' 'Of course,' replied Venerable Amritananda cheerfully, whereupon, very slowly and gingerly, Mohan Shamser inserted the key in the lock and gave it a single cautious turn. The reason for the Prime Minister's reluctance was that what to the pious Buddhist were 'Sacred Relics' to the orthodox Hindu were simply pieces of human bone and, as such, parts of a dead body, any contact with which automatically involved ritual pollution.

When, later on in the morning, Venerable Amritananda told me what had happened (at the time I was too far away to hear the exchange between him and the Prime Minister), I expressed considerable surprise that, even though he might want to oblige the Newar Buddhists for political reasons, an orthodox old Hindu like Mohan Shamser should allow himself to incur ritual pollution by touching the casket containing the Sacred Relics. Amritananda's almond eyes narrowed with amusement at my simplicity. Hindu orthodoxy was a very elastic thing, he explained, especially where the Ranas of Nepal were concerned. All Mohan Shamser had to do was to take a ritual bath when he got home, and get his household Brahmins to mutter a few Vedic mantras over him. At the worst, he would have to swallow the five sacred products of the cow – milk, clarified butter, curds, urine, and cow dung. Personally, he found it difficult to understand how it could be more polluting to touch the casket containing the Sacred Relics than to swallow some of these things. From the way in which Amritananda said this it was clear that he did not have much sympathy for the predicament in which the Prime Minister had found himself that morning. I even got the impression that, as a Newar Buddhist, he derived a certain amount of satisfaction from the thought that the former upholder of the anti-Buddhist laws had been obliged to show respect for the Sacred Relics even at the expense of his Hindu orthodoxy. Indeed, I got the impression that he derived a certain amount of satisfaction from the thought that by handing Mohan Shamser the key of the reliquary, and answering his question in the way he did, he had been personally responsible for scoring that particular tactical moral victory. Whether or not this was the case, there was no doubt that with the Newar Buddhists now on the winning side, and in favour with the King, Venerable Amritananda's star was in the ascendant. There was also no doubt that he was well aware of this and was taking full advantage of the fact.

Though the conversation that followed Amritananda's tactical moral victory over Mohan Shamser was the first we had been able to have since my arrival, I had known him since the beginning of 1950. We had met in Rajgir, when he accompanied Kashyapji and myself on our expedition to the Pippala Cave.[68] Since then he had been staying in Kathmandu (apart from a few months in Kalimpong, of course!), where despite the fact that he was permitted to preach only at the Ananda Kuti Vihara he had already become highly popular as a preacher among the Newar Buddhists. With the advent of the 'democratic revolution', and the collapse of the Rana autocracy, he had naturally been able to expand the scope of his activities considerably and do a number of things he had not been able to do before. Though by no means the seniormost of the Ceylon- and Burma-returned Newar monks, of whom there were about two dozen in Nepal, he was by far the most energetic and capable, and when a committee was set up to make arrangements for the reception of the Sacred Relics he was inevitably appointed Secretary. Since King Tribhuvan was Chairman of the committee, Amritananda frequently had occasion to meet him, and was in and out of the Narayanhiti at all hours. Indeed, he had become quite a favourite with the King, and on one occasion (it may have been on the King's birthday) had even been permitted to chant Buddhist verses of blessing over him in Pāli and tie a 'thread of protection' round his wrist – a thing that would have been unthinkable under the previous regime.

But success is rarely without its drawbacks. The fact that Amritananda had risen to a position of some influence, even though not of real power, had not unnaturally created a certain distance between him and the other Newar monks, with the result that, distance having led to mistrust and mistrust to misunderstanding, he was criticized on account of a number of things that might otherwise have passed without comment. He was particularly criticized for chanting verses of blessing over the King, and tying the 'thread of protection' round his wrist, while he himself was standing and the King seated on his throne. By performing the ceremony in this way, it was felt, he had lowered the dignity of the monastic order, members of which should neither remain standing when a layman is seated nor occupy a seat lower than that of a layman – even when the layman happened to be the incarnation of Vishnu. There had also been differences between Amritananda on the one hand and the Jyoti brothers and Mahanama on the other, though what these differences were about it was impossible for a non-Newar to tell. Nonetheless, they were sufficiently serious for Amritananda and Maniharsh Jyoti to have become the leaders of what were virtually two factions among the members and supporters of the Dharmodaya Sabha.

With the arrival of the Sacred Relics, however, a change had taken place. Mistrust and misunderstanding had been dissipated, criticism forgotten, and differences set aside, at least for the time being. All sections of the Newar community had been swept by a great wave of joy – a joy that had come surging up from the depths of their hearts. Whether rich or poor, men or women, high caste or low caste (for the Hindu caste system had been imposed on them centuries ago) they all rejoiced that they were able to pay homage to the memory of the two *arhants* who had been the Buddha's chief disciples. They rejoiced that they were able to welcome Buddhists from other countries. They rejoiced that the Sacred Relics had been kept at the Narayanhiti. They rejoiced that there had been a procession and a public meeting. They rejoiced that they were freer to practise and propagate their religion than they had ever been before. They rejoiced that public recognition had been given to the importance of Buddhism and, therefore, to the importance of the Newar Buddhists. They rejoiced that the Sacred Relics were being exposed for worship at the Ananda Kuti Vihara and that they were being looked after by relays of yellow-robed monks of their own community who were able to tell them about the lives of Śāriputra and Maudgalyāyana in their own language. As for the Newar monks themselves, they rejoiced that they were free to preach the Dharma, and that they could look after the Sacred Relics and minister to the needs of the hundreds of worshippers who poured into the vihara each day.

So much, in fact, did Amritananda and the rest of the Newar monks rejoice in looking after the Sacred Relics that they were glad to take on the entire responsibility for so doing. This left the visiting monks much freer than Sangharatana and I had been in Gangtok, Kalimpong, or Darjeeling. When not either going to the houses of lay supporters for ceremonial food-offerings, or giving lectures, or attending the various functions held in honour of the Sacred Relics, some of us therefore took advantage of the opportunity of doing a little sightseeing – especially as there were a number of English-speaking young men who were willing to escort us wherever we wanted to go. One of the first things I saw was Bodhnath, the great stupa to the east of Kathmandu that was said to contain relics of the former Buddha Kāśyapa, the third of the five Buddhas of the present or 'auspicious' aeon. About a hundred feet in height, it consisted of a three-tiered circumambulatory platform, a hemispherical dome, and a squared top-piece surmounted by a thirteen-stepped pyramid complete with ceremonial umbrella and 'sun-moon' finial. Though the white dome and gilded upper portion of the stupa were themselves sufficiently impressive as they loomed against the blue sky that afternoon, they were not the most remarkable feature of the vast structure. Its most remarkable feature was the squared top-piece, and the reason for this was that on each of the four gilded sides of the top-piece there was painted an enormous pair of eyes. These eyes regarded one steadily; they even followed one as one circumambulated the stupa and as one paused, every now and then, to peer into the shrines by which it was surrounded and which it completely dwarfed. Indeed, one had the feeling that they continued to follow one even after one had turned one's back on them and – in my case – had entered the two-storeyed Tibetan-style building that was the abode of the Chinia Lama.

I had not heard of the Chinia or 'Chinese' Lama before, but the young men from the Nepal Bank who were escorting me that day were eager that I should meet him and I gathered from their remarks that he was a well-known local character. The room in which he received us was not unlike the upstairs room at the Tharpa Choling Gompa in which the old eagle-abbot and I, with Thubden Tendzin as interpreter, had carried on our discussions earlier in the year. That is to say, it was quite a small room and furnished in the traditional Tibetan manner, though from the richness of the furnishings it was evident that the Chinia Lama was a much wealthier man than the abbot of the Tharpa Choling Gompa and lived in a much grander style. It was also evident that he lived in a much less monastic style, for his abode swarmed with women and children and servants and my interpreter on this occasion was a lively, attractive girl of fifteen or sixteen who introduced herself as the Chinia Lama's daughter. Since she had been educated at a convent school in India she spoke excellent English, but being of an extremely talkative disposition she kept breaking off in the middle of the sentence she was translating in order to tell me, at some length, what an extremely holy man her father was and how greatly he was respected by everybody. Meanwhile the holy man himself sat there in his brocade robes looking like a slightly depraved version of the original Laughing Buddha. Since very little of what I said to him, or he said to me, actually got translated by his talkative and admiring daughter, there was no question of any meeting of minds, but to judge from his continual nods, smiles, and winks he was pleased to see me, though whether he was pleased to see me because he saw in me a potential disciple or a potential customer it was difficult to tell.

Whatever the truth of the matter may have been, we did not stay long with the Chinia Lama and were soon on our way to the ancient town of Lalitpur (Patan), which was situated two or three miles south of Kathmandu. 'Lalita' means natural, spontaneous, or charming, so that it would be possible to render Lalitpur as 'the City Beautiful'. It would even be possible to render it as 'the City of the Fine Arts', for the term 'lalita' also means fine – as distinct from applied – in the aesthetic sense. In either case the rendering would be appropriate. As I saw when we entered the main square, the place was so beautiful as to be a veritable wonderland, and it owed its beauty not to nature but almost entirely to art. On all sides rose palaces and temples, and slender columns on the top of which knelt royal personages with hands folded in prayer. A few of the buildings were of white stone, delicately chiselled, but most were of warm red brick and wood and of these the majority were in the pagoda style of architecture, with tiered roofs and elaborately wrought doorways, trellis windows, and roof struts, some of them painted and gilded. In the case of one enormous palace the projecting eaves were supported by roof struts in the form of the fantastically elongated erect penises of gigantic monkey-like figures standing upright with their backs to the wall. Besides the palaces and the temples, though rising to a lesser height, there were the stupas (or *chaityas*, as the smaller ones were called), which I found not only in the main square but in all the squares and courtyards through which we passed. In some of these, indeed, they were as thick on the ground as the monuments in an English churchyard. So many buildings and stupas were there, in fact, and so much art of every kind, that the thought of the length of time it must have taken to produce them all was inevitably suggestive of the beginningless prehistoric past into which recede and disappear the few score centuries of the world's recorded history.

As I wrote in a rather lyrical article that I contributed to *Stepping-Stones* soon after my return to Kalimpong,

If the larger monuments of Nepal convey such an impression by their sheer antiquity, the smaller ones convey it more indirectly but no less effectively by their staggering multiplicity, and by their unbelievable richness of ornamentation. When one sees a geological formation miles high, and composed of innumerable strata; and when one reflects that hundreds, perhaps thousands, of years went into the making of a single inch-thick layer of rock, then one realizes how incalculably old the whole formation is, how ancient its mountains, how hoary with age its hills. And when one looks down through the clear blue waters which girdle some Pacific isle, sees the huge masses of delicately tinted pink and red coral branching up like great trees from the bottom, and considers how long it takes how many tiny creatures to add a single inch to their growth, then once again one's brain has to grapple with the thought of almost infinite duration, of millions of years of silent labour beneath the surface of the sea. Similar is the impression produced by the amazing multiplicity of the *chaityas*, viharas, and temples of Nepal; by the thousands of tiny shrines which cluster at the corners of the streets; by the tens of thousands of carved wooden windows, doors, and posts, by the millions of images, the miles of painted banners, the acres of hammered work in brass and copper, silver and gold. One feels that the production of such tremendous artistic wealth must have kept a whole nation busy for hundreds, if not for thousands, of years. So enormous, indeed, is the number of objects which have been accumulated, and so unmistakably does each bear the stamp of the same fantastic beauty, that the spectator even feels like attributing their production to the inexhaustible fecundity of some great natural force rather than to the labour of mere human hands. This impression is heightened by the minuteness, delicacy, and intricacy of much of the work. Leaving aside examples of craftsmanship in metal, ivory, and wood – materials which easily lend themselves to fine workmanship – and taking instead an example such as the Maha Bodhi temple at Patan, one finds that every single square inch of its exterior surface has been carved with a tiny image of the Buddha, on a scale so minute that it at once reminded me of a passage in one of the *sūtras*[69] which says that a Buddha together with His company of Bodhisattvas is contained in every grain of dust – a symbolical way of expressing the truth that every phenomenon in the universe contains indestructibly the potentiality of Bodhi.[70]

These somewhat extravagantly worded comments had reference to Nepalese art and architecture in general. But there was no doubting the fact that one could experience what the same article called 'this feeling of incredible ancientness' much more strongly amidst the glories of Lalitpur, which was a predominantly Buddhist town, than among the more hybrid splendours of either Kathmandu or Bhatgaon, the third of the three principal towns of the valley, which I visited about ten days later. In the meantime, I continued to do what sightseeing I could in the intervals between my other activities. With Dhammaloka and two young Nepalese for company I explored the curio shops in the Kathmandu bazaar, saw the temple of White Tārā, and paid a visit to the museum where, not surprisingly, we found a number of remarkably beautiful images, painted scrolls, and illuminated manuscripts. Dhammaloka and I also climbed the steps to the top of the Swayambhunath hill in order to take a closer look at the great stupa that crowned its summit. Here we found ourselves in another world. On all sides there were *chaityas* and pagoda-style temples and other shrines, belfries, and residential quarters, from the midst of which rose the enormous bulk of the Swayambhunath Stupa. Apart from the fact that the circumambulatory platform had not been incorporated into the general structure, it was built in much the same style as Bodhnath. There was, however, a difference in the relative proportions of the dome and the gilded upper portion of the stupa, the latter being at least twice the height of the former. Moreover, from the cornice of the squared top-piece – which was surmounted not by a thirteen-stepped pyramid but by thirteen tapering rings – there rose four gilded triangular plates that gave the top-piece the appearance of a head wearing a four-pointed diadem. All this had the effect of giving the top-piece much greater prominence, with the result that the enormous pair of eyes depicted on each of its gilded sides seemed to regard one even more steadily than at Bodhnath, as well as more intently.

As we made our way round the platform beneath their unblinking gaze, I noticed that strings of what from a distance looked like prayer-flags were stretched from the umbrella of the stupa to the roofs of the surrounding temples and other buildings. On closer inspection the 'prayer-flags' proved to be rectangular silver plates, each about twelve or sixteen inches in size, hinged together lengthwise so as to give flexibility to the string to which they belonged. Each string must have consisted of two or three hundred such plates. A similar inspection revealed that the open-work curtains hanging in front of some of the shrines, through which one had a glimpse of the image within, consisted of myriads of tiny metal rings fastened together in the manner of chain mail. Not that all the craftsmanship at Swayambhunath was on the same reduced scale. On a pedestal at the top of the stone-paved steps on the eastern side of the sacred hill lay a giant vajra or 'thunderbolt sceptre' – the Tantric symbol of irresistible spiritual energy and insight. It was about eight feet in length, and round it played a band of long-tailed grey monkeys, their quick, lithe movements contrasting in the most amusing fashion with the solidity and immovability of the vajra.

On another occasion I had the company not of Dhammaloka but of someone I had known in Kalimpong. This was Ratnaman, the round-faced, rose-cheeked young Newar who had taken over from Gyan Jyoti as Treasurer of the YMBA but who was now living in Kathmandu with his half-brothers and helping in the family business. He had come to see me on the very day of my arrival, having heard that I was among the monks accompanying the Sacred Relics, and had offered his services as cicerone. With him and four or five other young men, therefore, I went to see the Old Palace, as it was called, a pagoda-style building that was now unoccupied – except, it was said, by the ghosts of those who had been murdered there. Unfortunately, it was not only unoccupied but locked, and since the caretaker could not be found we had to content ourselves with gazing up at the intricately carved lattice windows and roof struts, some of which were so badly cracked as to be in danger of disintegration. From this scene of desolation and decay we drove to the Singha Durbar, stopping only to ascend a tower which, so my companions assured me, was 200 years old and 200 feet high. Whether it was really as high as that it was difficult to tell, but it was high enough, and from the top we had a fine view of the whole of Kathmandu, with Bodhnath to the east, Swayambhunath on its hill to the west, and the Himalayas far away to the north.

The Singha Durbar was built in the same neo-classical style as the Narayanhiti but on a much larger scale. I indeed had the impression – which may have been mistaken – that it was two or three times as big. If this was the case it was not surprising, for since the upper floors of the Singha Durbar comprised the official residence of the hereditary Rana prime ministers and the lower ones the secretariat, it had been, until very recently, the real seat of power in Nepal. But if it is true that 'uneasy lies

At the Swayambhunath stupa, Kathmandu

the head that wears a crown', that head lies all the more uneasy if the crown – or the power that the crown represents – has been usurped. On our approaching the Singha Durbar I noticed that there were no flights of steps as at the Narayanhiti. Neither were there any flights of steps within the building. In order to reach the upper floors, where the Prime Minister lived, we had to climb up a narrow, winding iron staircase at the top of which was an iron trapdoor. Access to the person of the Prime Minister had obviously been made as difficult as possible, no doubt as a precaution against assassination by an opponent of autocracy or a *coup d'état* by a brother or nephew impatient for power. On emerging from the trapdoor, which had been opened especially for us, we found ourselves in a series of state apartments which, like those of the Narayanhiti, were furnished in European style, but far more splendidly and luxuriously. The finest of these apartments was the vast reception hall, with its dozens of crystal chandeliers, from the broad balcony of which one looked out onto the courtyard. To this courtyard, in the days before the 'democratic revolution', would come – or be brought – all those who had any business with the Prime Minister, and at ten o'clock each morning he would appear on the balcony and deal with them. One of the young men told me that if the Prime Minister happened to be in a good mood a criminal who had been brought for sentence might be given a government job, whereas if he happened to be in a bad mood an innocent citizen who had come with a petition for a government job might be sent to gaol. Such were the ways of autocracy!

Having climbed down the spiral staircase and heard the trapdoor being closed and bolted above our heads, we drove from the Singha Durbar to another neo-classical Rana palace. This was the residence of the Commander-in-Chief, Keshab Shamser Janga Bahadur Rana. Though not nearly so big as the Singha Durbar, it was furnished in very much better taste and contained an excellent library consisting, for the most part, of finely bound volumes of the English classics. I was therefore not surprised to learn that Keshab Shamser was reputed to be the most cultured of the Ranas, that he was a liberal patron of the arts, particularly of Nepali literature, and that besides being Commander-in-Chief he was (or had been – the young men differed about this) a popular Minister of Education. Behind the palace there was a garden, or rather a series of gardens, one for each of the six seasons of the Indian year, and here too Keshab Shamser's good taste was very much in evidence. Since it was winter, it was the winter garden that was in bloom, principally with bronze, white, yellow, and pink chrysanthemums. The garden that appealed to me most, however, was the spring garden, though it appealed to me not on account of its flowers, which were not yet out, but on account of the verses that had been inscribed on a marble slab high up on the wall – verses with which I had been familiar since my boyhood and which now gave me, as they had given me a hundred times before, a keen thrill of delight.

Alas, that Spring should vanish with the Rose!
That Youth's sweet-scented Manuscript should close!
The Nightingale that in the Branches sang,
Ah, whence, and whither flown again, who knows!

> Ah love! could thou and I with Fate conspire
> To grasp this sorry Scheme of Things entire,
> Would not we shatter it to bits – and then
> Re-mould it nearer to the Heart's Desire!
>
> Ah, Moon of my Delight who know'st no wane,
> The Moon of Heav'n is rising once again:
> How oft hereafter rising shall she look
> Through this same Garden after me – in vain![71]

It was strange to find Omar Khayyám's verses inscribed, with such exquisite appropriateness, in the garden of a neo-classical Rana palace in Kathmandu. There was little doubt that Keshab Shamser's reputation as the most cultured member of his clan was well deserved.

Cultured or not cultured, however, a Rana was a Rana, and autocracy was autocracy, and the Buddhist Newars, at least, were glad to think that the moon that rose over the shrines and palaces of the Kathmandu Valley would in future look in vain not only for Keshab Shamser but for the whole tribe of Ranas. They were glad to think that even if the 'democratic revolution' had not actually shattered the existing scheme of things to bits it had in certain important respects remoulded it a little nearer to their heart's desire, for were not the Sacred Relics now being exposed for worship at the Ananda Kuti Vihara each day and were not their own Newari-speaking monks looking after the precious contents of the silver-gilt reliquary and explaining their significance? – things that would have been impossible under the Rana regime. While I was busy sightseeing in the company of Dhammaloka and my young Nepalese friends, as well as meeting people and giving lectures, the white-clad Newars therefore continued to pour into the vihara in their hundreds and to worship the Sacred Relics with a fervour which, by all accounts, was hardly second to that of the Tibetans whom I had seen paying their respects to the remains of the two *arhants* in Gangtok and Kalimpong a few months earlier. After a week, the flood of white-clad devotees having abated slightly, the Sacred Relics were taken first to Lalitpur and then to Bhadgaon, the Buddhist inhabitants of which were eager to have the opportunity of welcoming them to their own cities, which in ancient times had been the capitals of independent kingdoms. This meant that the visiting monks were again needed to help look after the Sacred Relics, especially when they were being taken in procession from the Ananda Kuti Vihara to the Gyabahal Vihara in Lalitpur and from the Gyabahal Vihara to the Old Palace in Bhadgaon, as well as needed to take part in the large and enthusiastic public meetings that were held in both places.

In Lalitpur, where the Sacred Relics were exposed for worship for four days, the public meeting was held under the presidency of Crown Prince Mahendra, while in predominantly Hindu Bhadgaon, where they remained for only a day and a night, it was held under the presidency of M. P. Koirala, the new Prime Minister, who had replaced Mohan Shamser a few days earlier. At each of these meetings, the first of which lasted for several hours, I spoke briefly in English. The rest of the time I spent simply studying the scene, particularly the faces of the other speakers, most of whom spoke either in Newari or in Nepali, neither of which I understood. One of the faces I studied most at the Lalitpur meeting was that of Crown Prince Mahendra, who sat listening to the various speakers without the slightest show of interest. Lok Darshan, the King's Private Secretary, and other friends, had hinted to me that the Crown Prince was quite stupid, perhaps even mentally deficient, and that he possessed no political influence whatever. He certainly lacked his royal father's openness of manner, and it was difficult to tell what he was thinking, if indeed he was thinking anything at all, especially as his eyes were concealed behind a pair of dark glasses. Years later, when he had succeeded to the throne, and when the name of King Mahendra of Nepal had become a byword for political astuteness throughout Asia, I wondered whether his former 'stupidity' had not been deliberately assumed. Lok Darshan, whom the new king eventually shut up in prison for a number of years, may well have wondered the same thing.

Whatever the truth of the matter may have been, the Crown Prince's presence at the meeting that afternoon hardly added to the liveliness of the proceedings, and I was not sorry when the long series of speeches came to an end. As soon as I decently could I left for Kathmandu, where I had to deliver a lecture, from thence returning to Lalitpur with Dr Soft and Devapriya Valisinha in time to attend a kind of religious service at the Gyabahal Vihara. Apart from the singing of the bands of worshippers who made their way up to the Swayambhunath Stupa every morning before dawn, and my brief and inadequate exchanges with the four young hermits of Santiniketan, this was my first real contact with traditional

Speaking in Patan (Lalitpur)

Nepalese Buddhism, as distinct from the 'reformist' Theravāda which Amritananda and his colleagues were seeking to introduce in its place, and the experience moved me deeply. Unlike the Ananda Kuti Vihara, the Gyabahal Vihara was not a modern structure but one of the oldest and most important, as well as most richly carved and decorated, religious foundations in Lalitpur and, indeed, in the whole Kathmandu Valley. Originally it had been a vihara in the stricter sense of the term, that is, it had been not only a temple but a monastery and had housed, besides images of the Buddhas and bodhisattvas, a community of celibate monks. Centuries ago, however, under the influence of a misunderstood and misapplied Vajrayāna or 'Tantric' Buddhism, these monks had not only given up their vows and married but had continued to live in the vihara with their wives and families and to conduct religious ceremonies there. The monks had thus in effect become priests, and occupied among the

Newar Buddhists a position analogous to that of the Brahmins among the Hindus. Indeed, like the Brahmins they had become not just priests but hereditary priests, for the present-day incumbents of the vihara claimed to be the direct descendants of the ex-monks of medieval times. A similar development had, it seemed, taken place at all the other viharas in the Kathmandu Valley, with the result that in the course of a few generations the character of Nepalese Buddhism had entirely changed.

What kind of spiritual life was being pursued in the secularized – or at least laicized – cloisters of the other viharas I had no means of telling, but the scene I witnessed at the Gyabahal Vihara that evening was sufficient to convince me that, degenerate though it undoubtedly was in certain respects, traditional Nepalese Buddhism was by no means dead. 'Aloft on the altar at the end of the chamber', I wrote shortly afterwards in the same lyrical article from which I have already quoted,

> stood a silver image of the thousand-armed Avalokiteśvara. Innumerable lamps were burning, and shed a soft lustre on the dark crimson pillars and yellow frescoed walls. A long row of yellow-robed figures, one of men, the other of women, sat on the right and left side respectively of the nave of the shrine. They chanted with half-closed eyes, their hands assuming various mudras, and the sound of their chanting was sweet as the music of birds in the trees of Sukhāvatī. At a signal from their leader, a stout, dignified old man who sat on a throne nearest the altar, holding the vajra in his right hand and the bell in his left, the deep-throated Tibetan trumpets would roar, and the drums beat, until the whole place trembled and shook with spiritual vibrations. Then again the brisk sweet chant would rise up like a wave, and the row of shaven-headed old women sitting opposite me would sway themselves gently to and fro, eyes closed, their wrinkled faces shining in the soft golden light of the lamps, absorbed within themselves and oblivious to the sights and sounds of the outer world....[72]

So deeply did that service at the Gyabahal Vihara move me that, as I stole from the shrine and crept down the uneven stairs into the darkened streets, and heard the sound of the chanting dying away behind me in the distance, I could not help thinking that it was in an atmosphere and environment such as this, profoundly peaceful yet full of hidden life and secret activity, rather than amidst the noise and bustle of the Ananda Kuti Vihara, that there might be engendered a spiritual impulse dynamic enough to bring about a revival of Buddhism in Nepal.

The public meeting that took place in Bhadgaon four days later marked the easternmost point of the Sacred Relics' peregrinations, as well as the virtual end of their visit to Nepal. Except that it was the new Prime Minister who presided and not the Crown Prince, the meeting followed much the same pattern as the one held in Lalitpur, and once again I studied the faces of the other speakers. On the way from Lalitpur to Bhadgaon it had, however, been my good fortune to see the Kumari or Virgin, as she was known, the young Newar Buddhist girl who was believed to be the incarnation of the bloodthirsty Hindu goddess Taleju, the tutelary deity of the royal house – one of the strangest examples of the way in which the Buddhism of Nepal had become contaminated with Hinduism. On my arrival in Lalitpur that morning with some of the younger Newar monks, the jeep in which we were travelling had been irresistibly drawn into the procession that had already begun escorting the Sacred Relics to Bhadgaon. As the mass of white-clad humanity by which we were soon surrounded slowly made its way through the narrow, winding streets of the ancient city I had plenty of time to look about me. On either side rose tier upon tier of elaborately carved windows, all slanting slightly outwards, and looking down at the procession from one of the finest of these I saw the inscrutable face of a young girl dressed as a Hindu goddess. Her almond-shaped eyes were enlarged with kohl and there was a third eye painted in the centre of her forehead. 'The Kumari!' whispered my young companions, momentarily awestruck despite their Theravāda training.

In Bhadgaon I had the opportunity of seeing the Old Palace, where the Sacred Relics were exposed for worship and where the monks were given a ceremonial meal before the meeting, as well as the no less famous Nyatapola or 'five-roofed' temple. The former residence of the Malla kings was an imposing but rather dilapidated building in which the warm red of the external brickwork made a pleasing contrast with the brown of the richly carved wooden string courses, doors, windows, and roof-struts, from which most of the paint and gilding had long since peeled away. As for the temple, it was dedicated to the bloodthirsty Hindu goddess Bhavani and was a perfect example of the Nepalese 'pagoda' style of architecture. Rectangular in shape, and consisting of five storeys of decreasing size, each with its own roof, it stood on the fifth and last of a series of rectangular stone terraces, also of decreasing size, which clearly were intended to duplicate the five roofs towering above. On account of this arrangement the structure gave an impression of both solidity and lightness. It was as though it was difficult to disturb but that it might, at the same time, fly away at any moment. Nor was this all. Running up the front of the terraces was a flight of stone steps, and on either side of the steps, on the edge of each of the terraces, sat or stood a pair of divine, or human, or animal figures – no doubt the guardians of the approach to the holy of holies. These figures were all of enormous size and brilliantly painted, and introduced into the front of the temple, at least, an element of life and animation that would otherwise have been lacking. On taking a closer look at them after the meeting, before leaving for Kathmandu with Anandji and some friends from Trichandra College, I also saw that the figures were extremely well executed. Flanking the steps at ground level were two seated sages or divinities (they could have been either), behind and above them two standing elephants, magnificently caparisoned, behind and above the elephants two lions, and so on, all gazing straight ahead and all seemingly oblivious to the swarms of men, women, and children who were constantly ascending and descending the steps between them.

So fascinating was the busy, colourful scene that had I been on my own I would probably have remained in the temple square for an hour or two more, simply observing, but the friends from Trichandra College had arranged for Anandji and me to give lectures that afternoon and we had to be on our way. The lectures were held at the Saraswati Sadan, a hall which, as its name suggested, was dedicated to the Hindu (and Mahāyāna Buddhist) goddess of learning and culture. Both Anandji and I had already spoken there several times. We were, in fact, the two most popular speakers among the visiting monks, especially with the students, who invariably gave us an enthusiastic reception. On the present occasion I spoke on 'Buddhism and Education'[73] and was followed by Anandji on 'Buddhism and Dialectical Materialism' – a subject that, as I knew, was very close to his heart. After we had given our lectures we answered questions, of which there were, as usual, quite a number. At first these were addressed now to me and now to Anandji, more or less alternately, but after some fifteen or twenty minutes they began to be directed exclusively to Anandji. Moreover, they all came out of the darkness at the very back of the hall, they all came seemingly from one and the same person (though who it was, I was unable to descry), and they all revolved round the same topic. This topic was the *ātman*, the unchanging immortal Self which, according to Hinduism, constitutes the inmost essence of man and is the subject of transmigration. The reason for the questions was that in the course of his lecture Anandji had touched on the Buddhist *anātma* doctrine, that is to say, that there is no unchanging immortal self, that the phenomena of consciousness arise in dependence on conditions, ceasing when those conditions cease, and that the process of 'transmigration' does not logically require an unchanging transmigrant. As the questions came out of the darkness, each one more insidious than the last, I realized that the unseen questioner could hardly be a student. Anandji was being seriously challenged on his own ground. The *anātma* doctrine was being attacked. Buddhism itself was being attacked – and being attacked in a manner that was all the more deadly for being so subtle. I also realized that Anandji – who was not at his best when dealing with topics of a purely philosophical nature – was simply parrying the questions rather than answering them and even, in some cases, trying to turn them aside with one of the witticisms for which he was so justly famous. Eventually the exchange came to an inconclusive end, the meeting broke up, and as Anandji and I stepped down from the platform the crowd parted respectfully to make way for a wizened little old man in traditional Nepalese dress who, emerging from between their ranks, slowly and deliberately limped towards us, his steps supported by a silver-headed cane. Friends hastened to introduce the newcomer, who clearly was none other than Anandji's unseen questioner on the topic of the *ātman*. In a deferential undertone we were informed that he was His Holiness Hemaraj, the Rajpurohit or Royal Chaplain, a personage who, as I already knew, was a pillar of Hindu socio-religious orthodoxy and moreover one who, until the collapse of the Rana autocracy, had been the second most powerful man in the country. Gravely and with an air of punctilious politeness he shook hands all round. When it came to my turn I perceived that his hand was not only withered with age but also cold and dry as that of a corpse. Nor was this all that I perceived. The truth of the matter was that I had met the Rajpurohit before, though not in the flesh, and that on his emergence from the crowd I had recognized him instantly – even as he, no doubt, had recognized me. He was not just a high-caste Brahmin, not just the Royal Chaplain. In reality he was a much more dark and dangerous figure, and in view of the nature of our previous encounter I did not find it at all surprising that on the present occasion he should have attacked the *anātman* doctrine and, in this way, have sought to undermine the foundations of the higher spiritual life.

The encounter in question had taken place in Delhi seven years earlier, only a few weeks after my arrival in India. I was meditating one night when there suddenly appeared before me, as it were suspended in mid-air, the head of an old man. He had a grey stubble on scalp and chin and his yellowish face was deeply lined and wrinkled as though with the sins of a lifetime. 'You're wasting your time,' he exclaimed, with a dreadful sneer. 'There's nothing in the universe but matter! Nothing but matter!'

'There is something higher than matter,' I promptly retorted. 'I know it, because I am experiencing it now.' Whereupon the apparition vanished.[74]

Why I should have encountered the old man a second time I do not know, but there was absolutely no doubt in my mind that the head that I now saw beneath a black Nepalese cap, and attached to a correspondingly wizened body, at the Saraswati Sadan in Kathmandu, was the very same head that I had seen suspended in mid-air before me in Delhi all those years ago. There was the same grey stubble, the same yellowish complexion, the same lines and wrinkles. Even the slightly high-pitched, sneering tone of voice was the same, so that the insidious questions that the Rajpurohit had put to Anandji about the *ātman* seemed to be identical in spirit and intent with the declaration of Māra or the Evil One – as I believed him to be – that there was nothing in the universe but matter. But though I recognized the old man, and though he must have recognized me, neither of us gave any sign of having done so, and after we had exchanged a few commonplace remarks he politely took leave of us all. Reflecting on the episode afterwards I felt more convinced than ever that if it was, in fact, Māra's head that had appeared to me in Delhi, and if that head was identical with the head I had seen beneath the black Nepalese cap, then in some mysterious way Māra and the Rajpurohit were a single entity, or at least were intimately connected. Nor was this surprising. The Rajpurohit was a pillar of orthodox Hinduism, and in Nepal the practice of orthodox Hinduism involved the rigid – and until recently the legally enforced – observance of the caste system, including Untouchability, together with the ritual slaughter of countless buffaloes, goats, and chickens to bloodthirsty male and female divinities – abominations which it was possible to support only if it was one's business to represent irreligion as religion and, in this way, to encourage people to follow the path that led downwards into Darkness rather than the path that led upwards into Light.

Besides lecturing at the Saraswati Sadan and other places Anandji and I also took part in the various meetings that were held in connection with the affairs of the Dharmodaya Sabha. From a purely monastic point of view the most important of these was a formal assembly of all the Nepalese and non-Nepalese monks at which two Newar *śrāmaṇeras* or novices were received into the Theravāda monastic order as *bhikṣus* or full monks. Narada Thera presided at this ceremony, which was held at the Ananda Kuti Vihara within a *sīmā* or '(ecclesiastical) boundary' that had been established some time earlier. Before they could perform the ordination ceremony the monks had to purify themselves by 'confessing their sins' in the technical sense of confessing any breach of the Vinaya or Monastic Code of which they had been guilty since last taking part in an assembly of that nature. In the earliest days of Buddhism the confession of sins had taken place at the fortnightly chapter meeting, but this practice had soon fallen into abeyance and among Theravādin monks, at least, confession was now not only less public but also, as I discovered, much more of a formality. At a signal from Narada Thera we all split up into pairs, squatting on our heels and facing each other. I was paired with Venerable Amritananda. Since I had not had an opportunity of 'confessing my sins' since my *bhikṣu* ordination the previous year, I naturally thought that it was incumbent on me to make a mental review of my conduct over the previous twelve months in order to ascertain whether I did, in fact, have something to confess. But Venerable Amritananda gave me no time. Hardly had we taken up our positions than he let fly at me a string of Pāli formulas, rattling them off with such rapidity that I could make out only part of the meaning. He then made me repeat the same formulas after him (for I did not know them by heart as he did), with variations appropriate to our different status within the monastic order. The whole business took no more than three or four minutes. All around us pairs of monks were already rising to their feet. We had 'confessed our sins' and purified ourselves and could now proceed to confer the higher ordination on the two *śrāmaṇeras*.

This was by no means the only time that I was made painfully aware of the extreme formalism of the modern Theravāda. Narada Thera had visited Kathmandu five or six years earlier, and on that occasion the Newar Buddhists had presented him with a considerable sum of money which he had, it appeared, deposited with Maniharsh Jyoti. Calling Maniharshji over to him one day, when the latter happened to be paying a brief visit to the Ananda Kuti Vihara, Narada Thera reminded the worthy trader how much money he had deposited with him, how much of it had since been disbursed in accordance with his (Narada's) instructions, and how much now remained. Having done this he not only directed Maniharshji to disburse various sums on his behalf for this and that purpose but also told him how much there would be on deposit after these instructions had been carried out. Either because he was very much a man of the world or because he was accustomed to the ways of Theravāda monks, Maniharshji attended to Narada Thera's behests without giving the slightest sign that there was anything unusual about them and, having assured him that everything would be done according to his wishes, quietly left the vihara. For my part, I was astonished at what I had heard. It was not that I was astonished by the power of Narada Thera's memory (for the amounts he had mentioned were not just round figures but exact to the last rupee and anna), or by his extraordinary capacity for mental arithmetic and even mental book-keeping. What astonished me was the fact that it was possible for the doyen of the English-speaking monks of Ceylon to receive and spend money through a lay intermediary and yet, at the same time, firmly believe himself to be a strict observer of the rule that a monk should not handle money (literally, 'gold and silver'). Evidently for Narada Thera, as for so many other Theravādins, observance of the Vinaya meant observance of the letter of the Vinaya, and only of the letter. There was absolutely no question of observing the spirit, or even of thinking in such terms.

On another occasion it was borne in on me that Theravāda formalism could sometimes coincide with Sinhalese cultural chauvinism, and for this insight too I was indebted to Narada Thera. A group of white-clad Newar Buddhists had come to pay him their respects, which they did in what was for them the traditional manner by first standing with joined palms, then kneeling, and then touching the ground with their foreheads, the whole procedure being repeated thrice. Though pleased with their devotion, Narada Thera could not resist the opportunity of striking a blow for 'the pure Dhamma' and therefore lost no time in taking them to task for prostrating themselves 'in the wrong way'. Turning to me he exclaimed, in his high-pitched voice, and with a bland unconsciousness that there could be any other way of doing things than his own, 'Tell them to prostrate themselves in the correct way – in the Ceylon way!' What I actually did tell them (in Hindi, which my elder brother in the Dharma did not understand) I no longer recollect, but it was certainly not what I had been told to tell them, and the Newars therefore withdrew from Narada Thera's presence unconscious of the *faux pas* they had committed and without having learned to prostrate themselves in the correct way.

A few days later Narada Thera was the central figure in an episode which took place in surroundings very different from those of the Ananda Kuti Vihara and which, while not illustrating Theravāda formalism, shed an interesting light on the methods by which Theravāda monks sought to ingratiate themselves with the laity, especially when the latter happened to be rich and powerful. The scene of the episode was the Narayanhiti, the 'Abode of Narayan', or Royal Palace. At Venerable Amritananda's suggestion the King had invited all the monks for a ceremonial food-offering and upwards of forty yellow- and orange-robed figures had gathered in the spacious apartment that had been selected for the purpose. Food was served in the Indian style, on *thalis* or circular trays. These trays were all of enormous size and all of massy silver, and there was an abundance of basins and ewers to match. After the meal Narada Thera, as the seniormost monk present, delivered the customary 'sermon of thanksgiving' as it may be called. For some reason or other he not only insisted on addressing the King in Sinhalese; he also insisted that Anandji, who had spent several years in Ceylon, should translate his remarks into Hindi, even though his royal auditor both understood and spoke English perfectly. On our return to Santiniketan that evening Anandji exploded. He had never been so embarrassed in all his life, he declared. As delivered in Sinhalese, Narada Thera's sermon had consisted of nothing but the grossest flattery of the King, whom he had unblushingly extolled as the modern Aśoka, as the embodiment of all the virtues, and so on. It made him positively sick even to think of the things he had had to translate. In fact, he had not really translated them: he had been unable to; he had paraphrased them and toned down the flattery as much as he could. Even so, the result was bad enough, and while speaking he had hardly been able to look the King in the face.

Anandji's explosion was, however, more of a mock explosion than a real one, for his sense of humour never deserted him for long and he was able to see the comic side of the episode. Soon we were laughing over what had happened and Anandji was regaling me with some of the choicer specimens of Narada Thera's rhetoric which, since he had not translated them at the time, I had been unable to appreciate. But though we laughed we both in fact felt more than a little sad and more than a little ashamed, for we were conscious that Narada Thera's performance – which he himself appeared to think entirely appropriate to the occasion – did not reflect much credit on the monastic order and in fact showed it in rather an unattractive light. We were also conscious that it raised some serious questions. Even granting that it was necessary not to give offence to the rich and powerful, and even to gain their sympathy and support, was it really desirable to flatter them so grossly as to overstep the bounds of truth and decency? Was it, in fact, desirable to flatter them at all and, if it was, how far could a Buddhist monk – or, indeed, any self-respecting person – permit himself to go in this direction? Moreover, where did honest praise end and flattery begin, and how was one to distinguish the one from the other? According to Anandji, flattery was a regular feature of the thanksgiving sermon of Ceylon, and in addressing King Tribhuvan in the way he had done Narada Thera was only following a well established tradition. Why, in Ceylon every petty village benefactor was eulogized as a modern Anāthapiṇḍika or a modern Viśākhā, and praises that had once been the reward of the giver of millions were now lavished on the donor of a few rupees! The reason for this state of affairs, Anandji went on to explain, was largely economic. Theravāda monks were like the lilies of the field: they toiled not, neither did they spin.[75] Consequently, they were dependent for their support on the laity, and since they were dependent on the laity they had to be careful to keep on good terms with them. What easier way of keeping on good terms with them could there be than by flattering them a little from time to time, and in particular flattering them on account of their generosity – especially their generosity to the members of the monastic order? In staunchly Theravādin Ceylon – so Anandji assured me – the monastic order was the basis of Buddhism. Since the monastic order was dependent for its support on the generosity of the laity, and since that generosity was not usually forthcoming without the help of a good deal of flattery, this meant that in Ceylon flattery was the basis of Buddhism. Perhaps Narada Thera had flattered the King because he wanted to make sure of his continued support for (Theravāda) Buddhism and the (Theravāda) monastic order!

Whether or not it was true that in Ceylon flattery was the basis of Buddhism (and I already knew Anandji to be capable of both cynicism and comic exaggeration), it was certainly true that without the support of King Tribhuvan and the Government of Nepal it would have been impossible for the Sacred Relics to visit Nepal or to be given such a lavish reception. It was also true that now that the Sacred Relics had been exposed for worship in Kathmandu, Lalitpur, and Bhadgaon their sojourn in the land of the Buddha's birth was beginning to come to an end. I had intended to pass my last two days immersed in the peaceful atmosphere of Santiniketan, but on the first of these days Venerable Amritananda succeeded in convincing me that before leaving the country I ought to see a little of Nepalese rural life, and I therefore accompanied him first to Bhadgaon and then to a pleasant valley entirely surrounded by beautiful green hills. Here we walked through the well-tended fields and market-gardens and I admired the methods of the sturdy Newar cultivators who, Amritananda informed me, belonged to the Jyapu caste, which was the lowest caste among the Newars. On the following day – my last full day in Nepal – I was able to immerse myself in the peaceful atmosphere of Santiniketan for at least part of the time. Having hunted for Nepalese hand-made paper with Ratnaman, and participated in a ceremonial food-offering at the Srighar Vihara, I returned to the Swayambhunath hill and 'the Abode of Peace' and spent the afternoon talking to the four young hermits, who by this time I had got to know quite well. In the evening their father, Yogaratna, came to see me and told me the story of his life and spiritual experiences, a brief account of which I included in the rather lyrical article that I contributed to *Stepping-Stones* soon after my return from Kalimpong and from which I have already quoted more than once. After describing his appearance and his manner of speaking, I wrote:

> It transpired that his wife had died many years before, and that not long afterwards he had resigned a lucrative government appointment in order to devote himself exclusively to the study

of religion and the practice of yoga. Sometimes living in temples, sometimes roaming about naked, and sometimes retiring into remote jungles and dwelling in inaccessible caves where (I heard later from one who had spent a few days with him in such a place) supernatural beings of frightful appearance visited him in such numbers that no other person dared to remain there with him, step by step he had advanced upon the hard and dangerous path of spiritual training, gradually acquiring in the course of his practice not only calm and illumination of mind but also various supernormal powers which, he told me one evening, had arisen spontaneously and become, as I could see for myself from the number of people who came to him for advice and instruction each day, the means of attracting numerous disciples and devotees.[76]

The next morning, after the singing of the bands of pre-dawn worshippers had awoken me for the last time, I said goodbye to Yogaratna and his sons and made my way to the Srighar Vihara. Here the other members of the delegation accompanying the Sacred Relics had already started assembling and it was not long before the final details of the last procession in which we would be taking part on Nepalese soil had been sorted out between ourselves and Venerable Amritananda. But before the procession could actually start the monks had to be fed, and at eleven o'clock my yellow-robed brethren and I therefore sat down to our last ceremonial meal at the hands of our warm-hearted Newar hosts. One of us no doubt delivered a sermon of thanksgiving, but it must have been a short one, for at twelve-thirty the procession left the Srighar Vihara and started winding its way towards the aerodrome. Once again the enthusiasm was immense. Once again the streets were lined with thousands of white-clad Newars and hundreds of khaki-clad Gurkha policemen. Once again there was a great crowd waiting at the aerodrome, including King Tribhuvan and the members of his government. This time, however, the crowd was waiting not to welcome the Sacred Relics but to bid them farewell, and although the atmosphere was one of rejoicing – for the time that the Sacred Relics had spent in Nepal constituted an epoch in the history of modern Nepalese Buddhism – the rejoicing was therefore not untinged with sadness. The vast majority of those present knew that they would not have another opportunity of paying their respects to the relics of the two *arhants*, and as the silver-gilt reliquary was carried across the tarmac and up into the waiting aeroplane many of them wiped tears from their eyes. Nonetheless, the last sound I heard, before the cabin door closed behind us, was that of the repeated triumphant shouts of 'Sadhu!' that rose spontaneously from the throats of the crowd, while the last sight that met my eyes, as I looked out of the cabin window, was that of a sea of upturned faces and frantically waving arms.

A few minutes later, shortly after midday, the aeroplane took off, and after a journey of little more than three hours, including a brief stopover at Patna, we landed at Dum Dum airport and soon were again breathing the smoke-filled atmosphere of Calcutta. The last but one of the Sacred Relics' journeys outside India was over, and sitting that evening in my dingy room at the Maha Bodhi Society's headquarters I felt the sharpness of the contrasts that I had encountered during the past two weeks already beginning to fade.

15
A BIG SETBACK

On my return to Kalimpong and the Hermitage one of the first things I did was go to the octagonal shrine-room at the end of the garden and pay my respects to the standing image of the Buddha which Lama Govinda had given me. There he stood, with his white sapphire sparkling in the middle of his forehead and his right hand raised in blessing, looking exactly as he had looked three weeks earlier. But though he looked the same as before I knew that he was not, in fact, the same. A subtle change had taken place. During my absence in Nepal he had been formally consecrated by a Tibetan incarnate lama. This incarnate lama was none other than the one who occupied the upstairs floor of the house in which Joe was living and who, the latter had informed me with considerable satisfaction, was studying English with him. Oh yes, even though he had received no education to speak of, and was only a humble *upāsaka*, he was now the honoured teacher of a prominent member of the Tibetan Buddhist hierarchy. Nor was that all. The Rim-POH-chee (as Joe insisted on calling the incarnate lama, deliberately mispronouncing the title so as to demonstrate his entire freedom from the taint of 'cleverness') was a model student. Believe it or not, he actually came downstairs for his lessons instead of allowing him, the humble *upāsaka*, to go upstairs. What could be more gracious and condescending than *that*, or more indicative of his respect for someone who, just because he wasn't 'clever', was generally looked down on? Moreover, the Rim-POH-chee always carried his exercise books and writing materials himself. He wouldn't allow his attendant monk to carry them for him, and he wouldn't allow him, a humble *upāsaka*, to carry them either. At the end of the lesson, though, he always invited him upstairs for a cup of delicious Tibetan tea, which he drank in the Rim-POH-chee's own private sitting room surrounded by the most gorgeous images and *thangkas*.

All this Joe had told me some time before my departure for Nepal, and I had naturally formed a wish to meet Dhardo Rimpoche, as the incarnate lama was called. On my mentioning the matter to Joe, however, the cantankerous *upāsaka* waved his beringed hand in the air in his most dismissive manner. It was out of the question, he declared. The Rim-POH-chee was very busy with his studies and meditations, as well as with the elaborate rituals which he was always being asked to perform, and it was extremely difficult to meet him. It was difficult even for Tibetans to meet him, especially as his old mother stood guard over him like a veritable dragon and turned away all those whose offerings were not, in her opinion, worthy of his acceptance. 'You come here to see such a big lama,' she would scold them, 'yet you bring such a small offering. Be off with you, and don't come again unless you can do better!' From the emphatic way in which he told me these things it was obvious that Joe was not at all keen on my meeting Dhardo Rimpoche and that his attitude towards his distinguished pupil was, in fact, quite possessive. Nonetheless I persisted, and after I had raised the matter with him two or three more times he reluctantly agreed to inform the Rimpoche that I wanted to meet him and, if possible, make arrangements for me to come up to Sherpa Building one day for this purpose. By the time of my departure for Nepal, however, these arrangements had still not been made, though Joe assured me that he had delivered my message and that the Rim-POH-chee had expressed his willingness to receive me. I therefore told him that one of the reasons for my wanting to meet Dhardo Rimpoche was that I had intended inviting him to visit the Hermitage and consecrate the standing image of the Buddha which Lama Govinda had given me. If the Rimpoche was agreeable, I added, I had no objection to this being done in my absence, since the sooner the image was consecrated the better, and in any case it would be a good thing for YMBA activities not to come to a complete standstill while I was away.

Thus it was that, some ten days before my return, Joe had brought Dhardo Rimpoche down to the Hermitage, where he had been received with all due ceremony and where, having been entertained to tea, he had consecrated Lama Govinda's image and blessed the shrine-room by chanting verses from the Tibetan scriptures and scattering grains of rice. Though not very largely attended, the function had by all accounts been a great success, the more especially since Dawa had been able to explain to the Rimpoche in Tibetan what the aims, objects, and activities of the YMBA were. Indeed, on his being shown over the premises the latter had evinced particular interest in the games room and the library and reading room, a fact that had delighted the regular users of those facilities. Dhardo Rimpoche was, it seemed, a very human kind of incarnate lama, and one who was by no means lacking in sympathy for the younger generation. As I heard all this from Lachuman and Dawa, both of whom were particularly enthusiastic about Dhardo Rimpoche's visit, I felt more sorry than ever that I had not been present and had not been able to meet the Rimpoche, especially as he had already left Kalimpong in order to take up an appointment in the same Ghoom Monastery which I had visited in the company of Lama Govinda and Li Gotami that autumn and where I had seen the colossal figure of Maitreya silently dominating the other images. Dhardo Rimpoche and I were in fact not to make each other's acquaintance for well over a year, and when we did finally do so it was thanks to the good offices of the young Tibetan in brown *chuba* and yellow sash whom I had met at Marco Pallis's bungalow. But though I was sorry that I had not been able to meet Dhardo Rimpoche I was glad that he had been to the Hermitage and consecrated Lama Govinda's image and glad that in my absence the Activities Committee had shown some initiative and organized at least one successful function. Nonetheless, I knew very well that such initiative was exceptional and that, partly on account of Joe's lack of enthusiasm for his duties as Chairman and partly on account of the inexperience of the other members, the Activities Committee was not functioning in the way that I had hoped it would. Obviously something would have to be done about this. No less obviously, however, it would have to be done later rather than sooner, for my immediate task, now that I was back in Kalimpong, was to bring out the next issue of *Stepping-Stones*, as well as to commit my impressions of Nepal to paper before they faded more than they already had done.

The next issue of *Stepping-Stones* was the November one. For some reason or other I had not been able to bring it out before my departure for Nepal, so that instead of appearing at the beginning of the month it appeared at the very end. This meant that as soon as I had sent the November issue to press I had to start putting the December one together, so that what with editing *Stepping-Stones* and writing my articles on Nepal – not to mention giving tuition every day and dealing with correspondence – I was kept quite busy. In these circumstances it was perhaps not surprising that the editorial which I contributed to the December *Stepping-Stones* should have been the shortest I had so far written, or that it should have been entitled '"Pauses" and "Empty Spaces"'. Anything of the nature of a 'pause' or 'empty space' must have been rather welcome to me at this time and it was no doubt with a certain amount of personal feeling that I wrote, *inter alia*:

> A life which consists of a frantic stream of external activities, without one moment of inward recollection, is like music which is an uninterrupted succession of sounds, or a picture which is crammed with figures: all three are not only meaningless, but positively painful.[77]

The other articles appearing in the December issue included the second instalment of Dr Guenther's 'Our Position in Life', which like the first one was peppered with quotations from recondite Tantric texts, both Sanskrit and Tibetan, and an unpretentious article entitled 'A Few Days in Sarnath' by Sarojani Guenther. It may in fact have been at about this time that the Guenthers paid their first visit to Kalimpong. Whenever it was (and it was probably during the Christmas holidays), Joe was at pains to make it clear that they were *his* guests and that he had no intention of sharing them with anybody, least of all with me, and I therefore saw very little of them. Indeed, I only saw them once, and then only for a few minutes, when we happened to meet on the road between the Hermitage and the bazaar. This rather saddened me, for I would gladly have heard more about the Vajrayāna from the brilliant if arrogant Austrian scholar, who in any case was a regular contributor to *Stepping-Stones*. Joe's attitude did not, however, surprise me, especially when I remembered how reluctant he had been for me to meet Dhardo Rimpoche. The truth of the matter was that the prickly *upāsaka* was not only taking less and less interest in the affairs of the YMBA and in his duties as Chairman of the Activities Committee but was also trying to form a little circle of his own in Kalimpong. Nor was that all. He evidently wanted to keep 'his' circle as distinct and separate as possible from what he chose to regard as 'my' circle, and unfortunately could think of no better way of doing this than by disparaging me and the YMBA as much as he could and discouraging people from having anything to do with us. It was as though he was afraid that if anyone from 'his' circle strayed into 'my' circle they would straight away become my friend rather than his, and henceforth think more highly of me than they did of him. Whatever the explanation of his shabby behaviour may have been, when I met the Guenthers on the road between the Hermitage and the bazaar they were noticeably less cordial than they had been in Lucknow, so that I had little doubt that Joe's vitriolic tongue had been at work with them too.

Before the year was out, however, it had become obvious that what Joe was saying about me and the YMBA was by no means the biggest of my worries. Though the January 1952 issue of *Stepping-Stones* appeared on time, it did not carry even a short editorial. For the first time in its history there was no editorial article at all and I had, therefore, no opportunity of striking, at the beginning of the issue, the unambiguously 'spiritual' note which I had always intended should characterize the magazine's entire contents in varying degrees. In place of the editorial there appeared an article bleakly headed 'An Appeal'. The appeal was, of course, for funds. Since my return from Nepal it had become more and more evident that, despite *Stepping-Stones'* modest success, both in India and abroad, we were getting deeper into debt with every issue and that it would be impossible for us to carry on without the help of our readers. In asking for that help I took the opportunity of making it clear that the publication of *Stepping-Stones* had been undertaken purely as an act of faith, that we had no wealthy backers, no permanent or regular sources of income, and that from the beginning of our existence we had to depend on the donations of friends and sympathizers. Having made this clear, I proceeded to strike a more personal note, though still using the editorial first person plural:

> Seeing us continually occupied with the collection of funds, frequently in debt, and moreover bearing the responsibility of running almost single-handed the various activities of the Association, our friends sometimes wondered why we should give ourself so much trouble, and even hinted that it would be better to

discontinue the publication of a journal on which so much money was being spent with apparently so little result. But we never heeded their suggestions. For the motive with which the publication of *Stepping-Stones* was begun, the fiery seed wherefrom it took its birth, was not the cheap desire that one more magazine might be added to the hundreds of literary and scholarly periodicals at present in circulation, but the lofty aspiration that the Wisdom and Compassion of all the Buddhas should be displayed before the eyes of beings as yet untouched by the beams of their glory. It was this thought which shed light on the darkest path we had to tread, which filled us with joy in the midst of difficulties. And when we reflected that our 'aspiration' was in truth a no-aspiration, and that there were in reality no 'beings' to whom the Wisdom and Compassion might be displayed, then our joy knew no bounds, and we worked more vigorously than ever at the task to which we had set our hand.[78]

What some of our readers made of this divagation into the metaphysics of the *Diamond Sūtra* in the middle of an appeal for funds I do not know, but I wanted as many people as possible to realize the kind of spirit in which, from an unknown town in a remote part of the eastern Himalayas, the little yellow-covered magazine had been sent forth each month to the four corners of the Earth. I wanted them to realize why it was so important that *Stepping-Stones* should continue to appear. Immediately after my divagation into the metaphysics of the *Diamond Sūtra*, however, I returned to the question of funds. We could no longer work unaided. If the publication of *Stepping-Stones* was to be continued, it could only be with the assistance of some at least of those who felt that its continuation would be of value not only to themselves but to all who prized the great treasure of Buddhist spirituality. Former sources of income, unreliable as they were, had in many cases been exhausted, and in others were no longer accessible. It was therefore imperative that new sources should not only be found but found immediately. There were now no funds with which to meet the monthly printing bills, to say nothing of building up a permanent fund for the journal, or of increasing its size or improving the quality of the paper on which it was printed.

It is for the bare existence of *Stepping-Stones* that we are making this appeal,

I therefore concluded.

> Those who wish to help us should do so by enrolling new annual subscribers, and by sending us *at once* the most generous donation that they can possibly afford. Having carried on the magazine for nearly two years without making any such appeal to our readers, in spite of the enormous difficulties which we have had to face, we feel that the cry for aid which in our present extremity we are compelled to utter will not go without prompt and generous response.[79]

As if to remind our readers of the kind of Buddhism for which *Stepping-Stones* stood, and make clear the ultimate source of the spirit in which the magazine was conducted, the January issue also contained an article by Lama Govinda entitled 'Origins of the Bodhisattva Ideal', as well as the first instalment of my own 'Glimpses of Buddhist Nepal',[80] a review of Dr Conze's recently published *Buddhism: Its Essence and Development* by Dr Guenther, and a translation of the famous episode from the *Vimalakīrti Nirdeśa* in which Vimalakīrti, in response to Mañjuśrī's enquiries about his health, says that he is sick because beings are sick and that a bodhisattva's sickness is caused only by his great compassion. At the very beginning of his article Lama Govinda pointed out that the bodhisattva ideal was inspired by the noble example of the Buddha's self-sacrificing career, for which reason he found it difficult to understand how such an ideal could arouse objections among those who professed to be followers of the Buddha. Yet some there were who looked upon the bodhisattva ideal as if it were either sheer foolishness or a most dangerous heresy. The Sinhalese monk Kheminda Thera, for instance, had written that with the acceptance of the bodhisattva ideal 'the Mahayanists and others who think like them have dared to go beyond the words of the Master.... What the Buddha, the World-Knower, did not say, that is said and propagated by these people, and often in a fanatical way.'[81] These objections Lama Govinda met head-on. 'Indeed', he retorted, 'the followers of the Bodhisattva ideal have dared to look beyond the "pointing finger" and have seen "the brightness of the moon" to which it pointed. Indeed, they have dared to follow not only the words but the example of the Master, – which is a great deal more than quarrelling about theories and haggling over scriptures. It is also a great deal more courageous, because it certainly involves more risks than sitting comfortably upon the pedestal of one's own virtuousness within the four walls of one's well-provided retreat, safely away from the polluting touch of the world.'[82] No doubt Kheminda Thera did not sit quite so comfortably on his pedestal after that. In the remainder of the article, which was written in the same trenchant style, Lama Govinda pointed out that one cannot help oneself without helping others, that the Buddhist virtues of selfless love (*maitrī*) and compassion (*karuṇā*) were not merely ratiocinations but emotions which involved our whole being, that motive was more important than external consequences, and that the bodhisattva ideal – which enjoyed the greatest popularity in all Buddhist countries – was not a dividing but a *uniting* factor in Buddhist life and thought.

Knowing that some copies of *Stepping-Stones* took several weeks to reach their destination I did not expect a uniformly speedy response to my appeal, and therefore brought out the February issue of the magazine as usual even though I knew that this would sink us deeper in debt than ever – at least for the time being. This time the editorial, which was entitled 'An Old Saw Resharpened',[83] was the longest I had written, and though the old saw in question was the one that 'charity begins at home' the article was in fact a vigorous attack on the spiritually disastrous habit of treating concepts as things-in-themselves and, therefore, as ends-in-themselves. There was also the second and concluding instalment of 'Glimpses of Buddhist Nepal', while the News and Notes section reported the holding of a highly successful ping-pong tournament, the finals of which had been played at the Town Hall under the presidency of the SDO,[84] and the presentation of an alabaster Buddha image by a pious Burmese couple living in Akyab. The most important feature of the February issue was, however, the first instalment of Dr Conze's 'Selected Sayings from the *Perfection of Wisdom*'. 'Roughly 25 Prajñāpāramitā Sūtras have been composed in India over a period of nine hundred years,' Dr Conze wrote in his brief Introduction, 'from ca. 100 BC to ca. 800 AD. The texts vary greatly in length, but their total bulk is considerable. They are in the form of dialogues between Buddhas, Bodhisattvas and Disciples.'[85] Since the Perfection of Wisdom *sūtras* were among the profoundest and most important of all the Mahāyāna scriptures, and since only a fraction of them had been translated into English, I was overjoyed that Dr Conze had entrusted the publication of his 'Selected Sayings' to *Stepping-Stones* and looked forward to our bringing out an instalment of the work every month until it was complete.

But this was not to be, and the remainder of Dr Conze's 'Selected Sayings' did not appear in print until the whole work was published in book form four years later.[86] The February issue of *Stepping-Stones* had not been out more than two or three weeks before it became obvious that my appeal was not meeting with the 'prompt and generous response' for which I had hoped – in fact it was meeting with no response at all – and that the February issue of *Stepping-Stones* would be the last. It was a big setback, and a great disappointment. It fact it was the biggest setback the YMBA had so far received, and probably the greatest disappointment I myself had experienced since the day when, in obedience to Kashyapji's behest, I had really started working for the good of Buddhism. The second of the two beautiful and iridescent balls that, twenty months earlier, had been invited to descend, was now floating away out of reach. Or rather it lay shattered into a thousand rainbow fragments on the earth, where it could no longer send out its brilliant flashes or be seen far afield. For a while I sought to piece some of those fragments together, trying to ensure the survival of *Stepping-Stones* in a form which, though it might be less pleasing to the eye and less convenient to handle, we at least could afford to produce. Thanks to the generosity of Thubden Tendzin I obtained a second-hand Gestetner duplicating machine from Calcutta and at once set to work to bring out the March issue of *Stepping-Stones* by this method, taking as my model the *Golden Lotus*, the beautifully duplicated Buddhist-cum-Theosophical magazine that we received each month from Philadelphia. But though typing the stencils was a simple enough matter, when it came to the actual business of printing I encountered serious difficulties. Either the special semi-absorbent duplicating paper would not feed into the machine properly or, if it did, the sheets more often than not failed to take the ink evenly. After several weeks of work I had still not succeeded in producing a single perfect copy of the March issue, let alone a thousand copies, and my wretched attempts bore no resemblance whatever to the immaculate products of the Golden Lotus Press. In desperation I therefore appealed for help to Joe, who I knew had had occasion to operate a Gestetner in his army days, when he had been in charge of the company office. Fortunately the unpredictable *upāsaka* was in a comparatively mellow mood (he had, in fact, not crowed over me quite so much as I had expected when I told him about the difficulties *Stepping-Stones* was facing), and actually spent two or three days at the Hermitage trying to get the Gestetner to work. But though he was, I suspected, not displeased to think that his headstrong and over-independent young friend could not get on without him, his efforts met with no greater success than mine had done and in the end he gave up in disgust. *This particular Gestetner was too much for him*, he declared, inhaling the smoke of yet another cigarette and coughing violently. With our hands covered in ink, and with the hundreds of sheets of duplicating paper we had spoiled lying on the floor around us, we therefore admitted defeat and eventually, over a cup of tea, concluded that the probable cause of the trouble was that the machine was adapted to the temperature and humidity of the plains, not those of the hills. Whatever the cause might have been, looking from Joe's haggard face to the recalcitrant Gestetner, and from the recalcitrant Gestetner to Joe's haggard face, I realized that there was no hope of my bringing out a duplicated edition of *Stepping-Stones* in Kalimpong – no hope of piecing any of the rainbow fragments together – and that the February issue of the little magazine on which I had lavished so much thought and so much love really would be the last to appear in any form.

Long before that, however, I had to face the fact that the first of our two beautiful and iridescent balls was in danger of floating away like the second, or of lying in a thousand rainbow fragments on the earth. Not only were there no funds with which to continue the production of *Stepping-Stones*. There were in reality no funds with which to continue running the Kalimpong YMBA. The annual Dewsay collection brought in only two or three hundred rupees, and the Activities Committee had never succeeded in contributing more than a fraction of the rent of the Hermitage, that is, of the main building, where the games room and the library and reading room were located, as distinct from the chalet at the other end of the garden where I lived. This meant that I had to subsidize the Kalimpong YMBA out of the donations I collected and even, on occasion, out of my own scanty resources, which were at that time very scanty indeed, consisting as they did of the tuition fees of one or two relatively wealthy Tibetan pupils (YMBA members did not have to pay anything for tuition), the payments I received from the *Illustrated Weekly of India* for poems and from the *Aryan Path*[87] for articles and book reviews, and the monthly allowance that I had been granted, on Kashyapji's recommendation, by Jugal Kishore Birla, the multi-millionaire Hindu philanthropist whose generosity had been responsible for the construction of Buddha Kuti, my teacher's residence on the campus of the Benares Hindu University.

I had met Birlaji some years earlier, when I was staying at Buddha Kuti with Kashyapji, and the meek and unassuming old man asked if there was anything he could do for me. No, I replied, there wasn't, since thanks to the kindness of my teacher I was already provided with everything I needed. Recollecting this exchange shortly after my removal from Burma Raja's guest cottage to the Hermitage, I had written to Kashyapji asking him to inform Birlaji that there was now something he could do for me, namely, help me financially. This Kashyapji had promptly done, adding that my work in Kalimpong was having the effect of counteracting the influence of the Christian missionaries, and Birlaji, who was the sworn foe of both Christianity and Islam, had at once given me a monthly allowance. It was for my *dudh-makhan* or 'milk and butter', the accompanying note explained. This allowance was to be my only regular source of income for nearly two years, and knowing that I would have to continue to subsidize the Kalimpong YMBA – which was in fact the only YMBA, our Ajmer branch having affiliated itself to a Buddhist organization in Delhi – as well as pay off our debts to the two presses, after the collapse of *Stepping-Stones* I therefore decided that there would have to be some drastic economies.

My first economy was to give up the chalet. I was very sorry to do this. For the last seven or eight months the greater part of my time had been spent inside the tiny wooden building, the exterior of which was already in need of a fresh coat of paint. There I had written and typed my articles and poems, edited *Stepping-Stones*, and given individual tuition to some of my students. There, too, I had sometimes lain awake at night listening to the sound of the bamboos in the *jhora*, only a few yards away, as the winds stirred their feathery tops and set their stems gently knocking one against the other. Normally I lived there alone, except for the company of Cleopatra, a stray tabby who had adopted us and who insisted on having her kittens on my bed. For a few weeks, however, I had shared my retreat with René de Nebesky-Wojkowitz, the young Austrian ethnologist who had arrived in Kalimpong with Dr Rock in 1950 and who had been a regular contributor to *Stepping-Stones* almost from the beginning.

Tall and fair-haired, and with a prominent beak of a nose, René was an exceptionally hard worker, and pursued his ethnological and allied researches with indefatigable zeal. His principal interest was the Oracles and Demons of Tibet, material on all aspects of which he was collecting for a book. Much of this material consisted of the detailed descriptions of the 'demons' which he had copied out from a variety of Tibetan religious texts (many of them supplied by Dhardo Rimpoche), and I spent a number of evenings helping him improve the English of his translations of these descriptions, which were often extremely vivid. During the day René was usually out. He was at that time working as Prince Peter's secretary, and immediately after breakfast used to set out on the long climb up to Krishnalok, the house in Ringkingpong to which the prince and princess had moved from Tashiding. Prince Peter, I gathered, was a very easy person to work for. Working for Princess Irene, however, was quite another matter. She was, in fact, an extremely difficult person to have anything to do with at all, and led poor René such a dog's life that he sometimes returned to the chalet in tears. When that happened I had to talk to him until his composure was restored, and on such occasions he sometimes spoke more freely about himself than his aristocratic reserve usually permitted. Though Austrian by nationality, he was of Czech descent, his family having possessed a castle in Czechoslovakia, as well as extensive landed estates. With the coming of Communism they had lost everything, and for the first time in generations had had to work for their living. He himself had not had an easy time getting through university, and he still had to help support his mother.

But though as a result of his sufferings at the hands of Princess Irene he sometimes opened up to me in this manner, René was by no means given to indulgence in either nostalgia or self-pity. A cheerful extrovert by nature, he was fond of the good things of life and saw no point in denying himself such of them as were within his reach – especially when they took the form of an attractive and complaisant Nepalese girl. His amorous escapades down at Seventh Mile were in fact notorious and on one occasion, so my students told me, he had actually been stoned by a party of villagers who had caught him misbehaving with one of the local beauties in a maize field and had had to flee for his life. The incident had taken place some time before he came to stay with me, and he naturally said nothing to me about it, or indeed about any of his amorous adventures, though he was not averse to hinting that he entertained a romantic passion for Kesang Dorji, the younger daughter of Raja and Rani Dorji. In any case, his exploits in the maize fields could not have occasioned the young ethnologist much uneasiness, for despite his (strictly scientific) interest in Tibetan Buddhism he was a practising Roman Catholic and on Sunday mornings generally went to confession and early mass at the Catholic Mission, where presumably he unburdened himself of his sins and made his peace with his Maker. Be that as it may, with his cheerfulness and sociability, and his keen interest in the life and culture of the area, René de Nebesky-Wojkowitz was a very agreeable companion, and despite the Lilliputian dimensions of the chalet I was glad to have him staying with me – the more especially since he was extremely scrupulous in money matters and always settled with me at the end of the week without demur or delay.

Besides being an agreeable companion, René also acted as an intermediary between the world of the Hermitage and the socially more brilliant world of Krishnalok, and during the time that he was with me I learned quite a lot about Prince Peter and Princess Irene, even as they, no doubt, must have learned quite a lot about me. Thus I learned that Princess Irene's jewel-box contained no fewer than seventy-three pieces of jewellery, including several magnificent tiaras, that she was an enthusiastic gardener, that she went for a walk with Dr Roerich every day and that they talked Russian together, and that she was devoted to her pet squirrel Krishna, after whom the house had been named. I also learned – in this case not by hearsay but by experience – that she was an excellent cook. From time to time René brought back with him samples of dishes she had prepared, from which I concluded she had forgiven me for not eating the cake she had made 'with her own hands' at the garden party nearly two years earlier. Indeed, from the time of René's stay with me at the chalet the Princess's dislike of me seemed to decrease, though it did not disappear entirely until Krishna died and I wrote an epitaph for him which she caused to be inscribed on his tomb.[88] More interesting than what I learned about the occupants of Krishnalok, however, was what I learned about the occupants of Crookety. On my first visit to Dr Roerich I had been conscious of a tremendous downward pressure, a pressure that was not physical but psychic, coming from the room overhead. René now informed me that this room was occupied by Mme Roerich, the Tibetologist's mother, and that the old lady was not only a Theosophist but a medium. Later on I discovered that she was, in fact, a 'spiritual medium', and that she had produced, in this capacity, a whole series of books that constituted the bible, so to speak, of a small occult group within the wider Theosophical movement. Dr Roerich was very devoted to his mother, René added – so devoted, indeed, that Princess Irene had once remarked of him that he had not yet been born.

By the time I gave up the chalet, however, the flow of information between the Hermitage and Krishnalok had virtually ceased, René having left on an ethnological expedition to the Bhutanese border some time previously. For the last few months of my tenancy I therefore had the place entirely to myself and was able to enjoy its peace and seclusion undisturbed – a circumstance for which I was sufficiently thankful when the time eventually came for me to move from the smaller to the larger building. Not that the latter was noisy, but only that it stood nearer to the road and that living there I was, of course, more easily accessible to visitors and had nowhere to escape to in the evenings if I wanted to be on my own. Yet despite these drawbacks the broken-down old bungalow was pleasant enough, and I soon settled down in my former room on the left of the games room, which was bigger and brighter than the corresponding room on the right, besides being farther away from the smoke of the kitchen. From the curtainless front and side windows of this room I could see a portion of the road below, as well as the foothills of Sikkim towering in the distance, and sitting at the rickety gate-legged table I would sometimes look up from my work to study the passers-by. This was especially the case when it happened to be raining heavily and I had no visitors, and when in any case I was in a reflective mood. Apart from the loudly chattering boys and girls on their way to – and from – school, most of the people who passed the bottom of the track leading up to my front gate (actually there was no gate but only two mildewed posts) were peasants and coolies bound for the bazaar, and many of these – women and bare-legged men alike – carried on their backs the traditional cone-shaped bamboo basket. On Wednesdays and Saturdays, which were market-days in Kalimpong, they would pass by earlier than usual, and in greater numbers, and their baskets would be heavily laden with charcoal, vegetables, and grain. Some of them would have chickens dangling head downwards from their wrists, legs tied together and wings feebly flapping, while others would be driving before them two or three protesting goats or even a whole herd of buffaloes.⁸⁹ Whatever it was that they were taking to market, I knew that they were taking it with the intention of selling it for the best price they could get and with the proceeds buying such things as paraffin, cooking oil, and matches, which they could not produce themselves. (Clothes were of course bought only once a year, at the time of the autumn pujas.) I also knew that regardless of what price they succeeded in getting, some of them were sure to end up spending a good part of the money in the liquor shops with the result that the next time they passed by, on their way home, they would be shouting incoherently and staggering from one side of the road to the other.

But even though most of the people who passed by the bottom of the track that led up to my front gate were peasants and coolies, this did not mean that those who did not fall into this category were not sufficiently varied in type. On looking up from my work I might see a Tibetan official in dark-coloured *chuba* and homburg out for a morning stroll – though most Tibetans lived at Tenth Mile, and were rarely seen in the vicinity of Eighth Mile or Ninth Mile. Or I might see a well-to-do Sikkimese nurseryman from Seventh Mile hastening to the bank, or a Muslim *roti-wallah* or bread man on his rounds, staff in hand and tin box balanced on turbaned head, or a white-shirted Bihari barber making his way to the house of a regular customer. Or I might even see a priest from the Roman Catholic Mission, or a pair of nuns. The priest would be wearing a white tropical soutane, and would generally have his nose in his breviary, while the nuns, whose habits were either black or blue in colour, would keep their heads well down and hurry past the Hermitage as though conscious that the place contained something – or someone – inimical to their faith.

When tired of sitting at the rickety table I sometimes walked up and down the path that ran between the Hermitage and the octagonal shrine-room, as I had often done when living in the chalet.⁹⁰ This path divided the garden into two unequal parts, in the more extensive of which – the one that lay farther back from the road – stood the majority of the ornamental trees that had been planted by the original owner of the property. With the exception of the forty-foot eucalyptus standing immediately opposite the front door of the Hermitage, the biggest of these trees were the magnolia and the tulip tree, both of which were now perfect specimens of their kind, as were most of the smaller trees by which they were surrounded. Since not all the trees bloomed at the same time of year, there was always a gleam of colour to be seen among the branches apart from the glossy green of the leaves. At one time it might be the cream colour of the enormous, globe-shaped magnolia blossoms, at another the mingled pink and white of the tulip tree's upward-pointing blossoms, conspicuous on their leafless branches, at yet another the deep red of the camellias or velvety-white of the gardenias. As well as the blooms of the ornamental trees there were those of the bamboo orchids and ginger lilies which grew in clumps at the foot of the bank to the rear of the garden. Though the former were partly pink and partly cerise, while the latter were wholly white, both looked more like butterflies than flowers and one half expected them to fly away. Yet whether the gleams of colour among the branches were many or few, as I slowly walked up and down the path, which sometimes was bordered with shocking-pink zinnias and bright orange marigolds, I nearly always experienced a deep sense of peace and harmony, of fulfilment and well-being. It was as though the trees were my silent companions – companions who could share my thoughts and feelings, and from whose tranquil presence I derived nourishment and inspiration. Indeed, as I walked up and down in their leafy neighbourhood sentences of articles and stanzas of poems would come unbidden into my mind, as well as feelings and insights for which I as yet had no words. When that happened I would experience an intense joy, the flowers above my head and at my feet would shine with an unearthly radiance, and to me it would seem that the garden of the Hermitage was a veritable Garden of Eden.

 The Adam and Eve of this Eden lived in a cabin near the front gate, halfway between the gate and the road. The official designation of the masculine and superior component of the aboriginal syzygy was *mali* or gardener (literally 'garland-man', the original function of the Indian gardener being to grow flowers for garlands), but neither he nor his wife ever did any gardening, except for occasionally sweeping up the dead leaves and growing a few vegetables for themselves. On the contrary, the so-called *mali* spent most of his time in town, working in a liquor shop, from which he would return at the end of the day with bloodshot eyes and uncertain step, the owner of the shop no doubt having found it more convenient to pay him in liquor than in cash. A Tamang – and therefore a Buddhist – by birth, as was his wife, he was an unkempt little man who always wore the same torn and filthy Nepalese costume, with a *kukuri* or Gurkha knife thrust into the cummerbund. His most striking feature, however, was his hair, which having been cropped a couple of years earlier now stuck out in all directions like the quills of a porcupine. Drunk or sober – and he was hardly ever sober – his face habitually wore an expression of sullen and stupid rage, a rage that, only too often, found an outlet in beating his wife, a fair-skinned, handsome woman nearly twice his size who apparently never attempted to retaliate, as some Nepalese women would have done. They had been married only a year or two, and their first child was born shortly after I had moved from the chalet to the main building. On looking out of my window on the day after the delivery – which of course had taken place in the cabin – I saw the *malini* or gardener-woman, as she was generally called, standing alone in the middle of their little vegetable patch. She was paler than usual, and in her eyes there was the blank, uncomprehending look of an animal.

Where Adam and Eve dwell, there Lilith will also be found – if not in the Garden of Eden itself, then certainly not very far away. On the terraced hillside above the Hermitage, but out of sight, there stood a wattle-and-daub hut, and in the hut lived a Nepalese woman and her three or four small children. Who the woman was, and what had happened to her menfolk, nobody seemed to know, any more than they knew how she managed to support herself and her brood. She was, in fact, something of a mystery, particularly as she spent most of her time either in the hut or on her own terrace and was hardly ever seen elsewhere. But if she was not seen she was certainly heard, especially on the night of the new moon. On that night I would be woken up by a kind of frenzied chant coming from farther up the hillside. What the words of the chant were I could not tell, but the woman shrieked them out at the top of her voice, and with all the strength of her lungs, as though her very life depended on it. Over and over again she shrieked them out, hardly pausing for breath, the feebler, shriller voices of the children sometimes accompanying her. Was she calling back a husband or a lover, or invoking a demon, or exorcizing the spirits of disease? I did not know. Whatever she was doing, she kept up the performance all night, and when dawn came her chanting was no less loud and no less frantic than it had been seven or eight hours earlier.

Though the mysterious woman woke me up with her chanting once a month her hut was situated several dozen yards away, and at other times she did not disturb me. The chalet stood a little nearer to the Hermitage than that, besides being situated on the same level, and knowing that my joint landlords would not allow the place to remain empty I naturally wondered who the new tenants would be and how great a disturbance their presence at the other end of the garden would constitute. One afternoon it seemed as though my worst fears might be realized. Hearing voices outside, I looked up from my work in time to see, passing in front of the building, the burly figure of one of the drivers who worked for my landlords' motor transport service. He was followed by his wife, his wife's sister, his mother, a servant girl, and an indeterminate number of children. There was even a baby, asleep in the arms of one of the women. On going out onto the veranda, and looking in the direction of the garden after the retreating figures, I saw them mount the steps of the chalet and, one by one, disappear inside. How they all managed to get in, and how they ever found room for all the boxes and bundles they had brought with them, I was unable to imagine. But get in they did and were still living there when, two years later, I myself had to leave the Hermitage. Since they found it convenient to make a footpath from the back of the chalet down to the road, I saw and heard very little of them, and it was only during the final months of my stay there that they gave me any cause for complaint.

16
THE NEAR AND THE FAR

'He that hath wife and children,' says Francis Bacon, 'hath given hostages to fortune.' I had neither wife nor children, but from the day that Gopal had entered my service as my first cook bearer I had been made increasingly aware of the fact that he that has servants has also given hostages to fortune, albeit to a lesser degree, and that even though servants might not be 'impediments to great enterprises' in a way that a wife and children were they could nonetheless be a source of as much inconvenience as convenience. At Burma Raja's guest cottage Gopal had been slow enough in everything he did, but since my removal to the Hermitage he had slowed down to such an extent that lunch was frequently not ready until three o'clock in the afternoon. Eventually he came virtually to a standstill, and I had no choice but to turn him away and look for somebody else. Either Sachin or Dawa found me a fellow in filthy Nepalese dress and with a face so dirty that it was difficult to make out how old he was. Though his smile was hardly less vacant than Gopal's, he was active and willing enough and might have suited me but for the fact that, as quickly became obvious, he knew nothing whatever about cooking. After putting up with his efforts for two or three days I therefore gave him a week's wages and dismissed him. Sachin or Dawa – whichever of them it was – had, it transpired, found him sitting at the coolie stand in the bazaar, had asked him if he could cook and, on his replying that he could, had straight away brought him along to the Hermitage! This was clearly not the best method of recruitment.

How I found Ang Tsering I no longer recollect. Probably he found me, for in a place like Kalimpong word that the English Buddhist monk was again in need of a cook bearer was not long in getting around. Not that Ang Tsering was really a cook bearer. As he frankly admitted in the course of our first interview he was not a cook at all but only a porter. In fact he had worked as a porter for Marco Pally (as Tibetan speakers always called my old friend Thubden Tendzin) and had accompanied that gentleman on more than one of his expeditions into Sikkim and Tibet. Being at present out of work, and without money, he was willing to work for me for whatever wages I chose to give him and was quite sure he would soon learn how to cook to my satisfaction. Impressed by his straightforward manner, as well as by the fact that he had worked for Thubden Tendzin, I decided to take him on and he gave me no cause to regret my decision. Within a very few days he was producing meals of rice and curry which, though they may not have been very tasty, I was at least able to eat, while within the month he succeeded in becoming a good, if decidedly plain, vegetarian cook. This was all the more creditable inasmuch as, being a Sherpa by birth, he was a non-vegetarian and, therefore, more familiar with the Tibetan than with the Indian style of cooking. But Ang Tsering possessed, as I soon discovered, all those qualities of adaptability and resourcefulness which had gone to make the Sherpas of Nepal an essential part of every Himalayan expedition and he could, I verily believe, have turned his hand to almost anything of an ordinary practical nature. In appearance he was the typical Sherpa, being of medium height, sturdily built, and with legs that were short in proportion to the trunk they supported. His dress was a version of the traditional Tibetan costume, though in cold weather he wore a Balaclava helmet on his bullet head and in hot weather went about in a species of Bermuda shorts. Perhaps not surprisingly in view of his history, he moved rather stiffly, as though carrying a heavy load on his back, and his forehead would often be puckered as if with the weight of this invisible burden. Sometimes, indeed, the open, honest face wore a deeply worried look, as if something was bothering him and he was trying to sort it out, but if asked if there was anything the matter he would quickly recollect himself and, with an embarrassed laugh, vigorously deny that such was the case. On these occasions his normally rather stolid features would light up with a delightful smile that made him look at least ten years younger than his actual age, which was about thirty-five.

Since he was a Sherpa by birth my new cook bearer was naturally bilingual, being fluent in both Nepali and Tibetan. He also spoke a little Hindi, in which language I generally communicated with him, though in communicating with me he sometimes lapsed into Nepali, which I was beginning to understand fairly well. The fact that Ang Tsering was bilingual was fortunate, for soon after he entered my service I acquired three Tibetan students, none of whom as yet knew a word of English, and when it came to settling terms and arranging times – for I taught each of them separately – his help as an interpreter proved invaluable. At this period in my career I generally charged my fee-paying students thirty rupees a month for their English lessons, which by Kalimpong standards was very little, but I had not yet realized that, as Joe was quick to grasp, the usefulness of a teacher's lessons tended to be judged – by the Tibetans at least – not according to the results achieved so much as according to the monetary value that the teacher himself placed on them. Thus, paradoxically, a bad teacher who charged high tuition fees might be more highly esteemed, and more eagerly sought after, than a good one who charged less. How one teacher originally came to charge more, and another less, seemed to depend either on accident or on the relative strength, or weakness, of his desire to make money.

Though my three Tibetan students began studying English with me within a few weeks of one another, they continued coming for their lessons for varying lengths of time and with widely varying degrees of success. They were also very different from one another. Tashi was sixteen or seventeen years old, more than six feet tall, proportionately well built, and handsome in a rather heavy sort of way. He was also extremely well dressed, invariably turning up in an expensive and – for Kalimpong – well-cut Western-style suit. Unfortunately, despite his good looks he was not very bright and had great difficulty in remembering anything from one week to the next, so that his progress was slow indeed. However, he seemed to enjoy his lessons, or at least his contact with me, and when he left for Calcutta with his parents after only three or four months of tuition I was genuinely sorry to lose him. I was less sorry to lose one of my two other students, who finally stopped coming for his lessons after a year of very irregular attendance. This was an official of the Tibetan government who lived just below Eighth Mile with two or three other officials, in a building known as Tibet House which seemed, in a shadowy, undefined sort of way, to be the seat of

Tibetan officialdom in the area. As befitted his position, he wore a black or dark-brown *chuba*, complete with red or yellow sash, and somehow contrived to give the impression of being an official of the Government of Tibet who happened to be studying English rather than a student of English who happened to be an official of the Tibetan government. Indeed, so much was the individual submerged in the official that I can no longer remember his name, and apart from the facts already mentioned there remains of him only a vague impression of a nervous and withdrawn individual of some intelligence who, if he had studied more regularly, would have made better progress than he did.

Brighter than Tashi, and incomparably more confident and outward-going than the Tibetan government official, Aggen Chototsang differed from my two other students even more than they differed from each other. He was a Khampa, and I was soon given to understand that a Khampa was not quite the same thing as a Tibetan. If he was a Tibetan at all, he was a Tibetan of a very special kind. Below average in height for a Khampa (some of those that I had seen swaggering up and down the bazaar were very tall indeed) and with a round, cheerful face, Aggen came for his lessons attired either in a rather nondescript Western-style suit, navy-blue in colour, or else in a black *chuba* which he wore, Khampa fashion, with one sleeve dangling empty at his side so as to reveal his white Tibetan shirt. Behind him there sometimes walked, carrying his books, a Khampa servant from whose belt hung a long Tibetan sword. Though brighter than Tashi, the third of my three Tibetan students was not *very* bright, but what he lacked in intelligence he more than made up for in perseverance, with the result that his lessons with me continued over a period of some eighteen months, on and off, and he eventually succeeded in acquiring enough English to be able to converse on most topics without much difficulty. Since he was of a communicative disposition I learned quite a lot about him. He and his two older and two younger brothers were traders who had been forced to leave their native Kham as a result of the Chinese invasion and were now carrying on the family business in Kalimpong. Not that they had given up hope of ever returning to Kham. Far from it. They would certainly return one day, perhaps quite soon, and if returning to Kham meant fighting the Chinese then so much the better. The idea of fighting the Chinese was something of an obsession with Aggen, as it was with so many of the other Khampas who had taken refuge in Kalimpong.

Whenever he spoke of it, which was not unoften, his eyes gleamed, and his round, cheerful face became rounder and more cheerful than ever.

Fortunately or unfortunately for Aggen, however, there seemed to be no immediate prospect of his fighting the Chinese, and he therefore remained in Kalimpong steadily improving his English – which he was learning mainly for business purposes – and not only thinking of his beloved Kham but making comparisons between the Khampa and the Indian way of life – comparisons that were invariably unfavourable to the latter. Indians, he once told me, had impressed him as being much less happy than his own people; they were also much less religious-minded, and did not know how to enjoy themselves. In Kham – he went on, waxing more and more enthusiastic – it was the custom for a family to divide its income into three equal parts. One part was for living expenses and reinvestment in the family business, one part was for pleasure, in the form of drinking, gambling, picnics, and parties, and one part was for the Dharma, as represented by monks, monasteries, and beggars. Here in Kalimpong, of course, it was not really possible for him and his brothers to distribute their income in this way: the cost of living was much higher and they had, therefore, proportionately less money to spend on pleasure and the Dharma. Nonetheless, they did their best to keep up the old customs, and even though their present standards fell far below those of Kham he was confident that he and his brothers all lived better, enjoyed themselves more, and accumulated a greater amount of religious merit, than did any of their Indian friends and neighbours.

References to himself and his brothers were, in fact, a regular feature of Aggen's conversation, and from the way in which he spoke it was clear that the five of them were bound by strong ties of mutual affection and common economic interest. At the same time, the fact that they were now living in India, under a totally different set of social conditions, inevitably had imposed a severe strain on those ties, which even before Aggen started studying with me had already begun to weaken in certain respects. Little by little I heard the whole story. Like many of their fellow countrymen, the five Chototsang brothers were polyandrous, that is to say, in addition to being what Indians called a joint family, and holding their inherited and acquired property in common, they had collectively married a woman who was the common wife of them all and to whom all of them enjoyed equal right of access. She and the children they had had by her had, of course, accompanied them to Kalimpong. But in Kalimpong a problem had arisen. Two of the brothers had entered into liaisons with local women and though this was not, in itself, a very serious matter, there was always the possibility that the women would want their paramours to marry them and live with them on a permanent basis. If this were to happen the brothers would have to divide their property, and probably carry on business separately, thus seriously undermining the economic position of each one of them. From the stumbling and shamefaced manner in which he told me all this it was evident that in Aggen's eyes, as in the eyes of most Tibetans, the break up of a polyandrous establishment in this way was more than just an economic disaster. It was a disgrace. Indeed, it was positively immoral, and had my faithful student then been familiar with the words there is little doubt that he would have been tempted to characterize the behaviour of his two brothers – behaviour that threatened the integrity and happiness of the whole family – as 'selfish' and 'individualistic'. As it happened, he was *not* familiar with them, which was perhaps just as well, for long before his lessons with me came to an end I concluded, from remarks he let fall from time to time, that a *third* brother had entered into a liaison with a local woman and that this brother was none other than himself. In the corrosive atmosphere of India the ties that bound the five brothers were, it seemed, in danger of being weakened more than ever.

Much though I heard about Aggen's brothers it was some time before I actually met any of them, and even then the only one I ever came to know at all well was his eldest brother, a personage of whom he stood very much in awe and whom he seemed to regard less as an elder brother than as a father. This brother was ten or fifteen years older than Aggen and in outward appearance, at least, did not resemble him in any way. Not only was he taller, but his face was thinner and wore an expression of sly good humour that was in marked contrast to Aggen's bluff cheerfulness. He was also much more conservative than Aggen, and invariably wore Tibetan costume, including a fur-trimmed hat. Since he knew no English, and I spoke only a few words of Tibetan, we were unable to communicate directly. Aggen therefore acted as interpreter and with his help we succeeded in achieving quite a good level of communication. This was particularly the case during the three or four days we all spent together in Darjeeling, for, thinking it was time they devoted some of their surplus wealth to pleasure and to the Dharma, the five brothers had not only decided to take a short holiday but had also invited me to accompany them. As I very quickly discovered, they were highly excited at the prospect of seeing Darjeeling, the main reason for their excitement being the fact that in Darjeeling they would be able to see a railway train, which was something they had not seen before. On the morning after our arrival, therefore, we all repaired to the railway station, where standing at the platform we found the tiny engine and no less tiny carriages of the Darjeeling Himalayan railway. Tiny as the engine was, however, it was far bigger than the biggest yak the five Khampas had ever beheld, and they gazed at it with undisguised astonishment and not a little awe. Eventually, plucking up their courage, they drew near and examined the monster more closely. One of them, greatly daring, even bent down and tried to peer beneath its belly. Just at that moment it let out a tremendous hoot, whereupon the inquisitive one fell back as though he had been shot while the rest retreated across the platform with many gesticulations and much excited discussion as to what the sound might mean. Before they could arrive at a satisfactory solution to the mystery there came a grinding of wheels and with a slow puff–puff–puff the engine steamed out of the station, pushing its three or four carriages before it until, with a final loud hoot, it disappeared round the hillside, leaving the five Khampas gazing after it in open-mouthed wonderment and with something to talk about for weeks afterwards.

Despite the fact that we were all staying together at the same hotel, a single-storey wooden building with cracked blue paintwork, I did not spend all my time sightseeing with Aggen and his brothers, especially as they wanted to visit the Lebong racecourse and other places of amusement in which I had no interest. Instead, I looked up some of the friends I had made on earlier visits to the Queen of the Hill Stations. One of these was Thubden Chodags, universally known in Darjeeling as the Yellow Monk. He was called the Yellow Monk for the obvious reason that, although born and brought up in Tibet, he wore not the maroon-coloured robes of the Tibetan branch of the monastic order, but the yellow robes that were associated, in the minds of Tibetan Buddhists, with countries like Ceylon and therefore with the Hīnayāna or 'Little Way' of Emancipation. Indeed, as if to emphasize that he was not a maroon monk Thubden Chodags' robes were not only yellow in hue but a bright mustard yellow that made him conspicuous even at a distance of several hundred yards. Moreover, instead of hanging in the customary voluminous folds his robes adhered tightly to his large, rather rawboned frame, which gave him a scantily clad look not at all in keeping with traditional Buddhist notions of decency. I had become acquainted with the Yellow Monk in the course of my first – or it may have been my second – visit to Darjeeling, and since then we had made a point of meeting whenever I happened to be in Darjeeling or he happened to be in Kalimpong. In this way acquaintanceship had developed into a sort of friendship, though it must be admitted that for one reason or other he seemed more anxious to keep up the connection than I was. Not long before he had, in fact, spent a few days with me at the Hermitage, and not long after my return to Kalimpong from my outing with the Chototsang brothers he came and stayed with me for several weeks. Thus at the very time when Ang Tsering was working for me as cook bearer, and when I had three Tibetan students studying English with me, I was also seeing quite a lot of the Yellow Monk, so that within the space of two or three months I had more to do with Tibetans or Tibetan-speakers than at any time since my arrival in Kalimpong.

But though I saw a lot of the Yellow Monk, and though he often talked to me at great length about himself, I soon realized that it was not easy to tell what he was actually thinking or what really motivated him and that he was, in short, a difficult man to know. In this respect he differed markedly from the Indians whom I had known in the plains, who tended to wear their heart on their sleeve, as well as from the Nepalese with whom I had more recently come into contact. The Yellow Monk's mind resembled nothing so much as a set of Chinese boxes, each one of which he opened very slowly indeed, only after a considerable period had elapsed since the opening of the previous box, and only after he had thoroughly assured himself that you could be trusted to look inside it and see the contents – which of course proved to be another box. Difficult as he was to know, however, there was no mistaking his dominant mood, for notwithstanding the smile that sometimes overspread his broad, flat features (though without ever reaching the narrowly slitted almond eyes), the Yellow Monk habitually exuded a sense of dissatisfaction, of bitterness and resentment, that was so strong as to be almost tangible. It was as though the Chinese boxes were all black, or at least dark grey, flecked with red. The principal object of his dissatisfaction was Tibetan Buddhism. At any rate, he was always running it down, and in fact seemed to have a personal grudge against it. Not that he was dissatisfied with its basic doctrines, which so far as I could tell he accepted unquestioningly. He was dissatisfied with its organizational structure. In particular, he was dissatisfied with the way in which members of the powerful feudal aristocracy were allowed to exploit the established religion for their own selfish purposes, as well as dissatisfied with the overbearing and contemptuous manner in which they habitually treated ordinary monks, that is to say, those monks who were neither abbots nor incarnate lamas. It was for this reason that he had left Tibet, gone on pilgrimage to the Buddhist holy places of India, visited Ceylon, and eventually taken ordination as a *śrāmaṇera* or novice from a Sinhalese elder monk, thus transforming himself from a maroon monk into the well-known Yellow Monk of Darjeeling, where he had now lived for several years. Even in Darjeeling, however, Tibetan Buddhism continued to give him cause for dissatisfaction. Recently arrived feudal aristocrats and officials of the Tibetan government (the two were practically synonymous), who did not know a word of English or any local language, were always pestering him to accompany them on their various shopping expeditions and act as interpreter. At first he had been happy to oblige them, especially as they asked him politely enough, but he had soon discovered that he was expected to do more than just translate. Having made their purchases the new arrivals would automatically hand them over to him to carry, with the result that he found himself in the ignominious position of following them round the bazaar with his arms full of parcels. So far as *they* were concerned, he commented bitterly, ordinary monks were no better than servants. He had therefore stopped accompanying them on their shopping expeditions, stopped acting as interpreter. He now had nothing whatever to do with them. If they saluted him when they passed each other in the street he returned their salutation; otherwise he ignored them.

From the controlled intensity of emotion with which Thubden Chodags told me all this it was evident that his dissatisfaction with Tibetan Buddhism ran very deep. Not only did he now have nothing to do with the recently arrived feudal aristocrats and officials of the Tibetan government; he had very little to do with Tibetans of any kind, preferring, by his own admission, to associate with Europeans and Americans or even with (Westernized) Indians. In the circumstances this was hardly surprising. As I already knew, Tibetan Buddhism and the Tibetan people were virtually inseparable, as least so far as the more ethnic aspects of the religion were concerned, so that one who was dissatisfied with Tibetan Buddhism to the extent that Thubden Chodags was would inevitably tend to avoid the company of Tibetans rather than cultivate it. There was, however, at least one Tibetan with whom the Yellow Monk did have something to do. This was an old woman who kept a vegetable shop in the heart of the Darjeeling bazaar. Since he passed by the shop nearly every day, the old woman had come to know him by sight, had got into the habit of greeting him, had stopped him for a little chat, and finally had invited him into the living quarters to the rear of the shop and offered him some light refreshments. By the time that he paid his long visit to me, after my return from the outing with the Chototsang brothers, he had got to know her quite well and the two of them had become something like cronies. He ate at her place at least once or twice a week, and they had long conversations in which she told him all her worries and troubles and he told her some of his.

As his custom was, the Yellow Monk communicated these facts to me very slowly, at great length, and with many significant pauses. Indeed, he communicated them so slowly that it was some time before I realized he was actually talking about the old woman quite a lot and that in talking to me about her he was, in fact, opening one of his Chinese boxes. Within the box there was, of course, another box. The old woman had a daughter, and this daughter, whose existence the Yellow Monk had not mentioned before, was not only her pride and joy but her biggest worry. What therefore could be more natural than that the old woman should, in the absence of husband or brother, confide in one whom she saw regularly and whom she had come to regard as a friend and seek his advice? It was not that the daughter was a bad girl. She was a very good girl. But although she was already twenty-five or twenty-six – the old woman was not sure which – she was as yet unmarried and it was proving extremely difficult to find her a suitable husband. The trouble was that having attended a convent school and being, as it were, English-educated, she did not want to marry an ordinary old-fashioned Tibetan who knew no language but his own, while the old woman herself did not want her daughter to marry a non-Tibetan. What was needed was, therefore, an English-educated Tibetan, and Tibetans of this type were difficult to find in Darjeeling, especially if one was looking for a husband

With friends in Darjeeling: (left to right) Sangharakshita, a Bengali school inspector, the yellow monk, and an RSS organizer

for a girl who, though beautiful and virtuous, was only the daughter of an old woman who kept a vegetable shop in the bazaar. When the Yellow Monk reached this point in his story – and he took so long in reaching it that, by the time he did so, it was really not a point at all – I started wondering just how simple the old woman really was and whether her mind, too, might not resemble a set of Chinese boxes. I even started wondering whether one of the boxes might not…

But the Yellow Monk did not allow me much time for wondering. Slowly and remorselessly, his story continued. Though the old woman confided in him about her daughter and even sought his advice, she was by no means so absorbed in her own worries and troubles as to be unwilling to listen to his. She in fact encouraged him to talk about them and gave him as much advice as he gave her. In particular she encouraged him to express his dissatisfaction with his present position in Darjeeling – and he was, he admitted, very dissatisfied with it indeed. He had no regular income, and therefore was forced to support himself by giving Tibetan lessons and by doing bits and pieces of translation work for the CID,[91] for he could not, of course, earn money by performing ceremonies for the Tibetan laity in the way that the maroon monks did. Poverty moreover obliged him to live in a single small room, in a noisy and overcrowded part of the bazaar, and to put up with the sneers of those who were richer and more successful than he was. In short, he was very dissatisfied and discontented indeed. Fortunately, the old woman sympathized with him in his predicament and not only encouraged him to express his dissatisfaction but also urged him to take steps to improve his position. She had, in fact, advised him to try for a full-time job as a CID translator and he was, even now, giving the matter his serious consideration. Once again a box was being opened, but this time I could not be sure whether it had been opened by the Yellow Monk himself or by the old woman. Perhaps they had both opened boxes; perhaps they had opened them at the same time; and perhaps their boxes matched. At any rate, in the course of subsequent instalments of his story the Yellow Monk slowly and cautiously opened one or two more boxes and by the end of his visit it was clear to me that he would get a full-time job in the CID, that he would cease to be a monk, of whatever colour, that he would marry the old woman's daughter, and that the three of them would live together in a small wooden bungalow in a less noisy and overcrowded part of the Darjeeling bazaar – which is exactly what happened. It did not, however, happen all at once. Indeed, it was only some years later that, having improved his position in the way that his mother-in-law had advised, the whilom Yellow Monk stood proudly before me wearing a smart Western-style suit and exuding a satisfaction that was somehow even more dreadful than his former dissatisfaction. Meanwhile, we continued to keep in touch and at each successive meeting he allowed me to look more closely at the contents of his Chinese boxes.

At about the same time that I was making new friends in the form of Aggen and his eldest brother, as well as deepening my friendship with the

Yellow Monk through the opening of the first of his boxes, I was also in process of losing two relatively old friends. Flossie and Esmond Crisp had had enough of Kalimpong. Or rather, Flossie had had enough of Kalimpong, and Esmond, as he always did, dutifully echoed his mother's sentiments. In fact, they had not only had enough of Kalimpong. They had had enough of India and were going to start a new life in a new country, and the country they had chosen was Australia. Whether the idea of their emigrating to Australia had originated with Flossie herself or with the Janssens was not clear, but I gathered that the Adventist Mission was helping them with their passage and that Mr Janssen had written to members of the church in Sydney on their behalf. Before they left Kalimpong I invited them to the Hermitage for a farewell cup of tea and they presented me with some of their goods and chattels. Among these was what Flossie called Esmond's desk, an unsteady piece of furniture that resembled nothing so much as a narrow washstand backed by double shelves like those of a dresser. Battered and ungainly though it was I was glad to have it, since I needed more space for my books, and Esmond's desk remained with me until the time of my own final departure from Kalimpong. Three or four weeks after they had left I received a picture postcard announcing their safe arrival in Sydney and a month or two after that came a letter. The Promised Land had not lived up to their expectations, Flossie wrote. She and Esmond had been ill, neither of them had been able to find work, and they were at present having to live in a disused chicken-house, where they were surrounded by wire netting. She was beginning to feel like a chicken herself, and would be glad when they were able to move into more suitable accommodation. Esmond was quite happy in the chicken-house, however, and had in fact adjusted to life in Australia better than she had expected. But whether my two friends ever succeeded in finding work, and whether they were able to move out of the chicken-house, I never discovered. My sympathetic and encouraging reply to Flossie's letter met with no response and I never heard from her again. In after years I often wondered what had happened to her and Esmond, and whether the cheerful and good-natured Irishwoman had remained faithful to her Seventh Day Adventist convictions or whether, as part of the business of starting a new life in a new country, she had thought it necessary to change her religion for the eighteenth time.

    Flossie Crisp's postcard and letter were by no means the only communications from overseas to reach me at the Hermitage. Though living in a remote corner of the eastern Himalayas, on the outskirts of a small town of which hardly anyone had heard before, I was now in regular correspondence with Buddhists and people interested in Buddhism in many different parts of the world. Most of these correspondents were former subscribers to *Stepping-Stones* who had first written to me in order to express their appreciation of our little 'journal of Himalayan religion, culture, and education', and most of them lived either in the United States or in England. Among those living in England the most important was one who was not simply a former subscriber and whom I had, in fact, known in London seven or eight years earlier. This was Clare Cameron, the editor of *Buddhism in England* (later renamed the *Middle Way*), the journal of the Buddhist Society, London. Though more than twice my age, Clare had been my closest friend within the Society and even after my departure for the East I had continued to write to her and she to me. During the time of my wanderings in South India and elsewhere our correspondence had naturally been interrupted, but two years ago I had sent her a copy of *Stepping-Stones*, which she had briefly acknowledged, and thereafter we had exchanged greetings from time to time. Now, in the middle of 1952, our correspondence was flowering once again and was soon to be in full bloom. She had relinquished the editorship of the *Middle Way*, she wrote, and now had a little magazine of her own called *Here and Now* which she had bought from a spiritually-minded young man called Derek Neville (had I heard of him?) who had founded it about ten years earlier. After four or five years spent on a farm in Suffolk she was back in London, living in the same small terraced house in East Ham in which she had lived as a girl, and looking after her blind father and ailing mother. Since East Ham was part of the East End of London this could not have been easy for her, and she sometimes admitted as much, yet from her letters and her editorials in *Here and Now* (she was now regularly sending me the magazine) it was clear that the readjustment to city life had served to intensify rather than to weaken the streak of poetry and mysticism that was so prominent a part of her character. It was also clear that she was less involved with Buddhism than before and was moving in the direction of a vague eclecticism that I did not find at all appealing.[92]

Since she was now less involved with Buddhism, Clare's letters contained little or no news of what was happening in the tiny British

Buddhist movement, in which she had once played such a leading role. For news of *that* sort I had to rely on my other Buddhist correspondents in England, most of whom were not only former subscribers to *Stepping-Stones* but also members of the Buddhist Society. As their warm appreciation of *Stepping-Stones* had indicated, they were all deeply interested in the Mahāyāna, though probably only one of their number, Richard Robinson, could be regarded as a serious student of the subject. Between them they had, however, formed within the Buddhist Society a group with which they studied translations of Mahāyāna *sūtras* and other texts, since they rightly believed that it was time for English Buddhists to acquaint themselves with the actual teachings of the Buddha and his Enlightened disciples rather than relying on misleading modern expositions of those teachings. This group, which had some ten or twelve members, was known as the Dharma Group, and there was little doubt that it constituted the main growing point of the Buddhist Society and, indeed, of British Buddhism. Unfortunately, Christmas Humphreys, the President of the Society and its main financial support, was unwilling to tolerate within the organization he had founded any group not under his direct personal control and guidance and the Dharma Group came to an untimely end. All this I learned from Richard Robinson and some of the other members of the Dharma Group, in particular from Jack Austin, the young bank clerk who for several years was one of the most regular and prolific of all my correspondents and my main source of information, or at least gossip, concerning the various things that were happening within British Buddhism.[93]

One of the things that happened within British Buddhism around this time, either shortly before or shortly after the demise of the Dharma Group, was the birth of Robert Stuart Clifton's short-lived Western Buddhist Order, about which Jack wrote at great length and with understandable enthusiasm. Robert Stuart Clifton (I had not heard the name before) was an American Buddhist who had paid a short visit to London, ordained a number of English Buddhists within the order which he had founded, or was in process of founding, and then departed as suddenly as he had arrived. Among those whom he had ordained were most of the members, or former members, of the Dharma Group, including Jack himself, who not only wrote to me about the ordinations but also enclosed newspaper cuttings of the actual ceremony which had, apparently, received a lot of publicity. One of the press cuttings showed Clifton touching an ordinee on the head with what was only too obviously a bread knife. According to Jack, from whom I tried to elicit details of the ceremony, this part of the proceedings represented a 'symbolical' head-shaving, the head-shaving being symbolical because no one was in a position actually to shave their head and give up the world. Besides those ordained in London and (I think) the United States by the Founder-Superior himself, Clifton's order consisted of Western Buddhists who had already received ordination at the hands of an Eastern Buddhist teacher and whose ordinations had been 'recognized' by Clifton without their having to undergo any further ceremony. Thus I was myself informed by Clifton that he 'recognized' my ordination as a Theravāda *bhikṣu* and subsequently received a certificate, signed by the Superior, attesting that I was a member of the Western Buddhist Order.

Though rather resenting his quite superfluous 'recognition' of my ordination, I wrote and thanked Clifton for the certificate and for some time gave his order whatever support I could, both publicly and privately. My feelings about it were, however, distinctly mixed. It was not that I disagreed with the idea behind the Order. Indeed, it seemed to me altogether a good thing that there should be established, in England and the United States, an organization of Western Buddhists which would be more than a collection of people simply 'interested' in Buddhism and which moreover would be adapted not to Eastern but to Western culture. It also seemed appropriate that such an organization should take the form of an order rather than of an association of the ordinary type. But while not disagreeing with the idea behind the Western Buddhist Order I was doubtful if Clifton was the man to give it concrete embodiment, and the more I learned about him the more doubtful I became. Indeed, I became increasingly convinced that he was almost the last person to be the founder and superior of a Buddhist order of any kind. Not only was his knowledge of the Dharma extremely superficial, but like my old friend Swale Ryan he seemed to think of Buddhism in almost exclusively organizational terms. Moreover, though he was probably well-meaning, in the more depreciatory sense of the term, he was brashly self-confident and by no means above making claims which were, it subsequently transpired, completely without foundation.

Such was the Venerable Dr Robert Stuart Clifton, as he then styled himself. A photograph that Jack sent me showed a man in his middle forties wearing a magenta-coloured robe over a lounge suit, and with a white haggard face not unlike Joe's and eyes that avoided the camera. What position in the Buddhist hierarchy the magenta robe signified I did not know, nor did Jack vouchsafe me any information, but since Clifton was understood to belong to the Zen school I took it to be a Japanese Zen robe or a version of such a robe. In the same way I assumed that the ordinations he had handed out so freely in London in fact were, as they purported to be, regular Zen ordinations and that he was fully qualified to confer such ordinations. This proved not to be the case. Clifton's position in the (Zen) Buddhist hierarchy was ambiguous, and the Supreme Patriarch of Sōtō Zen had certainly not authorized him to confer ordinations in the Western world as he claimed. His ordinations were therefore no ordinations at all; they were null and void, at least in the technical sense. Those whom he had 'ordained' in London, or such of them as still wanted to be ordained, were therefore obliged to seek ordination in one or other of the Eastern Buddhist orders. Some were ordained in Sōtō Zen, some in Jōdo Shinshū, while others, less fortunate, did not succeed in getting ordained at all. Clifton himself received ordination as a Theravāda *bhikṣu* in Laos in 1955, by which time his Western Buddhist Order had collapsed (though Jack bravely tried to keep the flag flying in London) and in 1957 went to live and work in Penang. Unfortunately, on his death in 1963 some of his Malaysian admirers published, no doubt in good faith, an obituary that repeated all his old claims. These claims were subjected to point-by-point refutation in the pages of the *Golden Lotus*, the editor of which had known Clifton during his two years as associate editor of the magazine and was well acquainted with the true facts of his career. It was during these two years that he had built up, with the help of the *Golden Lotus* address list, the contacts that had enabled him to establish his Western Buddhist Order and during the same two years that he had, apparently, paid his flying visit to London and conferred the ordinations about which Jack had written to me so enthusiastically.

At the time that Jack wrote to me about the ordinations, however, the true facts of Clifton's career had not begun to emerge, and indeed it was not until nine years later that, thanks to the editor of the *Golden Lotus*, I came to know them all. Yet even at that early stage of my contact with the Western Buddhist Order, before Clifton's breezy 'recognition' of my own ordination as a Theravāda *bhikṣu*, it was obvious to me that there existed among the newly ordained English Buddhists a good deal of confusion as to what 'ordination' actually meant and that this confusion extended to the Founder-Superior himself. They did not see ordination in terms of Going for Refuge to the Buddha, the Dharma, and the Sangha, nor did they see it in terms of going forth from home into the homeless life (the head-shaving was only 'symbolical'). For most of them ordination meant becoming a priest, and being a priest meant being entitled to style oneself Reverend, to wear robes, and to perform ceremonies, while still carrying on with one's secular occupation and one's family life. It meant achieving a higher religious status without actually having to renounce the world in the way that a monk did. Confusion about the meaning of ordination inevitably led to confusion about the meaning and function of the Order. The Order was not a spiritual community of those who had gone for Refuge to the Buddha, the Dharma, and the Sangha, nor was it a spiritual community of those who had gone forth from home into the homeless life. It was an association of priests. Indeed, there were times when I thought that for Jack, at least, the Western Buddhist Order was no more than the club, or even the trade union, of 'Buddhist priests' of Caucasian origin.

For this confusion the rank-and-file members of the Order were not altogether to blame. Perhaps Clifton himself was not altogether to blame, except insofar as the confusion was due to his own misrepresentations and false claims. Buddhism was still very new to the West, and confusion with regard to the true significance of some of its most basic categories, not excluding 'Buddha' and 'Dharma', was widespread even among scholars who had devoted the greater part of their lives to the subject. Little wonder, then, that a small band of youthful enthusiasts in London should have been confused as to the actual meaning of ordination (a confusion apparently shared by their unscrupulous and over-confident mentor), as well as confused about the true significance of the third of the Three Jewels, the Sangha or Order. Moreover, besides being very new in the West, Buddhism was also very old in the East, and in some parts of the Buddhist world the real meaning and significance of both ordination and the Order had been greatly obscured, in the course of the centuries, by various one-sided later developments. Ordination really meant Going for Refuge to the Buddha, the Dharma, and the Sangha. In the Theravāda countries of South-East Asia, however, it had come to mean becoming a monk, so that the Order now meant not the whole body of those Going for Refuge but simply the order of monks or monastic order. In Japan an exactly opposite development had taken place. There ordination meant becoming a priest. Since those members, or former members, of the Dharma Group who wanted to identify themselves more closely with Buddhism had no wish to become monks (a terrifying prospect for most of them!) they had no alternative, in the circumstances, but to become priests, and when Clifton descended on London and offered them a Japanese-style ordination as priests they therefore eagerly embraced the opportunity.

I myself was a monk, and wanted to be a monk. I was a monk because I wanted to identify myself with Buddhism and the spiritual life as fully as I possibly could, as well as to have the fact of my having so identified myself acknowledged by other Buddhists, and saw the monastic life as the best means of achieving this end. For me 'being a monk' certainly did not mean simply wearing a yellow robe and keeping my head shaved, as it seemingly did for so many other members of the monastic order. Nonetheless, even though I saw the monastic life as a means to an end, and therefore not as an end in itself, I at the same time tended to see the spiritual life as being – at least in its more intensive and demanding form – practically identical with the monastic life, which meant that I saw the monastic life not as a means to an end but, in effect, as virtually an end in itself. The reason for this contradiction was that although I was not confused about the meaning and significance of ordination in the way that the newly ordained members of the Western Buddhist Order were, I did not appreciate how absolutely central the act of Going for Refuge really was, its centrality having been obscured for me by the Theravāda's one-sided emphasis on the monastic life, as well as by the blindly mechanical way in which the lay followers of the Theravāda habitually repeated the Refuge-going formula on ceremonial occasions. True, I knew that Going for Refuge was important. I knew that it was Going for Refuge that made one a Buddhist. But I did not realize that being a monk was of significance and value – was a means of identifying oneself with Buddhism and the spiritual life – only to the extent that it was an expression of one's Going for Refuge. I did not realize that ordination – being a Buddhist – leading a spiritual life – Going for Refuge – were in fact virtually synonymous terms, and that whether one lived as monk or layman, *bhikṣu* or *upāsaka*, was a matter of comparatively minor importance. Indeed, in the absence of any real help from current Buddhist – especially current Theravādin – theory and praxis I did not realize these things until some time later, and even then it was only after many years that I succeeded in fully working out their practical implications.[94]

Meanwhile, I was a monk, and wanted to be a monk. Because I was a monk, and had gone forth from home into the homeless life, I considered it incumbent upon me to sever all connection with my relations in England. Consequently for the last five years I had not written to any member of my family, nor had any member of my family written to me. Indeed, so far as I was aware they did not even know whether I was alive or dead. However, around the time that Jack was writing to me about the newly born Western Buddhist Order I received a letter from my sister, who apparently had obtained my address from the Buddhist Society. She had recently given birth to a daughter, she wrote, and they were both well, as were the rest of the family. Though I was glad to hear from my sister, and though I replied to her letter, I must have made it clear that I had no intention of keeping up the correspondence, for she did not write again and it was twelve years before any communication passed between myself and any of my relations.[95]

Yet even though I had severed all connection with those who were nearest to me in blood, it was not so easy to escape worldly ties. I had students, some of whom were very close to me, those students had families, and with some of those families I had been on visiting terms ever since my days at the Dharmodaya Vihara. Among those families with which I was on visiting terms the one which I visited most frequently, and where I always received a particularly warm welcome, was Sachin's. Indeed, since my removal to the Hermitage the previous year I had been seeing his parents, and his brother and sisters, at fairly regular intervals, with the result that we were now well acquainted. In the course of the next year or two acquaintance was to develop into friendship, and friendship by imperceptible degrees into something like intimacy, until I had practically adopted the Singh family and the Singh family had practically adopted me. *Naturam expellas furca, tamen usque recurret.* Or, in the wise words of Francis Bacon, 'Nature is often hidden, sometimes overcome, seldom extinguished.'[96]

17
THE ENEMY OF THE CHURCH

During the eight years that I had so far spent in the East I had had very little contact with Christianity or with Christians, nor was I particularly desirous of having contact with them. In Calcutta I had taken a couple of monks belonging to the Ramakrishna Mission to hear Stanley Jones preach,[97] in Muvattupuzha I had made friends with two or three Indian Christians who were strongly drawn to Buddhism,[98] in Rajgir my teacher Kashyapji and I had discussed mysticism with a Roman Catholic priest who, on our departure, presented me with copies of Thomas Merton's *Seven Storey Mountain* and *Seeds of Contemplation*[99] – and that was about all. Now that I was living in Kalimpong, however, contact with Christianity and Christians was difficult to avoid, and to tell the truth though I was not particularly desirous of having contact with them I did not go out of my way to avoid it either. Christians, of several different denominations, were both numerous and ubiquitous in the little Himalayan township, and the external signs of their presence were, in fact, one of the first things that the visitor to Kalimpong noticed on crossing the municipal boundary. At Seventh Mile the extensive buildings of the Roman Catholic Mission covered much of the hillside above the road; at Eighth Mile, on turning a bend, one saw the square grey tower of the Scottish Mission church dominating the bazaar; while at Ninth Mile, just below the road, there squatted the comparatively modest premises of the Blind School which, during the time that it was under the direction of the Hon. Mary Scott, might be described as freelance Presbyterian. Behind and above the square grey tower of the Scottish Mission church, dominating both the tower itself and the saddleback on which the greater part of Kalimpong was situated, rose the thickly wooded heights of Dailo, which more often than not were half covered in cloud.

Dailo was the abode of Dr Graham's Homes, the principal stronghold of Christianity in general and Scottish Presbyterianism in particular in the Subdivision, though the Roman Catholic Mission, which had got off to a comparatively late start, was now running a good second in the Christian supremacist stakes. The Homes, as the institution was known in Kalimpong, had been founded by Dr Graham, a Scottish missionary and educator who subsequently became Moderator of the Church of Scotland. Originally it had been called The St Andrew's Colonial Homes, having been renamed in honour of its founder after his death. Dr Graham had founded the Homes in order to remedy, as he thought, a definite social evil. The Darjeeling District, of which the Kalimpong Subdivision formed a part, was full of tea estates: there were probably hundreds of them. In the days of the Raj the managers and assistant managers of these tea estates were nearly always British (many of them in fact were Scots), and of these British managers and assistant managers the vast majority were bachelors, at least in the sense of being temporarily separated from their lawful spouses. Since they were bachelors they naturally entered into liaisons with the younger and more attractive members of the Nepalese workforce, some of whom were very attractive indeed, and naturally these women sooner or later gave birth to half-caste children. Usually the children were not acknowledged by their fathers and lived with their mothers in the coolie lines, where they grew up dirty and neglected, without education, and with no better prospect before them than that of becoming coolies on the estate in which they had been born and to which, in a sense, they belonged. In the course of his pastoral and missionary visits to the tea estates Dr Graham had noticed these children, some of whom indeed had inherited the light-coloured complexion and even the blue eyes of their unknown fathers, and the kind-hearted clergyman had eventually arranged to take some of the more obviously European of them back to Kalimpong with him. In so doing he appears to have been actuated by two motives. One, no doubt, was purely humanitarian in character. He was distressed to see the sordid conditions in which the little half-caste boys and girls were living. The other motive was religious, even missionary. He could not bear to think that children of Christian, even Presbyterian, fathers, should grow up in total ignorance of the Gospel (the religion of their mothers did not, of course, matter). The result was the founding of The St Andrew's Colonial Homes, afterwards known as Dr Graham's Homes, where the unwanted offspring of the tea planters were decently clothed, housed, and fed, where they were given an English education, and where, above all, they were brought up as devout members of the Presbyterian Church of Scotland.

At the time of my arrival in Kalimpong the Homes occupied some three hundred acres of the wooded Dailo hillside, immediately above the Tharpa Choling Gompa, and had in its care about five hundred children of all ages. Among these children there were not only the unwanted offspring of the tea planters but also the second and third generation descendants of such offspring (as Mary Scott had told me, the system was self-perpetuating), as well as Anglo-Indian and even Indian Christian orphans and demi-orphans from as far away as Calcutta. The children were distributed, I believe according to age, among some twenty-five or thirty buildings and groups of buildings, each of which was in the charge of a house father and house mother or, in the case of the buildings occupied by the youngest children, of a house mother only. During the week the children attended the Homes' own junior school or the Homes' own senior school, as the case might be, and on Sundays they worshipped (twice) at the Homes' own church, a square building with a grey tower that dominated the Homes in much the same way that the Scottish Mission church dominated the Kalimpong bazaar. The institution also had its own hospital, its own meeting hall, and its own playing fields, besides numerous other facilities, some of which it owed to the generosity either of the tea planters themselves or of the companies for which they worked. It even had its own shop and its own magazine. Thus the five hundred children and their fifty or sixty house fathers and house mothers, as well as the Homes' hundred or more teachers, administrators, and maintenance workers, all lived very much in a self-contained little world of their own. But though they lived in a world of their own, they and the institution to which they belonged did, at the same time, exert a certain amount of influence – especially religious influence – on the larger and less highly organized world of Kalimpong. Both the house fathers and house mothers and the teachers, as well as some of the administrators, doubled as part-time missionaries, and on most days of the week four or five of them, either singly or in pairs, could be seen hastening along the High Street, Bibles beneath their arms and a look of determination on their faces, on their way to a 'personal testimony' meeting.

In the high and palmy days of the Raj the Homes and its representatives had done much more than just exert influence. They had practically ruled Kalimpong, especially during the heady period when the Subdivisional Officer, who of course was British, had been none other than the husband of one of Dr Graham's daughters, so that that lady reigned as undisputed Queen of Kalimpong by virtue of her double title as daughter of the town's leading citizen and the wife of the head of the administration. To such an extent was Kalimpong in the grip of the missionaries, indeed, that when the local Buddhists invited a visiting Buddhist monk to deliver a lecture on Buddhism at the Town Hall, those champions of the Gospel were able to prevail upon the Subdivisional Officer to issue an order prohibiting him from doing so. The monk in question was Bhikkhu Silachara (J. F. M'Kechnie), the *Scottish* Buddhist – perhaps *there* was the rub! – who had worked with Ananda Metteyya in Burma at the beginning of the century and whose translation of the first fifty discourses of the *Majjhima Nikāya* had been of such great help to me during my days in Muvattupuzha. Exactly when Silachara's visit to Kalimpong had taken place, and whether it had taken place during the reign of Dr Graham's daughter and her consort, I was unable to discover, but a year or so after the collapse of *Stepping-Stones* and, therewith, the Nepali section of the magazine, I brought out a Nepali translation of the Scottish monk's *Buddhism for the Beginner*. In my preface to this publication I described how he had been prohibited from speaking at the Town Hall, adding that it gave me great satisfaction to think that, through the medium of the little work now being brought out, he was at last able to give the people of Kalimpong – and, indeed, of the whole area – the message that he had been prevented from giving all those years ago.

Great as was the satisfaction it gave me to think this, however, it gave me still greater satisfaction to think that, now that India was independent, I myself was free to speak on Buddhism not only in Kalimpong but anywhere in India, and that Christian missionaries no longer had the power to prevent the followers of other religions from giving public expression to their own beliefs. During the year or more that I had been at the Hermitage I had, indeed, continued to lecture at the Town Hall and the Hillview Hotel, as well as deliver full-moon day discourses at the Hermitage itself. That I was able to do this naturally gave no satisfaction whatever to the missionaries. In fact it was a source of considerable dissatisfaction and disquiet to them, particularly to the Presbyterians, and I had little doubt that if only they had had the power they would have accorded me the same treatment that they had accorded Bhikkhu Silachara. Whenever they saw me coming along the High Street, especially after the visit of the Sacred Relics, in which I had played a prominent part, they would clutch their Bibles more tightly and hurry past me with averted faces.

Not all missionaries averted their faces, however. Even apart from Mary Scott, who was a brave woman (and in any case I had called on her at the Blind School, and she could hardly be uncivil), there were some missionaries who dared to look at me and some who even dared to speak to me. One of the latter, indeed, not only dared to pay me a visit but after we had talked for half an hour actually invited me to his home for a meal. This unprecedented event had occurred while I was still at the Dharmodaya Vihara, the courageous missionary in question being a young American Seventh Day Adventist who lived with his wife and two children about a mile down the road in a bungalow called Hegavus. Though I had always understood the Seventh Day Adventists to be fundamentalists and, therefore, intolerant even of other Christians, not to speak of the followers of heathen religions, the young American missionary showed no sign of either intolerance or bigotry and we were therefore able to have a quite amicable discussion on matters of religion. The discussion was all the more amicable in that we soon discovered there was common ground between us and concentrated on that rather than attempting to explore our differences, which in any case were sufficiently obvious. This common ground was vegetarianism and teetotalism, for the Seventh Day Adventists, I learned, abstained from meat, fish, and alcoholic liquors and, indeed, from all stimulants, including tea and coffee. Thus not only did the fact that we had common ground between us contribute to amicable discussion, but the fact that that common ground took the form of vegetarianism and teetotalism made it possible for my unusual visitor to invite me for a meal, which he could hardly have done had the Seventh Day Adventists been confirmed flesh eaters. Even if he had invited me I probably would have found it difficult to accept his invitation, knowing as I did the embarrassment that could result when my host discovered that I did *not* regard fish or prawns as vegetables. But on the present occasion there was no such difficulty. Whatever other differences might separate us, I the Buddhist monk and he the Seventh Day Adventist missionary could at least eat together, and thus it was that a few days later I found myself at Hegavus sitting down to an American-style vegetarian meal with my hospitable new acquaintance and his family. Though the meal did not include apple pie, the sight of the plump pink cheeks and healthy well-fed bodies, and the sound of the twangy transatlantic vocables, made me feel that I had suddenly been transported to America, the more especially since the family's standard of living seemed to be four or five times higher than that of their middle-class Indian counterparts.

Unfortunately, the acquaintanceship thus auspiciously begun did not continue. The young American missionary did not visit me again, nor did he invite me for another meal, and shortly before my own departure for Sarnath and higher ordination he left Kalimpong. Before leaving, however, he must have told his two successors about me, for they attended one or two of the lectures I was then giving at the Hillview Hotel under the auspices of the Institute of Culture. The younger of the two, who was likewise an American, did not remain long in the town, but his elderly Dutch colleague, Mr Janssen, was to stay for a number of years and become the real founder of the Seventh Day Adventist Mission in Kalimpong. But though he attended my lectures Mr Janssen did not speak to me, much less still invite me to his home for a meal, and it was not until the following year, when I moved from Burma Raja's guest bungalow to the Hermitage, that I had any further contact with the missionaries of Kalimpong.

This time my contact was not with Seventh Day Adventists but with Roman Catholics, and not with an American but with two or three Swiss and an Englishman. Whether I first visited them, or they first visited me, I no longer recollect. Since the Roman Catholic Mission was situated down at Seventh Mile, and since the white-clad priests often went into the bazaar, as I myself sometimes did, we must have passed one another on the road; when this had happened a few times we must have exchanged greetings, or spoken (the Roman Catholics were, on the whole, more civil than the Presbyterians), and in the end either I must have invited one of them to the Hermitage for a cup of tea or they must have invited me to come and see their church, about which I had already heard from a number of people and which was, in fact, one of the sights of the town. Whichever of us it was that took the initiative, there was a period of some two or three months during which I visited the mission, and one or another of the Swiss, or the Englishman, visited the Hermitage, fairly regularly. The mission consisted of two parts. Immediately above the road stood St Philomena's Convent and St Philomena's School, as well as the nuns' own church, a large and ornate Gothic building with, I believe, stained glass windows. Behind the convent, and on a higher level, stood St Augustine's Priory and St Augustine's School, which had their own separate entrance up a side road, though a flight of steps connected the two fiefdoms, between which, I subsequently learned, there was little love lost, the nuns particularly objecting to the priests and brothers playing football with the boys.

On my first visit to the priory (there was of course no question of my visiting the convent, the nuns from which averted their faces from me quite as sedulously as did the Presbyterians) I was shown the school, the library, and the cheese factory, where the priests and brothers, who were French- and German-speaking Augustinians, produced the excellent cheeses which were in such great demand among the European inhabitants of Kalimpong and Darjeeling and which found a ready market even in faraway Calcutta. Above all I was shown the church, of which the good fathers were justly proud. A low, rectangular building with a turquoise-tiled roof, it had been constructed on the model of a Tibetan *gompa* in order to make Catholicism more culturally acceptable to the local people, or at least such of them as had a Tibetan Buddhist background. In decorating the interior the same principle had been followed. Behind the altar there was a carved wooden panel depicting the Last Supper, Christ and the Apostles being represented with slightly Mongolian features and wearing the garb of Tibetan Buddhist monks, while on the floor in front of the table at which they were seated stood a teapot of characteristically Tibetan design. The carver of the panel, I was told, was a Lepcha Christian. There was also a life-size statue of St Augustine of Hippo, though the artist had resisted the temptation to make the African saint look like a Lepcha. When I had seen everything worth seeing I was taken to the refectory for a cup of tea. Though it was four o'clock, the remains of lunch had not been cleared away and half-eaten joints of meat and half-emptied bottles of wine still occupied the expanse of soiled white tablecloth. On my subsequent visits to the priory I spent most of my time in the library, where the more open-minded among the priests and brothers joined me for long discussions on Buddhism, comparative religion, and mysticism. Sometimes I borrowed a book, usually one of the Christian classics. For their part, my interlocutors were soon paying regular visits to the Hermitage, where we continued our discussions and where I lent them books on Buddhism.

In this way I got to know them quite well, particularly the two or three Swiss and the Englishman, who was known as Brother Peter. Tall, well built, pink-faced, fair-haired, and blue-eyed, Brother Peter was the very model of the pleasant young Englishman, and I was not surprised when I found him down at Glengarry one day having tea with Mrs Hamilton, who as a staunch member of the Church of England generally had no dealings with the Roman Catholic Mission (except when buying cheeses) but with whom Brother Peter was evidently quite a favourite – to the extent that that strong-minded woman could be said to have favourites. In the course of one of his visits to the Hermitage Brother Peter told me something of his religious history. Originally an Anglican, he had joined the Catholic Church only five or six years earlier and was thinking of entering the priesthood. From the interest he showed in Buddhism, however, and the eagerness with which he devoured books on the subject, I suspected that Brother Peter was still not settled in his views and that in the same way that he had moved from Anglicanism to Roman Catholicism he might well move from Roman Catholicism to something else. Be that as it may, when I had been visiting the priory for two or three months, and the three Swiss and Brother Peter had been visiting me at the Hermitage for a similar period, my contact with the missionaries of Kalimpong was again interrupted. Brother Peter and his colleagues suddenly stopped coming to the Hermitage and when I happened to meet any of them on the road they returned my greeting with an air of embarrassment and constraint and I realized that I was no longer welcome at the priory. Four or five months later I learned that Monsignor (of whose existence I had hitherto been unaware) had forbidden the priests and brothers belonging to the mission to have anything more to do with me. As for

Brother Peter, he had been transferred to another priory, and a year later I learned that he had left the Catholic Church.

Long before news of these developments reached me, however, contact between myself and the missionaries of Kalimpong had been renewed, though only to a very limited extent. During the two years and more that had elapsed since the Chinese invasion of the Land of Snows[100] the number of Tibetans in Kalimpong had steadily increased, as monks and laymen, aristocrats and traders, sought refuge in India from the miseries of life under Chinese Communist rule. As the number of Tibetans increased, so did the number of missionaries, as Christian missionary bodies around the world hastened to take advantage of the God-sent opportunity of converting the Tibetans, many of whom were known to have arrived in India with very limited resources and who might reasonably be expected, therefore, to be open to the appeal of the Gospel. Some of the new arrivals among the missionaries had spent many years in China, from which they had fled at the time of the victory of the Chinese Communist forces under Mao Tse-Tung over the Kuomintang forces under Chiang Kai-shek and the subsequent proclamation of the Central Government of the People's Republic of China.[101] A few of the more heroic of them had, indeed, made the journey to India by the perilous overland route via Tibet and had arrived in Kalimpong not very far in advance of the Tibetan refugees themselves. The other new arrivals came mainly from England and America, though considerable reinforcements for the Scottish Presbyterian Church also arrived from the land of John Knox. Since these additions to the missionary body belonged to a number of different denominations (some of them, apparently, to no denomination at all), and since they all had their own ideas as to the best method of converting the heathen, many of them were not interested in cooperating with any of the existing missions or even with one another. Some of them therefore came to be regarded by the other missionaries with suspicion and dislike, even with hostility – though not always for the same reasons.

Of none of them was this more true than of Father Morse, who so far as his fellow missionaries were concerned was the most unpopular – not to say the best hated – man in Kalimpong, with the possible exception of myself. Father Morse was a Cowley Father, that is to say, he belonged to the Society of St John the Evangelist, the oldest Anglican community for men, and had spent many years as a medical missionary in China, where his work had lain mainly among those afflicted with leprosy. Lepers were, in fact, Father Morse's special interest, not to say his passion, and on his arrival from China he had at once opened a leprosy clinic at Tenth Mile, in a small room on the ground floor of a squalid building that functioned as a kind of caravanserai for Tibetans of the lowest class, including prostitutes and criminals. In this room Father Morse also lived, with a leper boy as his servant and assistant. Here he happily looked after his lepers and anyone else who needed his help, and here he received his visitors, some of whom came out of genuine interest in his work and some simply out of curiosity. Those who came out of curiosity rarely came again, for more often than not they would be given tea in Father Morse's single chipped cup and the cup would be conveyed to them by the leper boy in what remained of his hands. Father Morse was in fact utterly indifferent to all that concerned his own creature comforts and did not bother overmuch, it seemed, about hygiene. Apart from the chipped cup (and his medical equipment) he possessed little more than a tin plate and spoon, a rickety chair, a saucepan in which the leper boy boiled potatoes for him once a day, and the shabby black cassock he stood up in. When he literally did stand up in it Father Morse was an impressive figure. An American by birth, he was quite a big man, with a full white beard that came halfway down his chest and made him look like a Father Christmas in mourning. Not that there was anything mournful about Father Morse, though, except when he put his hand into his pocket for some money to give to a beggar and found that there was nothing there for him to give. With his twinkling blue eyes, ruddy cheeks, warm smile, and gentle manners, the old man was in fact the very embodiment of cheerful asceticism, and Tibetans who happened to meet him on the road often sought his blessing as they would have sought that of an incarnate lama.

One would therefore have thought that the other missionaries would have been glad to have Father Morse living on their doorstep, so to speak, but this was far from being the case. They did not want him living on their doorstep at all, or anywhere near it. For one thing, they objected to his not living in the same comfortable European (or American) style to which they themselves were accustomed to live. (This was particularly true of the Presbyterians and members of other Protestant groups, who were fond of arguing that England and America were rich because God was pleased with them for being Christian, just as India and Tibet were poor because he was angry with them for being heathen. If one wanted to become rich one should become a Christian. Goodness and riches were inseparable. Father Morse's way of life had the effect of completely undermining this line of argument, which some of the poorer and more simple-minded Hindus and Buddhists found quite appealing.) The other missionaries also objected to Father Morse's living in a not very respectable part of the bazaar, among Tibetans of rather disreputable character. Above all, however, they objected to his refusal to convert anybody, for it was the old man's proud boast that in all his years of work as a medical missionary he had not converted a single person. To him, being a medical missionary did not mean doing a little doctoring when one was not engaged in the more important task of preaching the Gospel, much less still did it mean giving medical treatment on condition that the patient read a tract, or listened to a sermon, or even allowed himself or herself to be baptized. Being a medical missionary meant preaching the Gospel by ministering to the sick in the name of Christ and leaving the rest in the hands of God, and in any case had not Christ himself said, 'Inasmuch as ye have done it unto one of the least of these my brethren, ye have done it unto me,'[102] and was not this in itself a sufficient reason for ministering to the poor, the sick, and the afflicted?

This attitude the other missionaries of Kalimpong were utterly unable to understand. To them, being a missionary, whether medical or otherwise, meant converting people, and converting people meant baptizing them in the prescribed manner and adding their names to the list of 'souls won for Christ' that was sent each month to the parent body in Europe or America as proof that the Kingdom was spreading and that further financial support was, therefore, urgently needed. Since Father Morse refused to convert anybody, and even gloried in the fact, in the eyes of the other missionaries he was not really a missionary at all, whatever 'good works' he might perform. Nor was that all. Not only was Father Morse not really a missionary at all, in the eyes of his fellow missionaries, but his refusal to convert people was seen by them as constituting a direct criticism of themselves and their own work, for if being a missionary did *not* mean converting people then what were they all doing in Kalimpong? Their work was a waste of time, and their lives without meaning or value! Thus without his intending any such thing Father Morse's presence on the doorstep of the other missionaries had the effect of seriously undermining their confidence in themselves and what they were doing, even undermining their sense of identity, with the result that instead of considering seriously the questions that his presence among them raised they sneered at him, spoke disparagingly about him, avoided contact with him, and in short, in the case of the Presbyterians in particular, averted their faces from him – both literally and metaphorically – quite as much as they did from me.

To such an extent did the missionaries of Kalimpong, and the Presbyterians in particular, avert their faces from Father Morse that they refused to have anything to do with him even at that season of the year which was, supposedly, the season of peace on earth and goodwill towards men. Happening to look in at Father Morse's leprosy clinic on Christmas Eve, Joe found the old man almost in tears. Tomorrow was Christmas Day, he explained, but he had no food for the occasion and no money to buy any. Not that he really minded that. What hurt him was the fact that none of the missionaries had cared to invite him to have his Christmas dinner with them, even though they knew that he would be on his own, while they themselves would be sitting down to a sumptuous repast with their families. A little hesitantly, Joe suggested a solution to the problem. 'I am a Buddhist,' he said, 'but if you care to come to my place tomorrow I shall be glad to give you your Christmas dinner.' Father Morse brightened up immediately. 'Oh would you, Joe?' he cried eagerly. 'I should love to come!' The result was that next day Father Morse went to Joe's flat, where he was given a Christmas dinner consisting of roast chicken (Joe was not a vegetarian), potatoes, and peas, all of which he very much enjoyed and for all of which, no doubt, he gave heartfelt thanks to his God.

What would have happened if Father Morse had been in Kalimpong the following Christmas there is no knowing, but before he had been in the town a year his religious superiors (for whose instructions he had been waiting) recalled him to the United States. Since he had been hoping to be allowed to remain in Kalimpong, among his beloved lepers, the summons came as a great disappointment, but to him the voice of his religious superiors was the voice of God and he therefore obeyed it unquestioningly, though with obvious reluctance, and after saying his farewells sadly left for America, where there were no lepers for him to look after. But though his stay in Kalimpong had been comparatively short, Father Morse was remembered for a long time afterwards, and though the other missionaries might not have cared to mention him his name was pronounced in accents of affection and gratitude by many a Tibetan and many a Nepali, until time and distance eventually transformed the old medical missionary into an almost legendary figure whose benign presence had for a while shed a ray of light on some of the darkest places of the town.

A medical missionary of a very different type, whose presence shed no ray of light on the dark places of Kalimpong, and who was certainly not remembered in the way that Father Morse was remembered, was a bumptious red-bearded young Scotsman on whom Joe, in a moment of inspiration, bestowed the sobriquet of Springheel Jack. Springheel Jack had appeared in Kalimpong at about the same time as Father Morse, and thereafter reappeared at intervals for several years. Like Father Morse he had come from China and had, in fact, travelled to India by the overland route via Tibet. While in Tibet he had spent some time among the Khampas, for whom he had developed a great affection, the more especially since they were engaged in an armed struggle against the Chinese Communist forces, which had recently invaded their homeland in eastern Tibet. He had not, however, developed an affection for the Khampas' religion. To him Tibetan Buddhism was a species of demonolatry and its rites and ceremonies a form of black magic. Probably it was for this reason that he always gave me a wide berth and we never actually met (Father Morse had visited me at the Hermitage several times), though I saw him spring-heeling his way around the bazaar often enough, blue eyes fiercely blazing and the familiar black Bible tucked beneath his arm like a Sten gun, ready to spray anybody who crossed his path with texts. According to Joe, he had originally belonged to the Plymouth Brethren, but had left them because they were too liberal-minded and was now a freelance preacher of the Gospel, owing no allegiance to any religious organization and taking his orders direct from God. To do him justice, however, he spent very little time actually preaching, being mainly occupied either playing tennis or plotting against the Chinese Communists with his Khampa friends.

If Springheel Jack gave me a wide berth the Missionary Girls, perhaps less wisely, made a beeline for me. From what I subsequently heard about the two young Englishwomen thus denominated they were evangelical eager-beavers who, after spending two years at a Bible college in the West Country, had come out to Kalimpong full of the joy of the Lord and determined to do battle with the forces of evil and convert the heathen inhabitants of the town to Christianity. On their alighting from the Landrover that had brought them up from Siliguri, however, almost the first person they set eyes on was a European who had evidently been converted from Christianity to a heathen religion, namely, myself in my yellow robes. This was a terrible shock to them, since not in their worst moments had they imagined that there could be such a thing as a European Buddhist, least of all an English Buddhist. Undaunted nevertheless, after much searching of the scriptures, and much waiting on the Lord in prayer, they sent word that they would like to meet me, I responded by inviting them to tea, and at four o'clock on the appointed day, with their Bibles under their arms and rather fixed smiles on their faces, they accordingly ascended the steps of the chalet, where I had caused Ang Tsering to lay on a nice tea for them, complete with colourfully-iced little cakes from our itinerant *roti-wallah* or bread man. The minute I set eyes on the ill-assorted pair I mentally christened them Miss Long and Miss Short, and though subsequently I learned to speak of them as the Missionary Girls, as everybody else in Kalimpong did, it was as Miss Long and Miss Short that I continued to think of them for a long time afterwards. Miss Long was tall and thin, with a pale face and a thoughtful, even worried, expression. Miss Short, on the other hand, was of diminutive stature and decidedly plump, with round red cheeks and an expression of great cheerfulness, not to say heartiness. Both women had brown hair – straight in the case of Miss Long and curly in the case of Miss Short – and both were about the same age as myself, that is to say, not more than twenty-seven or twenty-eight.

As soon as we had exchanged greetings and they had taken their seats with me round the little table by the window at which I did my writing Ang Tsering entered with the teapot, held shoulder high in Tibetan fashion, and for the next ten or fifteen minutes I endeavoured to put my visitors at ease with a combination of small talk, cups of Darjeeling tea, and colourfully-iced little cakes. But though Miss Long and Miss Short each drank two cups of tea they only nibbled at the pink, mauve, and green cakes, and I realized that they would not be really satisfied or at ease until they had actually done battle with the forces of evil as represented by the yellow-robed figure on the other side of the table. I also realized that the reason they only nibbled at the cakes was that they suspected me of having muttered 'evil charms' over them. (Springheel

Jack and many of the other missionaries firmly believed that Buddhist monks were expert black magicians and often did that sort of thing.) When Ang Tsering had cleared the table I therefore gave them the opportunity for which they had, no doubt, been waiting by enquiring what had brought them to Kalimpong and why they wanted to meet me, though the fact that they had their Bibles open on their laps in readiness really made the question unnecessary. My visitors needed no further encouragement, and soon the bullets were flying thick and fast as now Miss Long and now Miss Short directed her fire power upon me or as – to speak less metaphorically – they between them treated me to the kind of text-citing evangelical spiel that might have been expected from two enthusiastic young women, both unmarried, who had just spent two years at Bible college and who possessed more zeal than discretion and no consciousness whatever of their limitations even as exponents of their own faith.

I made no attempt to interrupt them, much less still to argue with them, though in their eagerness to convert me they frequently interrupted each other and occasionally even disagreed on minor points. When they had finished, or at least were left with nothing more to say for the time being, I told them that while I had no wish to question the genuineness of their experience (for in the course of their joint harangue they had given their 'personal testimony' concerning the wonderful things that Jesus had done for them), I had no wish, either, to question the genuineness of the experience of the followers of other religions. Jesus had, no doubt, done wonderful things for them, but devout Hindus said the same thing of Rama and Krishna, and pious Muslims of Mohammed. Speaking personally, though I had no pretensions to either devotion or piety I could certainly say that the Buddha had done wonderful things for me, and I hoped that they would no more question the genuineness of my experience than I questioned the genuineness of theirs. In any case, no open-minded person could fail to agree that there was an element of truth in every religion, and that no system of belief to which men and women had sincerely dedicated their lives could possibly be regarded as nothing but a mass of falsehood.

This was very much the line of reasoning I had pursued with the priests and brothers of the Roman Catholic Mission, especially Brother Peter, and on account of which, no doubt, Monsignor had forbidden them to associate with me. In the case of Miss Long and Miss Short, however, I pursued it much more vigorously, and enlarged upon it to a much greater extent, than I had done previously; for whereas it had been possible for me to disclose my views to the priests and brothers gradually, in the course of a whole series of discussions, in the case of their less civilized Protestant counterparts I had to disclose my views all at once in response to what was, in effect, a frontal attack on my most cherished convictions as a Buddhist and as a thinking human being. So vigorously, indeed, did I pursue my more 'ecumenical' line, and to so great an extent did I enlarge upon it, that on the more intelligent and sensitive of my two visitors, at least, I eventually succeeded in making an impression. Not that Miss Long suddenly started doubting that Jesus had done wonderful things for her, but from the troubled, intent expression that appeared upon her pallid countenance, it was obvious that I had actually made her think and that, for one awful, dizzying moment, she had even contemplated the possibility that there might be something in what I said. Miss Short was made of sterner stuff, or perhaps she was only more obtuse. So far as she was concerned, there *could not* be anything in what I or any other Buddhist monk said and the question of contemplating, even for an instant, the possibility that there might be, simply did not arise. She had, however, wit enough to perceive that her friend had been somewhat disturbed by my words and needed, perhaps, an opportunity of strengthening her faith by more searching of the scriptures and more waiting on the Lord in prayer. A signal having passed between them, she therefore looked at her watch and announced that it was time they departed, and a few minutes later, after bidding me a rather constrained farewell, the two would-be proselytizers descended the steps of the chalet in a somewhat more chastened frame of mind than they had ascended them two hours earlier.

What account of their visit they gave to the missionaries of their acquaintance I never knew, but they did not come to see me again and whenever I happened to pass them in the High Street they did their best to pretend they had not seen me. When this was impossible Miss Long acknowledged my salutation with a look of mingled horror and reproach, as though I had brought her to the edge of the Bottomless Pit and had very nearly succeeded in pushing her in, while Miss Short gave me a grim smile and a barely perceptible nod. Nonetheless, despite their lack of success with me (and in my heart of hearts I could not help feeling quite sorry for them, especially for Miss Long), the Missionary

Girls were as determined as ever to convert the heathen inhabitants of Kalimpong to Christianity and apparently decided that if they were to make any real headway they would have to learn Tibetan. What better way of learning Tibetan could there be than living with a respectable Tibetan family and, at the same time, teaching the members of that family English or at least giving them practice in English conversation? Indeed, what better way of spreading the Gospel could there be? – for like many other enthusiasts Miss Long and Miss Short were convinced that except in the case of those who (like the English Buddhist monk) deliberately closed their hearts to the Truth their message had only to be heard to be believed. The only real difficulty lay in getting a hearing. A few months after their encounter with me, therefore, the Missionary Girls moved in with Mr and Mrs Shagabpa, an elderly couple who occupied the Western-style bungalow they had built for themselves below the road at Nine-and-a-Quarter Mile, next door to the Blind School. Tsepon or 'Treasurer' Shagabpa was a high official in the Tibetan government who invariably wore Tibetan dress and a gold-and-turquoise ear pendant and who, moreover, wore his long hair in braids coiled round his head, which gave him a curiously feminine look. I had known him virtually since my arrival in Kalimpong, and he had always been a generous supporter of the YMBA and *Stepping-Stones*, though since he knew little English and I less Tibetan communication between us had perforce been limited to an exchange of friendly smiles. Mrs Shagabpa, who knew no English at all, was a very large woman whose thick braids hung down to well below her rather high waist and the greater part of whose person was covered by an enormous expanse of rainbow apron. Though she hardly ever spoke, Mrs Shagabpa's rose-cheeked face was invariably creased in a beaming smile that appeared to betoken immense goodwill towards the whole world.

With Mr and Mrs Shagabpa, then, Miss Long and Miss Short domesticated themselves, though in what capacity or on what terms was far from clear. The Tibetans of Kalimpong were convinced that one could not possibly learn Tibetan or any other subject properly without a teacher to hit you over the head with a ruler (part of Joe's reputation as a teacher was due to the freedom with which he wielded that instrument of pedagogy), and still more convinced that no missionary could possibly succeed in converting a Tibetan – a real Tibetan born and brought up in Tibet, not the mongrel Darjeeling or Ladakhi variety – from Buddhism to Christianity. What, then, was the Missionary Girls' *real* motive for living with Mr and Mrs Shagabpa? It was not long before the collective intelligence of the Tibetan community succeeded in coming up with the solution to this problem, for, as I already knew, the Tibetans were a logically-minded people who firmly believed that there was a rational explanation for even the oddest behaviour and never rested until they had discovered it. The reason the two young Englishwomen had moved in with the Shagabpas was that they had their eye on Mr Shagabpa, who was not only a high official but extremely wealthy, and they had their eye on him because they wanted to establish themselves in life by becoming his secondary wives or concubines, it being well known that Mrs Shagabpa had so far borne him no child. The short, fat one, they collectively opined, would probably prove a good breeder, though they had their doubts about the tall, thin one.

Poor Miss Long! Poor Miss Short! If they had their eye on Mr Shagabpa at all it was only as a prospective convert, and had they known what the Tibetans were saying about them they would undoubtedly have been both shocked and horrified. Yet curiously enough, when I happened to call on Mr Shagabpa a few months later it was the frilly-aproned Missionary Girls who, under Mrs Shagabpa's kindly superintendence, carried in the heavily laden tea-trays and served tea (though without looking at me), for all the world as though they were concubines who were living in perfect harmony with both the master and the mistress of the house. After that I did not meet them – as distinct from passing them in the High Street – for several years, when I came upon them having tea with a Sikkimese Buddhist friend of mine and his European wife. By this time Miss Long had got over her horror of me, though both women continued to think of Buddhism in terms of demonolatry and black magic. This was evident from a story which Miss Long related for the benefit of our hostess shortly after my arrival. She had happened to pass a group of Tibetans who were performing some kind of ceremony, and a leaf from the officiating lama's book – Tibetan books were, of course, made up of bundles of loose leaves – had suddenly blown across her path. Since nobody seemed to want it she picked up the leaf and put it in her bag, intending to send it to her brother, who collected curios and was fond of such things. That night she had a most awful experience. A horrible hairy monster climbed on top of her and did its best to strangle her. For what seemed like an eternity she was unable to move or even to cry out. Eventually she managed to find her voice and with a supreme effort ejaculated 'Jesus!' – whereupon the monster fled, she awoke (if indeed she had been sleeping), and the first thing she did on getting up in the morning was to go to her bag, take out the accursed leaf from the lama's book with a pair of tongs, and burn it. 'What do you think of *that*?' she exclaimed, turning to me with an air of triumph, as though she had conclusively demonstrated the diabolical nature of Buddhism in general and Tibetan Buddhism in particular. 'I don't know what *I* think,' I replied, 'but I know what Freud would have thought.'

Sallies of this kind did little to increase my popularity with Miss Long and Miss Short, any more than my vigorous pursuit of a more 'ecumenical' line of reasoning had done when they visited me at the chalet. Indeed, shortly after that memorable visit I gathered that the well-meaning young women had been so upset and angered by my stubborn refusal to accept Jesus as my personal saviour and be converted back to Christianity that they had proceeded to give me an even worse name among the missionaries than I already possessed. Since it was at about this time that the missionaries started referring to me as the Enemy of the Church, I naturally suspected the Missionary Girls of having bestowed this sobriquet upon me, though the truth of the matter was that I was so unpopular – not to say infamous – with the missionaries that it could have originated with any one of them. Not that I minded being called the Enemy of the Church. On the contrary, I was proud of my new title, even though it did, at the same time, sadden me to think that any body of Christians could regard me as an enemy simply because I belonged to another religion. After all, I had done no harm to the missionaries or their work; I had not attacked Christianity publicly, much less still abused it in the vulgar and intemperate manner in which some of them abused Hinduism and Buddhism twice a week in the market place. All I had done was to live my own life as a Buddhist monk and explain Buddhism to those who were interested. But it was this that constituted my great offence; it was this that made me the Enemy of the Church. In fact it was not even necessary for me actually to do anything or say anything. All I had to 'do' was to be a Buddhist, and that I was a Buddhist my shaven head and yellow robe sufficiently proclaimed. It was therefore not just a question of my presence in Kalimpong rather than Calcutta, or West Bengal rather than East Punjab. I was the Enemy of the Church simply by virtue of my existence, even though that existence happened to be more perceptible in Kalimpong than elsewhere and constituted, therefore, a greater problem to the missionaries of that place. I had only to be seen walking through the bazaar, apparently, for doubts to arise in the minds of Nepalese converts to Christianity and for the faith of Western-educated Buddhists to be strengthened. It was as though I was a living testimony to the fact that Christianity was not the only religion, that an alternative existed in the form of Buddhism, and that there were Westerners who, despite their being brought up as Christians, nonetheless chose to follow the Buddha rather than Christ, the Dharma rather than the Gospel. Thus even without my intending it, my presence in Kalimpong had the effect of undermining the missionaries and their work to an even greater extent than Father Morse's presence had done. Father Morse's unwanted presence had only undermined their confidence in themselves as missionaries, whereas my own still more unwanted presence undermined their confidence in themselves as Christians. It was not surprising, therefore, that the missionaries should hate me even more, perhaps, than they hated Father Morse, or that they should start referring to me as the Enemy of the Church.

I had, of course, good reason to be the Enemy of the Church, whether by simply existing or in a more active manner. Indeed, I had not been in enjoyment of my new title for many months when, certain facts having come to my notice, I realized I had even more reason to be the Enemy of the Church than I had supposed. As I well knew, like their colleagues elsewhere in India the missionaries of Kalimpong, both Protestant and Roman Catholic, were concerned to make as many converts as possible. I also knew that they were not overscrupulous about how they made them: bribes, threats, and inducements all featuring among the methods of conversion, especially in the more outlying areas of the Subdivision. But there was a method of conversion of which I had not as yet heard, a method even more unsavoury than the others, if that were possible, and it was coming to know about this method that made me realize I had even more reason to be the Enemy of the Church than I had supposed. I called the method 'conversion through pregnancy'. At the beginning of September, when the rains were already abating and the sun shining forth, I learned from Lachuman and Dawa that three young men who were known to us were being subjected to tremendous pressure to become Christians. On my looking into the matter it transpired that all three of them had had affairs with local Christian girls and that, when the girls had become pregnant, the authorities of the mission where they lived had insisted that the young men should marry them. But this was not all. The mission authorities had not only insisted that the young men should marry the girls, which in itself was not unreasonable; they had also insisted that the young men should marry the girls in church and that, in order to be able to do this, they should become Christians. Only one of the young men, who happened to be the eldest son of the Long-Lived Deva, had had sufficient strength of mind not to succumb to the pressure that was brought to bear on him. He could not be sure, he declared, if the girl was really pregnant by him, since she was a girl of loose character and he was not the only young man in Kalimpong who had had to do with her. His two fellow culprits or fellow victims had, however, succumbed to the pressure exerted by the mission authorities, had agreed to marry their respective women, to marry them in church, and to become Christians. But one of them, at least, had reckoned without his mother. That short but formidable lady was not only a pious Buddhist but, what was more to the point, the proprietress of Gompu's Restaurant, a European-style establishment that stood a little apart from the other buildings at the far end of the High Street. He could become a Christian and marry the girl if he liked, she told her erring son, but if he did so he would cease to be a son of hers, she would disinherit him, and he would have no share in her property when she died. Pleasant, easygoing young Tashi Gompu was not long in making his choice. Like the youthful Edward Gibbon, he sighed as a lover, he obeyed as a son,[103] or rather he gave in to the stronger of the two pressures and bought off the mission authorities by promising to contribute to the support of the child.

This meant that, in the event, only one of the young men actually succumbed to the pressure exerted by the mission authorities and allowed himself to be married in accordance with Christian rites. Unlike the two who did not succumb, Dil Bahadur was neither Sikkimese nor Tibetan but Nepalese, and not Buddhist but Hindu. Moreover, unlike Karma Tsering he had no strength of mind and unlike Tashi Gompu he had no formidable and well-to-do mother to exert any counter-pressure. He was, in fact, in a quite vulnerable position. For one thing, the girl he had made pregnant was a Lepcha Christian, which meant that the well-organized and influential Lepcha Association had taken up her case and threatened him with all sorts of dire consequences, including a beating up on a dark night, if he did not marry her. For another, he worked in the Kalimpong Arts and Crafts, which – like the Lepcha Association – was controlled by the Scottish Mission, with the result that he had also been threatened with the loss of his job if he refused to become a Christian and 'do the right thing' by the girl. Dil Bahadur was, in fact, the same young decorator of lampshades and firescreens to whom Joe had become so strongly attached shortly after his arrival in Kalimpong, on whose account he had decided to settle in the township, and who had been living with him for the last two years, and the fact that his protégé had now succumbed to the pressure exerted by the mission authorities – not to speak of his having succumbed to the wiles of a Lepcha Christian girl – was a source of ill-concealed mortification to the hypersensitive *upāsaka*, the more especially since he was not in a position to exert the kind of counter-pressure that Mrs Gompu had exerted.

For my part, I was not very much concerned with the precise nature of the threats made against Dil Bahadur or with Joe's inability to prevent a development with which he was clearly unhappy. What interested me was the fact that in the case of all three young men there had occurred the same sequence of events. First had come the affair with the Christian girl, apparently with the approval, or at least the connivance, of the authorities of the mission where she lived. Then, when the girl had become pregnant, there had come the insistence of those same authorities that the young man should marry the girl – that he should marry her in church – that he should become a Christian. Moreover, this insistence had not been a matter of simple persuasion or exhortation but of the systematic exertion of every kind of pressure, not excluding the threat of physical violence. Knowing as I did how eager the missionaries were for conversions, and how unscrupulous they could be in bringing them about, I therefore found it difficult to resist the conclusion that, acknowledged or unacknowledged, conversion by pregnancy was one of the numerous methods by which they sought to win souls for Christ and enlarge the boundaries of the Kingdom. Something would have to be done to check the abuse. But what? I did not know. In any case, I was about to leave for Calcutta and had no time to give further thought to the matter. Perhaps my friends at the Maha Bodhi Society would be able to advise me.

18

DISCOVERING DHARMAPALA

Devapriya Valisinha and I did not know each other very well. We had met briefly in Gangtok and (I think) in Calcutta, and had spent some time together in Kathmandu, but the acquaintance had not really developed. Apart from the difference in our ages (he was nearly twice as old as I was), there was the fact that whereas I was a monk he was very much the Theravāda layman. More important still, though General Secretary of the Maha Bodhi Society he was of a somewhat shy and retiring, not to say nervous, disposition and did not make friends either very quickly or very easily. He was, however, an excellent correspondent, and ever since our exchange of letters concerning the bringing of the Sacred Relics to Kalimpong we had been writing to each other from time to time on topics of common Buddhist interest. Only a few months earlier, after the collapse of *Stepping-Stones*, he had written expressing his regret that I was unable to continue bringing out the magazine but remarking, at the same time, that it was not easy to propagate the Dharma in India and that, rather than trying to work on my own, I would perhaps be better advised to join forces with an established Buddhist organization. Now, towards the end of the rainy season, came a letter inviting me to come down to Calcutta and write a biographical sketch of Anagārika Dharmapala for inclusion in the Maha Bodhi Society's Diamond Jubilee Souvenir. The Society having been founded in 1891, Valisinha wrote, they should really have brought out the Souvenir the previous year, but there had been the usual delays and in the end it had been decided to bring it out this year instead, at the end of November, when the Sacred Relics of the *arhants* Śāriputra and Maudgalyāyana would be re-enshrined at Sanchi and the newly constructed Sanchi Vihara opened. Perhaps it would also be possible for me to accompany the Sacred Relics to Sanchi, just as I had accompanied them to Kathmandu.

Though I knew little more about Dharmapala than that he was the founder of the Maha Bodhi Society and that for years he had sought to wrest the Maha Bodhi Temple at Bodh Gaya, where the Buddha had attained Enlightenment, from the clutches of the mercenary Hindu Mahant, Valisinha's proposal appealed to me strongly. Since the demise of *Stepping-Stones* I had written little more than an article and a couple of short stories and welcomed the opportunity of putting my energies into a new literary project, as well as of getting to know Valisinha himself better. I therefore wrote to the shy and retiring General Secretary accepting his invitation and promising to come down as soon as I could. Thus it was that, at the beginning of September, I left Kalimpong for Calcutta for the third time since my arrival in the township with Kashyapji two-and-a-half years earlier. Though the rains had abated, landslides were still blocking the road between Teesta Bridge and the plains, so that my fellow passengers and I had to trans-ship three or four times and scramble – sometimes ankle deep in mud – over enormous piles of rock and earth, as well as over the trunks of uprooted trees. From Siliguri to Calcutta the journey was uneventful, except for the late afternoon crossing by paddle-boat from one sandy shore of the Ganges to the other, and by mid-morning the following day I found myself amid the clamour and bustle of Sealdah Station. Though five years had passed since Partition, thousands of refugees from East Bengal were still encamped in and around the station area; huts had sprung up, and from many of the huts flew the red hammer-and-sickle flag of the Communist Party. Extricating myself from the swarms of hawkers and beggars, I hailed an antiquated hackney carriage (on principle I tried to avoid using rickshaws),[104] directed the ancient driver to take me to College Square, and fifteen or twenty minutes later was alighting in front of the pink sandstone 'Ajanta style' façade of the Sri Dharmarajika Vihara – was haggling over the fare – was being humbly saluted by the *durwan* or doorkeeper – was being conducted along the narrow passage that ran down the side of the vihara and gave direct access to the Society's headquarters at the rear.

Within half an hour of my arrival I had been welcomed by Devapriya Valisinha, given tea and toast, and settled in a corner room on the second floor, immediately behind the vihara and at the opposite end of the veranda from Devapriyaji's own quarters. It was not, of course, the first time that I had stayed at the headquarters of the Maha Bodhi Society. Apart from the night or two that I had sometimes spent there in more recent years, on my way to or from Sarnath or Kathmandu, I had stayed there for a month or more in 1947, when I was still a layman, so that I was quite familiar with the place.[105] Unlike the Sri Dharmarajika Vihara, it had no architectural pretensions whatever, and was built round the three sides of a small square, one of the sides, on all three floors, being occupied by Indian-style bathrooms and toilets. Below me, on the first floor, were the library, the sitting room where important visitors were received, and the rooms reserved for students and resident monks, the most prominent among the latter being the High Priest, as Jinaratana liked to style himself. (At the time of my original stay it had been *His Holiness* the High Priest, I recalled.) On the ground floor were the general office, where an accountant and two or three clerks were employed and where Devapriyaji did some of his work, the dark and insalubrious kitchen and dining room, and the cheerless apartments in which pilgrims on their way to or from Bodh Gaya and the other holy places were allowed to put up for not more than three nights. On the same floor as my own room, and on the same side of the building, were four more rooms for students and monks, the last three of which gave off from the veranda that ran round the three closed sides of the square. Above me was the flat roof of the building, on which it had long been proposed to construct another storey. Yet though the place was familiar to me, and though outwardly nothing had changed, I was at once conscious that a very different kind of atmosphere now prevailed. Five years ago the atmosphere had been one of stagnation and decay, even of downright corruption; but now things were moving, there was a sense of purpose in the air, and it seemed as though it might, after all, be possible to regard the headquarters of the Maha Bodhi Society as a centre of Buddhism, which it had certainly not been in 1947, when Jinaratana was in charge and when I had shaken the dust of the place from my feet with feelings of disappointment and disgust. What, then, had happened? Was the fact that such a different atmosphere now prevailed due to the long-delayed return of Devapriyaji, who had been absent in Ceylon for some five or six years? Or was it due to the presence of the Sacred Relics, which in the intervals of their triumphant visits to different parts of India and South-East Asia had been exposed for worship in the Sri Dharmarajika Vihara? Or was the difference due simply to the fact that there were now more people living in the place, more visitors coming, and more pilgrims passing through on their way to or from the holy places? I did not know. Possibly the difference was due not to any one of these factors singly but to two or more of them in combination, or even to circumstances of which I was entirely ignorant. Or perhaps...

But there was no time for speculation. The Diamond Jubilee Souvenir had to be out by the end of November, Devapriyaji was keen that I should start work on my biographical sketch without delay, and before long we were sitting in his room, with a pot of Ceylon tea on the desk between us, discussing the project. The room was hardly wider than the desk, which was so placed as to divide it into two equal parts. Behind the desk, as though behind a barricade, and facing the door, sat Devapriyaji, while behind him, along the back wall of the room, could be seen the white-shrouded form of his bed, which was so lofty that it must have been difficult for him to observe the eighth precept on *poya* days.[106] Short, plump, and bespectacled, the little General Secretary wore a long Bengali-style shirt and a voluminous Bengali-style dhoti or loincloth, both of immaculate whiteness. Though born and brought up in Ceylon, he had spent the greater part of his adult life in Calcutta, and it was often said of him that in appearance and personal habits he was more like a Bengali than a Sinhalese. His features were certainly Bengali. Studying him as he did the honours of the teapot, I saw a face the colour of weak tea, with a prominent, high-bridged nose, a small chin and weak mouth, a pair of sad brown eyes like those of an ill-used but faithful dog, and a lofty but narrow forehead from which the hairline had receded to such an extent as to make him appear almost bald. When he smiled the tea-coloured face lit up, and it was evident that as a young man Devapriyaji must have been more than ordinarily handsome; but he did not smile very often, his expression usually being one of either nervousness or diffidence, and observing him from the other side of the desk as we discussed the projected biographical sketch, I could not help recalling what Swale Ryan had once told me about the circumstances that had led to his spending so long a period in Ceylon. In 1941 war had broken out with Japan, and on account of its close ties with the country the Maha Bodhi Society had fallen under the suspicion of the authorities. Devapriyaji and Dr Kalidas Nag (who was, I believe, the editor of the *Maha Bodhi* journal) were arrested and detained for five or six weeks, and during their detention both men were rather roughly interrogated. As a result of this unpleasant experience Devapriyaji suffered a nervous breakdown and had to be sent to Ceylon for treatment. Despite all the care he received, it was several years before he could again lead a normal life, and even after his return to Calcutta he still found it difficult to face the world and still spent much of his time alone in his room. For all his good qualities, Devapriyaji had never been a strong character, Swale had concluded, and though he was now more or less recovered and doing a good job as General Secretary – far better than that rascal Jinaratana could ever do – his little brush with the authorities had intensified his natural nervousness and he did not always find it easy to get on with people. If ever I went down to Calcutta and met the man I would see what he meant.

Now that I was in Calcutta, and discussing the projected biographical sketch with Devapriyaji in the privacy of his room, I could indeed see what Swale had meant. But notwithstanding the little General Secretary's undoubted nervousness, which showed itself in his expression and demeanour rather than in the way in which he conducted the Society's affairs, the two of us got on quite well together, and though we never became friends we nonetheless succeeded in developing a good working relationship – a relationship that was to endure for a number of years. That we were able to develop such a relationship was due to the fact that while he was anxious for me to write a biographical sketch of Anagārika Dharmapala for inclusion in the Society's Diamond Jubilee Souvenir, I was no less anxious to write such a sketch, as well as to the fact that, as the work progressed, I came to share his admiration for the man with whom he had been so closely associated, from whom he had gradually taken over the running of the Society, and whose spiritual heir he was generally considered to be. Not that the Anagārika's biography had not been written before. In the course of either our first or our second meeting Devapriyaji handed me the two bulky typewritten volumes which the Society had commissioned some years previously but which it had found unsuitable for publication. Why it had found them unsuitable for publication soon became apparent. I had not read more than one or two chapters of the work before I realized that the perfervid Sinhalese author would much rather have written a pornographic novel than the biography of a prominent religious personality, for on the pretext of giving an account of the social and economic condition of Ceylon at the time of Dharmapala's birth he had indulged in lengthy and highly detailed descriptions of the raping of black Tamil coolie women by lust-crazed white European tea-planters. This was not at all the kind of material for which I was looking, though Devapriyaji was right in letting me see the volumes, since I was able to glean from them at least a handful of relevant facts. More germane to my purpose were certain other volumes that Devapriyaji handed me. Stout and blue-bound, these were seven or eight quartos of Dharmapala's personal diaries, extracts from which had been regularly appearing in the pages of the *Maha Bodhi* for the past few years under the title 'Diary Leaves of the Late Anagārika Dharmapala'. Venerable Dharmapala had kept a diary all his life, Devapriyaji informed me, and there were altogether more than forty such stout blue-bound quartos in existence. Unfortunately, only a small proportion were actually with him in Calcutta. The rest were in the keeping of the Public Trustee of Ceylon. If I liked he would write and ask that functionary to send them all to Calcutta for my perusal. Naturally, I did like, since I wanted my biographical sketch to be as reliable as possible, and Devapriyaji accordingly despatched the necessary letter to Colombo without delay. For reasons which were never fully explained but which were, I gathered, mainly of a legal nature, the Public Trustee was unable to send to Calcutta more than ten or twelve inconsecutive volumes of the diaries, though a few even of these arrived too late to be of much use to me. Thus in writing the life of Dharmapala I had at my disposal upwards of twenty miscellaneous volumes of diaries, as well as being able to draw on the Anagārika's own 'Reminiscences of my Early Life', written shortly before his death, and on Devapriyaji's personal recollections of his master – not to mention such facts as I was able to glean from the bulky unpublished volumes of the perfervid Sinhalese. Though by no means complete, the material was more than sufficient for my limited purpose (I had, after all, been asked to write a biographical sketch, not a full-length biography) and I lost no time in settling down to the agreeable task of reading and assimilating it all as quickly and as thoroughly as I could.

Before many days had passed I had established a basic routine not too dissimilar to that which I normally followed in Kalimpong. My day began at about five, as – judging by the hawking and spitting noises that could be heard on all sides – most people's did in Calcutta. At six o'clock one of the Society's two Oriya servants, naked except for a white dhoti, swept my room out with a stiff reed broom, afterwards getting down on his knees and washing the floor with a rag which he dipped in a pail of filthy water. At seven the same servant brought my breakfast, which consisted of a cup of lukewarm but very strong tea and two slices of thinly buttered toast. This was the Society's standard breakfast, and it came not from the dark and insalubrious kitchen downstairs but from a nearby teashop. As soon as I had satisfied fleshly wants (and I had not, of course, eaten anything since noon the previous day) I barred my door against the world and settled down not, indeed, like the hero of Betjeman's well-known poem, to Norman fonts,[107] but to the bulky typewritten volumes of my Sinhalese predecessor and the earliest of the stout blue-bound quartos of the Dharmapala diaries and remained absorbed in them for the rest of the morning. Occasionally, when I felt stiff with sitting so long at my desk, or when I wanted to reflect on the information I had gathered, I strolled a few yards down the corridor and, resting my arms on the balustrade, looked out from the back veranda. Above me, there was only the intense blue of the unclouded autumn sky; below, the gloomy well formed by the first and second storeys of the building and the high wall that closed off the remaining side of the square round which it was constructed. On the other side of the wall could be seen the red-tiled, crazily irregular roofs of a cluster of huts that had sprung up, quite illegally, during the war years, and which were occupied by no less than seventy Muslim families, some of whom were engaged in criminal activities of various kinds. So closely were these little huts packed together that, from above, the area seemed covered by a single undulous roof on which the sun blazed down as on the petrified waves of a crimson sea. Some years previously the half-acre or so of land on which the huts stood had been acquired by the Society for its proposed Institute of Buddhist Culture, and the Calcutta Corporation had undertaken to re-house the occupants of the huts in one of its new colonies. So far, however, the Corporation had done nothing, and in fact was to do nothing for quite a few more years. Had the land been acquired by any other organization, the new owners would almost certainly have hired a gang of armed ruffians to drive out the unwanted tenants by force, as the Ramakrishna Mission had done in similar circumstances five years earlier,[108] and that would have been the end of the matter. But the Maha Bodhi Society was a Buddhist organization, and Buddhism was committed to the principle of non-violence, so that there was no question of its having recourse to methods of this kind – though I gathered that one or two Hindu members of the Governing Body were in favour of it so doing. Thus it was that, looking out from the back veranda, I could see below me the red-tiled roofage of the huts on the other side of the wall. I could also hear, rising and falling with monotonous regularity, the unearthly wail – more animal than human – of a madwoman who was confined in one of the back rooms of an adjoining building. The wail continued without intermission throughout the day and for part of the night, and if I listened carefully I could hear it in my room even with the door closed. Who or what the woman was I never discovered, but I heard that unearthly wail all day and every day for the whole of the three months that I stayed at the Society's headquarters. I also heard it on every one of my subsequent visits, so that – like the sight of the red-tiled roofage of the huts – the sound of the madwoman's wail came to be inseparably associated with my memories of Calcutta and of the Maha Bodhi Society.

At eleven-thirty I laid aside the volumes on which I had been working and went along to the bathroom-cum-latrine for a bath, taking good care to lock the door of my room behind me. The apartment in question, which was furnished with little more than a wall-tap and a convenient hole in one corner, stank abominably, while the floor was not only red with rust from the bottom of the buckets with which, Indian style, one doused oneself, but so slippery as to constitute a definite hazard to life and limb. Accidents were, in fact, always taking place there. When I had had my bath, shaved, and washed my robes by slapping and banging them on the floor in the approved fashion, I made my way downstairs to the dining room, a procedure which on some days felt more like making a descent into the infernal regions. According to the Theravāda Vinaya or Monastic Code a monk could not eat after twelve, but the monks of the Maha Bodhi Society were not very strict in their observance of the Vinaya, and lunch (as it may be called) usually did not begin until a few minutes before the clock in the library upstairs struck the fatal hour, with the result that more often than not we were still eating twenty and even thirty minutes after the prescribed period. Since the barred windows of the dining room were kept shuttered for greater security (two bent bars bore witness to a recent attempt at breaking in), and since very little light entered by way of the door, the dining room was quite dark, such illumination as there was being provided mainly by the dusty electric bulb that hung from the centre of the ceiling and shed a dim light on the table at which we sat. At that time there were no more than eight or ten monks staying in the headquarters building, and since they did not forgather for either morning or evening puja or, so far as I could make out, for any other purpose except to have lunch, it was only at lunch time that I saw anything of them. Most of them were Sinhalese and most were students at one or other of the city's educational institutions. (The lay students who stayed in the building came and ate only after the monks had vacated the dining room, the Theravāda convention that monks and laymen did not eat together being rigidly observed.) Among the non-Sinhalese monks there was one Bengali and one Newar. The Bengali monk was Venerable Silabhadra, the ex-Hindu lawyer who had become a Buddhist and a monk quite late in life and who now helped Devapriyaji edit the *Maha Bodhi*, while the Newar was Venerable Mahanama, whom I had last seen in Kathmandu and who was currently trying to get into Bengali films and had, in fact, already sent some very flattering photographs of himself (copies of which he showed us) to various leading producers and directors. As for the food with which we were served and which, at least in theory, constituted our one meal of the day, this consisted mainly of the same badly cooked rice and watery dal as in 1947 – which was hardly surprising, since it was cooked and served by the same black, hairy figure in the soiled white loincloth who had been in charge of the kitchen at that time and who was, it seemed, a permanent inhabitant of the ground floor, along with the bed-bugs and cockroaches. Venerable Jinaratana hardly ever ate in the dining room. On most days, however, he would come and sit with us for a while, crack a few jokes with the Sinhalese monks, wrinkle up his nose in disgust at the contents of our plates, scold Kristo for not feeding us properly and, if he was in a particularly good mood, send out for as many tiny earthenware pots of curd as there were monks in the dining room. Having gone through this little performance, he would go and have a leisurely massage and bath and then, retiring to the privacy of his own room, a no less leisurely lunch – a lunch that would be brought from a nearby Muslim restaurant and usually consisted of a roast chicken.

Since I had spent a night or two at the Society's headquarters several times during the last two years, and since Jinaratana and I had both been members of the delegation accompanying the Sacred Relics to Nepal, it was inevitable that after my higher ordination in November 1950 I should have met the self-styled High Priest on a number of occasions. It was also inevitable that now that we were in almost daily contact the feeling of awkwardness existing between us on account of the fact that, five years ago, I had witnessed some rather unmonklike behaviour on his part – an awkwardness that was still there at the time of my departure for Kathmandu the previous year – should at length be resolved, at least to some extent. At any rate, though Jinaratana did not exactly welcome me with open arms on my arrival at the Society's headquarters in my new character as Dharmapala's biographer, he at least made it clear, in his own abrupt and uncouth manner, that he was willing to let bygones be bygones and henceforth to regard me as a friend rather than as an enemy or rather – since for him friendship was a matter of mutual self-interest – as an ally rather than as an adversary. The first sign of this willingness came only a day or two after my arrival, and before I had established my routine. Four or five monks, including Jinaratana and myself, had been invited to the house of a wealthy supporter of the Society for a ceremonial food-offering and we had arranged to meet at the front of the building. As soon as I appeared Jinaratana's eyes opened wide in astonishment. 'Why are you wearing that shabby, patched old robe?' he demanded. '*What on earth will people think of us!*' In vain I protested that I had nothing better to wear and that, in any case, a shabby, patched robe was the best kind of robe for one who had given up the world and was, technically, a beggar. Why, the Buddha himself had worn just such a robe as this! But Jinaratana refused to listen. Seizing me by the arm, he hurried me upstairs to his room where he presented me with a brand-new cotton robe of the Sinhalese type, buttercup yellow in colour, and made me put it on. He himself, needless to say, was swathed in a magnificent robe of the finest yellow silk, and what with his bright new sandals and his polished scalp – not to mention his commanding air – looked the very model of a modern High Priest. In this he was not unrepresentative of the branch of the monastic order to which he belonged and it was not surprising that, writing three or four years later, I should have criticized the Hīnayāna for overattachment to the formal aspects of monasticism, or that in giving specific examples of such formalism I should have alluded to the fact that 'a [Theravāda] monk's outfit, technically the badge of poverty, can be four or five times as costly as that of a middle-class layman.'[109] At the time, however, I kept these thoughts to myself and, having exchanged my shabby, patched old robe for the brand-new one which, in Jinaratana's opinion, was less likely to bring discredit on the monastic order, I followed the glittering figure of my benefactor downstairs to the waiting taxi without a word.

But though I was relieved that Jinaratana was, as it seemed, willing to let bygones be bygones and to regard me as a friend rather than as an enemy, I felt I was entitled to let bygones be bygones only on my own behalf, that is, only in respect of my own past treatment at his hands, which in any case had not been so very bad. I was certainly not entitled to let bygones be bygones on behalf of other people, particularly insofar as his inhuman treatment of the aged and helpless Miss Albers was concerned – treatment I had witnessed with my own eyes and about which I had written a strongly worded letter of protest to Devapriya Valisinha,[110] who was at that time in Ceylon and whom I had not, of course, met. Moreover, even if the gift of the robe really was a sign of Jinaratana's willingness to let bygones be bygones, I could not ignore the fact that the immediate cause of his generosity was his fear of what people might think of Buddhist monks if one of their number was seen wearing a robe that was old, shabby, and patched. Thus the very gesture that was intended to demonstrate his willingness to regard me as a friend only served to show how great was the gulf that divided us and how little likelihood there was that anything remotely resembling friendship should ever exist between us. Our values were completely different, even opposed. Nevertheless, since we were living under the same roof and meeting almost every day, even if only at lunch time, I resolved that though I could not in honesty regard him as a friend I would at least try not to think of him as an enemy, and that those aspects of his behaviour which I was unable to condone – and there were some which filled me with unspeakable disgust – I at any rate would refrain from condemning. For the time being, at least, though I could not be cordial I could be correct. Let him follow his way of life, and let me follow mine. There was no need for us to clash or quarrel. At lunch I therefore tried to keep what was afterwards called a low profile which, since conversation was mainly in Sinhalese, I did not find very difficult. If Jinaratana gibed at me for my abstention from meat (for Sinhalese pilgrims would sometimes offer us fish and mutton dishes) I did my best to make light of my vegetarianism; or, if he made an indecent joke, I either affected that I had not heard or that I had not understood. In this way peace was preserved, much of the awkwardness between us resolved, and the beginnings of something like good relations established. When he had sat with us for a while, and had gone through his little performance, Jinaratana could therefore go and have his leisurely massage and bath, and his no less leisurely lunch, without anything having occurred to spoil his appetite, while I could return to my room relieved that another meal had passed without incident and that I was free to get on with my task of reading and assimilating the materials for my biographical sketch.

Not that I always got on with it immediately, however. Though Calcutta was not particularly hot at that time of year, it was hot and humid enough, and even though I did not sleep during the afternoon as everybody else in the building seemed to do, from humble Oriya servant to lordly High Priest, I usually lay down on my bed for a while, more often than not with a volume of English poetry in my hand. When sufficiently rested I rose, washed my face, and settled down once more to the bulky typewritten volumes and stout, blue-bound quartos that were now my constant companions, pausing only to go out onto the back veranda at four or five o'clock and, leaning as far out over the balustrade as I could, shout down into the well of the building for one of the servants to go and get me a cup of tea from the nearby teashop. At seven or eight I went out for a walk. By this time it would be quite dark, but not so dark that one could not see – and smell – the dense haze that was rising from the innumerable kitchens where fish was being fried in mustard oil – a haze that by nine or ten hung over the city like a pall and was at times so pungent as to make one's eyes water. Sometimes I walked round the tiny park in the middle of College Square, in one corner of which a game of volleyball would be in progress under the dim electric lights, and where the cracked marble statuses of bygone civic dignitaries rose white and solemn out of the shadows, some of them wearing Bengali dress and sitting with legs folded beneath enormous paunches at the top of crumbling pedestals faintly inscribed with their names, titles, qualifications, and achievements.

Sometimes, emerging from the park and crossing over onto the other side of College Street, I made my way along the row of second-hand bookstalls that, from six or seven in the evening until nearly midnight, displayed their wares on the railings in front of the Senate House. Here paraffin flares were the only illumination, so that it was not always easy to make out the titles of the books offered for sale. Most of them were, of course, in Bengali, but many were in English, with school and college textbooks predominating, though at one time or other I was able to pick up such bargains as the Bohn edition of the works of Sir Thomas Browne and an obscure American translation of Plotinus. At the time that I was preparing to write my biographical sketch of Dharmapala, however, and indeed for quite a few years afterwards, I had very little money to spare for books, so that I was perforce more often a browser than a buyer. Only occasionally did I return to the Society's headquarters with a slim volume of poetry or literary criticism that, to my great delight, I had succeeded in obtaining for a rupee or less. When that happened I usually stayed up quite late, devouring as much of my new acquisition as I could before sleep finally overpowered me.

Thus the warm autumn days passed quickly and pleasantly enough and I felt less and less inclined to interrupt the routine I had established. Indeed, I interrupted it only when Devapriyaji invited me to his room for a cup of tea and a chat, which he did every two or three days, usually after his breakfast or lunch. On these occasions, taking advantage of my opportunity, I would ask him to clarify anything of an obscure or controversial nature relating to the life and times of Dharmapala that I had come across in the material he had so far handed me, and also encourage him to give me his personal recollections of the great Anagārika, who had now been dead for nearly twenty years. In the course of our forth or fifth such meeting, however, the little General Secretary nervously opined that my preparations for writing the biographical sketch were taking far too long, especially in view of the fact that it did not have to be longer than ten thousand words in length, and that the sooner I got down to the business of actual composition the better. By this time it was late September or early October, and knowing that the Diamond Jubilee Souvenir had to be out by the end of November, and that the biographical sketch had to be not only written and typed but seen through the press, I had no choice but to agree. I therefore assured Devapriyaji, much to his relief, that I would start straight away and begin writing the first half of Dharmapala's life before I had finished going through the material relating to the second. This was not the most satisfactory arrangement, and probably a professional biographer would not have approved of it, but it was the only one that would enable the Diamond Jubilee Souvenir to be brought out on time, and since this was the main consideration I adopted it without hesitation.

Next morning I set to work. 'The prospects of Ceylon Buddhism in the sixties of the last century were dark indeed,' I wrote.

> Successive waves of Portuguese, Dutch, and British invasion had swept away much of the traditional culture of the country. Missionaries had descended upon the copper-coloured island like a cloud of locusts; Christian schools of every conceivable denomination had been opened, where Buddhist boys and girls were crammed with Bible texts and taught to be ashamed of their religion, their culture, their language, their race, and their colour.[111]

Having continued in this vein for a couple of pages, and painted a black picture of the religious situation in Ceylon at the time of Dharmapala's birth, I went on to describe the pious, well-to-do family into which he had been born, his early ethical and religious training, his education in various Christian institutions, and his growing awareness of the contradictions within Christianity and the extent of the difference between Christianity and Buddhism. Before many days had passed I was completely immersed in my subject and lived, thought, and felt Dharmapala – or Don David Hewavitarne, as he was known during the earlier part of his life. Practically all my waking hours were spent either writing or reading about him, and I grudged even the time I had to spend eating. To such an extent did I identify with him, indeed, especially after he passed from childhood to adolescence, that it was as though I was myself actually present with him throughout his career and witnessed each episode in his life as it occurred. I was with him when he met the founders of the Theosophical Society, with him when he accompanied Mme Blavatsky to Adyar and was told by her to study Pāli and work for the good of humanity, with him when he toured the villages of Ceylon with Col. Olcott, with him when he visited Japan, with him when he went on pilgrimage to India. Above all, perhaps, I was with him when, in January 1891, he visited Bodh Gaya and 'received the inspiration that was to change not only his whole life but the whole course of modern Buddhist history'[112] – the inspiration to stay and care for the sacred spot, then in a shamefully neglected condition. Thereafter I was with him when he founded the Maha Bodhi Society – when he visited England and America – when he attended the World's Parliament of Religions in Chicago – when he met Mrs Mary E. Foster, the most munificent of his supporters – when he visited the Far East – when he went on an extended tour of North India – when he battled for possession of Bodh Gaya – when he sought to reawaken the national spirit among his Sinhalese fellow countrymen – when he was interned in Calcutta – when he built the Sri Dharmarajika Chaitya Vihara and the Mulagandakuti Vihara – when he started a Buddhist mission in London – when he took first lower and then higher ordination as a monk. I was with him in the East and in the West, in youth and in old age, in his dreams and in his meditations, in success and in failure, in health and in sickness. Finally – when I had been writing for three weeks and had produced well over twice the number of words required – I was with him at the last stage of all when, as the assembled monks recited verses from the sacred texts, 'the Great Being's consciousness, radiant with a lifetime of wisdom, energy, and love, relaxed its hold on the worn-out body and flashed into new realms of service, leaving upon the face of the corpse it had forsaken a serene smile of happiness and content.'[113]

When I had written those words – the concluding words of my biographical sketch – I sat for a while 'like one that hath been stunned/ And is of sense forlorn.'[114] For three weeks I had not only been with Dharmapala, so to speak, but been with him throughout the whole of his latest earthly existence, and now that he was no more I experienced a profound sense of bereavement. I felt, in fact, as though I had lost a friend. The reason I felt like this was that, in the course of writing my biographical sketch, I had not only accumulated a good deal of information about the very extensive activities of the Founder of the Maha Bodhi Society and Reviver of Buddhism in India, as he was generally styled in the Society's publications; I had also got to know the man himself. *I had discovered Dharmapala.* Nor was that all. The Dharmapala I had discovered – the Dharmapala who revealed himself so vividly in the pages of the diaries – had turned out to be a very different kind of person from the Dharmapala hitherto known to me and very different, I suspected, from the Dharmapala known to the vast majority of the Society's members and supporters. Far from being an activist and organizer in the more superficial, even slightly perjorative sense, he was an idealist and a man of vision, a man of intense inner life who, from boyhood onwards, had been strongly inclined towards mysticism and asceticism and was always on the lookout for news about *arhants* and the science of *abhijñā*, or supernormal knowledge, even though, as he himself wrote in his 'Reminiscences', the *bhikṣus* of Ceylon were sceptical about the possibility of realizing arhantship, believing that the Age of Arhants was past and that the realization of Nirvāṇa by psychic training was no longer possible. Had circumstances been different, Dharmapala might well have spent his days not battling for Bodh Gaya and trying to revive Buddhism in India, or even 'girdling the globe with the Message of the Master', but meditating in a cave or forest hermitage somewhere in his beloved Ceylon. As it was, he grew up to be the most active and widely travelled Buddhist of his generation – so active and so widely travelled, indeed, that it was all too easy for one to see in him only the activist and organizer, overlooking the fact that 'beneath the dynamic activity of the selfless worker for Buddhism there lay the serenity and mindfulness of the yogi.'[115] It was all too easy for one to miss the Dharmapala who, during those memorable weeks, I had had the good fortune to discover and who was now the object of my fervent admiration.

The discovery of Dharmapala naturally led to the discovery of the Maha Bodhi Society. My sojourn at the Society's headquarters in 1947 had, of course, left me with an extremely unfavourable impression of that organization, and until I started going through the material Devapriyaji had handed me – until, more especially, I started writing my biographical sketch – little or nothing had occurred to modify that initial impression or to make me wish for a closer connection with the Society. On the contrary, I had wanted to have as little to do with it as possible. Now, however, I could see that the Maha Bodhi Society as it existed today was a very different kind of organization from the Maha Bodhi Society as it had existed during Dharmapala's lifetime. *Then* it had been an organization imbued with its founder's own idealism, his own spirit of self-sacrifice, so that it had been able to live up to its declared objects and to function as a medium for the dissemination of the Dharma. I could also see that since the Maha Bodhi Society was, in principle, no more simply an organization in the negative sense of

Anagārika Dharmapala as a young man

the term than Dharmapala himself had been merely an activist and organizer, it was always possible for it to change and be what it once had been. Perhaps the change had started taking place already. On my arrival at the headquarters building I had noticed that, though outwardly the place had not changed at all in five years, a very different kind of atmosphere prevailed, and having now lived and worked there for two whole months I was convinced that the difference was due largely to the presence of Devapriyaji. Though a lesser man than Dharmapala in every way, he had been closely associated with the Anagārika for sixteen years, and on the latter's death had become not only General Secretary for life but, what was even more important, 'the inheritor of his [master's] unfulfilled ambitions and the chief instrument for the perpetuation of the work and ideals to which he had dedicated his life'.[116] Devapriyaji thus stood for the Maha Bodhi Society as it had been in its founder's lifetime and, therefore, for the Maha Bodhi Society as it could be again, even as Jinaratana stood for the Maha Bodhi Society as it had come to be in more recent times. Devapriyaji stood for what the Maha Bodhi Society was in principle, Jinaratana for what, in the absence of proper leadership, it was possible for it to degenerate into. I therefore decided that I would do whatever I could to help Devapriyaji and in this way contribute, at least indirectly, to the restoration of the Society to a condition more appropriate to a Buddhist organization and, therefore, more in accordance with its founder's intentions.

Devapriyaji was certainly in need of help just then. Besides carrying on with his routine duties as General Secretary, he was busy organizing the Society's forthcoming Diamond Jubilee celebrations, a task that included the bringing out of the Diamond Jubilee Souvenir. He was also busy making arrangements for the re-enshrinement of the Sacred Relics of the *arhants* Śāriputra and Maudgalyāyana in their new vihara at Sanchi. Since Sanchi was situated near Bhopal and since Bhopal was more than six hundred miles distant from Calcutta, the making of these arrangements involved an enormous amount of correspondence, the more especially as Pandit Nehru was expected to attend the function, together with a host of other dignitaries, both Indian and foreign, Buddhist and non-Buddhist, monk and lay. So great was the amount of correspondence involved, indeed, that the clatter of Devapriyaji's typewriter could often be heard quite late at night, while there would be a light coming from beneath his door into the early hours of the morning. I was therefore not surprised when the little General Secretary asked me if I would mind taking over from him the responsibility for seeing the Diamond Jubilee Souvenir through the press and making sure that it was out on time. He himself, he added, would always be available for consultation. I certainly did not mind taking over the responsibility. In fact I was delighted to be of use, and spent the next few weeks checking galleys and page proofs, searching through old blocks for illustrations (there was no money for new ones), consulting with the young Bengali artist who was designing the cover, and somehow finding room for articles and messages that arrived late. Since the Souvenir eventually came to more than two hundred quarto pages, and since page proofs generally had to be read three or four times, all this involved more work than I had expected, but at last it was all done and a few days before the end of November Devapriyaji and I had the satisfaction of holding the olive and chocolate-coloured volume in our hands. Devapriyaji was relieved that the Souvenir had been brought out in good time, and pleased that a proper account of the life and work of Dharmapala and the achievements of the Society he had founded should at last be available. I was overjoyed that I had discovered Dharmapala, overjoyed that I had been able to share my discovery with others, and glad to see my first substantial piece of Buddhist writing in print.

As was only fitting, 'Anagarika Dharmapala: A Biographical Sketch' (to give my contribution its full title) and 'The Maha Bodhi Society, Its History and Influence' between them occupied the entire first half of the Souvenir, exclusive of introductory matter. The latter article was the work of Dr Nalinaksha Dutt, Head of the Department of Pāli at the University of Calcutta, whose scholarly *Aspects of Mahāyāna Buddhism and its Relation to Hīnayāna* I had long known and valued. Among the other contributions to the volume were articles on Buddhist history and culture by some of the leading Bengali savants of the day, as well as an article on 'Mrs Mary E. Foster, "Queen of the Empire of Righteousness"' (as Dharmapala himself had called her) which I had written almost immediately after completing my biographical sketch of the Anagārika.[117] Without Mrs Foster's unparalleled generosity Dharmapala would not have been able to achieve more than a fraction of what he actually did achieve; even before her death he had directed that her birthday should be celebrated at all centres of the Maha Bodhi Society, and I therefore felt that without a tribute to the memory of the great-hearted Hawaiian lady the Diamond Jubilee Souvenir of the Society which she had done so much to help would not be complete.

Be that as it may: on its appearance towards the end of November, only a few days before the Sacred Relics were due to leave for Sanchi, the Diamond Jubilee Souvenir met with a very warm reception both inside and outside the Society, my biographical sketch of Dharmapala being singled out for special praise. From some of the comments that reached me I indeed gained the impression that most members and supporters of the Society knew very little more about Dharmapala than I myself had known three months earlier, and that they were glad to have the man behind the activist and organizer brought to life for them. There was only one dissonant voice amid the chorus of praise, but the sound of that voice did not actually reach me until some time afterwards. Had it not been for an incident that had occurred while I was still checking page proofs there might, however, have been a few more such voices and their united sound might have reached me rather more quickly. Proofs were supposed to be delivered to me direct, so that I could set to work on them without delay. Sometimes, however, the printer's devil simply left them on Devapriyaji's desk in the general office downstairs, that particular desk being conveniently situated just inside the front door. If Devapriyaji happened to be in the office at the time he would send the proofs straight up to me by one of the servants; otherwise they might lie on his desk for hours. When too many hours had passed since the delivery of the last batch of proofs, therefore, I used to go downstairs to see if there were any lying on Devapriyaji's desk. On one such occasion I entered the general office to find the tall, safari-suited figure of Mr Sitaram, a South Indian member of the Governing Body, standing at the empty desk with an expression of apparent disinterest on his dark face. In his hands was a batch of page proofs, through which he was idly leafing, as it seemed, while waiting for Devapriyaji to arrive. Before I could take the proofs from him, however, his whole frame suddenly stiffened and his face became purple with rage, while his eyes remained riveted to one particular page as though unable to believe what they saw. 'This can't be published!' he roared, stabbing at the offending passage with a black forefinger. 'It's an insult to the memory of Swami Vivekananda! It's a foul slander! I shall complain to the Governing Body!' At this point Devapriyaji arrived, having been out for his evening walk, and there ensued a three-cornered wrangle in the course of which the incensed South Indian had a great deal to say, Devapriyaji quite a lot, and myself very little. The truth was that I had been taken aback by the violence of Sitaram's outburst and was at first at a loss to understand why he was so upset or in what way I had insulted the memory of Swami Vivekananda. But I soon understood.

Describing Dharmapala's return journey from Japan to Ceylon in 1889, I had referred to an incident which showed how faithful he was to his friends. The captain of the ship on which he was travelling happened to be a great admirer of Mme Blavatsky and Dharmapala was therefore soon on friendly terms with him, but when the captain confided that Col. Olcott was jealous of her and had engineered her departure from India the young Dharmapala hotly repudiated the suggestion and hardly spoke to the man again for the rest of the voyage. 'His loyal, affectionate, and grateful nature could never bear in silence an attack upon a friend,' I had written, commenting on the incident, 'and at this period especially devotion to the Colonel was one of the major passions of his life.'[118] Enlarging on the theme, I had then gone on to describe how a few years later, on his return from the World's Parliament of Religions, Dharmapala spoke publicly in defence of Swami Vivekananda when the latter was charged with having taken alcoholic liquors while in America, and when the citizens of Calcutta, scandalized by this departure from strict Hindu orthodoxy, were minded not to give him a reception on his arrival in the metropolis. So vigorously did Dharmapala speak in defence of Vivekananda – not in defence of his taking alcohol, of course, but of his whole 'heroic work' in America – that the cyclonic Hindu monk, as the Americans had dubbed him, was at once restored to popular favour. As in the case of the earlier incident with the ship's captain, my purpose in referring to these facts had been simply to illustrate Dharmapala's intense loyalty to his friends (he and Vivekananda had known each other in America) and thus to draw attention to an important aspect of his character. But Sitaram absolutely refused to see the matter in this light. Swami Vivekananda was a perfect monk, he stormed. He was a saint. He was a *jivanmukta*, one who had attained liberation in this very life. It was therefore utterly impossible that he should have taken alcohol, whether in America or anywhere else, and to suggest that he had ever done so would be nothing less than a foul slander. In vain Devapriyaji protested that Dharmapala had more than once seen Vivekananda drinking wine at dinner parties, and had recorded the fact in his diary. Sitaram refused to listen, and eventually stalked out of the general office declaring that unless the offending passage was removed from the biographical sketch he would raise the matter at the next meeting of the Governing Body. As he left the building I could not help wondering how he would have responded if Devapriyaji had told him that, as the diaries also revealed, Dharmapala had seen Vivekananda tipsy and that the cyclonic Hindu monk had wanted to marry an American woman with whom he had fallen in love and that his disciples had had to persuade him to give up the idea. No doubt he would have stormed that these too were foul slanders and that it was utterly impossible that his hero should ever have been tipsy or should have ever fallen in love with a woman, especially an American woman.

So obviously irrational was Sitaram's whole attitude, indeed, that despite the violence of his initial outburst I at first assumed that there could be no question of my having to remove the reference to Vivekananda taking alcoholic liquors. But the following morning, over our usual pot of tea, Devapriyaji regretfully disillusioned me. Sitaram was not a bad man, he explained: in some ways he was a very good man; but he was a staunch Hindu, and had been genuinely shocked by my reference to Vivekananda taking alcoholic liquors, true though it was. If I refused to remove the offending passage he would certainly complain to the Governing Body, and the Governing Body would certainly take the same view of the matter as Sitaram, since the majority of its members were Hindus and were, moreover, active supporters of the Ramakrishna Mission, which Vivekananda had founded. If I persisted in my refusal they might not allow the biographical sketch to be published at all, which would be a great pity. He therefore advised me, he continued, to remove the offending passage (after all, it was only a question of changing a few words!) before Sitaram had a chance to complain to the Governing Body and in this way save myself a lot of unnecessary trouble. Though pained by the idea that the life of a prominent Buddhist, written by a Buddhist monk, and due for publication by a Buddhist organization, should be subjected to what amounted to pre-censorship by a staunch Hindu, I could see that Devapriyaji's advice made sense and in the end reluctantly agreed to make the necessary sacrifice. Drastically shortening the passage concerned, I therefore described Dharmapala as defending Vivekananda *not* when the latter was charged with having taken alcoholic liquors while in America but simply when 'serious charges' were made against him in Calcutta. Strange to relate, when the amended passage was shown to Sitaram he approved it at once. Personally I would have thought that if it was objectionable to say of someone that he had been charged with taking alcoholic liquors it was at least as objectionable to say of him that serious charges had been made against him. The charge of taking alcohol related to the commission of a single specified offence, possibly not a very serious one at that, whereas 'serious charges' could refer to all manner of offences, from murder to bank robbery. But Sitaram did not see this. His sole concern was that in my biographical sketch of Dharmapala there should be no reference to Vivekananda taking alcoholic liquors, and once the words which (to him) represented the swami as actually committing this heinous offence had been removed he was satisfied.

Thus in the end my sacrifice was not a very big one. The changes I was forced to make did not really alter the meaning of what I had written to any material extent, even though without those changes there might have been, amid the chorus of praise with which my contribution to the Diamond Jubilee Souvenir was soon to be greeted, a few more dissonant voices than there actually were. All the same, I found the incident that had taken place in the general office, and its sequel, deeply disturbing. Besides showing how indifferent to considerations of objective truth an English-educated Hindu could be, it showed that although under the terms of Dharmapala's will Devapriyaji was General Secretary of the Maha Bodhi Society for life he was not in a position – or perhaps did not have the strength of character – to go against the wishes of the Governing Body. It also showed that the Governing Body was a predominantly Hindu body and that the affairs of the premier Buddhist organization of India were, therefore, effectively in the hands of people who were not really committed to the ideals of Buddhism. Above all, perhaps, it showed that, despite the fact that Devapriyaji had now been back in Calcutta for three or four years, the Society still had a long way to go before it could be regarded as fulfilling the objects with which it had been established by the Dharmapala I had recently discovered – the Dharmapala who, I hoped, I had caused to live once more in the pages of my biographical sketch.

19
A RE-ENSHRINEMENT AND A REUNION

Sanchi lay at a distance of twenty-five miles from Bhopal, the capital of the then state of Madhya Bharat, the hill on which it stood being an offshoot of the eastern Vindhyas – the celebrated mountain range separating the Ganges basin from the Deccan. According to one of the articles I had proofread for the Diamond Jubilee Souvenir, and which subsequently appeared in its pages, the history of 'Sanchi, the incomparable', as the author enthusiastically called it, filled a period of about twelve hundred years, from the reign of Aśoka down almost to the end of the Ancient period of Indian history. It thus coincided with what he termed the 'epic story' of the rise and fall of Buddhism in the land of its birth. During the six hundred years that followed the Muslim invasions of the twelfth and thirteenth centuries the stupas, monasteries, and temples of Sanchi fell into a state of increasing neglect and decay, and by the time General Cunningham visited the place in the middle of the nineteenth century many of the monuments were little more than a heap of rubble from which grew bushes and even trees. Besides surveying the area and carrying out excavations the great archaeologist sunk shafts into several of the stupas, and in the relic chamber of what was subsequently known as Stupa No. 3 he discovered the steatite boxes containing the tiny fragments of bone that were the sole mortal remains of the *arhants* Śāriputra and Maudgalyāyana. It was these same fragments of bone, these same Sacred Relics, that had lain in a London museum for ninety years and that, after being presented to the Maha Bodhi Society by the British Government, had been given such an enthusiastic reception by the people of India. Now, having concluded their visits to different parts of the Buddhist world with a visit to the Kingdom of Cambodia, they were about to be re-enshrined in their place of origin.

On 29 November 1952, therefore, the Sacred Relics were taken in procession from the Sri Dharmarajika Vihara to Howrah Station. Here a special train was waiting, and after being carried along the platform on the head of a civic dignitary the silver-gilt casket was placed in the specially decorated tourist carriage provided by the Government of India. At ten o'clock in the evening the train left, slowly drawing out of the great railway terminus to repeated shouts of 'Sadhu!' from the white-garmented devotees. During the final stages of my work on the Diamond Jubilee Souvenir it had become increasingly obvious to me that Devapriya Valisinha was taking it for granted that I would be accompanying the Sacred Relics to Sanchi, and as they set out on their homeward journey I accordingly found myself seated in a compartment of the specially decorated tourist carriage together with the familiar silver-gilt casket. With me in the compartment were Bhikkhu Silabhadra and four or five other monks, mostly Sinhalese. As the night wore on, however, the monks slipped away one by one until only Silabhadra and I were left. Having bolted the door, we therefore stretched out on the seats, being careful to lie with our heads towards the Sacred Relics, and soon were fast asleep.

We were not allowed to sleep for long. At Gaya the carriage was besieged by people wanting to 'take *darshan*' of the Sacred Relics, and we had to open the windows – a process involving much raising of gauze screens and wooden shutters – and hold the reliquary up against the iron window-bars so that they could see it and, if they were lucky, put their hand through the bars and touch it. In the course of the following day and night this procedure was repeated at most of the other stations at which the train halted. Silabhadra and I therefore spent the greater part of the journey sitting opposite each other in the window seats with the reliquary resting on the semi-circular ledge between us. Whenever people wanted to 'take *darshan*' we lifted it up a foot or so in order to give them a better view. Sometimes garlands of marigolds were thrust through the bars, as well as currency notes and handfuls of small change. Curiously enough, none of the other monks offered to take turns with us in looking after the Sacred Relics – Venerable Sangharatana was not, of course, among them, being busy with his own anniversary celebrations at Sarnath – and we in fact did not see so much as a flutter of their yellow robes again. By the time the train reached Sanchi my elderly companion and I were therefore feeling more than a little tired. But we did not mind. We had done our duty by the Sacred Relics, and in any case the thunderous shouts of 'Sadhu!' with which they were greeted by the waiting crowd were more than enough to revive our flagging spirits.

From the train the Sacred Relics were transferred to a lavishly decorated pavilion of the traditional Sinhalese type. As soon as they had been installed there I asked one of the volunteers to show me where my own quarters were and was at once conducted to a tent which I had no difficulty in recognizing as standard army issue. The fact was that the modern Sanchi consisted of little more than a tiny village and the archaeological area, so that there was no question of its being able to provide accommodation for even a fraction of the people who would be coming from all over India, as well as from the various Buddhist countries, for the re-enshrinement of the Sacred Relics and the opening of the new Sanchi Vihara. The Indian army had therefore been asked to help out, with the result that a veritable township of tents had sprung up in the vicinity of the archaeological area. Moreover, the township had been laid out in streets and lanes, as it were, and the individual tents consecutively numbered, so that the Maha Bodhi Society's invitees had no difficulty finding the tent they had been allocated. My own tent was situated not far from the centre of the township, and on entering I found that the monk with whom I was to share it had already arrived and was busy supervising the arrangement of his rather luxurious bedding. The monk turned out to be Narada Thera, whom I had last seen in Kathmandu almost exactly a year ago. Though I had little sympathy for his narrow and formalistic type of Buddhism, I was glad to see him again, while he on his part greeted me with evident cordiality and in a manner that suggested he was not sorry to have someone on whom to exercise his well known buttonholing proclivities. I was not ready to be buttonholed just then, however, and having arranged my own far from luxurious bedding went in quest of Lama Govinda and Li Gotami, who I knew would be attending the International Buddhist Cultural Conference that was being held that afternoon as part of the celebrations.

After a brief search I found their tent, which was not far from my own, and on lifting the flap had the satisfaction of being greeted by my two friends with exclamations of surprise and delight. Though a regular correspondence had been kept up between us, we had not seen one another since the autumn of the previous year, when they had stayed with me in Kalimpong and I had stayed with them in Ghoom, and our reunion – the reunion of three kindred spirits – was therefore a joyful one. Indeed, the prospect of seeing the mild-mannered German lama and his vivacious Parsee consort again had been one of the main reasons for my accompanying the Sacred Relics to Sanchi, and I had lived in pleasurable anticipation of the reunion for some days.

Having as much in common as we did, and having not met for so long, the three of us naturally had quite a lot to say to one another. Unfortunately we had very little time in which to say it. The eleven o'clock bell had already rung, and I had to go and join the yellow-robed figures who were streaming towards the dining area for the ceremonial food-offering which, in Theravādin eyes, was one of the most important parts of the day's proceedings. After the monks had eaten, and the 'sermon of thanksgiving' had been delivered, it would be the turn of the laity, and when *they* had been fed it would be time for the International Buddhist Cultural Conference to begin. Before hurrying off, however, I made arrangements with Lama Govinda and Li Gotami for us to spend some time together later on.

The Cultural Conference was held in a *pandal* or temporary structure of bamboo poles covered with white cloth, and its proceedings lasted for nearly eight hours, with only one short interval halfway through. Dr Radhakrishnan, the Vice-President of India, presided, Pandit Nehru, the Prime Minister, gave the opening address, and some twenty or thirty monks, scholars, politicians, diplomats, and people of local importance delivered speeches and read papers or simply spoke about whatever happened to be uppermost in their mind at that particular moment. So many contributions to the proceedings of the conference were there, indeed, that with the exception of Narada Thera's, Lama Govinda's, and my own, all recollection of them has long since faded from my mind. Narada Thera read a scholarly paper on 'Consciousness' in which, with characteristic aplomb, he took the opportunity of criticizing Dr Radhakrishnan for having misrepresented the Buddhist – that is, the Theravādin Buddhist – conception of *citta* in his well-known work on Indian philosophy.[119] The object of the criticism listened attentively, but did not seem unduly perturbed. Lama Govinda likewise read a paper, but unfortunately he read it without once raising his eyes from the manuscript and in a voice so low that he was seen rather than heard to read it. Only years later did I learn that at one point he had announced the establishment of the Arya Maitreya Mandala, the first Vajrayāna Buddhist organization to be introduced into the West.[120]

My own contribution to the proceedings was confined to a short speech in which I dealt with what I knew was a quite sensitive issue: the issue of Buddha Jayanti, or the fact that, five years after Independence, the Government of India had still not declared the Buddha's 'birthday' a public holiday. 'Jesus Christ was born in Palestine,' I told the conference, having worked my way up to the point, 'but his birthday is a public holiday in India. Prophet Mohammed was born in Arabia, but his birthday too is a public holiday. The Buddha, however, was born in India, but *his* birthday...' It was not necessary for me to complete the sentence, which drew a burst of laughter, followed by prolonged applause, from Buddhist and Hindu alike, and I thereupon concluded my speech with a strong appeal to the Government of India to take immediate action and honour India's greatest son by declaring his birthday, 'Buddha Jayanti', a public holiday. Dr Radhakrishnan could hardly ignore so marked an expression of popular feeling, and in his closing remarks adverted to what I had said. The request ought to have been made while the Prime Minister was present at the meeting, he observed, with an air of slight displeasure. Nevertheless, he would convey the request to his government for its consideration.[121] Pleased though I was to have achieved this much, at least, Radhakrishnan's observation that the request ought to have been made while the Prime Minister was present at the meeting struck me as distinctly unreasonable. I was not to know that Pandit Nehru would be leaving early, and in any case I had had no voice whatever in determining the order in which the different speakers should address the gathering.

Though the Cultural Conference was the longest of the events taking place during the two-day celebrations it was not, of course, the most important. The most important event – the one for the sake of which we had all made the journey to Sanchi – was the re-enshrinement of the Sacred Relics of the two *arhants* and, therewith, the opening of the new Sanchi Vihara. Such being the case it is strange that, though I was undoubtedly present on the occasion, recollection of the ceremonies that then took place has faded from my mind even more completely than has recollection of the various contributions to the proceedings of the Cultural Conference the day before. According to a report that appeared in the pages of the *Maha Bodhi* journal a few months later, 'Amidst chanting of Buddhist hymns, and recitation of suttas to the accompaniment of blowing of conch-shells and ringing of bells, the sacred relics of the two chief disciples of Lord Buddha were enshrined at 5.20 p.m. in the newly built vihara adjacent to the old stupa on the historic Sanchi Hill.' But of all this I remember nothing. I do not even remember the procession in which, according to the same account, the Sacred Relics were taken to the vihara from the pavilion in which they had been placed the previous day.

What I do remember, however, and remember very vividly, are the hours which, earlier that same day, I had spent with Lama Govinda and Li Gotami exploring the archaeological area. The sky was a deep, cloudless blue, and the sun shone warmly on ochre-coloured earth and pinkish-brown sandstone as reverentially we moved from one ruined or restored monument to another. The principal object of our attention was Stupa No. 1 which, since it was the biggest of the stupas in the area, was known as the Great Stupa. Originally built of brick by the Emperor Aśoka in the third century BCE, it had been encased in stone a hundred years later, during the Sunga period, when the stone terrace, balustrades, and flights of steps had also been added, so that from then onwards it had a diameter of over 120 feet and a height of 54 feet. With its four massive stone gateways, additions of the first century BCE, the Great Stupa towered above the surrounding monuments without appearing to dominate them, creating an extraordinary impression of dignity, harmony, and repose. After making our way round the upper terrace, thus circumambulating the stupa, we spent some time admiring the gateways, which stood at the four cardinal points of the ground terrace. Each gateway consisted of two square pillars with dwarf, elephant, or lion capitals, and these capitals were surmounted by a series of three architraves, all richly carved with human and animal forms, as well as with figures from Indian mythology. Originally the gates had been crowned by the symbols of Buddhism, the Wheel of the Dharma and the Triratna Trident, but of these only fragments now remained. Looking up at the panels of the architraves, twenty, thirty, and forty feet above our heads, we could make out not only separate figures but whole scenes. There were representations of events in the life of the Buddha and episodes from Buddhist history, as well as representations of the world of the gods, and Lama Govinda – more knowledgeable in such matters than either Li Gotami or myself – even managed to identify particular incidents from his beloved *Jātaka* stories. In the case of the scenes representing events in the life of the Buddha, the Buddha's own presence was indicated by the appropriate symbol, for in the first century BCE the Master was not depicted in human form and would not be so depicted for another hundred or more years.

Stupa No. 3, the stupa in which the steatite boxes containing the earthly remains of Śāriputra and Maudgalyāyana had been discovered, turned out to be situated in a village more than six miles from Sanchi proper, and we therefore did not see it. We did, however, see the monolithic Aśoka pillar that stood next to the Great Stupa. This had the usual round shaft and bell-shaped capital surmounted by four lions set back to back, and bore on its highly polished surface one of Aśoka's celebrated edicts. As I learned later on, the edict threatened with excommunication any monk or nun who created schism in the Buddhist community.[122] We also saw the four pillars which were, I think, practically all that remained of a small temple belonging to the Gupta period. These were of an almost Hellenic severity and simplicity, and served to remind me that between Buddhist India and Ancient Greece there existed a certain similarity of ideals. But whether ruined or restored, the monuments of the past were not the only objects to claim our attention. From time to time we lifted up our eyes to the nearby ridge, and to the dazzlingly white shape of the Chetiyagiri Vihara, as the new Sanchi temple was called. Architecturally speaking it was, I thought, a greater success than was the Mulagandhakuti Vihara at Sarnath; for whereas the Mulagandhakuti was impressive only when seen squarely from one side, the Chetiyagiri Vihara presented an impressive appearance regardless of the angle from which it was viewed.

At one point in our exploration of the archaeological area we were joined by Narada Thera. Lama Govinda was already well acquainted with him and had, as I knew, no more sympathy for his narrow and formalistic type of Buddhism than I had myself. In fact it was quite impossible for either of us to take him very seriously or to regard him as anything other than a figure of fun. So much was this the case, indeed, that we subsequently bestowed upon him the sobriquet of Auntie Narada, for with his high-pitched voice and his prim and pedantic ways the elderly doyen of the English-speaking monks of Ceylon was much more like somebody's maiden aunt than a real monk. Both his primness and his pedantry were evinced within minutes of his joining my two friends and myself. Lama Govinda had brought along with him a large, lavishly produced volume on Buddhist art, and among the illustrations to this volume there were some exceptionally beautiful Tibetan *thangkas* of different Buddhas and bodhisattvas. Thinking these would be of interest to him, Lama Govinda gave Narada Thera the volume to look at, but after turning a few pages the Sinhalese monk handed it back, remarking, 'No doubt the pictures are very nice, but as a Buddhist monk I am not allowed to appreciate beauty.' It was as though Govinda was a wicked Māra who, through the medium of Buddhist art, was trying to tempt him away from the right path with the lure of beauty – a temptation to which he, the virtuous monk, nobly refused to succumb.

But this was not the only experience of Narada Thera's type of Buddhism that I was to have that day. On entering the tent some hours later I found him – not to say caught him – hastily swallowing a handful of vitamin tablets. 'Oh Bhante, I did not know you took anything after twelve o'clock!' I exclaimed in genuine astonishment, for my elder brother in the sangha was well known for his strict adherence to the Vinaya rules and eating after twelve o'clock was popularly regarded as one of the most serious offences a monk could commit. As soon as he had finished swallowing the vitamin tablets Narada Thera hastened to put me right. They were *medicine*, he explained, and since they were medicine they could be taken after twelve o'clock without infringing the Vinaya rules. To me this did not sound very convincing. Vitamin tablets were surely taken not to cure disease but to provide nourishment. As such they were not medicine but food and as food they could not be taken after twelve o'clock. But Narada Thera was no more convinced by my arguments than I was convinced by his, and continued to insist that vitamin tablets were medicine. Indeed, by the time we went to bed he had, without realizing it, come very close to maintaining that if someone as strict in his observance of the Vinaya as *he* was took vitamin tablets after twelve o'clock then they could *not* be food and it *must* be all right to take them.

Narada Thera's type of Buddhism was not, of course, confined to Narada Thera. It was, as I had been made aware either that or the previous morning, well represented among the Sinhalese lay Buddhists attending the celebrations, and once again it was in connection with the vexed question of Buddhist art that narrowness and formalism manifested themselves. As part of the celebration an exhibition of Buddhist art had been organized, and among the artists contributing to the exhibition were Mme Brunner and her daughter Elizabeth. The Brunners, as their friends called them, were two highly unconventional, not to say eccentric, Hungarian Buddhists who lived together in Delhi and were, in fact, inseparable. Both women were extremely emotional, and it was said of them that whenever they failed to get their own way they would start screaming and tearing off their clothes – a tactic that was invariably successful with modesty-conscious Indians of every kind, from landlords to shopkeepers and from bank managers to railway booking clerks. Among Elizabeth Brunner's contributions to the exhibition there was a striking picture of the Buddha in meditation. It was quite traditional in conception, except that the Buddha was cradling in his hands not the more usual almsbowl but a human skull. When the Sinhalese lay Buddhists saw the picture they were shocked and outraged. The artist had committed sacrilege! She had polluted the Buddha! She had shown him in contact with a corpse! – and off they rushed to complain to the organizers, and to Devapriya Valisinha, and to demand that the picture be removed immediately. Devapriyaji, feeling rather out of his depth, for some reason came and consulted me, as did the unfortunate artist, who was in tears. The painting was not in the least sacrilegious, I declared. It could not even be said to be in bad taste. The skull obviously symbolized the truth of universal impermanence, and the fact that the Buddha was holding it in his hands meant that he was meditating upon that truth, or had realized it – and there could hardly be anything more truly Buddhist than that. Pollution was in any case a Hindu concept, and as such had no place in Buddhism. Devapriyaji was inclined to agree with me in this, as was Lama Govinda (Li Gotami admitted that the painting made her feel uneasy), but the Sinhalese lay Buddhists were not to be mollified and continued to clamour for the removal of the offending picture. As for Elizabeth Brunner, she made no attempt to start screaming and tearing off her clothes, probably because she knew that the Sinhalese Buddhists, being for the most part women, could scream louder than she could and would not, in any case, have been impressed by a display of female nudity. In the end the painting was removed from the exhibition.

Had the Sinhalese lay Buddhists known that before the celebrations came to an end I would be accepting an invitation to collaborate in the making of a Buddhist film they would have been doubly shocked and outraged; but such was indeed the case. In the course of my second day in Sanchi I was approached by a swarthy young man of about my own age who introduced himself as Arjun Dev Rashk. He was a writer, he explained. In fact, he added rather shamefacedly, he was a scriptwriter, and wrote scripts for Hindi films. At the moment he was working on the script of a film to be called *Ajanta*, after the famous cave temples. As yet there was no story, but the action would take place in and around the cave temples themselves, and the hero would be a young Buddhist monk. The part of the monk would be taken by Raj Kapoor, who would also be producing and directing the film. As a matter of fact, the young scriptwriter continued, Raj Kapoor had come down from Bombay with his aides for the re-enshrinement of the Sacred Relics and was even now in Sanchi. He had heard me speak at the Cultural Conference, and very much wanted to meet me. If I had no objection, he would take me to him straight away. Raj Sahib of course would have liked to come to me, but it was difficult for him to do so.

A few minutes later I learned why it was difficult. As we approached the actor's tent, which was situated somewhat apart from the rest of the township, I saw that it was surrounded by uniformed policemen and that the policemen were engaged in keeping back some hundreds of excited young men and boys who were, it seemed, hoping to catch a glimpse of Raj Kapoor when he came out. During the night, Rashk informed me with an indulgent chuckle, one young man, eluding the guards, had actually crawled underneath the canvas and emerged almost at Raj Kapoor's feet. Was Raj Kapoor very well known then? I asked. Rashk could not help smiling, goodnaturedly, at my ignorance. Raj Kapoor was very well known indeed, he replied. He was one of the best known male film actors of the day, and perhaps the most popular. Wherever he went people flocked to see him. He attracted more attention than the Prime Minister himself. At this point in the conversation I recalled that a week or two earlier Devapriyaji had told me, in confidence, that a famous Indian film star would be attending the Sanchi celebrations, but I had given no more thought to the matter. Evidently Raj Kapoor was the famous film star in question. But before I could recall what else Devapriyaji had said I had passed through the policemen, was inside the tent, and a figure in an open-necked shirt had stepped forward from among his aides and was greeting me with folded hands.

Later on Rashk told me that Raj Kapoor was popularly known as the Clark Gable of India, but so far as my vague recollections of *Gone With the Wind* enabled me to judge there was little or no outward resemblance between the American film star and his Indian counterpart. Like Rashk, Raj Kapoor was of about my own age, perhaps a little older, and of above average height, at least by Indian standards. Unlike Rashk, he was so fair-skinned that he could easily have passed for a European, the more especially since his cheeks were of a distinctly roseate hue. A smile played about his rather thin lips, though his habit of raising his eyebrows gave him a slightly quizzical expression, and I noticed that his eyes were cold. Needless to say, he radiated charm, and on the occasion of our first meeting that charm was turned exclusively in my direction. He was *delighted* to meet me, he declared, his voice vibrant with real or simulated emotion, and *so* grateful to me for taking the trouble to come and see him. As Rashkji must have told me, he was planning to produce a film called *Ajanta*. It would not be a Buddhist film, exactly, but it would have a Buddhist theme and the hero would be a young Buddhist monk who would embody all the noblest ideals of Buddhism, such as peace, love, and tolerance – though without ceasing to be very, *very*, human. He himself knew nothing about Buddhism, he confessed, with what was clearly intended to be disarming frankness. *That* was why he had been so anxious to meet me. He wanted *Ajanta* to be absolutely *authentic*, and the General Secretary of the Maha Bodhi Society had given him to understand that I would be the best person to consult in this connection. (Devapriyaji had, it seemed, already met Raj Kapoor.) *Would* I, then, be so *very* kind as to give him the benefit of my advice? He would be *immensely* grateful to me, and of course he would see to it that I was not a loser in any way. He would have liked to have a long talk with me there and then, but unfortunately he had to return to Bombay almost immediately. If it was not asking too much, would I come and spend a few days in Bombay as the guest of R. K. Films? Rashkji would escort me there, and book me into a first class hotel, and we could meet whenever it suited me. *Would* I be so kind as to accept his invitation? *Would* I?

After a minute or two's reflection I replied that I would. It was not that I found the famous film star's charm irresistible. It was not that, three-and-a-half years having passed since my last visit to Bombay, I was at all anxious to see the commercial capital of India again. It was not even that I was anxious to see the Maha Bodhi Society's two Bombay centres, about one of which I knew Devapriyaji was quite worried. From what Rashk and Raj Kapoor had told me about *Ajanta* it seemed more than likely that the film would seriously misrepresent both Buddhism and Buddhist monks, and the principal reason for my accepting Raj Kapoor's invitation was the hope that, by being involved with the production at an early stage, I might help him avoid some of the more obvious pitfalls. The following morning, therefore, Rashk and I boarded the crowded Delhi–Bombay Express and were ushered to the first class seats which R. K. Films had reserved for us. As Rashk remarked, not without complacency, R. K. Films had ways of doing things. Before leaving Sanchi I went and said goodbye to Lama Govinda and Li Gotami, who were delighted to learn that I was going to Bombay. When I had finished my work with Raj Kapoor, why not come and spend a week with them in Deolali? It was only a hundred miles away, and we would have more time to talk than we had had in Sanchi. Thus as the train hurtled towards Bombay I was able to look forward not only to a closer acquaintance with the film world but also to another reunion of the three kindred spirits.

20

DISCUSSIONS IN BOMBAY AND DEOLALI

The name of Ajanta was not new to me. I had been familiar with it from my boyhood, ever since the discovery of Mukul Chandra Dey's *My Pilgrimages to Ajanta and Bagh* had given me my first real glimpse of the colourful and inspiring world of Buddhist art.[123] From the pages of the book had looked out some of the divinest faces and forms ever conceived by the heart or executed by the hand of man – the faces and forms depicted on the walls, ceilings, and pillars of the cave temples of Ajanta. There was the Buddha sitting in the attitude of teaching the Dharma, his head aureoled as though by the outraying petals of a giant chrysanthemum, and the Buddha standing calm and majestic, almsbowl in hand, looking down at the diminutive figures of Yaśodhara, his former wife, and Rāhula, the child of his humanity. There were flying figures. There were celestial maidens with wonderful coiffures. There were tiaraed bodhisattvas with blue lotuses in their hands. There were palace scenes. There were wild geese with entwined necks. There were elephants and lotus flowers. During the eight years that I had lived in India I had seen these same faces and forms many times, for reproductions of the Ajanta wall paintings often featured in books on Buddhism and on Indian art, and as a result of this some of the faces and some of the forms that I had first seen looking out from the pages of *My Journeys to Ajanta and Bagh* were now deeply imprinted on my consciousness. As yet, however, I had not actually visited Ajanta or seen its paintings with my own eyes, and in fact was not to do so for quite a few more years.

Raj Kapoor had visited Ajanta only a few weeks before attending the Sanchi celebrations, and had been so overwhelmed by the experience that, as Rashk told me on the train, for several days afterwards he had been able to talk of nothing else. Ajanta had in fact become something of an obsession with him, and as was usually the case with his obsessions, apparently, he wanted to turn it into a film, with himself in the leading role. Before he could do this, however, there was another film to be finished and many questions about Ajanta that he wanted to ask. One of these questions in particular must have been very much on his mind, for on the occasion of our first meeting in Bombay he lost no time in putting it to me. It was generally understood, he prefaced, that the wall paintings of Ajanta had been executed by Buddhist monks. But some of those paintings were of an undeniably erotic character. They represented physically attractive young women in a state of almost complete nudity. How, then, was it possible for the monks who had executed those paintings to have been free from sexual desire?

I had not considered this question before and consequently had to think fast. Or rather, I did not think at all. The answer sprang to my lips as quickly and as spontaneously as though I had been inspired by the goddess Saraswati herself, the *veena*-playing patroness of learning and eloquence. To the monk artists of Ajanta women were simply part of the natural world, I replied. They depicted them in the same spirit that they depicted flowers, fruits, creepers, birds, animals, and other natural objects. They depicted them with sympathy but, at the same time, with complete detachment, and it was for precisely *this* reason that the women of the Ajanta wall paintings were so divinely beautiful. In other words, the ancient monk artists perceived women in purely aesthetic terms, and they were able to perceive them in purely aesthetic terms on account of their complete freedom from sexual desire. Had they *not* been free from sexual desire they could not possibly have depicted the women of the Ajanta wall paintings in the way they had done and the paintings would *really* have been of an erotic character.

Unpremeditated though my reply to Raj Kapoor's question was, the more I afterwards thought about it the more convinced I became that the explanation I had given him was correct and that, whether monks or laymen, the artists of Ajanta must have been free from sexual desire. Correct or not, the explanation appeared to satisfy Raj Kapoor, who proceeded to hold forth on the topic of Ajanta at great length and with the utmost enthusiasm. It was by no means always clear, however, whether he was referring to Ajanta the place or to *Ajanta* the film or even to both of them simultaneously. What gradually did become clear, though, was that *Ajanta* the film was at an even earlier stage of production than I had imagined. Indeed, it could hardly have been in a more embryonic condition, being little more than the gleam in Raj Kapoor's eyes and the stream of words that flowed from his lips. From what he then told me (and Rashk, who obviously had heard it all before) I gathered that during his visit to Ajanta it was as though the centuries had rolled away like clouds and he was standing not in the cave temples as they were today but in the cave temples as they had been in the days of their pristine glory. Moreover, he was wearing yellow robes. He was a young monk, perhaps a novice. Not that he had suddenly *remembered* being a young monk at Ajanta in a previous existence, he assured me, though the possibility could not be ruled out. (Did Buddhists believe in rebirth like the Hindus?... Yes, he had thought they did.) It was simply that he had *felt* what it must have been like to be a young monk at Ajanta all those hundreds of years ago. Perhaps the young monk was one of the artists who had decorated the walls of the cave temples. Perhaps he had executed some of the very paintings about which he had asked me at the beginning of our conversation – the paintings of physically attractive young women in a state of almost complete nudity. No doubt the monk artists who had executed the paintings *were*, in fact, completely free from sexual desire, as I had so clearly explained. But perhaps in the case of *this* young monk – just *this* young monk – there had been a little bit of sexual desire still remaining, and perhaps the women *he* had depicted on the walls of the cave temples were, in a way, the expression of that desire. Perhaps he had even fallen in love with the most beautiful of his own creations, or with one of the slave girls who waited on the monks and who had been secretly in love with him all the time. (Where Raj Kapoor had got the idea that the monks of Ajanta had slave girls to wait on them I did not know.) Perhaps the young monk and the slave girl had run away together. Perhaps the young monk wanted to *experience* the world. He had become a monk while still only a boy. He had been left an orphan at an early age and had been adopted by the head monk of Ajanta, a wise old man who loved him dearly. In the end, having experienced the world to the full, the young monk returns to Ajanta. The old monk, now very old indeed, clasps him to his breast. He is his best and truest disciple, he declares. He alone has understood his teaching. He alone has understood that Truth is to be found not by rejecting the world but by *experiencing* it. After the old monk's death the young monk – now not so young as he was – becomes the head monk of Ajanta, while the slave girl becomes his faithful disciple. Together they tread the path to Enlightenment.

By this time the gleam in Raj Kapoor's eyes had become brighter and the words were flowing from his lips in a more rapid stream. It was as though he could actually *see* the concluding scenes of the film: could see the young monk returning to Ajanta, see the old monk clasping the young monk to his breast, see the young monk becoming the head monk of Ajanta, and, finally, see the young monk and the slave girl – the hero and heroine – himself and his leading lady – slowly walking hand in hand into the sunset to the accompaniment of appropriate music. From time to time, in his excitement, he rose to his feet and not only supplemented the stream of words with extravagant gestures but even impersonated, one after another, the different characters whose experience he was describing. In my naivety I imagined that *Ajanta* now had a story, and wondered why Rashk was not writing it all down or at least making a few notes. But Rashk knew better. He had heard several versions of the story of *Ajanta* already, and in fact he and I were to hear several more versions of it in the next few days. In one of these later versions the young monk falls in love not with a slave girl but with a beautiful princess who has come to Ajanta on pilgrimage (or to pray for her sick father's restoration to health – Raj Kapoor could not make up his mind which), marries her, becomes king when her father dies, and returns to Ajanta only at the very end of his life. In another he is not an artist but a physician and marries the princess after curing her father of a serious illness. And so on. Eventually I realized that all the different versions of the story had certain features in common. They all began in Ajanta and ended in Ajanta, and they all featured a young monk who, having fallen in love and experienced the world, returns to the peace and seclusion of the cave temples where he has been brought up. I also realized that Raj Kapoor was in fact not interested in giving the story of *Ajanta* a definitive form. That would come later. What he was really doing, as he fantasized about what it must have been like to be a young monk at Ajanta in the days of its glory, was feeling his way into the film, especially into the role of the young monk, as well as trying to create the kind of scenes and situations that would enable him to exhibit his particular talents as an actor to their greatest possible advantage. Even when relating what was, for me, the first version of the story of *Ajanta*, Raj Kapoor portrayed the young monk so convincingly that it was evident he had been feeling his way into the role for some time and was, in fact, quite strongly identified with it already.

But what was the young monk's name? It was as though, being now quite strongly identified with the part, Raj Kapoor wanted to know what the young monk was called – wanted to know what *he* was called. The rest of our first meeting in Bombay was therefore spent trying to decide upon a name for the hero of *Ajanta* or, as Raj Kapoor saw it, trying to discover what the young monk's name actually was. For an hour or more I ransacked my memory for suitable names from the scriptures and from Buddhist history and legend; one after another I brought the names up, and one after another Raj Kapoor tried them out, so to speak, by repeating them aloud a number of times. Ānanda, Aniruddha, Mahānāma, Tissa, Kāśyapa, Aśoka, Upagupta – all were tried and rejected. Eventually I produced the name of Pūrṇa. This time Raj Kapoor not only repeated the name but repeated it with increasing satisfaction and delight. Poorna, he breathed, as his eyes shone and his whole face lit up. Yes, that was his name. Pooorna. Pooooorna. So extremely delighted was he with the name, and to such an extent did he seem to take it for his own, that I would hardly have been surprised if he had announced that in future he was to be called not Raj Kapoor but Purna. Had he actually done so Rashk would not have been impressed, even if I had been. In fifteen minutes time, the swarthy young scriptwriter observed as we drove off together afterwards, Raj Kapoor would be back on the set and immersed in a totally different role. True though this may have been, from the cordiality of the film star's *au revoirs* it was clear that so far as he was concerned our first meeting in Bombay had been a complete success and that in finding a name for the hero of *Ajanta* we had, in fact, done a good day's work.

The scene of this first meeting, as of most of my subsequent meetings with Raj Kapoor, was the lounge of his private quarters on the ground floor of R. K. Studios, immediately adjoining the production area. On our arrival in Bombay Rashk had booked me into a first class hotel, as previously instructed, and it was he who, a day or two later, drove me from the hotel to the studios for my meeting with Raj Kapoor, a service he was to perform several more times before the week was out. At the end of the week, however, I moved from the hotel to Ananda Vihara, the bigger and more centrally situated of the Maha Bodhi Society's Bombay centres, which at that time was without a resident *bhikṣu* and in fact almost empty. It was not that the hotel was uncomfortable. If anything it was rather too comfortable, and on the principle that 'a monk out of his cloister is like a fish out of water'[124] I thought it better for me to stay at Ananda Vihara, especially as there was plenty of room there and as, moreover, I would be more accessible to anyone who wanted to see me. Henceforth it was not from the hotel but from Ananda Vihara that Rashk drove me to my meetings with Raj Kapoor, usually stopping on the way so that we could have a cup of tea and a chat. On our approaching the R. K. Studios building, which was situated in Chembur, one of the more outlying parts of Bombay, I would invariably see a dozen or more young men hanging about the compound gate. They were all would-be film stars, Rashk explained, as he drove me through for the first time. They were all hoping to see Raj Kapoor and, if possible, persuade him to give them an audition. There was not one of them who would not sell his own grandmother for the sake of five minutes with the great man. Some of them could sing. Some could dance. Some were merely good-looking. Probably not one of them could act. But they all wanted to be rich and famous and they all believed – not without reason – that for a poor boy without connections or qualifications there was one road, and one road only, to riches and fame, and that was the films.

Since our meetings were always arranged in advance, on my arrival at the studios I usually found Raj Kapoor in his private quarters, waiting for me. Sometimes, however, he was still acting or directing or both, in which case Rashk and I would make ourselves comfortable in the lounge until, fifteen or twenty minutes later, he came to us straight from the set with his make-up on and with profuse apologies for his unpunctuality. That last scene had proved unexpectedly difficult, and it had taken them a long time to get it right. On such occasions he looked very tired and drawn but, at the same time, bright underneath and clearly ready to get back to *Ajanta*, and back into the role of Purna, without further delay. As soon as he had washed and changed, therefore, the meeting would begin. At all other times it began as soon as Rashk and I had arrived – sometimes even before the three of us were fairly seated round the coffee table in the centre of the room. Several meetings were devoted to

Buddhist monastic life, for I was concerned that this should be correctly represented in the film and that so long as the young monk wore the yellow robe there should be no love scenes between him and the slave girl, or the beautiful princess, or whoever else it had been decided the heroine should be. According to the Buddhist monastic law, I explained, a *bhikṣu* could not come into physical contact with a woman, or sit alone with her in a secluded place, or laugh and joke with her, and if Purna was shown doing any of these things while still a monk many Buddhists would feel deeply shocked, protests would be made to the Government of India, and in some Buddhist countries the film might even be banned. I also demonstrated the way in which Buddhist monks chanted such things as the Refuges and Precepts and the Salutation to the Three Jewels, at the same time suggesting that if any of the scenes in the cave temples called for congregational chanting it might be a good idea to enlist the cooperation of Venerable Sangharatana and the other monks of Sarnath – though in the interests of authenticity they would have to chant in Sanskrit and not, as they usually did, in Pāli.

To this and other suggestions of mine Raj Kapoor listened attentively with head bowed and hands clasped between his knees, only occasionally looking up to interpose a comment or question or to take up something I had said and make it the starting point for one of his own fantasizings. On the whole he found my suggestions acceptable enough, though he was not very happy with the idea of having to shave his head for those scenes in which Purna appeared as a monk – at least, he was not very happy with it until Rashk pointed out that it would not be difficult for the make-up man to provide him with an artificial scalp that would fit over his hair. With the idea that some of the scenes in the cave temples might call for congregational chanting, however, he was very happy indeed. On his visit to Ajanta he had, it seemed, been greatly impressed by the main *chaitya* hall, with its two rows of pillars and its stupa at the far end, and had no difficulty imagining it filled with yellow-robed figures, all chanting together, with Purna in their midst. Whether the scene was to take place before Purna ran away with the slave girl (or the beautiful princess), or whether it was to take place when he became the head monk of Ajanta (or when he returned to Ajanta at the very end of his life) was not very clear, but so vividly did Raj Kapoor describe the scene that, as he spoke, I saw the lamps shining on the lined faces of the monks and heard the sound of the chanting as, filling the hall with more and more powerful vibrations, it gradually rose to its tremendous climax.

In the course of our discussions Raj Kapoor, Rashk, and I would usually be joined by one or more members of Raj Kapoor's inner circle, as it might be termed. Besides the more shadowy figures of the art director and the music director this included Shanker and Jaikishen and Miss Nargis. Shanker and Jaikishen were two very unassuming young men of very ordinary appearance who were always seen together and who never said anything, unless it was to exchange a few words with each other. Despite their extreme youth (they seemed to be several years younger than I was) they were among the most celebrated names in the Bombay film industry. Between them they wrote the songs for Raj Kapoor's films, one of them being responsible for the music and the other for the lyrics. Some of their songs were very famous indeed and had, in fact, contributed greatly to the success of the films for which they were written. Miss Nargis was, of course, Raj Kapoor's principal leading lady, and just as he was popularly known as the Clark Gable of India so she (as Rashk told me, he being the source of my information about her, as of my information about Shanker and Jaikishen) was popularly known as the Greta Garbo of India. Since my recollections of *Marie Walewska* were even vaguer than my recollections of *Gone With the Wind* I had no means of telling to what extent the comparison was justified, but there was little doubt that so far as outward appearance, at least, was concerned, Greta Garbo might have taken it as a compliment to be known as the Nargis of America.[125] A few years younger than Raj Kapoor, and of medium height, Miss Nargis (the name meant 'Narcissus') had a clear brown complexion, a face elongated rather than round, a slightly prominent nose, and a pair of large, dark eyes. Though her look was one of intelligence, it was also one of extraordinary sweetness and charm, while the unstudied grace of her movements were a delight to see. She invariably appeared floating in layer upon layer of starched white chiffon, wearing little or no jewellery, and with the corner of her sari drawn modestly over her head. So much white chiffon was there, indeed, that she seemed to move in a cloud, and I was sometimes apprehensive lest she should trip over it or lest it should get in the way when she was pouring tea or handing round the cups; but she never tripped and it never got in the way. It was as though she was surrounded by invisible sylphs who bore up the edges of her draperies and prevented anything untoward from happening. Though she always followed our discussions with interest, she said hardly more than Shanker and Jaikishen, seeming perfectly content to sit and listen and to serve tea.

So quiet and so reserved was Miss Nargis, in fact, that when, towards the end of my stay in Bombay, Rashk wrote a scene that called for a violent emotional outburst on the part of the slave girl (or the beautiful princess) I could not help wondering whether such an outburst might not be beyond the Indian Greta Garbo's capacities. It was *well* within her capacities, Rashk assured me warmly. Nargis was a very great actress indeed. There was absolutely no comparison between her acting abilities and Raj Kapoor's. He could express only two different moods. She could express forty. On this occasion, as on others, I noticed that besides having the greatest respect for Miss Nargis in her professional capacity Rashk was inclined to think of himself as her champion. Not that this was really very surprising. As he explained to me over a cup of tea one day, she confided in him quite a lot, especially when there were tensions in her relationship with Raj Kapoor or when she was having trouble with her family. Probably he knew as much about her as anybody did. She was a Muslim by birth, as I must have realized from her name, and supported not only her mother but also her grown-up brothers, as well as a whole tribe of nieces and nephews. Though her brothers treated her very badly, even to the extent of beating her, she was extremely fond of her little nieces and nephews and was always buying things for them. She spent hardly anything on herself, he added, though privately I reflected that at some time or other she must have invested in quite a large quantity of white chiffon.

Be that as it may, she usually joined us at the coffee table only some time after our discussion had started, silently settling herself on the floor or on the settee beside Raj Kapoor with a smile of greeting for Rashk and myself. One day, however, I arrived to find her and Raj Kapoor bent over a tape-recorder. Apart from the pocket model with which Nebesky had recorded the recitals of a Tibetan bard this was the first time I had seen one and Raj Kapoor lost no time in showing me how it worked. It was a birthday present from Nargis, he told me proudly, and had cost two thousand rupees. Thereafter the tape-recorder was switched on for all our meetings and I believe Raj Kapoor also used it to record the lengthy monologues in which he was in the habit of indulging when alone. Probably the most interesting of our tape-recorded discussions related not to *Ajanta* but to a dream Raj Kapoor had had the night before. 'What do you think I dreamt last night, Reverend?' he demanded of me one day, as soon as I arrived. Of course I did not know, whereupon he proceeded to tell me how Jesus and the Buddha had been to see him, how one had sat on his right knee and one on his left, and how the three of them had had a long conversation. From the way in which he told me this I gathered that he took the dream to mean that Jesus and the Buddha had recognized him as their spiritual equal. This was not as surprising as it might seem. As I knew from my conversations with Rashk, Raj Kapoor was famous as a maker of 'social films', a social film being a film with a 'social message', usually of a vaguely left-wing kind. In these films he appeared in the role of the lovable and pathetic victim of social injustice who, after being made to suffer in various ways, eventually turns the tables on his oppressors and, in the course of so doing, delivers impassioned speeches on behalf of the poor and downtrodden. Apparently his best known scene was one in which, having pleaded not guilty to a charge of theft on the grounds that he was hungry, he proceeded to denounce the existing economic system at great length to a spellbound courtroom. Conveying the kind of message that they did, Raj Kapoor's films were extremely popular, not only in India but also, it was said, in the Soviet Union. Thus it was hardly surprising that he should regard his films as performing much the same function as the great religious teachers had performed of old and himself, therefore, as being the spiritual equal of those teachers. Another of our tape-recorded conversations related to literature. 'What do you think I did yesterday, Reverend?' he demanded of me on my arrival on this occasion. Again I did not know, whereupon he told me that he had actually *read a book*. From this I concluded that he was not a great reader, though later on Rashk told me that he did, in fact, read every day, but that he read only pornographic literature of the cheapest type. What he should really have said was that yesterday he had actually read a non-pornographic book.

Those of our meetings that did not take place in Raj Kapoor's private quarters at R. K. Studios took place at his own residence, which like the studios was situated at Chembur. Here I met his wife, his younger brother, his small son, his father, and various other members of the family, all of whom, it seemed, had been involved, were now involved, or were going to be involved, in the film industry. This was particularly true of his father, Prithviraj Kapoor, who had originally been a stage actor and, in fact, a leading figure in the movement for the revival of the Hindi theatre. With the virtual supersession of the stage by the screen, he had been forced to transfer his talents to the films and now generally took the part of king or demigod in the historical and mythological extravaganzas which were, if anything, even more popular with the cinema-going Indian public than were the social films. Though not nearly so famous as his son he was sufficiently well known and off the screen, at least, cut a far more impressive figure. Indeed, with his grizzled locks, regal bearing, sonorous voice, and carelessly draped *chaddar*, Prithviraj Kapoor looked every inch an actor of the old school. I also noticed that when he spoke to Raj Kapoor it was in a direct and authoritative yet, at the same time, essentially friendly and familiar manner which, I suspected, no one else could have adopted with him – certainly no one at R. K. Studios. Raj Kapoor, for his part, obviously stood very much in awe of his formidable parent, and in fact appeared quite diminished in his presence, the more especially since Prithviraj was the taller of the two by at least half a head.

Seeing Raj Kapoor as often as I did, and having so many opportunities of observing him at close quarters, I naturally tried to form an overall estimate of the character of the man. This was by no means an easy thing to do. Not only was it sometimes difficult for me to tell when the famous film star was acting and when he was not but, as I eventually realized, he did not always know this himself. In other words, he did not always know whether the feelings to which he gave such eloquent and even impassioned utterance were really his own feelings or were merely assumed for the occasion. So much was this the case, indeed, that there were times when I wondered if it might not be said of actors, as Pope said of women, that they were 'matter too soft a lasting mark to bear', and that most of them had, therefore, 'no characters at all'.[126] But this would probably have been going a little too far. In Raj Kapoor's case, at least, the actor was also producer and director, and in this latter capacity, so Rashk assured me, the Clark Gable of India was certainly not lacking in character. Intensely ambitious and of truly demonic energy, he demanded total loyalty from those who worked for him, in return for which he looked after them extremely well – so long as they remained working for him and showed no signs of wanting to leave for greener pastures elsewhere. If anyone actually did leave R. K. Films he took it very much to heart and might even turn quite nasty, with unfortunate consequences for the offender. Raj Kapoor was, in fact, an extremely vindictive person, Rashk added, besides being completely ruthless when it came to dealing with those who opposed him or who, whether intentionally or unintentionally, got in the way of his achieving his ambitions. In short, he was a dangerous man to tangle with, particularly as his popularity in the Soviet Union gave him entrée into the highest government circles and enabled him to pull all kinds of strings. Altogether it was not a very attractive picture, and one that I found difficult to reconcile with the impression I had formed of the film star in the course of our discussions. I was also left wondering whether Raj Kapoor the actor made use of Raj Kapoor the producer and director to achieve his purely artistic objectives or whether Raj Kapoor the producer and director used Raj Kapoor the actor to further his own very different aims. In the end I concluded that being, as he apparently was, both characterless and possessed of character, it was not really possible for me to form an overall estimate of Raj Kapoor without knowing him much better than I did and that he was, in fact, a quite complex person.

But if Raj Kapoor was a quite complex person Arjun Dev Rashk, on the other hand, was a relatively simple one and, therefore, much easier to get to know. Indeed, I had not been many days in Bombay before there sprang up between the swarthy young scriptwriter and myself a friendship that was to become quite independent of my connection with *Ajanta*. The main reason for this, apart from the fact that we happened to like each other, was a common interest in literature. As I soon learned, Rashk had started out as a poet – an Urdu poet. On discovering that there was, in his own words, 'no money in poetry', he had taken to writing scripts for Hindi films (an occupation he frankly regarded as a form of literary prostitution) and for the last two or three years had worked with Raj Kapoor, for whom he felt a strong but not uncritical admiration. An additional reason why a friendship had sprung up between Rashk and myself was the fact that we spent a lot of time together. In Sanchi Raj Kapoor had invited me to come to Bombay for a few days 'as the guest of R. K. Films', and even after my removal from the first class hotel to Ananda Vihara the guest of R. K. Films I most certainly was. Indeed, it was as though Rashk had not only been

Discussions for the film Ajanta *at Raj Kapoor's Bombay flat. Sangharakshita between Arjundev Rashk (left), and Raj Kapoor (right)*

instructed to escort me to Bombay and book me into a hotel but also instructed to keep me company, and look after me, for the whole of my stay in that city. It was Rashk who, nearly every day, collected me from the hotel or, after the first week, from Ananda Vihara, and drove me to R. K. Studios. It was Rashk who sat with me in restaurants and teashops discussing Buddhism, R. K. Films, Raj Kapoor, Nargis, the Bombay film industry, Indian politics, Mahatma Gandhi, sex, and the modern American novel. It was Rashk who accompanied me to the English bookshops in the Fort area and to the Prince of Wales Museum. It was Rashk who took me home with him to his flat in Khar to sample his wife's cooking. Finally, it was Rashk who, when I had been in Bombay for nearly three weeks, drove me all the way to Deolali for my second reunion with Lama Govinda and Li Gotami.

A few days before that, however, I had my first meeting with a man who, while hardly less known than Raj Kapoor, was in many ways his complete antithesis. This was Dr B. R. Ambedkar, the great Scheduled Caste leader, to whom I had written in June 1950 expressing my appreciation of his article on 'The Buddha and the Future of His Religion',[127] and telling him about the formation of the YMBA, and from whom I had received a friendly and encouraging reply. Since then no communication had passed between us, neither had we met. Prior to my leaving Calcutta I had, indeed, hoped that he would be in Sanchi for the re-enshrinement of the Sacred Relics and that it would be possible for us to have a talk, but in the event my hopes were dashed. The Scheduled Caste leader was not there. Quite possibly he had not even been invited to take part in the celebrations, for though I did not know it at the time he was at loggerheads with the government and Devapriyaji may well have thought that to have Ambedkar, who was nothing if not outspoken, occupying the same platform as Pandit Nehru and Dr Radhakrishnan, would be to invite almost certain trouble. Be that as it may, I had not been much more than a week in Bombay when I came to know, probably from an item in the newspapers, that Ambedkar was in the city, and at once decided to go and see him. As the telephone directory (I think) informed me, he lived at Dadar, a predominantly working-class district in the very heart of Bombay, and it was for Dadar that, on a day when I had no meeting with Raj Kapoor, I accordingly set out.

On my arrival at 'Rajgriha', the sizeable residence Ambedkar had built for himself ten or fifteen years earlier, I was shown into a large, rather sparsely furnished apartment that evidently served as both office and reception room. Here there were a number of people, including the ten or twelve members of what appeared to be a deputation, the leaders of which nervously clasped between them an enormous marigold-and-tinsel garland. Having dealt with the deputation, which seemed to have incurred his displeasure in some way, the grim-faced, heavily built man in the loosely fitting Western-style suit took his place at the desk before which, on my arrival, he had caused me to be seated. Like Raj Kapoor Ambedkar had a question, but unlike Raj Kapoor he put it without preamble and without the slightest attempt at charm. 'Why does your Maha Bodhi Society have a Bengali Brahmin for its president?' he demanded belligerently. It was not my Maha Bodhi Society, I retorted. I did what I could to help it, since it was the premier Buddhist organization in India, but I was not actually a member of the Society and was no more happy that it should have a Bengali Brahmin for its president than he himself appeared to be. (The Brahmin in question was Dr Shyamaprasad Mookerjee, who besides being the President of the Maha Bodhi Society was a former President of the Hindu Mahasabha, a right-wing Caste Hindu organization, and a leading opponent of Ambedkar's Hindu Code Bill.) My explanation having satisfied the Scheduled Caste leader, it was not long before conversation turned to Buddhism. Probably with his article on 'The Buddha and the Future of His Religion' in mind, I asked him whether he thought that Buddhism had a future in India. His answer to the question was an indirect one. '*I* have no future in India!' he exclaimed bitterly, his face darkening with something akin to despair. The fact was that at the time of our meeting Ambedkar's political career was more or less in ruins and his formidable energies had yet to be fully focused, as subsequently they were, on the conversion of his millions of Untouchable followers to Buddhism. It must have been one of the blackest periods of his life. I did not know this, of course, any more than I then realized the significance of our meeting, which was not only to be followed by further meetings but which, four years later, resulted in my coming into close personal contact with tens of thousands of ex-Untouchable Buddhists – a development that profoundly influenced the course of my life and work. Nonetheless, I was glad to have met Ambedkar, and glad I had had the opportunity of making clear to him where I stood as regards the Maha Bodhi Society and what I thought of that organization's having a Bengali Brahmin for its president.

But though I did not realize the significance of my meeting with Ambedkar, and indeed could not have realized it at the time, I was very much aware of the significance of my second reunion with Lama Govinda and Li Gotami. Kindred spirits that we were, the week that I would be spending with them in their new home would have the effect of strengthening our tripartite friendship and further defining what it was in our attitude to Buddhism that united us to one another and divided us from such as Tun Hla Oung and the militant Theravādins of Ceylon. On our way out of Bombay Rashk and I stopped off at Raj Kapoor's residence, so that I could bid the Clark Gable of India farewell, after which it was not long before we were on the dusty, tree-lined highway and heading for Deolali as fast as bullock carts and vagrant curs would permit. It was a glorious day, all blue skies and sunshine, and despite the stifling heat of the car I felt extremely happy, even jubilant. Behind me was a successful visit to Bombay, and now that it was over I could look forward to what would, I hoped, be a still more successful visit to Deolali. Moreover, on my bidding him farewell Raj Kapoor had not only thanked me, in his most ingratiating manner, for having helped with the planning of *Ajanta*; he had also handed me an envelope that proved to contain five crisp new one hundred rupee notes. This meant that my immediate financial problems were solved, and that I did not have to wonder how I was going to manage on my return to Kalimpong.

Barnes High School, Deolali, seemed to be situated miles from the cantonment, while the Gate Lodge itself, into which Lama Govinda and Li Gotami had moved some months earlier, seemed to be situated miles from the school. A grey stone building obviously dating from the time of the Raj, it straddled the road with what could only be described as an air of defiance. As Rashk and I drew up in its shadow, four or five hours after leaving Chembur, a door at the foot of one of its flanking towers flew open and Lama Govinda and Li Gotami issued forth to greet us and lead us upstairs to the range of spacious rooms that they occupied immediately above the road. Rashk was, I could see, a little taken aback by my two friends' colourful and exotic appearance, as it must have seemed to Indian eyes, and obviously did not know quite what to make of them at first; but so warm and friendly was their treatment of him that by the end of the meal which, at their insistence, he stayed and shared, the swarthy young scriptwriter was very much prepossessed in their favour. Before he left it was agreed between us that he should come and collect me in a week's time and drive me back to Bombay, whence I would make my way to Kalimpong. As soon as he had gone my hosts and I took up the thread of the talk we had been obliged to cut short in Sanchi and before long were deep in discussion. It was a discussion that not only lasted far into the night but continued, during the days that followed, almost without interruption. The only real interruptions, in fact, were when either Lama Govinda or Li Gotami had to go and take a class at Barnes High School.

As in Kalimpong and Ghoom, we ranged over practically the whole field of Buddhist life and thought, with particular reference to the relation between Buddhism and the spiritual life, on the one hand, and literature and the fine arts on the other. But though we ranged so widely there was one topic to which both Lama Govinda and Li Gotami came back again and again and which they both seemed, in fact, to have very much in mind. This was the topic of the Tsaparang expedition, the journey they had made in 1948–9 to the ruined temples of the former capital of Western Tibet. During the week that he and Li Gotami had spent with me in Kalimpong Lama Govinda had, of course, given a talk on the Tsaparang expedition, a talk he had illustrated by showing a number of his own paintings and sketches, many of them executed on the spot. Li Gotami, for her part, had shown the tracings she had made of frescoes depicting the life of the Buddha, tracings from which she hoped to produce copies of the frescoes, while Lama Govinda had given a running commentary on the different episodes in the Buddha's career that the frescoes depicted. Li herself had given neither talk nor commentary, being apparently averse to speaking in public; but she now made up for this by giving me *her* account of the Tsaparang expedition, dwelling in characteristically lively and entertaining fashion on difficulties at which Govinda had only hinted or of which he had made no mention – difficulties at which, in retrospect, both she and he could laugh, but which had been very serious at the time. One of their biggest difficulties, I gathered, was that of dealing with sullen, uncooperative porters and drunken, unreliable guides. The task of dealing with them had increasingly devolved upon Li herself, who spoke fluent bazaar Hindi and who, in the course of the journey, managed to pick up enough colloquial Tibetan for practical purposes – enough, that is, to give orders and bestow abuse. (Lama Govinda's Hindi was rudimentary, despite his long residence in India, and though he could read Tibetan religious texts he was unable to speak the language, as Dawa in fact had discovered in Kalimpong.) After hearing Li's vivid description of how, week after week, she had struggled with the logistics of the expedition, supervising the loading and unloading of mules and yaks, and organizing the crossing of rivers, I could not forbear asking 'But what did Lama Govinda do?' 'Oh, *he* did the cooking,' she replied, shrieking with laughter at the recollection as the lama himself smiled.

The reply did not surprise me. I had already noticed that at Deolali itself it was Govinda who did the cooking, while Li made the beds and swept the floor. He was quite a good cook, though as he explained to me one morning he never spent more than half an hour in the actual preparation of a meal. Having chopped his vegetables and washed his rice and lentils he popped them into the steam cooker and left them to boil while he carried on writing or painting. Long practice had, he assured me, enabled him to calculate exactly how much time was needed to cook a particular meal, so that lunch or dinner was always ready precisely when he and Li wanted to have it. As he explained all this to me, and indeed showed me just how he distributed the vegetables, rice, and lentils among the aluminium containers, and how he got the charcoal fire going in the little burner, I was reminded of those two solitary weeks at the Raipur Ashram when I myself had cooked with the help of a patent steam cooker – weeks during which my two friends were seeking permission to enter Western Tibet.[128] Li Gotami, by her own laughing admission, knew next to nothing about cooking. The Parsee family into which she had been born was a wealthy one, she had grown up surrounded by servants, and until her marriage to Lama Govinda she had had to make hardly so much as a cup of tea herself. (There had been a previous marriage, to a prominent Bombay lawyer and art critic, but of this she made no mention, either then or at any other time, and I learned about it only years later, after coming to know one of her Petit cousins.) Thus it was Govinda who did the cooking, and Li who made the beds and swept the floor. In their relationship there was, indeed, a certain reversal of the usual roles, with Li sometimes taking the more active, masculine role, and Govinda the more passive, feminine one. This may well have had something to do with the fact that Li was twenty years younger than her husband, whose student she had once been, and was possessed of an abundance of natural vigour. Whatever the explanation, there seemed to be little doubt that, on the mundane level at least, she had been the principal driving force behind the Tsaparang expedition, and that without her to cajole and bully on his behalf the gentle, retiring lama would never have seen Lake Manasarova and Mount Kailas, never have seen the Valley of the Moon Castle, never have seen the frescoes of Tholing and Tsaparang, and in all probability would never have written *The Way of the White Clouds*.

But often as Li might take the masculine role, she was by no means devoid of feminine qualities. On the Tsaparang expedition itself there had been occasions when these were very much in evidence. Some of the frescoes of which she wanted to make tracings were situated high up on the wall, just below the ceiling. In order to get at them she had to sit perched on a pile of stones that she and Lama Govinda dismantled and rebuilt at a slightly different spot each morning. It was bitterly cold. One day, Govinda recalled, he had looked up from his own work to see that Li was so cold and miserable that she was crying, and that her tears were actually freezing before they had time to reach the ground. Such was the vividness of his description that in my mind's eye I could see the unhappy Li perched aloft on her pile of stones like some latter-day female Stylites and weeping diamonds. Li laughed as Govinda told the story, but I noticed that there were tears in her eyes, as if she was re-experiencing rather than just recollecting the tribulations she had had to undergo in order to make her tracings. Oh yes, she exclaimed, dashing a stray drop of moisture from her cheek, her tears really had frozen. But that was not the worst of it. The Chinese ink she had been using to make the tracings had also frozen and she had had to keep on warming the tip of her brush with her breath.

In view of the enormous effort that had gone into the making of them, as well as on account of their intrinsic value to lovers of Buddhist art, it was not surprising that Li Gotami should be quite protective towards her tracings, as I had indeed observed in Kalimpong. She was even more protective towards the copies of the original frescoes on which she had been working for the last year or more, but especially after Lama Govinda and herself had settled in Deolali. Only one of these copies was actually finished – though there were two others on which she was working – and when I had been with them for two or three days Govinda prevailed upon her to show it to me, which with many protestations of its inadequacy she eventually did. Approximately three feet by two, which were the dimensions of the original fresco panel, it depicted the Buddha's victory over the hosts of Māra, immediately prior to his attainment of Supreme Enlightenment, and was remarkable for both richness of colour and delicacy of detail. As Govinda explained, the art of Tsaparang could be regarded as constituting a distinct stage in the evolution of Buddhist art, a stage that was intermediate between the latest frescoes of Ajanta and the earliest frescoes and painted scrolls of Tibet proper. The discovery of Tsaparang had, in fact, made possible the writing of a missing chapter in the history of Buddhist art and its importance could hardly be overestimated.

Li having shown me her first finished fresco-copy, and received my warm congratulations on what she had so far done and my strong encouragement to produce copies of all the frescoes of which she had made tracings (in the event she succeeded in producing only three altogether), it was Govinda's turn to show me the originals of what he called his 'cosmic abstracts' or 'meditation pictures'. I was already familiar with these, having seen reproductions of at least some of them in his little book on art and meditation (afterwards incorporated into *Creative Meditation and Multi-Dimensional Consciousness*).[129] But no reproduction could do justice to the glowing hues of the colour drawings he now carefully drew out from beneath their sheets of protective tissue paper. They were executed in oil pastels, a medium with which I was then unacquainted but which seemed to be a favourite one with Govinda. I must have commented on the fact, for he proceeded to explain how simple and easy oil pastels were to use and how convenient they were when one had no permanent studio and was forever on the move. Moreover, with oil pastels it was possible to obtain effects that could not be obtained with either oil paints or water colours. Unfortunately, they were effects that could not be reproduced by any mechanical means. None of the printers he had dealt with had been able to achieve more than an approximation to the colour values of his cosmic abstracts and other oil pastel drawings. Some had been unable to achieve even an approximation.

Talk about printers must have led to talk about publishers and talk about publishers must in its turn have led to talk about editors, especially magazine editors, for Lama Govinda proceeded to tell me about an unpleasant interview which he and Li had recently had, in Bombay, with the editor of the *Illustrated Weekly of India*. As I already knew, it was the *Illustrated Weekly of India* that had sponsored the Tsaparang expedition and they had agreed to sponsor it because, as Lama Govinda had explained to Mr Mandy at the time, the long-deserted temples of Western Tibet were unknown to modern scholarship, so that in visiting Tsaparang, and documenting its artistic treasures, he and Li Gotami would be doing something that had not been done before. They would, in effect, be discovering Tsaparang – discovering it for renascent India and for the world. Shortly before our reunion in Sanchi, however, Mr Mandy had summoned them to his office and virtually accused Lama Govinda of having misled him and obtained the sponsorship of the *Illustrated* on false pretences. The temples of Western Tibet had *not* been unknown to modern scholarship, and he and Li

Gotami had *not* done something that had not been done before. They had *not* discovered Tsaparang. Professor Tucci of Rome had discovered it. Professor Tucci, as he had recently learned, had led an expedition to Tsaparang a decade or more before they had done. He had visited the very temples that they had visited, had photographed the images and frescoes there, and had published the results of his researches in a book.[130] The news – and the accusation – had shocked and distressed Govinda and, as I could see from the way he spoke of the matter, distressed him still. It had not been difficult to convince Mandy that he had not intended to mislead him and that – strange as it might seem – he had been completely unaware of the fact of Tucci's having visited Tsaparang, but it distressed him to think that he had misled him even unintentionally. Moreover, it had not been possible to convince Mandy that he had not intended to mislead him without admitting that he was less than well informed in a field in which he had represented himself as being an authority. In order to salvage his credibility as a man he had had to sacrifice his reputation as a scholar. This too had distressed him, and distressed him still. But he was also puzzled. How could he *not have known that* Tucci had visited Tsaparang? he exclaimed, with more feeling than I had yet seen him exhibit. He simply could not understand it. He could only assume that owing to his reclusive existence (not to mention his internment) he had, over the years, become cut off from the international scholarly community to a greater extent than he had realized and that much was happening, in the way of exploration and publication, of which he had no knowledge.

Naturally I sympathized with Govinda. I sympathized with his distress at Mandy's accusation and at the harm that had been done (not permanently, I hoped) to his scholarly reputation. I also understood his puzzlement and sympathized with the predicament in which he found himself – the predicament of the artist-scholar who wished to live as a recluse but who, at the same time, wanted to know what was happening in the world, at least within the sphere of his own special interests. His predicament was, in a way, my own. Living in Kalimpong as I did I had cut myself off from the various cultural and religious movements then in progress in Western Europe – movements with which, had I returned to Britain after the war, instead of becoming a homeless wanderer in India, I might well have become involved. I had even cut myself off from the nascent British Buddhist movement. But I had no regrets, any more than Govinda really had. A reclusive existence, whether in Deolali or in Kalimpong, might indeed have its disadvantages, but the German artist-scholar and the English poet-monk were agreed that those disadvantages were far outweighed by the advantages.

Li Gotami must have been out when Lama Govinda told me about their interview with the editor of the *Illustrated Weekly of India*. She must have been out, either teaching at Barnes High School or shopping in the cantonment bazaar, because Govinda was able to tell me about the interview without being interrupted. When the three of us had been together in Kalimpong and Ghoom, and in Sanchi, the lively, pugnacious little Parsee woman must have been on her best behaviour, so to speak, for as far as I could remember she had never interrupted her husband while he was talking. In Deolali it was quite another story. Probably because she now knew me better, and felt less inhibited by my presence, she interrupted and contradicted the poor lama incessantly, this apparently being her normal way of relating to him. If he happened to recall how they had gone somewhere, or seen somebody, on a Thursday, she would be sure to interrupt him in mid-sentence with, 'No, it was on a Wednesday! I'm sure it was on a Wednesday!' 'No, darling,' he would reply, sometimes raising his hand in mild remonstrance, 'it was on a *Thursday*. It must have been on a Thursday because ...' And he would proceed to remind her that the visit or meeting in question had taken place under such and such circumstances and that, the circumstances being as they were, it *must* have taken place on a Thursday and could not possibly have taken place on a Wednesday. Sometimes it took Govinda several minutes to convince his argumentative helpmeet that he was right and she wrong, as was invariably the case. Once he had convinced her, she would lapse into silence and he would resume his discourse – until the next interruption. Li seemed not to mind being continually proved wrong in this way. For his part, Lama Govinda seemed not to mind her constant interruptions, and corrected her with his usual combination of firmness and gentleness. I noticed, though, that on such occasions he invariably addressed her as 'darling', as if this was as near as he could get to expressing his irritation. I also noticed, as I think I had noticed in Kalimpong, that Li usually addressed him as what sounded like 'Ken'. What did this mean? Was Ken the diminutive of Kenneth, in which case by what freak of feminine fancy had Li chosen so to denominate her spouse? Or perhaps it was not Ken but 'Khen', *khenpo* being the Tibetan word for abbot, though in that case Govinda would have been abbot of a very small cenobium indeed, consisting of himself and Li and the Gate Lodge cat. However, I did not think it proper to ask Li why she addressed Govinda as Ken (or Khen), either then or at any of my subsequent meetings with them. It was, perhaps, a delicate question, of the kind with which I was so familiar in Kalimpong, and the mystery remained unsolved.

Whatever mystery there may have been about the way in which Li Gotami addressed Lama Govinda, there was no mystery about the way in which she addressed me. She addressed me simply as 'Rakshita' or 'Rakshitaji'. (Govinda never permitted himself to shorten my monastic name in this manner, either then or afterwards.) Like the freedom with which she now interrupted her husband in my presence, her addressing me as Rakshita was no doubt due to the fact that she now knew me better. Since she knew me better she could speak more freely, and since she could speak more freely it was not surprising that one afternoon, when she was perhaps tired of the doctrinal discussions in which Govinda and I tended to become involved, she should have started talking about her schooldays in England. She had been educated at Roedean, the well-known public school for girls near Brighton, and had enjoyed her time there immensely. Indeed from what she said it was clear that the young Li Gotami must have been a 'jolly hockey sticks' sort of girl and extremely popular. Before her arrival, she related with hoots of laughter, the other girls had been told that a little Indian princess was coming to study with them. Though Li came from a wealthy family, and had an uncle who had been knighted, she was certainly not a princess, and the girls had been quite disappointed. Nonetheless, they made a great fuss of her and she soon felt at home among them.

Having been educated at Roedean Li was in some ways quite Westernized, even anglicized. Govinda, on the other hand, after twenty years of study and teaching at Santiniketan and Sarnath, Patna and Ghoom, was quite 'orientalized', even Indianized, though not so much in his personal habits as in respect of his philosophical outlook and religious beliefs. As for myself, I had spent only six years in India, two of them as a wandering ascetic, but I was already quite Indianized, in some ways perhaps to a greater extent than Govinda. Thus each of us represented a combination, in varying proportions, of the Eastern and the Western, India and Europe. Each of us had created – was in process of creating – his or her personal synthesis of modern culture and ancient spiritual tradition. As such we had a great deal in common, even apart from our common allegiance to Buddhism. It was therefore not surprising that the week I spent with Lama Govinda and Li Gotami in Deolali should have passed quickly, at least for me, and that by the time Rashk came to collect me I should have felt that our tripartite friendship was stronger than ever.

21

A FRESH BEGINNING

Almost the first thing I heard, on my return to Kalimpong towards the end of December, was that the missionaries – Catholic and Protestant alike – were extremely angry with me. They had good reason to be angry. During my stay in Calcutta I had not been so deeply immersed in the life and work of Dharmapala as to forget about the three young men, two Buddhist and one Hindu, who had been subjected to tremendous pressure to become Christians or to forget my resolve to do something about checking what I called 'conversion through pregnancy'. Devapriyaji, Dr Soft, and other friends whom I consulted were naturally horrified by my story, though hardly surprised, and it was agreed that the best thing I could do was to write to the newspapers exposing the evil. This I accordingly did, and shortly before my departure for Sanchi with the Sacred Relics a letter headed 'Conversion through Pregnancy' appeared over my signature in the correspondence columns of at least one of the leading English-language Calcutta dailies. Great was the indignation – not to say the fury – of the missionaries, not only in Kalimpong but also, as I subsequently learned, throughout north-east India, where the daily in question mainly circulated. But there was nothing any of them could do against me, at least not openly, and of course no denial of the allegations I had made was ever forthcoming. Whether the missionaries concluded that 'conversion through pregnancy' was more trouble than it was worth I never knew, but the fact was that there were no more cases like those of Karma Tsering, Tashi Gompu, and the wretched Dil

Bahadur, even though other unsavoury methods of conversion continued to be rife in Kalimpong, especially when the influx of Tibetan refugees into the town after the 1959 Lhasa uprising gave the missionaries of all denominations the opportunity for which they had been praying.

The checking of 'conversion through pregnancy' was not the only matter about which I had been concerned in Calcutta or about which I consulted Devapriyaji, Dr Soft, and other friends at the Maha Bodhi Society, nor was it the most important. I also consulted them about whether the Governing Body would be prepared to help me in my efforts to work for Buddhism in Kalimpong by giving regular financial support to the YMBA. They were unanimous that it probably would be – on one condition. The YMBA would have to affiliate itself to the Maha Bodhi Society as a branch. Devapriyaji, in particular, was very much in favour of such affiliation. There were definite advantages attached to being part of an old-established, internationally known Buddhist organization like the Maha Bodhi Society, and as *bhikṣu*-in-charge of the Kalimpong branch I would naturally have much the same freedom of action as before. Besides, he added, there were not many sincere Buddhist workers in India and they should work together rather than separately. In the end I applied for affiliation to the Society, the Governing Body accepted the application, and the Young Men's Buddhist Association (India) became the Kalimpong branch of the Maha Bodhi Society. Two months earlier, at the time of my arrival in Calcutta, I would not have been prepared to sacrifice the independence of the YMBA in this way, even for the sake of a grant many times bigger than the fifty rupees a month the Governing Body agreed to give the new branch. But since then I had discovered Dharmapala, and the discovery of Dharmapala had led to the discovery of the Maha Bodhi Society – not the corrupt and degenerate Maha Bodhi Society of Jinaratana and his toadies but the vibrant, idealistic Buddhist organization that had existed in Dharmapala's own lifetime and that, with Devapriyaji back at the headquarters building, might exist again. It was to *this* Maha Bodhi Society – the *real* Maha Bodhi Society – that, in my own mind at least, I had affiliated the YMBA. It was *this* Maha Bodhi Society that, as *bhikṣu*-in-charge of one of its branches, I represented, even though I never actually joined the Society as a member and never took so much as a rupee from it for my personal needs.

But whichever Maha Bodhi Society it was to which I had affiliated the YMBA, I had affiliated it without consulting our members, and it would not have been surprising if they had not been particularly pleased to wake up one morning, so to speak, to find that instead of being members of the YMBA (India) they were members of the Kalimpong branch of the Maha Bodhi Society. Fortunately this did not turn out to be the case. Lachuman, Dawa, and the other more active members to whom, in the course of the next few weeks, I spoke about the 'reorganization of our activities' as I called it, were inclined to welcome the change rather than otherwise. In any case, to such an extent were our members behind with their subscriptions, and so little had the Activities Committee done for so long, that it was less a matter of the YMBA (India) becoming the Kalimpong branch of the Maha Bodhi Society as of simply setting up a branch of the Society in the town, with myself and my work for Buddhism providing an element of continuity.

The only person who was *not* inclined to welcome the change was Joe. At the time of my return to Kalimpong the prickly *upāsaka* was away in Lucknow, having gone there to collect the last of his belongings, since he had recently moved to a spacious upstairs flat in the Development Area, not far from the bungalow once occupied by Thubden Tendzin and his companion Thubden Shedub. But although I could not see Joe I certainly heard a lot about him. According to René Nebesky, who came with his latest article on Tibet for me to correct and who was about to return to Europe, during my absence he had been running down the Western Buddhist Order, and Robert Stuart Clifton in particular, to all and sundry. Though I had my own reservations with regard to the Order I was annoyed that Joe, who knew nothing about it, should have been so foolish as to criticize it to people whom it in no way concerned and who, in fact, were unaware of its existence. The only explanation I could think of was that Clifton was an American and Joe, I knew, had a pathological hatred of America and Americans, as well as of Winston Churchill – a hatred to which he frequently gave expression in the most vitriolic terms. Dawa, who had just started working for the Central Intelligence Bureau as a translator, also had something to report. Mr Cann had taken a Tibetan boy from the bazaar to live with him, he told me, with a worried look. The boy was of *very* bad character, and he was at a loss to understand how a respectable gentleman like Mr Cann could have taken a boy of that type to live with him. He *must* have known what he was like. Naturally I wanted to know what Dawa meant by saying that the boy was of bad character. Was he a thief? But the question seemed to embarrass my former student and he would say no more.

A week later Joe was back in Kalimpong, and one afternoon I went to see him in his new abode, taking with me Sachin, Jungi, and Dawa, who had arrived at the Hermitage together a little earlier. We found the Chairman of the former Activities Committee busy decorating. He was not particularly pleased to see us and gave us tea with a very ill grace, glaring at us the while in his most forbidding manner. It was not the best time to speak to him about the reorganization of our activities, but I did so nonetheless. He responded with a marked lack of enthusiasm, and before long was making all kinds of cutting remarks about the YMBA, about the Maha Bodhi Society, and about headstrong, inexperienced young monks who were so foolish as to think they could change the world. The message seemed to be that while I was fully entitled to waste my time working for Buddhism, if that was what I wanted to do, I should not expect older, more sensible people to waste theirs. On my return to the Hermitage with my three young friends I was silent and gloomy, some of Joe's remarks having depressed me, and the following morning, feeling that no one understood me or sympathized with what I was trying to achieve, and that I had no earthly refuge, I composed a poem of seven eight-line stanzas entitled 'Taking Refuge in the Buddha'. When I transcribed the poem into my poetry notebook I placed at its head, by way of a motto, the words *N'atthi me saraṇaṃ aññaṃ, Buddho me saraṇaṃ varaṃ*, 'For me there is no other refuge, the Buddha is the supreme refuge' – the words being taken from the Pāli *Tiratana Vandanā* or 'Salutation to the Three Jewels', which I recited each morning before meditating.[131]

By this time I had been back in Kalimpong for more than a month and had spoken to most of our members, both active and inactive, about the YMBA's affiliation to the Maha Bodhi Society and about my plans for the future. On the full-moon day of Māgha,[132] therefore, two or three days after my encounter with Joe, there was held at the Hermitage not just the usual full-moon day celebration but the first general meeting of the Kalimpong branch of the Maha Bodhi Society. I did not expect Joe to come, but he in fact turned up early. Fortunately he was in a more positive mood, and I was able to give him an account of my experiences down in the plains. Someone must have mentioned the Tibetan boy, for the temperamental *upāsaka*, who was more accustomed to handing out criticism rather than receiving it, hastened to explain that he had taken the boy to live with him at the insistence of my old Khampa student Aggen Chototsang, who had in fact misinformed him about the young wretch. In what the misinformation consisted Joe did not say, and we talked of other things until it was time to repair to the shrine-room. A week or two later, however, he came to see me accompanied by the young wretch in question. Fifteen or sixteen years old, he was handsome in a ravaged sort of way and kept making eyes at me behind Joe's back.

The octagonal shrine-room, where Lama Govinda's Buddha image presided with hand raised in blessing, had been built as a summer house and it was not easy to squeeze everybody in for the puja and the short sermon, which as usual comprised, between them, the principal part of our full-moon day celebration. Latecomers had either to sit on the front steps or look in on the proceedings through the windows. Someone had brought along a harmonium, and after I had delivered my sermon Sachin and others sang to its not (to my ears) very pleasing accompaniment the melodious devotional songs that were so popular with religious-minded Nepalis, both Buddhist and Hindu, and which, even when sung by non-professionals, could bring tears to the eyes and a lump to the throat. Whether there were still tears in anyone's eyes when, emerging from the shrine-room, we made our way through the coolness and silence of the garden back to the Hermitage proper for our meeting, I cannot say, but certainly everyone seemed to be in an exalted mood, the meeting passed off smoothly, and a new – a Maha Bodhi Society – committee was elected, with Joe overcoming his lack of enthusiasm sufficiently to allow himself to be made an office-bearer. The reorganization of our activities had received the seal of general approval. A fresh beginning had been made.

Not that the reorganization was complete or indeed needed to be complete, or that a fresh beginning involved any real breach with the past. Members continued to make use of the games room, as well as of the library and reading room (which was given a government grant after a visit from a sympathetic inspector), students and others continued to come for private tuition, and visitors continued to turn up at all hours of the day and night, from Tibetan lamas to English professors, and from itinerant Indian magicians to Swiss journalists and German artists. The principal difference, now that we were a branch of the Maha Bodhi

Society, was that membership was no longer confined to young men and that we were taken more seriously by the older generation of local – mainly non-Tibetan – Buddhists and sympathizers with Buddhism, some of whom had their own connections with the Society and respected it as the leading Buddhist organization of India. We were also better off financially. Fifty rupees was not a large sum (it did not even cover the rent), but it came regularly and we could rely on it, and I hoped I would be able to persuade the Governing Body to increase it before long.

The fact that we had become a branch of the Maha Bodhi Society, and that I was *bhikṣu*-in-charge, made little or no difference to the pattern of my own life. It was more like the weaving in of an additional thread – a thread consisting mainly of the accounts and report of activities that had to be submitted to the Governing Body each month. Besides carrying on with my meditations and studies, I continued to entertain visitors, to see friends, to talk to enquirers about Buddhism, and to keep in touch with an ever-expanding circle of correspondents, some of whom had been writing to me since the early days of *Stepping-Stones*. The activity that took up the biggest slice of my time, however, was that of giving private tuition. As at most other periods, my students fell into two more or less distinct groups. There were those who came and took private tuition in English from me simply because they wanted to learn the language for business or social purposes, and there were those who came and took private tuition in English, or English literature, or logic, or rhetoric and prosody, as the case might be, in order that they could be sure of passing their school or college examinations in those subjects. The first group consisted mainly of Newar traders and Tibetan government officials (Aggen was now taking tuition from Joe). They came once a week and paid, or were supposed to pay, a small monthly fee. The second group consisted of school and college students, some of whom had studied with me, on and off, ever since the days of the YMBA tutorial classes at the Dharmodaya Vihara. They came several times a week, even daily, and did not have to pay anything.

One of those who came and took private tuition in English from me simply because he wanted to learn the language (or improve his knowledge of it) was Mr Bhumiveda. Plump and bespectacled, and with a gold-toothed smile, Mr Bhumiveda was neither a Newar trader nor a Tibetan government official but an elderly Thai who had left Thailand in a hurry for political reasons and was now staying at the Dharmodaya

Vihara. He did not come and take tuition with me alone. With him came the angry-looking Newar monk who had thrown me – and the YMBA – out of the Dharmodaya Vihara two years ago. Since his ostensible reason for throwing me out was my failure to pay him the hundred rupees a month for my room that he was demanding, Aniruddha could hardly have expected me to give him free tuition, and when he and Mr Bhumiveda came and announced that they wanted to study with me he indeed made it clear that his companion would be paying the tuition fees of both monk and layman. I at once agreed to teach them. In fact I was glad that Aniruddha and I were now on friendlier terms. At the same time I found it difficult to understand how, having treated me so badly, he could have the effrontery to ask me to teach him, even for a consideration – especially in the absence of any word of explanation or apology for his past behaviour. Eventually I concluded that for a person of his temperament even quite violent quarrels were nothing out of the ordinary, that he forgot them no less easily than he entered into them, and that even when making life at the vihara intolerable for me he had not, in all probability, wished me any real harm.

Aniruddha was not the only monk who studied with me. There was also Jibananda, the smiling young *śrāmaṇera* whom I had met in Calcutta and who, shortly after my return to Kalimpong, came and joined me at the Hermitage. Besides helping him improve his English, I taught him some basic Dharma, taking Dr Conze's *Buddhism: Its Essence and Development* as a text book, and introduced him to the practice of meditation. Unfortunately he was not happy in Kalimpong. A Bengali by birth, from the Barua community, he missed his Bengali friends and his Bengali fish diet, and left after staying only two months. I was sorry to see him go, since he was quiet and well behaved and I had hoped to train him up as my assistant. His departure left me with only one live-in student to teach. This was Man Bahadur, the diminutive young Nepali who had succeeded Ang Tsering as my cook bearer when the latter, having served me faithfully for a year and accumulated a small capital, left to set himself up in business as a pig breeder. Man Bahadur's most noticeable feature was his neck, which was of extraordinary length and gave his head the appearance of being set on a stalk. Otherwise he was unremarkable enough, cooked moderately well, sulked when reprimanded, and took English lessons from me last thing at night – no doubt with a view to getting a better paid job elsewhere later on.

If the giving of private tuition took up the biggest slice of my time, then by far the biggest share in that slice went to Sachin, Jungi, and Dawa, but especially to Sachin, who was now back in Kalimpong after an abortive attempt to do intermediate science in Darjeeling. My young Nepali friend had not wanted to do science, his interests being entirely literary, but his father, the jovial and popular Ravi Das Singh, was determined that his handsome and intelligent elder son should follow in the paternal footsteps and become a doctor, and to Darjeeling Sachin had accordingly gone, there being no science college in Kalimpong. Not surprisingly, he did not do well. In fact he did very badly – so badly that eventually his father relented and allowed him to return home and do intermediate arts at the local mission college. Being unwilling to lose the academic years he had spent doing science, he applied for permission to sit the IA examination the following year, but this the college authorities refused to allow. It was against Calcutta University rules, the principal told him firmly. I therefore wrote to Dr Snehamoy Datta, the Registrar of the University, whom I had come to know in Calcutta in his capacity as one of the editors of the Maha Bodhi Society's Diamond Jubilee Souvenir, explaining what had happened and asking if the rules in question could be waived in Sachin's case. Though friendly and sympathetic, Dr Datta's reply was unequivocal: the rules could not be waived. I then tried another tack. Could Sachin sit the IA examination next year as a non-collegiate candidate? But this also proved to be out of the question in the end, and as a last resort I wrote to the former Vice-Chancellor of the University, Dr Syama Prasad Mookerjee, who was also the President of the Maha Bodhi Society, appealing for his help.

All this took time. In fact I was in correspondence with Dr Datta until mid-June, since the question of who could and who could not sit the university examinations as a non-collegiate candidate required a good deal of sorting out. Meanwhile, Sachin attended college and took private tuition from me in English and logic, generally coming once a day in term time and twice a day during holidays, besides frequently dropping in at the Hermitage outside study hours for a chat or a game of ping-pong. Tuition in English meant tuition in English literature, especially as represented by the IA prose and poetry selections, both of which had obviously been compiled decades ago by someone whose preference was for the traditional rather than the experimental and for the romantic rather than the classical. Thus the prose selections included essays by Leigh Hunt and J. A. Froude, while the poetry selections featured such poems as Wordsworth's 'Immortality Ode', Keats's 'Ode to a Nightingale', and Shelley's 'Ode to the West Wind' and 'To Night', all of which I had read so many times since my rapturous first encounters with them in far away Tooting that I could repeat whole chunks of them by heart. Now, ten or fifteen years later, I was studying those same poems in the foothills of the eastern Himalayas, in the seclusion of a semi-derelict wooden bungalow set amid ornamental trees. I was studying them in the company of a gifted young Nepali who loved poetry no less than I did and whom I had promised, at the beginning of the year, to help obtain a good knowledge of English literature.

We studied each poem word by word and line by line, appreciating the appropriateness of an adjective and exploring the implications of a metaphor or simile, yet trying at the same time not to lose sight of the poem as a whole. Nor was that all. Whether it was a poem by Wordsworth, or Keats, or Shelley, or any other poet, as winter gave way to spring and bamboo orchids were succeeded, in the garden of the Hermitage, by camellias and gardenias, Sachin and I went through each poem not once but many times and I dictated him not paraphrases – one cannot really paraphrase a poem – but extensive critical notes. The greater the number of times we went through a poem the more deeply we were able to penetrate into its meaning – a meaning that seemed, in the case of some poems, to coincide with the meaning of Buddhism itself. Once again I realized what I had first realized three years earlier, namely, that in explaining a poem – a poem such as Shelley's 'The Cloud' or one of Keats's Odes – I was in fact teaching Buddhism, especially when I was explaining it to, or studying it with, a dear friend. It was therefore not surprising that at the time when Sachin and I were going through the IA poetry selections together I should have been impressed by Rilke's idea that poetry is not *about* existence but *is*, itself, a new kind of existence, or that I should have thought of writing an article on what I called 'the metaphorical nature of reality', as well as an article on the Buddhist element in the plays of Sophocles. (Next to Yeats, Rilke was my favourite poet at this time, and Sophocles I was rereading with great enjoyment after a lapse of some years.) Neither of the two projected articles was ever actually written, but the kind of ideas I had intended to express in them were henceforth to be a permanent part of my thinking.

Seeing as much of each other as we did, it was natural that Sachin and I should have experienced a deepening of our friendship. Such a deepening had not been possible during the two years that he was away in Darjeeling, though we met whenever he was in Kalimpong for his holidays or I in Darjeeling on *Stepping-Stones* business, and though we corresponded regularly and at some length. But now that he was back in Kalimpong, at least for the present, our friendship not only deepened rapidly but broadened out and became more solid, a development that was due partly to the fact that Sachin was more mature and responsible than he had been a year or two earlier and had a better understanding of the value of friendship. He was also happier than he had been for a long time. He was happy to be again surrounded by his family and his old friends, happy to be free from the hateful necessity of studying science, happy to be able to devote himself to literature. So happy was he, in fact, that he usually arrived at the Hermitage in a lively, frolicsome mood, with the result that the time we spent together passed in the most agreeable fashion. My young friend did, however, have occasional fits of depression, when he withdrew into himself and refused to speak to anyone, but these were not long of duration and tended, in any case, to be connected with quarrels within his family. Not that there were never any misunderstandings between Sachin and myself (we were, after all, of very different temperaments and from very different backgrounds), but our misunderstandings were *only* misunderstandings, and however hurt or upset one or other – or both – of us might have been they were soon cleared up and left our friendship stronger than ever.

Since I was seven or eight years older than Sachin, and a monk to boot, I could not help wanting to share with him the fruits of my experience of life, limited as Joe considered that experience to be, and from time to time gave him advice. Besides being concerned with ethical rather than religious issues, this advice was more general than specific in character, as I preferred to elucidate principles rather than lay down rules and liked to encourage my students to think for themselves. There was one area, however, in which my advice *was* specific, and in which Sachin wanted it to be specific. That was the area of poetry, or rather, of poetic composition. A poet in both English and Nepali, he wanted to know how to improve his poetry; this led to a number of discussions, and as a result of these discussions I thought of writing an article to be called 'Advice to a Young Poet'.

Unlike the articles on the metaphorical nature of reality and the Buddhistic element in the plays of Sophocles, this one did get written and was published in the *Aryan Path* later that year.[133] Apart from 'Krishna's Flute', an article on the poetry of Sarojini Naidu which I wrote shortly after my arrival in India in 1944,[134] it was the first article on a topic of literary interest that I had produced. Though intended for Sachin, in his capacity as Young Poet, it was written quite as much for my own benefit as for his. Poetry expressed the personality of the poet. It was the more or less complete embodiment of his whole experience of life. The poet therefore improved his poetry by improving himself, and he improved himself by cultivating certain emotional and intellectual qualities. In describing these qualities I cited a number of Western poets, as well as Plato. I did not cite any Eastern poet or thinker (though I advised the English poet to learn to appreciate Arabic, Persian, and Chinese poetry), nor did my references to the natural world so much as suggest that I lived in India. The article could just as well have been written in Tooting as in the foothills of the eastern Himalayas. Nonetheless I was deeply affected by my surroundings. They stimulated and inspired me, and without that inspiration I probably would not have written 'Advice to a Young Poet' at all, at least not in the same enthusiastic manner. I was inspired by the bamboos and the orchids, by the haze-softened foothills, gashed red here and there by the landslides, by the changing cloud formations, by the breadth and blueness of the sky. Above all I was inspired by the snows.

The snows were not visible from the Hermitage, but as one walked up the road, in the direction of the bazaar, they gradually hove in sight. By the time one reached the Dharmodaya Vihara, which was situated half a mile from the Hermitage, *there* was the dazzling white mass of Kanchenjunga, with its twin peaks, piled up on the horizon at an unbelievable height. For the best view of the snows one had to climb up to Dailo, the skull-shaped hill beyond Dr Graham's Homes, and one day, with three companions, Sachin and I did just that. The three companions were Jungi, Dawa, and Omiya, the cheerful Bengali proprietor of a small watch-repair business in Darjeeling with whom Sachin had become acquainted and who was now spending a few days with him. As agreed the night before, we met at Sachin's house after breakfast and from there set out. The climb was a stiff one, especially towards the end, and it was not until nearly midday that, having emerged from the pine forest, we found ourselves on the bare top of Dailo Hill. The sun was shining brilliantly. Below us was the River Ranjit, winding through silver sands towards the plains, while around us, and stretching away into the distance, rose innumerable hills, all covered in soft blue haze. Aloft on the horizon, and extending in an unbroken line from farthest east to farthest west, were the snow peaks of the eastern Himalayas. There must have been hundreds of them. Except for Kanchenjunga and Lama Yuru, a pyramidal mountain so called from its resemblance to a meditating monk, I did not know their names. Nor did I care to know them. For me it was enough to sit there in that intense stillness, five thousand feet above sea level, simply contemplating those silent white forms. Contemplating them in this way – taking *darshan*, as my Indian friends would have said – I could begin to understand why the Himalayas had such a hold on the imagination of the people of the subcontinent and why they occupied so prominent a place in the religious and cultural life of Hindus, Buddhists, and Jains alike. I could understand why Kalidasa, in an oft-quoted phrase, had described the Himalayas as 'the congealed laughter of Shiva',[135] and why the author of the *Skanda Purāṇa* had gone so far as to personify the Himalaya or Himachala, in the singular, and extol him as a deity, saying:

> He who thinks of Himachala, even though he should not behold Him, is greater than he who performs worship at Kashi. And he who contemplates upon Himachala shall have pardon of all sins. All things that die on Himachala, and in dying think of His snows, are freed from evil. In a hundred years of the gods I could not tell you of the glories of Himachala, where Shiva lives and where the Ganga falls from the feet of Vishnu like the slender thread of the lotus flower. Truly, as the dew is dried by the Sun so are the sorrows of mankind dried up by the sight of Himachala.[136]

I had contemplated Himachala, and though I did not feel that my sins had been pardoned I could well believe that my sorrows had dried up, at least for the time being. Sachin and the others, however, were growing restless. After a picnic lunch we had lain in the sun for a while, steeping ourselves in the silence and solitude, but now they were moving about and talking. It was time for us to depart. Having commemorated our visit with a poem, which we traced out on the ground in charcoal, we therefore started making our way downhill. The return journey took nearly as long as the outward journey had done, and by the time I reached the Hermitage, having halted for a cup of tea at Sachin's place, I was feeling extremely tired – and quite stiff.

The tiredness was gone by the morning, but the stiffness lasted for several days. It was also several days before I was able to re-engage properly with my regular activities, the *darshan* of the snow peaks that I had been vouchsafed on Dailo Hill having affected me deeply. Next to the giving of private tuition, the activity that took up the biggest slice of my time was probably correspondence. Letters came to me from all over the world and I did my best to reply immediately. There were letters from old friends and letters from new friends, from Buddhists and from non-Buddhists, from monks and scholars, editors and journalists.

One old friend who wrote to me was Buddharakshita. From earlier letters I knew that he was having a difficult time in Ceylon, his own brahminical conditioning having apparently collided head-on with the Theravādin conditioning of his Sinhalese preceptors, and he now wrote to say that he was going to Burma on a (Burmese) government scholarship. There were also letters from Raj Kapoor and from Arjun Dev Rashk. On my return to Kalimpong our younger members and friends had been greatly excited to hear of my contact with Raj Kapoor, in their eyes an infinitely more important figure than either Dr Ambedkar or Lama Govinda, and many were the requests I had received for a letter of introduction to the famous actor. They were even more excited when they heard that Raj Kapoor would be visiting Darjeeling, both he and Rashk having written to me to this effect. In the event the visit did not take place, much to everyone's disappointment, but almost to the day of my departure from Kalimpong, more than a decade later, young men who fancied themselves as film stars were in the habit of approaching me for a letter of introduction to Raj Kapoor or, at the very least, to Rashk. More often than not I did not give even the latter, being unable to forget either the young men I had seen hanging about the gate of the R. K. Studio buildings or Rashk's caustic comments on their abilities.

Now that the YMBA (India) was the Kalimpong branch of the Maha Bodhi Society, and I its *bhikṣu*-in-charge, one of my most faithful correspondents was Devapriya Valisinha. Early in March I received from him a letter that made me realize that it was not only English-educated Hindus who were indifferent to considerations of objective truth. This letter was not of Devapriyaji's own composing but was a copy of a letter that Dr Suniti Kumar Chatterjee, the (nominal) editor of the Maha Bodhi Society's Diamond Jubilee Souvenir, had received from C. Jinarajadasa, the octogenarian President of the Theosophical Society, challenging the accuracy of some of the statements in my biographical sketch and accusing the Maha Bodhi Society of hostility to the Theosophical Society. In his covering note Devapriyaji asked me for my comments. I had met Jinarajadasa at Adyar in the winter of 1946–7, when I was on my way to Calcutta from Singapore, and remembered him well, as I also did Rukmini Arundale and her lecture on 'Buddhism and Beauty', delivered in the open air beneath the spreading branches of Adyar's famous banyan tree. Probably Jinarajadasa did not remember me, or, if he did remember, failed to connect the young British serviceman who had come to see him in Adyar with the Buddhist monk who was the author of the offending biographical sketch. He was particularly incensed by a passage in which, describing Dharmapala's first visit to England in 1893, I had spoken of his being welcomed at Gravesend by Sir Edwin Arnold and 'several Theosophists, including Leadbeater and his young favourite Jinarajadasa, whom he had kidnapped and carried off to England.' He had *not* been kidnapped, he insisted, not without some harsh remarks on my failure to observe the fourth precept.

The Dharmapala diaries however showed that he incontestably *had* been kidnapped, Dharmapala himself having been personally involved in the subsequent fracas, in the course of which the father of the sixteen-year-old Jinarajadasa had wanted to shoot Leadbeater. When I wrote to Devapriyaji I was therefore emphatic that we should stand our ground. Jinarajadasa would have to be told that the statements whose accuracy he had impugned, including my reference to Leadbeater's kidnapping him, were based on the Dharmapala diaries and other contemporary evidence and that hence there could be no question of our withdrawing them. Devapriyaji accordingly drafted a letter to this effect for Dr Chatterjee to sign, and I heard no more of the matter. Nevertheless, it had disturbed me, and I continued to think about it. I was surprised and saddened by Jinarajadasa's evident desire to rewrite history, the more especially as the society of which he was President had taken for its motto a gnome from the Hindu scriptures which it translated as 'There is no religion higher than Truth'.[137] I was also surprised that Jinarajadasa should have accused the Maha Bodhi Society of hostility to the Theosophical Society. Dharmapala himself had been a member of the Theosophical Society, as well as a personal disciple of Mme Blavatsky, and in my biographical sketch I had made no secret of the extent of his indebtedness to Theosophy. I also made no secret of the concern and indignation with which the mature Dharmapala had viewed certain later developments in the Society, and it was perhaps for this reason, as well as because of my reference to his having been kidnapped by Leadbeater, that Jinarajadasa had reacted so strongly.

22

NEW ARRIVALS IN KALIMPONG ... AND DHARDO RIMPOCHE

If Darjeeling was the Queen of the Hill Stations then Kalimpong, smaller and situated at a lower altitude, was undoubtedly the princess, as least so far as north-east India was concerned. The town's importance was due to its position as a terminal of the Lhasa–India trade-route, which, having traversed the Chumbi Valley and negotiated the Julep Pass, cut across the south-eastern corner of Sikkim to wind its way round the foothills and finally peter out among the dust and mule-droppings of Topkhana, as the Tibetan quarter at Tenth Mile was called. Being the terminal that it was, Kalimpong had a sizeable Tibetan population that included, besides merchants and muleteers, officers of the Tibetan government and maroon monks. It was thus an ideal place to study the Tibetan language, in both its classical and its colloquial form, and over the years a dozen or more people must have come there from the universities of the West for just that purpose. Not that scholars were the town's only visitors. Artists, journalists, and students of the occult sciences also came, as well as ordinary tourists (though tourists generally preferred to go to Darjeeling). But whoever they were, and whatever their reason for being in Kalimpong, sooner or later they were bound to call at the Hermitage, the English monk, as I was generally termed, having apparently become one of the sights of the town, not to say one of its institutions. During the early months of 1953 there was a larger number of visitors than usual. What was more, several of them eventually settled in Kalimpong and became very much a part of my own life there.

The Honourable Helena Barclay was a middle-aged Englishwoman who, without being exactly a scholar, had come with the intention of making a serious study of Tibetan. She had not come alone. With her was her sixteen-year-old cat, who was to die in Kalimpong and whose remains I was to have the honour of cremating with full Buddhist rites. Miss Barclay, as she was always called, was fond of relating how she had paid for her pet to have a seat all to himself on the aeroplane and how her ticket had been made out to 'Miss Barclay and cat'. A little above average height, and inclined to corpulence, she had sandy hair, pale blue eyes, a pasty complexion, and a short nose on which perched a pair of gold-rimmed spectacles. Her expression was either one of amusement or one of annoyance for, as I soon discovered, Miss Barclay was the possessor not only of a sense of humour ('No, I'm *not* one of the banking Barclays,' she would say on being introduced to anyone) but of a truly fearful temper. She was also careless about her clothes to the point of slovenliness, wearing the same old skirt, and the same old sweater with the food stains all down the front, day after day and week after week.

By the time she called at the Hermitage she was quite well known in Kalimpong, for she was of a sociable disposition and mixed easily with people of all classes. Even Princess Irene held no terrors for her. 'She knows better than to act the princess with *me*,' she told me one day, shortly after we became acquainted, as she gave me an account of the dinner party she had attended at Krishnalok the evening before. '*I* know all about her and she knows that I know.' Miss Barclay did not tell me what it was that she knew about Princess Irene until some time later, but her father had been a diplomat, representing Great Britain at the League of Nations, and she was evidently well informed about all sorts of prominent people. Not that she spoke very much about her father. She spoke far more about her mother. Her mother – and her elder sister – had been the bane of her life, she assured me. Her mother actually hated her. She hated her because unlike her sister, who was the beauty of the family and whom her mother doted on, she was plain and awkward and stood little chance of making a good marriage. So much did her mother hate her that she used to destroy whatever she created. She would even pull up the flowers she grew. (Miss Barclay was a keen gardener.) During the Great War her only son, Miss Barclay's brother, had been killed in action. When the news reached her she had turned to her unloved younger daughter and said, 'It's a pity it wasn't you. We could have spared *you*.' Miss Barclay told me this sad story with a sangfroid that suggested it had all happened a long time ago and was really not worth bothering about, but I could see that she had been deeply wounded and that it was, in all probability, her mother's inhuman treatment that was responsible for her fearful temper and for the foul moods in which, only too often, she would arrive at the Hermitage – moods which it sometimes took me a couple of hours of patient listening to exorcize.

Within a month of her first calling on me the elderly Englishwoman with the gold-rimmed spectacles and food-stained sweater was, in fact, one of my most regular visitors, dropping in for a cup of tea and a chat at least three or four times a week. Rarely did she come empty-handed, bringing now a bunch of flowers, now a pair of vases for the shrine, and now a lettuce she had grown on the vegetable patch that adjoined the chalet she occupied in the grounds of the Himalayan Hotel. For my part I gave her some geranium cuttings and, on her birthday, a small clay figure of Shiva. One morning, when Sachin and I were studying logic, she brought her pendulum and showed us how it worked, holding it first over my outstretched hand, then over Sachin's, and finally over her own. Our vibrations all harmonized, she declared, with evident satisfaction. This was only the second time I had seen a pendulum, of the occult, radiesthetic variety (the first time was when the woman in charge of the Adyar library showed me the gem-studded gold pendulum she wore round her neck), and I was not sure if I believed that people's vibrations could be read in this way. I knew that Miss Barclay herself believed they could, for we had had several discussions on Mme Blavatsky and the occult sciences, as well as on Buddhism.

But whether or not it was because our vibrations harmonized, there was no doubt that the three of us – Miss Barclay, Sachin, and I – got on well together. There was also no doubt that Miss Barclay got on well with all the young men she happened to meet at the Hermitage, invariably treating them in a natural, friendly manner, and never talking down to them. One day she invited me, Sachin, Dawa, and five or six of our other more active members, to have tea with her at her chalet. Apart from Sachin, my young friends were not accustomed to mixing socially with their elders, especially when the latter happened to be pukka memsahibs, and they therefore looked forward to the tea party with a certain amount of trepidation. In the event they all enjoyed themselves immensely, and afterwards voted Miss Barclay a very kind and hospitable lady. On another occasion Miss Barclay and I hired a jeep and, with Sachin, went to the Pedong *mela*. This was the same government sponsored agricultural exhibition at which I had spoken on Buddhism three years earlier, shortly after my arrival in Kalimpong, and where a Christian preacher had told me that my fate after death would be worse than that of other people. Having looked round the exhibition we went to see the local (Bhutanese) *gompa*, as well as a smaller *gompa* I had missed on my previous visit. But they were both closed, and we had to be content with peering at the frescoes through the windows.

The only person in our little circle with whom Miss Barclay did not get on well was Joe, though this was more his fault than hers, the prickly *upāsaka* having regarded her with suspicion and dislike from the very first. In this connection he had, as he thought, a strange tale to relate. One day when he was walking home from the bazaar he and an elderly Englishwoman he had not seen before, but whom he afterwards realized was Miss Barclay, happened to pass each other on the deserted road. A few minutes later the Englishwoman turned round and started following him. She followed him for nearly a mile, then turned round again and walked in the opposite direction, that is, in the direction in which she had been walking originally. When I asked Miss Barclay why she had followed Joe she laughingly denied doing any such thing. He had imagined it all, she declared. But Joe was convinced that she *had* followed him, and not only persisted in his suspicion and dislike of her but avoided her as much as he could. When forced into contact with her, as he was on the occasion of our full-moon day celebrations, he usually betrayed extreme uneasiness.

Miss Barclay was of a sociable disposition not only in the sense that she enjoyed the company of other people; she also liked to act as peacemaker and to introduce her different friends to one another – in all this being the exact opposite of Joe. Thus she took it upon herself to tell Brother Peter that my letter to the Calcutta newspapers regarding 'conversion through pregnancy' was *not* intended to refer to the Catholic Mission. She also brought various people to see me, usually fellow guests of the Himalayan

Hotel or professors and professors' wives from Santiniketan who were staying either at Chitrabhanu with Mrs Tagore or at Manjula with Mrs Mitter. One afternoon she arrived at the Hermitage accompanied by a short, untidy Frenchwoman with an anxious expression whom I had already met in Calcutta. Miss Delannoy was studying Hindu temple architecture and Sanskrit but seemed to be more interested in Buddhism. At any rate, for the next two weeks she came to see me every day, and we had some interesting discussions on such topics as the Perfection of Wisdom *sūtras*, meditation, and the spiritual life, as well as on poetry and the relative claims of religion and art (she had written and published Surrealist poetry). Usually she came in the evening, for she liked to sit with me while I did my evening puja and meditation, and perhaps ask questions afterwards. Sometimes I was late, either because I had been out or because I had had visitors, and on entering the shrine-room would find her sitting there waiting for me. On such occasions she had a mournful, aggrieved look, as though by thoughtlessly preventing her from sharing my puja and meditation at the time she had expected I had done her a great wrong. In the years to come, when she had settled in Kalimpong and was studying Madhyamaka philosophy and Tibetan, I was to know that look only too well.

On the day of her departure Miss Delannoy brought a friend to see me. This was Mme Combastet, about whom I had already heard from Miss Barclay. According to Miss Barclay, Mme Combastet was 'of unconventional morals' (whatever that may have meant), but I found her to be sincerely interested in spiritual things and, in appearance at least, conventional enough. In marked contrast to the slovenly Miss Barclay and the untidy Miss Delannoy she was smartly dressed and had, moreover, a trim figure and a complexion so smooth as to seem enamelled. Her age I judged to be somewhere between forty and forty-five, but Joe, who insisted on referring to her as Madam Come-bust-it, assured me that she had had a face-lift and was at least sixty. A month or so after her first visit, having seen me only once in the meantime, she asked me to give her English lessons, mainly for the sake of conversational practice. Thenceforth she came twice a week and gave me, during the four months that the lessons continued, no cause for complaint. She always came – and went – exactly on time, was always in a good temper, always enjoyed her lessons, and always paid me on the dot. In short she was a model pupil. Her only fault (if fault it could be called) was that she made a point of telling me, in the course of every lesson, that all she ever had for breakfast was a cup of chocolate. 'Just *one* cup of *chocolat*,' she would say with a beatific smile, as though it was important that I should understand this. 'Just *one* cup. Just one.'

What with Miss Barclay, Miss Delannoy, and Mme Combastet, one would have thought that the English monk had quite enough Western females on his hands at this time, but there was another to come. Dr Irene Bastow Hudson, MD, whose stay in Kalimpong partly coincided with Miss Delannoy's, came equipped with a letter of introduction from Clare Cameron and the information that she was a life member of the Maha Bodhi Society, so that I felt doubly obliged to devote some time to her. A tall, gaunt woman in her early seventies, with scanty grey hair and pebble-lens spectacles, she had an aggressive manner and a loud voice that she was not afraid of using. She was, in fact, extremely talkative, and at our first meeting told me, among other things, that she was a Buddhist and a Theosophist (of the back-to-Blavatsky persuasion), that she had written several books, including one on the occult properties of blood, and that though born and educated in England she had spent most of her working life in Canada and was now a Canadian citizen. Besides being extremely talkative, Dr Hudson was very active and vigorous for her age and had no intention of passing her time in the lounge of the Himalayan Hotel. I therefore took her to see Dr Graham's Homes, the Tharpa Choling Gompa (where we missed the abbot but saw the Dalai Lama's new throne), St Augustine's Priory and the Blind School, and arranged with Dr Singh for her to visit the Charteris Hospital.

I also arranged for her to give a lecture at the Maitri Sangha (as Mr Indra's Institute of Culture was now called), where Miss Barclay had already spoken on 'Education in Europe'. Dr Hudson's subject was 'Fear in Relation to Health', fear being, apparently, a topic on which she considered herself to be something of an authority. She also considered herself to be something of an authority on sex, especially sex as viewed from the standpoint of Theosophy, and had written a pamphlet entitled 'The Secret Doctrine on the Evolution and Problem of Sex', a copy of which she gave me to read. It was a curious piece of work. Like her lecture at the Maitri Sangha, it jumbled together scientific facts and pseudo-occult fantasies in the most extraordinary fashion. It also contained a violent condemnation of masturbation, on the grounds that it was a form of black magic – this being apparently one of the author's favourite theses. A few years later, when she too had settled in Kalimpong, Dr Hudson had the pamphlet reprinted and gave me five hundred copies for distribution among the youth of Kalimpong. I distributed only one copy. This I gave not to a young Nepali or Tibetan but to Prince Peter, who returned it with extensive marginal comments one of which read 'The author must be mentally deranged.'

Since she had long thought of herself as the only Canadian Buddhist, Dr Hudson was astonished to find that in Kalimpong, of all places, there was another, Joe having awarded himself an honorary Canadian citizenship – presumably on the strength of his having spent part of his early life in Canada. But although Dr Hudson was anxious to meet Joe the latter, I knew, was not at all anxious to meet *her*. 'Don't have *anything* to do with her, Bhante!' he exclaimed when, two weeks earlier, I told him that I had heard from a Canadian Buddhist called Dr Hudson and that she would be visiting Kalimpong. 'Don't have *anything* to do with her! I know that woman. I've seen her name in the papers. She buys her way into organizations and then wrecks them!' But there was no way in which I could avoid meeting Dr Hudson and, having met her, no way in which I could avoid taking her to see Joe. The strong-willed woman would have gone to see him on her own anyway. As it happened, the meeting between the two Canadian Buddhists passed off quite smoothly. Joe received Dr Hudson in what he liked to call his boo-dwah and was all graciousness, while Dr Hudson had the satisfaction of holding forth for three hours on a variety of topics. On the way back to the Himalayan Hotel she kept repeating, half to herself, 'Cann, Cann, now where have I heard that name before? ... Ah, yes! His mother used to take in our washing. I examined him when he was at school. He had rickets.' The next time I saw Joe I retailed to him part of what Dr Hudson had said. He was not amused. 'She *didn't* examine me!' he spluttered indignantly, 'I *never* had rickets!' A few years later Dr Hudson was to have other reminiscences of Joe's early life, but to what extent she shared them with him I never knew.

Whether or not Dr Hudson had examined Joe when he was at school, during her stay in Kalimpong she certainly did not examine me; but she must have regarded me with a diagnostic eye, for when she came to say goodbye she gave me a hundred rupees, remarking, 'You look as though you are in need of a better diet,' at the same time adding, with reference to the donation, 'There's plenty more where *that* came from.' Apparently there was, for a week later I received a parcel of foodstuffs she had sent from Calcutta.

Though they may have taken up a good deal of my time, elderly Western females were not the only visitors to Kalimpong who called at the Hermitage, nor were they the only ones, among those who did call, who eventually settled in the town and became part of my life there. Returning to the Hermitage one evening, after attending Dr Hudson's lecture at the Maitri Sangha, I found on my pillow a note from Anand Kausalyayan, whom I had last seen in Calcutta after the return of the Sacred Relics from Nepal. He was staying at the Dharmodaya Vihara, the note informed me. This being as good as a summons, I accordingly retraced my steps and soon was knocking on the door of Anandji's room – the same upstairs front room that I had myself occupied three years earlier. My elderly Punjabi friend was not alone. With him was a Japanese priest, and since it transpired, when greetings had passed, that the priest would shortly be returning to Calcutta, I invited the two of them to come to the Hermitage the following morning for breakfast. Anandji not only came with the Japanese priest for breakfast. He also came by himself later on in the day and took me for a walk. Thereafter a walk with Anandji formed part of my daily routine whenever my elder brother in the sangha happened to be in Kalimpong, which he in fact was, on and off, for the next two or three years. Like Dr Hudson, he was active and vigorous for his age, so that our walk was usually a long one, and like Dr Hudson he was extremely talkative. Unlike Dr Hudson, however, he could be both witty and amusing, especially when he found himself in congenial company. At the Dharmodaya Vihara, I gathered, the company was not very congenial. Besides the irascible Aniruddha there was now his even more irascible father Dhammaloka, who also was a *bhikṣu*, as well as a lumpish young monk called Vivekananda and a thirteen- or fourteen-year-old novice called Sugatadasa. All four were Newars. Sugatadasa's parents, so Anandji told me, had given him to Narada Thera as *dāna* some years earlier, and Narada Thera had handed him over for monastic training to Aniruddha. As was obvious from his sullen, resentful expression, he was not at all happy at the vihara. Apart from the occasional Pāli lesson, his monastic training seemed to consist mainly in being jeered at by Aniruddha for wetting the bed every night – a charge the boy always vehemently denied. The only time I ever saw him smile was when, at my request, he was allowed to play carrom-board at the Hermitage. Thus with two irascible adults in residence, as well as one lumpish adult, not to mention an unhappy teenager, it was not surprising that Anandji should find the company at the Dharmodaya Vihara not very congenial. It was also not very surprising that, in the absence of any pupil of his own, he should come to the Hermitage virtually every day and take the young English monk whose acquaintance he had made in Nepal for a good long walk.

Seeing as much of him as I did, I soon learned quite a lot about the cynical, worldly-wise Punjabi monk, the more especially since he was so talkative – though I did not, I suspect, learn anything he did not want me to know. In the early thirties he and Rahul Sankrityayan had spent two years in London, staying at the vihara recently established by Anagārika Dharmapala, and many were the stories he had to tell about his experiences in Britain, as well as Germany, which he had also visited. One such story concerned a woman who had come to see him in Berlin. Since he had not quite finished writing a letter, he had asked her to wait in an anteroom. When ten minutes had passed, however, the door flew open and the woman burst in, exclaiming, 'I shall go mad if I stay there any longer! I've no one to talk to!' Anandji also had a fund of stories about Rahul Sankrityayan, the seniormost member of the once famous trio of Anandji, Kashyapji, and Rahulji. In the late thirties, when still a monk, Rahulji had gone to Lhasa in search of ancient Sanskrit manuscripts and had almost died owing to lack of proper vegetarian food. On returning to India he had joked that it was only the ants in the rice that had kept him alive.

Anandji himself had no interest in ancient Sanskrit manuscripts. Though well versed in Pāli, he was not a scholar like Rahulji, whom the pandits of Benares had hailed as one of their own. More journalist than monk, and more politician than journalist, his chosen field of operations was the world of linguistic politics. For the last twelve years he had been General Secretary of the Rashtrabhasha Prachar Samiti or 'Association for the Advancement of the National Language', a semi-governmental body that from its headquarters at Wardha organized the teaching of Hindi in the non-Hindi speaking areas of the country – often in the face of local apathy or antagonism. But now he was the General Secretary no longer. From what he told me, in the course of one of our walks, I gathered that there had been a prolonged bitter struggle for power between him, and his supporters, and a rival group within the Samiti. In the end Anandji's group had been defeated, after putting up a stiff resistance. At one point, suspecting that he was about to be removed from his post by unconstitutional means, he withdrew all the Samiti's funds – a matter of several *lakhs* of rupees – from the bank and kept the cash in a tin box under his bed. Unfortunately for him and for the nascent Indian Buddhist movement, he had emerged from the struggle not only without the General Secretaryship but with his personal reputation in tatters. As Devapriyaji afterwards told me, his opponents had sought to undermine his position by circulating a scurrilous pamphlet, copies of which were sent to the Maha Bodhi Society. 'We all have to hang our heads in shame,' Devapriyaji commented sadly. There had even been threats against Anandji's life. Feelings seemed to run quite high in the world of linguistic politics.

The presence of my Punjabi friend in Kalimpong was thus explained. He had come to Kalimpong because he had made Wardha – in fact the whole world of Indian linguistic politics – too hot for himself and because for the time being he was not particularly welcome at the Sri Dharmarajika Vihara and other centres of the Maha Bodhi Society. But whatever the reason for his being in Kalimpong (and it was only later that I learned the whole story), I was glad that he had come, and glad that a walk with him formed part of my daily routine. Though extremely talkative, Anandji was by no means a complete monologist, and I was able to share with him my thoughts on such topics as the relation between religion and art and what I termed the missionary menace. I also taught him to play ping-pong, borrowed his camera to take pictures of my students, and took him to see Joe's orchid collection. Thus relations between us were both close and cordial. Nonetheless, though I was glad he had come to Kalimpong, and though I enjoyed his company, I was conscious that there was something lacking. I missed in him that element of spirituality – of desire for the Eternal – that I still expected to find in one who was not just a brother monk but so very much my senior in monastic ordination. It was not surprising that I should have missed it. That element was simply not to be found in Anandji (except to the extent that it is found, as a potentiality, in all sentient beings), and it was not to be found in him because it was not to be found in Buddhism as he understood the religion. Anandji's Buddhism, I soon discovered, was an aridly rational – not to say rationalistic – teaching that, despite its Buddhistic terminology, was virtually indistinguishable from nineteenth century secular humanism or, for that matter, from eighteenth century Enlightenment philosophy. It indeed was his avowed ambition to be known as the Voltaire of India.

Fortunately for me it so happened that, less than two months after Anandji's arrival in Kalimpong, I met a monk of a very different kind. The meeting took place in unforseen circumstances. One morning, shortly before the Vaiśākha full-moon day, Joe arrived at the Hermitage in a state of great excitement. 'What *do* you think has happened, Bhante?' he exclaimed, in tones that in wartime England would have earned him a prison sentence for spreading alarm and despondency. 'There's been a tremendous dispute in Bodh Gaya between Dhardo Rim-POH-chee and that fellow Dhammaloka – *you* know, the monk in charge of the Maha Bodhi Rest House. The whole Tibetan community is up in arms about it. There could be a permanent breach with the Maha Bodhi Society.' Knowing the sensation-loving *upāsaka*'s penchant for dramatic exaggeration I did not take his report too literally, but it was clear that a dispute of some kind had occurred. The Maha Bodhi Rest House and the *gompa* of which Dhardo Rimpoche was abbot were, I knew, situated next door to each other, and there could well have been a disagreement over the respective boundaries of the two properties. I also knew that Dhammaloka was inclined to be hot-headed. (This was not the irascible Dhammaloka of the Dharmodaya Vihara but the young Sinhalese monk with the protruding ears and toothy smile with whom I had gone sightseeing in Kathmandu.) Since Dhardo Rimpoche was back in Kalimpong, and I was now *bhikṣu*-in-charge of the Maha Bodhi Society's Kalimpong branch, it was obviously incumbent upon me to do everything in my power to prevent the dispute from developing into an actual breach between the two Buddhist communities.

The following morning I therefore set out for Sherpa Building, on the upper floor of which the incarnate lama was again staying. Since I did not know Tibetan and since Dhardo Rimpoche, despite Joe's tuition, spoke hardly any English, I took an interpreter along with me. The interpreter was Lobsang Phuntshok Lhalungpa, the young monk-officer whom I had met two years ago at Thubden Tendzin's bungalow. He had given up the robe and married, and now lived with his wife and infant son in the upper part of the Manjula guest cottage. In recent months I had helped him improve the English of a political history of Tibet he was translating from the Tibetan and we were beginning to be good friends. Recently he had told me about the Tibetan school that he and his brother officers were hoping to establish in Kalimpong. The inspiration behind the project was Dhardo Rimpoche, with whom he

Dhardo Rimpoche

was closely associated, and whom he was anxious I should meet. I had not yet had the opportunity of meeting the Rimpoche, though while I was away in Nepal Joe had brought him to the Hermitage and he had consecrated the standing image of the Buddha given me by Lama Govinda. Indeed I had not, as I well knew, so much as seen him in passing. What I did not know, and was not to learn until quite a few years later, was that although I had not seen Dhardo Rimpoche he had seen me. He had seen me in Bodh Gaya in 1949.[138] Happening to look out of his window one day he was surprised to see on the flat roof on the Maha Bodhi Rest House a yellow-robed Englishman. So surprised was he, and so astonished and intrigued that a Westerner should be interested in Buddhism, that he called his monk-attendant to come and look. 'The Dharma has gone even so far as the West!' he declared.

Now, more than three years later, the same yellow-robed Englishman was coming to see him – coming to see him, moreover, in connection with a dispute that had arisen on the very spot where the Rimpoche had caught sight of him. Strange to relate, I have no recollection of my actual meeting with Dhardo Rimpoche at Sherpa Building that morning, possibly because it is so overlaid with memories of subsequent meetings. I have no recollection of the room in which we met and no recollection of what the thirty-five-year-old incarnate lama looked like on that occasion, though he must have been shaven-headed and have worn the maroon robes of a member of the Gelug order, with a triangle of gold brocade showing above the edge of the upper robe. What I do recollect – and recollect most clearly – is the impression of sheer goodwill, candour, and integrity that I received from Dhardo Rimpoche as he gave me a full account of the dispute between himself and Dhammaloka; a dispute in which the hot-headed Sinhalese had so far forgotten himself as to use expressions no monk should use to another. So strong was this impression that when, the following day, I wrote to Devapriya Valisinha, I had no hesitation in assuring him that the Rimpoche was in no way at fault and that the blame for the dispute rested solely with Dhammaloka. Predictably, the little General Secretary of the Maha Bodhi Society did not agree with me and was inclined to support his compatriot and fellow Theravādin. But this did not worry me. I had heard on the monastic grapevine that Dhammaloka had decided to disrobe after the Vaiśākha full-moon day and leave Bodh Gaya, which he did, and I never heard of him again.

As for Dhardo Rimpoche, he was from now onwards to spend most of his time in Kalimpong, and I was to be in increasingly close contact with him for the remainder of my stay in India – in a sense, for the rest of my life.

Dear Dinoo

LETTERS TO A FRIEND

WITH INTRODUCTION, NOTES AND APPENDIX BY KALYANAPRABHA

Dinoo Dubash

INTRODUCTION

Why publish letters? When there are five volumes of Sangharakshita's memoirs, Dharma books, and any number of lectures easily accessible on the Internet, why, you may wonder, should a volume of Sangharakshita's letters now appear?

Johann Wolfgang von Goethe had an opinion on the matter. 'Letters', he says, 'are among the most significant memorials a person can leave behind them'.[139] 'Memorial' conjures up, perhaps, an image in cold marble or stone. We might say rather that letters are among the most significant *communications* a person can leave behind them.

There is significance in the immediacy of a letter; a vivid record of someone's life, thought, and experience *at the time*. A memoir looks back, perhaps many decades. It is the younger self recalled across the passage of time by the maturer man.

A lecture is written for a specific audience, a memoir for one much larger and in a way more unknown, but a letter is written to a single friend. Sangharakshita once said, 'One can only speak the truth to one person. The larger the number of people to whom you are speaking, the more will what you say become an approximation to the truth.'[140]

John Donne also has something to say: 'Sir, more than kisses, letters mingle souls; for, thus friends absent speak.'[141] And here, I think, we have found the essence of the significance. Friends absent speak. There is a mingling of souls. In reading the letters, it is almost as if we are permitted to eavesdrop on a private conversation. In fact what we are afforded is a glimpse of a friendship.

༄༅

BOMBAY, 1955

She was middle-aged, Indian, with a Parsi background. She had founded one of the first Montessori schools in India. She painted and meditated and was interested in things spiritual. He was thirty, had grown up in England, and was now a Buddhist monk living in the foothills of the Himalayas. That autumn he was visiting Bombay to give lectures and to discuss the making of a film. In his spare time he was writing the last chapters of what would become his *magnum opus*.[142]

They met in 1955 at the Malabar Hill home of B. P. and Madame Sophia Wadia.[143] Sangharakshita was delivering the second of two lectures. On this occasion the theme was, 'Inspiration – Whence?' It turned out to be, in his own estimation, a particularly good lecture – perhaps because he was giving voice to ideas and experiences that he found especially important or significant. Whatever the reason, there was a buzz in the air at the end of the lecture and members of the audience pushed forward, eager to enter into discussion. One of them was particularly voluble and, managing to catch his attention, engaged him in conversation. She was 'a short, middle-aged woman in a Western-style frock,' and her excitement was due to the fact that in his lecture he had, as she now explained, given expression to some of her own deepest beliefs. This lady was none other than Dinoo Dubash; and that encounter the first event in a long-enduring friendship.

First impressions are sometimes to be modified on greater acquaintance; in this case the threads that wove the pattern of their friendship seem to have been present from the first. On the one hand Sangharakshita, with his exceptional understanding, able to give voice to those essential human values which others, hearing, could recognize – an experience which – as we see in their first meeting – gave rise in Dinoo to energy, excitement, and perhaps joy.

And then Dinoo, eagerly wanting to communicate, somehow managing to convey not only her response to the lecture, but also that she painted and meditated, that she considered herself a Buddhist, and that she wanted Sangharakshita to visit her and to meet a certain Dr Mehta. All these were to become vital threads in the tapestry of their growing connection.

Their second meeting took place a few days later at Dinoo's flat. Dinoo had a large ground floor flat in a block called 'Oceana'. Oceana was located in Marine Drive in western Bombay, one in a series of five- and six-storey blocks sweeping in a great curve along the bay, commanding magnificent views of the Arabian Sea. It was a fashionable address and home to a number of film stars and rich businessmen.

Dinoo, of course, was neither film-star nor businesswoman but a teacher. In fact she was principal of the Montessori school that she had founded in 1934, the second Montessori school in Bombay and one of the very first in India. Whether her school was located at Oceana from the outset is not clear, but it was certainly well-established when Sangharakshita came to know her in 1955. (It continues today at the same address, run by Dinoo's niece. On 6 August 2010 the school celebrated its 76th anniversary.)

It was a nursery school for children aged three to five. Necessarily they came from well-to-do families who could afford an upmarket education. Dinoo employed two or three teachers plus a cook, as well as other servants who lived with her. Her responsibilities were sometimes the cause of considerable headaches: 'I have had a hell of a time with the servants,' she writes in November 1957. 'I had no idea human nature could descend to such levels, & without a cause too. I suppose we have to live and learn.' It was not always easy, as a single woman, to gain their respect, and perhaps, as Sangharakshita hinted in one of our conversations, Dinoo herself did not always treat them with the sympathy or tact that would have fostered better relations.

But we are rushing ahead. Let us return to that first visit of Sangharakshita to Dinoo's flat at Oceana, where we find him being served with the best tea, and Dinoo trying out the sweetmeats which the cook brings forth from the kitchen, before handing them to her guest – no doubt returning them with a strong word of rebuff if they are not up to standard. (Dinoo's standards of housekeeping were high!) No doubt she talked and Sangharakshita listened, putting to her every now and then a question or remark or an anecdote of his own.

From then on, whenever he found himself in Bombay, Sangharakshita visited Dinoo to have tea with her and a good long chat. He would take his seat in her main room, a large room containing a good deal of furniture. Running along the walls were air-plants – a kind of green and white creeper which lives on air, popular in Bombay at that time. On the shelves were many well-read books. Looking around the room, the eye took in a couple of Buddha images. One was a beautiful Chinese porcelain, soft grey-green in colour, which, at the end of her life, Dinoo left to Sangharakshita's English disciple, Lokamitra. There was also a smaller Buddha image of a semi-translucent green stone in connection with which hangs a rather curious tale....

On one occasion when Sangharakshita was visiting Dinoo, after they had taken tea, Dinoo said, ' I just want you to sit in this chair and look at this image and tell me if you see anything.' She indicated the small green Buddha standing on the window sill, beyond it the open sweep of the sky. The chair was directly in front, just a few feet away. Sangharakshita took his seat.

Then, as he sat there looking at the image, he saw a green light slowly emanating from it. Gradually the light, a kind of neon light, filled the whole room.

'Do you see anything?' Dinoo asked.

'Yes,' he replied, 'I see a green light.' He tried to ascertain whether it could be coming from any source other than the image or whether it could be a trick of the light or a reflection. But no, it was clearly coming from the image itself.

'Yes, yes!' exclaimed Dinoo, 'I've seen it; and my servants have seen it.'

Then the light gradually faded away.

Dinoo asked Sangharakshita what he made of it. She said her servants – who were Goanese Christians – believed it was something to do with the devil and were therefore very afraid. But what did Sangharakshita think? He said he didn't know. Perhaps that small green Buddha figure had once been in the possession of someone who meditated. One could only speculate.

But such unusual happenings were the exception. Usually they simply talked. Dinoo was notable as a talker. 'If it were possible to meet I should let you talk for six hours without stopping (oh yes you could, quite easily!)' Sangharakshita teases her in one of his letters from Kalimpong. Sometimes Dinoo had with her a list of questions she wanted to put to her Buddhist monk friend, questions about meditation, about spiritual life, or perhaps about Dr Mehta and his Society. They talked about art and painting. But occasionally there were more personal exchanges and over the course of the years Dinoo confided something of her personal life.

A LADY OF SPIRIT AND DETERMINATION

Dinoo was born probably in 1902 into the Bombay Parsi community. (The Parsis were descendants of tenth-century Zoroastrian immigrants from Iran.) Literacy in that community was exceptionally high, and education for girls was valued as much as for boys. That Dinoo was well-educated for an Indian woman of her time is clear from her subsequent career; also that she came from a well-to-do family. We know she was the eldest of five sisters. More than this about her early life I have been unable to establish. Dinoo herself makes just one reference in the surviving letters to a conversation with her father. It took place when she was about twenty-two. She had been reading a book of her father's on the subject of Raja Yoga and had started practising the exercises she found described there.

'Talking ... to my father, I happened to mention the exercises.... My father looked so startled, and said he would never allow me to read any of his books if I dabbled in to things without a proper understanding of them. I was all confused and wanted to know why. The explanation he gave me seemed to me so sound that it has stuck in my memory.' We can see from these few sentences something of their relationship. Evidently he was used to the idea of his eldest daughter reading quite widely and discussing with him what she read. He seems to have communicated with her openly and intelligently in a way she could respect, but he did not hesitate to express his opinion firmly.

If this took place when she was twenty-two, then we must go back and mention a crucial event that had taken place a few years earlier. She married when she was seventeen. According to what she later confided in Sangharakshita, she left her husband, who was somewhat older, after just a few months. He had, she said, 'subjected her to indignities'. Though she did not spell it out, what Sangharakshita understood was that Dinoo at seventeen had had no idea about marriage, and her husband, perhaps much more experienced sexually, had shocked her. Something happened. The young woman returned to her parents and never married again. She did, however, have some sort of relationship with a man later on. She often referred to him in her conversations with Sangharakshita, though never very explicitly. His photograph was in her room, showing him to be a man of about forty. (At what period in her life she had known him was not clear.)

Whether Dinoo left her husband more in turmoil or in disgust we cannot know, but I think we can be sure she did not see the end of her marriage as the end of her life. She was a woman of spirit and determination and a decision she made in her early thirties shows exceptional boldness. She decided to study with the educationalist Maria Montessori (1870–1952). In the second half of 1933 she travelled to London for the three month duration of the course which was run by Mme Montessori herself. Returning to Bombay, she set up her own school, the second Montessori school to be established in Bombay, and among the very first in India. (Today there are scores of Montessori establishments in India. Seventeen are listed in the state of Maharashtra alone.)

MEDITATION, ART, AND FAITH

The next years of her life were taken up with her school. It was indeed, as Sangharakshita described it, her life's work. Zarin Malva recalls her dedication – not only to the school itself but also to promoting the Montessori method among the teachers. When, as a young woman in her early twenties, Zarin joined the school's staff, Dinoo would keep her back after school was over to talk to her, to teach and encourage her. This early encouragement shaped Ms Malva's life: she is now Principal of the RTI Montessori Training Course in Mumbai.

But though the school may have been her life's work, it did not prevent Dinoo from following other interests. She was an avid reader. Those who knew her remember the characteristic heavy underlining of passages that had particularly interested her. (We also find Dinoo highlighting certain paragraphs in the letters she received from Sangharakshita.)

As well as reading, she had two other particular interests. One was art. In her spare time, she painted. She also meditated regularly. And in the course of her life her meditations included visionary experiences which she tried to record with her paintbrush. In the letters, we find reference to paintings of Maitreya, 'the friendly one', traditionally regarded as the future Buddha. Sangharakshita recalls,

'She told me that she had seen Maitreya Buddha in her meditation and there were many portraits of him that she had painted in water colour ... a very Aryan Maitreya with white skin and rosy cheeks, blue eyes, a beatific smile and a lot of yellow hair ... quite well done.... She'd obviously had some training.'

The promise of one of these paintings for Sangharakshita's new vihara in Kalimpong is a topic that recurs in the letters. Eventually, after some procrastination on her part, and some encouragement and reassurance to 'take her time', on his, the painting was finished. Dinoo probably delivered it on her visit to Kalimpong in October 1958. In any case, Sangharakshita recalls it in its circular white frame, hanging for 'quite a while' in the vihara. I enquired whether it still exists and learned that unfortunately the white ants had got it – an Indian hazard.

Here, then, we find another common interest and source of connection for Dinoo and Sangharakshita. As a young man he, too, had painted – he had even considered becoming an artist – and had maintained a deep interest in the subject. It is perhaps not surprising that when he came to publish a number of pamphlets – which Dinoo funded – he chose to dedicate to her the one entitled, 'Buddhism and Art'.

As for meditation, he, too, had visionary experiences, as related, for example, in *The Rainbow Road*, when Amitābha, the Buddha of the West, appeared to him while he was meditating in a cave in southern India. That Dinoo had some personal experience of what one might call, 'higher realms of existence', was surely significant in the creation of a friendship between them and contributed to making it not just an ordinary friendship but also a spiritual one.

JAGDISH KASHYAP

A necessary condition for entering higher realms of experience is what Buddhists term *śraddhā*, that turning of the whole being, like a sunflower towards the sun, to that which is recognized as higher, in the sense of closer to reality or closer to the experience of Enlightenment. And if Dinoo found it in her meditation and sometimes in her reading, and gave expression to it in her painting, she also found it in her encounters with people. It is surely this that drew her in the first instance so strongly towards Sangharakshita. And this being drawn to those in whom she recognized a spiritual depth and understanding deeper than her own is also reflected in the trust and confidence she seems to have placed in the Buddhist monk, Jagdish Kashyap (one of Sangharakshita's own teachers, see Letter 5, notes 14 and 15). Here is Dinoo's account of their first meeting in a letter to Sangharakshita dated 18 December 1956:

> Mr & Mrs Birla took me to the Ananda Vihara on the 9th i.e. the day the Dalai Lama was coming to it.... Before the Dalai Lama arrived I asked the German monk if he was Jagdish Kashyap, and suddenly to my surprise I heard a voice on my right say, 'No, I am Jagdish Kashyap.' – 'Oh I am very happy to meet you' etc etc: and he asked me to come over to him on Friday the 14th between 4.30 and 5 p.m. so that was fixed.

The meeting duly took place and they had a long talk. Dinoo told him about the background to her interest in Buddhism, and talked about Dr Mehta and 'his present predicament'. Kashyapji told her about his studies, his travels, and how he had become a monk. A few days later he visited Dinoo at Oceana. She gave him one of Sangharakshita's letters to read, the highly significant letter written on 15 December 1956, just after the sudden death of Dr Ambedkar. Kashyapji was, she said, 'very pleased with your adventures in Nagpur'. He had come to say goodbye as he had been called away to Nālandā. How she wished she could go with him, Dinoo could not help saying. 'O, please come,' said Kashyapji – whether out of politeness or genuine interest, we cannot know. In any case, he offered to take Dinoo to various holy sites, as well as to Nālandā where he was expecting to meet Nehru, prime minister of India, and Zhou Enlai, first Premier of the People's Republic of China. (Kashyapji was in the process of raising funds for his Nālandā Vihara and presumably for this reason was meeting with the two statesmen.) 'Will be nice to see them both again,' Dinoo writes, rather surprisingly. (In what context she may have already seen them – other than in the newspapers – I have no idea.) Dinoo was highly excited by the prospect of the trip. But just over a week later, another letter is dispatched to Sangharakshita: 'Well, man proposes & God disposes! It seems I am not destined to do the holy places this year. J. K. got instructions from Delhi that he should go there....'

Although she was not to accompany Kashyapji to the holy sites, Sangharakshita is optimistic that his old teacher will be able to provide some study sessions for Dinoo and others in Bombay who are interested in Buddhism. However, by July 1957, Dinoo is writing that Jagdish Kashyap seems to have 'disappeared for good' and she does not refer to him again.

But if study with Jagdish Kashyap did not manifest, we know that earlier in the year she had enjoyed studying the *Dhammapada* with Dr N. K. Bhagwat (Letter 2, note 3). 'It is amazing how these verses stick in my head ... as if I had known them for generations.'

MEETING THE DALAI LAMA

An even briefer meeting, but one which seems to have aroused in Dinoo very deep feelings of faith and confidence, was that with the Dalai Lama. He visited the Ananda Vihara, as already mentioned, on 9 December 1956. Something occurred which passed Dinoo by, but which was recounted later by Jagdish Kashyap to Sangharakshita. It concerned the Dalai Lama's arrival at the Vihara. Being already acquainted with the Dalai Lama, Kashyapji stepped forward to greet him. Just as he did so, Aniruddha, the German monk, pushed him brusquely aside saying, 'I'm in charge here,' and went to greet the Dalai Lama himself! So much for *bhikkhu*-like humility!

Here is Dinoo's account of her encounter with the Dalai Lama – then a very young man, just twenty-six years old:

> The Dalai Lama prostrated himself before the shrine, & said some prayers, after which some presents were given.... I was standing right behind the Dalai Lama & held on to his warm brown garment, and also prayed to be liberated from all the hindrances. It was so nice to touch him & be so close to him. His expression as he prostrated was so different & spiritual. Then a little after he got up he winked & changed into his boyish smile. After prayers they were walking out. I kept by his side & asked 'Do you speak English'. He said, 'a little', then suddenly I do not know what came over me, I stepped in front of him took hold of both his hands, & put my head into them. Then after a while when I let go the hands and raised my head to look into his face, he smiled so sweetly & patted me on the head.

In his response to this confidence of Dinoo's, Sangharakshita shows his great capacity for empathy, recognizing, as he does, the real meaning of her actions (see Letter 10).

The next day Dinoo sees the Dalai Lama and his entourage again, this time at a function at the Convocation Hall.

'Poor fellows, they were boiling in their very warm clothes.... I could not help smiling when I saw the Dalai Lama wiping his head with his cloak. It seems they do not carry a kerchief.... It was all so sweet and innocent. I could not help loving him very much as if he were my own son. As I watched he suddenly gave me a look of recognition and smiled back. I was so thrilled.'

DINOO AND DR MEHTA

But if Dinoo's nature was one that sought out the Higher in experiences and in her encounters with people, inevitably she was at times disappointed in the latter, and nowhere more so than in her relationship with Dr Mehta whose name sounds like a constant bell, a rather clanging bell, through most of her early letters, answered by one a little more sonorous in the letters of Sangharakshita.

There is quite a lot to say about Dr Mehta and I refer the interested reader to the Appendix for a fuller account of him and his circle. Here let us take a look at him through Dinoo's eyes.

Her first contact almost certainly came about through a medical problem of some kind. We know that she suffered from chronic insomnia. ('It is 5 in the morning. Too tired to read over. Kindly excuse errors.' is scribbled hastily at the end of one letter.) That she may have suffered from other ailments we can surmise from the fact that at some point she became a patient of a naturopath – who was once personal naturopathic physician to Mahatma Gandhi – Dr Dinshah Mehta.

When, in the early 1950s, Dr Mehta set up his religious movement, The Society of Servants (renamed the Society of Servants of God when too many calls came for cooks and bearers!), like a number of his other patients and former patients, Dinoo went along – eagerly, we may imagine – to join in. Here she found people who, like her, had spiritual interests, in other words she found some kind of spiritual community; she found common practice in their group meditations; and she found teaching in Dr Mehta's 'guidance'. But if Dr Mehta believed himself to be guided directly by God, this did not go down very well with Dinoo, whose faith and confidence in the Doctor as a spiritual personality quailed quite quickly. Indeed, when Sangharakshita met her in the autumn of 1955, she was already expressing some reservations, and these grew into criticisms and even, eventually, denunciations. For one thing, she did not like the way he treated his wife, Gulbehn, who had become something of a friend. For another, she did not like his manner towards those in his circle – which seemed as time went by to become worse rather than better. 'The way he has taken to running down everybody, & holding himself up as a "Saviour of Souls",' exclaims Dinoo. 'There is of course no one to equal him, as so far no one [else] has been assigned such an onerous task.... This self-assigned Saviour of Souls had better be careful of his own soul before it gets too out of hand.' Looking back to the early days of his movement when no doubt she, too, had admired him, she recalls, 'our faith in D. [Dinshah] had completely blinded us & numbed our senses.'

Dinoo tried to communicate something of what she saw to Dr Mehta himself. '... no one so far had had the guts to speak to him with the candour that I did till I went to Poona, he felt quite smug. Now his feet tremble, the ground underneath feels very shaky.' Whether Dinoo's home truths really had such an effect on Dr Mehta's confidence is perhaps rather questionable. Sangharakshita suggests Dr Mehta would have dismissed any such criticism as the other person's problematic ego!

Just what Dinoo felt towards Dr Mehta is a question that cannot easily be answered. It was, perhaps, rather complex. It is notable that despite Sangharakshita's gentle encouragement to withdraw from the Society if she no longer found it helpful and his reminder that she need not continue her connection with either the Society or with Dr Mehta (Letter 8), she was not able to give up either so easily. In some sense, she had become attached, an attachment fuelled, perhaps, by disappointment and even some resentment. Perhaps Dinoo liked to have a reason for airing a little indignation, for 'letting off steam' which she was well able to do – and clearly felt free enough to do – in her letters to Sangharakshita. But when she wrote of Dr Mehta, she also showed some insight into his character. 'D. has a way of melting one,' she wrote once. 'That night after your talk when I said goodbye to him he gave me such a look before his customary embrace, that I thought he was going to burst into tears. It seems he does not like people to go away from him.'

Perhaps in the beginning, Doctor had succeeded in 'melting' Dinoo to some extent, which would account for the difficulty she had in giving up her connection with him and with the Society, even when it had deteriorated to something that no longer had any spiritual interest for her. One cannot help getting the impression that Dinoo's womanly heart was not immune to certain feelings, as her rather hard judgements of Sundri, Dr Mehta's chief disciple, may suggest.

'I do not agree with you that Sundri is entirely blameless,' she writes in December 1956. 'She is no ignorant lass mistaking intrigue for romance! She is a woman of mature years 34! & all her moves are well calculated!'

Gradually, however, Dinoo's involvement waned and her preoccupation with Dr Mehta and the Society faded. By the end of 1957 there is only a brief mention of the affairs of the Society. And by the time Sangharakshita has returned to England, Dr Mehta is no longer a significant theme in their correspondence.

DINOO'S ADVENTURES

Although Dinoo spent most of her time at home in Bombay, she was not without a spirit of adventure. Not only had she studied abroad; in 1956 she went on a pilgrimage to Ceylon and Japan from which countries she brought back the Buddhist images on display in her flat. She also passed through Bangkok where she met the 'sweet little monk' from Cambodia whom she hoped to introduce to Sangharakshita (Letter 12, note 6).

It is her account of this journey, an account warmly invited by Sangharakshita, quite early on in their correspondence, that seems to have brought the two into closer communion – perhaps because Dinoo gave a stronger and deeper expression to those things more essentially meaningful to her. In any case, Sangharakshita read her account 'with eager interest' and in his response speaks of her personal qualities with exceptional warmth and appreciation (Letter 5).

The following year comes her plan to go on pilgrimage with Jagdish Kashyap. When this falls through, and with Sangharakshita's encouragement and considerable practical help as regards her itinerary, Dinoo makes plans for a long journey, including a visit to Kalimpong.

The visit is postponed more than once but finally, in the autumn of 1958, the last plans are put in place. Despite the fact that he is keeping the rainy season retreat and therefore unable to leave his vihara, and despite the fact that viharas are not notable for such items, Sangharakshita promises to ensure there will be available to her a *long mirror* – without which, it seems, a proper visit cannot to be contemplated.

A BREACH

The long-awaited visit takes place and is followed by … silence. No letters survive (if, indeed, any were written) from the following four-and-a-half years. When the correspondence is taken up again in 1963, we can see from its content that something had occurred, some strain in their relations, some upset. Sangharakshita mentioned to me that Dinoo had been rather upset by the way the Kazini of Chakhung, a friend to whom he had introduced Dinoo (about whom more below), had not done all she could (in Dinoo's opinion) to help her find accommodation for her visit to Gangtok. But could this really have led to a break in relations with Sangharakshita (if such it was)? It seems Dinoo had seen this slight as an expression of jealousy on the Kazini's part of Dinoo's friendship with Sangharakshita – a suggestion Sangharakshita is inclined to dismiss. As we have seen in relation to Dr Mehta and Sundri, Dinoo herself was not immune to such feelings occasionally.

Whatever the cause (and there seem to have been subsequent misunderstandings relating to Dinoo's attending Sangharakshita's lectures in Bombay) we find in the next surviving letter, written by Sangharakshita in 1963 (in answer to one from Dinoo which did not survive) his concern to heal the breach, to find a reconciliation for, as he tells Dinoo, 'I never like to break with a friend.'

As is often the case in human relations, this effort to heal the breach, to find reconciliation, seems to bring about a greater trust and confidence. Perhaps Dinoo was convinced that Sangharakshita really did value her and their correspondence (doubts about which occasionally creep into her letters.) By the end of that year, 1963, Sangharakshita writes to Dinoo from his sick bed, 'I think that was the nicest letter you have ever written me – though all your letters are nice!'

A FRIEND'S SUPPORT

From the very beginning, Dinoo offered Sangharakshita support, giving him 1,000 rupees in honour of the Buddha Jayanti. In 1957, she is one of three friends who respond to his urgent request, when he is about to be made homeless, for money to purchase a building where he can finally settle and create a permanent vihara. Although a little later Dinoo goes back on a promise of money (perhaps part of the complications that arose subsequent to her visit to Kalimpong), her generous spirit is very much in evidence throughout their correspondence, whether in donations of money, her hospitality, or the gift of her painting. And Sangharakshita responds, dedicating one of his pamphlets to her, sending photographs, or making suggestions of books that he thinks may please or interest Dinoo. His last extant letter was sent along with a copy of a recently published book. Surely this ongoing exchange of gifts and kindnesses is part of the essence of friendship.

And there was what one might call 'moral support'. She intuitively grasped the significance of Sangharakshita's encounters with the newly-converted followers of Dr Ambedkar, about which he writes in December 1956. She responds with a burst of sympathetic joy: 'I had a feeling that Ambedkar's death would bring more people into the Buddhist fold. So over a lakh of people turned Buddhist! Within twenty years there will be a number of gems from among these lakh.' She continues, 'I wish more & greater successes to all your noble desires and endeavours! I am so happy, I can hardly contain myself!'

THE LAST YEARS

After Sangharakshita's departure for England in 1964, their written exchanges became less frequent. Nevertheless, they remained in touch. Sangharakshita visited Dinoo in 1966, along with his friend Terry Delamare, during his farewell trip to India before he settled in the West. At the time of the last surviving letter, written by Sangharakshita in January 1974, Dinoo was well into her seventies, had grown very deaf, and old age may have made writing more difficult. In 1979, on his way to New Zealand, Sangharakshita again visited India. While in Bombay, he naturally took the opportunity to visit his old friend, taking Lokamitra with him.[144] Lokamitra, one of Sangharakshita's senior disciples, had gone out to India the previous year and had decided to stay on, dedicating his life to helping the new Buddhist movement there. Now in his turn, when he was in Bombay he would visit Dinoo, enjoy her cakes, and, sitting close up (owing to her deafness), engage in long hours of conversation. Although there were no more letters, news of his Bombay friend continued to reach Sangharakshita.

Lokamitra told me Dinoo looked forward to her death with the curiosity that was one of her vital qualities. It seems in the end it did not come easily; there was suffering to be endured. Sadly, her efforts to get into contact with Lokamitra before she passed away were unsuccessful. He would have very much liked to have visited her. Her death finally came on 13 January 1991. She was nearly ninety. She left for Lokamitra her beautiful Buddha figure that had been present during so many conversations with her Buddhist friends, not only Lokamitra but of course, Sangharakshita too. Perhaps death was not the end of their connection.

THE LETTERS

In her last years, Dinoo photocopied twenty-nine letters from Sangharakshita that she had kept, and sent the copies to him. It is these letters that make up this book. The first is dated 21 December 1955. The address is Khar, the Bombay suburb where Sangharakshita was staying. 'Dear Upasika', it begins, showing us at once something of the nature of their connection. ('Upasika' is a term of address to a Buddhist laywoman and, as we have seen, that Dinoo saw herself as a Buddhist was surely an important aspect of their mutual interest.) But such formality did not last long. The following letter begins, 'Dear Miss Dubash' and already by the third letter, written in March 1956, Sangharakshita is addressing her as 'Dear Dinoo', the greater informality reflecting the growing friendship. As for Dinoo, though she liked to indulge in a little teasing from time to time, her basic respect for the much younger monk to whom she clearly looked up is reflected in her constant mode of address: 'Dear Bhante Sangharakshita.'

Dinoo and Sangharakshita corresponded for a period of almost twenty years. And while Dinoo's letters (nine of them survived) were written from her home in Marine Drive, the addresses that head Sangharakshita's letters reflect his exceptionally vigorous and active life. He wrote most of his letters from India: from Bombay, Poona, Calcutta, Delhi, and from two addresses in Kalimpong, the Himalayan town where he was based. The last few letters, though, came to Dinoo across thousands of miles, not only of land but of sea.

And what of the scope of the letters? While in this Introduction I look in particular at the friendship between the two correspondents, readers will see for themselves that there are many other seams to be mined. Sangharakshita's letters have many strata of interest which perhaps others will explore in the future. Or, to change the metaphor, you could say the letters are like so many snapshots of Sangharakshita's life and interests at that time so that we read of gardening and poetry, of lecture tours and politics, of visitors and meditation, of travel plans and rising housing costs. There are also a number of references to illness. We discover, for instance, that in the second half of 1957 – a hugely demanding year for Sangharakshita – he had been ill for three months – according to the doctor 'due to prolonged overwork and vitamin deficiency' (Letter 18) and had had to cancel his usual preaching tour in the plains. And we see during the years Sangharakshita is writing from India there is some change as of one moving from (worldly) innocence to one of much greater experience gained through the discharging of the responsibilities he undertakes, which prepares the ground for what is to come.

But if most of the letters have Indian addresses at their head, a very significant change takes place in 1964, the year in which Sangharakshita visits his native country. Before he embarks on his journey, he writes to Dinoo that he does not expect the visit to last more than four – or at the most six – months after which he intends to resume his life at his vihara. As it turns out, however – and as we learn from the letters – the visit changes the whole outer context of his life: he decides to settle in England and to continue his Buddhist activities from there. His last letters to Dinoo bear English addresses and tell of English winter and English spring and of the start of a new Buddhist movement in the West. As we read over Dinoo's shoulder, we catch just a glimpse of what it has taken to set that in motion:

'To be frank,' he confides, 'it was very uphill work indeed in the early days, but after seven years of hard work I think it can be said that we have at least the nucleus of a truly spiritual, and now rapidly expanding, Buddhist Movement in the West.'

This comes from his final letter. But if the correspondence between them came to an end it is certain that their connection did not:

'With one's real friends', Sangharakshita had written, 'I find, it does not matter very much whether one writes or does not write since they remain, as it were, a part of one's consciousness, so that it is impossible ever to forget them.'

THE ENGLISH MONK

Who was the English monk whom Dinoo came to know? In his memoirs, Sangharakshita adopts a style which is characterized, one might almost say, by understatement. Certainly he eschews anything of sensationalism. Yet anyone who has made even a cursory study of those volumes will have been left with the impression of a rather exceptional human being: exceptional from childhood in his interest in and prolific study of western and eastern art, literature, history, philosophy and religion; exceptional in his recognition of the profoundest truths of Buddhism when, aged sixteen or seventeen, he first encountered a Buddhist scripture; and exceptional in his confidence and clarity that he was a Buddhist 'and always had been', even when there was hardly any opportunity for meeting others of like mind.

In 1950, his first Buddhist teacher, Jagdish Kashyap (who makes an appearance in these letters), with whom he had spent nine months studying Pāli, Abhidharma, and Logic, took him to Kalimpong in the foothills of the Himalayas and left him there with the injunction to 'stay here and work for the good of Buddhism'. The capacity to turn this set of circumstances to the good shows again a man of exceptional creativity of mind and heart and an extraordinary ability both to 'go it alone' and to make friends with people from the most diverse backgrounds.

But what did – and does – working for the good of Buddhism mean for Sangharakshita? Without a doubt, for him it meant to teach the Dharma, to communicate the Buddha's teaching. 'Out of compassion for the world, for the benefit, welfare, and happiness of gods and men, teach the Dharma that is good in the beginning, good in the middle, and good at the end....'[145] So the Buddha had enjoined his own disciples 2,500 years ago. The insight that what the world most needs is the great wisdom, the understanding of the true nature of reality which alone gives rise to an unbounded compassion, we see expressing itself again and again in Sangharakshita's activities, whether in India or in the West. As he wrote five years before he met Dinoo:

> One need, and one need only,
> All earthly things above,
> This world hath now as ever –
> The need of boundless love.
> One way, and one way only,
> There is to outward peace –
> That Great Heart of Compassion
> Which bids all sorrows cease.[146]

It seems that for Sangharakshita the wish to spread the Dharma has been *the* driving force of his life and for this reason his move to the West was not for him a great watershed or change in the basic course of his life-stream as it might seem to others. 'To me it was just a single stream of activity, even though located in different places,' he recently explained.

Finding himself in 1950 in Kalimpong with the injunction to stay there and work for the good of Buddhism, he used his considerable talents (some of which he discovered in the process) to that end. He wrote articles, founded a magazine, *Stepping-Stones*, to which contributions were made by such well-known figures as Edward Conze and Lama Govinda, and in due course took over editing the Maha Bodhi Society's journal, one of the main Buddhist publications of the time, read both in the East and in the West, through which he became quite widely known in the growing Buddhist world of the second half of the twentieth century. He created a Buddhist youth organization in Kalimpong and he went on preaching tours. During the fourteen years he was based in Kalimpong he preached in almost every state in India. He discovered himself to be an inspired and fluent speaker who easily commanded the attention of his audience. Invitations to speak flowed in. With his wish to 'give the Dharma' – as he saw it, the duty of a monk – he responded to as many invitations as he could. In particular, he moved among the new Buddhists, the followers of that great figure of twentieth-century history, Dr B. R. Ambedkar. I refer the interested reader to Sangharakshita's book *Ambedkar and Buddhism* in which the significance of Ambedkar's life and work is painted in vivid colours, as well as his own involvement with the peaceful revolution that Ambedkar inaugurated.[147] The letter to Dinoo, written shortly after Dr Ambedkar's death, is of particular historical and spiritual significance (included here as Letter 9).

In trying to bring into focus the significance of Sangharakshita's life and work at that time, we need to bear in mind the state of Buddhism in both the West and in India in the mid-twentieth century. In the UK, Buddhism was hardly known. The Buddhist Society, founded in 1924, with which Sangharakshita came into contact in his late teens, had but a small membership. The English Sangha Trust emerged only in 1954. (The difference between then and now, when hundreds of Buddhist groups from all sorts of Buddhist traditions exist in Britain – and, of course, elsewhere in Europe and indeed the world over – is quite staggering.)

As for India, where once the Buddha himself had lived and taught, the Dharma had long since all but vanished under the onslaught of Muslim invasions in the twelfth and thirteenth centuries, other factors also playing a part. As the twentieth century dawned, there was a single figure illuminating the otherwise bleak and desolate landscape of Buddhism in India: Anagārika Dharmapala. His great contribution was his indefatigable efforts to reclaim from Hindu control the Buddhist holy sites. He also set up a Buddhist organization, the Maha Bodhi Society, whose branches later spread throughout the subcontinent.

Dharmapala was a great and inspiring figure (about whom Sangharakshita wrote a biographical sketch).[148] But, as he soon discovered, those who now ran the organization Dharmapala had founded did not share his great vision or his abilities. Some were downright corrupt. In addition, to some extent at least, the organization had come under Hindu influence. This, then, is the background to Buddhism in India in 1950 when Sangharakshita found himself alone in Kalimpong, determined to work 'for the good of Buddhism'.

FRIENDSHIP

In two areas, perhaps, he excelled above all. The first was in communicating the Dharma, which, as we have seen, he did through his writing, including his poetry, and his lectures. But perhaps even beyond this huge output, Sangharakshita's understanding of the essence of the Buddhist life was communicated through his friendships. The profound place of spiritual friendship in the Buddhist life is described in his essay, 'The Good Friend', originally an editorial for *Stepping-Stones*.

Friendship, he declares, 'is of the profoundest possible significance. Through it we perceive "through a glass, darkly" the pure and tranquil lineaments of Enlightenment itself.' I refer the interested reader to the full text.[149] Sangharakshita took to heart the Buddha's declaration to his friend, companion, and cousin, Ānanda, that spiritual friendship, *kalyāṇa mitratā*, was 'the whole of the spiritual life'.[150] It is the growing friendship with Dinoo as it communicates itself to us through their correspondence that is surely what most engages us in these letters.

Despite the differences in their ages, background, ethnicity, despite the fact that he was a monk and she a teacher, he a man, she a woman, the flower of friendship grew between them. Friendship is characterized by kindness, truthfulness, mutual interest, mutual helpfulness, by deepening trust, growing affection, and so on. We expect to find fidelity, as well as apology and forgiveness. Spiritual friendship is characterized by all of these as well as encouragement for human and spiritual growth. A spiritual friend must be able to see us for who we are, to empathize with us, while not always agreeing with us, and to encourage us in strengthening our virtues, while not condemning us for our faults, however clearly they may be seen. All this may be found in Sangharakshita's letters to Dinoo. His efforts to communicate to her his own spiritual understandings, e.g. about meditation, seem to arise from the wish to write to her about what might really have meaning for her. Nor does he neglect to tell her of his own life, in which she has a deep interest – not to say curiosity. And sometimes we find it is Dinoo who is the confidante. Their friendship, though not equal, was mutual.

SANGHARAKSHITA, WOMEN, AND FRIENDSHIP

At this point, I think I may need to address a certain related issue. I believe this particular topic has not been written about before – and some may say I am venturing where angels fear to tread! Among the various epithets that have attached themselves at different times to Sangharakshita (including 'Russian spy', 'American Agent' and 'narrow-minded Hīnayānist' – the inventor of the latter actually makes an appearance in these letters as 'the German *bhikkhu*', see Letter 15, note 7) – Sangharakshita has also been dubbed 'a misogynist'.[151] It seems the term was never applied to him in India and anyone who reads the memoirs relating to his time there will discover that he had many and varied contacts with women, a number of whom he came to regard as friends. (What this suggests more notably, given he was an ordained Buddhist monk, or *bhikkhu*, is his unwillingness to adhere rigidly to the letter of the monastic *vinaya*, or rule, when it seemed to have no bearing on spiritual life as he understood it. For instance, when he started his activities in Kalimpong, he realized it would not be possible to work for the good of Buddhism without handling 'silver and gold' which is, in fact, forbidden to monks.[152] In the same vein, he did not adhere strictly to the 'not eating after noon' rule when it seemed to him to get in the way of other more important matters. So, too, he did not hesitate to make friends with women, especially if they seemed to have a genuine spiritual interest. And though they were not permitted to stay overnight in the vihara itself – though in fact Sister Amita Nisatta stayed in the guest cottage in the vihara's grounds, (Letter 18, note 7) – they were welcome to join Sangharakshita and others at the Vihara not only for meditation, but also for meals – certainly not permitted by more traditional monastics – see the invitation to Dinoo in Letter 20.)

The epithet 'misogynist' did not arise in India but in the West. In fact it arose within the movement he had himself created. Did this mean that when he returned to his own country, Sangharakshita's relations with women suddenly changed? Reading *Moving Against the Stream*, it does not seem so. (Though I would suggest interested readers to find out for themselves.)[153] So where did the charge come from? I can only surmise. But I suspect it came from his contention that there is a difference in spiritual aptitude between men and women, meaning that although they equally have the potential for Enlightenment, other things being equal, men have some advantage in terms of realizing this potential.

If one suspects that the motive behind such a statement is the wish to denigrate women, one might easily come to the conclusion that Sangharakshita had some dislike of the female sex. (Even then 'misogyny' would be rather an extreme appellation, meaning as it does, according to Collins *Dictionary*, simply 'hatred of women', hatred being 'extreme dislike; enmity.') But if, in fact, it is simply an observation based on his own perception and experience, it need not be taken as an anti-woman attitude. One does not, after all, have to agree (though I know people, both men and women, who do – as well as others who do not). Perhaps most interesting is to observe reactions to the idea. For those who think there may be truth in it, if they are men, then they should not take it as licence for arrogance and those feelings of superiority which easily give rise to contempt, which certainly do not count as Buddhist virtues. In any case, one has to remember that a generalization can never be unthinkingly applied to any given individual. It is up to women not to let it undermine self-confidence but, confident that we do indeed have the potential for Enlightenment, to get on and make progress on the path.

I have heard in support of the idea that Sangharakshita has a somewhat jaundiced view of women references to his memoirs in which the description of certain women is not entirely flattering. But I think you will find that this is just as much the case for some of the male characters who make an appearance. It seems Sangharakshita combines a capacity for deeply-felt empathy with a keen perception that does not hesitate to see both virtue and folly. On occasion he gives voice to both.

But what about his younger days? Might he then have been something of a woman-hater? After all, what was the subject of his very first public talk? The subject (which he chose himself) was, 'The Inferiority of Women', and the talk – or rather paper – was read to a meeting of the Junior Staff Association of the London County Council (for whom he was working). He was sixteen and had taken a dislike to the Association's chairwoman.[154] One could, perhaps, write a whole paper commenting on this little episode and what it might tell us about men and women – but that is beyond the scope of this Introduction and must, perhaps, wait for another occasion.

If he sometimes took a dislike to certain individuals, including some women, he was equally capable of admiration. When he was nineteen, he wrote an article on the poetry of Sarojini Naidu. *Krishna's Flute* was to be a 'tribute from an admirer of her poetry and personality'. With his already exceptional powers of criticism, he shows the value – and heaps praise – upon her poetry. With all the passion of youth, he declares the lady herself an example of 'full and perfect Indian womanhood'.[155]

In fact it seems that throughout his life there have been women whom Sangharakshita admired. Charlotte Brontë's *Jane Eyre* was one of his favourite novels as a boy. Queen Elizabeth I is a figure in whom he took particular interest. His poems reveal his affection for and appreciation of some of the women he knew. In 1961 he wrote a long poem to honour Sophia Wadia on her sixtieth birthday from which here a single verse:

> As infant, girl and woman
> Into gracious middle age
> She has trod with step unfaltering
> Truth's arduous pilgrimage.[156]

In 1983 he wrote his 'Lines to Jayapushpa':

> Dear daughter of a tropic isle,
> For twice twelve months your radiant smile
> Has blessed our weary London streets....[157]

Enough said, I think, to show beyond the sphere of reasonable doubt that the term 'misogynist' simply does not apply. In any case, I think the letters to Dinoo speak for themselves.

OTHER FRIENDS

As we read Sangharakshita's letters to Dinoo, we find, of course, quite a number of other characters making an appearance. Dr Mehta is one. More on him and his circle can found in the Appendix. Here let us stay in the realm of Sangharakshita's friendships with women and take a look at two – very different – women with whom he became friends.

CLARE CAMERON

Sangharakshita's first encounter with Clare was in 1942, not long after he had realized he was a Buddhist 'and always had been'. He had sent her an article for the Buddhist Society Journal, *Buddhism in England* (later renamed *The Middle Way*), of which she was editor. She replied 'with kind words I did not really deserve.'[158]

Clare was born to an East London working-class family in 1896. Her early life, recounted in an engaging autobiography, *Rustle of Spring*, reveals her as the archetypal misfit, her interests at odds with those of all around her.[159] Early on she was drawn to things spiritual and began writing poetry:

If I could make a little song
    As lovely as the skylark's is
A simple music sweet and strong
    But soft and fleeting as a kiss;

A little song to truly tell
    All that I am and long to be,
The tender hopes and dreams that swell
    And so distress the heart and me;

Then would I come with quiet feet
    My song made perfect in my hand,
And nought on earth were then more sweet
    Than you should hear and understand.

Alas! 'tis crying for the moon
    And sun and stars, that I would be!
For I were God's archangel soon
    If I could sing such mystery.[160]

Eventually Clare found her way to the London Buddhist Society and it was here that she crossed paths with Sangharakshita. Although they had corresponded for some time, they actually met on his first visit to the Society premises in spring 1944, on which occasion she introduced him to Christmas Humphreys, the Society's founder and president.

Sangharakshita liked Clare immediately, seeing in her 'one of those rare spirits who, in the words of the Indian poet, are tender as a flower and hard as a diamond.'[161] She was the only person in the Society, Sangharakshita noted, who had the strength of character not to be dominated by Humphreys. Clare was one of those present in May that year when, in the middle of the Blitz, Sangharakshita first 'took' the Refuges and Precepts at the Buddhist Society's Vaiśākha Pūrṇimā celebrations, thus formally becoming a member of the Buddhist sangha.

Despite the discrepancy in age (he was eighteen, she in her late forties), their friendship grew – not only through their mutual interest in Buddhism but perhaps more especially through their mutual interest in poetry. By then she had had several volumes published and made him a present of *A Stranger Here*.[162] He went on to show Clare some of his own verses, and received 'some very sound criticism'. When, ten years later, he came to publish his own first volume, *Messengers from Tibet and Other Poems*, he dedicated it to Clare 'in token of my gratitude and admiration.'[163]

In August, Sangharakshita left for India. The two did not meet again for twenty years. But before following the fortunes of their friendship, let us briefly trace the contours of Clare's further life. She married the writer Thomas Burke and lived with him in London. He, it seems, was homosexual and their marriage was not a conventional one. She had a number of lovers. (She was an exceptionally beautiful woman.) In 1945, after several years of illness, Thomas died. The following year, Clare moved to a farm in the Suffolk countryside with Cuthbert Lambert where they tried, unsuccessfully, to form a community. In the early 1950s she returned to London to look after her elderly and sick parents. In rapid succession, both her younger brother and her mother died. She stayed on to care for her father and continued to write. She developed new interests: in Sri Aurobindo's teaching and in the dancing of Ram Gopal. She also edited a magazine, *Here and Now*, founded originally in 1939 by the poet and mystic Derek Neville, which Clare bought from him in 1950.

In 1956 Clare's father died. Whereas Sangharakshita at that time was working on his *A Survey of Buddhism*, concerned to see Buddhism in its full depth and breadth, Clare's interests had become universalist. She was a contributor to *Science of Thought Review*, a magazine founded by English mystic Henry Thomas Hamblin (Letter 24, note 8). Her contact with HTH (as he was affectionately known) became increasingly important and in 1958 she moved to Uckfield, Sussex, not far from his home. Later that year Henry Thomas Hamblin died. Two years later Clare took over from his son, Bert, the editorship of the *Review*. In 1964, on the death of Mrs Hamblin, Clare moved into Bosham House, where she remained until her own death in 1983. Others lived there with her from time to time. From 1981, she had a companion in her future biographer, Brian Graham. According to Graham, 'her last years were a mixture of fears and joy. At times she experienced being lifted into a higher state of consciousness where she walked hand in hand with God.... At other times she felt lost in a stormy sea full of the anxious and fearful....'[164] In the course of her life she made – and kept – many friends. There were many who admired her – for better or worse – as a mystic, and for others, no doubt, it was Clare's poetry that had most deeply spoken to them.

But what of her friendship with Sangharakshita?

Clare and Sangharakshita's friendship continued after his departure for India and over the twenty years, many letters were exchanged. Nor did they only write to each other; they exchanged magazines: he sent her *Stepping-Stones* and she sent him her magazine, *Here and Now*. In this way, Sangharakshita came to realize that his friend's thinking and attitudes were changing. Indeed, they were now dominated by a 'vague eclecticism' which he did not share nor did he find very appealing. As he was to write to Dinoo, 'Buddhism seems to give one a taste for intellectual precision, even though the limitations of the intellect are fully realized.' (Letter 24).

Clare included an essay from *Stepping-Stones* in an issue of the *Review*, but, with the magazine's readership in mind, she requested that the Buddha be referred to as 'a certain wise man'. Mention of the Buddha, it seems, would have put off some readers, who, though liberal-minded to an extent, were definitely Christian.

Notwithstanding that their outlooks had diverged, it was to visit Clare at her Sussex home that Sangharakshita hastened soon after his return to the West. He refers to his visits in Letter 27.[165] What he does not tell Dinoo, but relates in his memoirs, is the disappointment he experienced at their meeting – disappointment in Clare's 'vague, universalist mysticism'; and disappointment that she had no recollection of the three precious volumes and the notebook of his own verses which he had entrusted to her for safe-keeping before embarking for India.

So, it seems, their lives moved in different directions. Clare took only a little interest in the Buddhist movement which Sangharakshita went on to found. Nevertheless, his gratitude and admiration of her in his younger years shine through the first volume of his memoirs, and the 'pixie-like' editor of *The Middle Way* will surely be remembered as one of Sangharakshita's first good friends in the Buddhist and the literary world.

KAZINI ELISA-MARIA DORJE-KHANGSARPA OF CHAKHUNG

Should one find oneself wondering whether Sangharakshita's friendships with women were confined to a certain 'spiritual' type, encountering the Kazini soon dismisses any such supposition. She appears in this volume in the Notes. As already mentioned, the Kazini seems to have played a part in the complications that arose at the time of Dinoo's visit to Kalimpong in the autumn of 1958.

Almost two whole chapters of Sangharakshita's fourth volume of memoirs, *Precious Teachers*, are taken up with the lives, fortunes, and misfortunes of the Kazini and her Sikkimese husband, Kazi Lhendup Dorje of Chakhung, a Sikkimese aristocrat living in Kalimpong (later the first chief minister of Sikkim after it became a state of India in 1975). The two make a further appearance in *Moving Against the Stream*. I would refer the interested reader immediately to those fascinating, sometimes hilarious, sometimes sobering, as well as occasionally touching, anecdotes.[166]

Here we can only sketch briefly something of the life and times and the context of this friendship. It began in 1957 with the marriage of the Sikkimese Kazi to a Scottish woman. She was born in Dunoon, there were three older sisters, her given name was Ethel Maud Shirran. She later renamed herself Elisa Maria. She claimed to have studied law, probably in Edinburgh and perhaps elsewhere. She became Mrs Langford Rae in 1923 and lived with her husband in Burma, where she came to know Eric Blair, the English author better known by his pen name, George Orwell. She divorced in 1940. There was a son, Roderick Langford Rae, born in 1927. Roderick married but separated from his wife soon after his second child was born, 'due to religious differences'. This daughter, who was six years old at the time of her father's death in a road accident in Assam in 1965, recently published family research which includes fascinating details about her grandmother. 'After discovering that Ethel Maud had been going around telling people she was the daughter of Field-Marshal Mannerheim of Finland, I investigated her real origins in more depth and discovered that her true father was at least as interesting as the one she borrowed....'[167]

Sangharakshita was inclined to accept what the Kazini told him in the absence of evidence to the contrary. (Better to believe and discover oneself mistaken than commit the grave error of disbelieving someone who is speaking the truth.) Her granddaughter, on the other hand, having hard evidence at her disposal, concluded that Ethel Maud was both 'fabulous and a fabulist'.

No doubt more research needs to be done to untangle fact from fiction. What we can tentatively piece together is that the Kazini's life took her to many countries, both in the Far East and in Northern Africa. She may have lived for two years in the palace of Kemal Atatürk, founder of the modern Turkish republic. She told Sangharakshita that she had had a brief second marriage to a Dr Khan, a Muslim, but she refused to consummate it since he refused to follow the Islamic ceremony with a civil one.

Her third marriage, to the Kazi, hardly got off to a good start. She arrived in Kalimpong only to discover that the Kazi's former wife (of thirty years) was still living in his house! Sangharakshita was called in to participate in the serious discussions which took place to decide what was to be done.

The Kazini's greatest interest was politics and she threw all her considerable intellectual energies into furthering her husband's political ambitions. But she had some interest in Buddhism – perhaps partly because the Kazi was from a Buddhist family and had, in fact, once been head lama of a monastery. On 3 May 1958 she 'took the *pañca sīla*' at Sangharakshita's vihara, thus formally becoming a Buddhist. She saw herself as Sangharakshita's disciple.

What sort of a person was she? Sangharakshita describes her as a woman who was 'outspoken, tended to be sweeping in her judgements ... inclined to exaggerate and dramatize, though I never knew her to be untruthful.'[168] She was an excellent raconteuse, a good mimic, lively, intelligent, and articulate. Capable of intense political antagonism, her greatest enmity was reserved for her husband's rival, the Maharajkumar (later Maharaja) of Sikkim, who also happened to be a friend of Sangharakshita. It is remarkable that he was able to maintain his friendship over many years with both parties. As he writes in *Moving Against the Stream*, since both were Buddhists, 'I always sought to pour oil – the oil of the Dharma – on these very troubled waters, and if I could not bring the two of them together at least persuade them to moderate their hostility.'[169] (This effort to bring harmony – requiring at times surely all the wisdom of the serpent, as well as the gentleness of the dove, is apparent in his relations with

Dr Mehta, Dinoo, and others who were members of the Doctor's circle – see Appendix.)

For both the Kazi and the Kazini, the English monk was a trusted friend. He was called in to calm down the Kazini when she succumbed to outbreaks of fury and frustration towards her husband. After talking to her for an hour or so, peace would be restored and the three would sit together drinking tea (for Sangharakshita) or *thumbas*, a kind of beer (for the Kazi and Kazini).

It was Sangharakshita who confided in *them* when, towards the end of his farewell tour of India in 1966, he visited Kalimpong shortly after receiving the infamous letter from the English Sangha Trust asking him not to return to England. He told his friends of his decision to return notwithstanding, and to take forward the promising work that he had already begun there. They supported his decision. Sangharakshita had discussed his plans with other friends, including Dhardo Rimpoche and Yogi Chen. They had given their encouragement and blessing. But 'probably only the Kazini understood the kind of difficulties I would have to face.'[170]

Sangharakshita and the Kazini remained in touch by letter for many years. I have not been able to establish the year of her death. The Kazi outlived her, dying in Kalimpong in 2007 at the ripe old age of 103.

A WIDENING CIRCLE

Dinoo had contact with both Clare and the Kazini. It is possible Dinoo and Clare came into contact through a subscription to Clare's magazine, but more likely it was through Sangharakshita. Sangharakshita seems to have made a point of introducing his friends to one another when he had the opportunity. If Dinoo and the Kazini did not exactly hit it off when they met in Kalimpong (and who could be surprised at that!), Dinoo and Clare entered into a warm correspondence. Dinoo made Clare a number of gifts (see Letter 27) and there is reference to donations of money (possibly subscriptions to the magazine) which she asks Sangharakshita to pass on. Lokamitra's friendship with Dinoo has already been noted. So we see that the friendship between our two correspondents brought about further friendship and we now participate ourselves many decades later in those friendships, at least in imagination, and perhaps find ourselves invigorated, inspired, or moved by glimpses of that which another poet, William Blake, characterized as the most characteristic or essential activity of humankind: 'The bird a nest, the spider a web, man friendship'.[171]

A NOTE ON THE NOTES

Dear Dinoo is a book that will no doubt be read chiefly by Friends, Mitras, and Order members of the Triratna Buddhist Community.

'Friends' include all those who have any kind of contact with the movement and I am bearing in mind that some of you may know almost nothing about the Buddha, or Buddhism, or India, nor about Sangharakshita. Some of the notes are for you.

Mitras know at least something about Buddhism (or the Dharma, as Buddhists prefer to call the Buddha's teaching), something about the Buddha, and something about Sangharakshita, the founder of the movement of which they are a part. But very likely they want to know more. I hope some of the notes go some way to broadening your knowledge.

Mitras who have asked for ordination within the Order Sangharakshita founded, and of course those who have already joined the Order as *dharmacāris* or *dharmacārinīs*, men and women who see themselves as his disciples, or disciples of his disciples, they especially will want to know more about their teacher, more about his remarkable life dedicated to the communication of the Dharma, its spirit, and its letter. More, too, about the people with whom he came into contact and with whom he worked. There are quite a few notes for you.

There is, of course, a great deal of biographical material available – five volumes of memoirs, as well as poetry, plus additional material found in *The History of My Going for Refuge*[172] and other essays and papers, as well as Subhuti's biography, *Bringing Buddhism to the West*.[173] No doubt many of you have already turned to these volumes, but are not yet deeply familiar with them, while others have had them on their reading lists, perhaps for some time. Some of the notes are for you, referring, as they often do, to passages in the memoirs, and giving you, I hope, a glimpse of riches in store, making you eager to turn to their pages.

I imagine in the coming years and decades, when there will be, I think – and certainly hope – more awareness of Sangharakshita's stature, more people will want to engage themselves with researching his life. By fine-combing his memoirs to bring together facts, people, events and dates, I hope I will have saved some people some trouble.

Whether you are Friend, Mitra or Order member, or someone not connected with the Triratna Buddhist Community at all, you will be making Dinoo's acquaintance for the first time. (Even those familiar with *In the Sign of the Golden Wheel* will have only caught a brief glimpse of her entering and exiting the stage rather rapidly, mainly in order to introduce Sangharakshita to Dr Mehta.) Now Dinoo has a chance to take centre stage and for us to make her acquaintance a little more deeply. In the Introduction, through quoting from some of her surviving letters, I hope to have given you direct contact with this vital and warm friend of Sangharakshita, and most of all, through reading his letters, a glimpse of the friendship that existed between them.

Kalyanaprabha
Birmingham, UK
September 2011

EDITOR'S NOTE TO THE *COMPLETE WORKS* EDITION

Sangharakshita's letters to Dinoo were sometimes handwritten and sometimes typed. In neither case did they include Pāli or Sanskrit diacritics. In presenting the letters in this *Complete Works* edition we have tried as far as possible to maintain Sangharakshita's original epistolary style.

Notes in the *Complete Works* are usually listed at the end of each volume. We have followed this approach for the notes to the Introduction and the Appendix of *Dear Dinoo*. However, in the case of the Letters the notes appear, as they did in the original edition, immediately following each letter. The explanations they offer are sometimes essential to a proper understanding of the letters. We hope that leaving them in their original place will make them more readily accessible.

In the notes to the Letters, Sangharakshita's volumes of memoirs are abbreviated as follows:

RR: *The Rainbow Road from Tooting Broadway to Kalimpong*, covers the period August 1925 to March 1950. It is now published as *Complete Works*, vol. 20.

FMK: *Facing Mount Kanchenjunga* covers the period March 1950 to early 1953 and is included in this volume of the *Complete Works*.

ISGW: *In the Sign of the Golden Wheel* covers the period early 1953 to May 1957. At the time of going to press, published by Windhorse Publications, Birmingham 1996 (*Complete Works*, vol. 22).

PT: *Precious Teachers* covers the period spring 1957 to summer 1964. At the time of going to press, published by Windhorse Publications, Birmingham 2007 (*Complete Works*, vol. 22).

MAS: *Moving Against the Stream* covers the period August 1964 to April 1969. At the time of going to press, published by Windhorse Publications, Birmingham 2003 (*Complete Works*, vol. 23).

LETTERS

1

Khar,¹
Bombay²
21. 12. 55³

Dear Upasika,⁴

All right, you win. After consulting with my friends I have decided to leave Bombay by the Deccan Queen⁵ on the evening of 5th January. After lecturing on the 6th I shall leave Poona (for Bombay) on the morning train on the 7th. Would you please inform Dr Mehta⁶ of this arrangement when you meet. Somebody will have to meet me at the Poona station. There is only *one* station at Poona, I suppose. If there are two, please let me know at which one I should alight.

With best wishes and blessings,
Yours in the Dharma,
    Sangharakshita

NOTES

1. Khar is a suburb of Bombay. Sangharakshita is staying with Arjundev Rashk, a Punjabi poet and screenwriter whose unusual story is related in *ISGW*, pp. 262–3. It was in Rashk's flat earlier that year that Sangharakshita had written the last chapter of *A Survey of Buddhism* (Letter 15, note 5), conscious of a 'Presence' in the corner (see *ISGW*, chapter 19).
2. Bombay: the most populous city in India. Since 1996 known as Mumbai.
3. Dinoo and Sangharakshita met for the first time only a few weeks previously, at a lecture he had given in Bombay on the theme, 'Inspiration – Whence?' (See Introduction p. 458 and *ISGW* p. 255.)
4. *Upāsikā*: a laywoman in the Buddhist sangha or spiritual community.
5. The Deccan Queen was a popular train that then ran via Poona to Bangalore.
6. Dr Dinshah K. Mehta: see Appendix. Dinoo introduced Sangharakshita to Dr Mehta shortly before this letter was written. As a result of their meeting, Sangharakshita was invited to deliver a lecture at the Doctor's Nature Cure Clinic in Poona. In time Poona would become an important centre for his activities among the Ambedkarite Buddhists (see Introduction, pp. 470, 474).

2

Khar,[1]
Bombay
27. 12. 55

Dear Miss Dubash,

Thank you for your letter of the 25th.
Only one day after I had written to you agreeing to attend the Poona function[2] I learned from Dr Bhagwat[3] that it had been postponed. My thoughts were very similar to those which you have expressed.[4] As far as I know, I shall be leaving Bombay on or about 10th January, so that it will now be quite impossible for me to attend. But of course this does not in any way affect my high regard for Dr Mehta and the Society.[5] I owe you a debt of gratitude for your having been the means of my introduction to them both.[6]

I am glad that the idea of a Study Circle[7] has commended itself to you. Four or five people are quite enough to start with, provided they are seriously interested. Your place is, I think, ideal for such meetings.[8]

So I have to spend another day with you and stay for *both* meals. All right, I yield to the ultimatum. But you will have to allow me to fix the date a little later. Most likely it will have to be after another ten or twelve days – just before my departure. Perhaps we could *very tentatively* fix upon 7th Jan. Would this suit you? If it became necessary to change the date I should of course let you know in good time. Maybe 7th Jan. is one of your school days....[9]

Since our last meeting I have taken up the question of publications very seriously, and have entered into correspondence with some of my friends on the subject. I should like to provide each of the little pamphlets[10] with a beautiful frontispiece.[11]

One more thing you will have to do in honour of the Buddha Jayanti next year.[12] But about that I shall tell you when we meet.

Let me end with the orthodox Buddhist expression which it *is* proper for you to adopt, and remain very sincerely

Yours in the Dharma,
    Sangharakshita

P. S. I hope that your *lobha-carita* (artistic temperament) will overlook the inelegance of my stationery. S.

NOTES

1. Sangharakshita is again writing from the home of Arjundev Rashk (see Letter 1, note 1).
2. This was the inauguration of a Poona branch of the Society of Servants of God at the Nature Cure Clinic. It eventually took place at the end of January. Sangharakshita did attend and did deliver a lecture (see Appendix p. 603).
3. Dr N. K. Bhagwat, part of Dr Mehta's circle, was a member of the faculty at Bombay University. Though a Hindu, he was a Pāli scholar, and edited and translated several Buddhist texts, including the *Dhammapada*, which Sangharakshita had carried with him during his wandering days (see *RR*, p. 328). Dr Bhagwat's magazine, *Dharmachakra*, was read by Dinoo (see Letter 18).
4. The letter in which Dinoo expressed her thoughts has not survived. In all likelihood the meeting had been postponed due to the 'guidance' Dr Mehta had received in meditation. Neither Dinoo nor Sangharakshita gave any credence to this guidance.
5. The Society of Servants of God was founded by Dr Mehta some time between 1952 and 1954. It was originally known as the Society of Servants, but this produced enquiries for cooks and bearers so the name was changed.
6. See Appendix, p. 602.
7. For the study of Buddhist texts.
8. Dinoo lived in a ground floor flat

on Marine Drive in Bombay. Her pleasant sitting room was ideally suited for a small gathering such as this. See Introduction, p. 459.

9. Dinoo ran a Montessori nursery school from her flat. See Introduction, p. 459.

10. See also Letter 10. These pamphlets were (1) *Buddhism and Art*, later published as 'The Meaning of Buddhism and the Value of Art' in *The Religion of Art*, Windhorse Publications, Glasgow 1988, (*Complete Works*, vol. 26). (2) *Is Buddhism for Monks Only?*, a dramatic dialogue, which was translated into Bengali and performed in Bengali-speaking schools. It can be found in *Early Writings 1944–1954*, Ibis Publications, Ledbury 2014 (*Complete Works*, vol. 7). (3) a Nepali translation of the *Khuddakapāṭha*, a text which comprises five *suttas* including the well-known *Maṅgala Sutta* and the *Karaṇīya Mettā Sutta*.

11. The beautiful frontispiece for *Buddhism and Art* was a photograph of an ancient Japanese wooden image – probably Maitreya – seated, his head resting on his hand. The other pamphlets were produced more simply.

12. Buddha Jayanti is the most important festival in the Buddhist year, marking, according to different Buddhist traditions, the Buddha's birth, his attainment of Supreme Enlightenment under the bodhi tree, and his final passing into *parinirvāṇa* at his death. The Buddha Jayanti for the year 1956–7 was of especial importance, celebrated all over the Buddhist world as the 2,500th anniversary of the Buddha's *parinirvāṇa* (see *ISGW*, chapter 21).

3

Nature Cure Clinic,[1]
Poona[2]
3. 3. 56

Dear Dinoo,

(Please don't mind the informality – everybody here always calls you 'Dinoo' and it seems strange to call you 'Miss Dubash'.)

Yesterday at lunch time we were talking about you, and since you had not been along to the Society[3] for some time it was surmised that you were getting ready for your pilgrimage to Ceylon and Japan. This reminded me that I ought to write to you. In fact, I ought to have written before, as after all your kindness it no doubt seems ungrateful of me to neglect you for so long. But really my days have been so full – mostly with meditation and talks with Dr[4] – and the time has gone by so quickly that it has hardly been possible to keep up with correspondence.

No doubt you are very eager to know how I have been getting on here, and of course I am quite willing to satisfy your curiosity. But that cannot be done in a letter, or even in many letters. However, I shall be coming to Bombay on the 7th or 8th for one day only (as per instructions that have come in the scripts)[5] before flying to Calcutta. If you have not yet left for Ceylon we could probably meet for an hour. But you will have to have your questions ready in a neat list, as there will be very little time for discussion.[6] In any case, I shall send you a wire informing you of the date and time of my arrival in Bombay, and if you are still there you could meet me at the station (V.T.).[7] Should you have left, please write to me at the Kalimpong address,[8] and I shall continue to keep in touch with you.

Mr Davendra[9] has not replied to my letter. At least, no reply has reached me. But he might have written to either the Kalimpong or the Calcutta address,[10] as I had told him I would be leaving Bombay at the beginning of February.

Dr is keeping quite well. He has been reading several extracts from Buddhist books, and repeatedly refers to the Buddha's life and teachings. He is even thinking of making a small Buddhist shrine here. Gulbehn[11] is quite cheerful, and of course as active as usual. She and I have become well acquainted, and she too likes to hear about Buddhism. We chant the Buddhist prayers or verses from *Dhammapada* together every day before meditation. You would like it! Mrs Rasma Mistri[12] is coming every day. She too is very Buddhist-minded. Sundri[13] and Hira[14] are as busy as ever, and bear the main brunt of the work. Probably you have heard that the Society will be publishing a Journal called *Living Silence* and that Hira will be the publisher, Sundri editor, and myself associate editor.[15] Parvati[16] has not been keeping well and has been confined to bed for several days. On the whole the atmosphere here is very good, with everybody friendly and cheerful. In a way I shall be sorry to leave, though it will not be for long, as I have to come back – either here or to Bombay, wherever Dr is staying – after three or at the most four weeks.[17]

Well, the dinner-bell is about to be rung, so I think I had better close this long overdue letter. Should it not be possible for us to meet in Bombay I wish you 'Bon Voyage' and 'sukhi hontu'.[18]

Yours sincerely in the Dharma,
    Sangharakshita

NOTES

1. Sangharakshita is writing from Dr Mehta's Nature Cure Clinic in Tadiwalla Road where he stayed for several weeks (see Appendix p. 603).
2. Poona, since 1974 known as Pune.
3. The Society of Servants of God (see Letter 2, note 5). Dinoo would normally have gone to the Bombay meetings.
4. Sangharakshita's daily programme at the Nature Cure Clinic is described in some detail in *ISGW*, chapter 20.
5. While in a state of trance and with closed eyes, Dr Mehta received what he called 'guidance', which he wrote down at great speed and afterwards had read back to him, not knowing otherwise what he had written (see Appendix, p. 602 and *ISGW*, p. 272). The written texts were then known as 'scripts'. Dr Mehta believed this guidance came directly from God and expected his friends and followers to accept it. Sangharakshita, however, was not in the habit of following Dr Mehta's 'guidance'. (His remark here is meant ironically.)
6. Dinoo's questions were usually about meditation and Buddhism. She may also have had questions about Dr Mehta's guidance.
7. Victoria Terminus, the central station in Bombay, famous for its magnificent Gothic architecture.
8. Kalimpong is a hill station in the foothills of the Himalayas in the Indian state of West Bengal, not far from the borders with Sikkim, Bhutan, and Tibet. Sangharakshita arrived there in 1950 when he was twenty-four, and the town was his base for the next fourteen years. The majority population was Nepali but many other ethnic groupings, as well as a few Europeans, were resident in the town.
9. D. T. Davendra: a Sinhalese Buddhist from Colombo, editor of *World Buddhism*, a monthly to which Sangharakshita contributed articles. Davendra himself contributed to Sangharakshita's magazine, *Stepping-Stones* (see *ISGW*, p. 118). Sangharakshita may have given Dinoo a letter of introduction.
10. The Calcutta address would have been the Maha Bodhi Society headquarters (see Letter 9, note 1).
11. Gulbehn was Dr Mehta's wife. She lived in Poona at the Nature Cure Clinic with their two young children. (See Appendix, p. 615.)
12. Mrs Rasmi Mistri was an old nature cure patient of Dr Mehta's. (See *ISGW*, p. 282.)
13. Sundri Vaswani was Dr Mehta's chief disciple. (See Appendix, p. 616.)
14. Hira Vaswani, Sundri's brother, was for a short time involved with Dr Mehta and the Society. (See Appendix, p. 616.)
15. Sangharakshita subsequently refers to his being Joint Editor with Sundri.

16. Parvati was another of Dr Mehta's old patients. (See *ISGW*, p. 280.)
17. Clearly these are instructions from the Scripts! As it turned out, Sangharakshita was unable to visit the Doctor again until December.
18. *Sukhī hontu*: a Buddhist salutation: be well and happy.

4

'Everton Villa',[1]
Kalimpong
17. 7. 56

Dear Dinoo,

Some time ago I had told Sundri that I was writing to you, and you, apparently, had said you were going to write to me, so it seems that each of us was waiting for the other to set the ball rolling.

What I am most interested – indeed curious – to know is how you fared on your pilgrimage to Japan and Ceylon – what your impressions were, whether you were inspired or disappointed, what you saw and did, whom you met etc. etc. If it were possible to meet I should let you talk for six hours without stopping. (Oh yes you could – quite easily!) But since I am not likely to be in Bombay just yet you will have to write a long letter describing fully just what happened. The friend in Rangoon whom I asked to meet and help you wrote that he had been involved in a motor accident and was confined to bed. His letter arrived too late for me to be able to contact anybody else there. A couple of weeks ago the Singapore friends wrote that they had met you at the airport and accommodated you in the YWCA. I was sorry to hear that you and your cousin were too tired to go sightseeing. Mr Davendra never replied to any of my letters – not even to the last registered one. I wonder if you met him. He was usually so prompt in replying!

About Society affairs you will have received first-hand information, so there is nothing I need say about them. I should like to know, though, what you think of *Living Silence*. The first number horrified me,[2] but the subsequent ones are better. Now that the Jayanti celebrations are over I shall try to help Sundri more in the editorial work. Yesterday I sent her a review and a poem entitled 'The Voice of Silence'.[3] In case the poem is not printed you had better ask to see it.

Out of the money you gave me[4] I have had printed, so far, at a cost of Rs.260, one booklet, a Nepali translation[5] of the *Khuddakapatha** (translated as 'The Short Section' in your *Some Sayings of the Buddha*).[6] It looks quite nice. With the balance I shall be bringing out two or three English booklets.

Hoping to hear from you soon.
Yours in the Dharma,
  Sangharakshita

*with Pali text

NOTES

1. Sangharakshita moved to Everton Villa in September 1955. This was a bungalow on the Atisha Road, two miles from the Kalimpong bazaar, which commanded magnificent views of the hills. (For a more detailed description, see *ISGW*, p. 250.) The building was partially destroyed in a landslide after Sangharakshita's return to England.
2. Horrified because of its garish cover.
3. *Complete Poems 1941–1994*, Windhorse Publications, Birmingham 1995, p. 205 (*Complete Works* vol. 25).
4. This was probably the 1,000 rupees Dinoo mentioned when Sangharakshita visited her for the first time at the end of 1955 (see *ISGW*, p. 268).
5. For the local Nepali Buddhists.
6. *Some Sayings of the Buddha According to the Pali Canon*, edited and translated by F. L. Woodward, first published 1925.

5

'Everton Villa',
Kalimpong
21st September 1956

Dear Dinoo,

My heartiest thanks to you for your lengthy screed dated 25th July and your shorter letter of 14th September which reached me last night. Have I really kept you waiting two whole months for a reply? I certainly had never intended to do so. In fact, when I first heard from you, and read with eager interest what we might describe as 'Dinoo's Adventures in Buddhaland', my first impulse was to reply at once. But as you know, I was then in Calcutta,[1] and it was not long before the waves of my various duties submerged me – so much so, indeed, that it is only today that my head has emerged from the waters. However, before I start talking about myself, let me offer a few comments on your remarkable first letter.

The first thing of which I want to assure you is that I am not in the least annoyed at anything you have written, as in your rather pathetic second epistle you feared I might be. On the contrary, I am more than satisfied. In fact, one of the reasons for my not replying was that I felt quite unequal to dealing with it adequately in the intervals of other work. Even now I do not feel quite ready to reply to it, but I simply cannot keep you waiting any longer. What struck me most about your letter – I mean the part describing your various experiences in Buddhist countries – was the absolute freshness of your responses. This indeed is the most precious characteristic of your 'personality' and gives you an altogether exceptional honesty, directness, and integrity. Through your eyes one sees things as though for the first time, and therefore with all the thrill and wonder of novelty. It was quite clear to me that you had gone on your travels with a balanced attitude of emotional receptivity – perhaps I should say spiritual receptivity – and critical alertness of mind, and it was this, I think, which led to your receiving such valuable spiritual experiences. You got out of your trip what you put into it, just as we do in the case of life itself. If you found people friendly it was because you yourself radiated friendliness. This I say not to flatter you, but because I was – and am – really impressed by the quality of your letter as a whole, which I think very faithfully reflects your character.

About the details of your adventures and experiences I shall offer no comment now, in the hope that before long we shall have an opportunity to discuss them personally. I shall only say that they were all of very great interest to me, and from them I could understand that you are making progress on what according to the Buddha's Teaching is the Right Path.[2]

Regarding Dinshaw[3] I too have been rather puzzled, and I cannot claim that I have even now come to a final conclusion about his experiences and the work of the Society. To one principle – very clearly laid down by the Buddha – do I hold firmly: we are not to accept anything which is not in agreement with reason (not necessarily in the narrow logical sense of the term) and our own experience, both physical and superphysical. I therefore cannot agree that the 'guidance' which comes to Dinshaw, or to any other person, in meditation, can be accepted as infallible. As you yourself very clearly pointed out, in Hira's case the Divine seems to have made a mistake.[4] But was it really the Divine, in the sense of the highest Reality? This appears to be 'unproven'. According to the Buddha's Teaching, samadhi[5] is only a mundane experience of a higher kind, and does not in itself, in howsoever high a degree it may be present, constitute Enlightenment.[6] I admire Dinshaw very much, and I am convinced that he has very high experience of samadhi, but I am by no means convinced that he is Enlightened: some of the Scripts seem to prove the contrary. Therefore my advice to you still is that if you feel benefited by the atmosphere of the Society, which is certainly a very good one, you should certainly go there; but there is no need for you to accept everything you hear there – least of all the dogma (I can only call it that) of the infallibility of 'guidance' that comes in meditation. After all, we too are being guided by the Buddha's Teaching, are we not? and though our progress is not spectacular I feel that it is sure. Dinshaw would of course say that this sort of attitude springs from our egoism and refusal to surrender to the Divine. But does it? (Not that we have no egoism, of course.) Are we not justified in not surrendering when we are not convinced that it really *is* the Divine? One of the reasons for the confusion in Dinshaw's mind and in the minds of his followers is, I think, the fact that Hinduism,* unlike Buddhism, does not distinguish between samadhi and prajna, or experience on high levels of meditation and actual Enlightenment.[7] According to the Buddha's Teaching one may gain Enlightenment with the help of a very moderate degree of samadhi providing one makes that samadhi the basis for the development of Insight (vipassana), while on the other hand one may get stuck in very high meditative experiences and fail – at least for one life – to gain Enlightenment at all. The 'guidance' which comes from higher mundane planes is perhaps no more trustworthy than that which we get from our own common sense. My own feeling is that we should accept from Dinshaw whatever agrees with our own reason and experience and the Buddha's Teaching and reject the rest or at least leave it on one side. The fact that he can help us gain higher stages of samadhi, as I think he can, does not mean that as a teacher of truth he is infallible. The one simply does not follow from the other. As I have tried to point out – in a rather muddled way I am afraid – the important thing is clearly to distinguish between even the highest samadhi, which is mundane, and Enlightenment, which is transcendental. But this distinction only a Buddhist can appreciate. Hence the helpfulness to Dinshaw himself of the Buddha's Teaching. It can help him to realize that he should not accept uncritically whatever 'comes' in meditation, nor expect others so to accept it. Once he understands this the way may be open to further progress – perhaps even to Enlightenment.

Now let us come back to earth. Since leaving Bombay, or rather Poona, I have been extremely busy. April and August were both passed in Calcutta, and of course during the whole month of May there were the preparations for celebrating Buddha Jayanti in Kalimpong to be attended to.[8] Last month I spent a very pleasant week in Santiniketan,[9] where I gave a short series of lectures on Buddhism, and in May I had been on a similar mission to Gangtok.[10] With the increase of interest in Buddhism our work expands. There is much to do, but few to do it. I am hoping that a young Thai monk will be joining me here and cooperating in the work.[11] If it can be arranged I shall be freer for outside activities. But alas my literary work will suffer. This year I have written a whole volume of stuff but none of it of even relatively permanent value – all bits and pieces. As for poetry, it has been almost totally neglected. I am glad, by the way, that you now have a copy of *Messengers from Tibet*.[12] Since the publication of this volume I have written many poems – enough, I think, for three more volumes. But the difficulty is to get them printed in book form. The market for poetry is small here in India (publishers usually expect us to pay the cost of printing ourselves) and I have no connections with English publishing houses. Hence my output mostly appears in obscure magazines.[13] I am also glad to learn that you are painting, and very much look forward to seeing your work when I am in Bombay. As far as I know, I shall be coming again this Winter. I want to start the study classes about which we had spoken. My teacher, Bhikshu Jagdish Kashyap,[14] will be staying in Bombay for a few years (he is editing Pali texts in Nagari characters for the Govt.[15] and the press is in Bombay) and he could conduct the classes after my departure. So the future of Buddhism in Bombay seems full of hope. I warn you that I am expecting much from you in the way of active cooperation. Eventually you will have to take classes yourself.

Regarding your trip to Sarnath and other places, I think the idea is a good one. If you come to Calcutta why not visit Kalimpong? From Dum-Dum[16] to Bagdogra[17] is about a two hours' journey by air and will cost you only seventy-six rupees. From Bagdogra a car will bring you up to Kalimpong. If you write to me in time I will arrange your accommodation. It would not be possible for you to stay here of course,[18] but we could probably arrange a room for you nearby and give you your meals here. There is a hotel but it is rather costly (fifteen to eighteen rupees a day). Please write and let me know what you think of the idea.

Well, my letter is not yet as long as yours, but I think you will not mind if I close now. Believe me, I am deeply interested in your welfare and in your spiritual and artistic life, and you must never think that a long silence implies forgetfulness or indifference. In future, however, I hope to be more regular in correspondence. Please write again soon, and let me have your reactions to the ideas I have expressed about Dinshaw and also any news of interest that comes your way.

Ever yours sincerely in the Dharma,
Sangharakshita

*Though Dinshaw was born a Parsi[19] the mental climate in which he moves is Hindu and Christian.

NOTES

1. Sangharakshita was attending to *Maha Bodhi* journal work in Calcutta (see Letter 9, note 12) and giving a number of lectures at the Maha Bodhi Society headquarters (see *ISGW*, p. 302).
2. The Right Path is the Buddhist path of ethics and meditation. See, for example, Sangharakshita's *A Guide to the Buddhist Path*, Windhorse Publications, Birmingham 1996, pp. 119–20.
3. Dr Mehta's first name, more usually spelt Dinshah, but pronounced Dinshaw.
4. Hira (see Letter 3, note 11), originally part of the inner circle of the Society of Servants of God, got into serious financial trouble and disappeared. Clearly the Divine should have been aware that he was not honest!
5. Strictly speaking the term *samādhi* corresponds to 'one-pointedness' but in India it is used quite loosely to refer to higher meditative states of consciousness. Here it is equivalent to *dhyāna* (Pāli: *jhāna*), the four lower and four higher levels of meditative absorption. (For a detailed description of meditative states, see Sangharakshita, *A Survey of Buddhism*, ninth edition, Windhorse Publications, Birmingham 2001, pp.188–193 (*Complete Works*, vol. 1). For a shorter description see *A Guide to the Buddhist Path*, Windhorse Publications, Birmingham 1996, pp. 163ff.
6. Enlightenment is attained by direct insight into the true nature of reality.
7. *Prajñā* here is equivalent to Pāli *paññā* meaning transcendental insight or wisdom. For a full discussion of the important distinction between *samādhi* and insight see Appendix p. 611.
8. This was a magnificent occasion organized by Sangharakshita and his Thai assistant, Khemasiri (Letter 13, note 1). The procession included one hundred Tibetan lamas in ceremonial dress and

a thousand devotees bearing volumes of the Buddhist scriptures on their backs (see *ISGW*, pp. 299–300).

9. Santiniketan literally means 'Abode of Peace'. An educational and cultural establishment founded in West Bengal by the poet Rabindranath Tagore (1861–1941), it is known today as Vishva Bharati University. Sangharakshita first visited in December 1953 en route to Calcutta. He subsequently visited many more times, often giving lectures as well as meeting with the many cultured persons, Eastern and Western, who taught there. Famous pupils include Indira Gandhi, India's first female prime minister, and Satyajit Ray, the Bengali film-maker. Lama Anagārika Govinda (Letter 22, note 16) taught there in the 1930s, and met his future wife, Li Gotami, then a pupil. For Sangharakshita's account of his first visit to Santiniketan see *ISGW*, pp. 44–9.

   On the visit referred to in this letter, which took place during the first week of September, Sangharakshita gave three lectures whose titles reveal the breadth of his interests: 'Buddhism as a Religion for Life', 'Eastern Thought and English Literature', and 'The Philosophical Interpretation of the Buddha's Personality' (see *ISGW*, p. 303).

10. Gangtok is the capital of Sikkim, then an autonomous state with its own monarchy under the protectorate of India. In 1975 the monarchy was abolished and Sikkim became an Indian state. For further details of Sangharakshita's activities during these months see *ISGW*, chapter 21.

11. The Thai *bhikkhu* Khemasiri had arrived earlier that year (see Letter 13, note 1) and it seems there was hope that a second *bhikkhu* would join him. Sangharakshita was in touch with a number of Thai *bhikkhus*, some of whom did stay for short periods, though this was usually not long enough for them to be of much help. They usually stayed during the summer months when it was too hot in the plains.

12. See Introduction, p. 479.

13. Obscure magazines such as *Living Silence*!

14. Bhikṣu Jagdish Kashyap (1908–1976) was an Indian monk-scholar with whom Sangharakshita spent nine months in 1949–50, first studying Pāli, Abhidhamma, and Logic at the Hindu Benares University, and then on tour in the 'Land of the Great Disciples' (see *RR*, chapters 48 and 49). Their tour ended in Kalimpong where Jagdish Kashyap left his young disciple with the parting injunction to 'stay here and work for the good of Buddhism' (*RR*, chapter 50). Sangharakshita, obedient to his teacher's word, lived in Kalimpong for the next fourteen years. Jagdish Kashyap continued to be active in other areas. He established the Pāli Postgraduate Institute and Nava

Nalanda Mahavihara on the site of the ancient Buddhist monastic university, going on to become its director.

15. *Nāgarī*: i.e. *devanāgarī*. The Pāli scriptures of Theravādin Buddhism were at that time available only in the Royal Thai edition, i.e. in Thai script. Jagdish Kashyap was keen to make the Buddhist scriptures available to Indian scholars, who were familiar with the *devanāgarī* script in which Sanskrit is written. He had undertaken (and eventually completed) this enormous task for publication by the Government of Bihar.

16. Dum-Dum is a township in greater Calcutta (now Kolkata), some six miles north-west of the city centre. Dum-Dum airport is now known as Netaji Subhash Chandra Bose International.

17. Bagdogra is a town in the Darjeeling district with a small airport, fifty miles south of Kalimpong.

18. As a woman, Dinoo would not have been able to stay under the same roof as Sangharakshita, a *bhikṣu*. But see Introduction, p. 477.

19. The Parsis are said to be descendants of Iranian Zoroastrians who migrated to India in the tenth century CE. According to a 1950 census, there were then 111,791 Parsis living in India, the highest density being in Greater Bombay. The Parsi community was notable not only for having an exceptionally high literacy rate, but also for being generally quite well-to-do. Dinshaw and Dubash are both Parsi names.

6

'Everton Villa',
Kalimpong
30th September 1956

Dear Dinoo,

Thank you for your letter dated 27. 9. 56, which reached me this morning. As requested, I am replying to it immediately so that you may have enough time to make the necessary arrangements for your *pilgrimage*, as I shall insist on calling it.

The problem you have set me with regard to your itinerary is not an easy one, but I have thought the matter over carefully and will advise you as best I can.

The first part of your journey of course more or less works itself out. From Bombay you go to Sanchi,[1] then to Benares and Sarnath[2] then to Kusinara,[3] and from there to Lumbini[4] (via Gorakhpur and Nautanwa). This is all one direct journey, without any deviations or returning on your own tracks, and you simply go straight from one place to another. Regarding Kusinara, about which you have asked, it is in the Devria District of U.P.[5] There are two Rest Houses, in case you had to pass a night there, but the place itself can easily be seen in one day. The people in Sarnath will give you full information on how to reach it. In Sarnath you will be well advised to stay for one night, as it will take a couple of days to see the place *properly* and appreciate the atmosphere, though of course it is possible to rush round and 'see' everything – literally just that – in a couple of hours. In Benares there is nothing of Buddhist interest, but if you want to see the Hindu temples, ghats, etc. (picturesque but by no means beautiful) you had better put up at Clark's Hotel. Anyway, let us return to Lumbini, where we left you recovering from the effects of the first part of your journey.

As already described, you will have reached Lumbini from Devria (the station which serves Kusinara) via Gorakhpur. You will have alighted at Nautanwa (where there is a Maha Bodhi Rest House) and made the journey to Lumbini either by motor, by pony, or on foot. (Take your choice!) In Lumbini there is a small Dak Bungalow,[6] but as there is practically nothing to see except the Ashoka pillar[7] you will not want to spend the night there. Now whether it will be possible for you to go from Lumbini to Kathmandu[8] *direct* I am rather doubtful. There *is* some sort of air connection now between the two places but whether there is any regular plane service I do not know. You will have to ask the Asiatic Travel Co. to check up on this. (By the way, no visa is necessary for Lumbini though it is in Nepal territory, but I think you need one for Kathmandu.) If you can get from Lumbini to Kathmandu direct, all well and good; if not, you will have to come back to Benares, and go from there to Patna, where you can catch the plane for Kathmandu. Now at this point I am going to make a suggestion. You may not be aware of the fact, but from the 15th to the 21st of November, the World Fellowship of Buddhists will be having their fourth biennial conference in Kathmandu,[9] and there will be regular arrangements for taking people to places of interest. What is more important, delegates and visitors will be taken by special plane (visitors at their own cost) to Lumbini, where one session of the Conference will be held. In case you would like to participate in the Conference as an observer I am enclosing the necessary forms, which had been sent to me by the organizers, though unfortunately I am unable to go. At the Conference you will be able to meet Buddhists from many parts of the world. Many of my friends will be attending and if you mention my name it will be sufficient introduction. Should you attend the Conference it will not be necessary for you to go to Lumbini from Kusinara, as you will be taken there as part of the Conference programme.

Now that we have got you safely to Kathmandu let us try to settle the rest of your itinerary. To begin with, you cannot go direct from

Kathmandu to Darjeeling. You will have to return by air to Patna. From Patna you can either go by rail to Calcutta, in which case you could drop down at Gaya for a day or two (Buddha Gaya is 12 miles from Gaya station),[10] or else you could fly from Patna to Bagdogra, and from there take the motor up to Kalimpong.[11] If you choose the latter alternative, you could see Buddha Gaya on your way *back* to Bombay after finishing Assam. Should you choose the former alternative, you could come by rail from Gaya to Calcutta and then fly from Dum-Dum to Bagdogra (the journey takes only 2¼ hours and there are both morning and evening services). Once we get you safely to Kalimpong we can make arrangements for you to visit Darjeeling and Gangtok, both of which places are accessible only by motor. Two days will be sufficient for Darjeeling, and one or two for Gangtok. After finishing your programme in the hills you could return to Bagdogra and catch the plane for Gauhati, whence you could motor to Shillong.

The only difficulty is with regard to my own programme. It seems I shall be attending the Delhi Symposium at the end of November.[12] As I have to spend a week in Santiniketan and a week in Calcutta on the way it means I must leave Kalimpong not later than 1st November. If you start your pilgrimage *late*, so as to attend the W. F. B. Conference in Kathmandu, you will arrive in Kalimpong after I have left. If you start *early*, so as to be able to meet me here, then you will have to miss the conference, which means that you will have to go to Lumbini from Kusinara. I hope this is not getting too complicated. Needless to say, I should be very glad to see you here, but in any case we shall be meeting in Bombay, where I hope to spend the whole of December, so if you would particularly like to attend the Conference don't hesitate to do so. If you let me know when you will be in Kalimpong, and for how many days, I could make the necessary arrangements for you before leaving, and my friends here would be able to advise you about visiting Darjeeling and Gangtok. However, please think things over carefully and give me the details of the programme which you finally manage to work out.

Regarding temperatures here in the hills, Kalimpong has a moderate climate, but Darjeeling is rather cold in October–November, so you had better bring your fur-jacket and a few woollen things.

Darjeeling hotels are likely to be fully booked up for the Puja season.[13] Just now I sent a note to a friend of mine regarding the Central Hotel (where he had stayed last week) but he says it is fully booked up from the 9th October. The biggest and best hotel is the Everest, but it is very expensive. Other hotels are the Hotel Windamere, the Beechwood Hotel, and the Snow View. You could write to all of them, of course, but it will take some time to receive their replies. If the worst came to the worst you could always hire a car here in Kalimpong, leave very early in the morning, spend the day seeing the places of interest in Darjeeling, and then return at night; but this would be rather costly (no more, though, than three days at the Everest). Here in Kalimpong I would make arrangements for you to put up with a friend of mine, and if you came early you can have your meals with me (hope our cooking will suit you!)[14] If you do come early (that is, while I am here) try to spend a full week in Kalimpong.

This, I think, now answers all your enquiries. Please let me know the date of your arrival in Kalimpong, so that I can make the necessary arrangements. When you come up from Bagdogra, tell the driver to put you down at a house called 'Manjula'.[15] This is the place where, most likely, I shall make arrangements for you to stay. But even if arrangements are made elsewhere the people of that place will be able to direct you to our vihara, which is very near.

Hoping to hear from you again soon,
Yours sincerely in the Dharma,
   Sangharakshita

P.S. Write announcing your arrival in Sarnath to:
Ven. Bhikkhu M. Sangharatana,[16]
Jr. Secretary, M.B.S.,
P.O. Sarnath,
Dist. Banaras, U.P.
You may mention my name. S.

NOTES

1. Sanchi is a small village, then in Bhopal state (now integrated into Madhya Pradesh). It contains several Buddhist monuments dating from the third century BCE up to the twelfth century CE, including the ancient stupa from which British archaeologist Sir Alexander Cunningham took relics of Śāriputra and Maudgalyāyana (the Buddha's chief disciples) in 1856 and gave them to the Victoria and Albert Museum in London. In 1947 they were returned to the land of their provenance via the Maha Bodhi Society. Sangharakshita writes about the arrival of these sacred relics in India and the tour, which he accompanied, during which they were displayed to the public. See *FMK*, chapters 10 & 11.
2. Sarnath is one of the four chief Buddhist holy sites, being the location of the deer park in which the Buddha first taught the Dharma. It is located eight miles north-east of Benares.
3. Kusinara (or Kuśinagara) is the second of the four chief Buddhist holy sites, being the location of the Buddha's *parinirvāṇa* or passing away. It is now a town in Uttar Pradesh close to the Nepalese border.
4. Lumbini is the third of the four chief Buddhist holy sites, and is held to be the location of the birth of Siddhartha Gautama, the Buddha-to-be. It is in the Rupandehi district of Nepal.
5. U.P. is a standard abbreviation for Uttar Pradesh (under British rule, 'United Provinces'), the biggest and most populous state in India.
6. *Dak* literally means 'post'. *Dak* bungalows were established by the government at the time of British rule as guest houses, primarily for government officials on tours of duty, but other people could also use them, as Sangharakshita often did during his teaching tours.
7. The Aśoka pillar is one of many columns erected by the Mauryan king Aśoka throughout northern India in the third century BCE. This one indicates the place where Siddhartha Gautama, the Buddha-to-be, is believed to have been born.
8. Kathmandu is the capital of Nepal, and has a sizeable Buddhist population (though the majority are Hindu). The Boudhnath and Swayambhunath stupas are famous Buddhist sites.
9. The World Fellowship of Buddhists is an international organization founded in 1950. Its conferences have included representatives from all over the world. The 1956 conference was attended by Dr B. R. Ambedkar, less than a month before his death.
10. Buddha Gaya (or Bodh Gaya) is the fourth of the four chief Buddhist holy sites, the place where the Buddha gained Enlightenment. It is now a small town in the state of Bihar.

Sangharakshita describes his first visit to Bodh Gaya, in 1950, in *RR*, pp. 453–6. Deeply inspired by finding himself at the place of the Buddha's Enlightenment, he was shocked to find in the inner sanctuary of the Maha Bodhi temple a stone lingam (phallic symbol) of the Hindu god Shiva.

11. Motor here means a shared taxi.
12. The theme of the Delhi Symposium was 'Buddhism's Contribution to Arts, Letters and Philosophy' (see *ISGW*, p. 290). Papers from the conference were subsequently published in the *Maha Bodhi* journal. (For more on the *Maha Bodhi* see Letter 9, note 12.)
13. This is a season of important Hindu festivals during which pujas (devotional rituals) are conducted, dedicated to Hindu divinities such as Durga, Saraswati, etc.
14. Dinoo was accustomed to a professional cook with rather higher standards than the cook employed at the Vihara, where the food was very simple (see Khantipalo, *Noble Friendship*, Windhorse Publications, Birmingham 2002, p. 90).
15. Manjula was the summer residence of Mrs Charu Mitter, 'the Queen of Kalimpong' (see *FMK* above, p. 148). It was subsequently the home of Miss Barclay, who died there (see *ISGW*, pp. 75 and 80). Lobsang Phuntsok Lhalungpa and his wife and small son then took up residence (*ISGW*, p. 106). Lobsang was often present at meetings between Dhardo Rimpoche and Sangharakshita, acting as interpreter. He later emigrated to the USA where he became known as a translator of Tibetan Buddhist texts. The cottage was burned down during the Gurkha troubles of the 1980s.
16. Ven. M. Sangharatana Maha Thera (d. 1984) was *bhikkhu*-in-charge of the Sarnath branch of the Maha Bodhi Society (see *ISGW*, p. 121). A personal disciple of Anagārika Dharmapala (see Letter 9, note 1), Sangharatana appears on a number of occasions in Sangharakshita's memoirs. It was with Sangharatana, for instance, that Sangharakshita first visited Bodh Gaya (see note 10 above). In 1951 he was part of the Maha Bodhi delegation accompanying the sacred relics of Śāriputra and Maudgalyāyana, the Buddha's chief disciples, to Sikkim (as recounted in *FMK*, chapter 11. See also note 1 above).

7

'Everton Villa',
Kalimpong
4th October 1956

Dear Dinoo,

This is to let you know that I have arranged for you a very nice room, with attached bathroom, in 'Chitrabhanu', the Tagore's family house here in Kalimpong which is less than a furlong from our place with a marvellous view of the snows from your own window. Mrs Pratima Tagore[1] (daughter-in-law of the Poet) will be very glad to have you, as she is staying alone. Since I am not sure how long you will be staying I have not settled any terms, but I told Mrs Tagore that you would *probably* spend a whole week. So please do come. Your meals you will of course take with me (I hope our cooking suits you!!) Before you leave Bombay, please phone Sundri and ask if there is any message for me. By the way, when you near Kalimpong tell the driver of the car to put you down at 'Chitrabhanu', near 'Manjula' in the Development Area. *Don't* let him take you to the motor-stand in the bazaar, as from there you will have to come all the way back (about a mile). I shall ask Mrs Tagore to send word to me through a servant as soon as you arrive; then I shall come and bring you to our place for food.

Hoping to see *and* hear you soon,
Yours sincerely,
  Sangharakshita

NOTES

1. Mrs Pratima Tagore: see also
   ISGW, pp. 46 and 138.

8

New Delhi[1]
15. 11. 56

Dear Dinoo,

Many thanks for your urgent letter received last night, and for the long letter received much earlier in Kalimpong. The reason for my silence was that about three weeks ago I suddenly received an invitation to tour the Buddhist holy places as a guest of the gvt. of India (together with more than fifty other Border Area Buddhists) and had to leave at once. The tour was very strenuous, but inspiring.[2] I shall tell you all about it when we meet. On the 7th we reached New Delhi where, after four days of official receptions and sightseeing, the tour ended this week. After spending a few days in Sarnath[3] and Agra[4] (I leave for Sarnath today) I shall return to Delhi for the UNESCO seminar on Buddhism.[5] On the 29th November I leave for Bombay. At what time I shall arrive I do not know, but I shall send you a telegram so that you may be at the station to meet me. In case I miss you I shall come straight to your place so that we can have a good talk.

As far as Dr is concerned I will say only one thing now: even if you are disillusioned with him, it does not matter at all from the Buddhist point of view. First and foremost you are a Buddhist. You have been going to the Society only because you found it helpful to the leading of your own Buddhist life, particularly in the way of meditation. The minute you find the association no longer helpful you are justified in breaking it off. If the disillusionment is accompanied by any emotional disturbance it means there was some personal attachment of which you should try to free yourself.

Personally speaking, I have accepted Dr's guidance only to the extent that it accorded with the Buddha's teaching, which means that in his sense I did not accept it at all. What is discordant I reject. Before leaving Kalimpong I had written him a letter in which my position was made quite clear.[6] Perhaps that is why they no longer discuss me with you. More when we meet.

Sangharakshita

NOTES

1. Sangharakshita was probably staying at the Maha Bodhi Society's branch in New Delhi along with Dhardo Rimpoche and other 'Eminent Buddhists from the Border Areas'. See *ISGW*, p. 323. (For more on the Maha Bodhi Society see Letter 9, note 1.)
2. For an account of this tour, see *ISGW*, chapter 22.
3. Sarnath: see Letter 6, note 2. Sangharakshita's highly significant visit to Sarnath, for which he departs immediately after writing this letter, is recounted in *ISGW*, pp. 313–16. It takes place almost exactly six years after his *bhikkhu* ordination at the Sarnath Burmese temple (see *FMK* pp. 107 ff. above). His *bhikkhu* ordination had been arranged by the monk-in-charge, U Kittima, who had signed Sangharakshita's ordination certificate, testifying that he was properly ordained as a *bhikkhu* in the Theravadin tradition. Wishing to renew his ordination vows on this occasion, Sangharakshita went to the temple, only to be accosted by U Kittima's 'housekeeper' who, under threat of being thrown out by U Kittima, and in floods of tears, revealed that she had lived for twenty years as the monk's concubine and that her son was his son too. In this way Sangharakshita received a shock that reverberated for the next forty-three years: if a monk who had been part of the ordaining chapter had not, in fact, been a real monk, then his own ordination was, according to the *Vinaya*, rendered invalid. This shock caused Sangharakshita

to reflect over years and indeed decades on the true meaning of ordination. These reflections came together in the essay, *Forty-Three Years Ago: Reflections on my Bhikkhu Ordination*, Windhorse Publications, Glasgow 1993 (*Complete Works*, vol. 2).

4. Agra lies on the banks of the Yamuna River in Uttar Pradesh, and was formerly the capital of the Mughal emperors (1526–1658). Famous Mughal buildings include the Taj Mahal, Agra Fort, and Fatehpur Sikri. Sangharakshita visited the Taj Mahal (which far exceeded his expectations) with Dhardo Rimpoche (see *ISGW*, p. 321). He visited all three in January 1967 with his friend Terry Delamare during his farewell tour of India (see *MAS*, p. 362).

5. The UNESCO Seminar was part of the Buddha Jayanti celebrations organized by the Indian government (see *ISGW*, pp. 290 and 335).

6. For Sangharakshita's position on Dr Mehta's 'guidance' see Letter 3, note 4, Letter 5, and Appendix p. 604.

9

Calcutta,[1]
15th December 1956

Dear Dinoo,

So much has happened to me since leaving Bombay[2] that it is only with difficulty that I can pick up the threads of our discussions there.[3] But at least one or two things I must try to tell you.

First of all, as you no doubt already know or have guessed, I had several more discussions with Dr before my departure, but the more he tried to advance his own views the more clearly I saw that he was hopelessly wrong and that I was right. In the end I told Sundri (when she was talking about you) that you and I both had the same feeling about Dr and that we both thought it definitely wrong to accept 'guidance' of the sort that Dr offers unconditionally. Having made the position clear I felt much better.[4] I cannot help saying, however, that Dr spoke with me in a very gentle and friendly manner, and that I could not help feeling very fond of him. All the same, the whole basis of the Society will have to be changed if it is to survive. Dr's ideas about guidance are really fantastic.[5]

With Birla[6] too I had a long talk. He expressed his dissatisfaction even more strongly that you had done. It seems he is quite disillusioned and I should not be surprised if, after leaving Bombay, he discontinues his regular contributions. I was really surprised to learn how much money he had sunk in the Society – with really so very little result. He, too, is displeased with Sundri, and is inclined to put almost the entire blame on her.[7] Here I disagreed with him. As you know, the blame rests fairly and squarely on Dr's own shoulders. Please do not let Birla know that I have told you the details of our talk.

Before I left Bombay Dr was full of dark forebodings about what he thought was my failure to follow guidance and predicted that all my plans would come to nothing. From what happened in Nagpur, however, I could not help concluding that if anyone was guided it was me, and not Dr.[8] To begin with, I arrived exactly one hour before the news of Ambedkar's death was received.[9] Immediately on receipt of the news his followers came flocking to me. That same night I addressed a mass meeting of more than one lakh[10] of people – now all Buddhists. It was really a touching sight to see them all shedding tears for their lost leader. In my speech I emphasized the fact that his work must go on and Buddhism be propagated more vigorously than ever. To cut a long story short, in the course of four days I addressed nearly thirty mass meetings, and I think I can say without vanity that I created a tremendous impression. Dr Ambedkar's followers told me that they felt my being there at that critical juncture was a miracle and that I had saved Nagpur for Buddhism. Had I not been there, there is no knowing what would have happened. At first people felt that the end of the world had come. But after listening to my speeches – which were very strong indeed – they felt full of hope and courage and determined to work for the spread of Buddhism. On the last day of my visit I gave no less than eleven lectures. The last meeting was held at 1.30 in the morning, when fifteen thousand people were converted to Buddhism. My own spiritual experience during this period was most peculiar. I felt that I was not a person but an impersonal force. At one stage I was working quite literally without any thought, just as one is in samadhi. Also, I felt hardly any tiredness – certainly not at all what one would have expected from such a tremendous strain. When I left Nagpur I felt quite fresh and rested.[11] Now let us see about the rest of the programme.

Here in Calcutta I am busy with the *Maha Bodhi* journal[12] and other work, which will keep me busy probably until about the 6th or 7th January. From Calcutta I shall go to Santiniketan, where a lecture programme awaits me. Then follow two weeks in Kalimpong,[13] after which I shall most likely go up to Sikkim.

I am sorry to say I have not been able to find Bates's letter in my file.[14] It seems I must have left it in Kalimpong. I am really very sorry about this, as I know you wanted to reply. Anyway, as soon as I return to Kalimpong I shall post it to you. Please don't mind.

If you have time, please write to me. I shall be very glad to hear from you again. Let us hope that Bhikshu Jagdish Kashyap[15] will soon return to Bombay and that you will be able to take up regular studies with him.

Ever yours sincerely,
Sangharakshita

NOTES

1. Sangharakshita is writing from the Sri Dharmarajika Chaitya Vihara, the Maha Bodhi Society headquarters, where he is editing the *Maha Bodhi* journal (see *ISGW*, p. 342 and Letter 9, note 12 below, also Letter 20, note 9). The Maha Bodhi Society was founded in 1891 by Anagārika Dharmapala (1864–1933), who established its headquarters in Calcutta the following year. The aims of the Society were the resuscitation of Buddhism in India (where it had virtually died out centuries earlier) and the restoring of the Buddhist holy places which had been left to decay or fallen into Hindu hands (see e.g. *RR*, p. 455). The only existing English biography of this great Buddhist from Sri Lanka, *Flame in Darkness*, was written by Sangharakshita, originally for the Maha Bodhi Society's Diamond Jubilee Souvenir in 1952 (see *FMK*, chapter 18, 'Discovering Dharmapala'). On the death of Dharmapala, the Society swiftly deteriorated so that in 1947 when Sangharakshita first encountered it, the only representative of Buddhism he could find in India, he was greatly dismayed (see *RR*, chapter 17).

2. Sangharakshita left Bombay on 5 December, after a visit of four days or so.

3. On arriving in Bombay from Delhi, where he had just attended the UNESCO seminar, and before going to Dr Mehta's flat at Mayfair, where he was staying, Sangharakshita spent some hours with Dinoo. They talked about her disillusionment with Dr Mehta and his Society and Sangharakshita left his friend 'less upset by her disillusionment … and more confident that in ceasing to attend the Society's meetings she had done the right thing.' (See *ISGW* p. 335.)

4. For Sangharakshita's stay at Mayfair and discussions with Dr Mehta, see *ISGW*, pp. 336–7 and Appendix p. 602.
5. In the older sense of 'fantastic': fanciful and even preposterous.
6. Durgadas Birla was from the rich industrialist family. A founder member of the Society, he had provided substantial funds for its setting up (see *ISGW*, pp. 272 and 336).
7. Presumably because Sundri gave Dr Mehta unquestioning support, never doubting the 'guidance'.
8. In his memoirs, Sangharakshita recounts the imperative sense that came to him that he must leave Bombay and be on his way, though why he should be on his way he didn't know (see *ISGW*, p. 338).
9. On the afternoon of 6 December.
10. A *lakh* is 100,000.
11. Most of this paragraph – of such great historical significance – is cited verbatim in *ISGW*, p. 342. The events are described in more detail in *Ambedkar and Buddhism*, in *Complete Works*, vol. 9, pp. 21–4.
12. The *Maha Bodhi* was the monthly journal published by the Maha Bodhi Society. During the 1950s articles, book reviews, and poems by Sangharakshita appeared in its pages and in July 1953 he began a monthly column, 'In the Light of the Dhamma' written under the pseudonym Himavantavasi (see *ISGW*, p. 63). That autumn, Devapriya Valisinha, General Secretary of the Society and editor of the *Maha Bodhi*, invited Sangharakshita to take over the editorship (see *ISGW*, p. 57). Some of the editorials he went on to write are mentioned in *PT*, pp. 67–8; and his work for the journal features in many chapters of his memoirs. For the rest of his time in India, Sangharakshita continued to faithfully bring out the *Maha Bodhi* each month, an enormous feat given the bulk of his other work, and a major contribution to the revival of Buddhism in the land of its birth and to the growth of Buddhism further afield. He continued to work for the *Maha Bodhi* even after taking up residence in the UK. Gradually his connection petered out. The last time he is listed as a member of its editorial board is in the June 1969 edition. His *Maha Bodhi* editorials were collected together and published in 2012 as *Beating the Drum*, Ibis Publications, Ledbury 2012 (*Complete Works*, vol. 8).
13. Sangharakshita returned to Kalimpong in time for a reception of the Dalai Lama on 27 January.
14. Sangharakshita was unable to find this letter until the following summer when he returned it to Dinoo (enclosed with Letter 17). Dinoo had sent Bates's letter to Sangharakshita hoping for some advice on how best to respond to him. It appears that Bates was a European who had come to the East, taken the (Buddhist) robe, disrobed, and then re-robed. She may have met him through the Society of Servants of God. At any rate, we know

that Bates was keen that Dinoo consult Dr Mehta on his behalf. According to Dinoo's account, Bates suffered from extreme loneliness and eventually had a nervous breakdown. He had turned to Dinoo for support and advice. 'He has thrown too much on me and I hardly feel up to it,' she had written in February.

15. Bhikṣu Jagdish Kashyap: see Letter 5, note 14.

10

Calcutta,[1]
31st December 1956

My dear Dinoo,

Many thanks for your long letter dated the 18th and the shorter one dated the 27th. Thinking that you were away on pilgrimage[2] I had not replied to the first of these.

According to Tibetan custom, a blessing is given by placing the hands on the head. So it seems that you did get the Dalai Lama's blessings, after all.[3] Apparently you knew instinctively – or intuitively – what was the correct procedure.

Kashyapji,[4] it seems, will be spending several years in Bombay, and though the pilgrimage did not come off I am very glad that you have made contact with him. Perhaps you could arrange for him to give lectures in the Society. He might be able to influence Dr a little.

Birla apparently did not fully understand my words. Perhaps he did not want to understand. Though I told him that Dr's attainment in samadhi was in my opinion very high I made it quite clear that uncritical acceptance of samadhi experience was very dangerous and that Dr had fallen into this trap. I also said that the guidance he offered was not reliable. It seems that Birla is trying to bolster up his own collapsing faith.[5]

My work here has gone forward smoothly. One issue of the Journal has been brought out, and another is on the way. Out of the money you gave me I am bringing out two English pamphlets, one on *Is Buddhism for Monks Only?*, the other on *Buddhism and Art*.[6] The second I would like to dedicate to you. I hope you won't mind.

This will be all for the present, I am afraid.
With best wishes for the New Year.
Ever yours sincerely,
    Sangharakshita

P.S. Please give my New Year Greetings to all your teachers.[7]

NOTES

1. Written from the Maha Bodhi Society headquarters. See Letter 9, note 1.
2. In her letter of 18 December, Dinoo mentions that she has been invited to accompany Jagdish Kashyap on a pilgrimage to Nalanda and the Buddhist holy sites (see Introduction, p. 464).
3. In her letter of 18 December, Dinoo describes her first meeting with the Dalai Lama (see Introduction, p. 465).
4. The addition of 'ji' to his teacher's name is an expression of respect to which Sangharakshita meticulously adheres in his letters to Dinoo. In her letters, on the other hand, Dinoo sometimes refers to him simply as 'J. K.'
5. i.e. his faith in Dr Mehta and his 'guidance'.
6. See Letter 2, note 10 and *ISGW*, p. 342.
7. Sangharakshita had met the teachers of the Montessori school when visiting Dinoo during his trips to Bombay.

11

'Everton Villa',
Kalimpong
31. 1. 57

Dear Dinoo,

Probably you saw in the newspapers that the Dalai Lama had spent a week in Kalimpong. What you probably did *not* see was that he visited our own centre, where we had a really wonderful programme on the occasion. I had to fly up to Kalimpong on the same day as His Holiness in order to make all the necessary preparations, and I can assure you that although we had only four days at our disposal everything was done perfectly.[1] Before leaving Calcutta I managed to finish practically all my work and also to spend two days at Santiniketan, where, though there was no time for lectures, I did manage to do the business for which I had gone there.

Kalimpong is in one of its loveliest moods just now, cold but bright. After the hectic happenings of the last three months I am settling down to a little quiet routine work before embarking on further travels. The two Japanese vases have been duly installed in the Shrine, where they did duty on the day the Dalai Lama came. Oh yes, I forgot to tell you that His Holiness gave us, before leaving Kalimpong, a lovely brass Buddha image, two Tibetan sacred books, a signed photograph and a donation of Rs.1,000. Weren't we lucky! Next time I write I shall try to send you one or two photographs of the function.

What news of the Society of Servants of God? The January issue of *Living Silence*, which I received a few days ago, does not seem up to standard. In one of the poems Dr is threatening and fulminating in his best style.[2] Otherwise things are much as they were, except for the general all-round deterioration.

Kashyapji, I think, should now be back at work in Bombay. If you could give me some news of him too I should be glad, as I have to write to him. Your own studies are, no doubt, going on as usual. What progress have you been able to make with the picture you promised to do for me?

Please give my best wishes to all your teachers.
Ever yours sincerely,
    Sangharakshita

NOTES

1. The Dalai Lama's stay in Kalimpong, including his visit to Everton Villa, is recounted in *ISGW*, pp. 347–50. Of the reception at Everton Villa, to which local Buddhists were invited, Sangharakshita explained to me that 'The [local] Tibetans were very pleased that we had given him this reception because he was staying with Rani Dorje [which was rather] inaccessible even to the Tibetans. Whereas at our place they were able to see him and hear him. They were very pleased … that I'd made it possible for them to be with the Dalai Lama.'

2. Dr Mehta did not write original poetry as such. The reference is to one of his Scripts, written in a state of trance (see Letter 3, note 5 and Appendix p. 602).

12

'Everton Villa',
Kalimpong
19. 2. 57

Dear Dinoo,

Many thanks for your long and very interesting letter dated 8. 2. 57.
Tomorrow morning I have to go to Darjeeling[1] to see a dentist, as for the last five weeks I have been suffering from intermittent but very severe toothache. This, therefore, is merely an interim reply. On my return I shall write you the long letter for which you have asked and which you deserve.

Even before receiving your letter I had decided to sever connections with *Living Silence*, as all that you have said is very true.[2] Besides, I am terribly busy with other work. So as soon as I return off goes a letter to Doctor and Sundri.[3]

By now you must have received the small parcel of pamphlets I sent you. The Nepali *Khuddakapāṭha* (with Pali text), *Is Buddhism For Monks Only?* and *Buddhism and Art* have all been published out of the one thousand rupees you gave me last year.[4] There is now about one hundred rupees left, which I shall utilize for printing a leaflet. Thus you will have four Buddhist publications to your credit. Three more copies of *Buddhism and Art* will be sent you when I go to Calcutta, as the stock is there for the time being. (I flew up, so could not bring it with me.)

Please take your own time over the painting.[5] There is no hurry for it at all.

Bates's letter, I am sorry to say, has failed to turn up. Please accept my humble apologies. I shall search again when I return from Darjeeling.

To your sweet little monk[6] I shall write when I next write to you. You will be getting a really long and rather important letter from me, as I want to tell you about a plan of mine and ask your co-operation. Now *aren't* you curious!

Yours sincerely,
Sangharakshita

NOTES

1. Darjeeling was about two hours journey by jeep from Kalimpong.
2. Dinoo was highly critical of the content of the January edition of *Living Silence* going as far as to say that it should be renamed 'Living Terror'! (She was referring, presumably, to Doctor's 'fulminating', see Sangharakshita's comment in Letter 11.) Dinoo's criticisms refer to (1) a lack of critical judgement by the editor (Sundri) in choosing the material, (2) the 'pointless poems' which 'do not convey any novel thought or idea', and (3) to the 'travesty' of an article published as a 'Buddha-roar' written, she says, as a 'justification of temper or violence', i.e., entirely contrary to Buddhist teaching.
3. The letter to Doctor and Sundri was a letter resigning as joint editor (with Sundri) of *Living Silence* (see also Letter 14).
4. For more on the pamphlets, see Letter 2, note 10. The money had probably been given by Dinoo in honour of the Buddha Jayanti (see Letter 2, note 12).
5. This is the painting which Dinoo had promised to give to Sangharakshita. She had written, 'I haven't even started it. But I shall fulfil my promise, you may be sure. Are you in a hurry for it? If not, let me wait for the right mood – only then can the best results be achieved.'
6. Dinoo met this 'sweet little' Cambodian monk in Bangkok during her pilgrimage. She describes him as 'slim, tallish, olive in complexion, cutely Mongolian, with a very delicate, sweet mouth, nice cute eyes, attractive smile, regal neck and

bearing.' His name was Preah Maha Sokkhasobhano and they afterwards kept in touch. Dinoo copied out his whole letter when she wrote to Sangharakshita, in particular because she was worried that in beginning her letter, 'my dear little monk' she had offended him! What did Sangharakshita think? In addition, as becomes clear in subsequent letters, she hoped that Sangharakshita might take the young monk on at his vihara and offer him some training, not least in English.

13

'Everton Villa',
Kalimpong
26. 2. 57

My dear Dinoo,

Here I am back in Kalimpong. Yes, I have been relieved of my toothache, thank you, but I have to return to Darjeeling for further treatment in a few days' time. Meanwhile, I am rather busy. A few minutes ago I was out in the sunshine working in our garden – potting lilies and planting dahlias, but the thought that I had not yet written to you again as promised tickled my conscience and I came indoors, leaving my friend the Thai bhikkhu[1] manfully digging the ground alone. As you know, I had hinted in my last letter that I had something of importance to communicate to you. Well, here it is.

For the last seven years I have been carrying on Buddhist work with Kalimpong as my headquarters. For the first two or three years there were terrible difficulties; we were continually in debt, and sometimes there was no money even to buy food. Gradually, however, things improved. Through my writings, and in other ways, I became known, not only here in Kalimpong but also outside, and the more I became known the more our work expanded. Now we have a quietly flourishing centre which seems, from the number of people who come here, to be attracting an increasing amount of attention. I have an assistant (the Thai monk aforesaid), and apparently several more people are planning to join us on a permanent basis. Thus we shall be forming the nucleus not only of a Buddhist centre[2] but also a semi-monastic Buddhist community[3] which will both provide facilities for people wishing to lead a spiritual life and train up young men for Buddhist work, besides, of course, carrying on all the usual activities such as preaching and publishing.

So far, as you know, we have been functioning in rented premises. This was inconvenient in a number of ways. Every year or two we had to move, either because the house was sold or because the landlord wanted to live in it himself.[4] Then there was the fact that every month we were having to pay rent. For these, and other reasons, I have been driven to the conclusion that the time has come for us to have a place of our own. We shall then be able to place all our activities on a more permanent basis and the money which would otherwise have gone for rent can be utilized for the development of the centre. After much thought and meditation, as well as many consultations with friends, I have decided to acquire a small property on the outskirts of Kalimpong comprising about an acre of land and a small cottage.[5] After settling in the cottage, which we shall turn into a vihara, we shall one by one erect Nepali-style cottages round about for the accommodation of friends and visitors. This decision has been forced on me partly because our lease on 'Everton Villa', which is for sale (at Rs.45,000) expires on 15th September, when we have to move out, and because owing to the influx of Tibetans,[6] who have been buying up properties right and left, it has become quite impossible for us to find another suitable place to let. The property which I want to buy will cost about Rs.15,000 and since I have no resources of my own I am appealing for help to all those friends who I know are genuinely interested in my work.[7] I do not know what your present position is, nor even if you would be willing to help me, but if at all you do have a mind to contribute I can assure you that, so far as my own work is concerned, there will perhaps be no better time in my life than this. In all, there are about six or seven friends who I am asking to help me at this juncture. From one, about whom I might once have spoken to you, I am confident of getting about half the amount required; from the rest, including you, I am hoping to get the remainder. At any rate, I have resolved and am determined that whatever happens – whether my friends disappoint me or not – I am going to put our work here on a more permanent basis before 15th September, even if it means simply buying an acre of land and putting up a hut of thatch and bamboo. The time really has come when we must have a place of our own, and since you have always shown such a genuine and sincere interest in me and in my work I am hoping that you will be one of the friends who will assist me in making my dream come true. Needless to say, no pressure of any kind is being brought to bear on you; you must consider the matter dispassionately and decide first if you are willing and secondly if you are able to help me, and if able to what extent. But I shall not disguise from you or from any of my friends the fact that help received *now* will be of greater value than perhaps ten times the amount given next year or still later on. If there is any further information that you would like to receive before coming to a final decision of the matter I shall be, of course, only too glad to send it.

For obvious reasons, I am saying nothing about the matter to Dr. Some people have just come to see me, so in the hope of receiving an early reply, I remain

Ever yours sincerely,
Sangharakshita

NOTES

1. The Thai *bhikkhu*, Khemasiri, had been a student at Santiniketan (see Letter 5, note 9), one of a number of Thai monks studying there, they naturally spoke Thai among themselves. Concerned to find himself getting little practice at speaking English, Khemasiri decided to join 'the English monk' in Kalimpong (see *ISGW*, p. 296 and *PT*, pp. 122–3). 'Quiet, modest, and diligent' and 'easy to get on with', he had helped Sangharakshita organize the magnificent Buddha Jayanti festival in Kalimpong in May the previous year (Letter 5, note 8). He continued on as assistant, friend, and companion until sudden illness overtook him and he was forced to leave (see also Letter 16, note 6 and Letter 18).

2. This 'Buddhist centre' in Kalimpong can be seen as a precursor to the Buddhist centres

that were later established first in the UK and subsequently all over the world as part of the new Buddhist movement founded by Sangharakshita in 1967.
3. Semi-monastic in the sense of not following the minor monastic rules (which Sangharakshita had come to regard as unnecessary for leading a spiritual life) and, secondly, in the sense that it would not be just for monks: serious-minded lay people would also stay there. As recounted in his memoirs, all sorts of people did stay at the future vihara, including, for example, Amita Nisatta, a Swedish woman who wore the robe – although she was probably not ordained (see *PT*, pp. 129 and 140). Another sense in which it would be semi-monastic and thus not in accord with full Theravādin orthodoxy, was that everyone would eat together in the dining-room of the main building. Sangharakshita explains, 'Usually in the first Theravāda world monks – even *sāmaṇeras* [novice monks] – never eat with lay people. But at the Vihara we all ate together. In the West we see that as something quite ordinary, but within the Theravāda context it's revolutionary. When I came back to England [in 1964] and was at the Buddhist Society's Summer School and ate with lay people, that too was regarded as extraordinary!' (See *MAS*, p. 26.)
4. Sangharakshita started Buddhist activities from the Dharmodaya Vihara, his first place of residence in Kalimpong. He began by setting up the Young Men's Buddhist Association, Kalimpong, which held its inaugural meeting in May 1950, just two months after his arrival in the Himalayan town, and the following month he launched the magazine *Stepping-Stones* (see *FMK* above, p. 48). The fortunes of the association, and his other exceptionally varied work for Buddhism during the fourteen years of his residence in Kalimpong is recounted in *FMK*, *ISGW*, and *PT*. Due to serious difficulties at the Dharmodaya Vihara, in early 1951 he was given temporary residence at the guest cottage of Burma Raja, the nephew of King Thibaw, the last king of Burma (see *FMK*, chapters 6 & 7). In June 1951 a more permanent residence became available at the Hermitage (see *FMK* above, chapter 12). In October 1954 Sangharakshita was required to vacate these premises and moved to Craigside (see *ISGW*, pp. 176ff). In less than a year another move was forced upon him, this time to Everton Villa, where he moved in September 1955 (see *ISGW*, p. 250).
5. The property eventually purchased was considerably larger, comprising some four acres (1.6 ha.).
6. Tibetans were already fleeing their native country during the years prior to the full Chinese invasion of 1959. Though many were very poor, there were some

who came with considerable wealth, in silver and gold, and were able to buy up local properties, causing property prices in Kalimpong to rocket.

7. What follows – in effect a fund-raising letter – will be of particular interest to all those who have been concerned to raise funds for Dharma activities.

14

Calcutta[1]
28th March 1957

Dear Dinoo,

Many thanks for your letter dated 19th March, which reached me the day before yesterday after being redirected from Kalimpong.

I am truly sorry that you were disappointed at not getting a proper reply to your own letter.[2] As you know, I have always tried – and always will try – to deal with every point you raise; but once in a way this may for one reason or the other not be possible, and you must be generous enough to forgive me. My first note was written on the eve of my departure for Darjeeling,[3] and the second, long letter when I had my head full of the matter about which I wrote to you. So please don't take it too seriously if I seemed neglectful of matters which were of some interest to you. If you only knew how much there is to attend to nowadays I think you would easily forgive me for much more serious omissions, as I know that by nature you have an understanding and forgiving heart.

Now let me thank you very much for the promised help of one thousand rupees. You are the first of the friends to whom I have written to respond, and I am really grateful to you both for the financial help and the moral encouragement you are giving towards the materialization of my plans. If my other friends respond as promptly and as generously as you have done we shall soon have a flourishing permanent centre in Kalimpong. I too think that it will be better to buy a lot of land with a cottage ready built;[4] we can then expand and extend as funds become available. About the cost of building your dream cottage,[5] I can only give you a very rough idea, as a great deal will depend upon the materials used. If you build in modern style, using bricks or cement blocks, the cost would be in the region of ten thousand rupees. A wooden building would not, I think, cost more than three thousand, and one built in the local style, of bamboos and thatch (it can be made to look very nice) about fifteen hundred.[6] So you can take your choice. Incidentally, I do think it a very good idea that later on you should retire to the hills. Even if you do not settle there permanently, you could come up in the hot weather and spend your time in meditation or painting pictures. I am sure the idea is not so fantastic as it sounds. Once we are ourselves settled you could come up and see the place. In any case you have promised us a visit, haven't you? By the way, you need not send me a cheque just yet, as in any case I cannot pay it into the bank until after my return to Kalimpong, which will not be for at least another three weeks. So please hang on to it for the time being.

Your experience with Christian Science is very interesting.[7] I have not read *God Calling*[8] but I have heard of it and I seem to remember hearing Dr speak of it. It is quite likely that the book has influenced him, though probably he would not like to admit it.[9] From your remarks I infer that he must still be in Bombay. I still have not received any reply to the letter I wrote him and Sundri several weeks ago clarifying my position and resigning from the Joint Editorship of *Living Silence*, and since I have not seen the latest issue of the magazine I do not know if they have removed my name. Perhaps in your next letter you could throw some light on the matter.

At present I am busy with *Maha Bodhi* journal work. After leaving Kalimpong I spent a week in the Dooars, an area near the Bhutan-Assam border where there are many thousands of Nepali Buddhists. There too there is a great deal of work to be done.[10]

Hoping to hear from you again soon, and with all good wishes,
Yours sincerely,
    Sangharakshita

NOTES

1. Sangharakshita is once again in 'the city of dreadful heat' at the Maha Bodhi Society headquarters (see Letter 9, note 1).
2. Dinoo complained that neither the letter of 26 February (Letter 13), nor the one previous (Letter 12) 'contained a reply to my letter as such'. She is referring to her twelve-page letter of 8 February which covers a great variety of topics, some of which Sangharakshita refers to in his two letters, but others, such as the problem of 'Bates', about which Dinoo had written in detail, he had not responded to.
3. Departure for Darjeeling to receive treatment for severe toothache, as explained in Letter 12.
4. Dinoo had written with characteristic concern, 'it would be advisable to purchase the estate *with* the cottage, so that you would have something to live in right away, and also the vihara.'
5. Dinoo's dream cottage would have 'three or four rooms, two bathrooms and a veranda and a kitchen and a store room,' She might 'think of building one later.... This is purely a daydream [but] many a daydream has come true so who knows?'
6. In *PT*, pp. 44–5, Sangharakshita describes just such a cottage which he later had built in the grounds of the new vihara to serve as a guest cottage. Supervising the work himself, it was built to his own specifications and cost about 1,100 rupees.
7. Dinoo had written of turning to a Christian Science approach, particularly as outlined in the book *God Calling*, to help her deal with her own bout of severe toothache. For Dinoo, accepting Divine help through seeing the Divine in all things was, she explained, akin to the Buddhist idea of seeing the *dharmadhātu* (or ultimate reality) in everything.
8. A. J. Russell, *God Calling*, Arthur James, Evesham 1948. The book comprises 'teachings two ladies in England received from Jesus when praying together'.
9. Dr Mehta believed his 'guidance' came directly from the Almighty and was free from any other influences. In fact he had read many such books, as Sangharakshita knew, having seen them at the Doctor's residence.
10. Sangharakshita's teaching tour in the Dooars is mentioned in *ISGW*, p. 355. He was deeply concerned for these and other Buddhist communities who had almost no access to Dharma teaching. This included the Tamang Buddhists of the Longview tea estate in the Darjeeling district which Sangharakshita visited in 1953, recounted in *ISGW*, pp.13ff.

15

'Everton Villa',
Kalimpong
25th April 1957

Dear Dinoo,

Here I am in Kalimpong again! I was very glad to return, as the heat in Calcutta had become insufferable, and for the last ten days of my stay there I was suffering intermittently from fever.[1] Now I am feeling quite all right, as the weather in Kalimpong, though warm, in comparison with that of Calcutta is very enjoyable.

Since my return I have been exploring the possibilities of acquiring land etc., as the problem has now become acute. While in Calcutta I received a letter from our landlord requiring us to vacate these premises by the 15th May, as they have been bought by a Tibetan who insists on immediate occupation as one of the conditions of the sale. Fortunately, by the same mail that I received this news came a letter from a very good friend of mine promising very substantial assistance towards the realization of my plans.[2] What do you think of that for a coincidence? Yesterday I received another letter from the same friend saying that the money was being sent through the Bank and would be reaching me within ten or twelve days. The amount is not mentioned, but I gather it will be at least ten thousand rupees. This means that very soon I shall be in a position to realize my dream, and I have therefore set afoot enquiries concerning two or three suitable plots of land with small cottages which are being offered for sale. The housing problem has become very acute in Kalimpong recently, owing to the increasing influx of rich Tibetans, all of whom are buying up properties right and left.³ Consequently prices have gone up. We shall not be able to get anything at less than fourteen or fifteen thousand. I should like to ask you, therefore, to send your own contribution as soon as it is convenient, so that I shall be in a position to close the deal as soon as I can come to some agreement. If you would do this I should be more than ever grateful to you.

Now let me give you the rest of the news. I am rather surprised that since I wrote to Dr and Sundri some six or seven weeks ago severing my connection with *Living Silence* and making clear my position I have not received a word by way of reply from either of them. Neither have I received the April issue of the magazine, so I do not know if they have complied with my instructions and removed my name from the inside cover page. Perhaps you will be able to throw some light on the matter. I shall be interested to know what is happening. If I hear from you that my name is still appearing as Joint Editor I shall have to write them a very strong letter.

Herewith I am enclosing a leaflet about my *Survey of Buddhism* which has at last been published,⁴ though I have not yet received any copy. Copies have, however, reached London, and Dr Conze has written to me that he is very pleased with it and that he will be lecturing on it in London on May 3rd.⁵ If you think the book will interest you, then you may order either direct from the publishers or through the Bombay booksellers.

Do you go to the Ananda Vihara,⁶ and is the German 'bhikkhu' there?⁷ Are you still in correspondence with Kashyapji? Needless to say, I shall very interested to hear of the progress of your Buddhist life, and your thoughts and reflections. What of the picture you promised me? I wonder if you have yet been able to start it. I should very much like to have it for our new vihara. But as I said before, there is no hurry, and you must wait for the mood to come.

Nowadays the trees around our house are resounding with the cry of the cuckoo, so that I cannot help thinking of Wordsworth's famous poem. Do you remember it? The one beginning 'O Blithe newcomer …'⁸

But let me close this letter before wandering ever farther off the track, otherwise you will think that the cuckoo has made me 'cuckoo'.

With all good wishes,
Ever yours sincerely,
Sangharakshita

NOTES

1. In Calcutta Sangharakshita had seen the next edition of the *Maha Bodhi* through the press, given a number of lectures at the Sri Dharmarajika Vihara, and spent time with old friends (see *ISGW*, p. 355). For more on the *Maha Bodhi* see Letter 9, note 12.
2. The very good friend is Marco Pallis (1895–1989), *aka* Thubden Tendzin, author of *Peaks and Lamas*, mountaineer, and an expert in early music. Pallis was living in Kalimpong when Sangharakshita arrived there in 1950. Their growing acquaintance is recounted in *FMK* (pp. 159. above), where Sangharakshita hints at rather mysterious dimensions to Pallis's life: his involvement with the Khampas of Eastern Tibet who were resisting the Chinese. Pallis was secretly supporting them. For this reason, he had been asked by the Indian government to leave the country and was now writing to Sangharakshita from London.
3. On Tibetans buying up properties, see Letter 13, note 6.
4. *A Survey of Buddhism* began as a series of four lectures given in Bangalore in July 1954 at the invitation of the theosophist B. P. Wadia (1881–1958), and held under the auspices of the institute he had founded in 1945, the Indian Institute of Culture (see *ISGW*, chapter 9). It was also B. P. Wadia (to whom the book was subsequently dedicated) who requested that the lectures be written up in book form. Sangharakshita began this work on 31 August 1954 and continued writing during the very full months that followed (see *ISGW*, pp. 18 and 264–5), completing it in early 1956 (see *ISGW*, p. 265). It was finally published by the Indian Institute of Culture a year later, to considerable acclaim. Since then there have been no fewer than nine editions and the work has been translated or partially translated into Polish, Spanish, and German. See Letter 19, note 8. (The revised ninth edition is included in *Complete Works*, vol. 1.)

5. Dr Edward Conze (1904–1979) was an Anglo-German scholar and academic who mastered some fourteen languages, including Sanskrit. He eventually took up the study and practice of Buddhism – one of the first Western scholars to actually practise in the tradition. He is renowned for his outstanding translations into English of the Mahāyāna *Prajñāpāramitā* or Wisdom texts.

    To the great delight of the young editor of *Stepping-Stones*, Conze submitted the first instalment of his 'Selected Sayings from the *Perfection of Wisdom*' to the February 1952 issue of the magazine, with the promise of further instalments to come. Due to financial difficulties, no further issues appeared (see *FMK* above, p. 315). The association of the two men continued, however, with Conze submitting articles to the *Maha Bodhi* (of which Sangharakshita was editor, see *ISGW*, pp. 117 and 216, and Letter 9, note 12).

    Conze had a reputation for being outspoken, and forthcoming in his criticism. He was to write of the *Survey*, 'Without hesitation, without any reservation whatever, I recommend Sangharakshita's book as the best survey of Buddhism we possess at the moment.' (Dr E. Conze, *Further Buddhist Studies*, cited in endpapers to ninth edition of *A Survey of Buddhism*.)

6. The Ananda Vihara was one of the Maha Bodhi Society's two centres in Bombay, and stood in a corner of the Nair Hospital compound near Bombay Central Station. (For more on the Maha Bodhi Society, see Letter 9, note 1). Named after its patron, Dr Anandrao Nair, physician, and Buddhist (or at least 'a very good friend of Buddhism'), Nair had also founded the Buddha Society Bombay (see *ISGW*, p. 253). Sangharakshita stayed at the vihara on at least two of his early visits to Bombay. In fact, it was from here that Dinoo had collected Sangharakshita and taken him to meet Dr Mehta for the first time in November 1955 (see *ISGW*, p. 255).

7. The German *bhikkhu* was Aniruddha, a member of the Arya Maitreya Mandala founded by Lama Anagārika Govinda (see Letter 22, note 16). He wore the yellow robe although it is not clear if he had actually undergone Theravādin ordination. When the Dalai Lama visited the Ananda Vihara on 9 December, about which Dinoo had written in her letter of 18 December, it was Aniruddha who had managed the visit – 'hopelessly' according to Dinoo. Kashyapji had his own story to tell (see Introduction, p. 465) not, it seems, in Aniruddha's favour. Interestingly, it was Aniruddha who styled Sangharakshita a 'narrow-minded Hīnayānist'! (N.B. this Aniruddha should not be confused with the incumbent of the Dharmodaya Vihara in Kalimpong who appears first in *FMK*.)

8. *O Blithe Newcomer...*: From 'To a Cuckoo' by William Wordsworth, composed in 1802.

16

'Everton Villa',
Kalimpong
17th May 1957

Dear Dinoo,

Thank you very much for your kind and interesting letter dated 12. 5. 57. Yes, I have received your cheque, which was apparently posted quite a while after it had been signed. Thank you for this also.

You will be glad to hear that the principal donor[1] has sent me £1,100, which is equivalent to about Rs.14,300. The money is due in Kalimpong this week, having already reached Bombay. Since writing to you last I have agreed to purchase a small stone house, together with more than three acres of land, for nineteen thousand rupees, which considering the state of the market is a reasonable figure.[2] The place is ideal for a vihara,[3] and there is plenty of room for you to put up your koti[4] whenever you want to do so. As soon as we settle in I shall write to you in detail about the place. Just now, as you can well imagine, I am rather busy. But before closing this letter I must at least answer a few of the points raised in yours.

Bhagwat's article in the *Dharmachakra* did reach me and I thought it very much to the point. It seems, though, that he had thought I was responsible for the effusion originally published in the *L.S.* If you meet him please disabuse him of this idea as I have no time to write.⁵

Unfortunately I could not write to your little monk, you are not to suppose that I had just forgotten. At present I am sadly behind with all my correspondence and many of my friends are complaining that I do not answer their letters. So when you next write to the little monk please do tell him that I had not written because I was so busy but that he may certainly expect to hear from me as soon as I am settled in my new place.

The Thai bhikkhu who joined me as my assistant six months ago had an internal haemorrhage on 1st May and is now in the Kurseong T. B. Sanatorium. For about a week we had a really dreadful time, as there was danger of losing him if we did not take proper precautions.⁶

The Vaisakha celebrations went off very well indeed.⁷ No doubt you spent most of the holy day in meditation. At present I have a number of people staying with me, including five students from Santiniketan. So our place is full.

Please excuse me for writing such an inadequate letter. Write to me again as soon as you can spare time.

With all good wishes,
Yours sincerely and gratefully,
Sangharakshita

NOTES

1. The principal donor was Marco Pallis. (See Letter 15, note 2.)
2. The 'little comedy' that had to be enacted to procure its purchase is recorded in *ISGW*, p. 356.
3. An ideal place for a vihara because it was 'perched on a rocky spur ... faced due west and commanded a panoramic view.' (See *ISGW*, p. 356.)
4. *Koti* or, more usually, *kuti*: a hut or, here, small cottage.
5. During the course of this week, Sangharakshita and his friends were making habitable the newly-acquired property, which had been left vacant for more than a year. He took up residence on 23 May, just six days after writing this letter, and the following day

left Kalimpong to give a series of lectures in Gangtok. (See *ISGW*, p. 357.)

6. The Thai *bhikkhu* was Khemasiri (see Letter 13, note 1). Sangharakshita records: 'He was admitted to the T. B. Sanatorium in Kurseong, a small hill station situated between Siliguri and Darjeeling. He was not at all happy there, and in a long letter to me he complained bitterly about the noise and confusion of the place.... He spoke of his wish to return to Kalimpong to help me in my work,... but it was not to be. Khemasiri's condition deteriorated, and the Thai consul in Calcutta made arrangements for him to be flown back to Thailand. The next letter I received from him was dated from the 'Hospital for Monks' in Bangkok. His health had improved, he wrote, and he was thinking of returning to India. I did not hear from him again.' (See *PT*, p. 123.)

7. Vaiśākha Pūrṇimā (also known as Buddha Jayanti or Buddha Day) is the most important festival of the Buddhist year, marking the anniversary of the Buddha's Enlightenment, it falls on the full-moon day of April-May. In 1957 the full-moon day was on 13 May and Vaiśākha Pūrṇimā was celebrated at Everton Villa by members of the Maha Bodhi's Kalimpong branch. This marked the end of the Buddha Jayanti year celebrating twenty-five centuries of Buddhism, and a year which, in his personal life, Sangharakshita describes as an *annus mirabilis*. During that year he had visited the Buddhist holy sites in the company of Dhardo Rimpoche, forged a special link with the newly-converted followers of Dr Ambedkar, seen the publication of *A Survey of Buddhism*, received tantric initiation from Chattrul Sangye Dorje, and established at last a permanent vihara in Kalimpong. (For *annus mirabilis*, see *ISGW*, p. 357. For 'Buddha Jayanti' see Letter 2, note 12).

17

Triyana Vardhana Vihara,[1]
Kalimpong
12th July 1957

Dear Dinoo,

It seems such a long time since I heard from you that I could not help wondering if you had had the 'flu like everybody else, or whether there was any other trouble. Let us hope that it was just a case of no news being good news.

You will be glad to hear that we are now settled in our new permanent place, though there are still some legal formalities to be settled. My friend in London[2] contributed Rs.14,600 and another friend Rs.2,600,[3] so that with this and your contribution in hand we were able to agree on Rs.19,000 as the purchase price, which everyone seems to think very reasonable, as we have nearly four acres of land and a small building.

Since moving in we have been very busy trying to make the place look like a real vihara. At present three carpenters are at work repairing the woodwork, remodelling the room which will be used as the Shrine etc.

Herewith I am enclosing two photographs from which you will be able to get some idea of what the place looks like. Where would you like to build your own cottage?

Looking through my file the other day I came across Bates' letter. Though it is probably too late to be of any use to you, I am returning it.

How is your little monk? If you are still in touch with him I shall be happy to write to him now, as I shall be here in Kalimpong until the winter attending to correspondence and literary work etc. as well as to the improvement and development of this place.

The last issue of *Living Silence* was awful. All scripts. Since my letter of resignation (how glad I am I sent it!) I have heard neither from Doctor nor from Sundri. The Divine doesn't have very good manners, it seems.

How are you getting on with your studies, meditation, painting etc.? Are you keeping in good health? Please do write and let me know.

Hoping to hear from you soon, and with all good wishes,
Yours sincerely,
Sangharakshita

P.S. Did you receive my last letter? S.

NOTES

1. This is Sangharakshita's first letter to Dinoo from the Triyana Vardhana Vihara. The name means 'the vihara where the three *yānas* flourish', the three *yānas* (or 'ways') in question being the Hīnayāna, Mahāyāna, and Vajrayāna, regarded as the three great phases of Buddhism during its first 1,500 years of development. The name was bestowed by the celebrated Tibetan lama, Chattrul Sangye Dorje. Sangharakshita had met him for the first time on 8 March that year when they discussed, among other things, the phenomenon of Dr Mehta's 'guidance' and how one was to regard it (see Appendix p. 604).
2. Sangharakshita's friend in London was Marco Pallis. See Letter 15, note 2.
3. The other friend was Richard Nicholson, *aka* Thubden Shedub, Marco Pallis's companion in *Peaks and Lamas*, Sangharakshita had come to know the two friends at the time they lived together in Kalimpong. Like Pallis, Nicholson was an accomplished musician and an expert in early music. By the time of this letter, they had returned to live in London.

18

Triyana Vardhana Vihara,
Kalimpong
5th December 1957

Dear Dinoo,

Last week I was thinking of you quite a lot, and this week I get a letter from you, which I suppose means that you were thinking of me too!

Your earlier letter, dated 17th July, should and would have been answered a long time ago but unfortunately – you will be surprised to hear – for three months I was rather seriously ill. Now that I am better I won't bother you with the symptoms, which for a time were very painful,[1] but according to my doctor[2] they were all due to prolonged overwork and vitamin deficiency. Even now I am under treatment, and he has advised me to take rest for six months. For this reason I cancelled my winter tour, which this year was to have taken me to New Delhi, and in the course of which I had hoped to spend a few days in Bombay.

Here at the Vihara things are gradually getting organized. There has been a lot of outside work to do in the way of gardening and cultivation, as when we came here the place was rather a jungle.[3] Yes, we do have a view of the snows. Later on I shall send you some photographs better than the ones already despatched.

During the last few months we have had many visitors. The Head Lama of Sikkim has twice stayed here with one or two disciples and has now become a very good friend. He is a Tibetan by birth, and well versed in meditation. By temperament he is very simple and friendly.[4]

On the spiritual side I have several interesting encounters, and there is much that I would like to tell you.[5] However, it must wait until we meet.

As it seems likely that more and more people will be coming to stay with us, I have decided to erect, as soon as funds become available, three or four very simple cottages. If possible they will be put up this summer.[6] Then you could come and stay with us and decide, after seeing the place, whether you would like to construct your own cottage here. Though you could not, of course, stay in the Vihara,[7] there would be no objection at all to your staying within the compound.

At present I have with me for training two prospective samaneras[8] – one an American aged thirty, the other a Nepali boy of fourteen. A young Assamese bhikkhu[9] will be joining me as an assistant within a few days. Two other boys are also staying here.[10] So you will see that our 'family' is growing.

The Thai bhikkhu, you will be glad to hear, did not, after all, have T.B. But what was actually the matter with him the doctors were, apparently, unable to discover. At any rate it was something serious. He has returned to Bangkok, but hopes to join us again when he is better. I was sorry to lose him.[11]

You really do seem to have had a rough time with your servants.[12] I hope the two Parsi girls are proving satisfactory.[13] It is good, I think, that you did not yield to the impulse to flee from difficulties.[14] But of course that need not preclude the possibility of retirement after the difficulties have been solved.

What are you reading nowadays? Are you doing any more paintings? Please let me know. I am interested in all your activities. Once upon a time you had promised us a Buddha painting for the Shrine. Please remember your promise when you are in a painting mood.

The news about Dr and Sundri does not surprise me,[15] nor that about L.S.[16] When a monthly becomes a quarterly it means only one thing – that the magazine is on the point of extinction! For many months I have not seen the thing. So Dr wears his hair like the Buddha![17] In one of the Suttas there is a lion-roar about 'Fools who imitate me and die the death' like the young elephant who, seeing the elephant king eating lotuses, started eating them too, but without washing the mud from the stalks, with the result that they died.[18]

Bhagavat's 'buttering' of *L.S.*[19] was really disgraceful, especially after his attack on the 'lion-roar'.[20] It seems that he attacked the latter thinking, wrongly, that it had been written by me, as I had failed to persuade the Maha Bodhi Society to finance his *Dharmachakra*. On discovering that the lion-roar in question emanated from the gentleman in the top-knot[21] I suppose he wrote the 'buttering' article by way of compensation.

Kashyapji, it seems, is still at Nalanda. A few weeks ago I wrote to him about an urgent matter but so far have received no reply.

What news of Bates? Are you still in touch with your 'little monk' in Thailand? Please let me know. If you are not too busy, I shall expect a nice long letter from you.

Yours with Maitri,[22]
Sangharakshita

NOTES

1. In *PT*, p. 14 Sangharakshita writes of 'an extremely painful swelling of the gum' causing the right side of his face to become badly swollen.
2. Doctor Boral was a Bengali living in Kalimpong.
3. Sangharakshita set himself to making the most of the property's land (as recounted in *PT*, pp. 40–2). Orange trees, buckwheat, and maize were cultivated as cash crops. Bamboo was also sold, used locally for building construction and channelling water. Bananas and vegetables, especially pumpkins, prospered on the land, and Sangharakshita created a small garden that there might be fresh flowers for the shrine: marigolds, zinnias, gerberas, and geraniums, and on the bank behind the cottage, orchids.
4. The Head Lama of Sikkim was Kachu Rimpoche, one of Sangharakshita's eight main teachers. He was abbot of Pemayangtse gompa, the premier Nyingma monastery in Sikkim (see *ISGW*, pp. 307–8). Sangharakshita found him 'cheerful, straightforward, and down-to-earth' – at the same time, on two occasions the lama demonstrated the possession of

more than normal powers of perception. Kachu Rimpoche was a regular visitor at the Vihara, and Sangharakshita once visited him at his Sikkimese monastery. In 1962, directed by the great Nyingma guru, Jamyang Khyentse Rimpoche, Kachu Rimpoche bestowed upon Sangharakshita the Padmasambhava *abhiṣekha* (lit. 'blessing' or initiation) (see *PT*, p. 80).

5. Sangharakshita may well have been thinking of his meetings with Jamyang Khyentse Rimpoche and the initiations he received from him (see *PT*, pp. 14–19).

6. In fact Sangharakshita eventually had built – to his own specifications – a five-roomed guest cottage with accommodation for up to eight guests (see *PT*, pp. 44–5).

7. Dinoo could not stay in the Vihara because she was a woman. She was well aware of this and in her letter of 17 July, when thanking Sangharakshita for his invitation to come and stay, she added, 'Don't look so scared, I know I cannot stay at the Vihara.' See also Letter 13, note 3.

8. *Sāmaṇeras* are novice monks. There is no record of who these two may have been.

9. The young Assamese *bhikkhu* was Sugatapriya, a Theravādin monk who, like his predecessor Khemasiri, wanted to improve his English. Unlike Khemasiri, he was not very hard-working but nevertheless helped Sangharakshita in small ways (see *PT*, p. 123). He left after a year, unable to live without his familiar dietary staple of fish! (Thai *bhikkhus* were generally not vegetarian but the Vihara kept a vegetarian kitchen.)

10. One of these two boys was Dupchen, who had come from the Dooars in Assam, where Sangharakshita had given lectures and where he had suggested that the local Tamang Buddhists sent one of their young men to train at the vihara in Kalimpong. To this they had agreed, but instead of a young man, a ten- or eleven-year-old boy arrived. Learning that he was an orphan, Sangharakshita gave him a room in the guest cottage and sent him to the local government school (see *PT*, pp. 51–2). He stayed at the Vihara until he was sixteen. After Sangharakshita left for England, Dupchen ran away to Nepal, married a Nepalese girl, and became a taxi-driver.

11. The Thai *bhikkhu* was Khemasiri: see Letter 13, note 1 and Letter 16, note 6.

12. The Goanese servants, whom Sangharakshita had met, Dinoo had had to 'let go', and the new ones had proved 'most unsatisfactory' so she felt unable to leave the house in their care. She may also have been referring to one of her teachers who had married in February with the resolve not to have a baby for four years – but had returned from her honeymoon announcing 'the happy – or call it what you like – expectation'. This teacher expected nevertheless to stay on

until September but unfortunately developed a tumour requiring emergency treatment.

13. The two Parsi girls are mentioned in Dinoo's letter of 28 November and were due to take up residence with Dinoo as teachers in her school.

14. 'I had such a strong urge to leave everything and go and settle down in Kalimpong,' Dinoo had written on 28 November. But 'there were moments when I felt it would be like running away from my trials.'

15. According to Dinoo, Sundri had given up her job and was working on her own, having moved her office to Mayfair, Dr Mehta's flat in Bombay where formerly the Society of Servants of God had met. Someone who visited the place told Dinoo that there was not a soul there except for Doctor and Sundri – another sign of the failing fortunes of the Society.

16. In October Dinoo had received a letter from Dr Mehta's wife, Gulbehn, in which she related that *Living Silence* had become a quarterly. For more on *Living Silence* see Letter 3. For Dinoo's criticisms of the January edition, see Letter 12, note 2.

17. Dinoo had written: 'Dr now has his hair in the style of Lord Buddha. A bun on the top of his head.' Doctor's preoccupation with possible similarities between himself and founders of the great religions is recounted in the Appendix p. 614.

18. Vinaya Piṭaka ii.201 (*Cullavagga* 7.4); see I. B. Horner (trans.), *The Book of the Discipline*, vol. 5, Pali Text Society, London 1975, p. 282.

19. 'Buttering' is Dinoo's word, i.e. flattering. In her letter to Sangharakshita of 17 July, Dinoo wrote out part of an article written by Dr Bhagwat and published in his magazine *Dharmachakra* in which he lavished praise on *Living Silence* in phrases such as 'Ardent writers express their deep conviction and truer spirit of understanding by their little articles, poems or the scripts of the seer.' In Dinoo's estimation, Dr Bhagwat was showing himself to be a 'spunkless, unmitigated ass!' After all, Dr Bhagwat's praises were directed to the same magazine that she and Sangharakshita had agreed was deteriorating. (Sangharakshita had described the most recent issue as 'awful'. See Letter 17. For more on Dr Bhagwat see Letter 2, note 3, and Letters 16 and 19.)

20. It seems Dr Bhagwat had published an article in his *Dharmachakra* critical of an article in *Living Silence* that he assumed had been written by Sangharakshita. In fact it had been written by Dr Mehta. On discovering his *faux pas*, he tried to rectify things with the Doctor and the Society of Servants of God with a 'buttering' article.

21. The gentleman in the top-knot was Dr Mehta. See note 17 above.

22. *Maitrī*: Sanskrit for 'love' or, more accurately, loving-kindness (equivalent to the Pāli *mettā*).

Buddhist terms distinguish between different kinds of love so that *maitrī* is the love that exists in friendship as distinct from erotic love, *prema*, and 'sticky love' or *sneha* (applied for example to the relation of mother to child).

19

Triyana Vardhana Vihara,
Kalimpong
8th August 1958

Dear Dinoo,

As you see, I am being very bhikkhu-like[1] and *not* paying you back in your own coin.... As a matter of fact I almost *knew* that your long silence was to a great extent due to your being preoccupied by school affairs, though at the same time I could not altogether suppress the shadow of a doubt that you might be ill and unable to write for that reason. However, your very long and most welcome letter now sets my mind at rest and I am very happy to be in possession of such a comprehensive account of the events of the last few months.

Let me first of all say how sorry I was to hear of all the trials and difficulties you have had in connection with your teachers. It must have been a bitter experience for you, especially when one of the trouble-makers had the impertinence to tell you that she wished you could put into practice what you read. This is the sort of sneer that spiritually-minded people always have to put up with from the unspiritual. But I am glad to hear that you not only faced the unpleasant situation bravely, but also, which is far more important, without resentment, so that you were all able to part friends. But a devotee need not be a fool, as Sri

Ramakrishna used to say,[2] and I am glad to know that you were so wide awake and alert when the two people sent by Father[3] protested their honesty. Flowers don't have to proclaim how sweet they are. Self-advertisement always gives cause for suspicion. Anyway, it is a good thing that you are now settled, with two new and more reliable girls. Who would have guessed that behind the staid façade of a Montessori school such dramas were enacted![4]

Yes, I am indeed very pleased to know that the promised picture is at last ready, and that it has been admired even by Bendre,[5] about whom you did speak to me once or twice when I was in Bombay. I do hope, though, that you will follow his advice and put it behind glass at once, as I know what a dreadful 'fiddler' you are.[6] No, the Vihara does not yet have electricity, which it will cost at least a thousand rupees to install. We generally have Tibetan lamps and candles burning in the Shrine, which faces north-west and is inclined to be dark. We could, of course, hang the painting in the sitting room, which is a very bright room and where it will be seen by more people. Perhaps we had better wait for you to come to Kalimpong and let you decide yourself. How big is the picture? As I write it occurs to me that it *might* be possible to hang it in the middle of the Shrine behind and above the central image, where it would catch a certain amount of light.

Thank you for all the nice things you say about my *Survey*. I am really astonished at the warm reception it has received, and at the glowing reviews that have been written.[7] The publishers tell me that the first edition was sold out in six months, most of the copies being sold in London and New York. We are bringing out a second edition,[8] for which I am now preparing a Select Bibliography and Index – rather a boring job, especially as I have so much else to do. There is also some talk of the possibility of an American edition,[9] as well as of French[10] and Polish translations.[11]

What you tell me about the Maitreya picture[12] is extremely interesting, though I do not quite know what to make of some of it from the theological,[13] or rather Buddhological, angle. There is no doubt, though, that Maitreya possesses tremendous spiritual significance and influence at the present crisis in history, and that these will increase gradually as time goes on, culminating in another descent of an Enlightened One to our earth.[14] Your question about Dharmakara[15] I find very intriguing. It had certainly never occurred to me.[16] As the *Sukhavativyuha*[17] tells us, Amitabha[18] started his career as Dharmakara. We are also told, however, that Amitabha is the dharmakaya,[19] which is, of course by definition, birthless and deathless.[20] I am inclined to think that the solution to the problem lies in the fact that an individual Buddha is regarded as the symbol of Buddhahood, the realization of which makes Him a Buddha. Dharmakara, by reaching Buddhahood, becomes a symbol of the dharmakaya. The dharmakaya Itself has no name. In other words, strictly speaking Amitabha is not the dharmakaya, though by virtue of His having realized Buddhahood, and thus become one with the dharmakaya, He may be regarded as such. From another point of view, all Buddhas and Bodhisattvas whatsoever are manifestations of the Great Void,[21] the Reality, which is simultaneously Wisdom and Compassion, and we understand them best when we understand that in essence they are not different from one another – a point of view which you have expressed when you say that for you Sakyamuni, Maitreya, and Amitābha are one. Personally, though, I do not identify Christ and Maitreya, as according to Buddhist tradition Maitreya is yet to come whereas Christ came and went two thousand years ago. I rather suspect that certain interested persons are doing their best to persuade Buddhists that in worshipping Maitreya they are really worshipping Christ, so that instead of being Buddhists they ought to be Christians. I think you are right in saying that what you saw in your vision was not Christ, but Maitreya, and that you only thought it was Christ because to you it did not seem to have the appearance conventionally associated with Maitreya. All your spiritual experiences seem to me definitely Buddhist, not Christian at all. It is a fact that, according to Buddhist tradition the colour of Amitābha is red, which I am inclined to think is not a harsh bright red, but more like the soft rosy glow which you saw suffusing infinite space.[22] Needless to say, I shall be very interested to see the Maitreya picture, though when I shall have that privilege I do not know, as I am not sure when I shall be able to visit Bombay again. Meanwhile, I am very grateful to you for sharing with me your spiritual experiences.

From neither Dr nor Sundri have I heard since last writing to you. *Living Silence* no longer comes, but I do not know whether it is defunct or whether my name has been struck off the list because I did not renew my subscription. No doubt I am regarded as a lost sheep, wandering in the wilderness without 'guidance'. Birla wrote me a very nice letter, in reply to an invitation to our Buddha Jayanti functions which I had sent him (did you get yours?). He is still at Birlagram,[23] and seems to be quite out of touch with the Society. He again invites me to visit Madhya Pradesh.

I am very glad to know that the 'Lion-Roar' article was not directed against me, after all, as I should have been sorry to lose the friendship of Bhagvat. Now that you have cleared the air I shall write to him again.

Yes, my 'family' continues to grow. But since founding this Vihara and having such a success with my book[24] I am quite amazed to see how much jealousy my modest achievement has aroused. You would hardly believe it, but people whom I considered my friends, and who professed to be working for Buddhism, have developed a real grudge against me and at least one of them has stooped to all sorts of nasty tricks to put me into difficulties. However, like you, I try not to feel resentment, though it is not easy to be so forbearing. It seems that the more 'successful' we are the more jealousy is created.

Last April we managed to construct, at the cost of Rs.1,134 a very simple hut, thatched, with three rooms, in order to accommodate our growing family.[25] It is now fully occupied.[26] Walls are of mud-plaster, whitewashed. It should last ten or twelve years. I have also called for estimates for a permanent guest house, but this will cost us at least ten thousand, and at present we have no money at all. In fact, with so many mouths to feed, it is difficult to meet even the monthly expenses, which come to Rs.500 for eight persons. If you want to come and spend some time in Kalimpong, however, I shall arrange for a friend to take you as a paying guest. Please do try to come, at least for a short holiday. Why not come in October, which is our loveliest month?

There is a book which I very much want you to read – if you have not already done so. It is *Buddhist Himalaya*[27] by David Snellgrove.[28] In a way it is better than Conze.[29] Its account of Tantric Buddhism[30] is the best I know. You will be able to get the book, I think, from Chetana's.[31]

This morning it is raining heavily. For some reason or other I always feel more like writing long letters on rainy days. So you will have to thank the rain god for being so kind to you,

With very best wishes,
Yours with Maitri,
Sangharakshita

NOTES

1. *Bhikkhu* is the Pāli term for a monk, so *bhikkhu*-like means behaving like a true monk and not reacting with revenge (by not writing).
2. Sri Ramakrishna (1836–1886) was a Bengali mystic famous throughout India and beyond, whose disciple Swami Vivekananda (1863–1902) founded the Ramakrishna Mission at whose Colombo branch Sangharakshita spent much time in the later months of 1944 and early 1945 (see *RR*, chapter 11).
3. Father Mascarhenas was a disaffected Goanese Catholic priest associated with Dr Mehta and the Society of Servants of God (mentioned in *ISGW*, p. 272 and *MAS*, p. 307). Presumably he had been called on to intervene in the difficulties with Dinoo's servants, and had sent two people in his stead. Dinoo would have called on him because her servants, like the priest, were Goanese Christians – employed because they spoke good English, the language used by Dinoo and others of her class.
4. Dinoo ran a Montessori nursery school from her flat. See Introduction p. 459.
5. N. S. Bendre (1910–1992) was an Indian artist. From 1945 he worked with others from the Indian world of art and sculpture at Santiniketan, though he had left by the time Sangharakshita began his visits there (see Letter 5, note 9). The two never met.
6. 'Fiddler' – perhaps referring to Dinoo's habit of procrastination which, in a letter dated 8. 2. 57, she describes as 'one of my major foibles'.
7. Reviews e.g. see Letter 15, note 5 for Conze's estimation.
8. The second edition of *A Survey of Buddhism* was published by the Institute of Indian Culture in 1959.
9. The fifth edition of the *Survey* was eventually published jointly by Shambhala Publications in Boulder, Colorado, USA and Windhorse Publications, UK in 1980.
10. A French translation is still awaited. The Introduction and first chapter of the *Survey* were published in German in 1999 by Do Evolution as *Buddha-Dharma – Einheit und Vielfalt des Buddhismus, Band I*. A Spanish translation was published in 2008 under the title *Una panorámica del budismo* by Ediciones Dharma, Alicante.
11. It is not clear who may have shown interest in a Polish version at this time; Sangharakshita cannot recall. He had a Polish friend in Bombay, Maurice Frydman (mentioned in *MAS*, p. 329), who possibly showed an interest. Today, however, a Polish version does exist, published in Krakow in 2002 as *Wprowadzenie do buddyzmu*.
12. See Introduction p. 463.
13. The point here is that in Buddhism, a non-theistic religion,

one cannot talk of a 'theology'. Sangharakshita points out, however, that some scholars now use the term 'Buddhist theology' on the understanding that the original Greek term 'theos' did not refer to a singular God and theology meant something more like 'a science of the divine'.

14. Strictly speaking, the future Buddha Maitreya is not yet an Enlightened One (or Buddha) but will attain Buddhahood during a future rebirth on Earth. According to tradition, he currently resides in the Tuṣita god-realm. (Buddhist tradition describes thirty-three different realms of long-lived – but certainly not immortal – gods.)

15. Dharmākara was the name of the Buddha Amitābha in a former life. He was a monk whose great spiritual inspiration led him to make forty-eight vows, the most famous of which is that when he had attained Buddhahood, anyone reciting his name would be reborn into his Buddhaland (Sukhāvatī). See *A Survey of Buddhism*, ninth edition, Windhorse Publications, Birmingham 2001, pp. 366–8 (*Complete Works*, vol. 1). According to Mahāyāna Buddhist tradition, which emphasizes the compassionate and even salvationary aspect of Buddhahood, someone in training for Enlightenment, that is, a bodhisattva, is reborn over countless lives during which he or she accumulates the virtues and wisdom that eventually flower into Supreme Enlightenment for the benefit of all.

16. Dinoo's question about Dharmākara must have been a query about how the Buddha Amitābha, an archetypal figure symbolizing Buddhahood, who is said to be birthless and deathless, could at the same time be said to have had a former life as the monk Dharmākara. These very real philosophical problems concerning the Buddhist understanding of time and 'eternity' are dealt with by Sangharakshita in his 1969 lecture, 'The Buddha and the Bodhisattva: Eternity and Time'. An edited version of the lecture can be found in *The Bodhisattva Ideal: Wisdom and Compassion in Buddhism*, Windhorse Publications, Birmingham 1999 (*Complete Works*, vol. 4).

17. The *Sukhāvatīvyūha* (Sanskrit), lit. 'Array of the Happy Land', is one of the most revered and widely known Mahāyāna *sūtras*, composed sometime before the first century CE. Its teachings inspired the Far Eastern Buddhist schools. See *A Survey of Buddhism*, ninth edition, Windhorse Publications, Birmingham 2001, pp. 363ff (*Complete Works*, vol. 1).

18. Amitābha, lit. 'Infinite Light'. In the Mahāyāna tradition, Amitābha is one of many archetypal Buddha figures, each symbolizing Buddhahood viewed from a particular angle. Amitābha is the red Buddha associated with the western quarter. He sits on a great red lotus in meditation posture with the sun setting

behind him. He is associated especially with meditation, loving-kindness, and the purification of the poison of craving.
19. *Dharmakāya*, lit. 'body of truth'. In his following exegesis, Sangharakshita has in mind the *trikāya* doctrine that was developed in India during the centuries that followed the Buddha's *parinirvāṇa*, or passing away, as an attempt to give a philosophical account of the Buddha's true nature. The *trikāya* doctrine asserts that one can view Buddhahood as expressed on three planes: the ordinary phenomenal plane, where it is called the *nirmāṇakāya* or created body, the archetypal plane of the glorified Buddhas and bodhisattvas known as the *sambhogakāya* or body of mutual enjoyment, and finally the plane of absolute reality, the *dharmakāya*. See *A Survey of Buddhism*, ninth edition, Windhorse Publications, Birmingham 2001, pp. 282–97 (*Complete Works*, vol. 1), and *The Three Jewels*, Windhorse Publications, fourth edition, Birmingham 1998, pp. 38–40 (*Complete Works*, vol. 2).
20. Ultimately things are 'neither born nor are they destroyed' as stated, for example, in the *Prajñāpāramitā-hridaya Sūtra* (*Heart Sūtra*).
21. The Great Void or *śūnyatā* is 'the ineffable non-dual reality which transcends all apparent oppositions, such as being and non-being, self and others.'
A Survey of Buddhism, ninth edition, Windhorse Publications, Birmingham 2001, p. 24 (*Complete Works*, vol. 1).
22. The colour of Amitābha: Sangharakshita does not mention here his own vision of Amitābha that had occurred some years earlier, in 1949, in a cave on the slopes of Arunachala in southern India (see *RR*, p. 345).
23. *Gram*: lit. 'village'. Here a colony of housing that would have sprung up around one of the Birla industrial concerns, probably a suburb of Nagda in Madhya Pradesh.
24. The newly published *A Survey of Buddhism*. See Letter 15, note 5.
25. The guest house as Sangharakshita now recalls it had, in fact, five rooms. Possibly some were subdivided. See Letter 18, note 6.
26. As well as his assistant, Sugatapriya (see Letter 18, note 9), and the young Tamang boy, Dupchen (see Letter 18, note 10), the guests in the cottage included Jivaka, who arrived unannounced around the time this letter was written. A transsexual, his unusual and eventually tragic story is related in *PT*, pp. 45–56. See also Letters 23 and 24.
27. *Buddhist Himalaya* was subtitled *Travels and Studies in Quest of the Origins and Nature of Tibetan Religion*, Cassierer, Oxford 1957. The book was based on Snellgrove's experiences in Sikkim, Nepal, and the borders of western Tibet. Sangharakshita had especially noted it for its treatment of the Vajrayāna.

28. David Snellgrove (1920–2016) was a British Tibetologist who taught for many years at the School of Oriental and African Studies, University of London, until his retirement in 1982. Though deeply interested in Tibetan religion and culture, he was himself a convert to Roman Catholicism. During the Second World War he was stationed in India and afterwards stayed for a while in Darjeeling, visiting Kalimpong. Sangharakshita met Snellgrove without knowing it when he returned to Kalimpong from Calcutta in late January or early February 1954. He met him at Manjula cottage (see Letter 6, note 15) where Miss Barclay, one of Sangharakshita's Buddhist friends, had just died and where Mrs Perry of the Himalayan Hotel had arrived with an unknown Englishman (Snellgrove) to claim Miss Barclay's body for a Christian funeral (see *ISGW*, pp. 75–80).
29. Dr Edward Conze (see Letter 15, note 5). Conze had treated this subject (Tibetan Buddhism) briefly in *Buddhism: Its Essence and Development*, published in 1951.
30. Tantric Buddhism is here synonymous with Vajrayāna, the third phase of Buddhist development in India that was subsequently transported to Tibet.
31. Chetana's was a bookshop and publishing house in Bombay. It was to publish Sangharakshita's collection of essays, *Crossing the Stream* in 1960. (In *Complete Works*, vol. 7.)

20

                                              Triyana Vardhana Vihara,
                                                              Kalimpong
                                                                29. 9. 58

Dear Dinoo,

    Thank you for your letter, which took five days to reach me.

    It is indeed very good to know that you will be paying a long visit to Kalimpong. October is certainly the best time of year, and you will be able to see the place at its loveliest.

    The friend whom I had thought would be able to accommodate you is now unable to do so, but I have made arrangements for you to stay at 'Chitrabhanu', the Tagore family's Kalimpong residence,[1] which is only two furlongs along the road from the Vihara. One room, together with European style commode[2] and bathtub, will cost Rs.80 *per menoum* (including electricity), which in view of the great shortage of accommodation in Kalimpong is quite reasonable. Mrs Tagore (the poet's niece) says she will be leaving Kalimpong in a fortnight's time, which means that you will have the whole house – a very beautiful one, with a lovely garden – to yourself. The servants will be staying on. As regards meals, you can either give money to the servant, who will buy provisions and cook for you, or take them with us at the Vihara. The hotel charges Rs.14–18 *per diem*, but neither the food nor the general atmosphere of the place would, I think, suit you. At Mrs Tagore's place you could, of course, take any diet you needed.³

Being an Indian citizen you need no pass for Gangtok. Accommodation, though, is always a problem, as the Dak Bungalow is always full. However, after your arrival I shall write to someone and see what can be done.

Darjeeling will be rather cold by the time you go there, so you would be well advised to bring warm clothing.

There is no need to come by air from Calcutta. If you travel first class you should have no difficulty, though I would advise you to be very careful during the night, as you are travelling alone and there have been several reports in the papers recently of upper class passengers being robbed. At Haldibari you will have to cross the Ganges by steamer (which makes a pleasant interlude), but don't let the coolies rob you. They shouldn't get more than eight annas⁴ each.

On reaching Siliguri station⁵ (the train which arrives in the *morning* is the more convenient, since otherwise you will have to travel up to Kalimpong at night) take *one* seat in the taxi,⁶ which should reach Kalimpong not later than twelve noon. If I was not observing the Rainy Season Retreat⁷ I should come to meet you, but if you wire the date and time of your arrival I shall try to send a boy. But even if no one meets you, there will be no difficulty, I think. On reaching the Kalimpong motor stand take a local taxi to the Vihara. Ask for 'the English monk' at Chebo Busti.⁸

By all means go to the Dharmarajika Vihara, Calcutta.⁹ It is in College Square, immediately opposite to the University. It is difficult to give you a letter of introduction to anyone not jealous of me, as the Gen. Secretary¹⁰ means to have gone to Ceylon. However, the Joint Secretary¹¹ is coming to Kalimpong tomorrow, for one week, and should be back in Calcutta while you are there. I shall speak to him about you. Even if you are not able to meet anybody there it will not matter, as I think I shall be able to give you all necessary information and letters of introduction for your pilgrimage.

That settles everything, I believe – except the long mirror, which I am still trying to locate.¹² As during the Retreat I am not leaving the Vihara it is not very easy to arrange things. However, I shall do my best.

Looking forward to seeing you and the picture.¹³

Yours very sincerely,

Sangharakshita

NOTES

1. Tagore family i.e. the family of the Bengali poet, Rabindranath Tagore (1861–1941). The house was a close copy of Shyamali, Tagore's residence at Santiniketan (see Letter 5, note 9). Tagore visited Kalimpong many times, but only the poet's daughter-in-law, known as Pratima Devi, now lived there (see Letter 7, note 1, and *FMK* above, pp. 153).
2. European style commode: lavatory.
3. Any diet: see Letter 6, note 14.
4. An anna was one-sixteenth of a rupee. At the time of decimalization in India in 1957, the rupee was divided into 100 paise. However, people continued to use the more familiar term 'anna'.
5. Siliguri is the largest city in the Darjeeling district of West Bengal. Siliguri Town Station was one of two stations in the town at this time. Opened in 1880 under the British Raj, it was the terminus for trains from Calcutta.
6. It was common to pay for one seat and share the taxi with other passengers.
7. Since the time of the Buddha, as part of their discipline, Buddhist monks were expected to keep a three- or four-month rainy season retreat each year during which they would stay in one location and get on with more intensive spiritual practice. Sangharakshita especially enjoyed these times when he could devote himself not only to meditation but also to his correspondence and literary work. He continued to receive visitors.
8. Strictly speaking Chebo Busti referred to a Lepcha village just outside Kalimpong, although by extension it covered the surrounding area which included the Vihara. The Lepchas were the original inhabitants of the area, a small, fair people who lived mostly in the forest. Many who lived in the town had become Christians.
9. The Dharmarajika Vihara at 4a Bankim Chatterjee Street, Calcutta, was the headquarters of the Maha Bodhi Society (see Letter 9, note 1). Sangharakshita stayed here when editing the *Maha Bodhi* (see Letter 9, note 12). Four of his letters to Dinoo (Letters 9, 10, 14, and 26) are written from this address.
10. The General Secretary, Devapriya Valisinha (1904–1968), had been a personal disciple of Anagārika Dharmapala (see Letter 9, note 1). Like Dharmapala, he came from Ceylon. It was he who had invited Sangharakshita to edit the *Maha Bodhi* (see Letter 9, note 12). Sangharakshita commented of him that he was 'a very good man', respected by the Sinhalese monks. He also relates how his life ended rather sadly. He became infatuated with a Nepali woman, much younger than himself, whom he had met in Darjeeling. He took her and her mother to live at the Maha Bodhi

headquarters, creating rather an upset. There was also some sympathy, for it was evident to all that the woman had been interested in him only for his money. Being thus under great strain, he had sustained a stroke. It was then that Sangharakshita, on his farewell tour of India in November 1966, visited him in hospital and found his old friend with 'a tragic, haunted look', unable to speak, so that all he could do was 'sit with him in silent sympathy' (see *MAS*, pp. 326 and 359).

11. This Joint Secretary of the Maha Bodhi Society was Jinaratana who shared the post with with Sangharatana (Letter 6, note 16). Sangharakshita had first met him when he visited the Maha Bodhi headquarters in 1945 while still in the army (see *RR*, p. 162). When he visited again in 1947 with his friend Banerjee, he had been surprised to find Jinaratana, as monk-in-charge, styling himself 'His Holiness the High Priest'. Nor did Jinaratana's behaviour impress him as very monk-like (see *RR*, chapters 16 & 17). Jinaratana was managing editor of the *Maha Bodhi* with a seat on the editorial board, so Sangharakshita was required to work with him (see e.g. *ISGW*, p. 122). If he was to visit Sangharakshita in Kalimpong it was, in all likelihood, in connection with the journal. Sangharakshita does not recall whether the visit ever took place.

12. A long mirror was required by ladies for their toilette.

13. The by now long-awaited painting was first mentioned in February the previous year (see Letter 12, note 5). It was probably a round-framed picture of the future Buddha, Maitreya, that eventually did come to hang in the Vihara.

21

Triyana Vardhana Vihara,
Kalimpong
11. 10. 58

Dear Dinoo,

Thank you for your letter dated 6th October. If you were able to keep to your programme, you are now *en route* for Calcutta and no doubt feeling quite excited. Mrs Tagore has been informed of the proposed date of your arrival, and has promised to arrange at least a large mirror.

Our retreat ends on the next Full Moon Day, 27th October. I had been thinking of going up to Gangtok immediately afterwards, but nothing definite has been arranged. However, now that you will be coming up it would be a good idea, I think, to make the trip together. In this event, we should be there for the celebrations[1] which are being held in connection with the 40th anniversary of the Maharaja's[2] accession to the throne of Sikkim.[3] Regarding accommodation I shall do my best, but Gangtok is likely to be crowded. Rustomji[4] is a good friend of mine, but his place is small, and his mother, sister, and brother-in-law may be coming up. However, something will be arranged.

For the last few days Kalimpong has been overcast, and today it is actually raining! Hope it clears up by the time you arrive.

Looking forward to seeing you,
Yours v. sincerely,
Sangharakshita

NOTES

1. It seems that in the event Sangharakshita did not attend the 40th anniversary celebrations although Dinoo, who did travel to Gangtok after her visit to Kalimpong, may have done so. The difficulty of finding suitable accommodation seems to have been the subject of some misunderstanding between Dinoo and the Kazini (see Introduction p. 469).
2. Although a protectorate of India, Sikkim continued to be ruled by a monarchy until 1975.
3. See Letter 5, note 10. Sangharakshita made a number of teaching tours in Sikkim, see e.g. *ISGW*, chapter 16.
4. Rustomji, a Parsi, was the *dewan* or chief minister of Sikkim.

22

Triyana Vardhana Vihara,
Kalimpong
4. 3. 63

Dear Dinoo,

Thank you for your letter dated 23rd February,[1] which I was very glad to receive. It seems there has been some misunderstanding between us. I was certainly under the impression that, as I told Gool Mehta,[2] you were displeased with me since your visit to Kalimpong,[3] and that for this reason you had not come to my lectures.[4] Now that it transpires that this was not the case I feel very happy, for the thought that you were displeased had *troubled me*, as I never like to break with a friend.[5] At the same time, it was perhaps not unnatural that I should have got the impression I did. Whenever my lectures were arranged at the Society[6] I personally saw to it that you were sent an invitation and always looked for you among the audience. I knew, of course, that Doctor Mehta's ideology was unacceptable to you (as it is to me: having taken refuge in the Buddha, I need no other guidance),[7] but I thought that you would have no objection to coming to *my* lectures[8] (perhaps I flattered myself here) and therefore looked out for you, thinking you would come along and then, having renewed contact, invite me to your place as before. When, after several invitations had been sent, still you did not come, I formed the conclusion you were displeased. As for your own invitation sent through Mr Bo,[9] I have no recollection of it whatever, though I clearly remember his saying he had met you, I think it was at a wedding. Had I understood you to have invited me, I should most certainly have come – you can be quite sure of that. I should have been only too pleased to sit on the divan, amidst the whitewash and plaster![10] As for *my* being annoyed with *you* for going back on your promise, I certainly did feel a bit disappointed, as our Vihara is always in need of funds;[11] but in your letter you so clearly stated that the promise had been rashly made, and blamed yourself accordingly, that it was quite impossible for me to feel annoyed, and it was certainly not this which prevented me from contacting you in Bombay. With regard to your not seeing me in Lucknow,[12] I never went there, and cannot now recollect that I ever had any intention of doing so. It seems, therefore, that there has been misunderstanding on both sides, and in the same way that your letter has removed my misunderstanding I hope that this of mine will remove yours, and that we shall be as good friends in the future as we were in the past.

Now that we have re-established contact, let me bring you up to date with a few items of news. Since returning two years ago from my last visit to Bombay, which lasted for eight months[13] (most of which were spent in Poona, with visits to Ahmedabad,[14] Agra, Ajmer, Delhi,[15] and Almora[16] etc) I have hardly been out of Kalimpong at all. Much of my time has been occupied with the writing of a new book, called *The Heritage of Buddhism*,[17] which will cover even more ground than my *Survey*.[18] It is about three-quarters finished,[19] and until it has been completed I do not want to move out of Kalimpong. It has already been accepted by a London publisher.[20] Apart from this, I have been greatly occupied with the development of the Vihara, which has become quite well known, with the result that despite the restrictions,[21] this being a border area,[22] we get quite a lot of visitors, some of whom stay for longer or shorter periods for the study of Buddhism and practice of meditation.[23] Many of the local Tibetan lamas[24] also come here, some for the study of English.[25] Five young Tibetans,[26] two of them novice monks, are staying with me more or less permanently for the same purpose. So you will see my hands are full. There is also quite a lot of miscellaneous literary work, and unending correspondence. For every one letter I write I receive six, so you must not be surprised at my having neglected you, as many of my friends are in the same position. My health, I am sorry to say, has not been too good. Bombay suits me much better in the winter time[27] than Kalimpong. This winter I was down with 'flu three times, and confined to bed, which has left me feeling weak even now.

When I shall next be able to come to Bombay I cannot say, though I very much want to come. The newly converted Buddhists, Dr Ambedkar's followers, write to me constantly; but after finishing *The Heritage* I have to take up work on the biography of Anagārika Dharmapala,[28] founder of the Maha Bodhi, which has to be brought out in connection with the Birth Centenary celebrations next year. However, you may be quite sure that whenever I do come to Bombay I shall make tracks for 'Oceana' as soon as possible, without waiting for you to come to my lectures, and that I shall give you prior intimation of my visit.

Regarding the border situation,[29] I cannot tell you much more than you read in the newspapers, but I do not intend to leave Kalimpong unless absolutely necessary, and that necessity will, I hope, never arise.[30] All the same, the Chinese have shown themselves to be thoroughly untrustworthy and we must be prepared for any eventuality.

With the Society I now have hardly any contact. On the material, especially the business, side, it appears to be flourishing more than ever; but religious activities are practically nil. For some time past it has been my impression that Doctor's guidance has been sinking to lower and lower levels.[31] I am fond of him as a man, however, and would like to be able to help him.

Your letter, I assume, was written at night. This is being written in the afternoon, with the bright spring sunshine outside, and a strong wind shaking the trees and setting the signboard a-rattle. In a few minutes time I have to go to town, to attend to various little matters, so must bring this letter to an end. There is still much to tell you, but it will have to wait till next time. Meanwhile, I welcome more news from you, and hope very soon to receive from you an assurance that all causes of misunderstanding between us are now removed.

With all good wishes,
Yours sincerely,
Sangharakshita
(no longer a 'Stranger', I hope.)

NOTES

1. Some four-and-a-half years have elapsed since the previous letter. There may have been letters from either of them that are no longer extant. The letter Sangharakshita refers to from Dinoo has not survived.
2. Gool (Gulbehn) Mehta was Dr Mehta's wife. See Appendix p. 615.
3. The reason for Dinoo's displeasure is not clear. Sangharakshita recalls that she had been unhappy with her accommodation in Gangtok (see Letter 21, note 1).
4. Lectures given in Bombay, at Dr Mehta's flat in Mayfair, where formerly the Society of Servants of God had met. See Letter 18, note 15.
5. For more on Sangharakshita and friendship see Introduction pp. 469–70 and 475ff; and Appendix pp. 603–9.
6. i.e. the headquarters of the Society of Servants of God.
7. No other guidance: see Appendix p. 604.
8. No objection coming to Sangharakshita's lectures, since they would be on Buddhist subjects of interest to Dinoo.
9. Mr Bo was one of Dr Mehta's circle whom Sangharakshita had met on his first visit to the Nature Cure Clinic in Poona in March 1956 (see Letter 3). An Italian by birth and very anti-Catholic, he delighted in regaling his friends with stories and jokes told at the expense of the Roman Catholic clerisy. Being 'a militant atheist', he cheerfully dismissed Dr Mehta's claims to divine guidance (see *ISGW*, p. 282).
10. Evidently Oceana was undergoing some redecoration.
11. It seems Dinoo had offered to make a further donation but had then felt obliged to withdraw the offer. There is no record of this.
12. Lucknow is the capital city of Uttar Pradesh. Although he had not visited in recent years, and therefore had not seen Dinoo when she was there, Sangharakshita spent four days in the city in November 1950, immediately after his *bhikkhu* ordination, and gave lectures at the Bodhisattva Vihara and the University. Through the latter he had come into contact with the famous scholars Dr Herbert Guenther and Dr Surendranath Dasgupta (see *FMK*, pp. 109]ff. above).
13. This eight month tour was the fourth and longest of Sangharakshita's preaching tours, and lasted from October 1961 to May 1962, during which he visited more than half the states of India, gave nearly 200 lectures, and received 25,000 men and women into the Buddhist community (see *MAS*, p. 14).
14. Ahmedabad, the largest city of Gujerat state, was under Mughal rule from 1573 to 1758 (a major influence on its architecture of the city). Sangharakshita was in contact with a group of people

there, all Ambedkarites, and visited the city regularly to give talks. He spent five days there in 1966 during his farewell tour (see *MAS*, p. 295).

15. Delhi is the second largest metropolis (by population) in India. New Delhi, the capital of India, lies within its boundaries. It was just outside Delhi that Sangharakshita's army unit camped after arriving in India in September 1944 when he visited the city for the first time (see *RR*, pp. 110–15). In 1956, the Buddha Jayanti year, he was there again, this time with Dhardo Rimpoche (see Letter 8, note 1).

16. Almora is a Himalayan town in Uttarakhand state. Just outside the town runs the celebrated Crank's Ridge, associated with the names of many famous Western Buddhists, including the German-born Lama Govinda (1898–1985) and his Parsi wife, Li Gotami, who lived there for some three decades. Lama Govinda was an early contributor to *Stepping-Stones* (Letter 13, note 4). The three met when the Lama and Li visited Kalimpong in June 1951 (see *FMK*, chapter 13) and from then on their friendship blossomed. In Lama Govinda, in particular, Sangharakshita felt he had found a kindred spirit. He, too, was not only intensely dedicated to the Buddhist spiritual path, but was also an artist with a background in the western tradition who saw that artistic endeavour could be a part of spiritual life itself. Over the fourteen years of Sangharakshita's residence in Kalimpong, the friends met on a number of occasions: in Kalimpong, at Almora, and elsewhere (described in his memoirs). Clearly Sangharakshita's eight months away from the Vihara in 1961 had included a visit to his friends. He visited Almora once more, in 1966 during his farewell tour, taking Terry Delamare with him (see *MAS*, pp. 363–4).

17. *The Heritage of Buddhism* began as a series of contributions commissioned for the *Oriya Encyclopaedia*. (Oriya is the language of Orissa in eastern India. Sangharakshita's contributions were translated by the editor.) From this material, Sangharakshita planned to produce a series of five volumes (see *MAS*, pp. 41 and 194–5). The first appeared in 1968, published by Rider as *The Three Jewels: An Introduction to the Study of Buddhism* (more recent editions go under the subtitle, *an Introduction to the Central Ideals of Buddhism*) (*Complete* Works, vol. 2). The second volume was first published in 1985 by Tharpa Publications as *The Eternal Legacy: an Introduction to the Canonical Literature of Buddhism* (*Complete* Works, vol. 14). A third, covering the different sects and schools of Buddhism, was started but not completed, the first few chapters being published in India as a booklet. The fourth volume was to have been on Buddhism and Art, and the fifth

on Meditation, but due to the increasing volume of his other work, notably setting up the order and movement he went on to found in the West, they were never realized.

18. *A Survey of Buddhism* (see Letter 15, note 4, and Letter 19, notes 8 & 9) was an attempt 'to see Buddhism in its full *breadth* and in its ultimate *depth*' (see Preface to the sixth edition, reprinted in the ninth edition. *Complete Works*, vol. 1).

19. i.e. the first volume, see note 17 above.

20. The London publisher was Rider. See note 17 above.

21. Restrictions were put in place after the Chinese invasion of India in October 1962 to limit foreign visitors' access to the area.

22. Kalimpong lies near the border with Tibet, which had by then been claimed by China.

23. Visitors to the Vihara included monks from Thailand, Vietnam, Ladakh, and Tibet (see *PT*, chapter 12), as well as a number of Westerners such as the Swedish nun, Amita Nisatta (see Letter 13, note 3) and Jivaka (see Letter 19, note 26).

24. The local Tibetan lamas included Khemtul Rimpoche, a Kagyu incarnate lama and his lama brother (see *PT*, pp. 102–3), and Lama Lobsang from Sarnath (originally from Ladakh) (see *PT*, p. 128).

25. Since his arrival in Kalimpong, Sangharakshita had given English lessons, his first student being the young Bihari Tilakdhari Prasad Singh. Others included the young YMBA students studying for their matriculation exams, and even Aniruddha, the monk who had tried to throw Sangharakshita out of the Dharmodaya Vihara (see *FMK* above, p. 432).

26. The two novices were Lobsang Norbu, who had been a 'dubdor' or fighting monk in Tibet, and Thubden (see *PT*, pp. 131–3). A nephew of Kachu Rimpoche (see Letter 18, note 4) also lived for a time at the Vihara. It is not known who the other two were.

27. Winter in Kalimpong coincided approximately with the Christmas and New Year period.

28. On the strength of his biographical sketch of Anagārika Dharmapala (Letter 9, note 1), Sangharakshita had been invited by the trustees of the Anagarika Dharmapala Trust in Colombo to write a full-length biography. To do this, he required English translations of articles that Dharmapala had published in the Sinhalese newspaper he had founded, *Sinhala Baudhayya*. The commissioners of the biography being unable to supply these, and Sangharakshita being occupied with other matters, the project fell through, so that *Anagārika Dharmapala: A Biographical Sketch* remains the only English-language biography of Anagārika Dharmapala available (*Complete Works*, vol. 8).

29. After the Chinese invasion of India in 1962, there was much unease on the north-eastern border, and further developments

30. At this time Sangharakshita had no thought of returning to the West. In fact, he was approached by the local authorities who specifically requested him not to leave, as they believed that being a respected local figure, his remaining in Kalimpong would help maintain stability in the town. Many Indian officials did send their wives and children away. The local Nepalis, however, were not anxious about the possibility of a Chinese invasion (see *PT*, pp. 157–8).

were anticipated at any time. Sangharakshita writes about this period in *PT*, chapter 14.

31. i.e. more and more concerned with business, with buying up properties, and even creating a bank (see Appendix).

23

Triyana Vardhana Vihara,
Kalimpong
19. 8. 1963

My dear Dinoo,

There isn't really anything much to tell you, but I thought I should just let you know how glad I was to receive your long 'newsy' letter. You are one of those people who write exactly as they talk, so that as I go through what you have written I can hear your voice and see your face. You say that you look much older; but anyway, I see you as you were four (or is it five?)[1] years ago, and even if I *do* get a shock when we meet I shall have the benefit of all that extra wisdom! You are only two years younger than my mother,[2] from whom I heard the other week after an interval of fifteen years.[3] You see, I have accepted an invitation[4] to go to England next year for a few months (lectures, of course)[5] and the information reached her through the Buddhist Society.[6]

Your letter certainly tells a story of ups and downs, of experiences grave and gay. It must really have been a very heart-warming thing to find the teachers rising so wonderfully[7] to the occasion of the Silver Jubilee,[8] when you yourself felt so arid and blank, as you put it. At such times our faith in human nature revives. On the other hand, your experience of the shingles seems to have been really gruesome. I shuddered for you when I read your description. Though I had heard of this disease, I had no idea what it was, or that it could be so terrible. All the same, every cloud has a silver lining, and it seems that, in a very wonderful way, you were able to extract spiritual benefits even from this excruciating experience. Having never been so ill, I have no comparable experience to relate.

Jivaka was an odd – and a sad – case. He had plenty of money, and there was no need for him to have gone hungry, if he ever really did. The real trouble is that he had a morbid craving for love and affection. As I could not, or would not, give him enough of the sort of emotional slop he wanted he left me, got into the hands of the wrong people, who exploited him, and eventually died in mysterious circumstances. When we meet I shall tell you the whole story; it is very interesting.[9]

As for myself, I am still hard at work on my book, and I have no news for you. My only object in writing is to keep in touch, and if you think this a very poor return for your own magnificent epistle I must ask you to forgive me.

Ever yours sincerely,
Sangharakshita

NOTES

1. It was in October 1958, nearly five years earlier, that Dinoo had visited Sangharakshita in Kalimpong.
2. Dinoo was born c. 1900.
3. His mother had probably been in contact with Christmas Humphreys, the President of the Buddhist Society (whom she had once met), who had told her of the invitation to Sangharakshita and passed on his address in India.

    When Sangharakshita made the momentous decision to go forth from worldly life, as the Buddha had done before him, he understood this to mean severing all worldly ties, including those with his family. He also destroyed his identity papers (see *RR*, chapter 24). When he had written to his parents saying he was thinking of becoming a monk, his father had replied that his life was his own and he should do with it as he thought best. His mother hoped she would still see him sometimes (see *RR*, pp. 128–9).
4. This invitation came from the English Sangha Trust, a Buddhist

organization created in 1954 by Bhikkhu Kapilavaddho (formerly William Purfurst, see *MAS*, p. 37) with the aim of creating a monastic community for westerners in Britain. (The supporting body for lay-followers was called the English Sangha Association.) Sangharakshita had accepted the invitation, making it clear he did not intend to stay for more than six months. 'Prior to that,' he wrote later, 'I had not thought even of visiting the West; my life and my work lay in India.' Two considerations influenced his decision: that his presence might help resolve differences that had arisen between the English Sangha Trust and the Buddhist Society, the two principal Buddhist organizations in London, and that his parents were growing old and he ought to see them (see *MAS*, p. 15). Khantipalo, who was with Sangharakshita when the invitation arrived, had argued that he had a duty to help spread the Dharma in England, the land of his birth. 'I could not but recognize the force of his argument.' (see *PT*, p. 170). Khantipalo, an English-born monk, had stayed with Sangharakshita at the Vihara for two extended periods in 1961 and 1962. For an account of his experiences, see Khantipalo, *Noble Friendship*, Windhorse Publications, Birmingham 2002.

5. Through *A Survey of Buddhism* (Letter 15, note 4) and his editorship of the *Maha Bodhi* (Letter 9, note 12), Sangharakshita was by this time a well-known writer on Buddhism both in India and in the West and, in fact, the seniormost British-born *bhikṣu*, or monk. It was, therefore, natural that members of the English Sangha Trust, with their interest in creating a British monastic community, should have extended this invitation.

6. The Buddhist Society was founded by Christmas Humphreys in 1924 as the Buddhist Lodge of the Theosophical Society (from which it separated two years later). He was its president until his death in 1983. It is one of the oldest Buddhist societies in Europe (a reminder of how recent is the arrival of the Buddha's teaching in the West). It tended to an ecumenical approach to Buddhism, providing a platform for visiting Buddhist teachers of all traditions, as well as holding its own classes and summer schools (see *MAS*, pp. 36–7). Since 1956, the Buddhist Society has been based in Eccleston Square, Victoria, London.

7. As we know, Dinoo's teachers had not always given her so much cause for pleasure. See Letter 18, notes 12, 13, and 14.

8. Dinoo founded the school in 1934. It is unclear what this silver jubilee (25 years) was marking.

9. Khantipalo relates his version of the story of Jivaka in Khantipalo, *Noble Friendship*, Windhorse Publications, Birmingham 2002, pp. 17 and 134. See also *PT*, pp. 45–56.

24

Triyana Vardhana Vihara,
Kalimpong
31. 12. 1963

Dear Dinoo,

Thank you very much for your letter dated 23. 12. 63, which reached me yesterday, and which I think is one of the nicest letters I have ever received from you – though *all* your letters are nice. As a matter of fact, it came at a 'psychological moment'. A few days ago, returning very late at night from Gangtok after attending the Maharaja of Sikkim's funeral,[1] I caught a bad chill and had to stay in bed. When your letter came I had just had a very bad night, with fever and vomiting, and was feeling rather miserable. But after reading your letter (*twice!*) I cheered up considerably. This morning I am almost normal again, and am hastening to reply before getting back to my other work.

First of all about my plans for going to England.[2] I am going by boat from Bombay and have asked the travel agency to arrange a passage not later than the last week of March, in which case I shall probably be in Bombay some time during the first week of March. How long I shall be in England I cannot say, but most likely it will be not less than six months and not more than twelve months.[3] I am going at the invitation of the English Sangha Association, which is bearing all expenses. Though my headquarters will be in London, I shall be lecturing and holding classes in other parts of the country too,[4] and there is just a possibility that I shall go to the Continent and even to the U.S.[5] If anyone is interested in contacting me, the address will be The Sangha Association, 131 Haverstock Hill, London N.W.3. Telephone PRImrose 2618. This, as you probably know, is the Hampstead area, where many artists and writers now stay.[6]

Clare Cameron and I were very good friends and I look forward to meeting her again. If she is unable to come up to London I shall go down to Chichester, which is a town I know quite well, having visited it many times during the war.[7] It has a lovely old cathedral. That she was now editing the *Science of Thought Review*[8] I already knew, as I used to see this magazine at 'Mayfair'.[9] Henry Thomas Hamblin was, I believe, truly a great soul, though some of the other contributors, including Richard Whitwell,[10] often seemed to me rather too sentimental and wishy-washy. Buddhism seems to give one a taste for intellectual precision, even though the limitations of the intellect are fully realized.

Most of your other questions, I am afraid, will have to wait for an answer till we meet. Two of them, however, are quite straightforward and can be answered now. You are quite right in thinking that, the Buddha's 'death' having been voluntary,[11] we should always speak of His parinirvana.[12] The Buddhist scriptures always do so speak, and unless by an oversight I follow the same usage in my own writings. As for 'our going to hell for centuries on end for killing a few worms' I thoroughly agree with you that this is a gross exaggeration. While we must, according to the law of karma, suffer pain for the pain that we inflict, the effect is always proportionate to the cause, not disproportionate.[13] I can only suppose that the compilers of the *Mahavastu*.[14] (on the whole a fine and very important early work) simply wanted to impress the consequences of taking life on a rather obtuse audience and therefore had recourse to the rather unfortunate exaggeration you mention. Incidentally, the *Mahavastu* is held to reflect, on the whole, beliefs current among the laity, who perhaps would not be so precise in their doctrinal statements as the monks.

Yogananda's[15] *Autobiography of a Yogi* I read about fifteen years ago, but then it impressed me rather unfavourably. What my reaction might be now I cannot say. I understand, however, that the movement he started in the U.S.[16] is flourishing *mightily*, far more, in fact, than the Ramakrishna Mission.[17] If you are interested in autobiographies, you should read *The Ochre Robe* by Swami Agehananda Bharati.[18] It is available in Bombay.

Jivaka's is a long and rather sad story and the telling will have to wait until we meet. While he did turn over to me whatever cash he had on arrival in Kalimpong (about Rs.2,000) he also had, in England, about £20,000 in the bank, besides property and other assets. After leaving me he brought some of his money out to India, and gave several large donations (one of Rs.10,000) to several Buddhist organizations.[19] When I heard that you had bought him a pullover I thought it very mean of him to have asked you when he had all that money in England! What he really wanted, though, was not money but affection! He did not want a pullover so much as to be *given* something and to feel that somebody *liked* him enough to give. He also had the idea that since he was studying Buddhism he ought to be supported by the Buddhists.

Though I am aware that this is by no means an adequate reply to your nice, long, and interesting letter, I really must close now as it is nearly lunch time and after lunch I have to get back to my regular work. Literary work has gone very badly; several things started, but nothing finished!

If you have time, *please* write again. Otherwise, I shall simply let you know the date of my arrival in Bombay.

With all good wishes,
Yours very sincerely,
 Sangharakshita

NOTES

1 The Maharaja of Sikkim, Sir Tashi Namgyal (1893–1963), knighted by King George V, had ruled Sikkim since 1914. He died on 2 December 1963. Sangharakshita recalls that his funeral was 'quite a grand affair' with lamas from the four Tibetan sects or schools gathered around the cremation pyre at the four points of the compass, chanting. Many others were present, including the Maharaja's children, some of whom Sangharakshita knew well, including the Maharajkumar or Crown Prince. They were the

main mourners. Sangharakshita relates, 'The Maharani had been estranged from the Maharaja for many years after she had had an affair with a visiting high lama and given birth to a child. The Maharaja's private secretary, a rather traditional Sikkimese nobleman, had insisted that there be a separation, so she had a palace of her own outside Gangtok, but she came to Gangtok for the funeral which was held on ground behind the palace used for royal funerals. She didn't stand with her children and other members of the family; she was quite separate and on her own. I was quite close to her ... and she was weeping bitterly. She must have been thinking of the past.' Sangharakshita gave a series of lectures in Gangtok in connection with the funeral ceremonies.

2. These plans changed several times. Here, writing in December 1963, we see Sangharakshita is expecting to leave India by sea the following March. In the event he left by air in August.

3. In the event he returned to India after two years in the West – and then to make a farewell tour before establishing himself more permanently in Britain and founding the Friends of the Western Buddhist Order (now known as the Triratna Buddhist Order). These events are recounted in *MAS*.

4. Other parts of the country: during his first year in England, Sangharakshita visited many of the provincial Buddhist groups. In December 1965 he went north of the border to visit Glasgow (see *MAS*, p. 152).

5. Sangharakshita did not visit Europe or the USA on his first visit to the West, although in subsequent years he was to visit both.

6. Notable people who have lived in Hampstead include Samuel Taylor Coleridge, John Keats, John Constable, Florence Nightingale, Rabindranath Tagore, and Doris Lessing.

7. During the Second World War, at the time of the Blitz, Sangharakshita's younger sister, Joan, was evacuated to a farm near Chichester. He and his parents visited her from London from time to time.

8. The *Science of Thought Review* was a magazine founded by the English mystic, Henry Thomas Hamblin (1873–1958). Clare took over the editorship in November 1960. See Introduction, p. 481.

9. Mayfair was the apartment block that included Dr Mehta's flat. Sangharakshita often stayed there when his teaching tours took him to Bombay.

10. Richard Whitwell's style can be seen in, for example, *In the Desert a Highway*, a collection of articles contributed to the *Science of Thought Review*.

11. According to tradition, the Buddha could have prolonged his life if, for example, he had been asked to do so by his disciples. See *Mahāparinibbāna Sutta*, *Dīgha Nikāya* 16 (ii.104) in M. Walshe

(trans.), *The Long Discourses of the Buddha*, Wisdom Publications, Boston 1995, p. 246; and *Dialogues of the Buddha*, part 2, T. W. and C. A. F. Rhys Davids (trans.), Pali Text Society, London 1971, pp. 110–11.

12. *Parinirvāṇa* literally means 'beyond Nirvāṇa'. Sangharakshita is following Buddhist tradition in so designating the 'death' of a Buddha or Enlightened one. The Buddha himself insisted that it is not possible to say of an Enlightened one that after death he exists or does not exist, or both or neither. None of these predicates fit the case. Enlightenment is not to be expressed in these – or any – concepts. See *Anuradha Sutta, Saṃyutta Nikāya*, iii.257; Bhikkhu Bodhi (trans.), *The Connected Discourses of the Buddha*, Wisdom Publications, Boston 2000, p. 1033; or F. L. Woodward (trans.), *The Book of the Kindred Sayings*, part 3, Pali Text Society, London 1975, p. 204.

13. While the law of karma states that we must suffer pain for the pain we inflict, it does *not* state that all the pain we (or others) experience is due to past karma. This is an important distinction. For a discussion of the five *niyāmas* or causal relations, see *What is the Dharma?*, *Complete Works*, vol. 3, pp. 98–103 and 316–7.

14. The *Mahāvastu* is a biography of the Buddha compiled some five centuries after his *parinirvāṇa*. See *The Eternal Legacy*, Windhorse Publications, Birmingham 2006, pp. 59–61 (*Complete Works*, vol. 14).

15. Paramahansa Yogananda (1893–1952) introduced many Westerners to meditation and *kriyā yoga* through his *Autobiography of a Yogi*, published in 1946.

16. The movement he started was the Self-Realization Fellowship, founded in Los Angeles in 1925.

17. The Ramakrishna Mission was founded 1897 by Swami Vivekananda, chief disciple of Sri Ramakrishna, see Letter 19, note 2.

18. Leopold Fischer or Swami Agehananda Bharati (1923–1991) was born in Vienna and for thirty years was Professor of Anthropology at Syracuse University, USA. He spent seven years in India where he became a Hindu monk, and was known for his 'cultural criticism' of orthodox Hindus. In 1962 he published his autobiography, *The Ochre Robe*. Many years later, in 1976, he published, *The Light at the Center: Context and Pretext of Modern Mysticism*, which Sangharakshita reviewed in his essay, 'Hedonism and Spiritual Life', included in *Alternative Traditions*, Windhorse Publications, Glasgow 1986 (*Complete Works*, vol. 26).

19. Jivaka did not make any donations to Sangharakshita's vihara; he was by this time rather displeased with him. See *PT*, chapter 5.

25

Triyana Vardhana Vihara,
Kalimpong
23.3.1964

Dear Dinoo,

You will understand that I have been too busy to reply to your letter of 20th February before, besides which I was not in a position to give you any definite information about the date of my arrival in Bombay. For various reasons, my departure from India has been postponed, and now I shall not be leaving until 2nd June. I hope to be in Bombay by the first week of May,[1] but cannot be certain, as I may be detained in Calcutta by Reserve Bank formalities and other matters. If time permits, I shall make my first call on a Wednesday or Thursday after 3 p.m.; otherwise you will have to excuse me if I just barge in on you. In any case, I shall wire you from Calcutta before leaving that place, so that you will be on the alert. Even if you are free, please don't bother to come to the station, as it is not the best place to carry on a conversation, especially when one is tired and dirty after a long train journey. As usual, I shall be staying at 'Mayfair'. If you like, you may ring me; but I leave it to you. I shall not wait for a ring before contacting you.

It seems rather odd that Clare Cameron[2] does not, apparently, expect monks to be human, but perhaps she meant her remark more as a compliment to me than as a reflection upon other members of the Sangha. Though we haven't met for twenty years I still remember her very vividly. She is one of the best and sweetest persons I have ever met. In your next letter please give me her present address, as all I remember is that she now lives at Chichester, which is (or was) a sleepy old cathedral town.

As I am a U.K. citizen there is no difficulty about the duration of my stay, and in any case all my expenses are being met from that end. Some time ago I wanted to take Indian citizenship but it seems there is no provision for U.K. citizens to do this, only for foreigners.[3]

Now I have to get back to my work (preparing the Report of the Vihara) and will close with the hope that I shall be hearing from you again quite soon.

Yours very sincerely,
Sangharakshita

NOTES

1. In the following letter, Sangharakshita gives the date of his expected arrival in Bombay as 15th May.
2. Clare Cameron: see Introduction, p. 479.
3. Although India was now independent of the United Kingdom, she was still a member of the Commonwealth and apparently regarded British citizens in a different category to other non-Indian nationals.

26

Calcutta
10th May 1964

My dear Dinoo,

Many thanks for your letter dated 5. 4. 1964. Not having heard from me for such a long time you might have started thinking that my coming to Bombay was just another of those false alarms with which I am always plaguing my friends. But no. As you see, I am on my way. At present I am attending to *Maha Bodhi* Journal work in Calcutta and will be leaving for Bombay on the 13th which means, I believe, that I shall be at V.T. about noon on the 15th. As I shall not be in Bombay for more than a week, before proceeding to Poona for Buddha Jayanti,[1] I shall try to come and see you at about 5 o'clock on the day following my arrival, i.e. on the 16th. This is not a definite promise, of course; but if for any reason I cannot come along on that day I shall definitely turn up *very soon* afterwards.

With regard to my going to England there has been some change of programme. Instead of going by sea from Bombay I shall, most likely, be going by air from Calcutta. This means that after finishing my work in Poona I shall have to return to Kalimpong via Bombay and Calcutta and then come down to Calcutta again almost immediately afterwards after having made the final arrangements for my journey. Partly as a result of this change of programme I am faced by serious difficulties which are rather worrying me at present and I can only hope that everything will come out all right in the end.

As yet I could not write to Clare Cameron but will try to do so very soon. John Blofeld[2] is well known to me. He has been twice to Kalimpong and on his second visit stayed with me at the Vihara for about three weeks.[3] At the time of his first visit some kind person told him that I did not know anything about Buddhism[4] so he did not think it worth while making my acquaintance. However, shortly afterwards he happened to read my *Survey of Buddhism* and, as he told me afterwards, was astonished to find that he had been very seriously misled. Since then he has been one of my admirers though we have not corresponded for some time. His *Wheel of Life*,[5] an autobiography, is a very interesting and readable book. At present, I hear, he is preparing a new translation of the *I Ching*,[6] the old Chinese text of divination.

Calcutta is, as usual, stiflingly hot,[7] but since I started this letter the Monsoon has broken and the rains have come pouring down with such violence that I have had to close the window-shutters and turn on the electric light. The only thing I really like about Calcutta is the book-stalls.

As you say, we shall be meeting after an interval of five-and-a-half years.[8] Really, it does not seem as long as that. With one's real friends, I find, it does not matter very much whether one writes or does not write since they remain, as it were, a part of one's consciousness, so that it is impossible ever to forget them. Nevertheless, I look forward to seeing you 'in the flesh' and hope that I shall find you happy and in good health.

Till we meet,
Yours very sincerely,
　Sangharakshita

NOTES

1. To celebrate Buddha Jayanti, presumably at the invitation of the new Buddhists. For Buddha Jayanti see Letter 2, note 12.
2. John Blofeld (1913–1987) was a British writer on Asian thought and religion, especially Taoism and Chinese Buddhism. He also became interested in Tibetan Buddhism (see note 3 below). He married a Chinese woman and, after the Communist takeover of Beijing, lived with her first in Hong Kong and then for ten years in Bangkok, Thailand (his home at the time of his visit to Kalimpong). From 1961 until 1974, i.e. at the time of the writing of this letter, he worked for the United Nations.
3. This was in April 1959. John's two children were at school in Darjeeling, not far from Kalimpong, and he had come up into the hills to visit them. As related in *PT*, pp. 114–17, on this visit, John Blofeld, along with three others, joined Sangharakshita to receive initiation from the great Nyingma guru, Dudjom Rimpoche. He and Sangharakshita were to meet again in August 1964 at the Buddhist Society Summer School in Hertfordshire, England (see *MAS*, p. 25).
4. This was the eccentric Joe Cann (see *PT*, p. 114).
5. *Wheel of Life: The Autobiography of a Western Buddhist* was published by Rider and Co., London 1959, and more recently by Shambhala Publications, Boston 1988.
6. This translation of the *I Ching* was published by George Allen & Unwin Ltd in 1965 as *I Ching: the Book of Change*.
7. (c.f. Letter 15) Sangharakshita was to refer to Calcutta as 'the City of Dreadful Heat' (see *ISGW*, p. 113), after James Thomson's poem, *The City of Dreadful Night*.
8. Their last meeting had taken place in Kalimpong in October 1958.

27

Hampstead Buddhist Vihara
London N.W.3.[1]
20. 2. 65

Dear Dinoo,

I was delighted to hear from you, as though I could not write to you I certainly did not forget you, as I am sure you understood from the card.

The last six months have certainly been the busiest of my life, and much seems to have been accomplished.[2] As for my headquarters being now here, what I am really thinking of is trying to base myself as it were triangularly, with one foot in London, one in Kalimpong, and one in Bombay, as in all three places I have responsibilities which it is not easy for me to abandon.[3] Time alone will tell whether such an arrangement is possible or whether I shall have to choose.[4] In any case, I shall not be back in India before the Autumn,[5] and will most likely come straight to Bombay. Meanwhile, I am sending you a few reports (not complete) which will give you some idea of the sort of thing I am doing here.

You say I look healthy and happy in the photograph and I must tell you that I am definitely feeling so. A medical check-up (routine) has disclosed nothing worse than a minor complaint of the gall-bladder which is receiving attention. The only thing I am not happy about is the fact that I have no time at all for literary work, not even for writing letters! My book *The Three Jewels*, being the first part of *The Heritage of Buddhism*, has, however, been accepted for publication and will go to the printers as soon as I can make it ready.[6]

Just before Christmas I spent a few days with Clare Cameron[7] and greatly enjoyed the peace and quiet of her little country place.[8] On my first visit to her (before she moved)[9] she showed me the brass Buddha head and all the other lovely Indian things (so exotic here!) which you had sent her, and which she treasures greatly. Now they occupy various places of honour in the new house.

When I was in Calcutta, Valisinha and I got a bit muddled with our various amounts and accounts, and the various debitings and creditings, but it was all sorted out two months ago and your donation of Rs.100 towards the Dharmapala Institute of Calcutta[10] has now been credited where it belongs. I am sorry that your good intentions were temporarily frustrated, and hope that you have received the Society's official receipt.

Your friend Mrs Hilla Boyce has not yet contacted me but I shall be glad to meet her if she does.

At the moment of writing I am looking out of the window at a beautiful snowscape, as several inches of snow fell last night. Now it is beginning to melt away. Spring is coming! How pleasant it will be to see an English Spring!

With warmest good wishes, now and always,
Yours sincerely,
    Sangharakshita

NOTES

1. Sangharakshita writes from 131 Haverstock Hill, the premises of the Hampstead Buddhist Vihara and headquarters of the English Sangha Trust at whose invitation Sangharakshita had come to England (see Letter 23, note 4).
2. Sangharakshita arrived in England on 12 August 1964. Since then he had attended the Buddhist Society's Summer School, given lectures under the auspices of both the English Sangha Trust (see Letter 23, note 4) and the Buddhist Society (see Letter 23, note 6), as well various clubs and societies in and around London. He had also made

visits to a number of provincial Buddhist groups (see *MAS*, chapter 7). He continued with literary work and had contact with many new people who were drawn to the activities which his arrival on the British Buddhist scene had engendered.

3. These three places were in London with the English Sangha Trust and the Buddhist Society, in Kalimpong with the Triyana Vardhana Vihara which he had founded in 1957 (see *PT*, chapter 5), and in Bombay with the new Buddhists. The present letter shows Sangharakshita's 'thoughts in progress' concerning how he might best respond to the very great interest in Buddhism that he had discovered on his return to the land of his birth.

4. Time did tell and Sangharakshita did choose to base himself fully in the UK. At the same time, he maintained his links with his friends in Kalimpong, and with the new Buddhists in Bombay and Maharashtra, so that eventually, through the movement he founded, he was able to give more help than he ever could have done through his teaching tours alone. For instance, one of Sangharakshita's western disciples visited Kalimpong and found Sangharakshita's old friend and teacher, Dhardo Rimpoche, who ran a school for Tibetan refugee children, in serious financial difficulties. His teachers were leaving because he was unable to pay them. A fund-raising campaign was launched in London and £36,000 was very quickly raised which supported the school for some time. The school continues to receive support through a Triratna Buddhist Community charity, the Karuna Trust. For further details about the growth of the movement in India, see Letter 29, note 5, and Vajragupta, *The Triratna Story*, Windhorse Publications, Cambridge 2010.

5. In fact Sangharakshita did not return to India until September 1966, for a farewell tour, during which he took the opportunity to visit Dinoo in Bombay (see Letter 28).

6. For *The Three Jewels* and *The Heritage of Buddhism* see Letter 22, note 17.

7. Clare Cameron: see Introduction, p. 479.

8. Her little country place was Bosham House, near the Sussex Downs, just west of Chichester.

9. In *MAS*, pp. 30–1 Sangharakshita describes his first visit to Clare taking place at Bosham House. We may assume, however, that the account recorded in this letter is correct, i.e. his first visit was to the cottage where she lived before she moved to Bosham House.

10. At that time the Dharmapala Institute of Calcutta was being built next door to the Maha Bodhi Society headquarters. Its function was mainly as an institute of culture and it included a library and became a venue for lectures.

28

>Hampstead Buddhist Vihara,
>London
>17. 12. 65

My dear Dinoo,

 This is just to acknowledge the safe receipt, yesterday evening, of the beautiful cobra-skin wallet and the lovely card. By the same post I received a little book of poems from Clare Cameron. As you can well imagine, I am very much looking forward to receiving your next budget of news, after which I shall write you a proper letter. Meanwhile, my very best wishes for your health, happiness, and spiritual progress in the New Year.

 Yours affectionately,
 Sangharakshita

29

Tittleshall,¹
Norfolk
22nd January 1974²

Dear Dinoo,

Thank you for your card dated 19. 12. 1973, which reached me early in the New Year. I was very glad indeed to receive it, and it at once brought back very pleasant and interesting memories of my life in India in general and in Bombay in particular.

It is good to know that the *FWBO Newsletter*³ is reaching you regularly and that it is keeping you informed about the developments over here. To be frank, it was very uphill work indeed in the early days, but after seven years of hard work I think it can be said that we have at least the nucleus of a truly spiritual, and now rapidly expanding, Buddhist Movement in the West.⁴ Sooner or later I intend to establish a Centre of the FWBO in India,⁵ as I am sure that many educated Indians could benefit from our type of approach.⁶ In fact, to let you into a secret, I am selling the vihara in Kalimpong⁷ and buying – I hope – another place in a more accessible, less politically disturbed part of the country. Two or three of my pupils will, I hope, be able to reside there and carry on activities.

When I look back, it is difficult to think of you as being now 72, which is about the age of my mother (you are two years younger than she is). Anyway, I am really glad to learn that the operation was such a great success, as I remember how difficult it sometimes was for you to follow what people were saying and how you had to sit right up close to me when I came to see you.[8] I have certainly not forgotten our pleasant meetings and discussions at 'Oceana'. What wonderful teas you always used to give me, and how eager you always were to talk about the spiritual life and about Buddhism! Is the little green stone Buddha[9] still on your window sill, and do you still keep up your meditation practice?

A few months ago I received a letter from Dr Mehta's son Ardeshir.[10] He is now in Israel, studying Agriculture, and happened to meet a friend of mine from London. From Dr Mehta himself I never hear, though I send him the *Newsletter*,[11] but I gather from Indian friends that in recent years he has been out and about quite a lot, mostly in Delhi. Mme. Wadia[12] does not write any more, either. In fact, I do not even know if she is still alive.[13]

At present I am living in the country, in Norfolk, which is a very agricultural part of England, and do not hear much of what is going on in the world. When I went to see my mother recently[14] she spoke very feelingly of the sufferings of people in India (she had seen a television programme) and wanted to know when I was going back to help!

Well, Dinoo, I think I will close now. It is a cold, misty day, and looking out of the window of my cottage over the fields I can see bare trees beneath a dull grey sky. In Bombay, no doubt, you are enjoying plenty of sunshine. It is always good to hear from you, and to know that, though separated by several thousands of miles of land and sea, we are still very much in touch. By way of a little present for the New Year I am enclosing a copy of a little book of five talks on Zen, recently published,[15] which I hope will be of some interest to you. Please accept it with my love.

Ever yours sincerely,
Sangharakshita

NOTES

1. Tittleshall, Norfolk, is a village some 25 miles north-west of Norwich. Sangharakshita was staying with his friend, Vajrakumara, in a small cottage belonging to a friend of Mary Rawnsley (later Sulochana). They had stayed on after a week's study seminar on the great Mahāyāna text, the *Bodhicaryāvatāra*, which had taken place from 13–22 December 1973. It was the first such FWBO study retreat that Sangharakshita led (some 150 were to follow), and was held in Tittleshall at the Old Rectory, home of Mary Rawnsley. (The Old Rectory later housed 'Abhirati', one of the first FWBO communities.)
2. Just over eight years have gone by since Sangharakshita's last surviving letter to Dinoo. There were some letters in the interim. Two from Dinoo have survived, one dated 20. 12. 66, written after Sangharakshita and his friend Terry Delamare had visited her in Bombay during their farewell tour of India (September 1965 – February 1966) and a second one, dated 11. 11. 67, in which Dinoo thanks Sangharakshita for his 'prompt reply'. The 'prompt reply', however, did not survive.
3. The movement Sangharakshita inaugurated in London on 6 April 1967 was the Friends of the Western Buddhist Order (renamed the Triratna Buddhist Community in May 2010). The first *FWBO Newsletter* appeared in May 1968, and in the course of the following years sixty-eight issues were to appear, the last in the winter of 1985/6. The *Newsletter* was superseded by *Golden Drum* and in 1996 by *Dharma Life*. Currently there is no Triratna Buddhist Community newsletter, but regular news from the Triratna Buddhist Community is posted on thebuddhistcentre.com website.
4. The first Order Convention, which took place the year this letter was written, 1974, was attended by some 27 Order members.
5. Four years after this letter, the first FWBO activities led by Lokamitra and other disciples of Sangharakshita began in India. The movement expanded very rapidly, with a strong emphasis on the need for social change, especially in eradicating what Dr Ambedkar, the great leader of the former 'untouchables' had called 'the hell of caste'. Social projects to help the poor, the sick, and the illiterate were set up. Dhamma centres were established, as well as, in the course of time, retreat centres and the Nagarjuna Training Institute near Nagpur. For a fuller account of the development of the movement in India, as well as its expansion into many other parts of the world including New Zealand and Australia, Europe, America, etc., see Vajragupta, *The Triratna Story*, Windhorse Publications, Cambridge 2010.

6. In fact it was Sangharakshita's old friends, the newly-converted Ambedkarite Buddhists (see Letter 9), who, because of the disadvantages they had suffered under caste, were on the whole not educated but who were only too happy to attend the talks offered by Lokamitra and his friends (see note 5 above). It was they who became the nucleus of the Triratna Order and Community in India. These days, people from diverse Indian backgrounds are becoming interested in the Triratna Buddhist Community.
7. Sangharakshita is referring to the Triyana Vardhana Vihara (see Letter 17, note 1), whose purchase Dinoo had helped make possible (see Letters 13 to 17) and which she had visited in 1958. When he moved to England, Sangharakshita arranged for refugee Tibetan monks to stay in the Vihara. As they did not look after it, he decided to sell, and gave the money (about 20,000 rupees), to Lokamitra to support his work in Poona.
8. This was the visit with Terry (see note 2 above).
9. For the strange story of the green Buddha, see Introduction, p. 460.
10. Ardeshir Mehta visited the UK, probably in 1965, when Sangharakshita took him to see the Tower of London (see *MAS*, p. 98).
11. i.e. the *FWBO Newsletter*, see note 3 above.
12. Mme Sophia Wadia (1901–1986) was the widow of B. P. Wadia (see Letter 15, note 4). She was editor of *The Aryan Path* and head of the United Lodge of Theosophy from her husband's death in 1958 until the end of her life.
13. Mme Wadia died in 1986.
14. Sangharakshita's mother lived in Rayleigh, Essex, thirty miles east of central London.
15. *The Essence of Zen*, published the previous year by Windhorse Publications, was based on talks given at the Hampstead Buddhist Vihara in 1965 (*Complete Works*, vol. 13).

Appendix
THE MONK AND THE PROPHET

Sangharakshita and Dr Mehta

Two photographs: this one is black-and-white, and appears on the cover of a book published in Bombay. It shows a man posing as a Greek statue: the discus thrower of ancient Greece, his body youthful perfection. The second, in colour, takes up quarter of a page of *The Times of India*, Pune, 5 June 2010. It shows the head and shoulders of a much older man with a long, white, flowing beard, dark eyes, a rather bulbous nose, and an intense, not to say determined, expression. His mouth is almost lost under the dark moustache but there lingers something more of gentleness. Beneath the pictures we find the same name: Dr Dinshah K. Mehta.

In the course of his life and work, Sangharakshita came into contact with people from many different backgrounds and walks of life, people of many different nationalities, and people who held a whole variety of ideologies and philosophies. Of these, perhaps none was so colourful as the Doctor. Dinoo introduced them towards the end of 1955, and the Doctor went on to become a good friend, giving Sangharakshita – among other things – invaluable help in his work with the Ambedkarite Buddhists of Maharashtra. In taking a closer look at the Doctor and his life, we see something more of the milieu in which Sangharakshita's work for the Dharma took place during his years in India. The friendship between the two men is of intrinsic interest for it tells us not only more about Sangharakshita but more about Buddhism and perhaps something about the nature of friendship itself. In looking at that we shall have to try and resolve one or two apparent paradoxes....

DR MEHTA'S LIFE: THE EARLY YEARS

Dinshah Kaikhushroo Mehta was born in 1903 to a Parsi family. It seems that even as a boy he was preoccupied by the idea of attaining perfection, and as a young man he pursued his ambition of achieving the perfection of the body. At seventeen he began giving performances in which he posed – virtually nude – as famous Greek statues, playing to packed houses in Bombay and Poona and raising a great deal of money for charity. His physical prowess exhibited itself in his pursuits as a *shikari* or hunter. In his early years he shot tigers, leopards, and other game. (He gave up hunting after his 'conversion' in 1953.)[174]

In the early 1920s, still pursuing the perfection of the body, he read widely in anatomy, physiology, and related subjects and investigated naturopathy, an alternative medical system involving fasting and other regimes. He started his own naturopathic practice and it seems he achieved some remarkable cures. In 1929 he opened the Nature Cure Clinic in Poona. He set up three other clinics, including two in Bombay, and became well known as a naturopathic physician, treating many prominent figures of the time. His Nature Cure Clinic was visited by the likes of Pandit Nehru and his young daughter, Indira. (Incidentally, the only formal qualification the Doctor had was a BA in commerce – something he liked to joke about with Sangharakshita.)

In 1932 he met Gandhi, the world-famous leader of the Indian Independence movement, and became his personal naturopathic physician, supervising two of his three long, politically-motivated, fasts. Between 1944 and 1946, Gandhi used the Nature Cure Clinic in Poona as a base, often staying there with his entourage.

Dr Mehta told Sangharakshita several anecdotes about his association with Gandhi. The Doctor often used to massage his 'beloved patient',[175] and while he did so they would talk quietly together. On one occasion they were talking about the political situation. This was before Independence. Gandhi put forward his ideas and Dr Mehta – who was a relatively young man then – blurted out, 'You just think too much of yourself!' There was silence. Gandhi didn't say anything. After a little while the conversation resumed.

On another occasion, some years later, they were discussing a leading member of the Congress party, Morarji Desai, acting Prime Minister for a short time after Independence. He was known as a bit of a puritan. 'He may be narrow but he's straight,' remarked Gandhi to Dr Mehta. There was a pause. Then Gandhi spoke again: 'No, he's just narrow!'[176]

As time went on, Dr Mehta, whose political views were broadly in sympathy with Gandhi's, became one of his emissaries. Gandhi once referred to him as the 'Lawrence of India'. Not long after Partition, in January 1948, Gandhi sent Dr Mehta to Pakistan to speak to Governor-General Jinnah. Not only Jinnah, but other ministers of the new Pakistani government had been patients of Dr Mehta, and he continued to enjoy good relations with them. Dr Mehta at first refused to go, uneasy about leaving Gandhi, but the latter insisted. In his absence, Gandhi was assassinated. Dr Mehta told Sangharakshita more than once that had he not gone to Pakistan, had he only been with Gandhiji, he was sure he would have seen what was about to happen and, with his quick responses, jumped in front of the Mahatma[177] and saved him. After Gandhi's death, the room where he had stayed in the smaller building at the Nature Cure Clinic (known as Bapu Cottage)[178] was kept as a memorial with Gandhi's walking stick, spinning wheel, and other artefacts on display.

SPIRITUAL STRUGGLE AND THE BIRTH OF A PROPHET

From the 1930s, Dr Mehta, who had turned from the Zoroastrian faith of his childhood to agnosticism, went through long years of spiritual struggle. At one point, taken to the brink of desperation, he fasted almost to death until he heard a voice telling him to break his fast. Eventually, in 1953, he asked for a sign. In November that year, a sign came. From then on, Dr Mehta followed the 'guidance' that came to him in states of what he called, 'spiritual *samādhi*' or meditation, believing this guidance came directly from God. He founded the Society of Servants of God, styling himself the 'servant of servants'. He more or less ceased to practise as a naturopath, concentrating instead on what Dinoo called 'saving souls'.

How did this guidance arrive? The Doctor would sit and enter a trance-like state and, with eyes closed, unconscious of what he wrote, swiftly fill page after page with what he termed 'Scripts': edicts that, as far as he was concerned, came directly from the Almighty. They were of various lengths, written both in prose and in verse, the latter reminding Sangharakshita of the shorter suras of the Koran. They could be 'hortatory or consolatory, practical or deeply metaphysical'. The guidance thus received came not only for Dr Mehta but also for his followers, friends, and family. Should they doubt the divine provenance – as indeed some did, even his wife Gulbehn – or were reluctant to follow the guidance, Dr Mehta saw therein the dire workings of the ego, which it was his mission to help people to overcome. His followers – such as they were – consisted mainly of his patients and former patients for whom it was not necessarily so easy to regard their erstwhile naturopathic physician as a kind of prophet. Some, such as Durgadas Birla (see Letter 9), believed at first but rapidly became disillusioned. Dinoo, too, was very soon expressing scepticism.

It is at this point in Dr Mehta's story that Sangharakshita made his entrance.

FIRST MEETINGS

Dr Mehta's flat in Bombay was located on the ground floor of Mayfair, a block of luxury apartments not far from the Hanging Gardens. Sangharakshita went there for the first time in November 1955, shortly after his first visit to Dinoo. Entering the main room of the flat, he saw, 'a grizzled-haired, grossly corpulent figure' who welcomed him 'cordially, if with a certain solemnity, a smile of satisfaction on his grey, flabby features.' Dr Mehta was at this time still in his early fifties but seemed, perhaps, older, and whatever the state of his mind, he was no longer the epitome of bodily perfection.

Almost immediately the two men fell into discussion – mostly about meditation – which lasted several hours. Other members of the Society were present, as was Dinoo, but our voluble friend was the only one who occasionally joined in the discussions. After lunch, Dr Mehta read to Sangharakshita from the Scripts. Later on, some thirty people squeezed into the room to listen to Sangharakshita deliver a lecture on 'Love and Devotion in Buddhism', a talk that was well received by members of the Society of Servants of God and which was afterwards followed by a general discussion.[179]

Sangharakshita must have made a favourable impression – on God at least – for he was invited to give another talk a couple of weeks later, this time speaking on 'The Buddha and the Spiritual Life in Buddhism'.

'I spoke for nearly two hours,' he records in his memoirs, 'and whether on account of the concentrated, meditative atmosphere of the meeting, or because I was upheld by the sustaining power of the Buddhas and bodhisattvas, I gave what I afterwards thought was one of the best talks I had ever given, and probably the profoundest.'[180]

It was in this way that the connection between Dr Mehta and Sangharakshita began.

Perhaps not surprisingly, when plans were made to open a new branch of the Society of Servants of God in Poona, divine guidance arrived that Sangharakshita should be invited to attend and to give a talk. After consulting Dinoo, who thought the Society would benefit from 'a good dose of Buddhism', Sangharakshita accepted the invitation. It is at this very point that our correspondence begins! (See Letter 1.) The event is postponed (presumably due to further guidance from the Divine, and rather to Sangharakshita's inconvenience, as we read in Letter 2). Nevertheless, he is able to attend the inauguration a few weeks later, towards the end of January 1957, making his first visit to a city that afterwards became an important venue for his speaking tours among the Ambedkarite Buddhists. Having attended the inauguration and given his talk (to a rather smaller audience than expected, and alongside another speaker, the politician Gulzarilal Nanda – twice interim prime minster of India), Sangharakshita is invited to stay and stay he does for several weeks, living what seems to be an almost idyllic existence, as he describes it to Dinoo in Letter 3.

A KIND OF FRIENDSHIP

Several things contributed to this idyll. First there was the place: in the background, Poona, a city he found to his liking. Then the Nature Cure Clinic itself, a very pleasant place to reside. There was the communal life, taking meals together, meditating together, discussing spiritual matters together. And there was the generally cheerful atmosphere that seemed to pervade the place – in the creation of which Sangharakshita's presence played, I suspect, no small part.

He spent many hours in discussion with Dr Mehta. If with other people the Doctor was rather conscious of his role as God's Servant and the vessel through which God communicated to the Society, with Sangharakshita, it seems, he felt free to discuss matters both religious and secular, both general and personal. Their discussions ranged over a wide field. As well as meditation (about which more later) and Nature Cure, they spoke about topics such as the ethics of hunting, Indian politics (the Doctor was well informed and well connected), and the Moral Rearmament movement (he had known its leader, Frank Buchman). Dr Mehta was a mine of information about Maharashtra, the local people, their manners and customs, and so on. For Sangharakshita, new to that part of India, this was to be of great benefit in his work with the new Buddhists, most of whom lived in Maharashtra. 'These Maharashtrians', Dr Mehta had said one day, 'they're stickers. If they take a liking to you, they never give up, they stick with you,' which is just what Sangharakshita found.

Naturally, Sangharakshita did not accept Dr Mehta's view of the divine provenance of the Scripts. (As a Buddhist, he did not believe in God.) He seems to have regarded his friend's views at first with some puzzlement and later with a kind of tolerant amusement. But how, we may wonder, did Dr Mehta respond when Sangharakshita made it quite clear he could not go along with the guidance, obedience to which was, after all, the central principle of his teaching, indeed, one might say central to his very identity? Dr Mehta told Sangharakshita that there were three kinds of guidance: one that came directly from God to someone who was in a state of *samādhi*; he was an example of that. Then there was the guidance that came through a person like him from God to other people. He also believed in something he called 'guidance through circumstances'. Sangharakshita responded with his own take on the matter. 'I used to tell him that *my* guidance came to me through the Buddha and I found that guidance in the Buddhist scriptures, so I didn't feel the need for any other guidance. He accepted that, though not completely happily because he believed that the guidance which came, through him, directly from God was much more reliable. But he respected the Buddha and he liked me to talk about Buddhism, and of course to give talks on Buddhism for his Society. So we remained good friends despite these differences of opinion.'

A quality of Sangharakshita that stands out to those who know him is his appreciation of his friends, and this we see in his memoirs. He writes of the Doctor that while he could be 'a trifle portentous', at the same time 'there was a simple, human side to his character, and that whatever reservations I might have about the nature of the guidance he received he was, in fact, undoubtedly a man of broad sympathies, deep understanding, and great personal integrity'.[181]

We may be surprised to read this estimation of the Doctor's character, so much in contrast to Dinoo's (see Introduction p. 467). How can we account for this apparent discrepancy? And what other evidence do we have of Dr Mehta's positive qualities as Sangharakshita describes them?

To answer the second question first, we can see his 'broad sympathies' reflected in the tenor of his religious philosophy, which was more universalist than anything else. On the shrine at his Bombay headquarters were figures of Zoroaster, Krishna, and Jesus. Later he added the Buddha. Though broad, his sympathies were not uncritical. The Hindu god Krishna may have had his place on the shrine but the Doctor was strongly opposed to the Hindu caste system, especially untouchability, and made a point of employing 'untouchable' servants. His philanthropy was also expressed in his practice as a naturopath and in his interest in nutrition. (He invented a nutritious meal that, at a mere 25 paise, even the poorest could afford. It was eaten at Parliament House for eight years, in the hope that it would eventually become popular with the people.)

As for his deep understanding, perhaps Sangharakshita is referring to the fact that the Doctor had read widely and thought about many topics, as was evident in their discussions.

And what of his integrity? Integrity is the adherence to moral principles, and the Doctor scrupulously held to those principles in which he believed, most of all, of course, in following the guidance which he believed came directly from God. But his integrity is also evident in his refusal to follow social conventions in which he did not believe or which he found immoral, such as the dowry system or untouchability. He refused to employ any kind of bribery or for bribery to be used in his name. He was, in fact, scrupulously honest in money matters. Sangharakshita seems to have respected his integrity even while seeing quite clearly the delusion that sometimes lay behind it.

In December 1956 Sangharakshita was staying with the Doctor in Bombay. The Doctor and his chief disciple, Sundri (of whom more below), pressed him to stay on in obedience to the dictate of a newly arrived Script, but Sangharakshita insisted that he had to go (in obedience to his own inner dictates). The Doctor's response was to suggest this was nothing other than an exhibition of ego-assertion, that root of all evil, and it was this that was preventing Sangharakshita from surrendering himself to the Divine. Sangharakshita writes, 'I did not blame Dr Mehta and Sundri for putting this construction on my failure to accept the guidance.... Believing as they did, it was hardly possible for them to put any other construction on it. Far from blaming them ... I recognized that their efforts to persuade me ... to *accept God's guidance*, were motivated by a genuine concern for my spiritual welfare and were the expression, therefore, of true, if misguided, friendship.'[182]

Here is a clue as to why Dinoo and Sangharakshita may have responded so differently to Dr Mehta. While Dinoo became outraged by his insistence on people following the guidance, Sangharakshita saw, at least in relation to himself, 'true, if misguided, friendship'. In Dinoo, Dr Mehta probably saw a (former) patient and erring disciple, whereas in Sangharakshita he had found a friend.

But what was the nature of the friendship between these two men? In trying to shed some light on their relationship, one is conscious that both were quite complex figures so that their relationship, too, seems to have had a number of different facets and aspects.

But what, we may wish to ask ourselves once more, really is friendship? It is a relationship between two people obviously, but what makes it *friendship*?

When two people meet there is a sense in which two distinct universes come into contact. For each person, another world becomes visible, at least to some extent. Whether those worlds will come nearer through unconscious forces of attraction or be repelled by the forces of antipathy, whether there will be simply an exchange of goods and services, or whether the more human sympathies will come into play, mutual regard and mutual helpfuless which are the first spring shoots of friendship depend on many things. As to whether another, higher factor will emerge that is neither attraction nor repulsion, nor barter and exchange, and higher even than human sympathy, something that is more like mutual resonance through a deeper and stronger awareness, only time can tell, and only time will tell how deep that mutuality is actually able to go.

We might say these two were both rather large planets and perhaps that in itself brought a certain attraction. There seems also to have been something of the natural attraction that can exist between those of very differing character and background. But whatever the initial response, both were clearly interested in pursuing the contact and both no doubt had their reasons for wanting to do so.

Dr Mehta found in Sangharakshita a man of exceptional intellectual abilities with whom he could discuss his ideas and many interests, which Sangharakshita, with his own wide range of interests, also found stimulating. The Doctor found he had a sympathetic listener (as many others also found) to whom he liked to relate memories of his early life and recall the people he had known; and he had someone with whom he could speak freely on more personal matters. He had also found a gifted speaker who was willing to give talks on Buddhism – talks that were well attended by Society standards – which might help promote the growth of the Society.

To understand Sangharakshita's interest in pursuing his connection with Dr Mehta, we have, I think, to see it ultimately in terms of the context of his whole life at that time, in terms of what it was he was really trying to do, and see that deepest aspiration under which virtually all his activities seem to have been subsumed. We have, in fact, to look beyond the personal to the non-personal, the greater context of his life, to that wind that was blowing through it – as it seems from some other dimension and which in India took on clear direction to 'work for the good of Buddhism'. From this point of view he must have seen in his contact with Dr Mehta and the Society a possibility of spreading the Buddha's Dharma. When Sangharakshita decides to accept the invitation to speak at the inauguration of the Poona branch of the Society of Servants of God, he does so only when Dinoo has persuaded him that 'the Society could do with a good dose of Buddhism', and because he had heard there were Buddhists in Poona and he hoped to make contact with them.

During his stay at the Nature Cure Clinic in early 1956 he reports to Dinoo that, 'Dr has been reading several extracts from Buddhist books, and repeatedly refers to the Buddha's life and teachings. He is even thinking of making a small Buddhist shrine here' (Letter 3). Perhaps the Society could become a conduit for the Dharma? As time goes by, however, it is clear that it will not. Characteristically, Sangharakshita does not seem to be disappointed. Seeing that, although a welcome venue for giving talks on Buddhism, the Society itself is not going to be a means for spreading the Dharma (the principles on which it was founded being inimical to Buddhism), he simply focuses his energy on other activities through which he hopes the Dharma can flourish, such as founding his own vihara in 1957. But although he withdraws his involvement from the Society as such, resigning from the joint editorship of its magazine, he does not withdraw his friendship from the Doctor and Sundri – an important distinction. And although there is a period of silence (on their side) following the resignation, in due course contact is resumed.

For the Doctor, whose disapproval of caste and especially untouchability we have already noted, was happy to support Sangharakshita's work with the new Buddhists (the 'ex-Untouchables'). He invited Sangharakshita to use both the Nature Cure Clinic in Poona and his flat in Bombay as a base during his teaching tours in Maharashtra. There was always plenty of room and Sangharakshita found the venues most convenient, for his involvement with the followers of Dr Ambedkar was not without its complications:

> 'Among the ex-Untouchables there were great divisions after Dr Ambedkar's death, both politically and from a Buddhist point of view. [There were groups] hostile to one another.... Many of them used to organize my lectures and programmes but they always tried to get me just for themselves.... So it suited me to stay with someone who wasn't one of them. I did this in Nagpur too.... I always stayed with an old Brahmin whom I knew who was a good friend. [I would tell people] he was my friend from before the mass conversion. I'm not going to leave him now! So it was very convenient not staying with the new Buddhists which would have meant staying with one particular group. And in that way I could move freely among them all. So my friendship with Dr Mehta was very helpful from that point of view as well.'[183]

If the friendship gave both men opportunities for stimulating discussion and for furthering their own activities, it was also characterized by warmth and affection. Clearly Sangharakshita was fond of his old friend and remained so, but was he affected by the Doctor's 'way of melting people', as Dinoo called it? Or 'attaching people to him'? I asked Sangharakshita. He replied that he had been aware the Doctor could have that kind of effect but had not really let it influence him. Perhaps we may conclude that Dr Mehta, with his undoubtedly powerful personality, emitted a kind of charisma to which Dinoo had been susceptible and against which she later rebelled. In Sangharakshita's case, the charisma, if such it was, had no discernible effect, leaving him free both to empathize with the Doctor and to perceive him with some clarity – an unusual combination, perhaps a rare one – as we noted in the Introduction – and requiring no doubt, among other things, a rather exceptional strength of character. He remarked recently that in the course of his travels he had met quite a few 'gurus' without being too much affected by them!

The Doctor seems to have respected the much younger man. When others disobeyed the Scripts he would exclaim, 'They must be *made* to obey!' With Sangharakshita he spoke in very different tones: 'Dr spoke with me in a very gentle and friendly manner.... I could not help feeling very fond of him,' he reports to Dinoo after the discussions in which he had made clear his own (Buddhist) position on 'guidance'(Letter 9).

Sangharakshita was thus able to sympathize and agree with Dinoo in certain of her criticisms of the Doctor, whilst at the same time conveying to her his own basic warmth and regard for him. As we noted in the Introduction in connection with the Kazini and Maharajkumar of Sikkim, Sangharakshita had the rare ability to remain friends over many years with parties that were at enmity or, as in the case of Dinoo and the Doctor, in uneasy relations with one another. Not to inflame hostilities but wherever possible to bring harmony between differing parties is a fundamental injunction of the Buddha to his disciples and perhaps one of the most difficult to achieve. It is only too easy in gaining the confidence of one party to lose the confidence of the other. But in the cases here cited, it seems Sangharakshita managed to maintain the trust of both.

And if his relationship with the Doctor could never become friendship in its highest form, it certainly was friendship of a kind. Writing many decades later he recalled, 'something like a friendship developed between Dr Mehta and me.'[184]

DR MEHTA, MEDITATION, AND A CRUCIAL DISTINCTION

But let us return to the first year of their acquaintance. After Sangharakshita's extended stay at the Nature Cure Clinic in the early months of 1956, the two men did not meet again until the end of the year. In the interim Sangharakshita is reflecting on what he has come to know of the Doctor. His replies to Dinoo suggest that her letters from that time (which have not survived) expressed her doubts and dissatisfaction with the Doctor and his approach.

'Regarding Dinshaw I too have been rather puzzled,' Sangharakshita writes back in September. 'I cannot claim that I have even now come to a final conclusion about his experiences and the work of the Society' – characteristically taking his time before he is willing to form a judgement. Then he continues, 'I admire Dinshaw very much and I am convinced that he has very high experience of samadhi.' (Letter 5)

Here we find ourselves with a question and a conundrum. The question is, in what sense did Sangharakshita admire the Doctor? I put this question to him and he replied that he admired his qualities, the human qualities we have already mentioned. And then the Doctor had a much greater experience of life than Sangharakshita, who was more than twenty years his junior. It was, in a sense, natural that, as the younger of the two, and given that he was, in any case, of a disposition to admire wherever he could, that he should have in this sense looked up to and admired the Doctor too.

In the Introduction we noted that a characteristic of Sangharakshita, in writing about the persons he met during the course of his life and work, was to see both virtue and folly and at times not to hold back from putting a few darker brush strokes on the canvas of the story of his life, often with a touch of humour. Where someone has become a personal friend, has rendered personal service, or taken him into their confidence, the duties of friendship seem to give rise to a greater unwillingness to dwell on the weaknesses of character. So while he was not blind to the Doctor's faults, he makes little of them in the memoirs, and in his correspondence with Dinoo reminds her of the positive – even whilst acknowledging the less than complimentary. Writing at the end of January 1957, for example, he refers to the magazine *Living Silence*: 'In one of the poems Dr is threatening and fulminating in his best style,' with that touch of humour.

But what about the suggestion that Dr Mehta had very high experience of *samādhi*? This might indicate someone of great spiritual maturity – rather in contradiction to what Dinoo had to say of some of his behaviour. Here we have something of a conundrum. Of course, any argument hangs on the interpretation of the word '*samādhi*'. In a Buddhist context, the word can be synonymous with the Sanskrit *dhyāna*, meaning a deeply absorbed meditative state characterized by equanimity, and, in its lower manifestations, by joy, rapture, and bliss. High levels of *dhyāna* experience suggests high levels of psychic integration – but what we know of Dr Mehta does not seem to accord with that (see discussion below).

Can we shed any more light on the matter by looking at the context in which Sangharakshita uses the word? 'I am convinced that he has very high experience of samadhi,' he writes, but then continues, 'but I am by no means convinced that he is Enlightened: some of the Scripts seem to prove the contrary.' He then says, 'One of the reasons for the confusion in Dinshaw's mind and in the minds of his followers is, I think, the fact that Hinduism, unlike Buddhism, does not distinguish between samadhi and prajna, or experience on high levels of meditation and actual Enlightenment.' And in an explanatory footnote he adds, 'Though Dinshaw was born a Parsi the mental climate in which he moves is Hindu and Christian.' (Letter 5)

I find this a remarkable analysis given Sangharakshita's isolation as a Buddhist at that time. There was no one to talk these matters over with – he could refer only to his own experience and to the Buddhist scriptures. We find here the expression of his unswerving adherence to the Buddha's teaching and the ability to maintain clarity in the midst of 'a thicket of views'. (That he continues to reflect on the correct Buddhist response to Dr Mehta's teaching is borne out when we read in *Precious Teachers* that he raises the matter with the eminent Tibetan lama, Chattrul Sangye Dorje on his very first meeting with him in March 1957.)[185]

In this letter to Dinoo, we find Sangharakshita making a statement that contemporary meditators and followers of the Buddha's teaching would do well to remember.

'According to the Buddha's Teaching one may gain Enlightenment with the help of a very moderate degree of samadhi providing one makes that samadhi the basis for the development of Insight (vipassana), while on the other hand one may get stuck in very high meditative experiences and fail – at least for one life – to gain Enlightenment at all.' (Letter 5)

Sangharakshita is pointing to what in Buddhism is a crucial distinction between two kinds of spiritual experience. One is the experience of absorption, the *dhyāna* experience already referred to (also known as *śamathā*). The other is insight into the true nature of phenomena, most especially the true nature of 'self' (also known as *vipassanā* or, especially in Mahāyāna Buddhism, as the arising of wisdom or *prajñā*). It is towards this experience that all Buddhist practice leads. The complete penetration into 'the way things really are' is what constitutes Enlightenment (with its concomitant outpouring of what is usually termed 'compassion'). Sangharakshita points to the Scripts as evidence that the Doctor's view of reality does not conform with the Enlightened point of view – 'some of the Scripts prove the contrary.' His touchstone is, of course, the Buddhist scriptures describing, or indicating as they do – as far as that is at all possible in words – something of the Enlightened state.

In his letter to Dinoo, he emphasizes the importance of this crucial distinction using the terms *samādhi* and *prajñā*.[186] Of such great import is this that perhaps, concentrating on not losing sight of the distinction, not losing sight of the paramount place of transcendental insight in the Buddhist life, Sangharakshita does not subject the content of the Doctor's meditative experience to further scrutiny, and, rather uncharacteristically, does not scrutinize the Doctor's own use of the term '*samādhi*', a term the Doctor uses to describe the experiences of trance in which he 'received' the Scripts.

Now, more than fifty years later, looking back and considering the matter, Sangharakshita comes to the conclusion that in fact, 'his *samādhi* had nothing to do with meditation as I understood the term. It was more like the trance of a medium.' He compares it with the trance-like states of Tibetan oracles who received messages without being conscious of what they delivered, as well as Western mediums like Alice Bailey (1880–1949), co-founder of the Lucis Trust, who produced many 'channelled' teachings of this kind. Dr Mehta, too, recorded the guidance without being aware of what he was writing.

All this, though, only crystallized later. At the time, although it was clear that the Doctor's experiences had nothing in common with Sangharakshita's experiences in meditation, at the same time, the Doctor's interest in the subject and his dedication to entering what he called states of *samādhi* spurred on the younger man in his own exploration of this central Buddhist practice, and in fact his discussions with Dr Mehta in early 1956 bring about a significant deepening of his own meditation experience. He began keeping a meditation journal from which he quotes in his memoirs. Since people are often curious about the nature of Sangharakshita's experience in this field, I thought it worth quoting a paragraph in full:

> I made a special effort to deepen my meditation. Though I had been meditating for a number of years, my achievements in this field were far from commensurate with my aspirations. There were experiences of the bliss and peace of the lower *dhyānas*; there were visions, usually of the Buddha or Avalokiteśvara; there were flashes of insight, not always in connection with the meditation itself: and that was about all. What I now had to do, I felt, was to achieve a level of meditative experience which would enable me to receive whatever might be the Buddhist equivalent of Dr Mehta's 'guidance', for much as I rejected the possibility of guidance by God (a being in whose existence I did not believe) I was well aware that for real spiritual progress to take place the ego, or 'defiled mind-consciousness' (as the Yogācāra termed it) needed to open itself to the influence of what I was later to call 'the transcendental outpourings of the Absolute'.[187]

For an account of his progress, I refer the interested reader to the relevant chapter in his memoirs.[188]

THE MIND OF A PROPHET

Some of Dinoo's tales of the Doctor leave one with the distinct impression of someone suffering from gross delusions that in the West might easily come under the diagnosis of mental illness. Was the Doctor mad? I sometimes found myself wondering. I asked Sangharakshita how he saw it. In Dr Mehta one found, he said, 'a combination of madness and sanity in a very strange sort of way. He certainly had some delusions. For instance, sometimes I read in the newspapers that the government had taken such and such a decision. And ... he would say, "Yes, I know. My mind was in meditation on the members of the government and that is why they took that decision." He believed in that sort of thing.'

In one of her letters, Dinoo goes so far as to describe the Doctor as a 'megalomaniac'. What did Sangharakshita make of that?

'Well,' came the response, 'there are lots of megalomaniacs of that kind in India. Hindu teachers who believe that they're God-realized, that God is speaking through them. In Poona itself there was Meher Baba. I met one of his followers. A book of Meher Baba's teachings, which I read, was entitled *God Speaks*. Meher Baba had quite a following at that time.' And of course these kinds of claims are not unknown in the West. Only recently a book was published by someone claiming to be an *arhant*, that is, fully Enlightened. What is the Buddhist response to such claims? 'Well, use your common sense. And consult the Buddhist scriptures.'

Returning to Dr Mehta and his 'madness', I could not help recalling the Buddha's view of humanity: to the extent we are not Enlightened, we are all more or less deluded. Dr Mehta's delusions were perhaps just more visible, a little more extreme. Clearly, they were only part of the man. Indeed, a strange combination of sanity and madness.

One quirk of Dr Mehta was his concern with keys. He emphasized that it was important that one should always have one's mind on one's keys and always remember to lock up. He called it 'key-consciousness'. Another preoccupation was with possible likenesses between himself and the founders of great religions. In the photograph published in *The Times of India*, he looked, I thought, rather like an Old Testament prophet. Muriel Payne, another friend of that time, privately referred to the Doctor as 'Jehovah'! Sangharakshita commented to me with a twinkle in his eye that Dr Mehta probably thought he looked like Zoroaster. But it was not just likenesses with the founder of Zoroastrianism that concerned him. On one occasion he had said to Sangharakshita, 'You know, I've been thinking about early Christianity and about Jesus and do you know, according to the latest research he was quite short, like me.'

In one of her letters, Dinoo mentions she has heard that 'Dr now wears his hair in the style of Lord Buddha' (i.e. a bun on the top of his head). On this occasion, Sangharakshita replies quite forcefully, with reference to the Buddha's admonition to 'Fools who imitate me and die the death.' (Letter 18)

Nor was this the only way in which Dr Mehta likened himself to the Buddha. As Sangharakshita recounted to me,

> One day I was there with him, sitting in his sitting-room-cum-shrine and he said, 'I've been thinking. Yashodhara [the wife of Siddhartha Gautama, who was to become the Buddha] must have given the

Buddha a lot of trouble.' I knew what he was getting at, so I said, 'No. She became his disciple and gained Enlightenment.' So he said, 'No, she must have given him a lot of trouble!' He was thinking, of course, of his own wife.

DR MEHTA'S WIFE, GULBEHN

Dr Mehta did not marry in the ordinary Indian way, taking a wife with a dowry and holding a large wedding ceremony. He did not believe in marriage. He had tried to persuade Gulbehn to live with him as his partner. Understandably – given the Indian social milieu – she refused. So they came to a compromise. Dr Mehta agreed to marry her on the condition that the wedding cost no more than one rupee. This was his protest against the dowry system. She agreed, and in 1936 they were married. After the ceremony Dr Mehta bought one rupee's worth of sweets and distributed them.

By the time Sangharakshita met her, on his first visit to the Nature Cure Clinic in Poona, they had been married some twenty years and had two children, then about ten and eight years old. A difficulty had cropped up after her husband's 'conversion', for he had expected his wife, as well as others, to follow the guidance. Gulbehn, however, did not believe the guidance emanated from the Divine. To exert some helpful pressure on her, Dr Mehta decided he would not live with her until she had come round to the Divine's point of view. Thus she lived with the children in Bapu Cottage. When the Doctor – who was based in Bombay – visited, he stayed in the larger building.

Gulbehn was a follower of Vinoba Bhave, generally regarded as Mahatma Gandhi's chief disciple. (Vinoba Bhave was responsible for the Budhan movement through which landlords were persuaded to give part of their land to landless labourers.) As a staunch Gandhian, she wore *khadi*, handwoven cloth. When the first child came along, it was Gandhi who named him, Ardeshir. Her daughter, however, was named by Gulbehn after her mother: Shireen.

Sangharakshita was no less fond of Gulbehn than of her husband. 'She was a very good woman,' he recalled, 'a practical sort of woman. I became very good friends with her.' She would look after him during his stays at the Nature Cure Clinic and sometimes confided in him, including her distress that the Doctor refused to live with her and her disbelief in the guidance coming from God. Indeed, she thought he sometimes used it just to get his own way! No doubt it was a relief to Gulbehn to find that Sangharakshita believed in it no more than she did.

Dr Mehta's belief was, of course, unshakeable – or almost so. Every now and then he, too, confided in Sangharakshita that he had doubts in himself. But at such times, help was at hand. There was someone who never had any doubts, and should the Doctor express such, her unswerving faith in him would bolster his wavering belief. That person was his chief disciple, Sundri Vaswani.

THE CHIEF DISCIPLE: SUNDRI VASWANI

Sundri came from a Sindi Brahmin family, a number of whose members were quite famous. Sadhu Vaswani (1879–1966) was both an educationalist and widely revered as a 'holy man'. After Partition, when many Sindi Hindus left their homeland – now in Pakistan – to live in Poona, it was Sadhu Vaswani to whom they looked as leader. (There is, in fact, a statue of him in Poona.) There he founded the St Meera High School for Girls where Sangharakshita met him on being invited to give a talk at the school. By then he was an old man of about eighty. 'A bit like the conventional Indian idea of a saint, very, very kind, very gentle, very devoted,' Sangharakshita recalls, 'Dr Mehta was not quite so enthusiastic: "Yes, he's a good soul. He's a good soul," he would say if Sadhu Vaswani's name was mentioned. But of course,' Sangharakshita added, 'he wasn't in direct communication with God!'

Sundri's elder brother, Jashan P. Vaswani (b.1918) cut short a promising career as an academic to follow his uncle and in time took over leadership of the Poona mission that Sadhu Vaswani had founded. He, too, came to be regarded as a 'holy man'.

Hira, another of Sundri's brothers, was the black sheep of this Holy Family. For a short time he was part of the Society's 'inner circle' (see Letter 3 above), but he got into serious financial trouble and disappeared quite early on.

Of Sundri's own life prior to her involvement with Dr Mehta and the Society of Servants of God I have been unable to find an account. Apart from her family connections, we know only that she had a degree in statistics from the London School of Economics. She was clearly an intelligent and capable woman. Her fulfilment in life, however, came from dedicating herself to another's aims. This is not to say she was not remarkable in her own right, only that those whose life's work is devotion to another's cause do not often become the subject of a biography, nor do they necessarily have an entry in *Wikipedia*! Suvajra,[189] who met her much later on, in the mid-1980s, describes his first impressions:

> 'She was a very, very striking woman, past her middle age, but with very elegant bearing, very beautiful features. But it was her emotional character that struck you when you met her. She radiated something. She worked with a bunch of men and they were obviously absolutely devoted to her. There wasn't the kowtowing subservience you usually get from clerks and underlings to their boss. It was definitely something more like devotion.'

If Sundri could inspire devotion in others, at least in her later years, she expressed it unstintingly in her work for Dr Mehta. She attended to all the practical work of the Society, running the – highly successful – quality control business which was the Society's main source of income. (She gave all the considerable profits to the Society.) Later she oversaw the publication of Dr Mehta's *Fundamental Laws of Health* (1988) on whose cover (rather intriguingly) we find the photograph of the youthful body builder. She also edited Dr Mehta's *The Beloved Patient* (1992), which records his encounters with Gandhi, and was published only after her death.

In his memoirs, Sangharakshita describes Sundri on his first encounter with her simply as a 'youngish woman in a white sari'. But if in his memoirs he does not go into further detail, he later recalled his relationship with her by saying, 'She became almost like a sister.' (They were of a similar age.) 'We knew each other very well.' As for Sundri, years later when Suvajra met her, he noticed how she spoke of Sangharakshita – not as she spoke about Dr Mehta, who, after all, she saw as a great guru – but 'it seems she had a very high regard for [Sangharakshita]. Not just as a person but as a monk, as a spiritual teacher.'

Sundri was very much younger than the Doctor. We know from Dinoo that she was 34 at the end of 1956. Was she in love with Dr Mehta? Probably. Certainly Dinoo believed so. Did she ever marry? Sangharakshita: 'While I was once staying at Mayfair with them, at that time a young man who was her next-in-command, as it were, on the business front proposed to her and Dr Mehta urged her to accept and said it wouldn't make any difference to her spiritual development or her relationship with him. But she absolutely refused.' Both Dr Mehta and Sundri were very open on such matters with their English friend. 'I knew them both very well, they were both very frank about things.'

And what of relations between the two women, Dr Mehta's wife, with whom he would not stay so long as she refused to accept the guidance, and Sundri, his chief disciple, whom he had with him both in Bombay and Poona, and who never failed to believe in him? Although Gulbehn was upset when Dr Mehta stayed in the main Nature Cure building along with others such as Sangharakshita, and Sundri stayed there too, there was never any outright hostility between the two women. Probably they managed to operate mainly in different spheres. Dinoo, as we know, heartily took the side of Gulbehn and was not given to speaking kindly of Sundri. Sangharakshita, on the other hand, managed to remain the friend and confidant of all parties.

THE LAST YEARS

In the same year that the last of our letters was written, 1974, Gulbehn was diagnosed with cancer. Within seven months, she had died. Dr Mehta became particularly interested in the cure of this disease and tutored two German research students, Christian and Hella Bartsch, who went on to set up a research project in Tübingen, Germany.

Dr Mehta and Sundri moved to Delhi where they continued the Society's activities. Sundri died before the Doctor, probably in the late 1980s. The Doctor suffered a stroke and when Suvajra met him in the 1990s shortly before he died, he found the old man hardly able to speak and needing help even to take his food. His spirit, however, was very much alive and with some zest he recounted a tale. He recounted it with evident pride and satisfaction. His carer (who could understand his indistinct speech) explained it to Suvajra. It was the story of how he had wanted to make a donation of his Poona clinic to the Indian government but there were legal impediments. So he had sold it to them. Yes, he had sold it to them – for *just one rupee*!

Dr Mehta died in 1993. Branches of the Society he founded still exist in the USA, Canada, and Delhi as well as the research project in Germany.

Sangharakshita did not forget his friend when he returned to England in 1964. He visited him with Terry Delamare on his farewell trip to India in 1966; and in 1979, passing through India on his way to New Zealand, he visited the Bombay flat, meeting the old circle of the Society as well as Sundri. The Doctor did not come down from Delhi but the two men spoke on the phone. It was during one of his later visits that he visited the Doctor in Delhi, and he recalled him with warmth, humour, and appreciation when he came to write his memoirs, evoking something of his colourful life and character and recalling the particular benefits contact with him had conferred, especially in his work spreading the Dharma among Dr Ambedkar's followers.

NOTES

FACING MOUNT KANCHENJUNGA

1 See *The Rainbow Road from Tooting Broadway to Kalimpong* in *Complete Works*, vol. 20, chapter 47.
2 'Poetry is the record of the best and happiest moments of the happiest and best minds.' P. B. Shelley, *A Defence of Poetry* (1821).
3 See *Complete Poems 1941–1994*, Windhorse Publications, Birmingham 1995, p. 98 and p. 106 (*Complete Works*, vol. 25).
4 The temple-bells they say: Come you back, you British soldier; come you back to Mandalay!'

    R. Kipling, 'Mandalay' (1890).
5 *Stepping Stones*, vol 1, no. 1, July 1950, pp. 18–19.
6 See Sangharakshita's poem 'Rain', written at this time, which begins:

    How sweet it is, how sweet again
    To hear and see and smell the rain!

    Complete Poems 1941–1994, Windhorse Publications, Birmingham 1995, p. 43 (*Complete Works*, vol. 25).
7 The Buddha's teachings on how the *bhikkhus* should conduct themselves during the rains retreat is found at Vinaya Piṭaka, *Mahāvagga* 3 (i.137–56). See I. B. Horner (trans.), *The Book of the Discipline*, vol. 4, Pali Text Society, Oxford 1996, pp. 183–207.
8 *Macbeth*, Act V, Scene v, lines 27–8.

9   From 'An Old Saw Resharpened', first published as an editorial in *Stepping-Stones*, vol. 2 no. 10, February 1952, pp. 268–9. See also *Crossing the Stream*, second edition, Windhorse Publications, Birmingham 1996, pp. 101–2 (*Complete Works* vol. 7).

10 These great statues were blown up by the Taliban in 2001. See Sangharakshita's reflections 'The Big and the Great: Vandalism and Iconoclasm' in *A Moseley Miscellany*, Ledbury 2015, p. 101 (*Complete Works* vol. 26).

11 G. Roerich, *The Blue Annals*, Motilal Banarsidass, Delhi 1949 is a translation of a work whose full title is *The Blue Annals, the Stages of the Appearance of the Doctrine and Practices in the Land of Tibet* by the fifteenth-century Tibetan translator and scholar, 'Gos lo-tsā-ba gŽon-nu-dpal.

12 Founded in 1817 as *Blackwood's Edinburgh Magazine*, in its heyday it published the work of some of the greatest writers and poets of the nineteenth century. From 1905 the magazine was published in London as *Blackwood's Magazine* with a readership throughout the British Empire. It ceased publication in 1980.

13 Lama Kazi Dawa-Samdup (trans.), *Tibet's Great Yogī Milarepa*, ed. W. Y. Evans-Wentz, Oxford University Press, London 1928; and Lama Kazi Dawa-Samdup (trans.), *Tibetan Yoga and Secret Doctrines*, ed. W. Y. Evans-Wentz, Oxford University Press, London 1935.

14 'Mountains', in *Complete Poems 1944–1994*, Windhorse Publications, Birmingham 1995, p. 100. 'Messengers from Tibet', ibid., p.101, was first published in *Stepping Stones*, vol. 1, no. 1, July 1950, p. 3 (*Complete Works* vol. 25).

15   Alas! regardless of their doom,
     The little victims play;
     No sense have they of ills to come,
     Nor care beyond to-day.

   From Thomas Gray, 'Ode on a Distant Prospect of Eton College' (1745), lines 51–4.

16 IA stands for 'Intermediate Arts'. These were the final school examinations.

17 P. B. Shelley, 'The Cloud' (1820) has six stanzas, each between twelve and eighteen lines. The final stanza ends:

     I silently laugh at my own cenotaph,
     And out of the caverns of rain,
     Like a child from the womb, like a ghost from the tomb,
     I arise and unbuild it again.

18 'News and Notes', *Stepping-Stones*, vol. 1, no. 4, October 1950, p. 90. A talk given in 1966 soon after Sangharakshita's return to

the UK is entitled 'Evolution: Lower and Higher'. It was followed by two series on this theme, one in 1969 on 'The Higher Evolution of Man' and another, the following year, called 'Aspects of the Higher Evolution of the Individual'. Edited transcripts of these lectures appear in *Complete Works* vol. 12.

19 From Alexander Pope's long poem, 'An Essay on Man' (1734), Epistle iv, line 390:

> Come then, my friend, my genius, come along;
> Oh master of the poet and the song!...
> Shall then this verse to future age pretend
> Thou wert my guide, philosopher, and friend?'

20 Lama Anagarika Govinda, 'Look Deeper!', *Stepping-Stones*, vol. 1, no. 4, October 1950, pp. 78–9.

21 Lama Govinda, 'The Universal Perspective of the Bodhisattva Ideal' in *Stepping-Stones*, vol. 1, no. 5, November 1950, pp. 98–9.

22 'Unity', *Stepping Stones*, vol. 1, no. 2, August 1950, pp. 21–3. 'The Voice Within', *Stepping-Stones*, vol. 1, no. 3, September 1950, pp. 45–8. 'Everything That Lives is Holy', *Stepping-Stones*, vol. 1, no. 4, October 1950, pp. 69–72. 'The Problem of Desire', *Stepping-Stones*, vol. 1, no. 5, November 1950, pp. 93–6. 'The Awakening of the Heart', *Stepping-Stones*, vol. 1, no. 6, December 1950, pp. 117–19. The collected editorials from *Stepping-Stones* are included in *Crossing the Stream*, Windhorse Publications, Birmingham 1996 (*Complete Works*, vol. 7).

23 'Village India' in Sangharakshita, *Complete Poems 1944–1994*, Windhorse Publications, Birmingham 1995, p. 96. (*Complete Works*, vol. 25.)

24 'The Bodhisattva', ibid., p. 107.

25 B. R. Ambedkar, 'The Buddha and the Future of His Religion', first published in the *Maha Bodhi*, April-May 1950. See Dr Babasaheb Ambedkar, *Writings and Speeches*, vol. xvii (part 2), Education Department, Government of Maharashtra, Bombay 2003, p.105; also available at www.mea.gov.in/images/attach/amb/volume_17_02.pdf (April 2017).

26 'News and Notes' in *Stepping-Stones*, vol. 1, no. 5, November 1950, p. 116.

27 See Sangharakshita, *The Rainbow Road from Tooting Broadway to Kalimpong* in *Complete Works*, vol. 20, pp. 133–4.

28 R. Tagore, *Stray Birds*, Macmillan Company, New York 1916, verse 1 (translated from Bengali into English by Tagore).

29 'The Veil of Stars' was written between 1950 and 1953. The 'Introduction' by Lama

Govinda is dated 1954. A few copies of the poem were made while the author was in India. Later it was included in *The Enchanted Heart: Poems 1946–1976*, Ola Leaves, Norwich 1980; and then in Sangharakshita, *Complete Poems 1941–1994*, Windhorse Publications, Birmingham 1995, pp. 417–36 (*Complete Works, vol. 25*).

30 Kanchenjunga was first climbed on 25 May 1955 by Joe Brown and George Band, who were part of a British expedition. They stopped short of the summit in accordance with a promise given to the Chogyal (king of Sikkim) that the top of the mountain would remain inviolate. This has become a tradition with subsequent climbers.

31 At *Visuddhimagga* 102–7, Buddhaghosa describes the habits of those with angry, greedy, and deluded temperaments (and their corollaries – the faithful, intelligent, and speculative temperaments). Temperament can be recognized, he says, by someone's posture, way of eating, and so on. See Ñāṇamoli (trans.), *The Path of Purification*, Buddhist Publication Society, Kandy 1975, pp. 102–9.

32 ICS is the Indian Civil Service.

33 John Dryden, Epistle X 'To My Dear Friend Mr Congreve, On His Comedy Called "The Double-Dealer"', (1693), line 19.

34 H. Günther, *Das Seelenproblem im älteren Buddhismus*. Heinrich Hackmann, Konstanz 1949.

35 Teitaro Suzuki's translation, published in Chicago in 1900, and T. Richards' translation, published in Shanghai in 1907, attribute *The Awakening of Faith in the Mahayana* to the Indian Buddhist poet Aśvaghoṣa, the Chinese version being considered by Richards to be a translation by Paramārtha. Later scholars came to think the work was at least partly of Chinese origin.

36 'I will bestow ... a Dhāraṇī for the sake of preventing the loss of its memory': R. Emmerick (trans), *The Sutra of Golden Light*, Pali Text Society, London 1979, p. 44.

37 'The Awakening of the Heart' in *Stepping-Stones*, vol. 1, no. 6, December 1950, and *Crossing the Stream*, Windhorse Publications, Birmingham 1996, p. 87. 'Rights and Duties' in *Stepping-Stones*, vol. 1, no. 7, January 1951, pp. 141–5, and *Crossing the Stream*, ibid., pp. 35–40 (*Complete Works vol. 7*).

38 See Sangharakshita, *In the Sign of the Golden Wheel*, Windhorse Publications, Birmingham 1996, pp. 4–5 (*Complete Works vol. 22*).

39 Sangharakshita met Arnold Price at the Buddhist Society in London in 1944, see *The Rainbow Road from Tooting Broadway to Kalimpong* in *Complete Works*, vol. 20, p. 101. The letter recommending to Sangharakshita that he should read *Peaks and Lamas* is mentioned on pp. 150–1.
40 'L'Albatros' in C. Baudelaire, *Fleurs du Mal*, second edition, 1861. Baudelaire compares the ungainly albatross caught by mocking sailors on the deck of a ship with the albatross who flies majestic with great wings through the heavens. The final verse begins, 'The poet resembles this prince of cloud and sky'.
41 Sangharakshita's wanderings with Satyapriya are recorded in his previous volume of memoirs, *The Rainbow Road from Tooting Broadway to Kalimpong* in *Complete Works*, vol. 20, chapters 24–45.
42 Ibid., p. 453.
43 Ibid., pp. 458–9.
44 Marco Pallis, *Peaks and Lamas*, third edition, Woburn Press, London 1974, p. 303.
45 Thubden Tendzin, 'Sikkim Buddhism Today and Tomorrow' in *Stepping-Stones*, vol. 1, no. 10, April 1951, pp. 219–235.
46 Ibid, p. 233.
47 A traditional Tibetan reed instrument, similar to a shawm.
48 The *pie* was worth one-third of a *paisa*, and a *paisa* was one-hundredth of a rupee. The *pie*'s value dwindled to almost nothing and it had in fact been withdrawn from circulation in 1947.
49 See the section on Clare in *Dear Dinoo* above, p. 479–82.
50 The first issue of *Stepping-Stones* with a Nepali section was vol. 2, no. 2, which appeared in June 1951.
51 Lama Anagarika Govinda, 'Buddhism as Living Experience' in *Stepping-Stones*, vol. 2, no. 3, July 1951, p. 76.
52 'The Parable of the Raft' in *Stepping-Stones*, vol. 2, no. 3, July 1951, pp. 69–71, and *Crossing the Stream*, Windhorse Publications, Birmingham 1996, pp. 83–6 (*Complete Works*, vol. 7).
53 'The Good Friend' in *Stepping-Stones*, vol. 2, no. 5, September 1951, pp. 125–8, and *Crossing the Stream*, Windhorse Publications, Birmingham 1996, pp. 57–62 (*Complete Works*, vol. 7).
54 *Rhythmische Aphorismen*, Dresden 1926, and *Gedanken und Gesichte*, Dresden 1927. The titles translate as something like 'Rhythmic Aphorisms' and 'Thoughts and Visions'.
55 Presumably from Lama Anagarika Govinda, *Art and Meditation*, Allahabad Block Works, Allahabad 1936. What appears to be a revised version of this essay is included

under the title 'Parallelism Between Art and Meditation' in Lama Anagarika Govinda, *Creative Meditation and Multi-Dimensional Consciousness*, Unwin, London 1977, pp. 151–6.

56 Lama Anagarika Govinda, *The Way of the White Clouds*, Rider, London 1966. It was also published in German in the author's own translation, as *Der Weg der weissen Wolken*, Rascher Verlag, Zürich 1969.

57 This was Anne Habermann (1868–1950), photographer, author, and painter, whom Lama Govinda (or Ernst Hoffman as he then was) first met on the island of Capri. See K. Winkler, *A Thousand Journeys*, Element Books, Shaftesbury 1990, p. 7.

58 The story of Govinda's meeting with Tomo Geshe is told in Lama Anagarika Govinda, *The Way of the White Clouds*, Rider, London 2006, chapter 8.

59 See *The Rainbow Road from Tooting Broadway to Kalimpong* in *Complete Works* vol. 20, p. 134; and 'A Visit to a Tibetan Monastery' in Sangharakshita, *Early Writings 1944–1954*, Ibis Publications, Ledbury 2014, pp. 87–9 (*Complete Works*, vol. 7).

60 See Sangharakshita, *Through Buddhist Eyes*, Windhorse Publications, Birmingham 2000, p. 278 (*Complete Works* vol. 24).

61 'With the Newars in Nepal' in Sangharakshita, *The Rainbow Road from Tooting Broadway to Kalimpong* in *Complete Works*, vol. 20, chapter 47.

62 See 'Direct Action Day' in ibid., chapter 17.

63 'His head was bald and shone like any glass', from Geoffrey Chaucer, *The Canterbury Tales: The Prologue*, line 198. The *Tales* were composed between c.1387 and c.1400.

64 See *The Rainbow Road from Tooting Broadway to Kalimpong* in *Complete Works*, vol. 20, pp. 464–6.

65 This was when Sangharakshita was working for the Ramakrishna Mission in Calcutta, see ibid., chapter 16.

66 More than sixty years later this image of Vishnu appears in a poem composed in May 2015 called 'Vishnu's Dream'. See *Complete Works*, vol. 25.

67 See *Anagarika Dharmapala and Other 'Maha Bodhi' Writings*, Ibis Publications, Ledbury 2014 (*Complete Works*, vol. 8).

68 See *The Rainbow Road from Tooting Broadway to Kalimpong* in *Complete Works*, vol. 20, p. 462.

69 From the vows of Samantabhadra in *The Flower Ornament Scripture (Avataṃsaka Sūtra)*, see T. Cleary (trans.), *Entry into the Realm of Reality (Gaṇḍavyūha Sūtra)*, vol. 3, Shambhala, Boston 1987, p. 388: 'In a single atom, Buddhas as many as atoms / Sit.'…

70 'Glimpses of Buddhist Nepal' in *Stepping-Stones*, vol. 2, no. 9, January 1952, pp. 249–50, and *Crossing the Stream*, Windhorse Publications, Birmingham 1996, pp. 120–1 (*Complete Works*, vol. 7).

71 The *Rubáiyát* of Omar Khayyám, (1048–1131), translated into English by E. Fitzgerald, appeared in various editions from 1859. Quoted here are verses 72–4.

72 'Glimpses of Buddhist Nepal' in *Stepping-Stones*, vol. 2, no. 10, February 1952, p. 279, and *Crossing the Stream*, Windhorse Publications, Birmingham 1996, pp. 127–8 (*Complete Works*, vol. 7).

73 Although there is no further record of this lecture that we know of, a lecture on the same theme was given many years later, in May 1982, at Siddharth College, Bombay. See 'Lecture Tour in India 1981–2' in *Complete Works*, vol. 9, pp. 435–48.

74 See *The Rainbow Road from Tooting Broadway to Kalimpong* in *Complete Works*, vol. 20, p. 114.

75 Matthew 6:28: 'Consider the lilies of the field, how they grow; they toil not, neither do they spin.'

76 'Glimpses of Buddhist Nepal' in *Stepping-Stones*, vol. 2, no. 10, February 1952, p. 282, and *Crossing the Stream*, Windhorse Publications, Birmingham 1996, p. 132 (*Complete Works*, vol. 7).

77 '"Pauses" and "Empty spaces"' in *Stepping-Stones*, vol. 2, no. 8, December 1951, p. 209. (*Complete Works*, vol. 7.)

78 'An Appeal' in *Stepping-Stones*, vol. 2, no. 9, January 1952, p. 238.

79 Ibid.

80 'Glimpses of Buddhist Nepal' appeared in two instalments in *Stepping-Stones*, vol. 2, nos. 9 and 10, January and February 1952. See also *Crossing the Stream*, Windhorse Publications, Birmingham 1996 (*Complete Works*, vol. 7).

81 The footnote in *Stepping-Stones* attributes these words to an article by Kheminda Thera, 'Bodhisatta or Arahant', which appeared in *The Buddhist*, Wesak 1947.

82 Lama Govinda, 'Origins of the Bodhisattva Ideal' in *Stepping-Stones*, vol. 2, no. 9, January 1952, p. 238.

83 'An Old Saw Resharpened' in *Stepping-Stones*, vol. 2, no. 10, February 1952, pp. 265–270, and *Crossing the Stream*, Windhorse Publications, Birmingham 1996, pp. 97–104 (*Complete Works*, vol. 7).

84 The SDO, or Subdivisional Officer (the subdivision being Kalimpong, which belonged to the Darjeeling district) is noted as Dr A. K. Bhattacharya, M.A., P.R.S., S.D.O. The ping-pong tournament involved more than thirty competitors. See 'News and Notes', *Stepping-Stones*, vol. 2, no. 10, February 1952, p. 285.

85 'Selected Sayings from "The Perfection of Wisdom", chosen, arranged and translated by Dr Edward Conze', *Stepping-Stones*, vol. 2, no. 10, February 1952, pp. 271–6. This is reproduced, with some revisions to dates of composition, and referring not to twenty-five but to forty *Prajñāpāramitā Sūtras*, in the Foreword to E. Conze (trans.), *Selected Sayings from the Perfection of Wisdom*, second edition, The Buddhist Society, London 1968, p. 25.

86 In his Preface to *Selected Sayings from the Perfection of Wisdom*, (p. 9) Dr Conze writes, 'In 1952, in the last issue of *Stepping-Stones*, the Bhikshu Sangharakshita of Kalimpong began to print this collection of sayings.... Funds soon gave out and only the first instalment appeared.'

87 *The Aryan Path* was a theosophical journal founded in 1930 with B. P. Wadia as its first editor.

88 'Epitaph on Krishna, Princess Irene's Squirrel' in *Complete Poems 1941–1994*, Windhorse Publications, Birmingham 1995, p. 175. The four line epitaph begins, 'Now he's gone, the best of squirrels…' (*Complete Works*, vol. 25).

89 See 'Buffaloes Being Driven to Market' in *Complete Poems 1941–1994*, Windhorse Publications, Birmingham 1995, pp. 139–40 (*Complete Works*, vol. 25).

90 See 'Up and Down the Gravel Path…' in *Complete Poems 1941–1994*, Windhorse Publications, Birmingham 1995, p. 143 (*Complete Works*, vol. 25).

91 CID: Crime Investigation Department.

92 Sangharakshita writes about his friendship with Clare in *The Rainbow Road from Tooting Broadway to Kalimpong* in *Complete Works*, vol. 20, pp. 100 and 103. See also the section on Clare Cameron in *Dear Dinoo: Letters to a Friend* above, p. 479–82.

93 See *Moving Against the Stream*, Windhorse Publications, Birmingham 2003, pp. 42–3 (*Complete Works*, vol. 23).

94 See *The History of My Going for Refuge*, Windhorse Publications, Glasgow 1988 (*Complete Works*, vol. 2).

95 This was Sangharakshita's understanding at that time of what it meant to be a Buddhist monk and 'give up the world'.

96 Francis Bacon (1561–1626). Opening lines from Bacon's essay 'Of Nature in Men' in *Essayes or Counsels, Civill and Morall* (1625).

97 American-born Eli Stanley Jones (1884–1973) was a Methodist missionary who preached all over India in the early decades of the twentieth century. His book *The Christ of the Indian Road* (1925) was widely read.

98 See *The Rainbow Road from Tooting Broadway to Kalimpong* in *Complete Works*, vol. 20, pp. 284–5.
99 Ibid, p. 463.
100 This took place in the autumn of 1950. In 1951 the 'Seventeen Point Agreement' was signed giving China sovereignty over Tibet. (Its validity has long been questioned.)
101 The People's Republic of China was proclaimed by Mao Tse-Tung on 1 October 1949.
102 Matthew 25:40.
103 Edward Gibbon (1737–1794), author of *The Decline and Fall of the Roman Empire*. He writes about his relationship with Suzanne Curchod in his *Memoirs of My Life* (1796), chapter 4, 'Lausanne 1753–8'.
104 Rickshaws were pulled by men, which Sangharakshita considered degrading. It was well known that rickshaw-pullers died early.
105 See *The Rainbow Road from Tooting Broadway to Kalimpong* in *Complete Works*, vol. 20, Ch. 17.
106 *Poya* days are full-moon days on which, traditionally, the laity observes chastity and eight (rather than the usual five) precepts. The three extra precepts refer to not eating after midday, not listening to music or dancing and so on, and not sleeping on high beds. In other words they are days when a layman or laywoman lives more simply, a little more like a monk or nun.
107 See J. Betjeman, 'The Wykehamist' (1931):

> He gives his Ovaltine a stir
> And nibbles at a petit beurre,
> And, satisfying fleshy wants,
> He settles down to Norman fonts.

108 See *The Rainbow Road from Tooting Broadway to Kalimpong* in *Complete Works*, vol. 20, pp. 163–4.
109 Sangharakshita, *A Survey of Buddhism*, Windhorse Publications, Birmingham 2001, p. 259 (*Complete Works*, vol. 1).
110 See *The Rainbow Road from Tooting Broadway to Kalimpong*, in *Complete Works*, vol. 20, pp. 167–8 and pp. 170–72. The letter to Devapriya Valisinha is referred to on p. 213.
111 *Anagarika Dharmapala: A Biographical Sketch*, Ibis Publications, Ledbury 2013, p. 7 (*Complete Works*, vol. 8).
112 Ibid, p. 35.
113 Ibid, p. 68.
114 S. T. Coleridge (1772–1834), *The Rime of the Ancient Mariner* (1798), final verse.
115 Sangharakshita, *Anagarika Dharmapala: A Biographical Sketch and other Maha Bodhi Writings*, Ibis Publications, Ledbury 2013, p. 34 (*Complete Works* vol. 8).
116 Ibid., p. 63.
117 Ibid., pp. 69–78.
118 Ibid., p. 32.

119 S. Radhakrishnan, *Indian Philosophy*, a work in two substantial volumes, was published by the Oxford University Press in 1923.

120 According to the Arya Maitreya Mandala's magazine, *Der Kreis*, nr. 270, Oktober 2013, '80 Jahre Arya Maitreya Mandala', the organization was founded by Lama Govinda at a public meeting held in Darjeeling on 14 October 1933, curiously the same date (14 October) on which, twenty-three years later, Dr Ambedkar led the mass conversions to Buddhism in Nagpur. The development of the organization founded by Govinda would have been retarded by the intervening war years during which he was interned.

121 Today (2017) Buddha Purnima or Buddha's birthday is a regional public holiday celebrated in fifteen (about half) of the Indian states. The births of Jesus Christ and the Prophet Mohammad are public holidays in *all* Indian states. Interestingly, Dr Ambedkar's birthday (14 April) is a regional public holiday celebrated in twenty Indian states.

122 See the Sanchi Edict in N. A. Nikam and R. McKeon (trans.), *The Rock Edicts of Asoka*, Asia Publishing House, Bombay 1962, p. 62.

123 M. C. Dey, *My Pilgrimages to Ajanta and Bagh*, Thornton Butterworth Ltd., London 1923.

124 Geoffrey Chaucer (1343–1400), *The Canterbury Tales: General Prologue*, lines 179–80. Composed between 1387 and 1400, this was printed in 1477 by William Caxton, the first book to be printed in the English language.

125 *Marie Waleska* (or *Conquest*) (1937) is the story of a Polish countess (played by Greta Garbo) who became Napoleon's mistress in the hope of helping her homeland. *Gone With the Wind* (1939) is set at the time of the American Civil War (1861–5). The film starred Clark Gable as Rhett Butler who is romantically involved with Scarlett O'Hara (played by Vivien Leigh).

126 A. Pope, *Epistle to a Lady: Of the Characters of Women* (1743), lines 2–3. It seems the sentiment 'Most Women have no Characters at all' was originally expressed by the Lady to whom the Epistle is addressed.

127 B. R. Ambedkar, 'The Buddha and the Future of His Religion', first published in the *Maha Bodhi*, April-May 1950. See Dr Babasaheb Ambedkar, *Writings and Speeches*, vol. 17 (part 2), Education Department, Government of Maharashtra, Bombay 2003, p.105; available at www.mea.gov.in/images/attach/amb/volume_17_02.pdf (April 2017).

128 The two weeks Sangharakshita spent alone in the Raipur Ashram were in August 1947. See *The Rainbow Road from Tooting Broadway to Kalimpong* in *Complete Works*, vol. 20, chapter 23, especially p. 217.

129 Lama Anagarika Govinda, *Creative Meditation and Multi-Dimensional Consciousness*, Unwin, London 1977.

130 G. Tucci and E. Ghersi, *Cronaca della missione scientifica Tucci nel Tibet occidentale (1933)*, Roma, Reale Accademia d'Italia, 1934. It was published in English as *Secrets of Tibet. Being the Chronicle of the Tucci Scientific Expedition to Western Tibet*, 1933, Blackie & Son, London and Glasgow 1935.

131 'Taking Refuge in the Buddha' in *Complete Poems 1941–1994*, Windhorse Publications, Birmingham 1995, pp. 161–2 (*Complete Works*, vol. 25).

132 This is the eleventh month of the Indian national civil calendar. It corresponds to January/February of the Gregorian calendar.

133 This article can now be found in Sangharakshita, *The Religion of Art*, Windhorse Publications, Glasgow 1988 (*Complete Works*, vol. 26).

134 'Krishna's Flute' in *Early Writings 1944–1954*, Ibis Publications, Ledbury 2014 (*Complete Works*, vol. 7).

135 'The white lofty mountain appears as if it was accumulated out of the loud laughter of Shiva', C. R. Devadhar (ed.), *Works of Kalidasa*, vol. 2, p. xxxiv.

136 The *Skanda Purāṇa* is the largest of the eighteen *Mahāpurāṇas* of Hindu religious literature.

137 'There is no religion higher than truth' was H. P. Blavatsky's translation of '*satyān nāsti paro dharmaḥ*', the motto of the Maharaja of Benares. The Theosophical Society was founded, with this as its motto, in 1875 in New York City by H. P. Blavatsky, H. S. Alcott, William Q. Judge, and others. Jinarajadasa was president of the Theosophical Society based in Adyar from 1945 until his death in 1953.

138 Sangharakshita's account of this, his first visit to Bodh Gaya, can be found in *The Rainbow Road from Tooting Broadway to Kalimpong* in *Complete Works*, vol. 20, pp. 453–6.

DEAR DINOO

INTRODUCTION

139 'Briefe gehören unter die wichtigsten Denkmäler, die der einzelne Mensch hinterlassen kann': J. W. von Goethe (1749–1832), in his *Preface to Winkelmann und sein Jahrhundert, in Briefen und Aufsätzen*, Tübingen 1805, pp. xi–xii.

140 Sangharakshita in a seminar on *The Door of Liberation*, quoted in *Peace is a Fire*, second edition, Windhorse Publications, Birmingham 1995, p. 114 (*Complete Works*, vol. 26).

141 John Donne (1572–1631), the English metaphysical poet. Quoted here are the first two lines of his verse letter, To Sir Henry Wotton. Henry Wotton (1568–1639), poet and diplomatist, was a friend of Donne from his student days, and remained a close friend throughout Donne's life. Sangharakshita quotes these lines in his own verse letter, 'Letter to Ananda', published in *The Call of the Forest and other Poems*, Windhorse Publications, Birmingham 2000 (*Complete Works*, vol. 25).

142 i.e. *A Survey of Buddhism*, first published 1957 (*Complete Works*, vol. 1).

143 The Wadias had organized the lectures Sangharakshita gave in Bangalore the previous year (1954), which became the basis for *A Survey of Buddhism*.

144 There is a warm account of this visit in Travel Letters, Windhorse Publications, Glasgow 1985, p. 5 (*Complete Works*, vol. 24).

145 This oft-repeated formula appears for example in the *Kandaraka Sutta, Majjhima Nikāya* 51 (i.345). See I. B. Horner (trans.), *The Collection of the Middle Length Sayings*, vol. 2, Pali Text Society, Oxford 1994, p. 9; or Bhikkhu Ñāṇamoli and Bhikkhu Bodhi (trans.), *The Middle Length Discourses of the Buddha,* Wisdom Publications, Boston 1995, p. 448 where *kalyāṇa* is translated as 'good' rather than 'lovely'; and again in the *Dantabhūmi Sutta, Majjhima Nikāya* 125 (iii.134), I. B. Horner, ibid., p. 180; or Ñāṇamoli and Bhikkhu Bodhi, ibid., p. 993.

146 'The Only Way', *Complete Poems 1941–1994*, Windhorse Publications, Birmingham 1995, p. 89 (*Complete Works*, vol. 25).

147 *Ambedkar and Buddhism* (*Complete Works*, vol. 9).

148 See 'Discovering Dharmapala', *Facing Mount Kanchenjunga* above, chapter 18; and *Anagarika Dharmapalaw A Biographical Sketch*, Ibis

149   Publications, Ledbury 2013 (*Complete Works*, vol. 8).

149   'The Good Friend', in *Crossing the Stream*, second edition, Windhorse Publications, Birmingham 1996, pp. 57–62 (*Complete Works*, vol. 7).

150   *Upaḍḍha Sutta, Saṃyutta Nikāya* v.2; see Bhikkhu Bodhi (trans.), *The Connected Discourses of the Buddha*, Wisdom Publications, Boston 2000, pp. 1524–5; or F. L. Woodward (trans.), *Kindred Sayings*, part 5, Pali Text Society, London 1979, p. 2.

151   *My Relation to the Order*, Windhorse Publications, Glasgow 1990, pp. 26–7 (*Complete Works*, vol. 2).

152   See *Facing Mount Kanchenjunga* above, chapter 3, especially p. 42.

153   *Moving Against the Stream*, Windhorse Publications, Birmingham 2003 is the fourth of Sangharakshita's volumes of memoirs (*Complete Works*, vol. 23).

154   The *Rainbow Road from Tooting Broadway to Kalimpong*, in *Complete Works*, vol. 20, p. 83.

155   'Krishna's Flute', in *Early Writings 1944–1954*, Ibis Publications, Ledbury 2014 (*Complete Works*, vol. 7).

156   'To Shrimati Sophia Wadia in Honour of her Sixtieth Birthday', in *Complete Poems 1941–1994*, Windhorse Publications, Birmingham 1995, pp. 247–9 (*Complete Works*, vol. 25).

157   'Lines to Jayapushpa on her Return to Malaysia', ibid., p. 340.

158   See *The Rainbow Road from Tooting Broadway to Kalimpong*, in *Complete Works*, vol. 20, p. 87. The article was probably 'The Unity of Buddhism' which can be found in *Early Writings 1944–1954*, Ibis Publications, Ledbury 2014 (*Complete Works*, vol. 7).

159   C. Cameron, *Rustle of Spring: an Edwardian Childhood in London's East End*, second edition, Skilton & Shaw, London 1979, first published 1927.

160   Quoted in Brian Graham, *Clare Cameron, A Human and Spiritual Journey*, Werner Shaw Ltd., London 1984, pp. 11–12.

161   See *The Rainbow Road from Tooting Broadway to Kalimpong* in *Complete Works*, vol. 20, p. 100.

162   *A Stranger Here* was privately published in 1942.

163   *The Rainbow Road from Tooting Broadway to Kalimpong* in *Complete Works*, vol. 20, p. 103.

164   Brian Graham, *Clare Cameron, A Human and Spiritual Journey*, Werner Shaw Ltd., London 1984, p.172.

165   See also *Moving Against the Stream*, Windhorse Publications, Birmingham

166 *Precious Teachers*, Windhorse Publications, Birmingham 2007, chapters 3 and 9 (*Complete Works*, vol. 22) and *Moving Against the Stream*, Windhorse Publications, Birmingham 2003, pp. 176–7, 332, and 337–8 (*Complete Works*, vol. 23).

    2003, chapter 6, 'Rustle of Autumn', pp. 30–1 (*Complete Works*, vol. 23).

167 See Claire Jordan's article: http://members.madasafish.com/%7Ecj%5Fwhitehound/family retrieved May 2017.

168 *Precious Teachers*, Windhorse Publications, Birmingham 2007, p. 25 (*Complete Works*, vol. 22).

169 *Moving Against the Stream*, Windhorse Publications, Birmingham 2003, p.177 (*Complete Works*, vol. 22).

170 Ibid., p. 338.

171 W. Blake (1757–1827). This is proverb 27 from the 'Proverbs of Hell' in *The Marriage of Heaven and Hell*.

172 *The History of My Going for Refuge*, Windhorse Publications, Glasgow 1988 (*Complete Works*, vol. 2).

173 Subhuti, *Bringing Buddhism to the West*, Windhorse Publications, Birmingham 1995.

THE MONK AND THE PROPHET

174 These and other details of the Doctor's life can be found in *Fundamental Laws of Health*, Bharatiya Vidya Bhavan, 1988, compiled and edited by Sundri Vaswani.

175 *Mahatma Gandhi: The Beloved Patient* was the title of a book recounting Dr Mehta's encounters with Gandhi, edited by Sundri Vaswani.

176 In the absence of a footnote, the reader can assume quotations are from interviews with Sangharakshita conducted by the editor in 2010–11.

177 Mahatma: lit. 'great soul'. Rabindranath Tagore is said to have popularized this epithet for Gandhi.

178 Bapu: lit. 'father'. This title was commonly used by Gandhi's followers.

179 *In the Sign of the Golden Wheel*, pp. 269–7 (*Complete Works*, vol. 22).

180 Ibid., p. 271.

181 Ibid., p. 283.

182 Ibid., p. 337.

183 In the early 1960s, Sangharakshita visited Poona along with Khantipālo, an English bhikkhu who had stayed with him in Kalimpong. Using the Nature Cure Clinic as a venue, he held a month-long seminar. Thirty-five to forty people attended each day from 7–10 p.m. to 'take' the Refuges and Precepts, meditate, and study the *Dhammapada*, an early Buddhist text. Three of

those attending later became members of the order that Sangharakshita went on to found.

184 *Moving Against the Stream*, p. 297 (*Complete Works*, vol. 23).

185 *Precious Teachers*, pp. 5–6 (*Complete Works*, vol. 22).

186 In using these terms Sangharakshita has in mind two kinds of experience, i.e. absorption on the one hand, insight on the other. Readers should not be confused by the use of the term *samādhi* that in Zen tradition can refer to the experience of insight, e.g. in the *Sūtra of Huineng*.

187 *In the Sign of the Golden Wheel*, p. 284 (*Complete Works*, vol. 22).

188 Ibid., chapter 20.

189 Suvajra is a senior British disciple of Sangharakshita who has spent many years living and working in India.

INDEX

Advaita Vedanta 113, 157
'Advice to a Young Poet' 435–6, 631n
Agarwala, Banshilal 138, 141–2
Agra 519, 521n
Ahmedabad 572, 574–5n
Ahuja, Professor N. C. 55–6
Ajanta 71, 402–4, 408
Ajanta (film) 399–401, 404–6, 408
Ajmer 82, 146
Alaungyi 131–2
Almora 572, 575n
alms 9, 11–15, 41, 108, 183
Ambedkar, Dr B. R. xiii, 90, 415–16, 464, 474, 515n, 525n, 597n, 648–9
   birthday 630n
   followers of 90, 470, 494n, 523, 548n, 573, 575n, 598n, 599, 603, 608, 619, 648–9
   Sangharakshita meeting with 415–16
   writings 623n, 630n
Ambedkar and Buddhism 474, 525n, 632n
Amitābha 214, 463, 559, 562–3n
Amritananda 108, 120, 282–4, 294, 300, 304
Ananda Kuti Vihara 271, 281, 283
Ananda Vihara 407, 464, 543, 545n
Anandji, *see* Kausalyayan, Bhadant Ananda
Ancient Greece 396
Aniruddha
   of Arya Maitreya Mandala 465, 545n

of Dharmodaya Vihara 102–3, 115–18, 121, 123, 138, 158, 180, 210, 266, 432, 448, 545n
anna 301, 567n
annus mirabilis 548n
Anuradha Sutta 585n
Ariya Sangharama 107
Arya Maitreya Mandala 394, 545n, 630n
Aśoka pillar 396, 512, 515n
Aśvaghoṣa 624n
Atatürk, Kemal 484
Augustine, St. 351, 446
Austin, J. 339, 342, 628n
Autobiography of a Yogi 582, 585n
Avalokiteśvara x, 88, 214, 295, 613
Avataṃsaka Sūtra 626n
The Awakening of Faith 113, 624n

Baba, M. 614
Babu, G. 119–21, 124, 129–31, 133, 136, 138, 139–40, 142–3
Babu, M. K. 119–20, 121, 129, 138–42, 172
Bacon, F. 325, 344, 628n
Bagdogra 191, 507, 510n
Bagmati, River 275–6
Bahadur, D. 144, 231, 365, 427
Bahadur, M. (cook) 432
Bahadur, N. 36–7, 41–2
Bailey, A. 612
Bakula, K. 107
Banshi's Godown 138, 148
Banshilal 141–2

Barclay, Miss H. 442–5, 516n, 564n
Barnes High School 417, 423
Bartsch, C. and H. 618
Bates 525–6n, 532, 541n, 550
Baudelaire, C. 170, 625n
Beating the Drum 525n
Bendre, N. S. 558, 561n
Betjeman, J. 373, 629n
Bhadgaon 292–3, 296, 304
Bhagwat, Dr N. K. 465, 495, 496n, 546, 555n
Bhajuratna 272
Bharati, Swami Agehananda 583, 585n
Bhavani (goddess) 296
Bhave, Vinoba 615
bhikṣā (almsfood) 9, 10, 11, 12, 18
Bhumiveda, Mr 431–2
Bhutia, Dawa Tsering 72, 75, 309, 428
Birla, D. 522–3, 525n, 527, 528n, 559–60, 563n, 602
Birla, J.K. 317
Black Narcissus 73
Blake, W. 486, 634n
Blavatsky, Mme 380, 440, 631n
Blind School, the 34, 345
Blofeld, J. 589, 590n
Blue Annals, The 51, 622n
Bo, Mr 572, 574n
Bodh Gaya, *see* Buddha Gaya
Bodhananda Maha Sthavira 46–7, 111
Bodhicaryāvatāra 597n
bodhisattva ideal 88–9, 107, 114–15, 179, 245, 313–14, 562n, 623n, 627n, 648
Bodhnath 284–5, 515n
Bose, Miss 152–3
Bosham House 481, 593n
Boyce, Mrs H. 592
Brewster, Earl 261
Bringing Buddhism to the West 486, 634n
Brontë, C. 478
Brunner, Mme and Elizabeth 398
Buchman, F. 604
Buddha
    bodies of 214–15, 559, 563n
    images of 17–18, 56–7, 125, 217, 230, 232, 252, 261–2, 287, 307–8, 396–8, 402, 452, 568n
    parinirvāna of 584n, 585n
    visions of 563n, 613
Buddha Gaya (Bodh Gaya) 368, 380–1, 513, 515–6n, 631n
Buddha Jayanti 394, 469, 496, 497n, 506, 508–9n, 521n, 532n, 536n, 548n, 575n, 588, 590n
Buddha Purnima (birthday) 630n

Buddhaghosa 102, 624n
Buddhahood 83, 247, 559, 562–3n
Buddharakshita 191, 212, 263, 438; *see also* Satyapriya
Buddhism 244–8, 249–50
    and the arts 250–1, 434, 575n, 626n
    dynamic 114
    unity of xii, 89, 259, 633, 655
Buddhism and Art 463, 497n, 528, 531
Buddhism in England 338, 479
Buddhist, The 36, 627n
Buddhist Himalaya 560, 563n
Buddhist Society, The 233, 339, 475, 480, 537n, 578, 579n, 580n, 592n
Buddhist World, The 245–7
Burke, T. 481
Burma Raja, *see* Latthakin, Prince K. M.
Butaol 264

Calcutta 60, 367–8, 371–4, 378, 504, 508n
Cameron, C. 232–3, 338, 446, 479–82, 584n, 586–7, 594, 628n
    and Dinoo 633n
    in Sussex 582, 592, 593n
Cann, J. E. (Joe) 45–8, 56, 63–5, 75, 94–5, 109, 112, 150, 162–3, 166–7, 230–2, 257, 307–8, 310–11, 356, 428–30, 444, 447, 589, 590n
    and Ryan, Colonel J. W. (Swale) 81, 144–6
caste 69, 70, 75, 156, 168–9, 597–8n
caste system 20, 37, 67, 80, 169, 279, 284, 299, 605
Chandramani, U. 8, 98, 102, 107–8
Chattrul Sangye Dorje 548n, 550n, 611
Chaucer, G. 626n, 630n
Chebo Busti 566, 567n
Chen, Yogi 485
Chetana's 560, 564n
Chetiyagiri Vihara 172, 396
Chhawara, R. S. 82–3
Chichester 582, 584n, 587, 593n
Chinese invasion 104, 328, 353, 537n, 576n, 577n
Chinia Lama 285
'Chitrabhanu' 153–4, 517, 565
Chodags, Thubden (Yellow Monk) 331–6
Chototsang, A. 328–31
Christ 559
Christian Science 540, 541n
Chung, Mr 226, 240
Chung Building 210, 225–6
citizenship 587
Clifton, R. S. 339–42, 428
Combastet, Mme 445–6

638 / INDEX

Communist spy 54
Compassion 474, 559, 562n, 612
Convocation Hall 466
Conze, E. xi, 313–15, 432, 474, 543, 545n, 564n, 628n
Coomaraswamy, A. K. 161
cottage 540, 541n, 553n
Craigside 537n
Crisp, E. 223, 337
Crisp, F. 223–5, 253, 337
criticism 64, 481
Crookety 33, 49, 253, 319
Crown Prince Mahendra 293
cuckoo 543, 544n
Cunningham, General Sir A. 171, 172, 192, 198, 390, 515n

Dailo 346
Dailo Hill 13, 436–8
Dalai Lama 188, 191, 200, 209, 229, 545n
   Dinoo meets 465–6, 527, 528n
   in Kalimpong 525n, 529, 530n
Damodaran 25, 28, 152
Dantabhūmi Sutta 632
Darjeeling 91–2, 213, 233–5, 258, 259, 331, 335, 513–14, 531, 532n
Darshan, Lok 280, 293
Dasgupta, S. 112–15
Davendra, D. T. 499, 500n, 502
Dawa-Samdup, Lama Kazi 71, 622n
Deccan Queen 493, 494n
Delamare, T. 470, 521n, 575n, 597n, 618
Delannoy, Miss. 445–6
Delhi 299, 572, 575n
   Symposium 513, 516n
dentist 531, 541n
Deolali 417–25
Desai, M. 601
devanāgarī 18, 507, 510n
Devapriyaji, *see* Valisinha, Devapriya
Devayani, *see* Krishna, D.
Dewsay 100–2
Dhammajoti, Bhikkhu 26–7, 35, 79
Dhammaloka 274, 288, 451, 453
Dhammapada 9, 13, 237–8, 242, 465, 496n, 499, 634n
Dhammaratana 266
Dhardo Rimpoche xii, 307–9, 318, 441, 451–3, 520n, 521n, 548n, 575n, 593n, 631n
Dharmachakra 496n, 546, 553n, 555n
Dharmākara 558–9, 562n
dharmakāya 214, 559, 563n
Dharmapala, Anagārika xii, 98, 367–8, 371–2, 379–83, 385–9, 439–40, 475, 524n, 573, 576n, 593n, 626n, 632–3n, 648
Dharmapala Institute 592, 593n
Dharmarajika (Chaitya) Vihara 261, 381, 524n, 566, 567n
Dharmarakshita, Venerable 108
Dharmodaya Sabha 17, 20, 31, 37, 80, 103, 118, 120–1, 265, 271, 281, 284, 300
Dharmodaya Vihara 9, 17–19, 31, 41, 55, 58, 80, 115, 117, 120, 122–3, 125, 180, 206, 209–10, 537n
Diamond Sūtra x, 115, 312
Donne, J. 457, 632n
Dooars 33, 540, 541n, 554n
Dorji, R. C. 142–3, 174, 180, 182, 184–7, 208
Dorji, R. S. T. 142, 186–7
Dorji, T. 142–3, 191
Dubash, Dinoo xiii, 456, 458
   adventures 468, 504–5
   and art 461–2
   a breach 469, 571
   and Clare Cameron 485
   and cooking 459, 516n
   and Dalai Lama 465–6, 527
   and disappointment 539, 541n
   donations by 469–70, 485, 503n, 530, 531, 539, 572
   and Dr Mehta 466–8, 505, 519
   early life 461–3
   in Kalimpong 468–9
   last years 470–1
   and meditation 462–3
   and painting 462, 463, 532n, 552, 558
   and servants 459, 552, 554n
   and Sundri 468
Dudjom Rimpoche 590n
Dum-Dum 510n
Dupchen 554n, 563n

ecumenism 246, 360
Eightfold Path, Noble 83, 196
Elenjimittam, A. (Father Anthony) 37–8, 43–4, 86
elephants 552–3
Elizabeth I, Queen 478
'Emptiness,' Mr, *see* Sorensen, A. 88
English Sangha Association 580n, 581
English Sangha Trust 475, 485, 579–80n, 592n, 593n
Enlightenment 505–6, 508n, 611–12
Essence of Zen, The 596, 598n
Eternal Legacy, The 575n, 585, 662
Evans-Wentz, W. Y. 71, 622n

Everton Villa 502, 503n, 535, 537n
  sale of 542n
Evolution, Higher and Lower 83, 623n

faith (śraddhā) 197-8, 463-4
Flame in Darkness 524n, 576n
Fleurs du Mal 625n
Forty-Three Years Ago 521n
Foster, M. E. 381, 385
Foundations of Tibetan Mysticism 147
friendship 475-6, 575n, 589, 606-7
  Blake on 486
  with Clare Cameron 480, 482
  with Dinoo 458, 463
  with Dr Mehta 599-600, 603-9
  duties of 610
  with the Kazini 483
  with Lama Govinda and Li Gotami xii, 248-51, 392-3, 416-18, 422-5, 575n
  and love 556n
  with people in disharmony 484-5
  with Rashk 413
  with Sachin 74, 218, 344, 435
  widening circle of 485
  with women 476-7
  with the Yellow Monk 332
  in YMBA 74-6, 218
Fruit-Gathering 94
full-moon days 18, 77, 107, 218, 231, 349, 429-30, 444, 451, 548n, 629n
fund-raising letter 535-6, 538n
FWBO 595, 597n
  Newsletter 595-6, 597n

Gaṇḍavyūha Sūtra 147, 626n
Gandhi, I. 509n
Gandhi, M. K. xiii, 466, 600-1, 615, 634n
Gangeshwarananda, Swami 158
Gangtok 44, 188-9, 191, 193, 196, 234, 507, 509n, 584n
garden 534, 553n
Gauḍapāda 113
Gautam, J. B. (Jungi) 71, 75
Gazamair, (Lachuman). 71, 75, 77, 100, 309
Gelug order 177, 191, 453
Ghoom 91, 249, 256-8, 309
Ghosh, E. 156-7
Gibbon, E. 629n
Glengarry 220-1
Godden, Rumer 73, 74
God Calling 540, 541n
God Speaks 614
Goethe, J. W. 457, 632n

Going for Refuge 342-3, 648
Golden Lotus, The 315, 341
Gompu, T. 365, 426
'Good Friend, the' 475
Gopal (cook) 144, 212, 218, 325,
Gopal, R. 481
Gotami, L. *see* Govinda, L. G.
Govinda, Lama xii, 244-56, 257, 258-61, 392-3, 395-8, 401, 416-21, 423-5, 474, 509n, 575n, 625n, 626n
  and Arya Maitreya Mandala 394, 630n
  foster-mother 256, 626n
  and *Stepping-Stones* xi, 87-8, 146-7, 205, 244, 245, 246-7, 313-14, 474, 623n, 625n, 627n
  and 'The Veil of Stars' 624
Govinda, L. G. 244, 249, 251-6, 258-9, 261, 398, 416-18, 419, 420-1, 424-5, 509n, 575n
Graham, B. 481, 633n
Graham, Dr 34, 346-7
Gray, T. 622
Great Royal Mother, *see* Gyalmo Chenmo
'Great Wisdom' (Mahaprajna) 19-20, 32, 79-81, 101-2, 103, 120
Green Buddha 460, 598n
Guénon, R. 159, 161
Guenther, H. V. 111-13, 146, 310-11, 313, 574n, 624n
Guenther, S. 111, 310
Gurung, A. B. 33
Gyabahal Vihara 293-5
Gyalmo Chenmo 229
Gyan Jyoti 8-10, 18, 36, 52, 79, 118-19, 121, 175, 180, 182, 211

Hamblin, H. T. 481, 582, 584n
Hamilton, Mrs 220-3, 352
Hampstead Buddhist Vihara 592n, 598n
Harrer, H. 166
Hemaraj, His Holiness (the Rajpurohit) 298-9
Here and Now 338, 481, 482
Heritage of Buddhism, The 572, 575n, 592
Hermitage, The 216-19, 243, 261, 307, 321-2, 434, 441, 537n
Hettiarachchi, S. 168
Himalayan Hotel 29, 66, 87, 183, 443, 446, 564n
Himalayan Times 53-4
Hira, *see* Vaswani, H.
History of Indian Philosophy 113

History of My Going for Refuge, The 486
Hofford, D. 44–5
Homes, Dr Graham's 34, 232, 346–8
Hudson, Dr I. B. 446–8
Humphreys, C. 339, 480, 579n, 580n

I Ching 589, 590n
illness 551, 578, 581, 591
Illustrated Weekly of India 89, 90, 250, 252, 258, 261, 316, 421, 423
Indra, Mr 83, 446
Insight 289, 506, 508n, 611–12, 635n
Institute of Culture 82, 83–4, 157, 350, 544n
Irene, Princess of Greece 253–5, 268, 318, 319, 320, 442, 628n
Is Buddhism for Monks Only? 497n, 528, 531

Jagdish Kashyap, *see* Kashyapji
Jain, S. C. 53–4
Jamyang Khyentse Rimpoche 554n
Jane Eyre 478
Janssens, The 224–5, 337, 350
Jātaka stories 396
Jayapushpa 479, 633n
Jibananda 432
Jinarajadasa 439–40, 631n
Jinaratana 266, 275, 369, 375–8, 384, 568n, 626n
Jinnah, Governor-General 601
Jivaka 563n, 579, 580n, 583, 585n
Joe, *see* Cann, J. E.
Jones, E. S. 345, 628n
Jungi, *see* Gautam, J. B.
Jyoti, M. 24, 281, 284, 301

Kachu Rimpoche 552, 553–4n
Kalidasa 437, 631n
Kalimpong 8, 441, 500n, 576n
'Kalimpong, Queen of' (Mitter, C.) 148–55, 221, 255, 348, 516n
kalyāṇa 632
kalyāṇa mitratā 476 *see also* friendship
Kamalashila 85–7
Kanchenjunga ix, 7, 17, 40, 91, 98, 158, 173, 208, 436, 624n
Kandaraka Sutta 632
Kapoor, Raj 399–401, 403–6, 407, 408–9, 410, 411–13, 414, 417, 438
Karaṇīya Mettā Sutta 497n
karma, law of 582, 585n
Karuna Trust 593n
Kashyap, Bhikshu Jagdish (Kashyapji) ix, 7–12, 37–9, 85–6, 108, 196, 266, 283, 473, 507, 509n, 510n, 553
and Birlaji 317
and Dinoo 464–5, 468, 524, 527, 528n, 530, 543
disappointments with 202–5
and Sacred Relics 173, 188, 190, 192, 193, 194, 196
Kathmandu 269, 271, 274, 288, 290, 292, 299, 512–13, 515n
Kausalyayan, Bhadant Ananda (Anandji) 266, 271, 297–8, 300, 302–3, 448–50
Kawinda, Sayadaw, U 107–10
Kazi, L. D. of Chakhung 483–5
Kazini of Chakhung 469, 483–5, 634n
Keats, J. 78, 434, 584n
Keshab Shamser 292
Khantipālo 516n, 580n, 634n
Khar 471, 494n
Khemasiri 509n, 536n, 548n, 552, 554n
Kheminda Thera 313–4, 627n
Khuddakapāṭha 497n, 503, 531
Kipling, R. 25, 621n
Kittima, U 98, 106, 520–1n
Koirala, B. P. 278
Koirala, M. P. 277, 293
Krishna, D. 56–7
Krishna, K. 55–6, 134
Krishnalok 318
Krishnamurti 58, 134
Krishna's Flute 436, 478, 633n
Kristo 375
Kumari 296
Kusinara 8, 11, 263, 511, 515n

Lachuman, *see* Gazamair, L.
Lalitpur 286, 288, 293–4
Lama, K. B. (Karka) 71–2, 75
Lama, Mr 75, 92
Lama, old Mr 72
Lama, S. 143
Lambert, C. 481
Latthakin, Prince K. M. (Burma Raja) 117, 124–37, 143, 212, 218–20, 537n
Lawrence, D. H. 261
Lepchas xi, 190, 351, 567n
letters 457–8, 471–3
Lhalungpa, L. P. 163, 451, 516n
Li Gotami, *see* Govinda, L. G.
Living Silence 530, 532n, 550, 552, 555n, 559, 610
first issue 503n
inception 499
resignation from 531, 532n, 540, 543

Lokamitra xv, 460, 470-1, 485, 597n, 598n
London Buddhist Society, *see* Buddhist Society, The
Long, Miss 358-63
Long-Lived Deva, *see* Tsering, L.
Lucis Trust 612
Lucknow 46, 104, 109-12, 114, 572, 574n
Lumbini 11, 264, 511, 512, 515n

Macdonald, Mr 29-30
Māgha 429
Maha Bodhi, The 89, 474, 516n, 523, 525n, 540, 588, 623n, 648
Maha Bodhi Society 24, 26, 265, 367, 369, 373-4, 381-4, 416, 427, 475, 508n, 524n
  journal, *see Maha Bodhi, The*
  Kalimpong branch 427-31
  and Sacred Relics 171-2, 391
Maha Bodhi temple
  at Bodh Gaya 368, 516n
  at Patan 287
Mahanama 103, 118, 120, 274, 276, 281, 284, 375
Mahāparinibbāna Sutta 584n
Mahaprajna, *see* Great Wisdom
Maharaja of Sikkim 142, 191-2, 201, 484, 569, 570n, 581
  funeral of 583-4n
Maharani 35, 584n
Mahāvastu 582, 585n
Mahendra, Crown Prince 293
Maheshvara 270, 275
Maitreya 49, 51, 258, 394, 497n, 558-9, 562n, 568n, 626n
maitrī 314, 555-6n
Majjhima Nikāya 348, 632n
Malva, Z. xv, 462
mandala 259
Māṇḍūkya Kārikās 113
Mandy, C. R. 89, 421-2
Maṅgala Sutta 497n
Manjula 148-9, 514, 516n
Mannerheim, Field-Marshal 483
mantras 49, 202, 258
Māra 297-300
Mascarhenas, Father 558, 561n
Maudgalyāyana
  Sacred Relics 27, 171, 192, 198, 263, 390, 515n
  thangkas 230
'Mayfair' 524n, 555n, 582, 584n, 602
meditation 40-1, 86, 230, 508n, 562n, 567n
  and art 251, 625

Dinoo and 460, 462-3, 520
Dr Mehta and 466, 496, 505-6, 527, 601-2, 610-11, 612, 613
Lama Govinda and 259, 421
Mehta, A. 596, 598n, 615
Mehta, Dr D. (Dinshaw) xiii, 459, 493, 494n, 495, 496n, 506, 508n, 599-619, 634
  and Buddha's teaching 607
  and Dinoo 466-8, 524n, 532n, 606
  early years 600-1
  friendship 603-9
  and Gandhi 600-1, 617, 634n
  and 'Guidance' 496n, 500n, 505, 522-3, 524n, 530n, 541n, 573, 601-2, 612
    Buddha's 505-6, 519-20
    three kinds of 604
  last years 618-19
  and madness 613-14
  and meditation 466, 496n, 505-6, 527, 601-2, 610-11, 612, 613
  meeting Sangharakshita 498, 499, 602-4
  and religious leaders 552-3, 555n, 605, 614
  and 'Scripts' xiii, 498, 500n, 505, 530n, 550, 555n, 602, 604, 609, 611-12
Mehta, G. 499, 500n, 571, 574n, 615-16
  death of 618
  and Dinoo 467
  and 'Guidance' 602, 615
  marriage of 615
Messengers from Tibet 52, 481, 507, 622n
Middle Way, The 233, 338, 479
miracles 197-8
misogyny 477-9
Mistri, Mrs R. 499, 500n
Mitter, Mrs C. *see* 'Kalimpong, Queen of'
Moktan, D. 30-3, 143
monk, little Cambodian, *see* Sokkhasobhano, Preah Maha
Montessori, Mme M. 462
Montessori School 459, 497n, 528n, 558, 561n
Mookerjee, Dr S. P. 416, 433
Moral Rearmament 604
Morse, Father 353-7
mother, Sangharakshita's 578, 579n, 595-6, 598n
Mulagandhakuti Vihara 97-8, 104, 106, 381, 396
Munindra, Brahmacārī 191, 203-4

Nagarjuna Training Institute 597n
Nagpur 523–5
Naidu, S. 436, 478, 633n
Nair, Dr A. 545n
Nālandā 38, 85, 464, 528n
Nālandā Vihara 464, 510n
Narada Thera 267, 280–1, 300–4, 392–3, 396–8, 448
Narayanhiti 270–1, 302
Nargis, Miss 409–10
Nature Cure Clinic, Poona 496n, 500n, 574n, 600, 603, 608, 610, 615
  sale of 618
  seminar 634
Nebesky-Wojkowitz, R. de 87, 253, 317–9
Nehru, J. (Pandit) 171, 199–201, 384, 393–4, 415, 464, 600
Nepali Building 9–10, 13–14, 21, 24, 118, 121, 165
Neville, D. 338, 481
New Delhi 519, 575n
Nicholson, R. 160, 161, 550n
Nisatta, Sister A. 477, 537n, 576n
Nityaswarupananda, Swami 157
Norbu, L. 576n
Nyatapola 296

Oceana 459, 572, 574n
Ochre Robe, The 583, 585n
Olcott, Col. 380, 386–7, 631n
Old Palace, Bhadgaon 289, 296–7
'Only Way, The' 474, 632n
Order Convention 597n
ordination 106–10, 342–4
Oriya Encyclopaedia 575n
Orwell, G. 483

Padam, *see* Periyar, P.
Padmasambhava 93, 94, 214, 258, 554n
Pallis, M. 68, 142, 159–64, 175–6, 544n, 546, 547n, 550n, 625n *see also* Tendzin, Thubden
Palpa-Tansen 264
Panorama 125, 129–31, 133, 212–13
parinirvāṇa 37, 497n, 582, 585n
Parsis 461, 508, 510n
Parvati 499, 501n
Pashupatinath 274–5
Payne, M. 614
Peaks and Lamas 68, 142, 159–60, 178, 544n, 550n, 625n
Pedong 21
Pema Tsedeun, *see* Tsedeun, Princess Pema (of Sikkim)
People's Republic of China 353, 464, 629n

Perfection of Wisdom *sūtras* 314, 445
Periyar, K. 75–6
Periyar, P. (Padam) 71, 75, 76, 77, 100
Peter, Brother 352–3
Peter, Prince, of Greece 51, 88, 129, 253, 267–8, 318
Philomena, St. 351
Pines, The 257
poetry 77–8, 168, 250, 378–9, 433–6, 621, 658
  and Cameron, C. 479–80, 482
  and the Dharma 77–9, 147, 250, 434
  Sangharakshita's 23, 51–2, 89–90, 316, 319, 322, 429, 437, 478–9, 481, 503, 507, 525n, 623n, 626n
Poona 493, 500n
Pope, A. 623n, 630n
poya days 370, 629n; *see also* full-moon days
Pradhan, B. 236–7
Pradhan, G. 119
Pradhan, M. C. 58, 59, 134
Pradhan, M. K. 119, 174
Pradhan, P. 235
Pradhan, R. 20–21, 36, 182, 236–7
prajñā 506, 508n, 611–12
Prajnananda, Ven. 111
Prajñāpāramitā-hridaya Sūtra 563n
Prajñāpāramitā Sūtras 314, 545n, 628n
Price, A. 159, 625n
puja bowls 229
puja season 92, 98–100, 321, 513, 516n
pujas 86, 218, 229, 295, 445
  full-moon 77, 231, 430

Radhakrishnan, Dr S. 393–4, 415, 630n
Rae, Roderick R. L. 483
Rai, Sanumati 237
Rainbow, The 261
rainy season 40–1, 468, 566, 567n
Ramakrishna Mission 157–9, 561n, 583, 585n, 626n
Rana, K. S. J. B. (Keshab Shamser) 291–2
Rana, M. S. J. B. (Mohan Shamser) 277–9, 281–2
Rani, Princess 130–4
Rao, Miss and Mrs 225–8
Rashk, A. 399–401, 403–14, 417, 438, 494n
Ratana, Anagarika S. 36
Ratnaman 167, 289
Rawnsley, M. 597n
Ray, I. 156–7
Ray, S. 509n
Rilke 434
Ringkingpong 32, 253, 318

robes 12, 108, 177, 342, 374, 376–7
Robinson, R. 339
Rock, Dr J. 66, 87
Roedean 424
Roerich, Dr G. 33–4, 49, 51, 53–4, 253, 319–20, 622n
Roman Catholic Mission 345–6, 350, 359
Rustle of Spring 479, 633n
Rustom, Chief Minister 569, 570n
Ryan, Colonel J. W. (Swale) 24–8, 35, 37, 48, 51–3, 66, 79, 81, 103, 118, 124, 145–6, 150–3, 340, 370
and Cann, J. E. 81, 144–6

Sachin, *see* Singh, S. C.
Sacred Relics xi, 27, 146, 171–2, 179–82, 191, 192–3, 197–8, 207–8, 263, 267–73, 281–4, 292, 296, 305–6, 384, 390–1, 395
Saddhatissa 108
Sadutshang, Y. 166–7
Śākyamuni 57, 258, 559
samādhi 505–6, 508n, 523, 527, 611–12, 635
Samdup, Mrs R. 210–12, 225–6, 238–42
Sanchi 171, 172, 178, 390, 395–6, 511, 515n
sangha 203–4, 342
Sangha Association 582
Sangharatana, Maha Thera, Ven. M. 97, 98, 108, 173, 190–2, 196–8, 212, 516n
and the Sacred Relics 192, 193, 194, 196, 197, 206, 208–9, 210, 211–13, 214, 516n
Sangpo, Geshe 191
Śaṅkara 113
Sankrityayan, R. 75–6, 449
Santiniketan, Kathmandu 271
Santiniketan, West Bengal 154, 155, 507, 509n, 523, 529
Saraswati (Brahmin) 84–5
Saraswati (goddess) 113, 403, 516n
Saraswati Sadan 297
Śāriputra
Sacred Relics xi, 27, 171, 192, 198, 263, 390, 515n, 516n
thangkas 230
Sarnath 26, 49, 84, 98, 106–8, 110, 511, 514, 515n, 520–1n
Satyapriya 170, 625n; *see also* Buddharakshita
Science of Thought Review 481, 582, 584n
Scott, Dr Hon. Mary 33–5, 346, 349

Scottish Mission High School 62, 71
semi-monastic 535, 537n
seminars 634n, 649
Seven Years in Tibet 166
Shagabpa, T., Mr and Mrs 361–2
Shantabir 143
Shedub, Thubden 160, 550n; *see also* Nicholson R.
Shelley, P. B. 23, 78, 434, 621n, 622n
Shiva 275, 437, 443, 516n, 631n
Short, Miss 358–63
Shunyata, Shri, *see* Sorensen, A.
Sikkim 173, 191–3, 195–7, 509n, 553n, 569, 570n
Śikṣā-samuccaya 23, 89
Silabhadra 266, 375, 391
Silachara, Bhikkhu 348
Siliguri 8, 104, 143, 566, 567n
Singh, S. C. (Sachin) 73–4, 75, 76–7, 91, 94, 100, 101, 252, 255, 257, 344, 433–6, 443
Singh, T. P. (Tilakdhari) 15–16, 38–9, 576n
Singha Durbar 289–91
Sitaram, Mr 386–8
Snellgrove, D. 560, 563n, 564n
Society of Servants of God xiii, 466, 496n, 524n, 571, 574n, 601, 602–3, 607
Soft, Dr M. 173, 190–1, 196–7, 200, 209, 265, 426
Sokkhasobhano, Preah Maha 468, 532–3n
Sorensen, A. ('Mr Emptiness') 87, 88
spirit and letter 147, 244, 301, 486
Springheel Jack 357
śraddhā (faith) 463–4
Sri Dharmarajika Vihara 266–7, 368, 381, 390, 524n, 544n
Sri Ramakrishna 557–8, 561n
Srighar Vihara 304, 305
St Augustine's Priory 351
St Philomena's Convent 351
Stepping-Stones xi, 48–52, 80, 87–9, 146, 310–13, 315–16, 474, 482, 537n, 545n, 621n, 622n, 623n, 627n
and *Buddhist World* 246–7
and Clare Cameron 338, 482
and Dr Conze 314–15, 545n
and Dr Guenther 112, 310
and Lama Govinda 87–8, 147, 244, 246, 248, 313, 575n, 623n, 625n, 627n
Nepali Section 235–7
printing 234–5
Stranger Here, A 481, 633n

Stray Birds 94, 623n
Subba, Inspector 122, 123
Sugatapriya 554n, 563n
Sukhāvatīvyūha 558, 562n
Sulochana 597n
Sundri, *see* Vaswani, Sundri
śūnyatā 115, 187–8, 563n *see also* Void, the
Survey of Buddhism, A 494n, 543, 544n, 545n, 548n, 558, 561n, 572, 576n, 589, 632n, 648, 650
Sūtra of Forty-Two Sections 146
Sūtra of Golden Light 113, 624n
Sūtra of Huineng 635n
Suvajra xv, 617–18, 635n
Suzuki, D. T. 624n
Swale *see* Ryan, Colonel J. W. (Swale)
Swayambhunath 269, 272, 288–90, 515n

Tagore, Pratima Devi 153–6, 255, 517, 518n, 567n
Tagore, Rabindranath 43, 93–4, 509n, 567n, 584n, 623n, 634n
Tagore, Rathindranath 154–6
Taj Mahal 521n
'Taking Refuge in the Buddha' xii, 429, 650–1
Taleju (goddess) 296
Tamangs, the 30–1, 92–3, 554n
Tashi, T. 194–6
Tendufla, Mr 259–60
Tendzin, Thubden 159, 176–8, 195, 205, 208, 228–30, 315, 544n, 625n *see also* Pallis, M.
thangkas 29–30, 230–2, 258, 397
Tharchin, Mr 164–6, 180, 229
Tharpa Choling Gompa 32, 176, 177–82, 184–5, 207–8, 213, 228–9, 446
theology, Buddhist 562n
Theosophical Society 134, 380, 439–40, 580n, 631n
Thibaw, King 126–7, 537n
Three Jewels, The 575n, 592
Three Jewels, Salutation to the (*Tiratana Vandanā*) 17, 408, 429
Thubden 576n
Thubden Tendzin, *see* Tendzin, Thubden
Tibet House 327
Tibet Mirror 164–5
Tibetans 31–2, 180, 209, 321, 332, 353, 535, 537n, 543, 544n
Tilakdhari, *see* Singh, T. P.
Tiratana Vandanā 429 *see also* Three Jewels, Salutation to the
Tirpai 30, 208

Tirpai Gompa, *see* Tharpa Choling Gompa
Tittleshall 597n
Tomo Geshe Rimpoche 213, 258, 626n
tradition 161
Tribhuvan, King 269–70, 273, 276, 279–81, 283, 303–5
trikāya doctrine 214, 563n
Triratna Buddhist Community 486–7, 584n, 597n, 598n, 649, 656
Triratna Story, The 593n, 597n
Triyana Vardhana Vihara 550n, 553n, 595, 598n
Tsaparang 250, 252–3, 267, 418–22
Tsedeun, Princess Pema (of Sikkim) 24, 29, 35, 45, 142
Tsering, A. (cook) 326–7, 358, 432
Tsering, L. (The Long-Lived Deva) 70, 175, 182–3, 185–7, 206–8
Tse-Tung, Chairman Mao 164, 353, 629n
Tshering, T. 36
Tucci, G. 422, 631n
Tun Hla Oung, Major-General 245–7, 416
Turner, L. 44–5

UNESCO Seminar 519, 521n
United States Information Service (USIS) 57, 58
Universalism 159, 161, 482, 605
Upaḍḍha Sutta 633
Upāsaka 26
Upāsikā 471, 493, 494n

Vaiśākha Pūrṇimā 37, 480, 547, 548n
Vajrakumara 597n
Vajrapāṇi 230–2
Valisinha, Devapriya 24, 172, 263, 265, 280, 367–72, 379–80, 383–9, 438–9, 525n, 567–8n, 592
Vaswani, H. 499, 500n, 505, 508n, 616
Vaswani, J. P. 616
Vaswani, Sadhu 616
Vaswani, Sundri 468, 499, 500n, 523, 525n, 555n, 606, 616–18
and *Living Silence* 499, 503, 531, 532n
Vedanta Kesari, The 89
'Veil of Stars, The' 94, 623n
Victoria Terminus (V.T.) 500n, 588
Vimalakīrti Nirdeśa 313
Vinaya 177, 204, 300–1, 374, 397, 520n
Vinaya Piṭaka 555n, 621n
vipassanā 506, 611–12

Vishnu 270, 276, 437, 626n
Vishva Bharati University 509n; *see also* Santiniketan
vision 563n
Visuddhimagga 624n
Vivekananda, Swami 386–8, 561n, 585n
'The Voice of Silence' 503
Void, the Great 559, 563n

Wadia, B. P. 458, 544n, 628n, 632n
Wadia, Mme S. 458, 479, 596, 598n, 632n, 633n
Way of the White Clouds, The 252, 419, 626n
Wee 84–5
Western Buddhist Order of Clifton, R. S. 339–43, 428
    founded by Sangharakshita xiii, 584n, 597n, 649
Wheel of Life 589, 590n
Whitwell, R. 582, 584n
Wordsworth, W. x, 78, 434, 543, 545n
World Fellowship of Buddhists 512, 515n

Yatung 188, 200
Yellow Monk, *see* Chodags, Thubden
Yogananda, P 582, 585n
Yogaratna 304–5
Young Men's Buddhist Association xi, 35–7, 79, 82, 427, 537n

Zagaya, U 108, 110
Zhou, E. 464

A GUIDE TO THE COMPLETE WORKS OF SANGHARAKSHITA

Gathered together in these twenty-seven volumes are talks and stories, commentaries on the Buddhist scriptures, poems, memoirs, reviews, and other writings. The genres are many, and the subject matter covered is wide, but it all has – its whole purpose is to convey – that taste of freedom which the Buddha declared to be the hallmark of his Dharma. Another traditional description of the Buddha's Dharma is that it is *ehipassiko*, 'come and see'. Sangharakshita calls to us, his readers, to come and see how the Dharma can fundamentally change the way we see things, change the way we live for the better, and change the society we belong to, wherever in the world we live.

Sangharakshita's very first published piece, *The Unity of Buddhism* (found in volume 7 of this collection), appeared in 1944 when he was eighteen years old, and it introduced themes that continued to resound throughout his work: the basis of Buddhist ethics, the compassion of the bodhisattva, and the transcendental unity of Buddhism. Over the course of the following seven decades not only did numerous other works flow from his pen; he gave hundreds of talks (some now lost). In gathering all we could find of this vast output, we have sought to arrange it in a way that brings a sense of coherence, communicating something essential about Sangharakshita, his life and teaching. Recalling the three 'baskets' among which an early tradition divided the Buddha's teachings, we have divided Sangharakshita's creative output into six 'baskets' or groups: foundation texts; works originating in India; teachings originally given in the West; commentaries on the Buddhist scriptures; personal writings; and poetry, aphorisms, and works on the arts. The 27th volume, a concordance, brings together all the terms and themes of the whole collection. If you want to find a particular story or teaching, look at a traditional term from different points of view or in different contexts, or track down one of the thousands of canonical references to be found in these volumes, the concordance will be your guide.

1. FOUNDATION

What is the foundation of a Buddhist life? How do we understand and then follow the Buddha's path of Ethics, Meditation, and Wisdom? What is really meant by 'Going for Refuge to the Three Jewels', described by Sangharakshita as the essential act of a Buddhist life? And what is the Bodhisattva ideal, which he has called 'one of the sublimest ideals mankind has ever seen'? In the 'Foundation' group you will find teachings on all these themes. It includes the author's magnum opus, *A Survey of Buddhism*, a collection of teachings on *The Purpose and Practice of Buddhist Meditation*, and the anthology, *The Essential Sangharakshita*, an eminently helpful distillation of the entire corpus.

2. INDIA

From 1950 to 1964 Sangharakshita, based in Kalimpong in the eastern Himalayas, poured his energy into trying to revive Buddhism in the land of its birth and to revitalize and bring reform to the existing Asian Buddhist world. The articles and book reviews from this period are gathered in volumes 7 and 8, as well as his biographical sketch of the great Sinhalese Dharmaduta, Anagārika Dharmapala. In 1954 Sangharakshita took on the editing of the *Maha Bodhi*, a journal for which he wrote a monthly editorial, and which, under his editorship, published the work of many of the leading Buddhist writers of the time. It was also during these years in India that a vital connection was forged with Dr B. R. Ambedkar, renowned Indian statesman and leader of the Buddhist mass conversion of 1956. Sangharakshita became closely involved with the new Buddhists and, after Dr Ambedkar's untimely death, visited them regularly on extensive teaching tours.

From 1979, when an Indian wing of the Triratna Buddhist Community was founded (then known as TBMSG), Sangharakshita returned several times to undertake further teaching tours. The talks from these tours are collected in volumes 9 and 10 along with a unique work on Ambedkar and his life which draws out the significance of his conversion to Buddhism.

3. THE WEST

Sangharakshita founded the Triratna Buddhist Community (then called the Friends of the Western Buddhist Order) on 6 April 1967. On 7 April the following year he performed the first ordinations of men and women within the Triratna Buddhist Order (then the Western Buddhist Order). At that time Buddhism was not widely known in the West and for the following two decades or so he taught intensively, finding new ways to communicate the ancient truths of Buddhism, drawing on the whole Buddhist tradition to do so, as well as making connections with what was best in existing Western culture. Sometimes his sword flashed as he critiqued ideas and views inimical to the Dharma. It is these teachings and writings that are gathered together in this third group.

4. COMMENTARY

Throughout Sangharakshita's works are threaded references to the Buddhist canon of literature – Pāli, Mahāyāna, and Vajrayāna – from which he drew his inspiration. In the early days of the new movement he often taught by means of seminars in which, prompted by the questions of his students, he sought to pass on the inspiration and wisdom of the Buddhist tradition. Each seminar was based around a different text, the seminars were recorded and transcribed, and in due course many of the transcriptions were edited and turned into books, all carefully checked by Sangharakshita. The commentaries compiled in this way constitute the fourth group. In some ways this is the heart of the collection. Sangharakshita often told the story of how it was that, reading two *sūtras* at the age of sixteen or seventeen, he realized that he was a Buddhist, and he has never tired of showing others how they too could see and realize the value of the '*sūtra*-treasure'.

5. MEMOIRS

Who is Sangharakshita? What sort of life did he live? Whom did he meet? What did he feel? Why did he found a new Buddhist movement? In these volumes of memoirs and letters Sangharakshita shares with his readers much about himself and his life as he himself has experienced it, giving us a sense of its breadth and depth, humour and pathos.

6. POETRY, APHORISMS, AND THE ARTS

Sangharakshita describes reading *Paradise Lost* at the age of twelve as one of the greatest poetic experiences of his life. His realization of the value of the higher arts to spiritual development is one of his distinctive contributions to our understanding of what Buddhist life is, and he has expressed it in a number of essays and articles. Throughout his life he has written poetry which he says can be regarded as a kind of spiritual autobiography. It is here, perhaps, that we come closest to the heart of Sangharakshita. He has also written a few short stories and composed some startling aphorisms. Through book reviews he has engaged with the experiences, ideas, and opinions of modern writers. All these are collected in this sixth group.

In the preface to *A Survey of Buddhism* (volume 1 in this collection), Sangharakshita wrote of his approach to the Buddha's teachings:

> Why did the Buddha (or Nāgārjuna, or Buddhaghosa) teach this particular doctrine? What bearing does it have on the spiritual life? How does it help the individual Buddhist actually to follow the spiritual path?... I found myself asking such questions again and again, for only in this way, I found, could I make sense – spiritual sense – of Buddhism.

Although this collection contains so many words, they are all intent, directly or indirectly, on these same questions. And all these words are not in the end about their writer, but about his great subject, the Buddha and his teaching, and about you, the reader, for whose benefit they are solely intended. These pages are full of the reverence that Sangharakshita has always felt, which is expressed in an early poem, 'Taking Refuge in the Buddha', whose refrain is 'My place is at thy feet'. He has devoted his life to communicating the Buddha's Dharma in its depth and in its breadth, to men and women from all backgrounds and walks of life, from all countries, of all races, of all ages. These collected works are the fruit of that devotion.

We are very pleased to be able to include some previously unpublished work in this collection, but most of what appears in these volumes has been published before. We have made very few changes, though we have added extra notes where we thought they would be useful. We have had the pleasure of researching the notes in the Sangharakshita Library at 'Adhisthana', Triratna's centre in Herefordshire, UK, which houses his own collection of books. It has been of great value to be able to search among the very copies of the *suttas*, *sūtras* and commentaries that have provided the basis of his teachings over the last seventy years.

The publication of these volumes owes much to the work of transcribers, editors, indexers, designers, and publishers over many years – those who brought out the original editions of many of the works included here, and those who have contributed in all sorts of ways to this *Complete Works* project, including all those who contributed to funds given in celebration of Sangharakshita's ninetieth birthday in August 2015. Many thanks to everyone who has helped; may the merit gained in our acting thus go to the alleviation of the suffering of all beings.

Vidyadevi and Kalyanaprabha
 Editors

THE COMPLETE WORKS OF SANGHARAKSHITA

I FOUNDATION

VOLUME 1 A SURVEY OF BUDDHISM / THE BUDDHA'S NOBLE EIGHTFOLD PATH
A Survey of Buddhism
The Buddha's Noble Eightfold Path

2 THE THREE JEWELS I
The Three Jewels
Going for Refuge
The Ten Pillars of Buddhism
The Meaning of Conversion in Buddhism
The History of My Going for Refuge
Forty-Three Years Ago
Was the Buddha a Bhikkhu?
My Relation to the Order
Extending the Hand of Fellowship

3 THE THREE JEWELS II
Who is the Buddha?
What is the Dharma?
What is the Sangha?

4 THE BODHISATTVA IDEAL
The Bodhisattva Ideal
The Bodhisattva Principle
The Endlessly Fascinating Cry (seminar)

5 THE PURPOSE AND PRACTICE OF BUDDHIST MEDITATION
The Purpose and Practice of Buddhist Meditation

6 THE ESSENTIAL SANGHARAKSHITA
The Essential Sangharakshita

II INDIA

7 CROSSING THE STREAM: INDIA WRITINGS I
Early Writings 1944–1954
Crossing the Stream
Buddhism in the Modern World
The Meaning of Orthodoxy in Buddhism
Buddhism in India Today
Ordination and Initiation in the Three Yānas
A Bird's Eye View of Indian Buddhism

| VOLUME | 8 | BEATING THE DHARMA DRUM: INDIA WRITINGS II |

Anagarika Dharmapala and Other 'Maha Bodhi' Writings
Dharmapala: The Spiritual Dimension
Beating the Drum: 'Maha Bodhi' Editorials

9   DR AMBEDKAR AND THE REVIVAL OF BUDDHISM I
Ambedkar and Buddhism
Lecture Tour in India, December 1981–March 1982

10 DR AMBEDKAR AND THE REVIVAL OF BUDDHISM II
Lecture Tours in India 1979 & 1983–1992
Other Edited Lectures and Seminar Material

III THE WEST

11 A NEW BUDDHIST MOVEMENT I
Ritual and Devotion in Buddhism
The Buddha's Victory
The Taste of Freedom
Buddha Mind
Human Enlightenment
New Currents in Western Buddhism
Buddhism for Today – and Tomorrow
Buddhism and the West
Aspects of Buddhist Morality
Buddhism, World Peace, and Nuclear War
Dialogue between Buddhism and Christianity
Buddhism and Blasphemy
Buddhism and the Bishop of Woolwich
Buddhism and the New Reformation
Great Buddhists of the Twentieth Century
Articles and Interviews

12 A NEW BUDDHIST MOVEMENT II
Previously unpublished talks

13 EASTERN AND WESTERN TRADITIONS
From Genesis to the Diamond Sūtra
The FWBO and 'Protestant Buddhism'
Creative Symbols of Tantric Buddhism
Tibetan Buddhism
The Essence of Zen

IV COMMENTARY

VOLUME 14   THE ETERNAL LEGACY / WISDOM BEYOND WORDS
The Eternal Legacy
The Glory of the Literary World
Wisdom Beyond Words

15   PALI CANON TEACHINGS AND TRANSLATIONS
Dhammapada (translation)
Karaṇīyamettā Sutta (translation)
Living with Kindness
Living with Awareness
Maṅgala Sutta (translation)
Auspicious Signs (seminar)
Salutation to the Three Jewels (translation)
The Threefold Refuge (seminar)
Further Pāli Sutta Commentaries

16   MAHĀYĀNA MYTHS AND STORIES
The Drama of Cosmic Enlightenment
The Priceless Jewel (talk)
Transforming Self and World
The Inconceivable Emancipation

17   WISDOM TEACHINGS OF THE MAHĀYĀNA
Know Your Mind
Living Ethically
Living Wisely
The Way to Wisdom (seminar)

18   MILAREPA AND THE ART OF DISCIPLESHIP I
The Yogi's Joy
The Shepherd's Search for Mind
Rechungpa's Journey to Enlightenment

19   MILAREPA AND THE ART OF DISCIPLESHIP II
Rechungpa's Journey to Enlightenment, continued

V MEMOIRS

20   THE RAINBOW ROAD FROM TOOTING BROADWAY TO KALIMPONG
The Rainbow Road from Tooting Broadway to Kalimpong

VOLUME 21   FACING MOUNT KANCHENJUNGA
Facing Mount Kanchenjunga
Dear Dinoo: Letters to a Friend

22   IN THE SIGN OF THE GOLDEN WHEEL
In the Sign of the Golden Wheel
Precious Teachers
With Allen Ginsberg in Kalimpong

23   MOVING AGAINST THE STREAM
Moving Against the Stream
1970: A Retrospective

24   THROUGH BUDDHIST EYES
Travel Letters
Through Buddhist Eyes

VI POETRY AND THE ARTS

25   COMPLETE POEMS
Complete Poems 1941–1994
The Call of the Forest
Other Poems

26   APHORISMS AND THE ARTS
Peace is a Fire
A Stream of Stars
The Religion of Art
In the Realm of the Lotus
The Journey to Il Convento
St Jerome Revisited
A Note on the Burial of Count Orgaz
Criticism East and West
Alternative Traditions
The Artist's Dream and other Parables
A Moseley Miscellany
Adhisthana Writings
Urthona Articles and Interviews

27   CONCORDANCE AND APPENDICES

WINDHORSE PUBLICATIONS

Windhorse Publications is a Buddhist charitable company based in the UK. We produce books of high quality that are accessible and relevant to all those interested in Buddhism, at whatever level of interest and commitment. We are the main publisher of Sangharakshita, the founder of the Triratna Buddhist Order and Community. Our books draw on the whole range of the Buddhist tradition, including translations of traditional texts, commentaries, books that make links with contemporary culture and ways of life, biographies of Buddhists, and works on meditation.

To subscribe to the *Complete Works of Sangharakshita,* please go to: windhorsepublications.com/sangharakshita-complete-works/

THE TRIRATNA BUDDHIST COMMUNITY

Windhorse Publications is a part of the Triratna Buddhist Community, an international movement with centres in Europe, India, North and South America and Australasia. At these centres, members of the Triratna Buddhist Order offer classes in meditation and Buddhism. Activities of the Triratna Community also include retreat centres, residential spiritual communities, ethical Right Livelihood businesses, and the Karuna Trust, a UK fundraising charity that supports social welfare projects in the slums and villages of India.

Through these and other activities, Triratna is developing a unique approach to Buddhism, not simply as a philosophy and a set of techniques, but as a creatively directed way of life for all people living in the conditions of the modern world.

For more information please visit thebuddhistcentre.com